POLA
MAT
xxxxxxxx8021
6/21/2021

Item: ï¿½001010101852068 ((book)

ND
AL

RUIN AND RENEWAL

Civilizing Europe After World War II

Paul Betts

NEW YORK

BASIC BOOKS

Basic Books
Hachette Book Group
1290 Avenue of the Americas, New York, NY 10104
www.basicbooks.com

Printed in the United States of America
First Edition: November 2020

Published by Basic Books, an imprint of Perseus Books, LLC, a subsidiary of Hachette Book Group, Inc. The Basic Books name and logo is a trademark of the Hachette Book Group.

The Hachette Speakers Bureau provides a wide range of authors for speaking events. To find out more, go to www.hachettespeakersbureau.com or call (866) 376-6591.

The publisher is not responsible for websites (or their content) that are not owned by the publisher.

Parts of Chapter 2 were published in "The Polemics of Pity: British Photographs of Berlin, 1945–1947," in *Humanitarianism and Media: 1900 to the Present*, ed. Johannes Paulmann (Oxford/New York: Berghahn, 2018), 126–150.

Parts of Chapter 3 were published in "Religion, Science and Cold War Anti-Communism: The 1949 Cardinal Mindszenty Show Trial," in *Science, Religion and Communism in Cold War Europe*, ed. Paul Betts and Stephen A. Smith (London: Palgrave, 2016), 275–307.

Parts of Chapter 4 were published in "Manners, Morality and Civilization: Reflections on Postwar German Etiquette Books," in *Histories of the Aftermath: The Legacies of the Second World War in Europe*, ed. Frank Biess and Robert Moeller (Oxford/New York: Berghahn, 2010), 196–214.

Parts of Chapter 7 were published in "Humanity's New Heritage: UNESCO and the Rewriting of World History," *Past & Present* 228, no. 1 (August 2015): 249–285, and "The Warden of World Civilization: UNESCO and the Rescue of the Nubian Monuments," in *Heritage in the Modern World*, ed. Paul Betts and Corey Ross, *Past & Present* 226, supplement 10 (2015): 100–125.

Print book interior design by Linda Mark.

Library of Congress Control Number: 2020944635

ISBNs: 978-1-5416-7246-8 (hardcover); 978-1-5416-7247-5 (e-book)

LSC-C

1 2020

CONTENTS

Introduction

OLD WORLD MADE NEW

O NE OF THE MOST STRIKING FEATURES OF TWENTY-FIRST century international politics has been the widespread calls to protect civilization in danger. Since the shock of 9/11, the "fight for civilization" has suffused the speeches of American Republican Party presidents from George W. Bush to Donald Trump in connection with the "war on terrorism," and recent events in Europe have prompted numerous politicians to sound the alarm about European civilization under siege. In the wake of the November 2015 terrorist attacks in Paris, French prime minister Manuel Valls described the conflict with Islamic State of Iraq and Syria, or ISIS for short, as "a battle of values, a battle of civilisations." Hungarian prime minister Viktor Orbán has repeatedly proclaimed that refugees from Syria and elsewhere fleeing the conflicts in the Middle East imperil Europe's Christian roots and would forever alter "Europe's civilization." Political figures in Poland, Austria, Holland, Denmark, Serbia, Germany, and the UK, among others, have voiced similar anxiety about Europe's fragile frontiers, cultural identity, and "Christian civilization" under mortal threat. Russian president Vladimir Putin has enlisted the language of Russia's "distinct civilization" as a rebuff to American-style globalization and a means to justify military expansion in Ukraine. The attack on the National Bardo Museum in Tunis in March 2015 and ISIS's detonation of the Temple of Baalshamin in the ancient Syrian city of Palmyra in August 2015 were denounced as desecrations of "world civilization" by voices in Europe, the Middle East, and international organizations like UNESCO. No less disturbing, the last few years have witnessed the racist ramping up of the defense of "white civilization" as a clarion call for the radical Right across Europe and North America. The tagline of civilization in crisis is being regularly exploited, in part because its meaning is elastic enough to encompass secular, Christian, international, or national causes, depending on the context and identified menace. These developments are usually lumped together as fearful reactions to post–Cold War globalization, but the European politicking associated with repurposing cultural identities at risk goes back decades.[1]

Renewed interest in the defense of civilization is neither straightforward nor predictable, especially given the term's heavy historical baggage. Critics have long denounced the idea of civilization as one of the most unsavory elements of European politics and culture since the eighteenth century, a legacy infamously mixed with imperialist "civilizing missions," war making, and various domestic social engineering projects from the late nineteenth century onward. Civilization was central to nineteenth-century European self-understanding and a key ideological plank for overseas power and expansion before the outbreak of the First World War, and is now commonly dismissed by many commentators as an embarrassing relic from Europe's unwanted past that thankfully did not survive the mid-twentieth century. According to this view, the twentieth century's grim inheritance of two world wars, the Holocaust, and decolonization forever buried Europe's civilizing mission abroad, with its last rites read out at various low points during the last century, be it at Verdun, Auschwitz, or Algiers. British historian Tony Judt was certainly not alone when he wrote that Nazism and the Third

Reich's genocidal war rendered European civilization the "grandest of all illusions."[2]

However, the political language of civilization did not die with Germany's unconditional surrender. On the contrary, it reemerged as a potent metaphor to ascribe positive meaning to material and moral reconstruction after the war. In 1945, Europe lay in ruins. Some 50 million people were dead, cities were reduced to rubble, and large swaths of the continent languished in physical and moral defeat. Unlike World War I, which was mainly fought in the countryside between soldiers, World War II mercilessly blurred the boundaries between civilian and combatant, making it the first war in modern history in which civilian casualties far outnumbered soldier deaths. Law and order had collapsed, refugees were everywhere, and outside powers were in control. The liberation of the concentration camps exposed to a wide international audience the horrors of the Third Reich's racial war, pulling back the curtain on the depth and depravity of Nazi atrocities against Jews and other targeted minority groups. A continent that had long considered itself the measure of civilization for the world had turned into its barbaric opposite. That the international legal community felt compelled to devise novel terms to try to comprehend (and punish) German misdeeds—such as genocide and crimes against humanity—dramatized the stark sense of living in radically new times. Hannah Arendt's famous comment in 1945—that the "problem of evil will be the fundamental question of postwar intellectual life in Europe—as death became the fundamental problem after the last war"—resonated among contemporaries about the dark moral inheritance of Hitler's Europe. The discovery of the camps and the question of what to do with Germany and its captured leaders triggered widespread discussion about how the fate of civilization itself seemed to hang in the balance.[3]

While some contemporaries reacted by mourning civilization's demise, many more strove to remake it afresh. It was the very corruption and fragility of European civilization itself that stirred a diverse set of thinkers, politicians, activists, and reformers to try to salvage it from the ruins of war, destruction, and moral collapse. The mission to re-civilize Europe was by no means confined to conservatives, and was seized upon by a dizzying array of competing causes and interest groups from across the political spectrum and Iron Curtain. In the aftermath of the war, civilization served as a point of reference to grasp Europe's new postwar condition beyond the confines of the nation-state and Cold War division, and to reconsider its relationship to the past, the future, and the rest of the world.

This book gives voice to the many people who engaged in this reconstruction fever across the Cold War divide and even in various former colonies in the name of renewal and reform. Included among them were warmongers and peaceniks, preservationists and liberal modernizers, scientists and humanitarian aid workers, Christian conservatives and communists, nationalists and internationalists, as well as European imperialists and African anti-imperialists. In diverse ways, they all tried to make sense of Europe in defeat and division, and to forge a new understanding of civilization that would bring peace and progress to a broken continent. What follows is not just a story of how European intellectuals philosophized about their fundamentally changed fortunes since World War II, for the task of regenerating civilization prompted a variety of practical reform initiatives. Some saw civilization as singular and universal, others as plural and separate. Yet all parties set out to rebuild Europe anew from the debris of Nazism and the war. The contest for civilization inspired a mixed crowd of advocates on both sides of the Iron Curtain who mobilized support for the great issues of the day, above all war and peace, religion and science, rights and reconstruction, empire and anticolonial liberation, communism and anticommunism.

Pleas to defend civilization may be back today with shrill insistence, but there is little sense of how this came about. One of the reasons why we are so ill-equipped to get a grip on what is happening is because civilization is a term we love to hate. When mentioned in books and the press, it is almost always framed by ironic scare quotes or offset by the forbidding *so-called*—rhetorical strategies designed to deny any incriminating association between the speaker and the word itself. There is good reason for such distancing and moral disapproval, given the term's legacy of eighteenth-century elitism together with nineteenth-century imperialism, racism, and religious intolerance, which persist in myriad forms to this day. The strong emotions associated with the concept have animated public discourse in various ways for a century and a half, and were especially prevalent after World War II, as ideas of civilization fueled new political visions of how Europe's damaged cultural traditions could be revived and preserved. The breakdown of order in 1945 opened up the possibility of seeing and thinking about Europe differently; competing claims about the meaning and direction of civilization underlay the politics of reconstruction. Its radical appropriation by today's conservatives and neofascists obscures the ways in which civilization emerged as a rallying cry for building a better Europe after the war, often in the name of peace, justice, decolonization, and multiculturalism. Right-wing campaigns to reclaim civilization as their own were certainly present in the form of muscular Christianity, the defense of empire, and anti-Americanism, but these views were met by equally powerful counterclaims about the New Europe from liberals, Eastern European socialists, Third World radicals, UNESCO preservationists, and other reformers. The point is that the post–Second World War re-civilizing mission played host to a multiplicity of political storylines in which Europe was culturally imagined and reorganized, both on the continent and abroad. How and why this old, troublesome, and much-maligned principle was summoned to help redress Europe's crisis of identity—then and now—is the subject of this book.[4]

Another reason why we have lost sight of the rich and contradictory historical legacy of civilization is because it has been converted into crude shorthand for explaining the roots of post–Cold War political conflict. Civilization has never been just one thing, and variously serves as a contested idea, value, object of desire, and claim to power, and this book will attend to its different facets. In recent decades a selective reading of civilization has been advanced as a master key with which to interpret twenty-first-century war and violence. Such a view was famously put forward by American political scientist Samuel Huntington in his 1996 bestseller on international affairs, *The Clash of Civilizations and the Remaking of World Order*. His controversial ideas were first published as an article in 1993 in *Foreign Affairs* and then expanded as a full-length book three years later. Huntington's main argument is that future global conflict will not be so much about politics and economics, but rather will center on culture. "Global politics is the politics of civilizations," he wrote, in which the "rivalry of the superpowers is replaced by the clash of civilizations." In his telling, individual civilizations are essentially unchanging and unchangeable regional cultural identity blocs made up of shared religious and cultural histories, whose collisions of values perforce will fuel and frame political antagonism in a post–Cold War world. While there is no need to revisit the well-known pitfalls of the argument, Huntington does raise the issue of how the meaning of civilization was radically retooled after the Cold War.[5]

A more useful interpretation of the role and history of civilization as a global political force is the long-forgotten work of British historian Arnold J. Toynbee. His twelve-volume universal world history, *A Study of History*, published between 1936 and 1961, served as a standard reference for global history for decades. Toynbee is usually lumped together with Oswald Spengler as a gloomy prognosticator of Europe in decline. Yet such a characterization overlooks some of Toynbee's insights, which are important for this book. His principal point was to move beyond the modern historical preoccupation with the nation-state as the main unit of historical analysis. For him, the most "intelligible unit of historical study" is "neither a nation state nor (at the other end of the scale) mankind as a whole but a certain grouping of humanity which we have called a society," and "societies of this species are commonly called civilizations." In this view, civilizations are therefore essentially large societies that share common beliefs and values, and function as the last stand of diversity and plurality in the world. Toynbee was a devout Christian, and in the 1930s he repeatedly railed against the "new paganism" and "idolatrous worship" of state power, be it in the form of communism, nationalism, or fascism. He even criticized the myth of Western superiority and the "illusion of progress" that "proceeds in a straight line," which partly explains why he was often admired by non-European anticolonialists and Eastern European communists alike. But this was no defense of cultural relativism. Whereas individual civilizations may perish, so he argued, the shared global story of civilization as a constant through history remained firm. As he put it in his 1947 booklet, *Civilization on Trial*, "Civilizations have come and gone, but Civilization (with a big 'C') has succeeded, each time, in re-incarnating itself in fresh exemplars of the type." Abstract as some of this may seem, Toynbee's work struck a chord with countless readers around the world in the 1930s through the 1950s, to the point that he became the twentieth century's bestselling historian. His popularity derived less from his complex interpretations of the rise and fall of world civilizations than from his ability to give readers a sense of communal identity and broader historical purpose beyond the nation-state during the turbulent midcentury decades.[6]

That said, civilization escapes easy definition. The eminent British art historian Kenneth Clark opened his 1969 blockbuster BBC television series *Civilisation*—whose accompanying book was sold to over sixty countries—by confessing, "What is civilization? I don't know. I can't define it in abstract terms—yet. But I think that I can recognize it when I see it." Whatever one makes of his breezy patrician self-confidence in judging what does or does not count as civilization, Clark put his finger on the problem of identifying what civilization is. For him and many others, it is synonymous with a canon of venerable cultural artifacts in the arts and sciences, the unique material inheritance of a people or culture, in his case a Western cultural patrimony that stretched back to ancient Greece. For others, civilization was better understood as the cultural fruit of urban life—that is, roads and central states, food production and hospitals, cargo ships and cathedrals. German American theologian Reinhold Niebuhr, writing in the early 1950s, took up this view when he defined the difference between culture and civilization as one of scale, inclusion, and durability. Culture "would represent the sum total of the art, philosophy, literature and religion of a civilization, and civilization would represent the social, economic and political and legal arrangements by which the human community is ordered." Here Niebuhr alluded to the nineteenth-century distinction—most pronounced in Germany, as we shall see—between culture and civilization. By the 1950s, this once fiercely maintained dichotomy had lost much of its cultural power, apart from episodic expressions in the Federal Republic of Germany. French anthropologist Claude Lévi-Strauss, in his classic 1955 rumination on the limitations of anthropology, *Tristes Tropiques*, extended the scale even more broadly when he posited civilization as the last and most basic element of species-belonging in a connected world: "Being human signifies, for each one of us," he wrote, "belonging to a class, a society, a country, a continent and a civilization."[7]

But if some embraced civilization as a story of edification and inclusion, others were less sanguine. For more than a century, the West European Left summarily rejected the ideology of civilization as nothing but window dressing masking Western imperialism, domination, and barbarities of all sorts. German Jewish literary critic and philosopher Walter Benjamin sharpened the polemic in his 1940 "Theses on the Philosophy of History" when he wrote that there "is no document of civilization that is not at the same time a document of barbarism." For those on the receiving end of European expansion and colonial conquest, the line between civilization and barbarism was so thin as to be indistinguishable. Mahatma Gandhi's purported quip when asked what he thought about Western civilization—"I think it would be a good idea"—captured widely shared perceptions of the violence and hypocrisy inherent in the whole European enterprise itself. Nevertheless, these well-known objections miss two issues. The first is that Western civilization was never unified or consistent—its history has been marked by perennial doubt and self-criticism from various quarters since the eighteenth century, and most acutely so after World War II. Secondly, the claims of civilization were not completely dismissed by anticolonial intellectuals; as we shall see, the language of civilization was reformulated by elites in Asia and Africa in the aftermath of decolonization to showcase the glories of precolonial indigenous civilization as emblems of postcolonial sovereignty. Africa was a special case in this development, and thus the focus will be on that story. Of relevance here is that the early postcolonial critique did not reject the concept of civilization outright, but rather maintained that civilizations were multiple and equal, in which no continent—least of all Europe—enjoyed a monopoly or advanced position.

Civilization's protean but also multivalent quality is neatly captured by well-known French philosopher and former government official Régis Debray in his recent study of the global reach of American empire. In it he described civilization as a "vaporous, ethereal, shape-shifting word" that "sings and is sung in all sorts of scenes," a "wandering fairy that evaporates in an iridescent blur." While Debray rightly evokes the ever-changing nature of the term itself, he overlooks the ways in which civilization's power resides in the fact that it is both visible and invisible. Civilization goes beyond what meets the eye, serving as a myth of origins and development abstracted from the here and now. This stands in stark contrast to its less solemnly costumed cousin—heritage—which generally takes on

9

more flamboyant expression in the form of historical reenactments, patriotic pageantry, feel-good tourist attractions, and mass-produced souvenir trinkets. Unlike heritage, civilization has no obvious emblems or flags—crusader banners, cathedrals, and McDonald's outlets may signify Western civilization for many, but these examples never originated as such. The point is that civilization is elusive and hard to pin down, not least because it exceeds the nation-state, religious identity, or any singular people; it is at once material and transcendent, made real through belief, vision, and argument about the inheritance of history. Civilization is a way of seeing and a mode of action, what historian Mary Beard, in her copresented 2018 BBC television series *Civilisations*, called both "the eye of faith" and an "act of faith."[8]

Libraries around the world are full of learned histories of civilizations that chronicle the grand achievements of various empires, nations, regions, and peoples, often composed as glorified family trees of cultural bling and belonging. But it is worth remembering that the conjuring up of civilization more typically is a sign of rupture and plea for action. The breakdown of order in Europe in 1945 is an instructive example, as the continent became a vast theater of activity devoted to remaking Europe and Europeans, however differently understood and practiced. In this case, civilization functioned as a rhetoric of moral alarm announcing cultural breakdown, and the need to erect frontiers of inclusion and exclusion. It did not speak in a unified voice for a single cause, and instead was used to underwrite a range of diverse agendas and reforms. Just as democracy was subject to political wrangling after World War II—as seen in the proliferation of qualifying adjectives like social, Christian, liberal, socialist—so too did civilization fragment into multiple, overlapping, and antagonistic stories of Western, Christian, Atlantic, African, white, universal, and socialist civilizations. And precisely because discussions of democracy after 1945—in both West and East—betrayed a distinct present-mindedness that belied shallow historical roots, civilization was enlisted to bestow post-fascist Europe with a deeper sense of place and purpose.[9]

THE IDEA OF CIVILIZATION CAME TO REPRESENT SOMETHING new after 1945, and departed in significant ways from its traditional understanding. Chief among these is that unlike in the nineteenth century, the postwar understanding of civilization was shaped by insecurity, anxiety, defeat, and the daunting task of starting over. To better grasp this midcentury novelty, we need to backtrack to the history of the term. Etymologically, civilization is a neologism that originated in eighteenth-century France, and has long been associated with Guizot, Condorcet, Mirabeau, and Voltaire, as well as with those connected with the Scottish Enlightenment, such as Adam Ferguson, David Hume, and John Gordon. Its early eighteenth-century usage was connected with jurisprudence, to the extent that a criminal trial was turned into a civil proceeding. By the last quarter of the century, civilization became interchangeable with advancement, refinement, and humanity—the antithesis of barbarism. The history of the concept is greatly indebted to the influential German sociologist Norbert Elias, whose two-volume *The Civilizing Process*, published in 1939, analyzed its legacy in two strands—the first sees civilization as synonymous with civility, politeness, courtesy, manners, and the emergence of a law-based state and civil society; the second interprets the term as part of a broader project of state pacification and consolidation, to the extent that newly emerging absolutist states neutralized a rival aristocratic warrior class, along with others deemed hostile to the regime. Whether the "civilizing process" originates from civil society or the state depends on one's perspective. What both dimensions have in common is the idea that civilization was a call to action and quest for power. In fact, the term first existed as a verb (to civilize, or to be civilized) long before it became a noun in the late eighteenth century. But for all the

11

ideological differences, its eighteenth-century iteration presumed the idea of civilization in the singular, something closely linked to progress and the prospect of universality.[10]

The nineteenth century brought a new plurality of definitions, as pre-1789 ideas of a singular civilization fractured into various philosophies of difference that became increasingly nationalized and racialized in the second half of the century. This was especially pronounced with the expansion of imperialism, when civilizing missions based on a self-serving evolutionary hierarchy of races and cultures emerged as a primary justification for European enlargement and conquest. The French Revolution recast the secular mission of civilization as a French-led universalism predicated on republican progress, after which Napoleonic reforms imposed on vanquished territories assumed the equation of civilization with the French nation. There is a long and quite elaborate history of how civilization was defined differently in German, French, Italian, and English, and how it was suffused with hallowed national values and virtues. In Germany, much was made of how the inward, cultivated, and soil-bound German *Kultur* stood in proud opposition to the deracinated and superficial materialism of Anglo-French *Zivilisation*. But as culture was increasingly enlisted by all the Great Powers as a sphere of national competition, the realm of civilization conversely held out the possibility of broader allegiances that surpassed the nation-state, evidenced in the more abstract and far-flung terminology of European, Western, or Christian civilization. The linguistic differences between culture and civilization hardened along national lines during the First World War, as all transcendent philosophies of political community were pressed into national war service.[11]

The Great War spurred the militarization of civilization by all belligerents. H. G. Wells described the conflict as a "war of the mind" and "a conflict of cultures, and nothing else in the world." In his words, "We fight not to destroy a nation, but a nest of evil ideas." In October 1914 a group of ninety-three leading German intellectuals drafted *An Appeal to the Civilized World* that rebuffed allegations of atrocities committed by German troops in Belgium, insisting that the German army was the great guardian of German *Kultur*. Thomas Mann's *Reflections of a Non-Political Man*, published in 1918, cast the war as an existential struggle between the romantic ideals of German *Kultur* against the evils of a "democratic civilization-society of 'mankind'" and "the empire of human civilization." The kaiser's assault on Eastern Europe was justified as a Teutonic civilizing mission to export German values to the farther reaches of the continent. The French responded by denouncing the cozy union of German philosophy and military aggression, and couched their own military engagement as the defense of French republican principles. American war posters proclaimed that the war was a "call for civilization," while wartime Italian revolutionary journalist Benito Mussolini dramatically painted the war as an epic struggle between "Latin civilization" and "Germanic civilization."[12]

The war's industrialized killing and moral attrition occasioned profound soul-searching about the meaning of civilization itself, not least because science, technology, religion, and nationalism had been perverted to such destructive ends. An apocalyptic malaise associated with the loss of humanity and the imminent decline of the West pervaded the continent. Karl Kraus's *The Last Days of Mankind* captured the common sentiment of having forever left behind the old pieties of the nineteenth century. Nowhere was the ruin of civilization more powerfully described than by French poet Paul Valéry's 1919 letter to *La Nouvelle Revue Française*, in which he argued that civilization—like the bodies of the soldiers fighting in the trenches—now suffered the fate of its own mortality. "We now see that the abyss of history is big enough for everyone. We feel that a civilization has the same fragility as a life," one in which "the loveliest things and the most ancient, the most formidable and the best designed, are perishable by accident."[13]

Disillusionment with the alleged superiority of Western values sparked curiosity about other civilizations. The interwar years saw growing European interests in Islamic, Buddhist, Confucian, and Hindu civilizations, some of which dovetailed with nascent anticolonial movements based in Paris and other European capitals. The war all but did away with the idea of a single evolutionary model of civilization, after which a world composed of multiple civilizations became a new focus of international thought. While the appreciation of non-Western civilizations had been growing in the nineteenth century, especially in the fields of archaeology and the study of world religions, this interest developed dramatically after World War I. This could be seen in the writings of Okakura Tenshin, Rabindranath Tagore, Liang Qichao, and Mahatma Gandhi, to say nothing of Spengler and Toynbee. The breakup of the Habsburg, Hohenzollern, Russian, and Ottoman Empires, the prospect of communist revolution, the explosion of nationalism, and the rise of fascism occasioned serious reflection on the fate of Europe in a fast-changing new world. The Russian Revolution of 1917 deepened these anxieties, as interwar European thinkers, politicians, and religious leaders became increasingly preoccupied with the Red Menace and its impact on the mainstays of European traditional identities, be they religious or secular. Across Western Europe could be heard calls to defend European civilization at risk, as liberals, nationalists, Christian conservatives, and even socialists sounded the alarm about a continent in dangerous flux. The radical Right exploited the language of peril for their own purposes too. Italian fascists turned to the theme of civilization under threat to shore up Mussolini's political legitimacy and imperial dreams, especially in connection to the invasion of Abyssinia in 1935. Invocations of civilization spiked in World War II, during which the Allied cause was routinely trumpeted as a "war for civilization" against Nazism. Nazi Germany was no less outspoken in proclaiming itself as the great defender of both European *Kultur* and civilization in the face

14

of Anglo-American materialism, Soviet "barbarism," and a world supposedly dominated by Jews.[14]

What distinguished the twentieth-century notion of civilization from its predecessors was the explicit linkage to cultural crisis. It was no accident that the most serious commentators on the idea of civilization—Lucien Febvre, Joachim Moras, Norbert Elias, Toynbee, and, of course, Sigmund Freud in his late work—were writing in the 1930s. In interwar Britain, civilization was a common term of reckoning across the political spectrum, often tinged with the hue of belle epoque nostalgia. Its parlous state was invoked to describe the disorder after the Great War, the dangerous instability of capitalism, fears of racial degeneration, and the prospect of another war. A correspondence between Sigmund Freud and Albert Einstein on *Why War?* was published in 1933, with Einstein remarking that the threat of war was "a matter of life and death for civilization." The victory of Nazism in Germany in 1933 saw a number of books on "the return of barbarism." In 1939 a selection of Freud's writings was published under the title *Civilisation, War and Death*.[15]

Civilization in trouble became a central theme of European political commentary after both wars, though comparatively little attention has been paid to the post-1945 story. The new configuration after the war was also characterized by its relation to emotions. Traditional ideas of civilization pivoted on the control and self-control of emotions, especially violent passions. Unbridled feelings were equated with barbarism, forces that needed to be tamed and governed. It was a central theme for Scottish Enlightenment thinkers as well as for Thomas Hobbes, and resonated in various ways (notably among writers of manners manuals) through the 1950s. But whereas nineteenth-century Western notions of the enlightened self, society, and state were based on the strict management of emotions, this was less the case in the twentieth century, especially in Europe after 1945. The postwar reimagining of civilization was closely bound up with the sanctioned expression of overt emotion, including compassion and contempt, hope and fear, pride and shame, anger and grief. Civility and civilization, as they had been in earlier centuries, were still pleas for transformation, but it was the experience of utter devastation and dispossession that lent emotional power and moral weight to the dreams of reconstruction. While these reform initiatives took on a wide variety of forms, common to all was the unquestioned belief in both the possibility and necessity of refashioning Europe and Europeans after the defeat of Hitler.[16]

Postwar Europe played host to competing custody battles over what civilization was and could be after Nazism, the war, and empire. Civilization is the most European of ideologies and the most cherished of invented traditions, often most present in times of danger and disorder. Civilization can be understood as an inherited set of beliefs about the origins, achievements, customs, and values of a defined political community, whose fragility flashes up in moments of twilight and risk. Ideas of civilization therefore carry with them visions of history that situate communal experiences of radical upheaval in stories that connect past and present. While we generally think of the stuff of civilization as something durable, continuous, ever present, and even timeless, historical claims to its guardianship are typically sounded during periods of moral disorder, political upheaval, and existential threat. This was certainly the case in Europe following the French Revolution and Napoleonic Wars, and again after both world wars. Preoccupation with the fate of civilization is therefore less the product of peace and prosperity than the result of rupture, vulnerability, and the drive for reform. So for all the lofty claims of timeless continuity and inherited durability, civilization after 1945 was primarily a figment of hoped-for recovery, born of destruction and dislocation. It has been key to reconceptualizing Europe in the subjunctive mood, firmly located within the realm of wish, desire, and aspiration. The physical and moral collapse of Europe in 1945 was an extreme moment of cultural discontinuity and judgment, and the language of civilization was mobilized to help narrate Europe's new place in the world. In this way, this book seeks to show how the wide set of practices associated with re-civilizing the continent reflected the changing hopes and fears of postwar Europeans themselves.

A good example of how this played out is the birth of the United Nations in 1945. It was the harbinger of a new international order forged by "peace-loving states" after the defeat of Hitler, which kicked off the most ambitious experiment in twentieth-century internationalism. That spring a large assembly of people from around the world arrived in San Francisco to launch a new mission for world peace, under the auspices of the United Nations Conference on International Organization. An American venue was chosen to break Europe's long-standing dominance as perennial host of major international conferences since the early nineteenth century (Vienna, Berlin, and Paris), as well as to mark the arrival of American economic and military might. San Francisco in particular was selected to signal the growing place of Pacific power—China was one of President Franklin D. Roosevelt's "Big Four" and a UN charter member—and the city's direct connection to the war, "from whose hills and wharves," as one observer put it, "every visitor could see ships loaded with troops and materials departing for the Pacific theatre of war and others returning homeward with victims of that war." Delegates from fifty-one countries gathered in the coastal city's cavernous War Memorial Opera House from April 25 to June 26, 1945, flanked by representatives from some 250 international organizations. Hundreds of officials and their technical staffs were on hand, while newspaper and radio journalists generated wall-to-wall international coverage of the daily deliberations, churning out a half million sheets of paper a day. So big was the spectacle that over 2,600 US Army and Navy personnel, 400 Red Cross workers, 800 Boy Scouts, and 200 additional telephone operators were hired to service the diplomatic carnival. "Never before," American delegate

Virginia C. Gildersleeve remarked, "had a great international conference considering matters of the gravest import taken place in such a blinding blaze of publicity." The *New York Post* went so far as to call it "the most important human gathering since the Last Supper." The past, present, and future of civilization itself was very much on the minds of the delegates, as the fledgling United Nations doubled as both a military coalition and the bearer of civilization for a shaken postwar world.[17]

Field Marshal Jan Christiaan Smuts, the South African prime minister and one of the few delegates who had taken part in the creation of the League of Nations twenty-six years before, captured the solemnity of the occasion in his opening address. "For the human race the hour has struck. Mankind has arrived at the crisis of its fate, the fate of its future as a civilized world," for whom a new charter must be based on a "faith in justice and the resolve to vindicate the fundamental rights of man." During the war, Smuts had made several speeches about the crisis of civilization and the need for a new international organization to secure peace once the war was over. In one 1941 broadcast on "A Vision of the New World Order," Smuts remarked that "already the free Democracies representing the forward movement in our western civilization are grouping themselves under the pressure of the times." Smuts pushed for a soaring preamble to the United Nations Charter to make clear to the world what the UN was about. In his eyes, its mission was above all "to prevent a recurrence of the fratricidal strife which twice in our generation has brought untold sorrow and loss upon mankind," and to reestablish faith in "the sanctity and ultimate value of human personality, in the equal rights of men and women and of nations large and small." These "Smuts principles" served as the backbone of the preamble, with an American touch added by Gildersleeve, who aligned its global address with the famous opening of the American Constitution: "We the Peoples of the United Nations . . ." The stark novelty of that summer's frenzied work was neatly summarized by one Canadian report: "Since the United Nations began their work at San Francisco, Germany has fallen, Churchill has fallen, the atomic bomb has fallen, Japan has fallen. Things have moved quickly, and these are the days of new foundations."[18]

San Francisco was a mixture of political theater and technical planning, and set its sights on nothing less than the making of a new global order. Much of Europe was under military occupation, and its fate was being discussed by foreign powers in a distant foreign country. The organization was to deliver on Roosevelt's vision of global order based on the Atlantic Charter of 1941, which called for the creation of a "wider and permanent system of general security" that would "afford to all nations the means of dwelling in safety within their own boundaries." What made San Francisco special was that it was not a postwar conference to negotiate a treaty, but rather a wartime conference in which all nations represented were still officially in a state of conflict when the conference opened. Neither the defeated Axis powers nor neutral countries like Switzerland and Sweden were invited. In the words of US secretary of state Edward R. Stettinius Jr., who chaired the US delegation, the conference was at once a "peoples' conference and a soldiers' conference." After a war fought against Axis aggression and the evils of Nazism, hopes were raised about building a new world order founded on international justice, human rights, racial equality, and the end of colonialism. Delegates were inundated with letters from well-wishers from around the globe. Gildersleeve received 65,000 of them, and in her memoir described how the letters "urged me on to secure an international organization which would prevent war and they sent me their blessings and told me that they were praying for me." President Harry Truman's arrival from Washington was accompanied by great fanfare as each attending country paraded its national flag through the streets of the city, cheered by throngs of onlookers. At the closing plenary session, Truman intoned, "We must build a new world—a far better world—one in which the eternal dignity of man is respected" in a "friendly civilized community of nations." According to the conference's final report, the plenary finished in a kind of rapture in which "the delegates and the entire audience rose and cheered."[19]

The transition from the League of Nations to the United Nations marked the shift from the old language of civilization to the more concrete language of individual rights and collective security. The League's infamous distinction between the "family of civilized nations" and the rest of the world was dropped in all UN documents, and civilization as a foundational moral norm was expunged from conference resolutions. But while human rights may have moved to the center of discussion in 1945, the language of civilization scarcely disappeared. On the contrary, it enjoyed a surprising new lease on life far beyond Smuts's opening salvo. In part this was because its meaning was so elastic, and, reinvigorated, could be used for claim making of all kinds. Its moral authority attracted diverse interests and advocates, who all wished to exploit the term to advance specific grievances or concerns. Civilization was sometimes converted into a moral appeal among the European defeated. In a letter of September 10, 1945, to the *Manchester Guardian*, the renowned Italian philosopher Benedetto Croce worried about possible punitive measures taken by the Allies against Italy, reminding them that "in history Italy, France and England are the three countries to whom most clearly Western Europe owes its civilization," so "mutilating, humiliating and squashing Italy" after the war is not "the way to provide for a peaceful and civilised international order." In 1945 the Council on African Affairs, chaired by African American activist Paul Robeson, published a pamphlet, *The San Francisco Conference and the Colonial Issue*, stating that world security pivoted on the exercise of self-determination "of all dependent peoples," who must be "integrated with other peoples in the general progress of the world toward a higher and more stable civilization." African American intellectual W. E. B. Du Bois—who, like Smuts, was present at the

Paris Peace Conference in 1919—raised the stakes by saying that the United Nations Charter should "make clear and unequivocal" the "straightforward stand of the civilized world for race equality" in order "to save human civilization from suicide," since what "was true of the United States in the past is true of world civilization today— we cannot exist half slave and half free." In their hands, the appeal to civilization was political leverage to hold powerful states to account. Others saw the mission of civilization defensively. British delegate and Conservative politician Robert Arthur James Gascoyne-Cecil, also known as Viscount Cranbourne, insisted that a postwar set- tlement must be based on divisions between "peoples of different races, peoples of different religions and peoples of different stages of civilization." Varied ideas of civilization thus swirled around San Francisco, signifying anything from European to universal, radical change to conservative restoration, colonialism to anticolonialism.[20]

It is well known that the most ambitious dreams of renewal and regeneration of 1945 met with consternation and disappointment. Women's lobby groups at the conference such as the Commission on the Status of Women, chaired by Danish diplomat Bodil Begtrup, left frustrated by the ways in which "implementing the peace" in the name of security and welfare for all was severely circumscribed. The same went for those campaigning for self-determination and formalized racial equality. To its detractors—much like those dis- appointed by the false promises of the League of Nations back in 1919—the new Charter was equally hamstrung by issues of empire, nationalism, and race. That Smuts, the South African premier and longtime champion of segregation and white settler rule, was the figure most responsible for the UN's preamble was greeted by critics as ironic and hypocritical. Du Bois acidly remarked that "we have conquered Germany," but "not their ideas. We still believe in white supremacy, keeping Negroes in their place and lying about democ- racy when we mean imperial control of 750 million of human beings in colonies." So for all the augurs of starting anew, the UN—at least in its early years—was largely designed to steady a shaken imperial order. The disappearance of civilization from international law hardly spelled its demise as a term of engagement; rather, claims of civilization moved their way to the center of other domains of European public discussion, including humanitarianism, international justice, empire, science, religion, and material welfare.[21]

RUIN AND RENEWAL EXPLORES HOW AND WHY THE BRUISED concept of civilization fired the imagination of many Europeans acutely aware of living in a fundamentally new era. There was never any unitary or agreed idea of what civilization is, but this is precisely what accounts for its staying power. It was malleable, inconsistent, and contentious, at times restrictive and other times expansive, yet it never failed to spark wide public interest and political attention. The broad currency of the term was directly related to the contradictory condition of Western Europe in 1945. The imposition of order on the continent by foreign forces was accompanied by the impulse by those Western European imperial powers that had suffered under Nazi occupation—France, the Netherlands, and Belgium—to reclaim their empires once the Third Reich had been defeated. It is well known that the French were busy putting down an uprising in Sétif, Algeria, on V-E Day, May 8, 1945. Yet this was no isolated event, illustrating the way in which these defeated European powers sought to recoup their crumbling empires. While interpreting imperialism as a function of France's humiliating defeat in the Franco-Prussian War of 1870–1871 has long been a way of understanding its late nineteenth-century expansion into Africa and Asia, this will to reconquer lost colonies took on renewed expression after 1945. What makes this development so striking is that the restoration of empire took place at a moment when much of Europe itself had been physically destroyed by Nazi occupation and war. Europe had become a hive of international relief agencies, foreign religious charities, and philanthropic organizations across much of the continent. Germany dramatized the fate of Europe in these crucial years. Whereas its imperial power reached its zenith in 1942, it was laid low by total defeat, physical destruction, and military occupation just three years later. Germany's status as a divided country may not have been reproduced everywhere in Europe, yet its new "colonial" status was viewed as emblematic of the fate of Europe, now spanning two superpower-dominated half continents. What emerged was something unique: in the period 1945–1955, Western Europe was an empire and colony at the same time, and civilizing missions of all kinds colored both dimensions of Western Europe's postwar predicament.

Individual chapters take up various aspects of why the new mission of civilization meant so much to so many for so long. They shed light on how and why the cultural wars of the not-so-distant past continue to shape contemporary Europe and its relationship to the wider world. They look at how Europe was remade in the 1940s and 1950s, and take up the themes of ruins, refugees, and relief, as well as international justice and military occupation. Unsurprisingly, the fate of defeated Germany—its leaders, victims, and beaten empire—framed the early Allied discussion of the re-civilization of occupied Europe, whose pacification helped ensure that the Cold War stayed cold. No less important were the visions of reviving the continent from the perspectives of militant Christianity. In the 1940s the churches—driven by a resurgent Catholic Church under Pope Pius XII—led the charge in reasserting their role in redrawing the cultural geography of Cold War Europe around the frontiers of faith, Christian democracy, and a new identity of the West. The defense of Christian civilization—and even Judeo-Christian civilization—was central to this mission. Conservative Western European ideas of the revival of a neomedieval *Abendland*, or land of the West, helped to overcome confessional divides between Catholics and Protestants in the fight against "godless" communism, and to ward off the undue influence from America as well. Moreover, a secular ideal of Western civilization was exploited by American military and cultural authorities to bridge the United States and Western Europe in a new transatlantic alliance, best evidenced in Marshall Plan aid and intervention in the Greek Civil War in the late 1940s.

But civilization was not used only to demarcate Western Europe from its Eastern European counterpart. At times the language of civilization was drafted to overcome the Cold War divide. Science, peace movements, housing, and etiquette books are telling examples of similarity and even cooperation. The dawning of atomic warfare sparked lively discussion in Europe about the implications of Hiroshima for the meaning of civilization, and gave rise to a number of like-minded organizations and peace movements across the Iron Curtain that aimed to "civilize" science as a source of peace and international cooperation. Attention will also be devoted to popular understandings of housing, the primacy of the family, manners manuals, and anxiety about the coming of "American civilization" in both Western and Eastern Europe. International organizations also played a pivotal role in bridging Cold War divisions in the name of civilization. UNESCO in particular emerged as the principal international agency that brokered a new conception of "world civilization" based on the idea of a shared universalist past, social science, and world heritage. In all these cases, the postwar idea of civilization was transformed into a more peaceful and less elitist understanding of universal material progress, which set it apart from its eighteenth- and nineteenth-century forerunners.

While the first half of the book concentrates on the European continent, the second half takes up Europe's changing place in the wider world. There the focus will be on empire, decolonization, and the challenges to multiculturalism in the 1970s and 1980s across the Cold War divide. The loss of Europe's overseas possessions not only afforded a fundamental transformation of Asian and African history, but European history as well, and new ideas of civilization gave meaning to these political upheavals on both sides. Notable here is the fallout from the violent reclamation of empire in Africa immediately after the war. The old vocabulary of the civilizing mission became the language of defense for imperial Britain, France, Belgium, and Portugal, as well as for anticommunist authoritarian regimes in Spain and Greece, and shaped their confrontation with communists and nationalists from beyond the West at the United Nations. Nonetheless, fantasies of civilization continued to inform European-African cultural connections even after the end of empire. As we shall see, Africa played a special role in the shifting frontiers and understanding of Europe from both imperial, anti-imperial, and postimperial perspectives. Ghana, Algeria, and Senegal in particular will be analyzed as examples of the recasting of the legacy of Europe for their own purposes. Here and elsewhere, African national elites inverted the rhetoric of European civilization in their struggles for independence and new national identities. In their own ways, these countries recast precolonial Afrocentric civilization as a key dimension of African modernization and sovereignty, and as such pioneered the historic mission to build distinctly new postimperial civilizations.

These newly independent African countries were not the only non-Westerners interested in repurposing civilization for different political ends. The same went for the Soviet Union and its satellite states, whose use of the term civilization reflected evolving relations between Eastern Europe and the wider world. At first this may seem puzzling, given that the Soviet Union and the Eastern Bloc initially greeted the concept of civilization with skepticism and disdain. Given the overt Western exploitation of the term in the early years of the Cold War, communists tended to dismiss Western civilization as simply ideological cover for barbarism, hypocrisy, and imperialism. Communist regimes rarely used the rhetoric of civilization directly, preferring other terms of engagement—humanism, justice, dignity, and solidarity—to promote the virtues of socialist political culture.

Beatrice and Sidney Webb, leading lights of the British democratic socialist Fabian Society, were the first to apply the concept to the Soviet Union in their 1936 book *Soviet Communism: A New Civilization?* (the question mark fell away in the 1944 reprint), but civilization enjoyed comparatively little domestic resonance in the Soviet Union at the time. And yet, Soviet ideologues enlisted the language of civilization in peril during the Second World War, as well as in the Soviet press during the Nuremberg Trial. The neologism of socialist civilization thereafter emerged as a common self-description of the communist world's new global role during its encounter with Asia and Africa in the 1960s. At that time the Soviet Union and the smaller Eastern European states spearheaded a wide variety of "soft power" initiatives to build solidarity with prospective socialist partners in the developing world, especially in Africa. Eastern Bloc states forged their national identities and international mission around the socialist principles of peace, welfare, and gender equality as signal contributions to social betterment. Eastern Europe's modernization crusade became a socialist version of the civilizing mission, as the Soviet Union, Eastern Europe, and especially Yugoslavia developed a remarkable network of cultural connections across Africa in the wake of decolonization. There was another dimension to the modernization drive, as Eastern Europeans dedicated a great deal of energy to championing the preservation of indigenous Third World traditions (from folk art to archaeology) in the name of anti-imperialism and international fellowship. Socialist humanism and socialist civilization became bridge concepts to convey anti-imperial kinship with Third World counterparts. In Eastern Europe, civilization also surfaced in discussions about science and the coming of industrial society, and was embraced by dissidents like Václav Havel to analyze socialism's "technological civilization." Socialist conceptions of civilization drove archaeology campaigns in the 1970s and later shaped Gorbachev's understanding of "European civilization" and his reform-era "return to Europe."

To be clear, this book is no "spot the word" exercise, in which the political usage of civilization is plotted in a kind of crude "*n*-gram" analysis of broad linguistic trends. The departure point is rather how various social groups understood and acted to protect civilization in a threatening political world, often in relation to cognate terms like heritage, tradition, humanity, and even democracy. The geographical scope of analysis has also been widened beyond the typical, exclusively Western history of concepts to trace how the term traveled across the continent as well as to Europe's former African colonies, where it was inverted and recast for fresh political objectives by independent African states. In the late 1960s, the ideology of civilization rebounded back to continental Europe in new and dangerous guises.

For decades, studies of civilization have been the preserve of intellectual historians and international relations theorists, who mostly use the term to describe the rise, expansion, and justification of European power abroad. What attention has been accorded to the subject is usually confined to the history of ideas, and in particular to the rise and fall of international law as the "gentle civilizer" of international relations. This book removes the story of civilization from the confines of international law to show how it figured prominently in public discussions of postwar Europe more generally. My approach also diverges from standard histories of the period, and does so in several ways. Unlike the impressive political surveys of post-1945 European history by Tony Judt, Mark Mazower, Konrad Jarausch, and Ian Kershaw, I will include not only Western and Eastern Europe, but also empire, international organizations, decolonization, and multiculturalism in the broader discussion. Accounts of post-1945 Europe that rely exclusively on stories of economic recovery, political stability, and Cold War division neglect these key cultural developments, as do those that focus solely on the Americanization and Sovietization of Cold War European culture. What follows is a blend of political, intellectual, and cultural history, one that includes religion, science, photography, architecture, and archaeology. New notions of civilization meant new cultural maps of Europe, ones that redefined the relationships between Western Europe, Eastern Europe, and European overseas territories both before and after decolonization. *Ruin and Renewal* does not approach postwar European history as a tale of superpower domination or as a collection of discrete national stories; instead, it tracks the ways in which the language of civilization enabled elites and ordinary citizens to reshape the very meaning of Europe amid political conditions often not of their choosing.[22]

This book is no self-congratulatory story of Europeans learning to live peacefully with their neighbors, having built a shiny peaceable kingdom atop the charred ruins of the past. No doubt the pacification of Western Europe is a remarkable story in itself, and the awarding of the Nobel Peace Prize to the European Union in 2012 as the keeper of the peace is only the latest installment in this affirmative account of a re-civilized Europe. To this day many studies of twentieth-century Europe tend to be tales of two halves—the first half characterized by war, destruction, crisis, and revolution, with the second half depicted as a narrative of imposed peace, political stability, and widening prosperity across the blocs. This characterization is too simple, however, for the postwar period itself can be divided into two halves, and the changing usage of civilization points up larger political transformations. By the 1970s, civilization had migrated from progressive campaigns of moral reconstruction, anticolonialism, and anti-Westernism to the shoring up of various conservative regimes and causes under threat. In the final two decades of the Cold War, civilization became closely aligned with counterrevolutionary nativism in the form of anti-immigration, the Christian West, and the retreat from multiculturalism. The right-wing co-optation of civilization has only intensified in the wake of 9/11, as international terrorism and the refugee crisis have weaponized the civilization-in-crisis theme in ways not seen since the early Cold War.

This book is by no means advocating the rehabilitation of its mission for our time; instead, it seeks to show how and why it has rested at the heart of Europe's fractured identity and history since 1945. The reinvented legacy of civilization in each postwar decade, as we shall see, remained deeply indebted to both strands of its Enlightenment heritage—civility and violence.

Ruin and Renewal is a different history of the remaking of Europe after 1945 that places the continent's damaged and disputed heritage center stage. Whereas Europe's civilizing mission had once been exported to all corners of the globe in the name of progress and development, this mission boomeranged back to Europe with the cease-fire. By the late 1940s Europe had become a primary testing ground for the "re-civilizing process" in an era of division and decolonization. The political and cultural makeover of the continent may have been spearheaded by the superpowers in uneven manners, but Europeans found ways to recast their place in history and in the world from new angles. Civilization provided a means of thinking about Europe and its postwar condition beyond the nation-state, Cold War division, and empire, and offers us a useful lens today through which we can reinterpret European history after World War II. The deep tensions that bedeviled the San Francisco conference in 1945 have animated the development of European affairs ever since. In an era in which the headlines are about the disintegration of Europe, this book returns attention to the radical reconstruction of Europe in the shadow of a much bigger crisis exactly three-quarters of a century ago. How and why the old and much-maligned faith in civilization helped map and maintain Europe's inheritance after World War II is the main theme of this book.

one

CALL TO ALMS

IN JULY 1945 ENGLISH POET STEPHEN SPENDER JOURNEYED from France to Germany on special assignment. He had lived in Hamburg and Berlin during the dying years of the Weimar Republic, and hadn't been back since. This time, Spender arrived in Germany as an officer for the Allied Control Commission in the British Zone of Occupation with an unusual six-month task, namely "to inquire into the lives and ideas of German intellectuals, with a particular view to discovering any surviving talent in German literature" and "of inquiring into the condition of libraries." He kept a diary of his mission, which was quickly brought out in 1946 as *European Witness*, one of the earliest firsthand reflections on decimated Europe. A few years earlier, in 1942, Spender had published a cycle of poems called *Ruins and Visions* that combined private experiences with the themes of air raids, the Nazi takeover of France, and death itself, yet nothing prepared him for the shock and scale of the ruins and visions that awaited him in Germany. The Cologne cityscape—or what was left of it—overwhelmed him: "My first impression on passing through was of there being not a single house left"; the charred, broken walls "served as a thin mask in front of the damp, hollow, stinking emptiness of gutted interiors." No less unsettling was that the ruins equally characterized the survivors: "The ruin of the city is reflected in the internal ruin of its inhabitants" who "resemble rather a tribe of wanderers who have discovered a ruined city in a desert and who are camping there, living in the cellars and hunting amongst the ruins for the booty, relics of a dead civilization."[1]

For Spender, the smoking remains of the bomb-blasted cities signified much more than the immolation of Hitler's Third Reich. These "corpse-towns" had become "an achievement of our civilization" whose ruins were "the shape created by our century as the Gothic cathedral is the shape created by the Middle Ages." Spender's admitted depression about the obscene "shape created by our century" was inseparable from his more nagging concern about "the potentiality of the ruin of Germany to become the ruins of the whole of Europe." Just as disturbing to him was the growing "sense as I walked along the streets of Bonn with a wind blowing putrescent dust of ruins as stinging as pepper into my nostrils" that "the whole of our civilization was protected by such eggshell walls which could be blown down in a day."[2]

Spender was hardly alone in his descriptions of the collapse of civilization in Zero Hour Europe. For him and others, the invocation of civilization was far removed from Romantic-era meditations on crumbling cultural inheritance from the early nineteenth century. As we shall see, these were narratives of overwhelming shock and rupture, ones that spelled the dramatic collapse of European power and cultural might. The magnitude of destruction was also a call to action. This chapter will look at how foreign observers, charity workers, and international relief agents from the newly created United Nations Relief and Rehabilitation Administration (UNRRA) bore witness to a Europe in ruins, and were at the front line of material and moral rehabilitation in the immediate aftermath of war. This was no small historical development, to the extent that it marked the full reversal of Europe's nineteenth-century civilizing mission. Europe, long the energetic missionary power in all parts of the globe, had now become a site of busy missionary activity and outside influence. Foreign relief agencies—both religious and secular—dispensed aid to those who had suffered under Axis occupation; UNRRA established missions in sixteen countries across Europe and cared for displaced persons (DPs) in Germany, Austria, and Italy. These massive and internationally coordinated missions were bold experiments in internationalism in the wake of the war, and became a source of conflict and controversy. The Cold War—whose beginning is usually attributed to the 1947 Truman Doctrine or the Berlin Airlift of 1948–1949—was already assuming form in the DP camps. Attention will be paid to the diaries and photographs of these international aid workers confronted by ruins, refugees, and what was commonly called the crisis of civilization. Foreign volunteers who staffed the religious charities and intergovernment agencies were among the first narrators and builders of postwar Europe, whose work was central to the moral and material reconstruction of the continent.

THE YEAR 1945 WAS A CALAMITOUS ONE OF RECKONING, EVIdenced by the mountains of rubble, ash, and dead bodies disfiguring the continent. Whole cities had been wiped out, and flattened Guernica, Rotterdam, Caen, Dresden, and Warsaw became the architectural signatures of the age of total war. Over 90 percent of Warsaw's dwellings were damaged beyond repair, and Minsk, Budapest, Kiev, and Kharkov suffered a similar fate, as did many German cities by the end of the war. Even so, Berlin occupied a special place in the geography of destruction. American war correspondent William Shirer described Berlin as "a great wilderness of debris, dotted with roofless, burnt-out buildings that look like mousetraps with the low sun shining through the spaces where windows had been." Death, eerie silence, and a sense of finality dominated contemporary accounts of defeated Germany. One British soldier in Berlin was struck by the "silence over everything," in which people "talk in low voices as if they are afraid to wake the dead below the debris." Soviet war correspondents noted, often with satisfaction, that Berlin was "a chaos of huge craters and smoke-blackened stone, shattered concrete, twisted girders and broken glass."[3]

Observers experienced the sheer incomprehensibility of destruction, not least in terms of the radically changed fortunes of Germany and Germans. Shirer recorded in his Berlin diary on November 3, 1945—almost six months after the cease-fire—about the impossibility of finding "words to convey truthfully and accurately the picture of a great capital destroyed almost beyond recognition," of the total defeat of the once-brazen "master race" now "poking about in the ruins, broken, dazed, shivering, hungry human beings without will or purpose or direction, reduced like animals to foraging for food and seeking shelter in order to cling to life for another day." *New Yorker* journalist Janet Flanner underlined how the Second World War differed from its predecessor—defeat "in the last war did not cost Germany a stone. This time the destroyer of others is herself destroyed." Cornelia Stabler Gillam, a young Quaker from Philadelphia who came over to Europe to play piano concerts in US Army canteens, described the destruction of the cathedral city of Aachen in a June 1945 letter to her parents: "People crawling likes rats out of the ruined buildings where they live," and "I was afraid several times that I would cry, and I knew that it would be misunderstood. I would not be weeping for the Germans but for all the world."[4]

German writers registered shock and bewilderment too, especially those returning from exile. Klaus Mann recorded his confusion and despair as he revisited his beloved Munich, on this occasion as a reporter for the American military newspaper *Stars and Stripes*: "What used to be the fairest town in Germany" had been "transformed into a vast cemetery," and "I could hardly find my way through the once familiar streets." Theodor Plievier, who journeyed from Moscow to Germany in the spring of 1945, recounted the "strangely ghostlike" atmosphere of Dresden, with "wave after wave of rubble and masonry frozen into immobility." In his essay "A Journey through the City of Ruins," Arnold Zweig interpreted the ruins of Berlin as the "backkick of total war," a gruesome quid pro quo: "it was here that it was unleashed: a hundred thousand throats yelled their assent in the Sport Palace—and so a hundred thousand houses here are reduced to rubble, including that very Sport Palace," as "Berlin paid dearly for Hitler and Goebbels' rhetorical sport." For Zweig and others, the destruction of Berlin was fitting payback for the violence unleashed by the Third Reich's war machine that rebounded onto Germany in the last two years of the war.[5]

Berlin inspired historical reflections on the fate of Europe in total disarray, drawing links to classical history to make sense of the destruction. Spender approached the ruins of the Reichstag and Chancellery "with the same sense of wonder, the same straining of the imagination, as one goes to the Colosseum at Rome." Peering through his airplane window over Berlin in 1945, Harry Hopkins, longtime advisor to President Franklin D. Roosevelt, likened Berlin to a "second Carthage." The Polish émigré historian living in England Isaac Deutscher compared the bombed-out former capital of the Third Reich to the ruins of antiquity, writing in *The Observer* in 1946 that "Berlin evokes the impression of a miraculously preserved ruin of classical antiquity—like Pompeii or Ostia—on a gigantic scale." This romance with ruins is something that had been envisioned during the Third Reich itself, as Albert Speer wistfully anticipated the noble beauty of his Berlin monumental architecture shimmering in a state of natural decay centuries later. By 1945 Speer's infamous ruin theory of value had been fulfilled with savage realization, as the remnants of the Thousand-Year Reich had become the mute rubble of total defeat.[6]

Foreigners noted how German survivors responded to this destruction. One Quaker relief worker recorded that "I have seen a sort of numbed despair, that so many beautiful cities, that one has known once, are now no more—one can hardly yet realise the extent of irreparable loss." This sense of despair did not go away quickly. Another English Quaker, describing an art exhibition in Berlin in May 1946, found a "staggering revelation of the state of chaos and depression of the German mind at present," which "all added up to a tale of horror and downfall and nothingness." While Londoners celebrated Germany's unconditional surrender with "wild excitement in Trafalgar Square, half London seemed to be floodlit," as one diarist put it, Germany was plunged in darkness and silence. German diarists used the terms "point zero" or "zero hour" (*Stunde Null*) to convey the utter collapse of their world. An entry from a Königsberger on V-E Day tallied up the effects of the war by saying that the "upshot of the dream of a world-dominating Greater Germany was Europe in ruins with a vastly enlarged sphere of influence for the Soviet Union." The scale of ruination was perhaps best captured by one fourteen-year-old boy from Berlin who in May 1945 observed corpses "lying around in parks, at the roadside, often looted to such an extent that it was impossible to tell whether a body belonged to a shot soldier or a murdered civilian." "Raped women," he continued, "with their mouths wide open, their gold teeth torn out by robbers. Some half charred in the ruins of burnt-down houses. It wasn't lilac, it wasn't hyacinths that gave this spring its sweet scent."[7]

Nowhere was this sense of physical and moral ruination more evident than in the accounts of the liberation of the concentration camps. In his 1948 memoir *Crusade in Europe*, Supreme Commander of Allied Forces in Europe Dwight D. Eisenhower recalled how the liberation of Ohrdruf, a subsidiary camp near Buchenwald, brought him "face to face with indisputable evidence of Nazi brutality and ruthless disregard of every shred of decency," adding that "I have never at any other time experienced an equal sense of shock." So affected was Eisenhower that he dispatched an immediate communiqué to both Washington and London about his impressions, urging them to send "a random group of newspaper editors" and elected representa-

36

tives from both countries to Germany to "leave no room for cynical doubt." Twelve American congressmen and eighteen newspaper editors—along with eight members of the House of Commons—toured Buchenwald in April 1945 to see for themselves what one of the accompanying American reporters called an "organized crime against civilization." One British Labour MP, Mavis Tate, elaborated on the point in a *Spectator* article: "I have returned from Germany" and witnessed "the deep streak of evil and sadism in the German race, such as one ought not to expect to find in a people who for generations have paid lip-service to Western culture and civilization."[8]

British witnesses recounted the discovery of the Belsen "horror camp" as the grimmest expression of Nazi cruelty and suffering humanity. BBC war correspondent Richard Dimbleby reported that "I passed through the barrier and found myself in a nightmare. Dead bodies, some of them in decay, lay strewn about the road and along the rutted tracks." On April 24, 1945, the German mayor of Celle and other mayors from the area were summoned as representatives of the German people to view the atrocities of Belsen, with a message in German read over the loudspeaker: "What you see here is such a disgrace to the German people that their name must be erased from the list of civilized nations." One mayor covered his eyes and wept, while another became sick. Jewish rabbi Leslie Hardman of the British VIII Corps simply asked that British officers treat liberated inmates with patience, for they had been subjected "not only to a deliberate extermination of themselves as a people, but to a disintegration of their souls."[9]

Belsen survivors recounted how "eerie silence marked the moment of our liberation. We were too weak, and had experienced too much, to feel joy." One British soldier recorded that liberated prisoners "seemed beyond articulate speech, even supposing we had found a common language." The way in which Belsen marked both an end and turning point of civilization itself was acidly conveyed by the opening sentence of Sergeant W. J. Barclay's Belsen report: "Belsen.

It is the 21st of April in the year of civilization 1945." An accusatory sign at the entrance of the Bergen camp before it was burned down on May 21, 1945, was posted by the British authorities, ending with: "10,000 unburied dead were found here, another 13,000 have since died, all of them victims of the German New Order in Europe and an Example of Nazi Kultur."[10]

The language of the end of days was commonplace, as were apocalyptic descriptions of Germany in total defeat and destruction. At the Yalta and Potsdam conferences a vanquished Germany—and its former capital—was quartered into zones and occupied. Germans had no rights or authority of their own, and were at the mercy of the Allies. While some observers then—and many historians since—have disputed this tabula rasa sentiment for obscuring many continuities with the past, Zero Hour parlance revealed a great deal about the perceived historical moment, one in which past and future seemed to dissolve into a permanent present. Other major historical upheavals from the past—like the French and Russian Revolutions—proudly proclaimed the messianic significance of their national political revolution as a major global rupture, literally rewriting the calendar of history in such a way that modern political time began in 1789 or 1917. While the Nazi Revolution of 1933 did not bring with it the same millennial sense of calendrical caesura, the self-description of a "thousand-year" Third Reich was widely circulated. Goebbels and other Nazi ideologues never tired of boasting that Hitler's unpredicted assumption of power in 1933 served as the twentieth century's French Revolution both in power and scope, more far-reaching than its hated Soviet forerunner.[11]

The term "zero hour" signified utter disaster and destruction, the obverse of the hopeful revolutionary proclamations of the past. It was a description of negation, the emptying out of historical time. The experience of living through dark times was nothing new to Central Europe—similar apocalyptic sentiments were recorded during the Black Death and the Thirty Years War, as well as at the beginning and end of the Great War. The harrowing Great Inflation of the early Weimar Republic was often characterized by the explosion of zeroes in everyday life, most dramatically with its ever-diminishing currency—at one point in 1924, 1 trillion Reichsmarks were equivalent to a single American dollar. The carnivalesque stories of the inflation years when people hurriedly trundled wheelbarrows of paper notes to the bank for deposit before they depreciated even further encapsulated the topsy-turvy quality of economic life in the early Weimar Republic. German Bulgarian Nobel laureate writer Elias Canetti chronicled how a whole world based on thrift, rational exchange, and above all psychological predictability—to say nothing of the sturdy presence of the past and optimism toward the future— had suddenly vanished for individual and nation alike "under the sign of Zero." In 1945 the meaning of *zero* was radically different, as total defeat led to a shortage of food, shelter, political stability, and moral order not seen since the Thirty Years War. Unlike during the Weimar Republic, 1945 was not the mass production of zeroes and ever-diminishing material worth; rather, it signaled the fall of value and civilization itself, a kind of Ground Zero of European culture. Ruins and DPs now characterized the continent, as cigarettes, misery, and blaming others became the common currency of exchange in Central Europe.[12]

FOR ALL THE MEMORABLE ACCOUNTS OF DEVASTATED CENTRAL Europe by writers and other observers, a great deal needed to be done on the ground. Civilization was more than simply reference to a shaken set of values, it was a matter of urgent practical organization. Under these circumstances, civilization shifted from its traditional status as a lexicon of elites to a call to alms for the victims of war. Much of the daily administration of the displaced persons camps was carried out by foreign relief workers from abroad, mostly from Britain, France, Canada, and the United States. Millions of DPs, expellees, and POWs peopled the continent, huddled in makeshift relief camps dotted around the former war zones of Central and Southern Europe. Swedish novelist Stig Dagerman, in his 1946 *German Autumn*, portrayed refugees as both witnesses and emblems of the times: "Ragged, staring and unwelcome, they crowded in the dark, stinking station-bunkers or in the giant windowless bunkers that look like rectangular gasometers, looming like huge monuments to defeat in Germany."[13]

By the end of the war, there were over 40 million displaced persons in Europe. In Germany alone, there were 8 million civilians who qualified as DPs in 1945, 10 percent of them Jewish. While wartime planners had done their best to anticipate the crisis, the scale of dislocation and population transfers was overwhelming. Already in 1944 Assistant Secretary of State Dean Acheson remarked before the US House of Representatives that "I believe that not since the Middle Ages has there been any such movement of population as this war has brought about." Everywhere the breakdown of stable society, moral authority, and basic infrastructure was visible. The scope of emergency went beyond the pressing problems of repairing bombed-out buildings and roads, usable water supplies, sanitation systems, hospitals, and schools. Malaria and tuberculosis stalked the continent, and famine was rife, especially in Vienna and Budapest. No less challenging were the often violent and unbalanced survivors themselves. Their behavior was attributed to psychological trauma associated with wartime violence, the disintegration of family life, and the collapse of moral order. Postwar Europe was often described as a continent of women, but it was also a continent of children orphaned or separated from their families. In 1946 there were some 180,000 vagrant children living in Rome, Naples, and Milan. In the DP camps there was wide discussion of the troubling presence of so-called wolf children, who, in the words of British American writer Alice Bailey, "lack all moral sense and have no civilized values."[14]

Humanitarianism was coordinated in new ways to aid the tens of millions of DPs. Many of the organizations were private and religious charities founded during the Second World War to carry out relief work in Europe and Asia. The Unitarian Service Committee was established in 1940, Catholic Relief Services in 1943, the Lutheran World Relief in 1945, and perhaps most famously, the Cooperative for American Remittances to Europe, or CARE, in 1945. The presence of foreign relief workers in Europe was hardly novel. The Red Cross was founded in 1864, after which national branches were set up in many countries to aid victims of natural and man-made disasters. They were joined by other services, such as the American Jewish Joint Distribution Committee (est. 1914) and the American Friends Service Committee (est. 1917). After the Great War, the social reformer Eglantyne Jebb founded the British Save the Children Fund, and a number of other private agencies were created during the Second World War to help civilians under siege. The Jewish Relief and Rescue Committee was active in Budapest in 1944–1945, and a 1942 report by the American Jewish Joint Distribution Committee on "Aiding Jews Overseas" chronicled some of its relief efforts amid harrowing conditions. While the report grimly stated that even if "all in all, the record is one of destruction, of death, of despair," the JDC managed to "bring help and hope to hundreds of thousands," and was the single largest provider of aid in the American occupation zone in Germany.[15]

Relief workers bore witness to a destitute Europe. The growth of privately organized humanitarian outreach after 1945 was often interpreted—especially in relation to Christian groups—as part of a new mission to "re-Christianize" postwar Europe in the wake of war and political violence. Certainly, this was a key issue for some church authorities, as we will see in Chapter 3. But for most relief workers, the main task at hand was simply to assist those in need. Missionary Europe became the target of foreign care and consolation.

Catholic relief workers arrived in force in 1945. Vatican relief missions sent Catholic aid workers to all three western zones of Germany after the war in order to give spiritual and medical relief to the displaced. Catholic Relief Services was among the first to arrive in Italy after the war, after which they established relief operations in Germany, Poland, and Czechoslovakia. While Catholic relief groups had tended to focus on helping Polish Catholics in the last two years of the war, and then German Catholics after the war, they soon expanded their charity to all those at risk. As the head of the Vatican Mission in Belsen, Abbé Regnault, made clear, Catholics would administer aid to all, with "no distinction between race or religion," since we "are at the service of mankind." Such Catholic outreach was in part to make good on international criticism that the Church had done little to help Jews in their time of need, and to signal that Rome would play a more active role in postwar European affairs.[16]

Protestant humanitarians were equally present. Among Lutherans there was deep concern that more than a fifth of all Lutherans worldwide were refugees after the Second World War, especially in Germany, and were in desperate need of material assistance. Scandinavians and Swiss brethren lent their support, and a Canadian Lutheran World Relief was formed in 1946. In the first three months of 1946 alone, Lutheran World Relief sent over 2,260 bales of clothes and bedding, plus 245 crates of shoes, to Germany, Finland, Holland, Czechoslovakia, Belgium, and Yugoslavia. Quakers were particularly active on the ground in 1945, building on their tradition of dispensing relief in war zones. They were not the biggest relief outfit—numbering around 1,200 volunteers in 1945—but they were highly experienced and efficient. The Society of Friends had been aiding victims of war since the Crimean War, and in the Second World War the Quakers' Friends Ambulance Unit had engaged in Egypt, Greece, El Alamein, France, China, Burma, Syria, Ethiopia, and India. After 1945 their European presence was felt from Sicily and Greece to Yugoslavia and Austria, and of course in Germany. What distinguished the Quakers was their policy of providing aid to all those in need, including former enemies, which did not always endear them to the military authorities or their national publics back home.[17]

Foreign aid workers were some of the first narrators of Europe after the war. In notebooks and memoirs they gave voice to the plight of Europe in the aftermath of World War II, and their accounts of the brutality, unfamiliarity, and lack of moral direction of Europe are revealing sources of everyday life just after the capitulation. Many of them were seasoned relief workers, having cut their teeth during the First World War and later the Spanish Civil War. But even they were overwhelmed by Europe's new circumstances. That their diaries carried titles like *The Wild Place*, *By the Rivers of Babylon*, and *Europe Without Baedeker* reflected a sense of bewilderment about how Europe now appeared alien and unfamiliar. Many felt the strain from the heavy demands of ministering assistance, and some admitted to not being kindly disposed toward the Germans. Red Cross worker Robert Collis could not help seeing the devastation of Osnabrück as just deserts for the German attack on Rotterdam in 1940, since "they started it." A French relief worker, mourning the death of her brother in the war, recorded her rage toward Germans by saying, "I hate them ferociously!" and "No civilized people would ever have accepted the effects of such a dreadful dictatorship." One English relief worker assigned to the German Wildflecken DP camp laconically admitted: "Since I've seen a poor creature's number tattooed on his body I don't feel so friendly."[18]

This humanitarian sensibility suffused the photographs taken by Quaker and Catholic relief workers. They usually captured informal scenes of philanthropic service, camaraderie, and even friendship. The accent fell on moments of communion between donor and receiver, often invoking the traditional iconography of Christian charity. This can be seen in Figure 1, in which Monsignor Alfred Schneider, the Catholic Relief Services director for Germany, is pictured giving

Figure 1. Monsignor Alfred Schneider, Catholic Relief Services director for Germany, giving aid to homeless German children, 1945. *Credit: Eileen Egan,* Catholic Relief Services: Beginning Years: For the Life of the World *(New York: Catholic Relief Services, 1988)*

food to a homeless child in a German DP camp, or in Figure 2, depicting a nun embracing an elderly refugee in an unnamed camp. Here and elsewhere Catholics are portrayed as offering alms to the poor and downtrodden in classic missionary style. Quaker images are slightly different, in that they tended to be less-staged celebrations of comradeship with DPs, taken during meals, at play, and even at weddings. In part this had to do with the media and audience of communication. Catholic images of almsgiving were sometimes reproduced in church publicity outlets, whereas Quakers rarely intended to publish their photographs, and those that did appear were reprinted in published diaries only decades later.[19]

The accounts of Quakers captured their understanding of the relief mission in Europe. A number of them chronicled the shock of discovering the "very many unburied dead lying all over the place and the living dead crawling through the muck." British Quaker

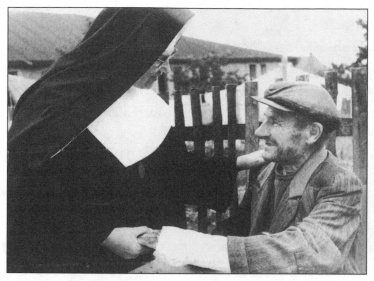

Figure 2. Catholic Relief Services nun, giving aid to expellees, Germany, 1945. *Credit: Eileen Egan,* Catholic Relief Services: Beginning Years: For the Life of the World *(New York: Catholic Relief Services, 1988)*

Roger Wilson recounted his relief work from 1940 to 1948 in France, Germany, Italy, Holland, Austria, and Poland. Like many others, he documented the maddening lack of provisions, as well as the difficulty of requisitioning clothes, mattresses, towels, food, and milk. Things became more grave when he moved from Greece to Germany and was faced with countless POWs, refugees, a flourishing black market, and rampant crime. For him, improving German perceptions of non-Germans and attending to the bodies and souls of forlorn Europeans were noble expressions of Christian charity. As he put it, the "worst damage of war lies not in its infrequent spectacular episodes, but in the slow, steady corruption of the human spirit." For many Quakers, the Friends Relief Service found its vocation in acting on "a wonderful sense of common responsibility before God that gave happiness, peace and strength." While many DPs and expellees reportedly found Quakers strange, and were particularly puzzled by their pacifism, the Friends managed to build lasting relations of trust, sympathy, and mutual understanding in the camps.[20]

British Quaker Margaret McNeill's memoir, *By the Rivers of Babylon*, is a particularly revealing source. The title of her book refers to the biblical passage, "By the rivers of Babylon there we sat down / Yea, we wept when we remembered Zion," and her account of Europe's "unhappy exiles," told with sympathy and compassion, captured the confusion and insecurity of DP life in Germany and Poland. She recounted how the Quakers' work often challenged the cool and detached relationship between military occupier and desperate refugees. On her first day in a DP camp in Germany on July 1, 1945, McNeill wrote that "amidst all the filth a group of people were busily engrossed in scraping a dead pig prepatory to some cooking orgy. There was an absolute babel of Polish and other lesser-known tongues and through it all walked the British Army with an expression of jaundiced endurance." Like other aid workers, she saw her task as going beyond simply doling out food and provisions, including helping to explain to Germans why the Allies were hostile toward them. "Again and again we were amazed at the ignorance of the ordinary German of the reason for the hatred and contempt shown toward Germany by those countries which her armies had occupied," and most of them "looked upon the privileges, such as they were, which the Allies extended to the DPs as nothing more than a deliberate taunt to humiliate the Germans." Other accounts noted how German civilians looked enviously at assistance offered to Jews by foreign aid workers, sometimes to the point that many "began to weigh Auschwitz against Dresden and to compare the forced emigration of Germans from the East with the persecution of the Jews." Such views jibed with what Hannah Arendt, in her 1950 "Report from Germany" for the journal *Commentary*, called the Germans' "escape from responsibility" and refusal to "come to terms with what really happened." Tales of denial and victimization became the dominant war stories of German survivors through the

1950s and beyond, and McNeill was one of the first foreigners to record its articulation.[21]

Striking too were McNeill's views on the problems with reintroducing culture as civilizing comfort for the DPs. It is well known that the DPs enthusiastically set up libraries, theaters, newspapers, craft exhibitions, song evenings, competitive sporting events, and orchestras in the camps in an effort to undo years of cultural deprivation. Relief workers carefully documented these initiatives, but they also noted the outbreak of "competitive nationalism" in the camps around cultural events. In response, Quaker charity workers promoted traditional dance performances in the camps—rather than craft shows or sports—in the belief that dance encouraged curiosity and cooperation with other national cultures. Sometimes the resuscitation of culture even caused grief. McNeill drew attention to the mismatch between the missionary zeal of foreign relief workers to use cultural activities as a salve of war and the damaged psychology of war survivors. A "love of culture does not necessarily draw people together," since for many DPs culture was "something inextricably associated with their shattered past" and "the outcome of a stable and self-respecting society" before the war, which made it "something far too delicate and complex to be goaded into living growth by tournaments and discussion groups." Here and elsewhere relief work exposed the limit of cultural regeneration and the need to scale back expectations. In the end, McNeill concluded, we "no longer tried to organize culture for the DPs, but simply shared with them the things that gave us so much pleasure ourselves." Such accounts of the interaction between religious charity workers and the DPs provided an early indication of the dreams and limitations of the new civilizing mission.[22]

IN THE WORLD OF RELIEF WORK, THE MOST CONSPICUOUS NEW-comers to Europe were those associated with the UN's newly created special relief organ, the United Nations Relief and Rehabilitation Administration, which differed from the religious charities in fundamental ways. UNRRA was created in 1943, when representatives from forty-four associated nations met in the East Room of the White House to sign an agreement pledging cooperation to administer aid—in the words of President Franklin Delano Roosevelt—to the "victims of German and Japanese barbarism." Though it was called a United Nations special agency, UNRRA actually preceded the official creation of the UN by two years. The Americans took the lead with funding and organizing UNRRA's relief efforts, which one commentator described as "the first blueprint of the postwar order." Offices were set up in China, the Philippines, Korea, and the Middle East to help with the transition from war to peace, providing a "gateway to recovery." What distinguished the new agency was the accent on international cooperation, for out of World War II, as one brochure phrased it, had grown "the idea of nations united in action, pooling their resources for the common good."[23]

The urgency of food and housing in wartime Europe led to debates on both sides of the Atlantic about the bare minimum of civilized life across Europe, and helped give shape to the development of new international organizations and European welfare states. Influential in this respect was a wartime conference organized by the International Bureau of the Fabian Society at the University of Oxford in December 1942, dedicated to the theme of the relief and reconstruction of Europe. It was a star-studded event, featuring the likes of British public intellectuals Leonard Woolf, Julian Huxley, and Harold Laski. Labour MP Philip Noel-Baker opened the conference by drawing attention to the portentous historical moment, saying that "the Armistice will begin the greatest opportunity for collective progress which mankind has ever had." No one dramatized the high stakes involved more than the eminent Victorian Leonard Woolf. Notwithstanding "burnt and bombed cities," he said, the "real problem will be the ruin and wreckage of human life, of civilization itself," because "these people are the real ruins and wreckage of our civilization which the Nazis and war have wrecked and ruined." For Woolf, the re-civilization of Europe must begin with a blend of democracy and international planning, so that "out of the ashes of barbarism, Hitlerism, and war, there may rise a new order, the civilized society of free men." Huxley spoke along similar lines about the need to move beyond the "Wilsonian fiction of the equality and sovereignty of all nations" so as to coordinate a new international relief mission; Laski went so far as to say that what was needed was a new associative "machinery of relief" that would "recreate the atmosphere in which civilized life again becomes possible." These English Fabians were not alone, and there was a great deal of international discussion in the early 1940s within government circles, international organizations, and charity groups about what to do with Europe once the Nazis had been defeated.[24]

UNRRA was to make good on Article 6 of the Atlantic Charter of 1941, which set out American and British war aims, including the hope that people everywhere might lead their lives "free from fear and want." Of paramount concern was to avoid a repeat of the epidemics that afflicted Europe after the First World War. The Spanish influenza pandemic of 1918–1919 killed more civilians in four months of peace than all combatants killed in battle in four years. UNRRA's main task was to help feed, clothe, and house war victims across Europe and Asia, with a focus on providing water, food, public health, clothes, shelter, technical expertise, consumer necessities, and communications. It was driven by practical concerns, as legions of doctors, nurses, and care workers were dispatched to fight disease and want. The new UN agency was thus the humanitarian face of the wartime Grand Alliance, but it was much more besides. It undertook to locate missing people, oversee refugee centers, and repatriate children. What also set it apart from other aid organizations was that it was neither private, national, nor religious. In fact, UNRRA was a kind of coordinating operation, entrusted with uniting the relief efforts of more than forty national governments and private philanthropic groups across Europe and Asia, marking a new departure in the history of what historian Jessica Reinisch has called "missionary internationalism."[25]

Such internationally organized aid raised questions about the relationship between humanitarianism and national sovereignty. These issues were hardly new—humanitarian crises had long been considered pretexts for undermining the sovereignty of the nation-state targeted for aid. British Liberal statesman William Ewart Gladstone's 1876 pamphlet on *Bulgarian Horrors and the Question of the East* is a famous example, in which the British prime minister, outraged about the alleged atrocities committed by the Ottomans against Christians there, effectively rejected Ottoman sovereignty and the doctrine of noninterference in another state's domestic affairs. The unconditional surrender of Germany and Japan in 1945, together with the devastated state of both countries, provided a unique opportunity to expand international relief in previously unimagined ways.[26]

Tensions between sovereignty and relief animated discussion in France. France was not represented at the 1943 Tehran conference of the wartime allies, nor at the 1945 follow-ups in Yalta and Potsdam, where many of the practical details about the postwar military occupation of Germany and Austria were discussed. At war's end, France's place within UNRRA was unclear, given its double status as having been occupied by the Nazis—which according to UNRRA guidelines, rendered the country eligible for aid—and as one of the victors over defeated Germany. However much the country was in desperate need of relief, French authorities would not permit international aid to compromise its newly regained national sovereignty. For French UNRRA officials (as instructed by political economist and diplomat Jean Monnet in 1944), the overriding priority was to make sure that France was not classified as a "receiver" country, for fear of its implications for national sovereignty. One French official remarked that France "was in no mood to be beholden to anyone and would prefer to see its people starve than to have to ask for charity." As late as autumn 1944 General Charles de Gaulle even signed a treaty of alliance with the Soviet Union to weaken his country's forced dependence on his British and American allies. After the war, the French did come on board, identifying UNRRA as crucial for strengthening ties to the Western bloc and for securing badly needed supplies and foreign currency. Issues of sovereignty arose in other contexts—for example, the restored right-wing government in Greece was suspicious of communist infiltration into UNRRA and insisted on taking over the program within its borders, after which UNRRA was left in an advisory role.[27]

Another example was the Soviet Union. The USSR, which had been invaded by the Nazis along a broad front and bore the brunt of the fighting against Hitler's troops, was in urgent need of aid after the cease-fire. Under Secretary of State Dean Acheson was not keen to divert American money to help communist countries rebuild after the war, but because UNRRA assistance was already committed to ex-enemy states like Germany, Austria, and Italy, the Soviets could not be refused according to the agency's charter, and thus received their share of food and aid as victims of Nazi aggression. Missions were created in Belorussia and Ukraine, and were staffed almost entirely by Americans. Upon arrival they were overwhelmed by the scale of devastation in cities such as Minsk and Poltava, and starvation and tuberculosis were rampant. The operation in these areas was massive, so much so that, according to one 1946 report, "virtually every Byelorussian—peasant, factory worker, government official or party leader—had some contact with the UNRRA program." Under difficult conditions, American relief agents and local Soviet authorities and staff developed warm relations, as American agency officials noted universal goodwill among Soviet citizens toward the American contingent. It was there that the director of the UNRRA mission in Ukraine, the New York attorney Marshall MacDuffie, formed a lasting friendship with the head of the Communist Party in Ukraine, Nikita Khrushchev, as recounted in *The Red Carpet*, his memoir of his time in Russia and Ukraine. While agency workers in the Soviet Union were under no illusion that sharp ideological differences could be wished away, they did believe—as noted in one UNRRA report—that a workable collective of sovereign nations could be built by people "who know how to live and work together peacefully."[28]

Cold War anxieties about control and sovereignty developed around the administration of aid. On the one hand, the Soviet Union grew increasingly suspicious. While the 1944 brochure *War and the Working Class* praised UNRRA's humanitarianism, the Soviets voiced concern that the agency was primarily advancing the "interests of some political and business circles in the US and Britain." Certainly the financing was uneven—the Americans footed 73 percent of the UNRRA bill, while the British contributed 16 percent to the overall budget. In Soviet eyes, UNRRA represented Anglo-American encroachment disguised as humanitarianism, and the agency was barred from operating in the Soviet zone of Germany. On the other hand, the Americans were equally apprehensive about UNRRA's mission creep and internationalist camaraderie on the ground, especially in communist countries. A *Life* magazine editorial in November 1945 fumed that the relief agency "has become an Anglo-American Administration for the Relief of Russian Europe." Rumors swirled that the missions in the Soviet Union were riddled with spies and communist sympathizers who had been hoodwinked into diverting American relief funds for Russian military purposes. The cloud of suspicion that hung over UNRRA officers for being too internationalist and soft on communism could be seen in the way that those who had been deployed in the Soviet Union and Yugoslavia were rejected from any future employment with the United Nations or the Marshall Plan. While such espionage claims were wildly exaggerated, the accusations were at times confirmed: in 1947 six high-profile American UNRRA staff members were unmasked as spies for the Soviet Union, further deepening American skepticism toward the organization.[29]

Nevertheless, the agency mounted an impressive operation under testing circumstances. Aid ships arrived in Southern Europe as early as March 1945, a good two months before V-E Day. UNRRA's livestock fleet was made up of seventy-two vessels that transported over 300,000 farm animals overseas, described in one publication as "the most important waterborne migration of animals since the time of Noah." Its European operations were at first restricted to a narrow band of countries in the southeast—Greece, Yugoslavia, and Albania—but were expanded to include Poland, Ukraine, Belorussia, and Czechoslovakia, and then to Germany, Italy, Austria, and Hungary. Over 300 DP camps across Europe were administered. At times it was a derring-do enterprise, with relief workers forced to use warfare techniques to administer relief. In Sardinia relief agents fought off swarms of locusts by using gasoline flamethrowers and jeeps, deploying the new chemical Gammexane to destroy insects and salvage the grain harvest there. The agency distributed aid to seventeen countries staffed by 10,000 trained employees who oversaw what was hailed as the largest peacetime shipping business in history. By the end of 1946, its fleet of 6,000 vessels shipped over 25 million long tons of goods to Europe and Asia—more than three times the level of post–World War I relief. Although it faced constant bottlenecks and administrative snafus, the agency could claim that it did much to overcome "homelessness, hunger, raggedness and cold, enforced exile, despair" for many DPs, serving as an affirmation to those waiting behind German and Japanese lines that, according to one agency publication, they had not been forgotten.[30]

A formidable roll call of volunteers—pacifists, conscientious objectors, religious activists, nurses, and social workers—came together to assist war victims. Most staff hailed from Britain and the US, but others came from France, Canada, the Netherlands,

Italy, Czechoslovakia, and the Baltic States. Canadian officials and nurses tended to be comparatively better qualified than the others, offering distinguished service for attending to those in need. Many volunteers were women—by mid-1946, 42 percent of staff were female, rising to almost 50 percent by the end of that year. A large number of agency nurses and relief workers operating in Europe after 1945 first earned their stripes as Quaker relief workers in Spain in the 1930s, and often joined UNRRA because the pay was better at both executive and field levels. The tough conditions, competing government budgets, and overlapping staffs led to some divisions within the organization, with American workers coming in for special criticism from other nationalities, who judged them as distant and careerist. British writer Iris Murdoch, an agency volunteer in 1945, lampooned do-nothing American officials who sit "behind enormous desks and chew gum and call their fellow citizens by their Christian names."[31]

Agency workers confronted the breakdown of civilization in the form of overcrowded camps, inadequate housing, and makeshift sanitation facilities, but it was the human cost of war in the form of infirm and unbalanced survivors that dominated the memoirs. They recorded the radical sense of rupture and loss among DPs, what one called the "despairing cry of homelessness, the unanswered cry of fearful and lonely people." Their accounts described how DPs were suffering from a so-called liberation complex, a mix of despondency, mood swings, and the desire for revenge, which made them difficult to manage and control. So common were the DPs' difficulties in adjusting to postwar life that their condition was designated by experts and relief workers as "DP apathy," or even "Belsenitis." Attending to their needs was seen as a first step in the psychological reconstruction of Europe, where the site of diagnosed trauma had moved from the battlefield to the displaced persons camp.[32]

Straitened circumstances steeled missionary purpose, as evidenced in Francesca M. Wilson's memoir of her relief experiences,

Aftermath. What she liked about the new agency was that it did "not spend its time round a table, uttering platitudes and splitting hairs," rather, "its function is executive." It was composed of wily adventurers dedicated "hard to the mission" who provoked the ire of many military officers skeptical about their motives, competence, and occasional use of black-market scrounging to secure under-resourced supplies. As a British Quaker career welfare worker, Wilson had worked with French, Serbian, and Montenegrin civilians during World War I, then was active in famine relief in Russia in the early 1920s and later in Spain during the civil war. This time Wilson "felt exhilarated by being with so many" engaged in the task of liberating "their own and other countries' deportees from enemy territory." At the DP camp at Feldafing, Bavaria, she was taken aback by the state of "walking skeletons" with "the furtive look and gestures of hunted animals," whose "years of brutal treatment" and "the constant fear of death" meant that "all that was human had been taken away from them." Like others, she was convinced that the "Nazi concentration camps will throw their shadow over Europe for centuries," and will "take away one's pride in being European."[33]

Kathryn Hulme's *The Wild Place* recounts her experiences as deputy director of UNRRA's Polish displaced persons camp at Wildflecken, Germany. In her memoir, the American volunteer noted that Wildflecken meant "wild spot," which for her served as a "perfect description for this end-of-the-world place." In her eyes, UNRRA was a kind of "United Nations in a test tube," as she handed out food and made do in the surreal conditions of chronically scarce materials and never-ending waves of refugees: "The DP world turned into an Alice-in-Wonderland world," in which "we were the appointed guardians of a small lopsided corner of earth where things quite definitively were growing queerer and queerer." She conceded how at times welfare workers cracked under the strain. Faced with yet another arrival of several hundred desperate Poles clamoring for food parcels, Hulme admitted that at that moment "I despised the insanity of international relief that imagined something could be done with this ruin in the human soul, so much more fearful than all of the mountains of rubble strewn over the face of Europe." Susan T. Pettiss's memoir carried on in a similar vein. Pettiss was a social worker from Mobile, Alabama, who volunteered to go to Europe to escape a crumbling marriage back home. She enlisted with the hope of helping to create "a true world community with new social systems and international relations." Pettiss recorded the incessant demands of the homeless along with the round-the-clock rotation of work, with occasional fraternization and dancing with black soldiers, even noting that as a white southern woman it was the first time that she had ever socialized with African American men. Pettiss also documented Europe in moral crisis, disfigured by revenge, repatriation, and violence, all of which challenged her own beliefs. Relief workers were unavoidably drawn into the catch-as-catch-can world of scrounging and "moonlight requisitions"—stealing from Germans to feed the hungry—which taxed her conscience: "I felt my values jolted," "constantly faced with the dilemma of distinguishing between stealing, capturing, confiscating and appropriating enemy material."[34]

What distinguished UNRRA from traditional religious aid organizations was the way that the care of the body replaced care of the soul, with the aid worker standing in as the new modern missionary. This could be seen in some of the humanitarian agency's photographs. For almost a century and a half, humanitarians have used photography to draw attention to human suffering, much of which is closely associated with the effects of war, dislocation, and poverty. While such humanitarian photography originated in the nineteenth century, it exploded in the wake of the First World War as a means of politicizing injustice and atrocity and to mobilize popular support for various international moral causes. A humanitarian photographic sensibility returned after the Second World War, and UNRRA was at the heart of the revival. Most of its photog-

Figure 3. Fresh milk on the dock, Gdansk, Poland, 1946.
Credit: UNRRA/4459, photo by John Vachon, United
Nations Archives and Record Management

raphers were American, usually former soldiers who had worked
for the US Army Signal Corps. The manner of depicting DPs was
inspired by the well-known documentary work of the US government's Farm Security Administration, or FSA, whose portraits of
American migrant workers in the 1930s elicited a strong plea for
social reform. It was no accident that the two most famous UNRRA
photographers—John Vachon in Poland and Arthur Rothstein in
China—were former FSA photographers. Vachon's bleak pictures
of devastated Warsaw depicted destroyed buildings, blasted urban
life, and helpless children, all represented with great sympathy and
compassion, as seen in Figure 3.[35]

UNRRA photography betrayed a distinct political agenda. In
part this was because the agency was under attack back in the US.
American under secretary of state Acheson grumbled that most of
the relief went to Eastern Europe and "was used by governments
bitterly hostile to us to entrench themselves, contrary to agreements

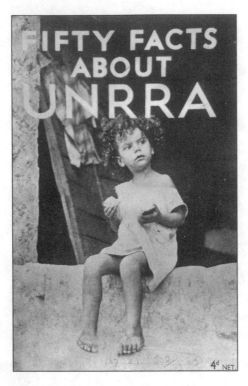

Figure 4. Cover of *Fifty Facts About UNRRA* (London: His Majesty's Stationery Office, 1946). *Credit: United Nations Archives*

made at Yalta." That the two biggest beneficiaries were Poland and Yugoslavia did not endear the agency to the American public. Henry R. Luce, publisher of *Life* magazine and an ardent conservative, was highly critical of UNRRA's mission in Europe for aiding in the reconstruction of communist-controlled countries there, and would not publish positive images of agency activity abroad. As a result, UNRRA devoted significant resources to publicizing its good works through film and photography. Gene Fowler's 1946 documentary film *Seeds of Destiny* lovingly chronicled shipments of food to various world destinations, and the agency's photographic media recorded families energetically boarding ships to head back to their country of origin or en route to Palestine. Standard before-and-after photographs of malnourished children were taken to celebrate effective work in the camps. The 1946 brochure *Fifty Facts About UNRRA* was widely distributed to receiver countries in Europe and

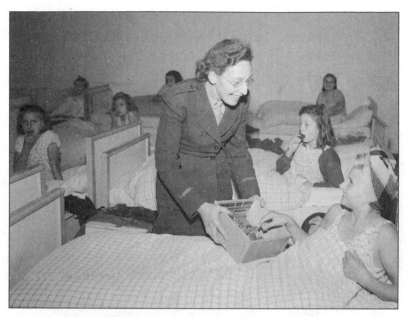

Figure 5. Kloster Indersdorf DP camp, Germany, 1945.
Credit: Getty Images

Asia (Figure 4). Its cover featured a vulnerable child in need of care, while additional images depicted relief workers aiding children in Yugoslavia, Germany, and Italy, as noted in Figures 5, 6, and 7.[36]

Whereas the experience of many DPs and relief workers was often one of chaos, despair, and frustration, official agency photos conveyed an orderly world of well-run camps and well-organized refugee repatriation. One relief worker admitted that Ukrainians— "strong well-built men"—"figured large in the photographs we used to send home to show the DPs at work." Pain, suffering, and distress went unrepresented, with emphasis instead placed on positive moments of refugee life—eating and being looked after; receiving medicine; children playing; and refugees boarding ships or trains to head back home, as noted in the image of Jewish refugees receiving food at a UNRRA-run DP camp outside of Linz, Austria.

Many photos featured adults at work, given that part of the agency's mission was an updated colonial-era idea of rehabilitation

Figure 6. UNRRA aid distributed to Italian children, 1946.
Credit: United Nations Archives

through labor. Pictures also underscored the proclaimed mission to "help those to help themselves," on the assumption that the DPs' repeated exposure to Nazi brutality would be overcome through self-reliance. Above all, agency photographs were used to justify the good deeds (and spiraling costs) of this sprawling international humanitarian undertaking, as well as to present a story of progress to other refugees stuck in these camps. Photographers were given clear instructions to portray the UN's relief mission in this positive light, what Vachon cynically called "UNRRA's angle."[37]

Agency photographs reflected the inherent tensions of its mission. Unlike the imagery of Christian charity work, UNRRA photographs conveyed a discernible air of emotional disengagement. At first this may seem surprising, given that UNRRA was set up as the humanitarian face of global governance. Agency officials had to work with presiding military authorities, and often chafed with them over the administration of the DP camps. Relief workers complained that the military forces were uncaring and callous toward

Figure 7. Jewish DPs receiving UNRRA food at Bindermichl DP camp in US zone, near Linz, Austria, most likely 1946. Photographer: Lepore. *Credit: United States Holocaust Memorial Museum, courtesy of National Archives and Records Administration, College Park, MD, 111–SC–234939*

their charges, preoccupied above all with getting the DPs billeted, fed, and deloused. One relief agent despaired that "there seemed to be no recognition of, or respect for, the emotional ties engendered by the actual work," because the "Ford Assembly Line was held up as a model of organisation to be followed," making us feel like "chessmen in the hands of our superior officers, and this was one of the causes of our endless frustration." The language of civilization often framed their frustration. One British relief worker expressed his irritation in a diary entry from June 17, 1945, writing that if these "blasted people in high places" would "only realise that these people are human beings who were in a war while we were sitting pretty at home and that here in Hanau they have had their first opportunity for years to set up something like their own civilisation."[38]

UNRRA's world was one of medical assistance and intergovernmental administration, quite removed from the more informal intimacy of care carried out by the religious organizations. UNRRA even condescended toward the religious charities' "amateurish and well-meant efforts." Quakers in turn chided the agency's obsession with routines, inflexible feeding schedules, and military-style provisioning, while other religious charity workers derided UNRRA's "high pay and people with no ideals." The frequent presence of disease in the camps and the need to keep a strict hygiene regimen were also factors in the distancing between the giver and receiver of relief. Decisive too was that the agency was under attack back in the US and suspected of going native in terms of internationalist inclination and communist sympathy; the photographic representation of professional distance and interpersonal detachment was used to communicate the agency's self-image of corporate efficiency. In this way, official photographs of staffers handing out food and administering medicine captured the broader objective of trying to direct the viewer's sympathy and support toward the relief organization itself, and less toward the recipients of aid.[39]

Positive photographic representations could not obscure the fact that UNRRA was saddled with real problems. For one thing, it was wholly dependent on the priorities of national governments and military occupation commands, and therefore subject to the fast-changing international political scene. The Allied military command preferred to work with established charities like the Red Cross, not least because many UNRRA officers were inexperienced and underqualified. Lorna Hay, a London *Picture Post* reporter covering Germany in 1945, noted that UNRRA was "gradually but insidiously made to feel that it was nobody's baby, that nobody quite expected it, and that it was rather a bore that it should have arrived at all, and should have to be given billets." Relief workers noted that DPs—especially if they were grouped with fellow nationals—tended to guard their autonomy and were chary of relief workers as intrusive do-gooders insensitive to their wartime struggles and sacrifices. UNRRA was also put in competition with other relief charities, whose workers sometimes sniffed that the agency's acronym really stood for "U Never Really Rehabilitate Anyone." Some officials reportedly had mistresses selected from Polish DPs, all of which undermined its mission and moral legitimacy.[40]

Repatriation represented the thorniest issue. In Europe some 40 million noncombatants were displaced during the war, and UNRRA's brief was to repatriate them as quickly as possible. It was part of a much broader organized transfer of peoples after the Second World War, and was being driven forward with the blessing of the international community. Historian Peter Gatrell has rightly argued that "far from bringing an end to organized deportation, the defeat of Nazism helped to popularize the idea." Feeding, housing, and repatriating DPs was already a major discussion point during the war, but it became a huge problem after the cease-fire. At first the top priority was sending back Russians—6 million of whom were outside the USSR at war's end—who were seen as posing a danger to public order in divided Germany. The Russians were expensive to feed, since they were entitled, according to the Yalta agreements, to the same rations as Allied soldiers. The agency was told that the faster they were returned, the faster Moscow would send back Allied POWs still in the Soviet Union.[41]

Equally complicated was what to do with those displaced persons—especially from Poland, Hungary, Czechoslovakia, and the Soviet Union—who did not want to return to their former countries. A significant number of them had lost everything, felt unwelcome in their homeland, feared the consequences of Red Army retaliation, and hoped to start a new life elsewhere. "A very large proportion," observed Hannah Arendt at the time, "will regard repatriation as deportation." Relief workers were well aware of the ambiguous situation, but were under strict instructions to prepare the DPs for repatriation. Despite early idealism about building a new world community from the ruins of the war, UNRRA was obliged to classify recipients according to nationality and to return them to their country of origin. Such work distinguished UNRRA from the religious charities and caused grief and roiled consciences for many aid workers. Kathryn Hulme was shaken when she learned that some Russian refugees "had slashed their wrists, stripped naked and hanged themselves rather than get into the repatriation train." How typical such despair was is hard to know, but the Soviets certainly took resistance to repatriation very seriously. Soviet films such as *The Road Home* and *Home for the Homeless* were produced to broadcast positive images of life in liberated Poland and the Baltic states, and Soviet repatriation officials working in Iran, Greece, Egypt, and elsewhere published newspapers that supported DPs returning to their countries. Some of the religious organizations, in particular the Quakers, objected to these forced transfers on moral grounds. UNRRA by contrast was obliged to repatriate all expellees, and repatriate them it did. The statistics are quite staggering: of the approximately 7.7 million DPs in Germany in May 1945, more than 4 million had been "replaced" by the end of July. In the shocked words of relief worker Rhoda Dawson, agency policy had shifted from being "absolutely non-committal" about whether refugees stayed or returned to one in which "welfare comes last, the main object is repatriation." By the end of 1946, Dawson wrote, UNRRA "Repatriation Officers" and a "Repatriation Team" had been equipped with a "loud-speaker van, records and film" to encourage people to go home, communicating the message in Polish, Russian, and Yiddish. Agency workers reportedly even threatened to withhold rations from those who refused to return. Still, the Soviets suspected Western foot-dragging when it came to repatriating DPs. In UN debates about the fate of DPs, the defense of the refugee's individual human rights against nefarious states deepened Cold War conflict, making humanitarianism a new dividing line. Eleanor Roosevelt, who chaired the UN's Human Rights Commission, described the arguments over the fate of the refugees as "the scene of one of the early clashes between the Soviet Union and the West."[42]

No less intractable was how to handle groups that were not nationals, above all Jewish survivors. Given the horrors of World War II, there was great concern among Jewish groups that there was neither a UNRRA-recognized central Jewish body within each national government nor a Jewish central agency coordinating Jewish relief efforts. Calls were made for the establishment of specifically Jewish agencies, but UNRRA firmly rejected any special treatment of Jewish war victims on an international basis on the grounds that the "Jewish problem" had to be dealt with within each afflicted nation. Back in 1944 the American Jewish Congress and World Jewish Congress pleaded for more Jewish representation at UNRRA, not least because Nazi terror against the Jews dramatized the urgency and distinctiveness of Jewish relief and rehabilitation. The unclear fate of Jewish survivors became an opportunity to persuade Jews to emigrate to Palestine. For camp survivors with nowhere to go, Zionism became an ideology of hope and escape. Relief workers noted the growth of a "Jewish ethnological nationality" in the DP camps in Germany, and with time UNRRA acknowledged Jewish nationhood claims to emigrate to Palestine. David Ben-Gurion, executive head of the World Zionist Organization and later Israel's first prime minister, toured Europe five times between 1945 and 1946, giving passionate speeches to recruit Jewish survivors to emigrate to Palestine. Positive reports of Jewish Palestine were produced and distributed in the camps to win over European Jews to the Zionist cause, whose message was framed in the terms of a new civilizing mission in the Middle East: "At the edge of Tel Aviv, I saw the first houses. There was a marked improvement. I thought to myself: Here before your eyes is proof that Palestinian Jewry is bringing civilization to the Middle East." The recruitment drive proved successful, as reportedly some 25 percent of all Jewish DPs ended up in the newly founded state of Israel, while others were repatriated back to Eastern Europe. For some aid workers, the growth of nationalism and Zionism in the camps did not square easily with the agency's self-styled internationalism. Arriving with "the idealistic sense of 'one world,'" UNRRA worker Pettiss grew disillusioned when that "unity didn't materialize right away," as she realized "that for both psychological and practical reasons, national grouping was best during the insecure and traumatic times in the lives of the displaced."[43]

There is another crucial issue that distinguished secular humanitarianism from the religious charities. UNRRA's brief did not extend relief or assistance to ex-Axis soldiers or civilians, but only to the "victims of German and Japanese barbarism." No aid was to be given to Germans, other than to those designated as "victims of Nazi terror." Such measures were not unprecedented. In 1945 the Polish Red Cross refused to serve hot drinks and food to Germans in railroad stations. However, these discriminatory practices set off UNRRA from most other religious relief groups—especially the Quakers—who fed, clothed, and looked after all people in need, regardless of nationality, race, or political status, in the name of political neutrality and Christian service. The huge influx of German refugees from the East in 1945 created pangs of conscience among agency officials about extending relief to needy Germans on the ground, though policies were not modified. As a result, Germans remained excluded from UNRRA's humanitarian assistance and human rights advocacy, pointing up the agency's—and the international community's—conditional understanding of humanity and humanitarianism after the war.[44]

The agency's discriminatory policy toward Germans stirred fierce moral discussion back in the US around the issue of charity and civilization. American Roman Catholic bishop Aloisius Joseph Muench (later apostolic nuncio to West Germany, 1951–1959) led the charge in urging reconciliation between Germans and non-Germans through alms. In his widely circulated 1946 pastoral missive *One World in Charity*, Muench pleaded for mercy toward the Germans and for an end to America's "cold, calculated policy of revenge." Muench expressed great dismay that for "the first time in the history of Christian nations, powerful governments are making the exercise of Christian charity impossible," and explicitly condemned the "official inhumanity" of prohibiting UNRRA from dispensing aid to Germans. "Charity," he continued, "has been civilization's most successful builder." His missive exonerated Catholics, hardly mentioned Jews by name, and denied any notion of collective guilt. It was widely reprinted in the US and became a sensation in Germany when it was translated and published the following year, after which it served as an affirmation of the myth of Christian victimization in early postwar Germany. Muench went on to organize large-scale charity drives for the American zone of Germany and helped rebuild spiritual and material bonds between American and German Catholics.[45]

In January 1946 the US Senate engaged in passionate debate about starvation conditions in Germany. A number of senators argued that UNRRA and American relief forces should reverse their discrimination policy against Germans. The language of civilization in crisis was invoked to justify new action. A senatorial petition had been sent to President Truman on December 15, 1945, drafted by Senator Kenneth S. Wherry of Nebraska and endorsed by thirty-four senators from both parties. They demanded the end of the "appalling famine in Germany and Austria," which are "today facing starvation on a scale never before experienced in western civilization." Colorado senator Eugene Millikin interjected that "it is not a question of having sympathy for the Germans; it is a question of having sympathy with our own civilized principles." Opponents of clemency toward the Germans cited a recent letter from President Truman in which he insisted that "no one shall be called upon to pay for Germany's misfortunes except Germany itself." But the opponents of aid were outnumbered, as a majority of senators rallied around the idea that

American and UNRRA policy not to aid Germans was leading to a "world catastrophe" of mass starvation. Religious groups lent support to the cause. A November 1945 plea published in *Christian Century* and signed by a joint committee of the World Council of Churches, the International Red Cross, the World Jewish Congress, and the Save the Children Fund proclaimed that current American policy "being followed in Central Europe is ghastly" and "a repudiation of Christian charity and a defiance of Christian morality." With such cross-faith unity and grassroots lobbying, American aid began to be dispatched toward Germany and the Germans outside UNRRA channels. By 1947, 60 percent of US CARE packages were going to Germany. Such a shift in policy was increasingly deemed both morally appropriate and politically expedient. General Lucius D. Clay, then deputy military governor of Germany, added his view that "we could not hope to develop democracy on a starvation diet." The debate reflected shifting sensibilities among humanitarian activists about the moral mission of international relief work and the treatment of defeated enemies, as we shall see in the next chapter.[46]

All told, UNRRA posted remarkable achievements under demanding conditions. By the time it terminated operations in June 1947, it had helped curb famine in Austria, Yugoslavia, and Greece, and supervised hundreds of camps in the American and British zones of Germany, twenty-one in Austria, and eight in Italy. In Eastern Europe nearly 10 million DPs were assisted in two years. Recipient countries expressed their gratitude in various forms. Thousands of thank-you letters were written to local agency missions, a monument to the aid agency was unveiled in Poland, and a college in Czechoslovakia was named in its honor. Parades and exhibitions were organized across Central Europe and Asia, and peasants thronged to cheer the arrival of requisitioned UNRRA jeeps in Chinese villages. Children, horses, and livestock in Central Europe were supposedly named after UNRRA. The agency marked a first foray into global governance under emergency conditions, shaped by a new blend of compassion, technocracy, and American-led liberal internationalism. While its legacy is mixed, UNRRA did forge a new language of civilization and the civilizing mission for postwar Europe. Its short history demonstrated the power and problems of coordinated international assistance and the ideological belief that the unmixing of peoples (in the form of forced repatriation) was the precondition to political peace. International aid ended up strengthening nation-states and a nation-based international system. The two guiding principles that drove intergovernmental relief and rehabilitation in the wake of the war—the restoration of family and nation—went on to serve as the moral foundation of political order in Cold War Europe, West and East. In many ways, UNRRA was out of sync with growing Cold War tensions on the ground. Ukraine mission leader Marshall MacDuffie was not wrong to say that the missions in the Soviet Union were "just about the brightest signs throughout the world in Anglo-American relations with the Soviet Union." An *Economist* article made a similar point in deeming the aid agency as "the only organization or activity still bridging the gulf between East and West." Washington's European Recovery Program, which began in April 1948, would mark the moment when Americans rejected UNRRA-style internationalism and took control of aid to Europe with overriding national interests in mind. In the words of one US State Department official in 1947, "We must avoid getting into another UNRRA. The United States must run this show."[47]

THESE NEW HUMANITARIANS HELPED BRING PEACE TO THE continent, and in so doing gave form to a new idea of Western Europe in the aftermath of war. Relief workers engaged in frontline encounters with the victims of war and with former enemies. Wartime antagonism was supplanted by a new kind of civilizing mission driven by care, compassion, and the desire to bind the wounds of war for countless DPs across Europe. The unprecedented scale of international relief work was organized in the name of humanity and humanitarianism, one in which the basic material needs of survivors trumped all; even for the religious charities, bellies—not Bibles—were the chief source of concern. Missionary Europe saw the tensions between nationalism and internationalism around the relief and rehabilitation of war victims; it also marked the end of American peacetime isolationism and the forging of new American-driven transatlantic links in Western Europe.

The year 1945 was one of both fevered destruction and reconstruction, during which the prospects of peace and civilization were hashed out on the ground by volunteer relief workers toiling in the shadow of Allied military authorities. The crisis of civilization was noted everywhere, and for some the deep past—including classical civilization—was summoned to cope with the breakdown of cultural meaning and moral compass. For Stephen Spender and others, the ruins and refugees of Central Europe symbolized the end of one world and the uncertain beginning of the new. The sense of zero was by no means limited to the defeated, but suffused the rest of Western Europe too. The surprising story of 1945 is how quickly the crisis of civilization moved from confusion and despair to coordinated international action to confront the damage of war and to care for its victims. For those humanitarian workers on the ground, civilization was not an idea linked to past glories or inherited heritage, nor to historical progress or even the future. It was a Zero Hour term of ruin and rupture in the here and now, as well as a call to action amid harrowing conditions to help the most needy, one relief parcel at a time. The sprawling relief efforts marked a new kind of secular international mission after the war, with the DP camp as its principal site of activity and purpose.

These humanitarians were also among the first witnesses and builders of postwar Europe, dedicated to the continental conversion of war to peace, killing to care. They were a mix of secular and religious volunteers, men and women. Their experiences were generally recorded in private diaries, letters, and photographs not intended for publication. There were exceptions—Hulme's *The Wild Place* was published in 1953 and won the *Atlantic Monthly* Nonfiction Award that year. The experiences and stories of relief and rehabilitation in the early postwar period have largely been overlooked in European history writing, which tends to skate over the 1945–1950 period as an interregnum between the end of Hitler's empire and the onset of the Cold War. This narrative absence is in marked contrast to the iconic status of the so-called rubble women of Germany, who worked around the clock after the cease-fire to clear away the massive debris from Germany's bombed cities and towns so as to start life again. In reality these women weren't as selfless and self-sacrificing as legend had it, in that many of them cleared the rubble for rations or as punishment by the Allies. Even so, the marveled "Hour of the Woman" was celebrated and universalized by newly licensed national newpapers as a symbol of (West) German resilience and recovery, one in which these women's contribution to reconstruction was elevated as a parable about the rebirth of the nation.[48]

Nothing equivalent happened with the international aid workers, either in terms of their actions or storytelling. In part this is because they often labored under the shadow of occupying military regimes, and usually returned home once the mission was declared accomplished. Many UNRRA workers continued their careers as international public health servants in other crisis-ridden areas of the world, often in connection with the World Health Organization. Their experiences and stories also have faded because the larger cause—emergency internationalism and coordinated foreign welfare assistance—found little narrative space in a world increasingly defined by the restoration of nation-states and deepening Cold War division. International aid, of course, did not disappear, as the coming Marshall Plan for European economic recovery made plain. What first-person narratives exist on the workaday world of Marshall Plan assistance were written by politicians, businessmen, and elite go-betweens, mostly as tales of the Americanization of Western Europe. By contrast, the demanding experiences and modest recollections of ordinary aid volunteers in Europe from 1945 to 1947 were not penned by elites. Many were written by female volunteers who recounted the dramatic changes of Europe through the care and consolation of the hungry and displaced. They were Western Europe's hidden civilizers who improved the lives of millions of DPs and war victims, vanishing mediators of a continent rapidly moving from war to Cold War. The ironic effect was that their actions in the DP camps inadvertently intensified the breakdown of both the wartime Grand Alliance and the prospects of internationalism several years before superpower relations turned even more frigid and confrontational.

What this meant for the future of Europe was unclear at the time, for 1945 marked the collapse of Hitler's empire as well as the expansion of American and Soviet power. The radical newness of the moment was captured by celebrated American writer and literary critic Edmund Wilson, who, like Spender, toured Europe in the summer of 1945. Wilson had been a frequent visitor to Europe before the war, but wherever he went, the Europe he encountered this time unsettled him. His profound disorientation was reflected in the very title of his travelogue, *Europe Without Baedeker: Sketches Among the Ruins of Italy, Greece and England.* In it he noted the dramatic decline of "the little European nations" in relation to the new superpowers, and he spent time talking to frustrated UNRRA officials in Italy and Greece. In Italy they confessed that their worthy work was just "a drop in the bucket" and that they were consumed by a "futile feeling." Even if their efforts "met with the applause" of locals, these workers confessed to feeling embarrassed for "doing so little and living so well themselves." The discomfort of the privileged among the powerless was a common refrain, but Wilson sensed that this sentiment hid a larger issue—the burden of empire and a recast civilizing mission in Europe under radically changed circumstances.

"Where the enemy are roofless and starving, where we have reduced their cities to rubble, we get now not even useful plunder or readily exploitable empire," he observed, "but merely an extension, a more wearisome load, of harassing demands and duties." As we shall see in the next chapter, the terms and expectations of foreign military rule changed, yet the problems of control, justice, and the moral price of reconstruction—like international aid—would continue to bedevil all the occupiers of Central Europe.[49]

two

PUNISHMENT AND PITY

O N November 21, 1945, Robert H. Jackson, US Supreme
Court justice and chief counsel for the Allied prosecution,
opened the "Trial of the Major War Criminals Before the International Military Tribunal" in Nuremberg's Palace of Justice. The
bombed-out medieval city was identified as a fitting venue to stage
the trials, given its role as home to the Nazi Party's rallies and the
notorious Nuremberg Laws, which forbade marriages between Jews
and Germans and barred Jews from citizenship in the new Reich. In
the courtroom sat twenty-two high-ranking German leaders on trial
for a catalog of gross misdeeds and war crimes (Figure 8). Most of
the ringleaders of the Third Reich, including Joseph Goebbels, Heinrich Himmler, and of course Hitler himself, had committed suicide
some six months before. But others, including Hermann Göring, Albert Speer, and Hans Frank, had been apprehended and over the next
few months become the subjects of international media fascination.
In the end, twelve were condemned to death, three acquitted, and the
rest sentenced to various prison terms, ranging from ten years to life.

Yet the significance of the trial went far beyond passing judgment on the accused. Above all, the tribunal was designed to help
the international community draw the Second World War to a close

Figure 8. Nuremberg Trial, 1946. *Credit: Fred Ramage, Getty Images*

in a new way—not just through definitive military triumph and occupation, but also through the victory of law and justice. The Allies
tried the defendants according to a division of juridical labor agreed
in the Charter of the International Military Tribunal of August 8,
1945: the United States assumed responsibility for conspiracy, the
British for crimes against peace, the Soviets for war crimes in Eastern
Europe, and the French for war crimes in Western Europe. While
some legal scholars were uneasy about some of the novel charges
brought against the accused, such as conspiracy against peace and
especially crimes against humanity, the atrocities committed by the
regime were deemed of such depth and depravity that they had to
be dealt with in an international war crimes tribunal. Summarily
executing the captured Nazi leaders would, in the words of John
McCloy, Washington's assistant secretary of war and US high commissioner for Germany after 1949, represent a "descent to the methods of the Axis." Conducting the trials as a kind of theater of justice
was especially important to the Americans, but the British, French,

and Soviets played their part too. The world had never seen anything quite like it both in scope and reach, and the courtroom was abuzz with international press, especially at the beginning and end of the hearings. It was reportedly the largest gathering of journalists ever for a single event, with some 60,000 visitors' permits issued over the tribunal's ten-month life.[1]

Whereas the previous chapter looked at the role of international humanitarian aid as a new civilizing mission, this chapter shifts attention to how the goal of re-civilizing the defeated enemy found expression in the administration of international justice and military occupation. Not surprisingly, the trial opened with a bouquet of superlatives in an attempt to capture the uniqueness and grandeur of the proceedings. Jackson called the tribunal the "first trial in history for crimes against the peace," and said "no litigation approaching this magnitude has ever been attempted." Hersch Lauterpacht, the Polish Jewish legal theorist who helped Jackson and his team shape the new legal principle of "crimes against humanity," was overwhelmed by the unprecedented nature of the trials, writing in his diary that "it was unforgettable to see, for the first time in history, a sovereign State in the dock."[2]

The concept of civilization framed much of the proceedings. In his opening speech, Jackson raised the moral stakes in stating that "the real complaining party at your bar is Civilization," with a capital *C*. "The wrongs which we seek to condemn and punish have been so calculated, so malignant, and so devastating," Jackson continued, "that civilization cannot tolerate their being ignored, because it cannot survive their being repeated." Lead French prosecutor François de Menthon intoned that Nazism was best understood as an explosion of "all of the instincts of barbarism, repressed by centuries of civilization, but always present in men's innermost nature, all the negations of the traditional values of humanity." Toward the end of the trials British prosecutor Hartley Shawcross solemnly added that the Allied nations felt it "proper and necessary in the interests of civilization" to say that these Nazi crimes—even if committed at the time "in accordance with the laws of the German state"—surpassed "domestic concern" and were "crimes against the law of nations." In Japan in late April 1946, Joseph B. Keenan, chief prosecutor for the International Military Tribunal for the Far East, christened the Tokyo War Crimes Trials with almost identical words: "Mr. President, this is no ordinary trial, for here we are waging part of the determined battle of civilization to preserve the entire world from destruction." In both venues, Allied lawyers and judges took these trials into uncharted waters by interpreting acts of aggression and war crimes as unprecedented breaches of civilization that demanded new concepts of international justice. In them, civilization was enlisted as a community of values that gave humanity its spirit and meaning, one now being summoned to the bar in collective judgment.[3]

This chapter looks at how the fate of defeated Germany—its leaders, victims, and ruined empire—framed the early Allied discussion of re-civilizing occupied Europe. Attention will be devoted to the ways in which the International Military Tribunal at Nuremberg exposed Allied tensions about the relationship between international justice and civilization. The focus will then move to military occupation, with an eye toward how the Anglo-American policy of nonfraternization provoked wide public debate about how victors should engage with the vanquished. The British Zone of Occupation played host to the most controversial discussions in the media (driven in part by photojournalism) about the role of pity and humanitarianism in occupied Europe, and thus will receive special attention. The grassroots campaign to properly feed, provision, and even forgive the Germans (led by figures such as the London publisher Victor Gollancz) quickly turned into a national debate about the very meaning of British civilization. At issue is how Allied understandings of international justice, reeducation, and gradual accommodation with former enemy countries reflected the victors' changing visions of post-fascist Europe.

THE YEAR 1945 WAS NOT THE FIRST TIME THAT THE NAZI RE-
gime was put on trial. A mock trial of Hitler's government was held
in New York City's Madison Square Garden on March 7, 1934,
before no fewer than 20,000 spectators. It opened with the words
"All those who have business before this court of civilization give
your attention and ye shall be heard." Twenty representatives from
various trade unions, Jewish associations, churches, sports organizations, and state governments presented "The Case of Civilization
Against Hitlerism" for human rights violations, religious persecution, the imprisonment of labor leaders, and intellectual censorship.
The indictment accused the Third Reich of "compelling the German people to turn back from civilization to an antiquated and barbarous despotism which menaces the progress of mankind toward
peace and freedom." It went on to say that the German government
"stands convicted by its own acts of a crime against civilization,"
a verdict that met with a "great swelling roar" of approval. Later
that same year a group of writers, politicians, journalists, lawyers,
and rabbis published a volume called *Nazism: An Assault on Civilization*, in part to "marshal the conscience of mankind against
the brutal treatment of minority groups." Such gestures may have
seemed helpless howls of despair from across the Atlantic, but they
did point up the ways in which civilization became a language of
outrage and cultural shock, years before it would resurface in the
courtroom at Nuremberg.[4]

The Second World War saw a flourishing of the term. Predictably, Nazi Germany was routinely held up as the embodiment of
barbarism for its racism, anti-Semitism, and political violence—
punctuated by the drip-feed revelations about the horrors of what
we now call the Holocaust—and eventually became the global
benchmark for radical evil and the end of civilization. The Nazi
annexation of Czechoslovak territory in 1938, the Nazi invasion
of Poland in 1939, and the Japanese attack on Pearl Harbor in December 1941 sparked interest in law journals about the defense of

civilization against fascist "lawlessness." The Western Allies had elevated the "rights of man" and human rights as the highest moral
cause of the war, perhaps best evidenced in H. G. Wells's 1940
booklet *The Rights of Man, or What Are We Fighting For?* Here Wells
highlighted the defense of the "Rights of Man" as the moral mission
of the united "Atlantic civilizations" during the war. General Charles
de Gaulle, leader of the Free French, delivered a lecture at Oxford
University on November 25, 1941, on the "crisis of civilization," in
which he argued that only deepened military, political, and spiritual
collaboration between Britain and France—the two great "homes"
of the "liberties of man"—"can ensure that victory will bear fruit"
for "the cause of civilization." The 1941 Atlantic Charter and the
1942 United Nations Declaration (signed by twenty-six countries)
to create a "great union of humanity" based on "faith in life, liberty,
independence and religious freedom, and in the preservation of human rights and justice in their own lands as well as in other lands"
were pressed into ideological service as a response to totalitarianism.
While Theodore Roosevelt was the first US president to link the
country's imperial foreign policy to the expansion of Western civilization, it was his cousin Franklin Delano Roosevelt who deployed
the term the most, in particular in the run-up to and during the
Second World War, to underline the global moral stakes in the fight
against Nazism. But for him civilization was not synonymous with
isolation and nationalism, but rather was collaborative. As FDR put
it in a 1938 speech, "civilization is not national—it is international."
In a wartime private letter, Roosevelt described the war as a "crusade" to save "civilization from a cult of brutal tyranny, which would
destroy it and all of the dignity of human life."[5]

The Soviet use of the term also intensified during the war to
help shore up 1930s Popular Front antifascism. At first this may
seem odd, not least because the early Soviet Union had served notice to the world of its fundamental break from the corrupting influence of Old Europe. Even if Lenin and Stalin rarely used the

term civilization, they did not hesitate to condemn the tsarist regime as "Asiatic barbarism" and "Asian reaction." In Soviet parlance, civilization was used negatively to denounce the West and in turn to extol the world-historical role of the Soviet Union as a pioneering and progressive civilization in solidarity with the downtrodden of the world. In 1927 Stalin inveighed against the West's tendency to classify the world in a strict hierarchy of races in which non-Europeans were deemed uncivilized while the white races were presented as the carriers of civilization. One of the great results of the October Revolution, Stalin wrote, was the full destruction of these "legends," one that has inspired "liberated non-European peoples" to become a "genuinely progressive culture, a genuinely progressive civilization." A few years later, the exiled Soviet revolutionary Leon Trotsky went further in couching the legacy of the Russian Revolution in the language of civilization. In his 1932 "In Defense of October" speech, Trotsky insisted that the revolution was not the antithesis of civilization, but rather the birth of a new one. "The fact alone that the October Revolution taught the Russian people, the dozens of peoples of Tsarist Russia, to read and write stands immeasurably higher than the whole former hot-house Russian civilisation," concluding that the "October Revolution has laid the foundations for a new civilisation which is designed, not for a select few, but for all." While the revolutionary democratization of civilization was hardly a central plank of Soviet ideology, Stalin and Trotsky's views neatly dovetailed with the Soviet Union's broader message of anti-imperialism and solidarity with the colonial world.[6]

The threat of Nazism shifted the ideological landscape. The Nazi attack on the USSR in June 1941 prompted an English-language propaganda response from the Soviet Union, *In Defence of Civilization Against Fascist Barbarism: Statements, Letters and Telegrams from Prominent People*, published to help mobilize the West to support the Soviet Union in the battle against Nazi Germany. Civilization was the chosen language of defense and threat. "The union of all the forces of progressive humanity for the fight against fascism is absolutely vital" because "at stake is the salvation of culture and civilization, of science and art; it is the future of humanity." Statements from such prominent Soviet cultural luminaries as Alexey Tolstoy, Dmitri Shostakovich, Sergei Prokofiev, Sergei Eisenstein, and Valeria Barsova were included to solicit assistance from "our friends in England and America" for the coming battle against the "Hitlerite gravediggers of civilization." Western cultural figures like Theodore Dreiser, Upton Sinclair, H. G. Wells, Heinrich Mann, and Jules Romains lent their support, topped off with Dean of Canterbury Hewlett Johnson's cued affirmation that the "great Soviet peoples" are "carrying civilization's banner against the fascists."[7]

This rhetoric also played a domestic role within the Soviet Union. Just two days after Hitler's invasion on June 22, 1941, the Soviet press extolled the Red Army's mission as the "defense of the fatherland, the salvation of civilization"; a few months later *Pravda* claimed that the "Red Army defends world civilization"; even the victory in May 1945 was described in the press as the great triumph of "the victorious Red Army" in staving off Nazism's "mortal threat to all mankind, to world civilization"; and in another *Pravda* article a few months later, the Soviet people were praised for having "saved the civilization of Europe from fascist pogromists." The stress on the "Soviet defense of civilization" gave broader meaning to the Allied military alliance, not least because Marxism-Leninism had little emotional appeal outside the USSR, or even within it during the war.[8]

Some have interpreted the revival of civilization at the Nuremberg Trial as the last gasp of a late nineteenth-century logic to unite law and morality, one that stretched back to the Hague Conventions on warfare. Certainly it is true that the Hague Peace Conferences of 1899 and 1907 frequently referred to civilization under siege, as noted in the wide usage of "civilized countries," "civilized nations," "civilized states," "world-wide civilization," and "civilized humanity."

Yet the invocation of civilization at Nuremberg was more recycled Popular Front antifascism from the 1930s and 1940s.[9]

Even so, the prevailing mood among the Allies at the end of the war was hardly one of cool-headed courtroom justice. Churchill famously quipped that justice for Nazi leaders ought to be nothing more than to "line them up and shoot them." Stalin was initially very skeptical about the point of the war crimes trial. He reportedly gave a toast half in jest to his British and American colleagues on the eve of the trial's opening, asking those present to raise a glass to the execution of the German leaders before the trial had even started. Others demanded revenge more directly. In a 1945 publication called *We Come as Judges*, Soviet writer Ilya Ehrenburg claimed that if "there is a man who forgets what the Germans have done [then] he will be cursed by the graves of the innocents." American secretary of state Cordell Hull (who was awarded the Nobel Peace Prize in 1945) darkly told his British and Soviet counterparts that he'd like nothing more than to "take Hitler and Mussolini and Tojo and their arch accomplices and bring them before a drumhead court-martial," after which "at sunrise the following day there would occur a historic incident."[10]

Calls for revenge against Germans were standard fare across Europe during the war, ranging from Lord Robert Vansittart's 1940 booklet *Black Book: Germans Past and Present*, in which he denounced Germans as a "race of hooligans" which "from the dawn of history has been predatory and bellicose," to Ehrenburg's exhortation that "nothing can save Germany from inexorable retribution." In the aftermath of the war, Europe descended into a violent orgy of revenge and reprisals, lawlessness and chaos, as local communities were purged and brutalized. States and political authorities had either collapsed or been discredited, giving rise to massive theft and looting. Arrests and torture were typical means of settling local scores with collaborators and other accused enemies. In Italy, fascists were summarily rounded up, punished, and occasionally killed after the liberation. There was also a good deal of German-on-German violence in the form of countless reprisals, denunciations, and acts of retribution. Mass rapes took place on a shocking scale. In Vienna, 87,000 women were reported by clinics to have been raped in the aftermath of the liberation; in Berlin, the numbers were much higher, and across Germany it was reported that as many as 2 million women had been brutally victimized. Most of these assaults took place at the hands of Red Army soldiers, though it is often forgotten that the US Army was reportedly accused of raping as many as 17,000 women in North Africa and Western Europe between 1942 and 1945.[11]

Whole populations were terrorized as payback for alleged crimes. There were bouts of violent expulsions conducted in the name of state security and ethnic purification, effectively finishing the work that Stalin and Hitler had started during the war. Ethnic Germans were forced out of Poland and Czechoslovakia for their loyalty to the Führer; Sudeten German women in Czechoslovakia were made to eat pictures of Hitler, and sometimes their hair was hacked from their heads and stuffed into their mouths. Hungarians were kicked out of Slovakia and Romania, Romanians expelled from Hungary and Ukraine, and Italians from Yugoslavia. As late as the 1950s Bulgaria expelled 140,000 Turks and Gypsies across its border with Turkey. Rough forms of popular justice were being practiced in makeshift "people's courts" hastily put together to mete out punishment toward accused collaborators. Some 57,000 people were prosecuted in court for collaboration in Belgium, and another 50,000 collaborators sentenced in the Netherlands; in Hungary the figure was around 27,000, with another 50,000 in Greece. In France, over 6,000 people were killed in l'épuration sauvage in 1944 as alleged German collaborators. Around 2,000 French women were killed as "horizontal collaborators," or violently and publicly humiliated in ritualized pageants of shame, with those accused stripped, shorn, and forced to march through the streets of their hometowns as designated traitors to the community and nation. These events were proudly photographed by onlookers as a kind of grim spectacle of justice, with women's bodies serving as sites of vengeance and national purification. The sad fate of these *femmes tondues* was not limited to France, but had counterparts in Holland, Belgium, and Norway as well.[12]

The Nuremberg Trial was partly an effort to put an end to such brutal versions of local justice, and to help restore law and order across the continent. As Jackson famously put it, "That four great nations, flushed with victory and stung with injury, stay the hand of vengeance and voluntarily submit the captive enemies to the judgement of the law is one of the most significant tributes that Power has ever paid to Reason." But the constant invocation of civilization at the trial—far more redolent than human rights—was also a means to find common cause with the Soviet Union. While Stalin was initially reluctant to have the Soviet Union involved in the trial, he changed his mind. A large team of Soviet lawyers, journalists, photographers, and filmmakers was sent to Nuremberg to take part in and document the proceedings for a Soviet domestic audience. Soviet state prosecutor Andrey Vyshinsky recognized that the International Military Tribunal at Nuremberg would become a kind of show trial of international proportion. That the Soviet legal team was mainly composed of judges and prosecutors from the infamous Moscow show trials of the late 1930s (including Vyshinsky), in which members of the so-called Trotskyite "Left Opposition" and "Right Opposition" of the Communist Party were tried and executed, alarmed Western legal observers, yet the Soviets did play a key role in developing the legal concept of "crimes against the peace." The Soviet prosecutors often used "freedom-loving nations" and "great democracies" as terms of solidarity with their Western counterparts. They also endorsed the language of civilization as the trial's larger moral purpose. *Pravda* articles readily employed the Russian term *tsivilizatsiya* to frame Nazi crimes. On January 9, 1946, *Pravda* commented that "with the adoption and propagandisation of *Mein*

Kampf, the Hitlerists deliberately pushed civilisation into the abyss of war"; a few months later *Pravda* reported that German fascism "had become a mortal threat to human civilisation"; and in August 1946 *Pravda* made known that Soviet chief prosecutor at Nuremberg General Roman Rudenko "spoke on behalf of the entire Soviet people" in accusing the "fascist executioners" of "horrendous crimes against humanity, civilisation, and law." The Soviet co-optation of the term was significant: whereas older communist understanding of civilization saw fascism, capitalism, and civilization as of a piece, the new rendition recast civilization in the language of antifascism in solidarity with the West.[13]

Before the Nuremberg Trial, the legal usage of civilization was mainly negative, that is, to exclude designated uncivilized nations from statehood and self-governance. After the First World War, Western legal theorists put Germany, the Ottoman Empire, and the new Soviet Union beyond the pale of civilized Europe, as evidenced in their conspicuous absence from the negotiating tables at Versailles. Peacemaking in 1919 was based on a redrawn cultural map of civilization and barbarism. But lawyers and judges at Nuremberg invoked civilization expressly to keep Germany within the community of civilized nations, a community that could be separated from Nazi practices of barbaric lawlessness. The court thus interpreted Nazism as a lapse of civilization on the grounds that the Weimar Republic had developed "a civilized and enlightened system of jurisprudence." As a consequence—and this was pivotal to the tribunal's finding—it was held that the "accused knew or should have known" that they were "guilty of participation in a nationally organized system of injustice and persecution shocking to the moral sense of mankind." In other words, the very existence of Germany's pre-1933 legal system and its "norms of civilization" meant that these men standing trial could and should have known that their actions were illegal. The point was to separate the criminal regime from the German people, and to honor its pre-1933 international legal standing.[14]

There was another understanding of universal civilization at the trial. The repetitive usage of the term helped fortify one of the weakest aspects of the prosecution's case, namely the absence of legal norms regarding crimes against humanity. Declaiming a breach of civilization was not enough—it needed to be shown, and this is where the union of media and law was so decisive. At Nuremberg the Allied prosecution relied on written documentation and visual material, especially photography and film, for its evidence. Some 25,000 captured photographs were reviewed, and no fewer than 1,800 were prepared as trial exhibits.[15]

Arguably the real star of the trial was film itself, as it was used as a substitute for witnesses to authenticate Nazi crimes. While crime scene photography had been employed sparingly in Anglo-American courts for decades, the introduction of atrocity film footage in a trial had no precedent. Toward the end of the war, the Americans and the British were already putting together films to help maintain domestic support for the war and to ready public opinion for possible postwar occupation. As one British cameraman put it in 1944, the atrocity films offered "the most revolting proof of what we are fighting for." Likewise, Soviet films about the liberation were designed to incite Soviet soldiers and the home front against Germans and to speed punishment. All the Allies produced their own documentary films about Nazi misdeeds and used them in the proceedings. The American film *Nazi Concentration Camps* served as a key witness for the prosecution, and its screening had a sensational effect. While some lawyers and journalists were uncomfortable with the incorporation of "horror films" into the trial, their use was justified to expose the horrors of the Third Reich and to prick the cocoon of denial and proclaimed non-complicity.[16]

No less striking is that these atrocity films were shown to catch the conscience of the accused in a purpose-built theater of public retribution and coerced contrition. Much of the American camerawork homed in on defendant reactions to the gruesome footage shown in the courtroom. Faint lights were used to illuminate the faces of the accused once the room was dimmed for film viewing so that observers could study the effects on the defendants. Foreign journalists often squinted at the prisoners through opera glasses or army binoculars in an attempt, as journalist Janet Flanner put it, "to discover enlarged signs of shame, alarm or guilt on their features." This gave way to a new genre of reporting in which journalists commented on the responses of the Nazi criminals to the films. Historian Ulrike Weckel has argued that the visible signs of shame were interpreted by the Allies (especially the Americans) as proof that Germans could be reeducated. For this reason the Allies set great store on the potency of images in their broader project of rehabilitating Germans after defeat.[17]

The trial largely succeeded in both the short and long terms. The sight of German leaders in the courtroom did not, as feared at the time, provoke sympathy among Germans, nor incite dreams of revenge. Quite the opposite. One German remarked that "we are simply too hungry" to concern ourselves with their fate, and for these figures "even a death sentence is too lenient." So in that sense, the trial was a triumph, inspiring new confidence in the rule of law and helping to create the conditions for political order and stability. Even the notoriously unreliable star witness, Albert Speer, later admitted that the trial was a "step on the road to re-civilisation, despite its flaws." The trial also led to other tribunals of transitional justice, first by the Allies and then by the occupied countries themselves. At Nuremberg there were twelve trials in all, involving 184 senior military, industrial, and medical officials. In the American Zone of Occupation, 1,600 people were tried in 489 trials, and German judicial authorities conducted 24,000 hearings in the British Zone alone, though most of the 3.66 million Germans subjected to denazification measures were not prosecuted. And like the Atlantic Charter, the Nuremberg Trial began to take on a life of its own by serving as an inspiration to other freedom fighters around the world.

The American National Negro Congress, moved by the words of Jackson, the chief counsel for the Allied prosecution, wrote a "plea of justice" to the United Nations in the spirit of his lofty phrases regarding the breach of civilization and humanity, to draw attention to the 13 million "oppressed black human beings" living in the US.[18]

The broader understanding of civilization at the trial began to drop away toward the end of 1945 as Cold War hostilities intensified. By the end of the trial, the Americans had begun working to define civilization as synonymous with liberal values. That they played underhanded tricks on the Soviets in the trial was evidence of this growing antagonism. At one point US prosecutors allowed the German defense to cite incriminating evidence of Soviet crimes against peace, in clear breach of the pretrial agreement that such connections would not be raised; by contrast, no evidence or discussion was brooked about American or British war crimes, including aerial bombardment of civilian targets. Such a move undermined the Allied consensus at the trial. And as the Soviet prosecution was finishing up its presentation against the "Hitlerites," American newspapers circulated the text of Churchill's "Iron Curtain Speech" on March 5, 1946, with the headline "Unite to Stop the Russians," in which the former British prime minister brazenly yoked communists and fascists as twin threats to "Christian civilization." News of Churchill's speech caused such a stir in the courtroom that one commentator reported that "unconcealed hope shone" among the Nazis on trial that their sentences might be commuted. It was at this point that the Anglo-American interpretation of the trial as liberalism triumphant began to take hold.[19]

Carl Schmitt, interwar Germany's foremost legal theorist and early apologist of the Nazi legal order, noted the political shift. In his influential 1950 *The Nomos of the Earth in the International Law of the Jus Publicum Europaeum*, Schmitt argued that until the early twentieth century the concept of international law, much like "universalist concepts of humanity, civilization and progress," was "Eurocentric to the core," with civilization denoting "self-evidently only European civilization, and 'progress' the linear development of European civilization." For Schmitt, this was sadly no longer the case. While some of this was due to the shaken power of Europe after the Great War, it was the post-1945 ascendancy of the US as a new superpower that accelerated these developments. With it came a new international order that did away with the *res publica christiana* of medieval Christendom. Schmitt may have underestimated the Christian underpinnings of post–World War II liberal civilization, as we shall see in the next chapter, but he was right that the mission of civilization was being remade as an Anglo-American joint venture.[20]

DEFEATED GERMANY AND AUSTRIA WERE PARTITIONED INTO four zones of military occupation by the US, the United Kingdom, France, and the Soviet Union, with the Western Allies administering the western flanks of the countries, while the Soviets controlled the eastern sectors. Berlin and Vienna were similarly subdivided, though Vienna's central district was jointly commanded by the Allied Control Council. International justice was a key form of encounter between victor and vanquished, but so too was the highly charged interaction between the occupying powers and ex-enemies in Germany and Austria. The Western Allies devoted special attention to reintegrating the vanquished back into the charmed circle of what was commonly called the Atlantic Alliance, with the Americans and the British taking the lead.

At the 1945 Yalta Conference, Churchill, Roosevelt, and Stalin declared that "it is our inflexible purpose to destroy German militarism and Nazism and to ensure that Germany will never again be able to disturb the peace of the world." Radical reform first focused on the so-called Four Ds—denazification, decentralization, decartelization, and democratization. Such an attitude reflected Roosevelt's comment at the 1943 Tehran conference that "Germany was less dangerous to civilization when it was in 107 provinces." In Germany, much of the reeducation initiative aimed to extirpate Prussia and Prussian militarism as the root of all German evil, and the official dissolution of Prussia in 1947 was shaped by this logic. Such "deprussianization" was as important to historians as military men. With characteristic bluntness, the well-known British historian A. J. P. Taylor described the landed nobility of Prussian Junkers as "ruthless exploiters of conquered lands" who were "untouched by European civilization." To this end, all military schools, clubs, and associations were prohibited, as were all memorials, monuments, and posters glorifying Germany's military tradition; public spaces all over the country were expunged of swastikas, and street names, postage stamps, and official seals were changed. Similar policies were implemented in occupied Austria, as disarmament directives banned all signs of paramilitary activities, from veterans' associations to martial music. This applied to civil society as well, as a number of volunteer Austrian organizations, such as youth groups and ski clubs, were dissolved.[21]

For the Americans, reeducation became the centerpiece of their mission on the Rhine. Imposing democracy on other people was considered by some as a paradox, but military authorities felt it was a necessary step. While most surviving school buildings were initially used as billets, military hospitals, or DP camps, they managed to reopen as functioning schools by October 1945. A good deal of time and resources went into creating West Berlin's Free University (opened in 1948) as an institution of free inquiry, buttressed by the creation of numerous cultural exchanges between the US and Germany for students, cultural figures, and church leaders. Across West Germany, the State Department created several Amerika-Häuser, or America Houses, in the early 1950s as cultural centers showcasing American books, magazines, music, and films. Military authorities established a Seventh Army Symphony Orchestra in Rhineland-Palatinate, and choirs and jazz ensembles performed across the American zone; bilingual church services were led by German and American clergy; and friendship committees and dances were organized to forge better relations between occupiers and occupied. American authorities made sure to translate military signs into German in an attempt to portray themselves as allies, not occupiers. With time they even initiated so-called Open Houses so that local Germans could tour American military bases annually. Some Germans continued to grouse that "Europe meant old culture and America meant [new] civilization, refrigerators, and jazz music," but there was growing appreciation for American culture and the military government's effort to cater to local cultural tastes.[22]

Conditions in the British zone were not so dissimilar. Early on, the British were criticized for their bearing and arrogance, sometimes described as behaving like the Raj in mudboots who "settled in the ruins as if they were in the White Highlands of Kenya." Like the Americans, the British authorities generally made the distinction between Nazi leaders and the misled people. In the British zone the focus was also on health, hygiene, and schooling, and there were careful purges of Nazi teachers. By the time all elementary schools had officially reopened on October 1, 1945, some 11,467 teachers had been arrested, dismissed, or refused employment as part of denazification. The British also devoted a good deal of resources to censoring German book, film, and music production, all the while promoting cultural works, often through the British Council, which promoted the British way of life, along with writers Elizabeth Bowen, Graham Greene, Virginia Woolf, and D. H. Lawrence.[23]

Life in the Soviet zone of Germany was dominated by the chief concerns of imposed reparations, economic exploitation, and military occupation. Here denazification was synonymous with political control and the construction of Stalinist-style socialism. Schools were reorganized and secularized, with "new teachers" peddling Marxism-Leninism and antifascism. Given their mission of turning fascists into socialists, the Soviets committed even more resources to culture and education than the British or Americans. Johannes Becher founded the Kulturbund zur demokratischen Erneuerung Deutschlands, or Cultural Association for the Democratization of Germany, which was officially dedicated to the "rebirth of the German spirit guided by an assertive democratic world-view." Chess tournaments and Pushkin festivals (especially around the 150th anniversary of the writer's birth in 1949) were organized, and German writers like Anna Seghers and Günther Weisenborn were invited to Moscow as "progressive intelligentsia." A House of Culture of the Soviet Union was opened in Berlin, which showed films, mounted exhibitions, ran children's programs, arranged guest lectures, and offered language courses. The Soviet Union's All-Union Society for Cultural Relations with Foreign Countries, or VOKS, sent folk and classical music and ballet troupes, theater performers, and Russian writers to Berlin. For the bicentennial of Goethe's birth in August 1949, the Soviets endeavored to transform Goethe into a German Pushkin, an exponent of "progress and democracy," a precursor of Marx, and a champion of the Volk. Much of this was an attempt to block the makeover of Goethe in the West as an emblem of "Atlantic culture," and to claim him as their own. Even Thomas Mann was invited from California to accept a Goethe Award from the Kulturbund in East Berlin.[24]

Unlike the British and Americans, the French were less engaged in denazification. There was no infamous *Fragebogen*, the political questionnaire produced by the Americans and the British that asked people to recount their Nazi involvement, and the general perception was that ex-Nazis were treated more leniently in the French zone than elsewhere. The French view of how to administer their occupied zone was illustrated by the remarks of General Jean de Lattre de Tassigny, the first commander in chief of the French Zone of Occupation. In March 1945—a full two months before V-E Day— he claimed that participating in the final victory over Germany was the "surest means of demonstrating" France's "resurrection," one that was "as much to raise our world prestige as to lay out the basis of our postwar position on the Rhine."[25]

The French initially promoted a policy of vengeance and economic exploitation to undo the sense of bruised honor associated with the humiliation of Nazi occupation. French political economist Jean Monnet and minister of finance Robert Schuman saw the occupation of Germany as a vital means of French economic recovery. The French occupation army was supposedly a haven for Vichy collaborators who were escaping punishment at home. Lattre and his cronies ruled in a grand manner, consciously organizing the French occupation to rival and even surpass Nazi displays of grandeur and spectacle. Lattre's staff took over most of the luxurious villas in the French zone, organized gala banquet evenings, and conspicuously enjoyed the high life as imperial viceroys. Kurt Schumacher, leader of the Social Democrats in the British zone and later in the Federal Republic, caustically called the French the "Russians of the West," equally as loathed in their zone as the Russians were in theirs. Lattre's successor, the Free French officer General Pierre Koenig, was less punitive and prestige obsessed, and more interested in Franco-German rapprochement, especially in the realm of culture. Koenig's administration poured resources into educational facilities and cultural activities as a part of the French mission of re-civilization, in the form of schooling, university renovation, and art exhibitions. His idea was that Prussian militarism could be overcome by accentuating French universalism, which included resuscitating the "true humanism" of Goethe, Kant, and Beethoven. Germans in the French zone complained that they were served more culture than food, and many of them bristled that they were on the sharp end of an updated colonial *mission civilisatrice*. With time the seeming "colonial" spirit gave way to more successful cultural exchanges and education programs.[26]

Germans were busy reviving cultural life themselves, with the Allies' help in terms of arranging licenses and venues. Already by

May 13, 1945—just five days after the cease-fire—the first public concert performed by the Berlin Chamber Orchestra took place in the Bürgersaal of the Schöneberg city hall, while the Berlin Philharmonic played its first concert in the Titania-Palast in Steglitz a few days later. The first football match took place on May 20 in Berlin, watched by some 10,000 spectators. Cultural exhibitions were mounted, bookstores were reopened, and Weimar modernism was back in vogue as cultural compass. In the frigid winter of 1945–1946, the Berlin theater world put on forty-six plays ranging from Shakespeare to Brecht, playing to huddled audiences in unheated halls.[27]

The terminology of re-civilization resurfaced in the more daily interaction with Germans on the ground, and in particular in relation to the strict imposition of so-called nonfraternization in the British and American zones during the first few months of military occupation. This anti-integration policy applied to both Germany and Austria, though most of the attention was trained on Germany. Non-socialization policies were motivated by concerns of security and terrorism, health and hygiene. But there was a key moral dimension too. According to one American officer stationed in Vienna in 1945, such restrictions would "avoid the lax morals and numerous temptations present in a country whose social codes had been overturned by Nazism and the influx of refugees." Restrictions were numerous and far-reaching: Germans and Austrians were forbidden to converse with American or British soldiers except when necessary; could not travel, send letters, or receive newspapers or books from abroad; were subject to curfew; could not use telephones; could be searched or questioned at any time, and have their property requisitioned. In the British zone, things were sometimes so severe that German bureaucrats were even threatened with appearing before a military tribunal if they did not stand up when a British officer entered their workplace. At the beginning, the Americans were even stricter: GIs were forbidden to shake hands with Germans, visit their homes, play sports with them, exchange gifts, or take part in social events with Germans present. It was also a policy of segregated social space. Brits and Germans were required to travel in separate cars in the subway, while British troops could not attend services in German churches with Germans present. They were not even allowed to listen to music together, which often meant that orchestras had to play the same concert twice. Many Germans found such directives puzzling, expressing what one called "regret that there is little contact between British and German officials outside the office," which led to "very little confidence and so much stiffness."[28]

Nonfraternization measures had been drawn up during the war, and social distancing between victors and vanquished was seen as a vital part of moral reconstruction. The regulation was announced the day after American troops entered Germany on September 12, 1944. In a 1944 circular on the conduct of Allied soldiers in Germany, General Dwight Eisenhower insisted that there was to be no billeting among civilians, no marriage or common religious services, no playing games or attending dances—in his eyes, "the Germans must be ostracized."[29]

British general Bernard Law Montgomery issued a *Letter by the Commander-in-Chief on Non-Fraternisation* in March 1945, instructing all British troops that "you must keep clear of Germans—man, woman and child—unless you meet them in the course of duty." This Allied assumption of German collective guilt had not been widely shared at the beginning of the war. In a broadcast to the German people a few days after the outbreak of war, British prime minister Neville Chamberlain assured that "we are not fighting against you, the German people, for whom we have no bitter feelings, but against a tyrannous and forsworn regime which has betrayed not only its own people but the whole of western civilization and all that you and we hold dear." As late as 1944, Deputy Prime Minister Clement Attlee wrote that impending victory should not "enjoin the treatment of all Germans as sub-human by occupying troops and the exhibition by them of behaviour indistinguishable from that of the

Nazis." The shocking death toll between January and April 1945—more people died in this four-month period of ferocious fighting on the Eastern Front than during the first five years of the war—altered political opinion. For now "a guilty nation," Montgomery's letter continued, must "realise its guilt," for only then "can the first steps be taken to re-educate it, and bring it back into the society of decent humanity." Nonfraternization was therefore both a punishment and a security measure. The failed peace of 1919 was the ready reference: "Last time we won the war and let the peace slip out of our hands. This time we must not ease off—we must win both the war and the peace." Imposing distance between victor and vanquished was to make sure that the occupying forces did not engage in too friendly a way with Germans after the war, as they supposedly had done during the occupation of the Rhineland after the Great War.[30]

By 1944, as the British and Americans were preparing for military occupation of Germany, their armies produced guidebooks for soldiers on how to behave and engage with defeated Axis nations. The new premium placed on civilization was part of it. Take the 1944 *American Pocket Guide to Germany*, put together by the War Department. This pamphlet insisted that American soldiers must stay on guard, for "you are in enemy country! These people are not our allies or friends." The Germans have "sinned against the laws of humanity and cannot come back to the civilized fold merely by sticking out their hands and saying 'I'm sorry.'" Exhortations to "keep your distance" were uppermost. To what degree this was ever enforced is of course debatable, and the guide even featured a section on "marriage facts" stating that "you should know that marriage to a foreign girl is a complicated procedure." The British counterpart was a sixty-four-page booklet called *Germany: The British Soldier's Pocketbook*, produced in 1944 by the Political Warfare Executive, a branch of the Foreign Office. The booklet opened with "You are about to meet a strange people in a strange, enemy country." Here too the need to stay vigilant against defeated Germans was paramount—"you may be tempted to feel sorry for them," yet their "hard luck stories" "will be hypocritical attempts to win sympathy," especially from women who will "make themselves cheap for what they can get out of you." The British government clearly expected its soldiers to stay in Germany for quite a long time, as the guidebook was also a kind of soldier's Baedeker complete with tips on local German food, architecture, language, and customs.[31]

Nonfraternization was not imposed consistently. In occupied Japan, by contrast, there was no strict ban on consorting with former enemies. In Europe, British and American military governments were aware of "fratting" between soldiers and civilians in Italy, Belgium, Holland, and France, and it was deemed acceptable and even encouraged. An "Operation Fraternization" was initiated under the auspices of Princess Juliana and Prince Bernhard of the Netherlands as a way of offering English-speaking female company to over 100,000 Canadian soldiers in Holland in 1945. No doubt fraternization took place, as there were high levels of illegitimate births with military occupations, including 7,000 in Holland in 1945 alone, three times as many as in 1939.[32]

There were also different attitudes among the victors toward nonfraternization in Germany. Comparatively few nonfraternization measures existed in the French zone, as the French generally kept to themselves and imposed fewer curfews. While in the French zone, Germans were not allowed to ride bicycles and faced penalties if French orders were not heeded, they were permitted to live in the same houses with the French, and contacts were generally good, so much so that Germans were often treated as what one historian described as "welcome partners in a common cultural inheritance." Nonfraternization was even less of an issue in the Soviet zone. While from mid-1947 onward any Soviet officer found living with a German woman was to be sent back to the Soviet Union, there were otherwise few restrictions. In fact, early Soviet leniency became an awkward point of competition. One American memo written in

May 1945 nervously admitted that while the Russians were under-taking a "vigorous plan of winning over Germans, we may be going on a tack which will result in estranging them."[33]

Soldiers on the ground voiced a good deal of misgivings, especially in the British zone. The main criticism was that the social ban drove a wedge between soldiers and civilians, and made communication difficult. British officer Leonard O. Mosley raised the political stakes, saying that how British soldiers got on with local Germans "will prove once and for all whether there is hope for European civilisation or not." He sympathized with German resentment, writing that such negative reactions were "not of a people angry that they had lost the War, but of a friendly people who felt that, without reason, they had been sent into purdah over-night, and snubbed and humiliated." In his estimation, "I found Germans—good Germans, sincere Germans—eager and ready not only to make amends, but to work their passage back to civilisation." The fraternization ban also made things uncomfortable for the newly arrived wives of the British officers, and some of them made a political point about it. A jointly signed letter to the editor of the London *Times* from twenty "British Wives in Germany" on October 10, 1946, complained that it was not unusual for up to twenty Germans to be evicted from their homes to provide rooms for one British officer and his wife, while "special transport facilities" were arranged "to save the British wife from sitting near a German." The letter icily finished by saying that such "injury to British popularity and prestige will only add to the numbers of soldiers required, and to the length of their stay."[34]

The debate about nonfraternization pivoted on a gendered understanding of Germany after the war. In part this was due to the so-called female surplus of German civilians in the military zones in 1945, as the presence of women was three times that of men at the end of the war. The "feminization" of Germany after the war altered the way that Allied soldiers saw their mission, one that shifted from fighting fierce enemies to providing for a captive civilian population. Anxiety surrounding fraternization could be seen in the fact that even before the war was over, the American *Pocket Guide* discussed above was withdrawn quite soon after the conquest of German territory, lest it encourage more contact (it contained a section on conversational German). This meant that soldiers were bereft of clear guidance in Germany, and often had a lot of time on their hands. The editors of the American newspaper for overseas soldiers, *Stars and Stripes*, tried to fill the void, furnishing stories that warned soldiers about the dangers of "getting chummy with Jerry" and "Jerry's deadliest V weapon—VD." Fraternization was a very elastic term, and touched on issues ranging from prostitution, rape, sexually transmitted diseases (VD was commonly referred to as *Veronika Dankeschön*), the informal system of food distribution, as well as a spike in the births of "occupation children" as the consequence of American-German liaisons.[35]

Further complicating the fraternization issue was race, particularly relations between African American soldiers and local German women. Older Germans recalled the shock and humiliation associated with the billeting of French African soldiers during the occupation of the Ruhr in the early 1920s as punishment for Germany's reneging on its reparation payments. After 1945 many felt threatened by the presence of supposedly "racially inferior" African American soldiers in their towns and cities. Hostility was directed toward African American GIs in Austria. Local Austrian press published numerous stories of unruly and unwanted black soldiers, to the dismay of the US Army, which took pains to confront this worrisome press coverage. Warm relations between black GIs and local German women also caused friction between white and black soldiers within the army. Moreover, the army faced an equally awkward issue in Germany—African Americans openly admitted that they often enjoyed their time there, generally got along well with locals, and remarked on a new sense of freedom experienced in Germany. Mixing with locals was a welcome relief from the segregated social world of army life on the base. The flagship African American monthly magazine *Ebony* published a report in 1946—complete with photographs of interracial fraternization—that "here where Aryanism ruled supreme, Negroes are finding friendship, more respect and more equality than they would back home," provocatively concluding that "democracy has more meaning on Wilhelmstrasse than on Beale Street in Memphis." President Truman would begin desegregating American armed forces only in 1948. By 1952, a mere 7 percent of black American soldiers in Europe were serving in integrated units. As late as the mid-1960s, 64 percent of black GIs claimed that they found more racial equality in Germany than in the US. Liaisons between African American soldiers and German women scrambled militarized hierarchies and cultural identities, as both victor and vanquished contributed to the racial reconstruction of post-fascist Germany.[36]

German reactions to nonfraternization were mixed. Some preferred the Allied policy of social segregation for specific reasons, ranging from racism to leftist anti-Allied resistance. Allied observers often interpreted German atittudes toward the ban more politically. According to one US Army lieutenant, the level of German acceptance of "fratting" between Allied soldiers and local German women was "the thermometer which registers the degree to which they accept defeat," in that "the sight of a German woman with an American conqueror enrages an 'unreconstructed' German more than a German who is anxious to cooperate with us." Defeat was bound up with demasculinization, as seen with the comparative absence of men in Germany in 1945 as well as the inability of German men to protect and take care of their families and communities.[37]

With time, Allied attitudes toward their German charges began to soften. In part this was due to the experience of encounter, as Germans in the flesh were not quite what the Allies had expected. Once they arrived in Germany, American soldiers were often surprised to discover that there were few defiant supporters of Nazism; what they faced was a nation of people largely sunk in denial and self-pity. In November 1945 a survey of American soldiers' opinions revealed that 80 percent of those polled reported positive impressions of Germans; only 43 percent blamed Germans for the war, and no more than 25 percent judged the Germans responsible for the atrocities committed in the concentration camps. Perhaps relatedly, more than 56 percent admitted to having spent time "talking" with German locals in defiance of the nonfraternization ban.[38]

By late summer the ill-starred Allied nonfraternization measure was rescinded, as all the occupation zones judged it unnecessary, unenforceable, and obstructing broader reconstruction. Some observers remained concerned that the military authorities were becoming too friendly and gullible toward German tales of non-culpability. American journalist Martha Gellhorn lampooned this new softness toward Germans, saying that apparently "no one is a Nazi. No one ever was. It should, we feel, be set to music. Then the Germans could sing this refrain and that would make it even better." In a tellingly titled book, *The Embers Still Burn: An Eye-Witness Account of Our Get-Soft-with-Germany Policy*, Ira Hirschmann, former special UNRRA envoy to Germany, likewise interpreted the "shameful conduct of our soldiers and German fräuleins" as symptomatic of a growing go-easy attitude toward Germany, which he felt was undoing Roosevelt's One World vision and accelerating the division of Europe along Cold War lines. Yet these were relatively isolated voices. The direction of travel was clear, as occupation policy was shifting from punishment to Cold War alliance.[39]

THE END OF NONFRATERNIZATION IN THE AUTUMN OF 1945 coincided with the arrival of unprecedented numbers of ethnic German expellees from Czechoslovakia and Poland, especially in the British Zone of Occupation. It was not just a question of how to cope with the staggering influx of refugees from the East; at stake was a larger moral issue associated with zonal occupation and unconditional surrender. By the autumn of 1945 British public opinion toward the Germans was starting to change, and photography played a key role in brokering a new attitude toward their ex-enemies. British photo-journalism of Germany—and the ensuing broad public discussion about the images—reflected a shifting British attitude toward their German charges that carried wide implications for the development of postwar humanitarianism. Feeding and forgiving the Germans became a surprisingly widespread topic of public debate about the very meaning of British civilization.

How did British opinion go from disdain and distance toward German survivors to inclusion and cooperation in several short years? The simple answer is that things had changed dramatically in those early postwar years, during which the main political experience moved from war to peace, and from combat to occupation to Cold War alliance. However, this still does not tell us much about how this change of sensibility actually took place, and here British photojournalists played their part. It is worth recalling that most of the initial pictures of defeated Germany were taken by the victors. The link between the media and the war was a direct one for the Allies: no fewer than 558 writers, reporters, photographers, and cameramen were embedded in the Allied invading forces, and were recruited precisely to chronicle military triumph. By contrast, the Third Reich prohibited images of material destruction and social chaos in the endgame of the war. Bombing damage was extensively photographed, especially around Cologne, but such images were censored, and mostly not shown until after the war. The Soviet occupiers required all Germans to turn in their cameras to the authorities. The upshot was that Germans were rarely the ones who took photos of their own decimated country in the immediate aftermath of war. The few who did, such as August Sander, Friedrich Seiden-stücker, and Willi Saeger, tended to focus on destroyed cityscapes and ruined statues as allegories of the fate of the country and its citizens more generally. By the early 1950s there was a brisk trade in the photographic imagery of blasted German cities on the commercial market, as before-and-after so-called ruin-books of bombed German cities (especially Berlin, Cologne, and Hamburg) became a bestselling genre.[40]

Allied photographers left a dramatic visual archive of war action, and most of the first photos of defeated Germany concentrated on the taking of German prisoners of war. The Soviets had been documenting Nazi atrocities with their cameras since 1941, yet their wartime focus on the horrors of German misdeeds was soon replaced by celebratory pictures of conquest and heroism—the seizure of the Reichstag and Reichkanzlei were favorite photographic trophies. While there was some initial Allied sympathy toward captured German soldiers in 1944 and early 1945, especially among the British, such compassion soon evaporated with the shock resulting from the liberation of the concentration camps. Allied soldiers photographed Bergen-Belsen, Dachau, and Buchenwald in great detail, after which these images were splashed across the national media in both the US and Great Britain. American antipathy toward Germans under occupation could be seen in Signal Corps pictures of a black-and-white moral world of perpetrators and victims. American troops commonly forced Germans to confront their heinous misdeeds, and on several occasions compelled local Germans to hold corpses (in staged photographs) as punishment for their sins.[41]

American photographs reflected a distinct physical and moral separation between occupier and occupied. Margaret Bourke-White's 1946 photo book, *"Dear Fatherland, Rest Quietly": A Report on the Collapse of Hitler's "Thousand Years,"* is a famous example of this genre of using the camera to cast judgment on the German people, depicting concentration camp victims, destroyed cities, shameless looting, and even the moral scourge of fraternization. Lee Miller's June 1945 article in *Vogue* magazine entitled "Germans Are Like

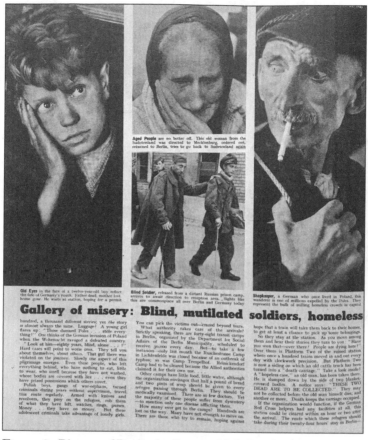

Figure 9. Photos of Berlin by Leonard McCombe, *Illustrated* (London), September 22, 1945. *Credit: Odhams Press, London*

This" was equally unforgiving. In the accompanying text, Miller wrote that "we claimed to be waging war on the Nazis, only. Our patience with the Germans has been so exaggeratedly correct that they think that they can get away with anything." Other journalists welcomed Allied efforts to force Germans to face up to the evidence of war atrocities.[42]

Compassion toward the Germans remained a delicate issue. A good example is an October 1945 piece, "Gallery of Misery," in London's *Illustrated*, with accompanying photos by British photographer Leonard McCombe (Figure 9). The editors felt obliged to add a contextualizing caption beneath the moving photographs of gruesome destitution and misery, lest the reader feel too much sympathy for German survivors. As they put it: "These displaced Germans are being treated callously but not with the deliberate cruelty which their government once inflicted on others. They are, at least, allowed to live."[43] Such moral tension was evident in Humphrey Jennings's short film *A Defeated People*, shot in the British zone in the autumn of 1945 and released in 1946. It exhibited great compassion toward the suffering of Germans, featuring crowds of POWs, forlorn civilians, and destitute children. But again, there was a marked disjunction between image and word, picture and policy. The film's stern voiceover jarred with the more sympathetic images on offer, admonishing the Germans and mocking the deserved fate of the defeated "master race of men," concluding that "we shall stay in Germany until we have real guarantees that the next generation will grow up sane and Christian again."[44]

The American military government was much stricter than the British about peacekeeping imagery. Just after Yankee soldiers landed in Germany, US Army press photographers snapped what they thought were non-controversial pictures of German civilians offering warm welcome to American soldiers. Eisenhower reacted angrily to this undue fraternization on display, after which his press staff was told in no uncertain terms that any images of fraternization would be censored. This strict policing of images of American-German interaction gave British photographers an opening, as they took the lead in framing new and more ambiguous images of Allied encounters with German survivors.

By the second half of 1945, British photographers were parting company from their American allies and provided strikingly sympathetic press toward the Germans. Sad and pitiful scenes at Berlin's railway stations and transit camps were favorite subjects of British photographers, and helped shape British views of life in Germany that year. This could be seen in outlets such as the *Daily Herald*, the Labour Party's mass circulation newspaper, and *News Chronicle*, a liberal daily. Like their counterparts in the American Signal Corps, most of the British photographers were War Office photographers working within the Army Film and Photographic Unit, and those who shot photographs for British illustrated magazines after the cease-fire usually had been army photographers during the war. Eyewitness reports by British journalists on special assignment often took up the humanitarian crisis afflicting the "homeless hordes" across Germany. Numerous accounts circulated about the deplorable conditions of Germans in the British zone, living in squalor, malnourished, and badly suffering from illness and disease. A 1945 *News Chronicle* piece sensationalized Berlin's shocking scenes of "the dead and dying and starving flotsam left by the tide of human misery that reaches Berlin."[45]

In a *Picture Post* article in September 1945 called "Report on Chaos," journalist Lorna Hay and photographer Haywood Magee reported on the 2.1 million displaced persons in Germany. They wrote that their diet consisted of 1,000 calories a day, compared to British rations at 2,000 calories a day, and US Army rations of 3,500 calories a day. They grimly concluded that "Germany's misery this winter will be on a scale unknown in Europe since the Middle Ages." "They may say: 'The Germans deserve it. Why should we worry?' Maybe they do deserve it. But do our armies of occupation deserve to be set down in such a country, or to be asked to face the consequences of the breakdown of civilised life among a population of 90,000,000?" Other newspaper pictures depicted the chaos of checkpoints and train stations, trucks full of refugees and scavengers on the road huddled in "ragged camps" in a "gallery of misery." While the style was still quite matter-of-fact, there was a discernible sense of compassion too.[46]

The difficult moral issue of expressing pity toward former enemies was neatly captured by one *Daily Herald* journalist: "Today I have seen thousands of German civilians—old men and women and children of all ages—reduced to the depths of misery and suffering that the Nazis inflicted on others during their beastly reign." For this journalist, the plight of Germans was nothing less than a test of British values and the very fiber of Britishness: "But if we are to prove to the German race, that our methods, our civilisation, our creed were right and theirs wrong, and if we are to keep faith with those who died, were maimed and suffered intolerable hardship, then these problems have got to be solved and have got to be solved quickly." Such views reflected a growing British sensibility about seeing suffering in universal terms visited upon all Europeans, and the disturbing photographs in the *Times* and *News Chronicle* spurred broad discussion in the British press.[47]

Various British politicians entered the debate. In one *Picture Post* article called "Wanted: A New Policy for Germany," Labour Party MP Maurice Edelmann wrote that he was tired of the "you brought it upon yourselves" theme, countering that "we should treat fellow human beings, not by Nazi standards, but by the standards of Christian civilization." Violet Bonham Carter, president of Britain's Liberal Party, raised the moral stakes of the debate still higher. In her Conway Hall speech of October 9, 1945, Bonham Carter described the food crisis in the British zone of Germany as "perhaps our greatest, most critical and testing hour, as a nation, since 1940. Now, as then," she continued, "we stand alone for certain values," for "there is not one of us who has the right to ask 'Am I not my brother's keeper?' to whatever race he may belong."[48]

The campaign to take better care of the Germans in the British zone enlisted the support of the Anglican church. Bishop George Bell set the tone and made his views known to the public. Bell had established good ties with the dissident German Protestant Church during the war, the so-called Confessioning Church, and sought to reach out to German Christians under Hitler. He voiced his criticism of British bombing of Germany, writing in the *Times* in April 1941 that "if Europe is civilised at all, what can excuse the bombing of towns by night and terrorizing non-combatants?" Other Anglican leaders expressed similar views toward the end of the war. Bell's 1946 tract *If Thine Enemy Hunger* argued that British enmity toward its former enemies undermined Christian principles. For Bell, the pretext for intervention was the announcement by the British occupation government in Berlin in late February 1946 that the British zone would make a "drastic cut" in the rations for Germans, whose effect in Bell's eyes would be that "very large numbers will certainly die of starvation." Bell appealed to the Christian conscience of British citizens, asserting that German suffering served "as a challenge to their humanity," because the "world can be saved" only—and here he addressed the reader directly—by "harnessing your soul to the energy of love." Notably, Bell spearheaded Anglican opposition to further war crimes tribunals after the Nuremberg Trial, arguing that it was time for forgiveness rather than endless retribution.[49]

Nowhere was the shifting sentiment toward the Germans more evident than in the debate about the morality of expulsion in the autumn of 1945. Once the war had ended, Czechs and Poles made a concerted effort to expunge ethnic Germans from their homelands as an act of national purification and peacemaking. Czech president Edvard Beneš, in his first speech on May 16, 1945, demanded the "liquidation" of the country's Germans and Magyars "in the interest of a united national state of Czechs and Slovaks." For Beneš, "our Germans" have "betrayed our state, betrayed our democracy, betrayed us, betrayed humanness, and betrayed mankind." The Polish and Czech governments-in-exile had been discussing the expulsion of the Germans from their countries almost since the war broke out, and looked to the transfer of Greeks and Turks as a result of the 1923 Treaty of Lausanne as a model. Sudeten Germans were fifth columnists in Czechoslovakia, and the Nazi takeover after 1938 brought brutal exploitation, forced labor, and executions, culminating in the infamous killing of 192 civilians at Lidice. Revived nationalism was considered a key step toward state-building, and

Czech leaders made the case that expelling Germans and expropriating their land would help ease the surplus agricultural population. Stalin supported this move in numerous conversations with both Polish and Czech leaders; Churchill, in a House of Commons speech on December 15, 1944, agreed that the political effects of the expulsion "will be the most satisfactory and lasting." Such policy was also agreed in the Potsdam Treaty by the leaders of Britain, the US, and the Soviet Union. In both Poland and Czechoslovakia the doctrine of collective guilt was applied against Germans, after which pillage and expropriation were rife as part of the broader campaign of de-germanization. The backs of Sudeten Germans were often painted with swastikas, and Germans were forced by Czechs to wear white armbands affixed with *N* for *Nemec,* or "German." Makeshift people's court trials, revenge killings, and population transfers dominated the aftermath of war. The newly established United Nations turned a blind eye to the expulsions, for fear that it would appear too sympathetic toward ex-Nazis. Expulsions too were seen as part of the broader logic of postwar peacemaking—whereas after the Great War, efforts were made to draw the new state borders of post-Habsburg Central Europe so as to accommodate ethnic groups on the ground, post-1945 planners opted for moving people to suit newly drawn-up national borders. The point is that the Great Powers and the United Nations all gave Poland and Czechoslovakia their blessing to unmix their national populations in the name of modernization and nation-building.[50]

However, international groups voiced their dismay. In the autumn of 1945 British and American press decried the expulsions as violating Article 12 of the Potsdam Protocol, which demanded "orderly" transfers to be put in place. *New York Times* correspondent Anne O'Hare McCormick called the organized expulsions of ethnic Germans from Poland and Czechoslovakia "the most inhuman decision ever made by governments dedicated to the defense of human rights." The *Manchester Guardian* condemned the Czech treatment of Germans as "reminiscent of Hitler's pan-Germanism" and racial politics "unworthy of the country of Masaryk." Roman Catholics denounced Beneš and his "new secular Puritans" for taking their country down the road of "post-Christian barbarism." In February 1946 a committee of the World Council of Churches meeting in Geneva, which included Archbishop Bell and prominent German Protestant minister and anti-Nazi activist Martin Niemoeller, implored the victorious nations to combine justice with mercy, because to "seek vengeance against former enemies" "can only bring fresh disaster."[51]

An American 1947 pamphlet called *The Land of the Dead: Study of the Deportation from Eastern Germany* sounded the moral alarm. It was published by the New York–based Committee Against Mass Expulsion, and was signed by public intellectuals including Varian Fry, Dorothy Thompson, John Dewey, and Norman Thomas. They protested the brutal expulsions that "[offend] against the basic principles of our civilization," and that brazenly flouted the Atlantic Charter. For them, these developments challenged the very foundation of civilization itself, and they concluded that "what happens to Sudetens and Eastern Germans today could happen tomorrow to Moslems in India; to Jews in Palestine; to Whites in South Africa; to Negroes in the United States." Not least, various German groups communicated their outrage to the United Nations and the international community, arguing that their treatment at the hands of the Czechs and Poles was a human rights violation of the first order.[52]

The Czechs and Poles reacted angrily to international criticism of their expulsion measures against the Germans. One Pole wrote an "Open Letter [to] the British Labour Party" in May 1946, saying, "Who has any right to condemn us for our attitude? Where is the one 'without sin,' who would do otherwise in our situation?" Beneš defended his country's policy in terms of the defense of civilization. In an interview with a Moscow correspondent of the *Times*, he insisted that the expulsions were necessary, darkly adding that the alternative "would not be humane. It would be a pity if we were penalized for being civilized." In a speech at the Czech National Assembly in March 1946, Czech foreign minister Jan Masaryk intoned that "we have a good name as a civilized people. We are going to keep that good name."[53]

While their expulsion policies initially received international blessing as a necessary step toward political peace, the Polish and Czech governments were suddenly targeted by the new moral politics of Anglo-American public opinion. British photojournalistic images shaped this debate, and shifted the moral attitude toward ex-enemies. Even hardened British reporters began to change their minds, as newspaper photographs of German expellees suffering in the British zone evoked pity. George Bilainkin, a longtime Germanophobe and reporter for the *Daily Mail*, was at first sympathetic toward the Czechs and Poles for expelling the Germans. Yet in his diary, and almost despite himself, he admitted that "the picture of elderly women, and young girls, with children almost dying on the railway stations of Berlin after long journeys from their former homes, provides [a] test of political convictions. Humanitarian, not soft-hearted, considerations rise unwillingly to the surface." Bilainkin was scarcely alone, as media coverage of the expellees—especially in Britain—continued to move British civil society in new directions.[54]

IT WAS AT THIS STAGE THAT VICTOR GOLLANCZ ELECTRIFIED the debate. Gollancz was a brash Jewish London publisher who used the proceeds from his successful Left Book Club in the 1930s to peddle his own controversial views on contemporary political problems. In that decade and the early 1940s, he published a series of pamphlets chronicling Nazi terror, such as *The Brown Book of the Nazi Terror* (1933); *The Yellow Spot* (1936), about the cruelties inflicted on Jews in Germany; and *Let My People Go* (1943), which attempted to incite public opinion about the plight of Polish Jews. Even so, he was no Germanophobe. In fact, Gollancz was outraged by Lord Robert Vansittart's infamous and bestselling *Black Book: Germans Past and Present*, and challenged the dangerous effects of "Vansittartism" and what he felt was unjustified antipathy toward Germans. In his 1942 booklet *Shall Our Children Live or Die? A Reply to Lord Vansittart on the German Problem*, Gollancz sought to show that the problems of German history were not unique to Germany, and that Germany and Germans were not especially aggressive. In April 1945 Gollancz waded into further controversy with his booklet *What Buchenwald Really Means*, in which he rejected charges of German collective guilt as ill-judged and vindictive. He went on to castigate Britons for doing nothing to save Jews, which provoked a good deal of hate mail directed toward him in response. For him a much bigger issue was at stake: "This Judeo-Christian tradition is our inner citadel. We have been fighting to preserve it for our children: are we now to surrender it in the very moment of victory?"[55]

Over the course of that year Gollancz became increasingly out-raged by the harrowing press reports from the British zone, and used missives, pamphlets, and photographs to plead for better treatment of Germans. In a letter to the *News Chronicle* in August 1945, he lamented the emergence of a dangerous "new morality" that regarded mercy and pity as "not merely irrelevant, but positively disgraceful." A May 1945 poll found that 54 percent of Britons said they "hated the Germans," with 80 percent in favor of harsh peace terms; Gollancz felt that this augured badly for any durable postwar peace. Gollancz ratcheted up the rhetoric still further in his 1946 pamphlet *Leaving Them to Their Fate: The Ethics of Starvation*. He felt compelled to write it out of a "mounting sense of shame" about conditions in the British zone of Germany, and accused the English of "starving the German people." In Gollancz's eyes, Germany's unconditional surrender rendered this a supreme moral issue of noblesse oblige for Britain: "Germans were required to place themselves utterly in our hands," he intoned, and "if that does not impose a special obligation on a nation that calls itself civilised, then what does?" Britain's "special obligation" was the duty of the "liberal or Christian conqueror to his enemy" and "the preservation of western values."[56]

Gollancz took up the broader moral dimension of the poor treatment of Germans inside the British zone most pointedly in his 1947 book, *Our Threatened Values*, which sold over 50,000 copies. Here he cited extracts from a speech made by Viscount Montgomery, in which he was reported to have said that "German food-cuts have come to stay." For Gollancz, Montgomery's words revealed "the moral crisis with which western civilisation is faced." Gollancz denounced British nonfraternization policies precisely because they undermined the very values for which the Allies had supposedly fought the war.[57]

Gollancz's campaign to treat the Germans more humanely was vividly reflected in the photographs in his publications. In late 1945 he rushed out a pamphlet before Christmas called *Is It Nothing to You?*, demanding relief for German expellee children. He was scandalized when the British minister of food, Sir Ben Smith, had announced that Britain's own rations were to be increased before Christmas, in crass contrast to the harrowing situation in the British zone in Germany. Gollancz's pamphlet featured images of emaciated German expellee children in hospital beds languishing in pain and hunger, photographs that he took himself. The cover—featuring a starving German child—exhorted British readers to show sympathy toward their former enemies (Figure 10).

Such imagery was in itself nothing new, recalling as it did the 1919 poster by Save the Children Fund founder Eglantyne Jebb, "A Starving Child," which famously sought to draw British attention to the plight of Viennese children suffering from the consequences of the Allied blockade during World War I. Jebb focused on children as a means of building goodwill toward former enemy nations, and

Figure 10. Malnourished young boy, Berlin, on cover of pamphlet by Victor Gollancz, *Is It Nothing to You?* (London: Victor Gollancz, 1945). *Credit: Orion Books, London*

led the campaign to send food supplies to help children in Russia in the aftermath of the 1921 famine there.[58]

Gollancz's imagery in this sense was both old and new. Those sympathetic to the plight of Germans often used expellee children as a means of eliciting pity. Gollancz's strategy dovetailed with humanitarian relief films produced after World War I by the League of Nations and the International Red Cross, and echoed the photographic documentation by international agencies of relief assistance during the Spanish Civil War. His imagery also recalled that used to publicize the wartime campaign to assist starving children, as noted in Thérèse Bonney's 1943 photo book, *Europe's Children*, which became an overnight sensation. But of course in 1945 the main reference was the mass-produced pictures of starved Holocaust survivors spread across the newspapers of the West following the liberation of the camps, and here Gollancz was trying to extend the story of humanitarian neglect and cruelty across the 1945 divide to blur the perpetrator-victim distinction. Gollancz's report of his 1946 visit to

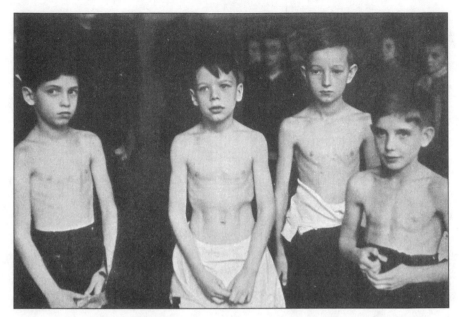

Figure 11. Malnourished schoolboys, Germany, 1947. Victor Gollancz, *In Darkest Germany* (London: Victor Gollancz, 1947). *Credit: Orion Books, London*

Germany, *In Darkest Germany*, included harrowing photos of squalid living conditions and malnourished children, with the aim of showing that Germany was not recovering from the war (Figure 11).

He appended more than a dozen pages of photos of dilapidated childrens' footwear to dramatize poor care in the British zone (Figure 12). Gollancz often appeared in the photos himself as a kind of solemn witness, standing behind the forlorn children in a sort of paterfamilias pose. Some have argued that his main motive behind the book and pictures was to draw attention to the expense and difficulty of administering the British zone, so as to encourage handing over the zone to the Germans as quickly as possible. On this point it is worth remembering that there were initially fewer than 100 British public health officials in a British zone made up of around 22 million people. Even so, these were shocking images. What made them so unusual was the way that they sought to provoke shame and pity in a war-weary British public unaccustomed to sympathy toward

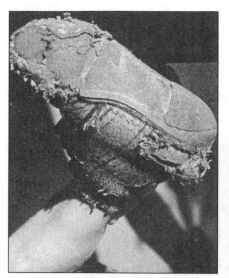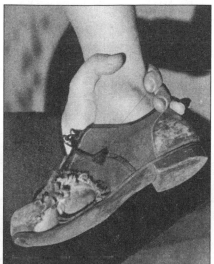

Figure 12. Delapidated shoes of German children, 1947. Victor Gollancz, *In Darkest Germany* (London: Victor Gollancz, 1947). *Credit: Orion Books, London*

the Germans. Like Jebb's Save the Children Fund after World War I, Gollancz's campaign was directed toward former enemies in the wake of war. But whereas Jebb was arrested for her poster on charges of public indecency, Gollancz's scandalous photographs found a supportive audience, especially among the churches, prompting many to donate humanitarian aid toward Britain's former enemy.[59]

Given the positive support from readers, Gollancz launched his "Save Europe Now" scheme in 1945, which asked the British public to voluntarily cut their rations to help feed needy German children. The first appeal was issued in early September 1945, and within ten days some 5,000 cards were received by mail, and after another week over 20,000 people had responded positively. On one level, this sentiment was not altogether new. In an August 1940 speech, Churchill had argued that "we shall do our best to encourage the building up of reserves of food all over the world, so that there will always be held up before the eyes of the peoples of Europe, including—I say it deliberately—the German and Austrian peoples, the certainty that the shattering of the Nazi power will bring to them all immediate food, freedom and peace." Toward the end of the war there was growing willingness in Britain, from groups ranging from the churches to organized labor, for further rations to aid the decimated continent. The revelations of Nazi atrocities and the discovery of the concentration camps reversed British and American attitudes toward the Germans as popular opinion stiffened against aid or sympathy. What is so striking is how quickly the case for helping German civilians after the cease-fire took wing.[60]

In this regard, the British media campaign in 1945 and 1946 proved remarkably successful. The German refugee crisis was the dominant issue in the daily press and especially in the illustrated print media, and figures like philosopher J. B. Priestley and Violet Bonham Carter supported aid for Germany. Minister of Education Ellen Wilkinson went so far as to say that Gollancz's "Save Europe Now" was "carrying on in the Dunkirk spirit." Some MPs supported the campaign strictly out of national interest, arguing that starvation in Europe might lead to disease and epidemics that could affect British troops stationed in Germany. Gollancz's charity sent a large number of parcels of rationed food donated by British families, which were distributed by Red Cross relief teams. By the end of 1948 more than 35,000 parcels had been sent to the continent, half of which were dispatched to Germany, whose "spiritual and psychological importance," according to one report, were "far greater than their calorie value." Feeding Germans properly in the British zone—however difficult this was to countenance after the war—served as the very marker of British civilization.[61]

With time, the tone of the British zone photographs changed too. The more strident military photography that initially demarcated the British military personnel from their German subjects softened by the late 1940s, as the occupying forces began to get used to living in Germany, and with Germans. With the stabilization of the situation, photographers increasingly turned to everyday life and

Figure 13. Photo by Sergeant Wilkes, Berlin, July 1945. *Credit: BU8610, Imperial War Museum, London*

civilian reconstruction. The heroism of the so-called rubble women, or *Trümmerfrauen*, who worked tirelessly to clear the debris from Germany's bombed-out cities became a favorite subject of British photographers. What was new was that British photographs now featured Germans alongside Brits. The overcoming of social distance was part of the increasing relaxation of the once-stern nonfraternization policies, and could be noted in some of the photographs of German women and children, often in interaction with Allies, which went a long way toward "humanizing" the former enemy by the late 1940s (Figure 13).

Not everyone was on board with helping Germans. Few in the Labour cabinet shared Gollancz's sympathetic views toward their former enemy. Prime Minister Clement Attlee, an infantry officer in World War I, held long-standing anti-German attitudes, and Foreign Secretary Ernest Bevin once colorfully remarked that "I try to be fair to them but I 'ates them, really." Attlee and Bevin would not visit Berlin until the Berlin Airlift in 1948. Nöel Coward's famous 1943 song "Don't Let's Be Beastly to the Germans" was a satire of Britain's "excessive humanitarians" who were "taking a rather too tolerant view of our enemies," including J. B. Priestley, Bertrand Russell, and Gollancz. Attlee supposedly dismissed a delegation led by Gollancz and the economist William Beveridge, who pleaded for more money and leniency. One British soldier countered that "I have not seen anybody starving in Germany yet, at least not in the British zone and in Berlin," and "people in Westphalia live better than many people in Britain." A German concentration camp survivor, Franz Burger, objected to Gollancz's "bold flight of British conscience" in his effort to place "the British in the dock," thereby making every Briton guilty, and hoped that other Brits will "stand up to their stern prosecutor Gollancz." Gollancz was severely criticized in both the British Jewish community and the right-wing press as unpatriotic, arrogant, and anti-Jewish, and many felt that his moralizing was excessive and inappropriate just after the war. Others too were alarmed by such English pro-German sentimentality. The Polish poet and Nobel laureate Czesław Miłosz remarked to a British visitor in 1945 that "I don't understand your people. . . . You have hearts, yes, but do you think with them?"[62]

Gollancz's romantic views of former enemies predictably met with adulation in West Germany. Konrad Adenauer, who became the Federal Republic's first chancellor in 1949, acknowledged that "Germany owes Victor Gollancz a great debt of gratitude, a debt which is all the greater in view of his Jewish descent." At an official gathering at the Nuremberg Opera House in 1950, Gollancz was hailed by the mayor as a "modern Nathan the Wise" who "never preached hatred and revenge against the German people." In 1953 Gollancz was given the Order of Merit by the German ambassador as the first non-German recipient of the award. No doubt there was an ever-present air of moral self-righteousness in Gollancz's press crusade, yet his campaign did force people to see Germans differently, and spurred great popular interest and support for British operations in Germany.[63]

THE ANGLO-AMERICAN CAMPAIGN TO FEED AND FORGIVE THE Germans was the expression of a broader transatlantic civic voluntarism that initially challenged harsh military government policies, and with time even helped transform them. While some of these movements were relatively short-lived, such as Gollancz's "Save Europe Now" campaign, they did mark a decisive shift of moral sensibility. The media campaigns to visualize the pain of others were efforts to forge new ways of seeing the ex-enemy, and the British took the lead. Like the nineteenth-century abolition crusades, postwar humanitarianism was designed to forge a new moral community of sympathy from a distance. Most scholars locate this shift of attitude with the food crisis associated with the Berlin Airlift of 1948–1949, during which Berlin was transformed from the capital of Nazi militarism to the vulnerable outpost of solidarity between the Western allies and West Berliners. Yet it really started in the autumn of 1945.

The relationship between the Allies and their ex-enemies ran the gamut of emotions in 1945 and 1946—from vengeance to shame, hatred to pity. The international war crimes trials were an effort to stay the hand of vengeance and reassert the role of law in international affairs after the total collapse of European society. Controversial as it was, the Nuremberg Trial did help establish political peace in the Western zones of occupation, and helped kill off any fantasies of fascist revenge. The "civilizing mission"—the nineteenth-century motor and framework for Europe's engagement with the non-European world—was now turned toward other Europeans, primarily Germans, underwritten by new norms of international order and moral regeneration based on material welfare. This remaking of civilization after

1945—especially in dealings with Germany and Germans—pivoted on the expression of pity and compassion as markers of the West.

This is why photojournalism was so critical, for it brokered a new universalist sensibility after the war. Just as romantic novels in the early nineteenth century helped engender a new sensibility of humanity toward suffering distant strangers, these photographs played a similar role in helping to spur a new phase of humanitarianism after 1945. Such sentiment is usually associated with other landmark photography shows in the late 1940s. A UNESCO photo book produced two years after the war, *The Book of Needs*, marked a new tone by focusing on children, education, and reconstruction. A similar spirit could be seen in UNESCO's 1949 *Children of Europe* book, with photos by David "Chim" Seymour. While the lone suffering child became a visual staple after World War I as a rallying cry of humanitarian assistance from the British Save the Children Fund through the Spanish Civil War, such imagery was revived as a crucial moral compass after 1945. In *Children of Europe*, Europe's orphans were depicted as victims of war against ruined European landscapes, irrespective of background or nationality, and as such helped create a new inclusive European sensibility (Figure 14). This sentiment found supreme expression in the 1955 blockbuster show *The Family of Man*, conceived by Edward Steichen in collaboration with the Museum of Modern Art in New York. It was the most popular international photography exposition of all time, seen by over 9 million people in thirty-eight countries. *Family of Man* aimed to show what Steichen called "the essential one-ness of mankind throughout the world," portraying peoples from across the world in a kind of intimate family album of post-fascist humanity. Yet these British photographs of defeated Germans played a forgotten role in forging this new visual language of humanity and inclusivity, and were used to enlist moral and material support from a quite hostile British public toward Germans living under British dominion.[64]

Figure 14. From *Children of Europe*, photograph by David Seymour (Paris: UNESCO, 1949). *Credit: Magnum Photographers, New York*

What made British views of the Germans so unique was that they turned the criticism on themselves as occupiers, to the extent that they saw the proper treatment of Germans in the British zone as an instance and test of British civilization. And even if this moral crusade was often motivated by Christian principles, it was the care of the bodies (not souls) that spurred calls for action. The history of early postwar interaction between Allies and their German charges recalls a time when the expression of humanitarianism was still severely rationed, precisely because it included defeated enemies in a new moral universe of common humanity so soon after the fighting.

The shift toward sympathy for Germans and their inclusion in the story of wounded humanity came at the expense of the victims of Nazi crimes. It is striking that the campaign to aid the Germans took place precisely during the opening of the Nuremberg Trial, when discussion and images of Nazi atrocities were covered in the press on a daily basis. The shocking photos of the liberation of the camps six months before were apparently old news by that autumn, despite the widespread discussion of Nazi misdeeds during the trial and after. The polemics of pity had shifted focus. The issue that stirred the conscience of the American and British publics was less the tragic fate of the Jews, but rather the plight of German refugees—all in the name of humanity, Christian charity, and a new moral universalism. Gollancz's media campaign played a vital role in making these shifting views palatable to a British audience, not least because it was couched in notions of "Judeo-Christian civilization." The universalization of victimhood espoused in these famous photography exhibitions of the 1940s and 1950s unwittingly erased the specificity of Jewish victimhood and suffering, as Nazi genocide against the Jews was marginalized in public consciousness as simply a subchapter of the broader story of World War II. It was not until the 1980s that the Holocaust and Auschwitz moved to the center of the history of World War II and even the century itself.

With the intensification of the Cold War in Europe, the moral relationship between friend and foe took on a new geopolitical expression. Civilization was again used to map and narrate the changing understanding of the continent, but by the late 1940s the new frontiers of identity centered on religion.

three

FAITH AND FRONTIERS

O N THE DAY AFTER CHRISTMAS 1948, CARDINAL JÓZSEF
Mindszenty was arrested by the Hungarian state police. The
communist leadership had kept a close eye on the outspoken conservative leader of the Hungarian Catholic Church for several years, and
had grown tired of the prelate's uncompromising nature and defiant
attitude. At the end of 1948 the Hungarian People's Republic banned
all religious orders as treasonous, and accused Mindszenty of being
an enemy of the state. The prosecution took a month to prepare its
case, after which the cardinal, his secretary, and several close ecclesiastical associates became the subjects of a high-profile show trial in
Budapest starting on February 3, 1949. After two days of relentless
denunciations and sham proceedings, they were all found guilty and
sentenced to life imprisonment. It was a scripted showdown between
the Church and the communist state, and the Hungarian Communist Party wished to make a dramatic example of the cardinal. Much
of the trial was broadcast live on Hungarian radio and received wide
coverage in the Party-controlled print media.[1]

Mindszenty's name may remain largely forgotten today, yet his
case provoked remarkable international controversy at the time. No
issue exercised the international Catholic community more in the

125

early Cold War, as Roman Catholic leaders and publicists around the world raised their voices in protest and numerous Catholic demonstrations were organized on both sides of the Atlantic. While the trial mobilized the transnational Catholic community in unique ways, it had equally important effects for the postwar formulation of human rights and the cultural frontiers of the Christian West. A particularly keen follower of the cardinal's plight was none other than the US government, and in particular the CIA became fascinated by how the trial seemed to showcase the Soviet Union's new brainwashing techniques to extract confessions. Mindszenty's fate was central to widespread discussions about the crisis of civilization in the late 1940s and early 1950s, and this chapter will focus on the trial and its impact on the redefinition of the Christian West. In a variety of ways, the 1949 Budapest trial emerged as an international flashpoint for organized religion, human rights, and the Cold War geography of Christian civilization.

WHAT MADE MINDSZENTY'S CASE SPECIAL WAS IN PART HIS biography. He had been a key figure in the Hungarian Catholic Church for decades, and was arrested just after the First World War by the short-lived Béla Kun communist government in 1919 and then again by the fascist Arrow Cross regime in 1944 for protesting the continuation of war on Hungarian soil. Mindszenty came from a small village in western Hungary and had been a rural pastor for almost thirty years, after which he was elevated as the head of the Hungarian church by Pope Pius XII in 1945 largely on the strength of his outspoken anticommunist views. He possessed impeccable antifascist credentials, was a sworn enemy of the left, and did not shrink from a fight. In his inaugural sermon after being named cardinal-prelate, Mindszenty boldly described himself as the "pontifex, bridge builder, and first dignitary of the state, vested with 900-year old rights." He was pitted against a formidable figure in his own right—Mátyás Rákosi, the Hungarian communist leader, who was committed to destroying the remnants of old Hungary to erect a new revolutionary order along the Danube.[2]

While church-state relations in the early postwar years were relatively peaceful, Mindszenty and his church were increasingly seen as an obstacle to communist political plans and social engineering. This was especially so in regard to the regime's desired land reform, nationalization of children's education, and the dechristianization of the national press. Against these plans the cardinal fought back in various ways. For instance, he refused to declare any loyalty to the Hungarian state unless the communist regime guaranteed freedom for all Catholic associations; permitted the publication of a daily, not just weekly, Catholic newspaper; and resumed diplomatic relations with the Vatican. In a 1947 pastoral letter, Mindszenty employed the new language of human rights to challenge government legitimacy: "We must publicly declare that no Christian voter can support a party that rules by violence and suppression, and tramples underfoot all natural laws and human rights." And in an effort to beat back the communist state's encroachments, he declared the period between August 1947 and December 1948 the "Year of the Virgin," with the slogan "Hungary Is the Virgin Mary's Country." The Marian Festival was designed to energize the besieged Hungarian Catholic community through mass sermons, parades, pilgrimages, and marches in a show of resistance against state incursions into traditional Catholic cultural territory. By all counts, the festival was a huge success—the clergy led several pilgrimages, with estimates of up to some 1.5 million people participating.[3]

The festival was a shrewd move by Mindszenty, and not just against the state, for he also aimed to help reunite the Church with popular religious sentiment. Here it is well to remember that the Cult of Mary enjoyed a dramatic comeback across the war-ravaged continent in the wake of World War II, punctuated by a rash of religious sightings, roaming faith healers, pilgrimages, and miracles that attracted hundreds of thousands of believers in a number of countries. It was part of an explosion of popular religiosity that is still largely unremarked in histories of the postwar era.

It is well known that the modern pattern of Marian witnesses originated in France in the mid-nineteenth century, with the sightings in 1858 at Lourdes as the most famous. Pilgrimages to Lourdes began in 1872 after France's defeat by the Prussians, a defeat that was interpreted as divine judgment for the sins of the Republic and Paris Commune.[4] The immediate post-1945 period saw a bounty of miracles and apparitions across Europe, ranging from Spain, France, and Ireland to West Germany, Austria, and Hungary. Between 1947 and 1954 dozens of apparitions of the Virgin Mary were reported to church authorities across Europe each year, more than three times the average both during the preceding and in the following decades. The old pilgrimage sites, such as Lourdes and Marpingen in Germany, maintained their place after World War II, but now new ones arose in other places too, drawing crowds of tens of thousands for weeks or even months on end, as a new populist Catholic evangelism gripped post-Nazi Europe. Some of these sightings took on Cold War dimensions: the famed Fatima apparitions in Portugal in 1917—whose apocalyptic visions had supposedly revealed the sorrows and scourges of the Russian Revolution—became a touchstone of Cold War commentary about the heightened fears of the new specter of communism after 1945. In fact, an International Pilgrim Virgin Statue—a copy of the Fatima image blessed by the bishop of Leiria in Portugal—embarked on a world tour in 1947, reportedly accompanied by miracles and the mysterious presence of doves. The 1943 Oscar-winning film *The Song of Bernadette*, based on Franz Werfel's 1941 novel of the Lourdes story, was released in Western Europe in 1948, and was the biggest box-office film that year in Western Germany. In 1949 there arose in West Germany the Apparition Cult of Heroldsbach-Thurn, a village in southeastern Germany, accompanied by widespread reports of daily divine visitations to a group of young female seers. By 1952 some 1.5 million pilgrims had visited the site and its four female visionaries to witness its frequent apparitions, and the town's proximity to the Czech border during the 1948 communist consolidation of power was understood to have heightened the Cold War fears of apocalypse. Such sightings were not confined to Western Europe. In Poland's Lublin Cathedral, it was reported that the statue of Mary began to weep, drawing crowds of up to 100,000 a day. The wider point is that the postwar period—routinely characterized as an era of economic and political miracles—was awash with religious miracles as well.[5]

In 1950 Pope Pius XII sought to harness this new popular religiosity to the Church. His declaration of the International Marian Year in 1954 was broadcast by television to diffuse what he proudly called the "further triumphs of Jesus and Mary." As he saw it, this renewed cult was born of the difficulties of wartime, reflecting a common Catholic view that Nazism was the extreme extension of a secular anthropocentric worldview that began with the Renaissance and French Revolution. Across the Cold War divide there was widespread feeling among Catholic churchmen that their parishioners were susceptible to the sirens of totalitarian ideologies because they had abandoned the Church or were being distracted by secularism, materialism, and individualism. Turning toward the Blessed Mother was thus a step toward peace, grace, and the restored authority of the Church.[6]

Not surprisingly Hungarian communist authorities interpreted Mindszenty's Marian Festival as subversive activism, and local police were given orders to crack down on the faithful. They disrupted the celebrations by means of curtailing water and electricity, refusing to run railroad facilities, seizing microphones and loudspeakers, as well as forcing believers to go elsewhere. Mindszenty's arrest was the final act of imposing order.[7]

The communist case against Mindszenty hinged on several allegations. According to the minister of the interior, the police confiscated a metal cylinder at the cardinal's palace in Esztergom, which allegedly contained documents written in Mindszenty's hand "urging Western powers to intervene in Hungary." It was also suggested that the cardinal was the founder of a royalist movement in 1945, and that he was plotting with none other than Otto von Habsburg of the ancient royal family formerly based in Vienna for the overthrow of "the democratic State order and the Republic." Most incriminating was an alleged handwritten confession that he "expected the restoration of the Monarchy after the conclusion of a third world war by an American victory." Mindszenty was further accused of embezzling funds and engaging in black marketeering with foreign currency. A so-called Yellow Book of documents on the case was quickly prepared by the regime for the foreign press (in English and French editions) in order to win over the international community shocked by the cardinal's arrest. Crude accusatory photos were included: one featured Mindszenty in unusually dashing clothes about to leave for Rome on an airplane "put at his disposal by the American mission"; another portrayed his secretary and archivist with the infamous aluminum tube of damning documents supposedly found under the floorboards of the prelate's residence.[8]

The cardinal was then forced to confess publicly at the trial. While Mindszenty later recounted in his autobiography that he had been drugged and coerced in the form of imposed sleeplessness and beaten with a rubber truncheon, no one knew what was happening at the time. What captured immediate attention among his supporters was that Mindszenty's oral confession was delivered in a manner unfamiliar to his friends, as he appeared exhausted and drooling. Equally disturbing was that his written confession was riddled with basic grammatical and spelling errors uncharacteristic of him, demonstrating what one outside commentator called the "devilish techniques employed by the faithful imitators of Goebbels and of Himmler." According to the *New York Times*, two handwriting experts hired by the government escaped the country and later admitted that they had been forced by the police to forge documents for the trial.[9]

That the sham trial spurred such international outrage is less obvious than it first appears, not least because the cardinal's case was quite typical for the period and region. It is worth recalling that 1948 had been a delicate year in Eastern Europe, as Stalin ordered a major wave of arrests of internal enemies in the wake of the Berlin Blockade and the dramatic break with Tito and the Yugoslav Communist Party. Stalin was alarmed by the role of church officials as fifth columnists, and condemned the Holy See's appointments of prominent American prelates to key diplomatic posts behind the Iron Curtain, such as in Romania and Yugoslavia. Not that religious persecution was anything new to Eastern Europe in the aftermath of World War II. The 1946 arrest and imprisonment of Archbishop Aloysius Stepinac of Zagreb by Marshal Tito's secret police on charges of fascist collusion during the war was a kind of dress rehearsal of Mindszenty's trial. In his case, Stepinac was accused of fascist collaboration with Germans, Italians, and the Croatian revolutionary movement Ustasha during the Second World War, fomenting anti-Yugoslav views in the Catholic press and forcing conversions, as well as conspiring against authority. Stepinac was judged as the treasonous ringleader of a group of Ustasha friars and priests, and was sentenced to sixteen years imprisonment.[10]

International outcry followed Stepinac's trial and intensified the ideological split between East and West. Letters of protest filled the Western press, and the pope excommunicated Tito and those responsible for Stepinac's arrest and conviction. American bishops attacked what they saw as communist disregard for human rights and the rule of law in Eastern Europe, pleading that the West must stand by its Yalta pledge to defend Eastern Europeans in the face of religious persecution. Catholic leaders around the world condemned the arrest, and Archbishop Francis Spellman of New York called Stepinac "but one of thousands of martyrs of every faith whom corrupt, ruthless dictators daily betray and befoul as they wield poisoned power and force to achieve their goal of godless government throughout the world." Spellman raised money for the creation of Archbishop Stepinac High School in White Plains, New York, and organized a rally in New Jersey that attracted 140,000 people. The Vatican's *L'Osservatore Romano* even claimed that this trial represented "a tactical moment in a war of vaster proportions whose operations are not directed from Belgrade and in which are competing the two civilisations which are vying for control of the world." The scandalized fate of the Eastern European churchmen enabled the Church to deflect communist press attacks about the Vatican's pro-fascist sympathies in the 1930s, and helped turn Western European public opinion against the Soviet Union. With it, Archbishop Stepinac was converted into what one historian called the "first martyr to communist expansionism." Persecution against the Church in the late 1940s did not stop there, as a range of other religious leaders faced the wrath of the communist regimes across the Eastern Bloc. The head of the Lutheran Church in Hungary, Bishop Louis Ordass, was seized in late 1948 on charges of misuse of currency; in Bulgaria fifteen Protestant ministers were indicted on charges of espionage. The archbishop of Prague, Josef Beran, was arrested and sentenced in 1949 for similar charges, and Cardinal Stefan Wyszyński of Poland was placed under house arrest for four years between 1953 and 1956. Their causes also became rallying points for Catholic mobilization.[11]

Show trials became prevalent across the Eastern Bloc as vehicles for communicating these regimes' broader message of communism under siege. With time the focus of these pedagogical spectacles of justice moved from religious leaders to government officials, in a pattern more reminiscent of the Moscow Purge Trials of the 1930s. Leading Hungarian Communist official László Rajk was put on trial in Budapest in September 1949, followed by the similar trials of Traïcho Kostov in Bulgaria (1949) and Rudolf Slánsky in Czechoslovakia (1952). The new Eastern European communist regimes sought to use these show trials to garner support for the communist cause by unmasking internal enemies of the state. They were part of the battle against the dangers of "Titoism"—seditious separatist, anti-Moscow agitation—and the encroachments of the West. All the suspects were accused of plotting armed insurrection with American aid, and usually were linked to Hitler and fascism for dramatic effect. As such, the trials helped advance a new politics of fear across Eastern Europe built on cleansing and defending the socialist body politic from internal and external dangers. In effect they also reinforced the idea of the Iron Curtain and the divisions of Cold War Europe based on differing conceptions of dissent, danger, and political community.[12]

The Mindszenty case, however, was of another magnitude. The Hungarian government's effort to dampen down international alarm through the production of the Yellow Book had precisely the opposite effect, as the West expressed outrage toward the arraignment, not least because the Hungarian state's published account against the prelate actually appeared a month *before* the trial began. Mindszenty's fame as an international media event soon extended far beyond the Roman Catholic faithful, as his plight became a Cold War cause célèbre of Soviet aggression, religious persecution, human rights violation, and an affront against Christian civilization. Books covering the imprisoned prelate's trial were produced by the dozens across the Western world, and were translated into Japanese, Chinese, Spanish, and Arabic.[13]

THE IDEOLOGICAL DIFFERENCES BETWEEN EAST AND WEST have long been—and often still are—portrayed as a colossal confrontation between rival secular utopias, conventionally characterized as a half-century face-off between America's Empire of Liberty and the Soviet Union's Empire of Justice. In this reading, the spheres of economics, politics, and culture emerged as fierce superpower battlefields, as each bloc worked to present itself as uniquely capable of providing the good life to the masses and delivering on promises made to weary home fronts during World War II. Yet religion was fundamental to the Cold War from the very beginning, and shaped Cold War antagonism in surprising ways.

The nexus of Christianity and American Cold War politics is a good example. While Roosevelt did not invoke religion much during the war, in part to keep good relations with the Soviet Union, the invocation of God and religion became a hallmark of early Cold War American politics. The muscular Christianity of Presidents Truman and Eisenhower, and of Secretary of State John Foster Dulles, shaped a good deal of US foreign and domestic policy in the early Cold War and helped build a strong case for new American engagement around the world after 1945. In August 1947 Truman took part in a high-profile epistolary exchange with Pope Pius XII, published in all the major Western newspapers and translated into six languages. In it, they expressed the shared need to defend what was perceived as an imperiled Christian civilization. Truman, a devoted Baptist and collector of Bibles, opened his first letter by saying that "no peace can be permanent which is not based upon Christian principles," and that the American "quest for righteousness" could win only if "in St. Paul's luminous phrase, [we] put on the armor of God." While some Protestants bristled about America's new alliance with the papacy, the larger message was of a new Western alliance underwritten by strong Christian values.

No wonder that the exchange was widely seen as the spiritual corollary of the Marshall Plan. Eisenhower too made no bones about his belief that, as he put it, "spiritual weapons [are] our country's most powerful resource." His high-profile baptism a few weeks after his inauguration in January 1953—the first and only presidential baptism in American history—set the religious tone of his presidency, during which he supposedly began all cabinet meetings with a few moments of silent prayer. In 1955 the American Congress passed a law adding the phrase "under God" to the Pledge of Allegiance that all American schoolchildren recite, and two years later the US government changed its official motto from "E pluribus unum" to "In God we trust," which was thereafter inscribed on all paper currency after 1957. The stepped-up activities of the notorious red-baiting House Un-American Activities Committee (founded in 1938, but expanded in the 1950s) were in large part driven by its sense of communism's hostility toward religion.[14]

Things were not so dissimilar in Western Europe, though in this case Catholicism—and less so Protestantism—was the preferred language of Christian transnational solidarity and moral mission. The Italian electoral contest of 1948 highlighted the new West European marriage of religion and politics after 1945, culminating in the Vatican's own stark electioneering slogan: "Either for or against Christ, this is the principal question." West Germany's Christian Democratic chancellor, Konrad Adenauer, was not shy in speaking about "spiritual weapons" and the urgent defense of a Christian *Abendland*. For Adenauer, the "world cannot exist without a Christian and Occidental Europe," and thus the postwar era's chief task was "saving Occidental Christian Europe" from the "moral disease" of Marxism's "materialist philosophy." Catholic pro-Europeanist political leaders, such as Adenauer, Alcide De Gasperi, and Robert Schuman, saw the budding European Economic Community as in part a Christian bulwark against Soviet atheism. No less than Britain's Labour foreign secretary Ernest Bevin called for a "spiritual union" of nations in 1948, based on shared Western European values.[15]

Mindszenty's trial served as a lightning rod for the international Christian community. The trial incited a torrent of protest across the Catholic world, from Western Europe to the United States to South America. The Vatican led the way by proclaiming that the conviction of a member of the College of Cardinals was an "act of violence committed against a strenuous defender of the rights of the Church and of the human person." On February 20, 1949, Pius XII denounced the trial in a speech delivered to some 300,000 people in St. Peter's Square, after which the Holy See decreed that no modus vivendi with communism was possible, so much so that those involved in prosecuting the cardinal were formally excommunicated. In the US, Archbishop Spellman mounted the pulpit of St. Patrick's Cathedral in New York City for the first time since V-E Day to speak before 3,500 listeners. He opened by saying that the US needed to unite in prayer and protest for the imprisoned cardinal victimized by the "world's most fiendish, ghoulish men of slaughter." For him and other churchmen, the trial was nothing less than "the crucifixion of mankind." In London more than 6,000 Catholics filled Albert Hall to protest the indictment of Mindszenty, and in Paris "tens of thousands of demonstrators" reportedly demanded the cardinal's release. In Dublin some 150,000 people, including trade union representatives, protested the cardinal's imprisonment on May Day. As far away as India special masses were held in Catholic churches throughout the country to honor the imprisoned prelate. A similar sentiment extended to the Protestant communities across the world; the Anglican archbishop of York, for example, "denounced the mockery of justice" and felt the trial should be used to bolster a sense of transatlantic alliance under siege. Truman himself dismissed the trial as "the infamous proceedings of a kangaroo court." *Life* magazine summed up the sentiment: "Communists Make Martyr of Cardinal." Such outrage found expression among the Eastern European émigré community in the West as well; one book concluded by saying that "in the most stupendous spiritual battle of world history, Cardinal Mindszenty is the embodiment of Western Christianity to-day."[16]

The case enjoyed great coverage in the mainstream press. The international media launched defenses and counterattacks, published in French, German, and English, often accompanied by supporting documents. So vociferous was the international attack against the sham trial that the Hungarian government felt compelled to publish a sequel to the Yellow Book, dubbed the Black Book, to try to refute the Western press's crusade against the trial. The regime's text blasted Western states and the pope for excoriating Hungary in such a manner "uncommon in international relations and almost forgotten since the fall of Nazi Germany." Particular ire was evoked by the Western charge of the "devilish drug"-induced confession, whose intellectual level was derided as "far below an Edgar Wallace murder mystery." The Hungarian government hoped to defuse Western criticism by portraying the cardinal as a fascist and anti-Semite instead of religious martyr and human rights hero. Different photos were appended to give an alternative image of the trial, one with the prelate sitting in quiet consultation with his counsel and another depicting an orderly trial setting.[17]

Mindszenty became a reference point in popular culture in the West, especially in the US. Numerous American television programs in the late 1940s and early 1950s (e.g., *Studio One*, *Crossroads*, and most notably Bishop Fulton Sheen's popular and rabidly anticommunist show, *Life Is Worth Living*) took up the theme of religion and devoted considerable airtime to Mindszenty's plight. Cinema also registered the importance of the trial. The first film that addressed the cardinal's fate was Felix Feist's 1950 *Guilty of Treason*, which recounted the story of the torturing to death of a Hungarian music teacher who refused to let her primary school class sign petitions for Mindszenty's arrest. Peter Glenville's 1955 film, *The Prisoner*, starring Alec Guinness, was an adaptation of a 1954 West End play by Bridget Boland with the same name. The film was a box-office success and garnered good reviews in the UK and the US, clearly striking a chord with audiences.[18]

The trial helped popularize the idea of Eastern Europe as an enslaved half continent among politicians and thinkers in the West during the late 1940s and early 1950s. The "captive peoples" behind the Iron Curtain was a favorite term of description, ranging from John Foster Dulles's pronouncements to Czesław Miłosz's classic account, *The Captive Mind*, published in 1953. Such a view was perhaps most famously expressed in Siegfried Kracauer and Paul Berkman's 1956 study of Eastern Europe, *Satellite Mentality*, based on interviews with émigrés. In it they often used loaded terms like "thought control," "mind manipulation," and "indoctrination" to make their polemic points, even claiming that these "satellite non-communists" living in Eastern Europe saw their countries as colonies of Moscow.[19]

Another effect of the trial was the tightening relationship between Catholicism and politics in the early Cold War, especially between the papacy and European states. The Mindszenty trial steeled Pius XII's resolve to abandon the Church's usual neutrality and to engage more directly in world affairs to defend Christian Europe and its institutions. The cardinal's conviction prompted the pope in a 1948 speech to entreat "the great nations of the continent" to form a "large political association" in self-defense, and it was in this context that the pope gave his blessing to the Western Union, which was a European military alliance formed by France, the United Kingdom, and the Benelux countries in September 1948. And on July 1, 1949, for the first time in the twentieth century, the pope excommunicated all members, supporters, and followers of communist parties, supposedly even extending the ban to readers of communist newspapers. One commentator was not wrong to say that "never before had the Pope identified so unequivocally with the western alliance." His opponents dismissed the Holy See as the "chaplain to NATO," and not for nothing was Pius derided by the Soviet Union as the "Coca-Cola Pope" for his ardent support of an American-led Western Europe.[20]

THERE WAS A SCIENTIFIC ASPECT OF THE TRIAL THAT ATTRACTED international attention, and this too touched on the issue of civili-

Figure 15. Cardinal József Mindszenty show trial, Budapest, February 8, 1949. *Credit: Getty Images*

zation. What transfixed the international community the most—whether religious or lay—was the forced confession at the trial, and in particular the apparent use of drugs to extract it. The Catholic press was the first to break the story. The British Roman Catholic weekly, *The Tablet*, reported that "a tablet of the potent nerve-destroying Actedron" had been used on the cardinal to induce his self-incrimination.[21]

It was the shocking appearance of the skittish, wild-eyed archbishop that observers found so disturbing. The trial was not filmed, and there were very few photos taken. As a result, the mass-circulated photograph of the prelate at the trial, shown above, became emblematic of the whole trial itself, and one of the most reproduced images of early Cold War culture (Figure 15). (A dissident Hungarian politician later claimed that the release of the photograph was "one of the greatest mistakes of Soviet propaganda.")

Archbishop Spellman protested that Mindszenty had been the victim of "torture and drugging," and contrasted photographs taken at the trial with those taken of the Hungarian prelate during his visit to the US two years before. The use of the mysterious drug had supposedly rendered him defenseless and devoid of his faculty of memory and judgment, furnishing sobering "evidence of his broken, tortured mind, the unhingeing of his mental balance and loss of his self-control." One inside contact at the trial remarked that actedron was the "dread weapon of Communist tyranny against which there is no defense."[22]

Public interest in Mindszenty's psychological state was closely tied up with two other events that caught the imagination of the Cold War West at the time. The first was the 1949 espionage trial in Budapest of the American ITT business executive Robert Vogeler, just months after the Mindszenty trial had concluded. The Vogeler affair, as it became known, was an international diplomatic crisis between Hungary and the US. At the trial, Vogeler surprised international followers of the case by pleading guilty to espionage, after which he was sentenced to fifteen years in prison, though his sentence was commuted to just two. International journalists roundly condemned the trial as yet another Stalinist "diabolical puppet show." What generated huge media attention was Vogeler's 1952 tell-all memoir of mental torture and drugging published after his return to America, called *I Was Stalin's Prisoner*. Vogeler's story caused an overnight sensation, as his tale of dark psychic manipulation received wide press and became fodder for fiction writers, most famously Paul Gallico in his 1952 novel *Trial by Terror*.

The second episode was the 1951 publication of Edward Hunter's *Brain-Washing in Red China: The Calculated Destruction of Men's Minds*. Hunter was a CIA propaganda operator and undercover journalist who coined the term "brainwashing" as a translation of the Chinese colloquialism *hsi nao* (literally "wash brain"), which supposedly came from Chinese informants who described its diabolical use. With it, Hunter gave a new name to a growing fear of devious communist subterfuge. In his account, Hunter aimed to show the sinister ideological makeover of citizens taking place in Mao's China. For Hunter, such psychological warfare represented a new and dangerous phase of the Cold War. Anxiety further intensified when the Chinese government launched a propaganda initiative in 1952 that featured recorded statements by captured American pilots supposedly confessing to having committed war crimes in Korea during the war there, including participation in germ warfare. By end of the war it was reported that some 70 percent of the 7,190 American prisoners in Korea had either confessed or signed petitions demanding an end to the American war effort in Asia; only 5 percent were openly resistant. Worse for many observers is that most of those who had confessed stood by their confessions even after returning to America once the war was over. Such uncomfortable stories prompted a new round of American government worry about communist techniques of brainwashing.[23]

The blended media coverage of Mindszenty, Vogeler, and the Korean War confessions spurred a range of new scientific studies on psychological manipulation, mostly in the United States. Popular fear about the destruction of individualism was registered in American pulp fiction, ranging from Robert Heinlein's *The Puppet Masters* (1951) to Jack Finney's *The Body Snatchers* (1955) to A. E. van Vogt's *The Mind Cage* (1957), and found cinematic expression as well. Lewis Seiler's 1954 film *The Bamboo Prison* exploited the brainwashing theme related to American involvement in the Korean War. What catapulted the issue into American popular mythology was Richard Condon's bestselling 1959 novel, *The Manchurian Candidate*, which was turned into a box-office smash in 1962 by director John Frankenheimer. In this setting it was no accident that films on Mindszenty's ordeal centered on drugs and brainwashing: *Guilty of Treason* drew attention to the cardinal's confession as a form of evil hypnosis, while *The Prisoner* depicted the interrogator's use of modern psychological techniques as part of communism's dark arts.[24]

Disquiet about the sinister science behind Mindszenty's confession was scarcely confined to film and fiction. The danger of malicious "truth serums" was extensive enough to warrant attention at the United Nations, and again the Mindszenty trial was the principal reference. In April 1950 the UN put forward a motion to get such serums banned on the grounds that they represented a breach of human rights. Even if the endeavor failed when the international commission, according to one *New York Times* journalist, "could not agree to include 'confessional drugs' under an approved provision forbidding torture or inhuman treatment," its coverage at the UN reflected how prominent the trial was internationally in terms of coupling "dark psychiatry," the breach of civilization, and human rights abuses.[25]

Nevertheless, the most ardent student of the trial was the CIA. Like fiction writers and filmmakers, the CIA also believed that brainwashing was a form of modern witchcraft, whose evil spell (and spellbinders) needed to be studied and counteracted. Even by the late 1940s there was concern within the CIA (fueled by defector testimonies) that the US had fallen behind the Soviet Union in medical intelligence, and the cardinal's confession was widely regarded as indicative of new advances in Soviet psychological techniques. CIA operatives were keen to develop new means of both extracting key information quickly from captured Soviet agents and to help US personnel resist Soviet truth serums or other psychochemical agents if they were captured. The cardinal's trial, the detonation of the Soviet Union's first atomic bomb later that same year, and the "confessions" of captured US soldiers in the Korean War all heightened the urgency for the newly created CIA to step up research into psycho-medical science. Later interviews with retired CIA agents recalled that they had looked into the "vacant eyes" in the photograph of the Hungarian prelate at his treason trial and "had been horrified"; they were convinced that his confession had been extracted under the influence of "some mysterious mind-bending drug" reminiscent of Soviet show trials from the 1930s.[26]

Internal CIA documents made clear the depth of agency apprehension about Mindszenty's appearance in court. In February 1949 the CIA was already gathering reports from abroad about the Mindszenty trial. Speculation abounded that the cardinal was under the influence of "some unknown force," and the mysterious power of actedron (also known as Benzedrine) was suspected. By 1952 there was a growing fear of "Soviet interest and research in this direction" and its "threat to US National Security."[27]

The CIA then created a new secret program, Project Bluebird, to conduct new scientific research into fending off communist mind-control techniques. The first field operation was set up in 1950 to test-drive behavioral techniques and drug experimentation (sodium amytal and Benzedrine), ostensibly in order to induce amnesia on suspected double agents. The project's secret brief was further expanded in its renamed guises as Project Artichoke (1952) and MKULTRA (1953), with virtually no governmental oversight or accountability, as first revealed in John Marks's classic 1977 exposé of CIA secret programs, *The Search for the "Manchurian Candidate": The CIA and Mind Control*. Scientists associated with the shadowy programs were especially keen to study the world of occult "black psychiatry"; while many of their ideas thankfully never left the drawing board, the CIA continued its research into psychochemicals aimed to get people to talk. The trial spurred a new round of worry (and funding) inside the American intelligence community to engineer its own version of what it called at the time the "Mindszenty effect," leading to the agency's infamous LSD research in the mid-1950s. While a "mind-control gap" may have been as illusory as "missile gaps," by the early 1950s mind control took on a momentum of its own. In The Hague an International Documentation and Information Center, or Interdoc, was established in February 1963 as a kind of French–West German–Dutch joint venture to confront the "ideological threats" posed by Soviet and Chinese communism, and to build Western European intelligence networks outside American control. Eastern European intelligence agencies, such as the East German Stasi and Romania's Securitate, also developed an interest in psychology and social science to monitor dissidents and to control informants.[28]

The Mindszenty trial and Korean War confessions kicked off a cottage industry of new social science studies on Soviet social science. In part this had to do with what was perceived as the perverse inversion of psychology—where the original impetus behind Freudian psychoanalysis had been to liberate people from their mental afflictions and "restore their personality" to them, this new "black psychiatry" was conversely geared toward manipulation, control, and the destruction of individual personality. Western observers were aware of the show trials of the 1930s in which older Bolsheviks were targeted and disgraced by the Party; what made the post-1945 trials distinctive was that they featured hardened anticommunists, thereby making their confessions all the more troubling. This was what one observer called the "Iron Curtain mystery," one that warranted serious scientific attention. New scholarly interest emerged in how "Pavlovian" psychology had been turned to new political ends. Examples included George S. Counts and Nucia Lodge, *The Country of the Blind: The Soviet System of Mind Control* (1949); Joost Meerloo, *The Rape of the Mind: The Psychology of Thought Control* (1956); and most famously, Robert Jay Lifton's *Thought Reform and the Psychology of Totalism: A Study of "Brainwashing" in China* (1961). By the late 1950s the brainwashing fear had generated hundreds of social science books and articles about the dangers of what FBI director J. Edgar Hoover called the communist "thought control machine." The proliferation of books on the subject reflected growing concern in the 1950s that the Cold War was moving on to new terrain, and the new battleground was the science of suggestion and mind control. The Mindszenty trial was thus a milestone in the politicization of psychology and social science in the early Cold War.[29]

THE EFFECTS OF THE MINDSZENTY CASE COULD ALSO BE SEEN in the realm of human rights. From the very beginning, human rights talk was subject to the ideological rivalry between East and West, wherein issues of discrimination and injustice were sensationalized on both sides of the Iron Curtain to showcase the superiority of each respective system. On the one hand, Westerners used human rights as a cudgel with which to bash Soviet despotism behind the Iron Curtain, and in so doing helped consolidate a new Cold War anticommunist consensus. The Council of Europe was founded in May 1949 by ten Western European countries with the express aim to uphold human rights, democracy, and the rule of law in Europe. It was a response to the crushing of democracy in Czechoslovakia in 1948 (otherwise known as the Czech coup) by the Czech Communist Party, with Soviet backing. Thereafter the Council made membership conditional upon respect for human rights and democracy. On the other, the USSR never tired of pointing out the hypocrisy of the West, depicting Western poverty, unemployment, and welfare neglect as human rights violations of various kinds. The parlous fate of African Americans in the South during the civil rights struggle became a favorite communist reference point in drawing attention to American racial politics during the 1950s and 1960s.[30]

Over the course of the 1940s and early 1950s in Western Europe human rights were being reworked from a decidedly Christian perspective—so much so that human rights were often understood as a distinctly Christian project. Leading intellectuals within various Christian churches (especially Catholics in France and Britain) viewed such rights as a blend of spiritualism, individualism, and humanism— what was called "personalism" at the time—that supposedly predated and transcended the world of politics. Catholic thinkers during the

Second World War often used human rights as a language of resistance and antifascist solidarity, and much human rights talk just after the war emerged from progressive Catholic circles. Recall that Roosevelt and Churchill's signing of the Atlantic Charter in 1941 on a US naval warship off the coast of Newfoundland, a declaration of Anglo-American principles based in part on the pledge to protect human rights, ended with a religious service and anthem to Christian soldiers. It has even been argued that Christian lobby groups from the US and Western Europe were responsible for making sure that the 1948 UN Universal Declaration of Human Rights provided a robust affirmation of religious liberty at its core. The postwar rise of human rights was closely bound with the construction of Christian democratic Western Europe, and such moral politics were very much part of the broader conservative campaign to recast bourgeois Europe in a Christian spirit. In this rendition, human rights emerged as a fixture of the anticommunist consensus across Western Europe.[31]

A pivotal figure in this shift was the Frenchman Jacques Maritain. In his influential work he helped fuse rights and religiosity, and served as one of the principal architects of the Universal Declaration of Human Rights. Maritain had been an exponent of Catholic humanism, personalism, and human rights since the 1930s, and helped conjoin Christianity and democracy at the time. This could be seen in his *Integral Humanism* (1936), which served as a touchstone text for the small Christian democratic movements in the 1930s. In it he claimed that what was needed was a new anti-secular spiritual humanism—that is, a "New Christendom"—"inseparable from civilization or culture, these two words being taken as synonymous." His widely distributed 1943 pamphlet *Christianity and Democracy* heralded this union as the best path for moral regeneration after the war, and thousands of copies of the pamphlet were dropped by warplanes over Nazi-controlled territories in 1943 as part of the Allied assault on occupied Europe. He elaborated on the moral meltdown affecting Europe in his *Twilight of Civilization*, published in France in 1939 and then translated into English in 1943. Here Maritain saw the crisis of civilization in terms of the world's tragic turning away from God toward a false faith in the "anthropocentric concept of man and culture," which for him led to "materialism, atheism, anarchy bearing the mask of State-Despotism," culminating in "Nazi racism" and communism. What was needed, he continued, was a "new humanism" based on the "dignification" of the "created being" opened up "to the universe of the divine and the super-rational"—what Maritain called "the humanism of the Incarnation." Maritain then sounded the Christian mission: "It is not Europe alone, it is the world, it is the whole world which must resolve the problem of civilization. It was too late for the Europe of yesterday. For the crucified Europe of today it is not too late."[32]

The language of human rights suffused the West's condemnation of the Mindszenty trial. Given that the Universal Declaration had been signed just a few months before, the Mindszenty trial was its first real test case. The pope drew on the recast understanding of human rights in his February 14, 1949, speech on the trial before the College of Cardinals. In it he intoned that the sad fate of the prelate "inflicts a deep wound not only on your distinguished college and on the church, but also on every upholder of the dignity and liberty of man." The linkage of Catholicism and the "dignity of the person" had been around since the social encyclicals *Rerum Novarum* (1891) and *Quadragesimo Anno* (1931), but was now updated to suit a new political world. Charles Malik, the Lebanese philosopher of Greek Orthodox faith and coauthor of the United Nations Charter, supposedly drew on these Catholic encyclicals in framing the Universal Declaration. Catholic publicists were quick to recognize the power of linking human rights and Catholic causes. While other non-Europeans present such as Chinese delegate P. W. Chang made a strong case for the place of non-Christian Confucian thought in the formation of human rights concepts, the christianization of human rights earmarked Western political thinking.[33]

147

Connecting the Nuremberg Trial and Mindszenty's trial further cemented this early Cold War Western understanding of human rights. In October 1949, Sir Hartley Shawcross, the British attorney general and, four years before, the British prosecutor at the Nuremberg Trial, condemned the treatment of the Hungarian churchman. In a speech before the United Nations in 1949, Shawcross claimed that "exactly the same techniques were being pursued to-day as the Nazis themselves pursued—in these ex-enemy countries the red flag has been hoisted in place of the swastika." Even more important in this linkage was David Maxwell Fyfe, who had been one of the British judges at Nuremberg, and afterward was one of the framers of the 1950 European Convention on Human Rights. For Maxwell Fyfe, the Mindszenty affair was a kind of extension of the Nuremberg Trial. In April 1949 he was interviewed about the Mindszenty trial in the British Roman Catholic weekly newspaper the *Catholic Herald*. In it he made the connection explicit: "At Nuremberg I learnt in detail and by admission out of their own mouths how human rights and all that civilisation stands for can be destroyed by poisoning the fountain of justice," and this "is one of the things that Cardinal Mindszenty fought against in Hungary. May his martyrdom not be in vain." Such views reflected the extent to which human rights, religion, and civilization were being integrated into anticommunist Christian democratic projects.[34]

The West's reception of the Mindszenty trial put Rákosi's government on the defensive. Special venom was directed at the way the Western press twisted the case as about the "curtailment of religious freedom," presenting Mindszenty as a "Catholic martyr" and "defender of human rights and freedom of speech." Hungarian authorities insisted that the trial was never about attacking Roman Catholicism or religious rights, but rather about the treasonous activities of an "ordinary criminal." That the Hungarian state's Black Book version of the trial felt compelled to rebut British foreign secretary Ernest Bevin's claim that the trial was "utterly repugnant to our conception of human rights and liberties" made clear that the Rákosi government was losing the debate internationally. In fact, the issue gathered enough momentum and international media coverage to be brought before the UN. The day after the trial ended, US secretary of state Dean Acheson went to the United Nations to condemn the cardinal's sentence as a "conscienceless attack upon religious and personal freedom" and a shameless effort to "remove this source of moral resistance to Communism." In another speech delivered at the UN, Acheson protested that the persecution of religious figures in Hungary, Bulgaria, and Romania meant that the Danubian states were in violation of human rights enshrined in the 1947 peace treaties with these countries.[35]

The trial played a powerful role in the creation of the European Convention of Human Rights in 1950, which departed in significant ways from the UN's Universal Declaration of Human Rights passed two years before. The 1948 Declaration offered an inclusive raft of rights that went far beyond classic liberal rights protecting the individual citizen from an overbearing state. These more expansive rights included the right to work, the right to education, and the right to health care, thanks in large measure to the presence of the Soviet Union in these discussions. This European Convention was expressly conceived as anticommunist in tone, one in which the social and economic rights featured in the 1948 Universal Declaration were quietly dropped. Enshrined instead were the new hallmarks of a Western European understanding of human rights: the sanctity of law, the prohibition of compulsory labor, due process in court, freedom of thought and conscience, as well as the new clause specifying that "everyone has the right to respect for his private and family life, his home and correspondence"—all patent liberal principles that communists interpreted as bluntly directed at their regimes. The European Convention was crafted by a group of powerful conservative thinkers, including Winston

Churchill and Maxwell Fyfe, and was largely an effort to curb both the threat of domestic leftist political parties at home and Soviet hegemony abroad by forging a new West European consensus around an understanding of human rights based on individual liberty. The broader point is that in conservative hands, human rights no longer originated in 1789, but rather were a Christian creation to be defended against the legacy of the French Revolution and the revolutionary threat of communism.[36]

For the Council of Europe, religious freedom and "Christian civilization" were the cornerstones of the European Convention on Human Rights, and the fate of the captive cardinals in the East—and in particular Mindszenty—underscored their significance. Mindszenty's case helped forge the intimate relationship between human rights and anticommunism to such a degree that freedom of religion became the most prominent human rights issue in the West during the early Cold War. In April 1949—that is, several months after the trial—the UN debated the convictions of both Cardinal Mindszenty and several Protestant pastors in Bulgaria as violations of UN member states' obligation to respect the human rights of their citizens. The Eastern Bloc representatives at the UN General Assembly argued passionately that such issues should not come under the UN's purview, but instead should be subject to domestic jurisdiction; the accused, so they continued, were common criminals whose cases had nothing to do with human rights concerns, and thus they rejected what they claimed was the UN's affront to their national sovereignty. After ten days of debate, the UN adopted a resolution (30–7) in April 1949 condemning the show trial convictions as egregious human rights violations. The fallout was that Hungary, Bulgaria, and Romania were excluded from membership in the United Nations, on the grounds that they had abjured the respect for "human rights and fundamental freedoms." The Mindszenty affair spurred the diplomatic isolation of three countries from the international community.

IN CERTAIN RESPECTS CHRISTIAN ANTICOMMUNISM IN THE late 1940s was a rerun of the Catholic Church's interwar crusade against the Russian Revolution and the "spirit of 1917." The dangerous albeit short-lived Hungarian and Bavarian Soviet Republics after 1918, the "Two Red Years" in Italy (1919–1920) with its factory occupations and peasant strikes, the Mexican Revolution (1910–1920), and of course the Spanish Civil War (1936–1939) caused deep concern for Christians about a rising red tide of Bolshevik anti-clericalism threatening traditional Christian strongholds around the globe. In response, the Vatican launched a large transnational offensive in the 1930s as a kind of Catholic International to offset the power and reach of its communist rival. It did so by means of a well-organized media campaign through radio and print, traveling exhibitions, and film to reconquer Catholic territories under threat. Rome was portrayed as the great bulwark against Moscow. Pope Pius XI's March 1937 encyclical *Divini Redemptoris* denounced atheistic communism as "the all too imminent danger" undermining "the very foundations of Christian civilization." Such strong anticommunism would dominate Vatican thinking for a generation, as the 1937 encyclical served as official Catholic doctrine until the Second Vatican Council in the early 1960s. Protestants undertook similar initiatives—in the 1920s Protestant activists founded the Swiss International Anticommunist Entente and the German Church's Campaign Against the Alienation from God and Anti-Divine Forces, which likewise became clearinghouses of publications and conferences devoted to the communist menace, providing a firm basis of cross-Christian solidarity in the Cold War.[37]

In its train came a new geography of Christian Europe. What was sometimes called Atlantic civilization, Western civilization, or Christian civilization was predicated on the identification of Western Europe as the principal battleground of a new cultural war, with certain states to the east and south emerging as key flanks against the danger of communism.

The persecution of captive cardinals behind the Iron Curtain helped give shape to this new cultural map of Europe. Mindszenty himself was not shy in placing the Hungarian Catholic fight against communism in a broader historical Christian struggle against the infidel. The Hungarian Kingdom had long been considered the Eastern outpost of Western Christendom, and Mindszenty now updated the struggle to suit Cold War concerns. For him, the confrontation with communist authorities was only the latest round of antagonism with anti-Christian forces that originated in the Hungarian battles against Islam in the sixteenth and seventeenth centuries. On October 4, 1948—several months before his December arrest—Mindszenty delivered a sermon for the rosary feast before some 35,000 faithful Catholics in Budapest. On this occasion he reminded his listeners that the origins of the feast lay in the victory of Europe's Christian states over the Ottoman Turkish fleet in 1571, which "Christians won with the rosary in their hands at Lepanto." Budapest had been under Turkish occupation since the capture of Constantinople in 1453, and for Mindszenty this great triumph of universal Christendom was coupled with a more direct Hungarian episode, namely the victory of the Habsburg army over the Ottoman Turkish enemy at the battle of Temesvár in 1716. In Mindszenty's eyes, the reason why the Habsburg general Prince Eugène defeated the Turks was primarily because he was a "man of prayer." Europe had therefore found political unity and moral strength in the face of a common infidel enemy.[38]

Mindszenty was not alone in interpreting the Counter-Reformation as a moment when Christian civilization, as he put it, was "restored from within and defended against hostile outside forces." This view had become widely held among nineteenth-century Hungarian Catholic churchmen, as they welcomed a reinvigorated Roman Catholicism as the most important transnational cultural force across the continent. Such an interpretation received new vigor in the 1930s, especially from Cardinal Eugenio Pacelli, who later became Pope Pius XII. At the Thirty-Fourth International Eucharistic Conference in Budapest in 1938, Pacelli praised what he called the "invincible courage of the Hungarian armies" in their defense of Christian civilization against the "proud crescent of Islam" in previous centuries. He concluded by saying that he hoped their deeds would inspire today's Catholics to "defend the church and Christian civilization against the leaders of religious negation and of social revolution by opposing them, as did Hungary of the seventeenth century." On October 7, 1947, Pacelli, now Pope Pius XII, referred to the high historical stakes of this battle with communism in a speech to a group of touring American senators. In it he reminded them that "October 7 is a memorable day in the calendar of Occidental Europe," for it was on this very day in 1571 that the "powers representing Christian civilization united to defeat the mortal threat from the East" and thus saved Christian Europe from the invasion of the Turks. The battle of Lepanto became a favorite symbol for European conservatives in the Cold War against the "New Turks" from the East, and helped define the church's role in world affairs after 1945. So by the time Mindszenty was rewriting history in this way, he was following the views of Catholic leaders from the 1930s about the world-historical stakes of the clash between communism and Catholicism. Communist Hungary now emerged as the front line of this new international Christian struggle.[39]

Equally striking is that the Mindszenty case prompted the expansion of this new transatlantic solidarity to include other religious groups. In fact, the American reception of the Mindszenty trial served as an impetus to unite Christian faiths as well as to garner Jewish support for the larger political cause of religious liberty. Although the term "Judeo-Christian civilization" originated in the late nineteenth century, it is more commonly associated with the work of the National Conference of Christians and Jews, founded in 1928 and active through the 1930s to promote interfaith harmony. During the war, the cause of Judeo-Christian civilization was championed by major Christian intellectuals such as Reinhold Niebuhr, Jacques Maritain, and Paul Tillich as a means of building a united cultural front against Nazism. After the shocking revelations of the Nazi death camps, the defense of Christian civilization appeared too partial and noninclusive, so "Judeo-Christian civilization" emerged as a preferred moniker to describe the shared spiritual underpinnings of American life. But it was during the Cold War when this rhetoric intensified. In a speech in New York a few days before Christmas in 1952, President-Elect Eisenhower asserted that "our form of government has no sense unless it is founded in a deeply felt religious faith, and I don't care what it is," though "with us of course it is the Judeo-Christian concept, and it must be a religion that all men are created equal." By the early 1950s, so-called Judeo-Christian values were elevated as the moral foundation of what was called "tri-faith" liberal America. While this campaign in part aimed to counter anti-Semitism, it also helped solidify the ideological links between organized religion, anticommunism, and political liberalism.[40]

A more open-minded American Protestantism that reached out to Catholics and Jews in the name of Judeo-Christian civilization emerged as one of the hallmarks of American political culture in the 1950s. Illustrative of this trend was the ubiquity of so-called prayer breakfasts in American national politics in the 1950s, in which a priest, a rabbi, and a minister were routinely called upon to open all major political conventions to consecrate the new union of religion and Cold War liberalism. Such broad-tent ecumenicalism even briefly extended to the Muslim world at the time. American opposition to the British, French, and Israelis during the Suez Crisis of 1956 generated goodwill toward America among the international Muslim community, and Eisenhower sought to capitalize on this in his address during the opening ceremony of the newly created Islamic Center in Washington, in which he praised Islam's contributions to world civilization and the "peaceful progress of all men under one God." That said, Christian and Jewish unity remained the heart of this new Cold War religious sensibility. In this understanding, the values of Western civilization were seen as resting on a new religious consensus that included Christians and Jews.[41]

Articulations of a transatlantic Christian West committed to Judeo-Christian values were partly brokered by a number of prominent émigrés from Central Europe. The idea that the United States must serve as the defender of a distinctly Judeo-Christian civilization had gained expression during the Second World War, especially among liberal German emigrés from the Weimar Republic who moved to the United States in the 1930s. This could be seen in the work of the German Catholic theologian Waldemar Gurian, whose highly influential 1935 *Bolschevismus als Weltgefahr*, translated in English as *The Future of Bolshevism*, electrified Catholic readers around the world. In it he argued that communism was not really committed to any higher ideals, but rather was a totalitarian regime bent on destroying all traditional sources of authority, including the churches and religious liberty. His wartime writings went so far as to say that the Second World War in Asia and Europe "is not an economic or political war, it is a war of civilization," and since "it involves the spiritual and religious principles of the civilized order, it is also a religious war." Another influential émigré was Carl J. Friedrich, who served as a bridge figure between Weimar and American liberalism in the 1950s. Friedrich was chief advisor to General Lucius Clay, the US military governor of Germany, and thereafter set up Harvard University's famed Graduate School of Public Administration; in his work Friedrich argued that the origins of democracy lay not in the Enlightenment but rather in seventeenth-century Protestant thought. This was important not only because he espoused a close affinity between democracy and Christianity, but also because he claimed that democracy had homegrown German roots that migrated to America with the Puritans. In Friedrich's eyes, only the United States had the capacity to safeguard the "common religious heritage of modern civilization," a heritage that needed to be defended by Protestants, Catholics, and Jews alike as a sacred "Judeo-Christian" tradition under siege from Nazism. Over the course of his postwar American career he trained a number of powerful American Cold War statesmen, including Henry Kissinger and Zbigniew Brzezinski, who all championed America's role as the defender of Western civilization in the face of communism. These émigrés thus helped fortify the links between the US and Western Europe as part of the new religiously inflected liberal mission against Moscow.[42]

While Mindszenty helped draw the United States and Western Europe together as part of a new transatlantic Christian West, the Catholic Church was busy redrawing the cultural map of Europe in other ways. The political frontiers of Catholic Europe were not simply to the East—no less decisive were the southern borderlands of Europe. The initial line of southern defense was Italy. The Italian electoral contest of 1948 was the first case of the new West European marriage of religion and politics after the war. The election became a closely observed testing ground for Catholic anticommunism in Europe, and conservatives were intent on neutralizing the popular hold of the Italian Communist Party and its close ties to Moscow. In 1944 Italian Communist Party leader Palmiro Togliatti had triumphantly returned from Moscow with his mission to build an "Italian road to socialism," which sent shock waves across the Catholic community. The conservative Catholic press, led by *L'Osservatore Romano* and the influential Jesuit journal *La Civiltà Cattolica*, or *Catholic Civilization*, spearheaded the anticommunist campaign against "Soviet totalitarianism" through numerous articles and booklets. Though the Jesuit journal championing "Catholic civilization" was originally founded in 1850 to confront the dangers of secular liberalism and freemasonry, it was now directed toward the threat from Moscow. The Vatican and the CIA swayed the election in favor of the Christian Democrats. The election victory marked the revival of anticommunism as a mobilizing cause that ideologically bridged fascism and post-fascism, with Italian Christian Democrats couching themselves as frontline defenders of Western values and Christian civilization. The triumph of Christian democracy in Italy inspired like-minded parties across Western Europe in their effort to fend off the domestic threat of communism.[43]

Safeguarding the southern flank of Christian Europe could also be seen in the recasting of fascist Spain as a bulwark against the Red Menace, with Spain's dictator Francisco Franco serving as the valiant defender of Christian civilization on the Iberian Peninsula, designating himself as "El Generalisimo Cristianísimo de la Santa Cruzada." Franco had repeatedly exploited the language of civilization during the Spanish Civil War from 1936 to 1939, justifying political violence as an epic defense that pitted "Western civilization against Muscovite barbarism," "Christian civilization" against republican "satanic hordes." The French Catholic Church along with leading French conservatives such as Paul Claudel and Henri Massis praised Spain as a beacon of Catholic values and Western civilization under threat. After 1945 Franco resuscitated this language to fit Cold War imperatives. In his new rendition, the abandonment of traditional Catholic national values in the run-up to the Spanish Civil War had thrown Spain into sin, chaos, and destruction, and the westward march of communism into Central Europe made the red threat all the more urgent. Portugal's similar blend of authoritarianism and Catholicism was integrated into this self-styled Iberian flank of Christian civilization. As a consequence, Italy, Spain, and Portugal were reconfigured by Christian publicists as vital salients in the new Cold War cartography of a rejuvenated Christian Europe.[44]

There were also important outposts to the northwest. Indeed, Britain played a key—if underappreciated—role in trumpeting the Christian foundation of Western Europe as post-fascist moral compass. A notable Anglo-American bridge figure in the international defense of Western civilization was Arnold J. Toynbee, the well-known London School of Economics polymath historian and director of the Royal Institute of International Affairs. His twelve-volume *A Study of History* (1934–1961) used the theme of civilization to decipher the broader patterns of world history. His books provided a colorful pageant of the genesis, growth, and disintegration of twenty-six world civilizations on the global stage—sixteen of which were dead and another nine moribund, with only "Western Christendom" in a state of development. The first three volumes were hailed as timely interventions about the malaise of civilization, and the final three appeared just before the outbreak of World War II and were greeted as a trenchant diagnosis of a world on the verge of another major conflict. The abridged versions of his books sold hundreds of thousands of copies in Britain and across the world. So popular was his work that Toynbee has been described as one of the century's "most read, translated, and discussed living scholars," who provided a timely explanation about the widespread sense of the West's "de-civilization." After the war Toynbee enjoyed remarkable celebrity status in the United States. American publishing mogul Henry R. Luce touted Toynbee as a new Christian prophet, and promoted his views in a cover story for the March 1947 edition of his bestselling *Time* magazine. The British historian's image was superimposed over the caption "Our civilization is not inexorably doomed." The *Time* cover story coincided with the publication of an abridged version of Toynbee's 1936 *Study of History*. In *Time*'s rendition of Toynbee's ideas, the place of America in world history hung in the balance. The article asserted that the contemporary "crisis of Western civilization" necessitated that the US must become "the champion of the remnant of Christian civilization against the forces that threaten it." The cover story inspired a torrent of American interest in Toynbee's work—churchmen, educators, and politicians all wrote to *Time* to request reprints for local distribution, and Toynbee's lecture tours across the country attracted capacity crowds wherever he went.[45]

Another key intellectual broker of this new European dream was none other than Winston Churchill. After his election defeat in July 1945 he devoted considerable energy to his pet "European Movement" in support of European unity, though it found little traction, either domestically or in Europe. After all, campaigning for European unity was hardly a popular position in 1945. During the Axis occupation of Europe, the fight against fascism was primarily directed toward the liberation of the nation-state from Nazi occupation. The end of the war on the continent brought little appetite for internationalism, let alone Europeanism. In fact, "Europeans unite!" had been a favorite rallying cry of collaborationists during World War II. Churchill saw things differently. In a March 1943 broadcast, Churchill had called for a Council of Europe, along with a Council of Asia, and phrased his Europeanist convictions thus: "In Europe dwell the historic parent races from whom our western civilisation has been so largely defined. I believe myself to be what is called a good European, and deem it a noble task to take part in reviving the fertile genius and in restoring the true greatness of Europe." In 1945 Churchill went on the road with his European Movement to rally support for anti-Bolshevik Western European unity. Western civilization was his go-to term of cultural regeneration for Western Europe. In his "Europe Arise" speech, delivered to thousands gathered in the Royal Albert Hall for the European Movement's inaugural mass rally on May 14, 1947, Churchill referred explicitly to the "spiritual conception of Europe." He stressed that the "real demarcation between Europe and Asia is no chain of mountains, no natural frontiers, but a system of beliefs and ideas which we call Western Civilisation."[46]

Churchill provided more substance to his European ideal in a Zurich speech of September 19, 1946, on the "tragedy of Europe." "This noble continent," so he argued, remained the fountain of Christian faith and Christian ethics, and "the origin of most of the culture, arts, philosophy and science both of ancient and modern times." For Churchill, the "re-creation of the European family" must be based on a "partnership between France and Germany," a suggestion that Churchill knew would court controversy. "I am now going to say something that will astonish you," he said, asserting that there "can be no revival of Europe without a spiritually great France and a spiritually great Germany." No less provocative was that Churchill's European Movement began with the speedy integration of Western Germany into this designated European family, predicated on a new call to forgive and forget. In his eyes, the conclusion of the Nuremberg Trial meant that "there must also be an end to retribution. There must be what Mr. Gladstone many years ago called 'a blessed act of oblivion,'" for if Europe "is to be saved from infinite misery, and indeed from final doom, there must be an act of faith in the European family and an act of oblivion against the crimes and follies of the past." So intent was Churchill on this message of forgiveness that he personally contributed to the defense fund of German officers accused of war crimes, such as Field Marshal Erich von Manstein. Needless to say, such views were not widely shared in 1946. British historian E. H. Carr grumbled that Churchill's speech would only further threaten relations with the Soviet Union, as "many will see in his speech a call, not for a United States of Europe but for a United States of western Europe." But even if Churchill's "forgive and forget" attitude may have been a highly unusual position at the time, he did serve as one of the forgotten champions of Western European political integration.[47]

The politics of forgetting could be seen in other ways too. One instance was the extent to which Catholics and Protestants successfully buried their interwar legacy of antiliberalism and confessional fighting in favor of a new ecumenical Christian front dedicated to upholding a new liberal version of Christian democracy. Serious theological differences between Catholic and Protestant theologians still persisted, perhaps best noted in the fact that the Roman Catholic Church was never invited as a member of the World Council of Churches, the massive interdenominational faith organization founded in 1948. Even so, the Cold War threat of "godless" communism spurred church leaders and conservative Western European political elites to make common cause in the fight against Moscow. With it, Europe's long-standing wars of religion seemed to have come to an end.[48]

The Catholic Church undertook the campaign with particular gusto. Already in his 1945 Christmas message Pius XII asserted that true peace was to be found "in the internationalism of Christian democracy and not in the internationalism of atheistic communism." The pope's backing of the Western European Union served as an alternative to Atlanticism, and helped counter the common perception that the Vatican was too closely aligned with American policy. The European Coal and Steel Community, founded in 1951, was of course dedicated to the pooling of vital material resources, but the cultural and Christian dimension was no less present. Such a view of the Western European supranational club was part of a larger effort to give the New Europe a spiritual framework and higher cultural purpose. While some Protestant observers complained that the European Coal and Steel Community was really a Vatican-sponsored organ spearheaded by Catholic-led France, Belgium, West Germany, and Italy, they played their part in helping bring about the economic union in a show of Western European cultural unity. Even leftist politicians came on board. Socialist Belgian foreign minister Paul-Henri Spaak repeatedly saw the integration of Western Europe over the course of the 1950s in terms of the need—as he put it in one 1950 *Foreign Affairs* article—to "defend a certain civilization, a certain way of life and a certain philosophy," based on what he called in a 1957 *Foreign Affairs* piece "the respect for the human person." In a December 1947 letter to US general and secretary of state George Marshall (the architect of the famous 1948 European recovery plan associated with his name), Britain's Labour foreign secretary Ernest Bevin called for the formation of a "spiritual consolidation of western civilization," and in talks with French foreign minister Georges Bidault he went so far as to insist that our chief task "is to save Western civilization."[49]

By the mid-1950s, the defense of Western civilization had become a foundational element of Christian democracy across Western Europe. Christian democracy was animated by the idea of Europeanness and the Christian West, building on interwar German Catholic discussions of the *Abendland*. The concept of *Abendland* (literally "evening country") was originally based on a premodern medieval notion of the Catholic West from the eras of Charlemagne and Pope Gregory the Great. The term first entered German in the sixteenth century as an antithesis to Martin Luther's conception of the Orient as a *Morgenland*, or "land of the rising sun." The understanding of *Abendland* as a nostalgic hankering for the medieval Christian West assumed heightened meaning in the wake of the French Revolution, as Catholic counterrevolutionary intellectuals like Novalis and Chauteaubriand sought to devise a Romantic counterpoint to the Enlightenment, secularism, and revolutionary violence. Over the course of the nineteenth century, German Catholics tended to prefer the term *Abendland* to Europe, since Europe to them was too closely associated with Protestant-ism, nationalism, and the nation-state system. Oswald Spengler's bestselling 1918 *Der Untergang des Abendlandes*, or *The Decline of the West*, popularized this historical interpretation for a large German readership after the military defeat of the Great War. The need to bolster a weakened *Abendland* gained intellectual credence in the 1920s in response to the Russian Revolution, fascism, and the per-ceived decline of Christian culture across Europe. The flagship Ger-man journal *Abendland: Deutsche Monatsschrift für europäische Kultur, Politik und Wirtschaft* (*Abendland: A German Monthly for European Culture, Politics and Economy*) was founded in 1925 by Hermann Platz to capitalize on growing Franco-German concern about de-fending a common *Abendland* under siege. After 1945 Christian

Democrats looked to the "neo-Carolingian" dream of Western European unity as a moral bedrock for post-fascist Europe. A number of journals and organizations were founded to promote the defense of *Abendland* as the true history and identity of European alliance.[50]

In the 1950s *Abendland* was frequently used by various Western European politicians to help give form to Western European solidarity. French statesman Robert Schuman tirelessly described Europe as "a spiritual and cultural community" and "common destiny" coterminous with the heritage of the Christian West. In a 1954 speech at the European Parliaments Conference, Italian prime minister Alcide De Gaspieri asserted that "Christianity lies at the origin of this European civilization," and undergirds "our common European heritage." For his part, West German chancellor Konrad Adenauer maintained that there were two Germanies, the Roman Catholic Western half and the Prussian-Protestant Eastern half, from which sprung the forces of materialism, atheism, and militarism originating with the Reformation and continuing through to the Third Reich and the "Prussian" Soviet Zone of Occupation. De Gaulle also endorsed the idea of a common European civilization based on a shared cultural and spiritual heritage "from the Atlantic to the Urals," as he famously put it in a speech in 1963. For de Gaulle, united Europe rested on Franco-German Christian democracy, what he reportedly likened to "resuming Charlemagne's enterprise." Observers at the time were quick to point out that the geographical contours of the European Coal and Steel Community closely matched Charlemagne's "Frankish" Europe over a millennium before.[51]

The fledgling Federal Republic of Germany had a special investment in this conservative *Abendland* identity. Stressing West Germany's central place in the history and mission of the Occident effectively blended continuity with rupture, and helped unite Catholics and Protestants as well as liberal and Christian political parties in the name of national renewal. West Germany's Christian

Democratic Party explicitly based its program on the maintenance of "Christian and occidental values of life." In so doing the concept of *Abendland* helped bind West Germany to the United States as part of the Cold War geography of the Christian West. Even if anti-Americanism remained a strong feature of West German elite culture, Adenauer and his fellow Christian Democrats made no bones about praising America's "Occidental Christian spirit." In fact, the union of German Catholicism and American liberalism emerged as one of the most distinctive features of West German political life. In its celebration of membership within the Christian West, West German *Abendland* ideology shelved any fantasies of German unification to the distant future, and in part aimed to delegitimate leftist nationalism and the politics of self-determination advanced by the rival Social Democratic Party. The crowning event enshrining this remaking of Christian Western Europe was when de Gaulle invited Adenauer to Reims Cathedral in July 1962, during which the two Catholic statesmen prayed together for peace, amity, and reconciliation. This was the West European version of Cold War containment policy.[52]

Here and elsewhere the preservation of Christian civilization assumed material form. While the urgent need for reconstruction shaped all discussions about provisioning war survivors with food, shelter, medicine, and schooling, the ruins of war took on heightened symbolic expression for many Europeans. This was especially pronounced among Christians, who often saw the cityscapes of catastrophe as divine punishment for Europe's turn away from God. The feverish rebuilding of damaged cathedrals and destroyed churches across Western Europe received a great deal of cultural attention as a necessary step in the "re-Christianization" of the continent after the war.

Not surprisingly Germany occupied a special place in this story. In the midst of sifting through the rubble and imagining what a new Germany might be and look like, much attention early on focused

Figure 16. Christ in the rubble, Cologne, Germany, 1945.
Hermann Claasen, *Gesang im Feuerofen* (Düsseldorf: L. Schwann,
1949), 29. *Credit: L. Schwann Verlag, Düsseldorf*

on the restoration of damaged cathedrals and churches as a badly
needed moral compass after the war. The task was daunting, and the
figures sobering: in Aachen, for example, only 43 of the 498 churches
survived; in the Rhineland, some 400 churches had been totally destroyed. Rebuilding churches was thus considered an urgent dimension of postwar moral and physical reconstruction. The high-profile
restoration of Aachen and Cologne cathedrals—to say nothing of the
conspicuous display of the ruins of the Kaiser-Wilhelm-Gedächtnis-
Kirche in West Berlin—are famous instances of the Federal Republic's *Abendland* cultural policy as a bulwark against both the Nazi past
and potentially communist future. Scores of books published in the
wake of the war lavishly chronicled the damaged state of cathedrals
set against the backdrop of mountains of rubble. The earliest and perhaps most famous example—Hermann Claasen's 1947 photo book

Figure 17. Life among the ruins, Cologne, Germany, 1945. Hermann Claasen, *Gesang im Feuerofen* (Düsseldorf: L. Schwann, 1947), 31. *Credit: L. Schwann Verlag, Düsseldorf*

about Cologne, *Gesang im Feuerofen*, or *Songs from the Furnace*—drew on a long tradition of romantic ruins to drive home the pathos and prospect of Christian rebirth (Figures 16 and 17). Claasen's book was one of the first attempts at German public remembrance about World War II, and like-minded photo books were made about Dresden, Berlin, and Stuttgart. Herbert Mason's celebrated 1940 photograph of London's St. Paul's Cathedral under assault from German bombardment was used for similar purposes, serving as a symbol of Christian rectitude and perseverance (Figure 18). Likewise, France, Holland, and Belgium showcased damaged churches as metaphors of Western civilization under assault. In Germany, the Allies (most notably the Americans) welcomed the revival of the churches and religious life as positive signs of denazification and progress. Jewish ruins and restitution, by contrast, played no role in the symbolic re-

Figure 18. St. Paul's Cathedral during London Blitz. Photo by Herbert Mason. *Credit: Getty Images*

construction of postwar Europe, and it was only during the 1980s that synagogue restoration emerged as a political matter of national atonement across the Cold War frontier, especially in divided Germany and Poland.[53]

Such a view of Western Europe's common values, heritage, and civilization was soon written into the moral foundation of key postwar institutions. A good example is the Council of Europe, which came into existence on May 5, 1949, through a treaty signed by ten countries, and was dedicated to defending human rights, democracy, and the rule of law in Europe. It was in part the fruit of the Congress of Europe, which took place the year before in The Hague. On hand were twenty-two former prime ministers, twenty-eight former foreign ministers, and several hundred guests, including representatives from trade unions, women's movements, and religious organizations. There was some controversy about whether to admit the delegates from Franco's Spain, but in the end the council decided to take on the "semi-official" Spanish delegation in the name of European unity, marking the first time that Spain participated in an international meeting since 1945. The Christian underpinning of the new council was stressed in the final resolution, which proclaimed that "unity even in the midst of our national, ideological and religious differences is to be found in the common heritage of Christian and other spiritual and cultural values."[54]

The new Council of Europe's ecumenical spirit of Western European humanism was on display in other ways. Officials from the Council closed their 1949 conference by laying a wreath at a statue of Goethe at Strasbourg University, honoring him as the symbolic patron of Western Europe's reborn Christian civilization. The event was designed as a contribution to the bicentennial celebration of Goethe's birth around the world at the time. That year Goethe was the subject of transatlantic adulation in the United States and in both Germanies. The feting of Goethe the humanist animated the inauguration of the Goethe Bicentennial Convocation and Music Festival in 1949 in Aspen, Colorado, which featured José Ortega y Gasset and Albert Schweitzer among the star-studded roster of keynote speakers to lionize the "anti-totalitarian" German thinker as a bridge between old and new, Western Europe and America.[55]

Not everyone was enamored by the conservative tenor of this new Council. The *London Daily Worker* condemned the Congress of Europe "as a front of the War Bloc, of the campaign for a third world war." *L'Unità*, the Italian communist daily, lampooned the congress as "the new Holy Alliance" of illiberal counterrevolution. In Britain some conservatives worried that the Council was a "step in the consolidation of the Catholic 'black international,'" while Labour MP James Callaghan predicted that "such a Federation would be Catholic, Liberal and Reactionary." Even so, the declamation of Western civilization had become a marker of identity, mission, and borders for Western Europe by the late 1940s. Such language permeated not only so-called soft power institutions, but sometimes hard ones too. The preamble of NATO's charter, signed in April 1949, pledged its twelve signatories to remain "determined to safeguard the freedom, common heritage and civilization of their peoples, founded on the principles of democracy, individual liberty and the rule of law."[56]

THE NEW MISSION OF CHRISTIAN CIVILIZATION EARMARKED the 1940s and 1950s in Western Europe, and the scandal surrounding the Mindszenty trial gave purpose to it. But by the early 1960s, Mindszenty and his place within Cold War cosmology was becoming more and more marginal. The close relations between Washington and Rome peaked in the early 1950s, and the Vatican did not exert any comparable political power in Europe until the accession of the Polish pope John Paul II in 1978. By the mid-1960s, the CIA's secret psychological programs were winding down, as the obsessive 1950s interest in brainwashing and mind control declined from prominence. With time Mindszenty's star had also faded among international politicians and even Catholic activists. However, the Mindszenty saga took one more dramatic twist—he surprisingly resurfaced during the Budapest Uprising of 1956, in which thousands of protesters marched against the Hungarian People's Republic and its Soviet-imposed policies. After some confusion, Premier Imre Nagy freed the cardinal, allowing him to return to Budapest as a liberated man. Mindszenty wasted little time in praising the insurgents, and delivered speeches and radio addresses calling for the restoration of Christian public life. Yet four days later Soviet tanks cracked down on the protesters; the cardinal—seen as one of the leaders of the uprising—escaped to the American legation in Budapest, where he would remain for no less than fifteen years in political asylum until 1971. His temporary release in 1956—after spending seven years in jail—and further confinement in the US legation attracted a fresh round of worldwide condemnation. So vociferous was the anger that a militant Cardinal Mindszenty Foundation was founded in 1958 in the US, which elevated the Hungarian prelate as the masthead martyr of the American anticommunist cause. But within Christian circles in the Eastern Bloc, Mindszenty was seen as a growing liability, in that his inflexible position toward the communist state had made things difficult for the Church and its parishioners both in Hungary and across the region. In Eastern Europe, Catholics interpreted Mindszenty's showy defiance as simply a pretext for communist repression, and opted for a more accommodating line toward communist regimes in the name of preserving the Church's semi-independence. Heinrich Grüber, a high-ranking authority in East Germany's Evangelical Church, went so far as to say that Mindszenty "the schemer, avid for power" was responsible for the bloodshed in Budapest in 1956.[57]

In the US legation, Mindszenty was not allowed to pursue any activity construed as provocative and was forbidden to interfere in the operation of the Roman Catholic Church in Hungary or issue any orders. His frustration was often expressed in letters to American presidents and secretaries of state, pleading for Western assistance toward Hungarian liberation. On November 8, 1957, the one-year anniversary of the uprising, Mindszenty ratcheted up his rhetoric in a letter to Secretary of State John Foster Dulles: "As the Hungarians have withstood the forces of the Tatars, the Turks, and the Russians in defending Western Civilization throughout ten and a half centuries—and even most recently opened the eyes of the West to their struggle—this will be their mission in the future, too, while standing in the front ranks of all people." Even if these letters invariably went unanswered for fear of causing diplomatic tension with the Soviet Union, they did reveal Mindszenty as a Hungarian nationalist and anticommunist Christian crusader.[58]

But while Mindszenty had not changed, the Cold War had. For one thing, Pope Pius XII died in 1958 and was succeeded by Pope John XXIII. His 1963 encyclical *Pacem in Terris* left open the possibility of cohabitation with communism, setting in motion a Vatican *Ostpolitik*. Over the course of the 1960s the Hungarian church eventually made its peace with the communist state, as had the other churches across the Eastern Bloc. In fact, the communist states' relatively successful effort to suppress the transnational dimension of Catholicism both across the Bloc and across the Iron Curtain meant that these churches were effectively nationalized. By the late 1960s a new pope, Paul VI, went further in this spirit of détente: he declared the cardinal "a victim of history" (significantly, not communism) and annulled the ban imposed by Mindszenty on his political opponents. In response, the Hungarian communist government was prepared to let him leave the country. By the early 1970s the US felt that Mindszenty had become an obstacle and embarrassment to warming Soviet-American relations, since his presence, as the primate himself admitted, "stood in the way of the policy of détente." In 1971 he was thus pushed out unceremoniously from the American legation as Nixon's unwanted guest, after which the cardinal went into his second exile at the Pázmáneum seminary in Vienna. Though his old supporters expressed anger toward the Church for having lost its fighting spirit from the early days of the Cold War, Mindszenty was now a relic from a bygone age.[59]

In his memoirs the former socialist Belgian foreign minister Paul-Henri Spaak famously remarked that Stalin was the true father of the European Economic Community in that the fear of the Soviet Union spurred the unity of Western Europe. This is valid to an extent in providing a negative foil against which Western European consolidation could take place. Certainly, the communist takeover of Czechoslovakia in March 1948 was read as an ominous omen of the Soviet designs on Europe, and the Western European reaction to the coup cemented the idea of Western Europe as made up of states committed to religious freedom, human rights, and other liberal values. But this negative definition of Western European unity was never enough, nor was the EEC only about the pooling of industrial resources. The martyrdom of Cardinal Mindszenty played a fundamental role in providing moral direction to budding Western European solidarity. His high-profile trial helped spur and shape the early Cold War revival of Christian civilization in the form of a rebooted church, resurgent Christian democracy, christianized human rights, and Judeo-Christian values, as well as a new map of the cultural frontiers of Europe—all of which undergirded a new Western European identity that transcended the framework of competing nation-states. The shifting understanding of psychological research and social science endeavor—in part driven by the widespread concern with brainwashing as the "de-civilization" of science—could also be traced back to the cardinal's trial. The defense of Christian civilization provided a language of solace, engagement, and militancy for a newly formed Western alliance. So even if the deposed cardinal may have ended his captivity largely as a forgotten figure, the ideological refortification of the western half of the continent after 1947 was very much a part of his legacy.[60]

The battle for civilization was waged not just in the world of the spirit, nor only in the pulpits, streets, news offices, and courtrooms of Western Europe. As we shall see in the next chapter, the material reconstruction of the continent sparked lively debates about the meaning of peace, prosperity, and even decency in post-fascist Europe, and ideas of civilization were central to them on both sides of the Iron Curtain.

four

SCIENCE, SHELTER,
AND CIVILITY

D URING THE LAST WEEKEND OF AUGUST 1948, OVER 450
writers, artists, and intellectuals from forty countries gathered
in the newly renamed Polish city of Wrosław (formerly Breslau)
to take part in the World Congress of Intellectuals in Defense of
Peace. The event was organized by the new Polish People's Republic
and featured a star-studded array of leading leftist international figures, including Graham Greene, Bertolt Brecht, Paul Éluard, Anna
Seghers, Fernand Léger, Irène Joliot-Curie, Pablo Picasso, and Aldous Huxley. Its objective was to build a "tenuous bridge" across
the hardening geopolitical and ideological gulf between West and
East, and to create a spirit of cooperative exchange to discuss the
prospects of world peace. British filmmaker Ivor Montagu praised
those speakers who rejected the "division of the world into 'Atlantic'
or 'European' or 'Western' culture" from its Eastern counterpart so
as to affirm "the inseparable inter-influences" of cultural life across
the continent. Of particular concern to many delegates—as noted
in the congress's resolution—were the ways in which "the sublime
mission of science" was "being used for the secret production of instruments of destruction" and the "abrogation of the cause of peace."

173

The congress summoned the champions of "progressive culture" everywhere to help develop "mutual comprehension between cultures and peoples" in the "interest of world civilization."[1]

Nevertheless, the causes of peace and world civilization did not fare very well at the congress. Proceedings quickly degenerated into grandstanding and mutual recriminations, especially between the Soviet and English representatives. This was mainly because the Soviet delegates used the opportunity to condemn repeatedly Western warmongering and the evils of American nuclear weaponry. Polish-born British artist Feliks Topolski described the congress as "a huge cry of faith-declaring" among the Soviet contingent. The atmosphere soured when Aleksandr Fadeev, the head of the Union of Soviet Writers, claimed that "the shackles of US imperialists have turned the world into a police precinct and its people into slaves of capital," and then called for a "lightning war against the decadence of literature and art in the West." Fadeev poured scorn on several celebrated Western writers in colorful language: "If jackals could learn typing, if hyenas knew how to wield a pen, what would come out would certainly resemble books by Miller, Eliot, Malraux, and Sartre." Participants were taken aback by the tone and content of the attack, spurring the prominent British historian A. J. P. Taylor to fire back: "The task of intellectuals is to preach tolerance and harmony rather than hatred. And here is proclaimed war, not peace." To many Western delegates Fadeev's tirade made a mockery of the congress's quest for peace and cross-cultural understanding, and several walked out in protest. Even though the conference finished with honeyed words of future cooperation, it was plain that bipolar cooperation on peace issues—even among the international left—was not going to be easy. Several spin-off international conferences were dedicated to rallying "peace-loving humanity," but these too generally fell along Cold War lines. The Soviet Union attempted to seize control of the issue by spearheading the peace campaign of 1949–1951, which was originally based on the World Committee of Partisans of Peace under the auspices of the Information Bureau of the Communist and Workers' Parties (the so-called Cominform) created in 1947. In 1950 the group adopted the new name of the World Peace Council and tirelessly lobbied the international community about the dangers of American warmongering. Peace, like Europe itself, was divisible.[2]

While the ill-starred conference was certainly an important symbolic event marking the breakdown of Allied wartime military and cultural alliance, the dream of international peace did not disappear with the onset of the Cold War. There were a number of initiatives to build a better world for the sake of peace and civilization, some of which united activists across the Cold War divide. Two surprising areas of convergence were science and humanitarian law. The previous chapter discussed how these fields, as seen in the antagonistic bipolar understanding of human rights and the Western debate about the "black science" of brainwashing, had become embroiled in Cold War politicking. Yet in other ways, science and humanitarian law still held out the possibility of cooperation across ideological and national boundaries, often around the theme of secular civilization. Housing, domesticity, advice book literature, and anti-Americanism were related topics that found similar manifestations on both sides of the Iron Curtain. These material expressions of civilization were neither linked to religion nor region, nor tied explicitly to defending cultural borders or imperiled heritage. For these broad-minded scientists, peace advocates, and domestic modernizers, the cause of civilization was taken up to promote the material welfare of citizen and society.

THE AMERICAN DETONATION OF TWO ATOMIC BOMBS ON HIROshima and Nagasaki in August 1945 may have sped the end of fighting in the Pacific theater and kept the Soviets out of the endgame of war in Japan. Yet the effects of what American secretary of war

Henry Stimson predicted a few months before would be the "most terrible weapon ever known in human history" immediately caused widespread soul-searching in the West about the ramifications of what had happened. The instantaneous decimation of two Japanese cities and their civilian populations introduced a new dimension of industrialized death in a war that had already far surpassed the moral and technical conventions of mass killing in Europe. The magnitude of nuclear war meant that the tragedies of Hiroshima and Nagasaki transcended Japanese history to serve as grim signatures of a new age, as the iconic mushroom cloud marked the birth of a planetary consciousness about the shared fate of humanity in the face of unprecedented technological power. The advent of nuclear war animated debate around the world, especially for an American public uneasy about what its government had done in its name. "Seldom, if ever," announced the American radio commentator Edward R. Murrow on August 12, 1945, "has a war ended leaving the victors with such a sense of uncertainty and fear, with such a realization that the future is obscure and that survival is not assured." Moral disquiet was especially pronounced among scientists, religious groups, women's organizations, and the mass media, and everywhere the crisis of civilization seemed ominously at hand. Japanese emperor Hirohito's declaration of August 1945 to his subjects in the aftermath of nuclear destruction solemnly grasped what was at stake: "Should we continue to fight, it would not only result in an ultimate collapse and obliteration of the Japanese nation, but also it would lead to the total extinction of human civilization."[3]

Hiroshima and Nagasaki marked a fateful marriage of science and warfare, and drove a new urgency to bring nuclear science under civilian control. For many observers, Stimson's hope that "if the problem of the proper use of this weapon can be solved, we would have the opportunity to bring the world into a pattern in which the peace of the world and our civilization can be saved" was too important to be left to the whims of the American government. New political

176

engagement and proper international oversight were now desperately needed, and the language of civilization framed the discussion. In November 1945 British prime minister Clement Attlee argued that "without a moral enthusiasm equal to that which savants bring to their researches, the civilization built over the centuries would be destroyed." French writer Albert Camus condemned the bombing of Hiroshima as "organized murder," one in which modern civilization had reached such a "degree of savagery" that it was now necessary to choose "between collective suicide or the intelligent utilization of scientific conquests." American journalist Dorothy Thompson worried about its political fallout, arguing that the Hiroshima blast "did more than blow up landscapes, buildings and populations. It blew up the San Francisco Charter [of the United Nations] and made it as obsolete as the Holy Alliance created after the Napoleonic wars."[4]

Atomic warfare sparked wide interest in the creation of a world government that would manage nuclear weaponry, most notably in Japan, Scandinavia, Holland, the United States, and Great Britain. A new World Federalist Movement strove to put nuclear technology under careful international control for peace. The scientific community took the lead, since many scientists felt that there was insufficient management of the global atomic threat. In October 1945 Albert Einstein published a letter in the *New York Times* saying that the United Nations was ineffective because it was too beholden to the "absolute sovereignty of the rival nation-states"; what was needed was a "Federal Constitution of the world, a working worldwide legal order, if we hope to prevent atomic war." The hope of harmonizing science, peace, and morality was a prevalent theme in political discussions across the Cold War divide in the late 1940s, ranging from Attlee to Stalin. But it was in the realm of civil society where support was the strongest, and by 1949 the World Federalist Movement counted as many as 47,000 members across the globe. A petition was signed in 1950 by a range of celebrity advocates, including Camus, American writer John Steinbeck,

French philosopher Jacques Maritain, Italian filmmaker Roberto Rossellini, Senegalese poet and politician Léopold Sédar Senghor, and German writer Thomas Mann. "Confronted by the means of destruction that are now in the hands of men," their statement read, "all differences of politics, race and creed are beside the point," since they "will virtually cease to exist along with the human race unless mankind agrees to the establishment by peaceful means of a world government"—the choice, they concluded, is now "between one world or none." While the World Federalist Movement faded from prominence in the face of Cold War division, it did reflect a new mode of international thinking at the time that strove to forego the framework of nation-states.[5]

But if the world government movement failed, the campaign to civilize science was more successful. The *Bulletin of the Atomic Scientists* was founded in 1945 by prominent physicists Eugene Rabinowitch and Hyman H. Goldsmith, who were part of the famed Manhattan Project to develop the first nuclear weapons. In the early years the *Bulletin* devoted great energy to publicizing the dangers of atomic energy and the goal of banning atomic weapons. According to Rabinowitch, the atomic scientists' movement "was part of a conspiracy to preserve our civilization by scaring men into rationality." In March 1946 the *Report on the International Control of Atomic Energy* raised the hope of agreement between the superpowers as a step toward a world constitution. A 1946 booklet made up of short articles by leading atomic scientists called *One World or None* opened with a preface by Danish Nobel Prize–winning physicist Niels Bohr titled "Science and Civilization," calling for the demilitarization of science. Further cooperative steps were taken with the creation of the Geneva-based European Organization for Nuclear Research, or CERN, in 1954, initially conceived as an endeavor to win back European scientists who had gone to the US to work for the American "military-industrial complex." Renowned for its particle physics research, CERN played a key role in distinguishing European science from its more military-oriented American counterpart, and saw itself as instrumental in taming science for peaceful purposes. Yet scientists around Europe continued to voice their concern about nuclear physics being weaponized. On April 12, 1957, eighteen West German nuclear scientists—the so-called Göttingen Eighteen, which included four Nobel laureates—published a manifesto rejecting the arming of the West German army with tactical nuclear weapons. International interest in the peaceful application of science for the material benefit of humanity found supreme expression in the 1958 World's Fair in Brussels, which was the first such exhibition since the Second World War. The domestication of science was the international show's main theme, and a giant model of a unit cell of an iron crystal—the Atomium—served as the emblem of the international event. All the national pavilions addressed the peaceful and domestic uses of modern science in various ways.[6]

National governments spearheaded their own public education campaigns about the potential benevolence of nuclear energy. In 1947–1948, Attlee's government sponsored an "Atom Train" traveling exhibition, in which a special locomotive journeyed across Britain to inform the public about the peaceful windfall of atomic science for domestic energy usage (Figure 19). It was organized by various government offices, private industry, and the Atomic Scientists' Association to allay public fear and to help promote the international control of nuclear energy, reportedly attracting some 168,000 visitors over the course of its 168-day tour. A few years later, the American government offered its own version of how atomic energy was to be civilized, best captured in the "Atoms for Peace" initiative announced by President Eisenhower in December 1953. Eisenhower's campaign was explicitly designed to manage international fears of American atomic power by publicizing the benefits of the "friendly" atom. This was no easy sell, not least because the US had exploded its first hydrogen bomb the year before, with the Soviet Union doing the same in August 1953. Eisenhower

179

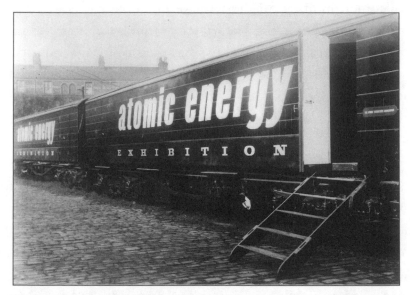

Figure 19. "Atom Train" traveling exhibition, London, 1948. *Credit: Churchill Archive, London*

announced the Atoms for Peace program in a speech at the United Nations General Assembly, and pledged that the US would "devote its entire heart and mind to find the way by which the miraculous inventiveness of man shall not be dedicated to his death, but consecrated to his life." The US Information Agency stepped up its media campaign by distributing the speech to all major international newspapers. Walt Disney even produced a short film titled *Our Friend the Atom*, which was shown on American television and in American schools in 1957. Over 16 million posters and booklets were produced about "Atoms for Peace," and equipment and teaching materials were sent to schools, hospitals, and research centers across the US and to other countries. Large mobile exhibits (notably with no mention of bombs or weapons) were mounted on truck trailers and sent to major cities in Western Europe, Asia, and Africa to convey the message that atomic energy was safe and beneficial. These shows reportedly attracted over 100,000 viewers each in Frankfurt, Buenos Aires, Rome, Stockholm, Kyoto, and Accra; one American report boasted that in India the "horror and assumed anti-Asian tinge of our Hiroshima drop still lingers but our efforts to 'civilize' the atom have moved us to the plus side of the ledger." Whether this was true remains an open question, but the Atoms for Peace campaign amply underscored America's interests to counter both its belligerent reputation and the fear of atomic energy around the globe.[7]

The most celebrated attempt to overcome the dangerous politicization of science in the Cold War was the famed Pugwash Conference. Pugwash was an international movement that started in 1957 and involved some of the most famous scientists of the day, whose aim—in the words of founder Joseph Rotblat—was to "ensure that mankind will not destroy itself." Its chief task was to provide informal contacts between the US and USSR during the Cold War in the hope of confronting the threat of nuclear war, and possibly of getting both East and West to renounce nuclear weapons altogether. The idea of the East-West conferences was first suggested by British philosopher Bertrand Russell, who in a speech in the House of Lords on November 28, 1945—just several months after the Hiroshima detonation—suggested that a meeting between Western and Soviet scientists would be the best means to avert the further destruction of civilization. In his 1953 speech at the United Nations, Eisenhower had warned that nuclear war would mean the "probability of civilization destroyed," and in March of the following year Soviet premier Georgy Malenkov concurred that "a new world war with nuclear weapons" would spell "the end of world civilization." But little was being done about it, prompting Russell and Einstein to draft a manifesto calling on the international community to abolish war and renounce nuclear weapons to avert the very real "risk of universal death"; the petition was cosigned by other prominent scientists, many of whom were Nobel laureates.[8]

The first meeting took place in Pugwash, a fishing village in Nova Scotia, Canada, and the birthplace and summer home residence of American industrialist Cyrus Eaton, who funded the conference in the early years. At the first meeting were twenty-two eminent scientists, including seven from the US and three each from the USSR and Japan. It led to the creation of the Soviet-American Disarmament Study Group, which directed its attention to arms control and as such became a primary forum for informal discussions about military de-escalation. First Secretary of the Communist Party of the Soviet Union Nikita Khrushchev became a great supporter of Pugwash, and repeatedly extolled its work in advancing peace and disarmament in order to avoid the "destruction of civilisation." Although the conferences eventually became embroiled in power politics between the US, the USSR, and China, they did serve as an important stimulus for international cooperation and helped to pave the way for the Limited Test Ban Treaty of 1963, the Nuclear Non-Proliferation Treaty of 1968, and the Biological Weapons Convention of 1972, and culminated with the 1972 SALT I agreement and the Anti-Ballistic Missile Treaty.[9]

Another surprising example of cooperation across the Cold War divide was the campaign to civilize war itself. This was most dramatically evidenced in the ratification of the Geneva Conventions of 1949. In August of that year, representatives from fifty-nine countries gathered in Geneva to discuss and formalize a new international code of military conduct in armed conflicts of the future. Its double objective was to protect soldiers captured in combat from ill treatment at the hands of the enemy, as well as to safeguard civilians from the brutality of armed enemy forces. As such, it went beyond earlier Hague Conventions (of 1899 and 1907) by making the civilian the focal point of the new laws of war, as opposed to soldiers, nurses, and Red Cross agents, who had been the main subjects of protection in previous conventions. The Red Cross was founded in 1864 by Swiss businessman Henry Dunant with the express aim of administering humanitarian aid to all wounded soldiers irrespective of nationality in the name of Christian charity, universalism, and neutrality. The Red Cross led the way in devising comprehensive wartime conventions following the harrowing civilian experiences of both the Great War and the Spanish Civil War; nevertheless, the expanding technology of war (including aerial warfare and the targeting of civilians) continued to outpace the international community's ability to protect innocents caught in war zones. The 1949 Conventions attempted to reinstate this distinction so as not to repeat the tragic fate of unprotected civilians in the Second World War. The wider goal was to repair the worrying divergence between humankind's military and moral progress, which the framers felt was responsible for the crisis of civilization itself. Jean S. Pictet, head of the International Red Cross and the most celebrated commentator on the Conventions, proclaimed that robust new international norms would be a vital "safeguard for countless persons and the last refuge of civilization and humanity." Another legal commentator ratcheted up the rhetoric by saying that the two world wars signaled "the total crisis of Western Christian culture, a crisis which threatens the very survival of our civilization," exposing the fact that the "cultured man of the twentieth century is no more than a barbarian under a very superficial veneer of civilization."[10]

The 1949 Geneva Convention for the Protection of Civilian Persons in Time of War was a milestone in the history of warfare, and pivoted on the demarcation between civilization and barbarism. This was not altogether new, as the etymology of civilization—to make civil—referred above all to transform a criminal matter into a civil one, as forcefully argued by seventeenth-century legal theorists. This broad understanding of civilization as linked to the state's moral and legal comportment toward its citizens became standard by the late eighteenth century, and Jeremy Bentham was the first writer to use the term civilization in the context of international law. By the mid-nineteenth century, civilization was increasingly interpreted as an expression of restraint in warfare. This was best illustrated in the preambles of nineteenth-century humanitarian law documents, such as the 1863 Lieber Code governing the actions of Union soldiers in the American Civil War and the 1868 Declaration of St. Petersburg that outlawed the use of certain projectiles "in times of war between civilized nations." In a twentieth-century world in which peace treaties became less common conclusions of armed conflicts, and as wars more typically ended with cease-fires and truces with or without the benefit of international peacekeeping forces, the Geneva Conventions were identified as an essential retaining wall against further barbarism. Pictet captured his generation's mixture of hope and anxiety about the utility of international law after the Second World War when he wrote that the Conventions primarily aimed "to safeguard respect for the human person, the fundamental rights of man and his dignity as a human being, in the hope that universal peace—the desire of all men of good will—may one day be established." The Geneva Conventions were therefore central to a new international politics about the laws of war.[11]

What is often forgotten is that the Soviet Union exerted an important influence on the Conventions. At first this may seem puzzling, given the USSR's long-standing characterization of the Red Cross as a Western puppet organization. The Soviets had accused the Red Cross of being too sympathetic to White Russians during the Russian Civil War that followed the Revolution, as well as harboring pro-fascist loyalties during the Second World War. But by 1949 the Soviet Union had officially rescinded its boycott of the Red Cross and even recognized some of its landmark conventions from the interwar years, such as the 1929 Convention Relating to the Treatment of Prisoners of War. To the surprise of the other international delegates, the Soviets arrived in full force in 1949, as they and their allies pushed hardest for having the more far-reaching Conventions universally applied to all wars and to all civilians. The Soviet Union even accused those states that aimed to limit the definition and protection of civilians as "enemies of humanity." While such maneuvering was largely motivated to embarrass a Western coalition led by the United States and the United Kingdom, the Soviet

Union managed to position itself as the leader of the international campaign to "humanize" the laws and customs of war.[12]

It is easy to dismiss this engagement as nothing but Soviet grandstanding, given the ways in which we have already seen how the Soviets politicized the cause of peace during the early Cold War. But in Geneva the Soviets were serious in their efforts. The first major test case of the Conventions concerned the question of atomic weapons, and this debate exposed the problems of peace politics across the Cold War divide. The Soviet Union was a cosignee of the 1948 Convention on the Prevention and Punishment of the Crime of Genocide that formed the international protection umbrella of civilians, and now advocated the 1949 Conventions as an extension of the Geneva Protocol of 1925, which had outlawed the use of chemical and biological weapons. To the list of prohibited and punishable offenses against civilians agreed to by all parties at Geneva in 1925—such as murder, torture, and medical experimentation—the Soviets wished to include indiscriminate bombing and atomic weaponry. They then drafted a resolution calling for a full ban on atomic bombs on humanitarian grounds, in direct criticism of the American and British delegates. The reception of the Soviet motion fell along Cold War lines: it was duly supported by Bulgaria, Romania, Belarussia, and Czechoslovakia, while the US and its allies roundly rejected it. The motion to include the clause was defeated, on the grounds that such a debate was better handled by the UN and that more time was needed to digest the issue. Nevertheless, the Soviet claim to speak in the name of peace and humanity put the United States and its allies on the back foot. The Soviets continued to apply pressure, and posted some lasting achievements. In the early 1970s, for example, they led the way in drafting the Convention on the Prohibition of the Development, Production and Stockpiling of Bacteriological and Toxic Weapons and on Their Destruction, ratified in 1975, which the US refused to sign lest it would have to acknowledge the illegality of US military operations in Vietnam. With it the Geneva Conventions became a testing ground for giving form to a new international civilization after Auschwitz, Hiroshima, and "total war."[13]

Soviet peace politics were not restricted to international diplomacy, and had domestic resonance. In the late 1940s the "struggle for peace" became a common phrase in Soviet popular press, and enabled citizens to engage more directly with foreign policy objectives. Predictably, *Pravda* made much of the idea that Moscow was leading the global movement of peace against Western aggression, and that peace was thus synonymous with protecting the Soviet Union from Western encroachment and warmongering. The Struggle for Peace media campaign was intensified to mobilize popular support against the West after the outbreak of the Korean War in 1950, and to drive home the point that the USSR was a champion of the oppressed and the global defender of peace. Many letters by factory workers, housewives, and ordinary citizens were sent to the Committee in Defense of Peace in support. Such public endorsement of Soviet foreign policy may be brushed off as just another example of how people learned to speak socialist and perform outward conformity. While there is no doubt some truth in this, these letters can be viewed differently. For example, the Struggle for Peace campaign—and its reception among ordinary people—may have helped cultivate a new superpower consciousness among Soviet citizens about their country's custodial role in global affairs in the name of peace and protection, linking the Soviet cause to world affairs. These letters of sympathy with the Korean people at war have also been read as unique if indirect instances of citizens acknowledging their own painful wartime experiences in the broader cause of international peace.[14]

Elsewhere in Eastern Europe, peace politics integrated foreign and domestic policy. State-led solidarity initiatives generated significant activity across the region. In East Germany, Hungary, and Poland, peace committees organized mass rallies to condemn the encroachment on North Korea and independent Vietnam by the US and France, and factories collected donations and organized extra work shifts to send military and humanitarian aid. In June 1950 East German peace committees choreographed mass demonstrations across the country and launched campaigns to support the Korean People's Army with donations of medical supplies. Following the armistice in July 1953, the Czechoslovak Communist Party launched the "Let's Help Korea!" initiative, which included raising funds through cultural performances. Just as in the Soviet Union, shows of solidarity with North Korea and Vietnam appealed to many who had experienced the horrors and destruction of World War II in Eastern Europe. As one Polish newspaper put it in reference to American aggression in North Korea: "We Poles know this style. In such a way and in such a tone, the Nazi occupiers addressed the Polish nation. Because the American occupiers of Korea also showed that they differ from the Nazis only in style of uniforms." And a speaker at the 1950 demonstration of the Hungarian Women's Federation against the Korean War claimed that "we hold our ground in the peace front as we battle for each and every seed of grain." Such militant language was designed to raise awareness about the linkage of foreign and domestic policy, and ideologically helped prepare the ground for Eastern Europe's turn outward to the Third World in the 1960s, as we shall see in Chapter 8.[15]

Such peace politicking animated Western Europe too, and shaped public understandings of the postwar welfare state. Whereas the nineteenth-century European state was concerned with turning civilians into soldiers, the post-1945 West European state distinguished itself by its effort to transform soldiers back into civilians. After the war, death itself was no longer part of the social contract. Charles Tilly's well-known aphorism that "war made the state and the state made war" seems to have been rejected after 1945 in both halves of Europe. The transition from war to peace was neither quick nor comprehensive—Europe was hardly demilitarized, as evident in the presence of American and Soviet soldiers conspicuously encamped across their respective Cold War spheres of influence. Furthermore, many of the most prominent postwar European leaders were former military heroes, including de Gaulle, Churchill, Stalin, Tito, and Franco, who often appeared in full military uniform. While the leaders of the winning side of the war regularly dressed in military attire as reminders of wartime valor and national mission, the losers did not do so in an effort to showcase the full break from fascist military pasts, most plainly witnessed in Italy and West Germany. Much commentary in the Federal Republic noted that Adenauer was the first modern German head of state who commanded respect without appearing in uniform.[16]

The large Western European demonstrations in the 1950s against nuclear power—both religious and secular—recast social politics in a new way. The development of the hydrogen bomb in the early 1950s sparked international concern about the prospect of global annihilation, and across Western Europe peace and disarmament movements mushroomed as grassroots initiatives. While such political engagement took place from Denmark to France to Greece, Britain's Campaign for Nuclear Disarmament (CND) and West Germany's "Easter marches" and Campaign Against Atomic Death (*Kampf dem Atomtod*) were the most prominent. Many members came from pacifist Christian backgrounds, and were often involved in the labor movement in their home countries. The early days of the movements took on the hues of a moral crusade, not unlike the antifascist movement across Europe during the Spanish Civil War. But the stakes were higher, since the prospect of planetary nuclear death prompted new international activism. One CND member described the first Aldermaston protest in April 1958, when thousands marched through the Berkshire countryside in song and with "Ban the Bomb" placards, as a kind of anti-American "civilizing mission, a march away from fear toward normality, toward human standards." Bertrand Russell, the figurehead of disarmament in Britain, described the movement in terms of the defense of civilization, saying that in the early days "our mood was like that of St Jerome and St Augustine watching the fall of the Roman Empire and the crumbling of a civilization which had seemed as indestructible as granite." CND's inaugural meeting attracted 5,000 people, and by 1959 it had 270 branches throughout Britain; the 1962 Easter march counted 150,000 protesters. Striking, however, was how quickly the vocabulary of peace and civilization disappeared from this movement, in part because ideas of "partisans for peace" had been co-opted by the communists. This was even more palpable in the continental peace movements, as the goals and self-descriptions of the movements shifted from peace to security. The West German peace movement grew out of grassroots engagement within civil society, and its effort to raise awareness of the new global condition of nuclear threat drew on a language of victimhood in being at the mercy of superpower decision-making. In all these movements, the once-common analogies to the horrors of the Second World War faded with time, as did references to history and civilization in crisis. But there were fundamental differences between East and West. By the late 1950s the Western European movements directly confronted the policies of their governments as complicit in these new existential dangers, whose solution lay in challenging the broader Cold War politics of *pax atomica*. Simply put, the Western European peace movements agitated against the state, while the Eastern European counterparts supported it.[17]

There was also a gender dimension to the international peace movement. In 1958 British CND activist Dora Russell organized a Women's Caravan of Peace as a joint peace initiative across the Iron Curtain. It was composed of nineteen women who set out on a fourteen-week tour in an old bus and Ford truck to take the message of peace through Central and Eastern Europe, ending up in Moscow, where they met the Soviet Peace Committee. Yet there were bigger operations afoot. To advance the cause of world peace, the Women's

International Democratic Federation (WIDF) was founded in 1945 in Paris, with strong links to the Soviet Union. The WIDF pushed for peace issues, women's rights, anticolonialism, and antiracism on a number of fronts. National chapters were set up in some 40 countries in 1945 and by 1958 the figure rose to over 70 countries, and again to 117 by 1985. The federation organized fact-finding missions to Latin America and Southeast Asia to research women's lives there and to cooperate with local women's organizations in the developing world, and engaged in peace initiatives around the globe. However, the WIDF soon fell foul of Cold War politics. In 1950 it spear-headed an investigative mission during the Korean War to look into war crimes against Korean civilians, especially women and children, committed by American and South Korean soldiers in the conflict. Its report caused a furor, and the organization became a target of an anticommunist campaign within the UN, led by the US and Great Britain. In 1951 it was forced to move its headquarters from Paris to East Berlin, and became increasingly linked with the World Peace Council, strengthening the perception that the WIDF was a Soviet front organization. Still, it remained involved in a range of gender and peace causes, particularly in Asia, as well as in relation to the Algerian and Vietnam Wars.[18]

These peace movements helped reshape the language of civilization. In the 1940s, civilization was usually invoked to narrate death, loss, and danger as the underside of war and mass destruction, as noted in the discussion of both atomic warfare and humanitarian law. These were by and large secular discourses that encompassed all of humanity, and provided a moral framework of what was being risked and what needed to be protected. Pacifism and peace—seen as treasonous during the war—now returned as the very expression of continental virtue. But the language of civilization was not always nostalgic or backward-looking—the 1950s and 1960s also gave rise to energetic European efforts to build shiny new material civilizations in the here and now.

In 1951 THE FRENCH COMMUNIST POET LOUIS ARAGON caustically described the United States as a "civilization of bathtubs and Frigidaires," views about the American cultural menace that were common fare among leftists at the time. Aragon was right to the extent that by the late 1950s, most Western Europeans identified America as a powerful consumer culture of appliances, youth fashion, jazz, rock 'n' roll, and film stars, whose modernizing influence on postwar culture was everywhere palpable. By the mid-1960s the emblems of American modernity had made significant inroads into the everyday fabric of Western European society. While a number of European intellectuals routinely denounced the "American way of life" as a form of cultural imperialism, America's "civilization of bathtubs and Frigidaires" was mostly welcomed by war-weary Western Europeans as sources of comfort and pleasure.[19]

This was especially the case with home life. After 1945, having a warm, dry, and quiet home emerged as the most cherished object of desire. Running water, gas, indoor plumbing, and electricity in the first instance, followed later by the acquisition of radios, televisions, and cars, were milestones in the lives of many citizens and shaped the dreams and wishes of the so-called reconstruction generation. According to a poll conducted in France in 1961, which asked one thousand women what they needed to be happy, only 22 percent mentioned love, whereas 54 percent plumped for "a comfortable life and material conveniences." In 1954 only around 7–8 percent of French households had a fridge or washing machine, and only 1 percent had a television. By 1962, more than a third had a fridge and washing machine, and a quarter a TV. By 1975, the figures were 91 percent, 72 percent, and 86 percent, respectively. Such patterns were comparable in Eastern Europe. Housing was central to social policy in every European country after the war, despite extremely divergent experiences of material decimation, housing shortages, social dislocation, and refugee crises. It attracted a remarkable amount of public attention, ranging from national governments to municipal policy makers, welfare workers to women's organizations, architecture and design circles to advertisers and consumer activists. Common to all was a powerful yearning to begin things afresh—so much so that for many Europeans securing a home of one's own signaled the real conclusion of the war and its subsequent hunger years, as registered in the period's memoirs and oral histories across Britain and Europe, including among displaced persons and refugees.[20]

At first glance, the primacy of the home and home life after 1945 may seem a recycled version of developments and sentiments following the Great War. Homes took on heightened political significance after 1918, and this was particularly true of worker domiciles. Even if worker housing first emerged as a new pet issue among social reformers in the mid-nineteenth century, as schemes about improving worker housing made their debut at the Great Exhibition in London in 1851, the European housing reform movement did not really take wing until the 1920s. It was in the interwar years that housing moved to the center of social politics and often served as a litmus test of new European welfare states to make good on pledges made during the war. The British promise to build new "Homes Fit for Heroes" is a celebrated example, but similar initiatives were undertaken across Europe. The results were often quite spectacular for their day, as a coterie of avant-garde architects, city planners, and progressive mayors came together to give mass housing a fresh face and new political priority.

Housing acquired a very different meaning in the wake of the Second World War's legacy of mass death and destruction, genocide, and forced population transfers. It is no surprise that the home became a favorite theme of exhibitions in the immediate postwar era. Across Europe there was renewed interest among state officials, industrial leaders, educators, and museum curators to mount housing shows as markers of national recovery, social improvement, and aesthetic education. This was certainly the case in Western Europe, whose tone was set early on by the 1946 Britain Can Make It and

1951 Festival of Britain shows. In each fair, the accent fell on patriotism and production. What distinguished the post-1945 shows from
their interwar predecessors was the soft-pedaling of references to
empire and class; the focus was squarely on the national community,
the national economy, and national domestic culture.[21]

Similarly, the political significance of the home was greatly am-
plified by the Cold War. In the late 1940s, Marshall Fund administrators in West Germany and Italy mounted housing exhibitions to
showcase the "American way of life" to destitute West Europeans,
and to give material expression to the idea of Western civilization
that connected the United States and Western Europe. The term
often used was the Atlantic Community, which served as a cultural corollary to NATO's American-led military alliance. Many
of these exhibitions were about idealized domestic life complete
with the latest consumer appliances available from America, un-
derscoring the perceived connections among reconstruction, individualism, consumerism, and domestic happiness, based on a clear
gender division of desire and duties. Occupied Berlin was awash
with competing exhibitions about postwar renewal and the good
life, most of which focused on material bounty and modern living.
The particular circumstances of divided Germany fostered an early
politicization of the home as an ideological symbol on both sides of
the Iron Curtain. The 1952 Marshall Fund–sponsored West Berlin exhibition, We Are Building a Better Life—which featured a
two-bedroom single-family dwelling along with some six thousand
objects freely "available to our Western civilization"—attracted some
500,000 visitors, 40 percent of whom came from the Eastern part of
the city. In the exhibition, actors were hired to demonstrate the won-
ders of American-style domestic modernity, with onlookers watching the consumer spectacle from above (Figure 20). The redemptive
power of consumer goods to draw a line under the Nazi past was
strikingly displayed in the West German industrial town of Essen,
whose destroyed synagogue (what the small Jewish community

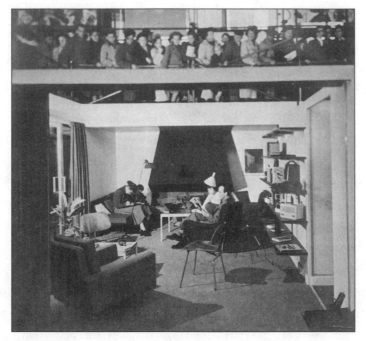

Figure 20. We Are Building a Better Life exhibition, West Berlin, 1952. *Credit: Alfons Leitl, "Die Wohnung der westlichen Völker,"* Baukunst und Werkform *4, no. 12 (1952), 39*

there described in a letter to city officials as the "the most beautiful and dignified in Europe") was repurposed and reopened in 1961 as the House of Industrial Design, which proudly showcased the shiny consumer accoutrements of West German economic recovery. At the occasion Mayor Wilhelm Nieswandt intoned that the "dedication of this desecrated former synagogue to this new dignified purpose" should "make us aware and resolute that such events of blind intolerance must never happen again in a free and democratic Germany" (Figure 21). Similarly, East German architects, planners, and ideologues worked hard to convince socialist citizens of the merits of the ruling party's ambitious housing policy. East Berlin's Stalinallee—a boulevard of grand "worker palaces" initiated in 1952—was the first major building scheme in the country's much-publicized "national reconstruction program," and was hailed as an ideological

Figure 21. House of Industrial Design (exterior above; interior below), Essen, 1961. *Credit: Ruhr Museum, Essen, Germany*

elixir that would instill a new collective socialist consciousness and help curb the allures of the West.[22]

Khrushchev's Soviet Union also put housing at the heart of attempts to garner support for his renewed vision of socialism. From the late 1940s on, the importance of the home as an emblem of personal security, socialist progress, and material prosperity emerged as a primary concern after the war. While mass housing was an important indicator of socialist achievement and prosperity from the 1930s, Khrushchev set in motion an enormous building program that aimed to fulfill promises made at the Twentieth Congress of the Communist Party of the Soviet Union in 1956 that each Soviet family would be housed in its own apartment. The proposed solution to the Soviet Union's dire housing shortage was the construction of a new domestic landscape featuring the mass production of squat five-story apartment buildings in the 1950s and then high-rise tower-blocks in the 1960s. Design reformers mounted campaigns through a wide variety of channels, ranging from government committee papers to design journals, social policy initiatives to home decoration magazines, all of which encouraged dwellers to abandon old antiques and other bourgeois possessions in favor of objects that better represented socialist modernity. Across the Soviet Union and the Eastern Bloc the promotion of modern design and modern domesticity with its emphasis on utility and technology was hailed as a step closer to the realization of communism and the end of the misery and poverty of the past.[23]

The housing boom in West and East Europe was fueled by a Cold War desire to build more and better dwellings than its ideological counterpart as a key litmus test of political legitimacy. The Cold War battle over the domestic sphere found dramatic expression in the infamously ill-tempered "kitchen debate" between US vice president Richard Nixon and Soviet premier Khrushchev at the American National Exhibition in Moscow in 1959. Standing next to a model kitchen in a modest ranch-style home before the cameras and microphones of the world's press, Nixon took the opportunity to extol that "American superiority in the cold war rested not on weapons, but on the secure, abundant family life of modern suburban homes." The debate made clear that Atomic Age existence itself—home, hearth, and family—was at stake. It also highlighted the growing desire in both West and East to make the modern home the very emblem and yardstick of civilization.[24]

For Western European conservatives, the defense of the family was construed as a necessary deterrent against state socialism, to the extent that it provided a healthy division of state and society, public and private, work and leisure, along with segregated gender roles and activities. That women were the targets of domestic modernization was nothing new to this period. Much of this can be traced back to the late nineteenth century and interwar years, and found intensified expression across liberal, fascist, and communist regimes during the 1930s and 1940s. The post–World War II Western European idealization of the modern middle-class home complete with elegantly dressed (that is, nonworking) housewives and high-tech kitchens was a favorite self-image of the leisured West. But this is not to say that this postwar restoration of family life was without new features. Much was made in the Western European media—and advice literature, as we shall see—of the shifting understandings of fatherhood, one in which traditional images of the stern, formal, and patriarchal head of household gave way to more informal depictions of fathers at home in house slippers playing with the children and even helping with the housework. This was hailed as the civilization of men and fatherhood, with wartime images of martial masculinity increasingly being replaced by peacetime depictions of relaxed domesticity and familial intimacy.[25]

The home and the restored nuclear family served as Europe's romanticized sphere of postwar moral and aesthetic idealism. This was especially true in West Germany and Italy, as stable home life, traditional gender relations, and the private virtues of individual propriety and decency were hailed as the strong sinews of a post-fascist social order. Such initiatives are commonly associated with the ruling Christian Democratic conservative parties, but policies to shore up families enlisted wide support across the political spectrum from churches, women's organizations, Social Democrats, and socialists. For their part, Western European socialists labored to marry socialism and material civilization. In 1950 the Fabian Society of Great Britain devoted a lecture series to "Whither Socialism?," with several talks addressing the problem of civilization directly. In one, member of Parliament Richard S. Crossman, best known for his 1949 anticommunist edited volume *The God That Failed*, devoted his lecture to "Socialist Values in a Changing Civilisation." For him socialism could never be reduced to economic materialism and scientific socialism; in his estimation, "moral values"—including Labour's push for "fair values" such as the National Health Service—were "the real achievements of socialism in the last five years." "Our mission is to civilize the Cold War," Crossman continued, just as "the working class had in its long process of civilizing British Capitalism." For many Western European Social Democrats and socialists, the advanced welfare state was the very fulfillment of civilization itself.[26]

The ideological significance of the family was not confined to the West. Throughout the Eastern Bloc, a modernized home life was also broadcast as the proud realization of its socialist humanism. As in West Europe, the picture of the modern socialist family relaxing together amid the latest goods and consumer technology became a mass-produced symbol of security and prosperity in Soviet and Eastern Bloc lifestyle magazines. It was under Stalin that radical reforms of the family in the early days of the revolution had cooled off, as the 1930s were characterized by comparatively conservative notions of domesticity. By the mid-1950s, there were surprising similarities between West and East European domestic ideals in terms of the cultural representations of happiness and the good life. So much so that the 1950s image of East European home life—despite party rhetoric about the full equality of the sexes—betrayed its own myth of the "new woman in socialism" based to a large degree on old bourgeois assumptions of proper female behavior and duties.[27]

Such ideology bumped up against the demands of women, especially under socialism. Women in socialist societies were forced to juggle the competing demands of waged work, housework, and political involvement, and this so-called triple burden became a source of mounting frustration. The ever-present queues that marked socialist consumer society consisted largely of women, while women wrote most of the complaint letters to local authorities and often campaigned as working mothers to secure better social services from the state. The expanded scope of welfare policies into the home was largely introduced in the name of relieving overburdened mothers saddled with the lion's share of child-raising and housework. Domestic reform initiatives were spearheaded by various groups of women who successfully made the case to their governments that family residential problems deserved urgent state attention. Across the socialist world (and not unlike their counterparts in the West) women increasingly demanded labor-saving household appliances, cleaning supplies, better furniture, easily prepared foods, and more attractive clothing for themselves and their families. This meant that the domestic sphere—the perennial blind spot of traditional socialist theory and practice—came back with a vengeance in the 1960s and 1970s, as female activists agitated for more state welfare assistance at work, at home, and in the family. In the end, this reformist campaign served as the socialist world's answer to the 1968 feminist slogan in the West that "the personal is political."[28]

Sweden was often invoked as a model of progressive civilization that might satisfy householders' needs for comfort and accommodate design reformers' interests in affordable housing and social justice.

Sweden did not suffer much loss or damage during the war, and its social democratic domestic culture harked back to the prewar years. Not only did interwar Swedish Social Democrats use the idea of the *folkhem*, or "people's home," as a unifying national symbol, they also developed a particularly Swedish concept of modernity that linked domesticity to democratization and modern life. Modern Swedish homes furnished with modest, well-constructed wooden furniture, plain walls, and natural textiles were commonly invoked in ways that drew connections between modern citizenship and modern aesthetics, as noted in the 1955 Helsingborg Exhibition, an internationally successful housing show. The appeal of neutral Sweden was shared on the other side of the Iron Curtain in the wake of de-Stalinization, as Eastern Bloc architects, designers, and writers admired Swedish domesticity too. Sweden's domestic ideal served as the cultural embodiment of a Third Way alternative across the Cold War divide during the 1950s and 1960s. In the mid-1960s the translation and republication of the eminent Swedish sociologist Alva Myrdal's *Nation and Family*, first published in 1941, became a standard reference for European policy makers regarding the need to link welfare planning, family policy, and gender equality as the bedrock of social order and political stability. (The American translation was published in 1968 as a hoped-for antidote to the rash of race riots that erupted across the country in 1967). Such views underpinned the social and moral foundation of peacetime Europe.[29]

The fascination with the Scandinavian welfare state reflected substantive shifts in the Western European conception of the state after the war. As opposed to the development of modern European states until 1945, the new polities of Western Europe did not devote much of their budgets toward weapons or massive standing armies. The presence of young European men in military uniform was no longer a common feature of city life after 1945, as it had been since the eighteenth century. Those who were in uniform were often foreigners, be it Americans in Western Europe or Red Army soldiers in Eastern Europe, though conscripted citizens in army kit were still present across Europe at the time. The pacification of Europe by external armies was part of the re-civilization of the continent, and made it possible for European states to devote much more of their resources to peacetime civilian matters. For France, the Netherlands, Belgium, Britain, and later Portugal, decolonization—as we shall see—greatly accelerated this demilitarization of state budgets and international engagement. The post-1945 shift from warfare to welfare states reflected new circumstances, as well as the changing attitudes of citizens. An influential study by American social scientist Ronald Ingelhart on changing European values published in 1977 showed that postwar Western Europeans identified the state's chief political goals as promoting economic growth, education opportunities, affordable housing, and health care, less so national defense, political participation, or even civil rights. On the international level, this shift in mentality about the purpose of the state was a striking instance of the pacification of the old warring continent, and the primacy of social welfare and stable family life reflected these postwar trends.[30]

RELATIVE PEACE AND PROSPERITY ACROSS EUROPE PRODUCED new anxieties about the hidden dangers of civilization, and this often took the form of growing anti-Americanism, especially among European elites. Critiques of modern civilization had been a hallmark of European cultural commentary since the late nineteenth century, and were especially prevalent in the Weimar Republic in debates about "Amerikanismus" and mass culture. Such commentary is usually associated with the so-called Frankfurt School thinkers, but concerns about the threats of American-style technological modernity were common on the right too. Although there was great discussion about the threat from America, especially in terms of the new power's ability to loosen traditional class and social hierarchies, many Western European critics in the 1960s worried about the cultural consequences of American modernization. In March 1964 French political scientist Maurice Duverger informed his readers in *L'Express* that communism was no longer the real threat, instead "there is only one immediate danger for Europe, and that is American civilization." Soul-searching about the dark side of prosperity first arose as a cottage industry in the United States. The 1950s saw the publication of numerous books on alienation, unbridled materialism, the breakdown of community, and the machinations of Madison Avenue advertisers in corrupting American society, as noted by the popularity of commentators like Vance Packard, David Riesman, and John Kenneth Galbraith. Such criticism was perhaps most sharply addressed in the work of the German exile and eventual guru of the American New Left Herbert Marcuse, whose *Eros and Civilization* (1955) and *One-Dimensional Man* (1964) captured the growing apprehension that civilization itself had imposed repressive "Establishment values" on modern society and smothered the expression of true liberty. Betty Friedan's 1963 bestselling polemic, *The Feminine Mystique*, gave the purported pleasures of comfort a feminist twist, arguing that for women the much-touted suburban home was a "gilded cage" and "comfortable concentration camp." For these critics, the ruse of material civilization—and its advertising culture—was that while it held out the allure of liberation, its main effect was to transform the emancipatory power of freedom into the never-satisfied quest for creature comforts.[31]

Western European elites soon articulated their own homegrown version of the anxiety of affluence, not least because their continent seemed to them so defenseless before the onslaught of Americanization. The early postwar decades thus gave rise to a transatlantic clash of civilizations between the US and Western Europe. Whereas the 1940s version of the European crisis of civilization mostly pivoted on the need to restore the damaged prewar heritage of European culture and values as moral guidance, Western European jeremiads of the late 1950s and 1960s focused more on the dangers of the modernizing present. In Western Europe, American military and economic hegemony were essentially fait accompli by the late 1940s, with the result that the sphere of culture emerged as a favorite site to voice European misgivings and resistance. Ruminations about the negative side of industrial modernity were mostly confined to Western Europe, though concerns were voiced in the East as well. In large measure such common criticism was made possible by the republication of the young Karl Marx's classic *Grundrisse* in the mid-1960s, which explored the themes of alienation and subjectivity. What took place in both sides of Europe, as we shall see in Chapter 8, was a rediscovery of humanism and civilization as terms of engagement for a critique of a machine-centered world of work, life, and culture.[32]

In the 1950s and 1960s, plenty of Western European intellectuals and cultural critics took umbrage with ordinary citizens for pursuing the false idols of abundance and self-enrichment, subjecting them to schoolmarmish finger-wagging about what to desire and how to live. Austrian-born essayist Jean Améry began his 1964 *Preface to the Future* by lamenting that "Euro-American civilization, as seen at the end of the destiny-laden decade of 1950–1960, had only one point of reference—consumption. The rest is illusion." And in her 1966 book *Les Belles Images*, Simone de Beauvoir chided her fellow Frenchmen for "seeking an abundance which does not exist, and may have never existed," and said they should instead content themselves "with a vital minimum, as is still the case in certain very poor regions in Sardinia and Greece, for example, where technology has not penetrated and money has not corrupted." De Beauvoir then concluded that "only a moral revolution, not a social, political or technological one, can bring man back to his lost truth." In her view, some degree of poverty should be embraced as a means of protecting the masses from the moral hazards of prosperity and modernity. Here and elsewhere Western European elites—to say nothing of their Eastern European counterparts—commonly invoked the stereotyped image of American consumerism as a rhetorical foil against which to forge a more moral European lifestyle.[33]

But there were alternative voices. Indicative in this respect is the French thinker Jean-Jacques Sevran-Schreiber, whose 1967 book, *Le Défi Américain*, or *The American Challenge*, was France's biggest postwar bestseller. He trained as a pilot in the US and then joined the Free French Air Force. After the war Sevran-Schreiber founded *L'Express* news magazine and later was indicted for his hard-hitting exposé on Algeria, *Lieutenant in Algeria*, for allegedly undermining the morale of the French army. Servan-Schreiber's *American Challenge* was about the American economic invasion of France, but his views were no garden-variety anti-American pessimism. Rather, his was a call to action for Europeans—not just Frenchmen—to learn from American managerial ingenuity as well as its democratic culture, social system, and application of technical know-how. In his eyes, American business had already taken over Western Europe, and Europeans needed to adjust if they wished to maintain any independence at all. What is striking is that he couched his argument in terms of the defense of civilization as Europe's last refuge; he suggested that Western Europe, like Japan in the late nineteenth century, was at a crossroads in which state planners had to decide whether to fight in vain against American commercial might or find ways of tailoring American modern civilization to their own advantage. Here the defense of civilization was no misty nostalgia for days gone by, but rather a hardheaded prognosis for reconstituting a new and autonomous European civilization for a new era. If the moment was not grasped, he concluded, then Europe, "like so many other glorious civilizations, will gradually sink into decadence without ever understanding why or how it happened."[34]

Others were less sanguine. Some of the more interesting thinkers saw America's post-1945 legacy as one that combined atomic power with consumer society. Influential in this regard was the Austrian philosopher Günther Anders, whose book *Die Antiquiertheit des*

Menschen, or *The Antiquated Nature of Humanity*, caused a great stir when published in 1956. Anders had been a longtime critic of technology, and his book was composed of short essays and diary entries, many of which originated from his exile in the US in the 1940s. For Anders, one of the most dangerous developments of the Atomic Age was the growing gap between humanity's technical ability to create and destroy and its underdeveloped capacity to imagine, interpret, and avert that destruction. Hiroshima figured as the prime example of this phenomenon, and Anders became one of the intellectual leaders of the West German peace movement. But it was the thingliness of modern society that really agitated him. In one provocative section, Anders framed the changing relationship between people and things with reference to the "shame of Prometheus" for having produced such "'humiliating' (*'beschämend'*) high quality manufactured goods." For Anders, Prometheus's shame derived from the fact that humans, by contrast to these objects, "were born and not manufactured." What Anders abhorred was an object-driven world in which people have less and less of a place, let alone the means to control it, yet are psychologically numbed to the horror because of the beauty and comfort that these goods bring. The great tragedy of modern civilization, he concluded, was that it was killing off the capacity of reason to avert—let alone interpret—global disaster. In some ways, Anders's jeremiad echoed German Expressionist critiques of urban life from the late nineteenth century, but such anxieties took on meaning in an age of atomic warfare, rapid scientific advancement, and unbridled consumerism.[35]

Perhaps the most trenchant thinker about the prospect of civilization was Hannah Arendt. Arendt, of course, was one of the most celebrated political thinkers of the twentieth century, and is often associated with her controversial views put forward in her journalistic work for the *New Yorker* magazine, *Eichmann in Jerusalem*. Yet she also developed far-reaching and often unusual ideas of civilization in the 1950s. First of all, she analyzed contemporary states (especially the United States) in relation to the Roman Empire. In a number of essays, Arendt approvingly identified the hallmark value of ancient Roman civilization as being a law-based republic that enabled it to integrate foreigners and the conquered into its imperial body politic, thus preserving the distinctiveness of their own cultural identities in a "civitas." For her, this was the moral foundation of the American and French Revolutions, making possible the development of liberal civilization based on old Roman republican virtues that still needed to be defended. Secondly, in her 1958 book, *The Human Condition*, she made clear that the division of public and private was the very foundation of the liberal polity and the construction of a peaceful social order. Of grave concern to her, however, was how mass society was undermining both the public and private spheres. For her, mass society "deprives men not only of their place in the world but of their private home, where they once felt sheltered against the world" and where "even those excluded from the world could find a substitute in the warmth of the hearth and the limited reality of family life." Mass society not only had the capacity to upend the liberal political order, but also its material and moral foundations. She developed this idea later in the book, as the relationship between people and things—including the desire for durability—assumed heightened importance. As she put it, "it is this durability which gives the things of the world their relative independence from men who produced and use them." "From this viewpoint," she went on, "the things of the world have the function of stabilizing human life, and their object-ness" rested in the fact that "men, their ever-changing nature notwithstanding, can retrieve their sameness, that is, their identity, by being related to the same chair and the same table."[36]

What is striking about Arendt's passage is its inherent half-truth in regard to the postwar generation. For if anything, the war exposed the utter fragility and dispensability of people, places, and things—even humanity itself, as she wrote elsewhere—in the face of total war and mass destruction. Durability, identity, and existence itself were no longer givens, but had to be reconstructed and defended like everything else. It was this background of moral and material catastrophe that separated postwar European domestic life from its American counterpart, and made the longing for shelter and security all the more intense and distinctive there, transcending as it did regions, classes, and Cold War divisions. This is the common thread uniting these diverse thinkers on the fate of civilization, who all in their own way called attention to the broader connections among home, everyday life, and political community in Reconstruction Europe.

In the end, however, such Western European anti-Americanism and critiques of industrial civilization did not find much popular traction, as most citizens welcomed American-style modernity and its creature comforts with open arms. In the 1950s Aragon's derisive "civilization of bathtubs and Frigidaires" was broadly conceived by ordinary people as inherently anti-elitist in its promise of material improvement for everyone; postwar states enjoyed electoral support precisely in relation to their ability to make good—or not—on ambitious welfare policies. The result was that civilization started to shed its eighteenth- and nineteenth-century legacies: the coming of material civilization was not associated with domination or exclusion, but rather with democratization and the overcoming of old elite barriers, as witnessed with the rapid postwar expansion of mass education, health, and housing. Delivering on the promise of material well-being emerged as a chief source of policy competition among national political parties, as well as between East and West. It marked out the material identity of the West, in which the "porcelain whiteness of its new material civilization," as historian Victoria de Grazia has argued, was "viewed against the darkness of Third World poverty and the dinginess of state socialism." The socialist world had its own version of this bright new consumer culture, and competed on the same terrain. Unlike in the sphere of military buildup and confrontation, no one was directly threatened in this battle over kitchens and cars; in principle all benefited, rendering civilization a newly inclusive discourse for all classes. At issue then was not the shame of Prometheus, but rather its opposite. Prometheus the mythic maker emerged as the great civilizer of the continent, the symbolic patron of postwar Europe across the Cold War frontier.[37]

POSTWAR VISIONS OF MODERN CIVILIZATION WERE NOT LIMited to the remaking of national states and domestic spaces, but also included the makeover of self and society. These changes were perhaps best illustrated with the explosion of manners manuals after 1945 across the continent. Given the harrowing conditions under which Europeans had to meet basic questions of food and shelter during the "hunger years," advice books may seem a far cry from the pressing demands of the day. Historically they have been creatures of peace and prosperity, speaking more to the powdered anxieties of the drawing room than to the horrors and homelessness of bombed-out cities and makeshift shelters. And yet the immediate postwar period saw a remarkable flourishing of etiquette books spanning Europe and North America, beginning in the late 1940s and reaching its apogee in the late 1950s. Advice literature even attracted prominent historians, such as Arthur Schlesinger Jr. and Harold Nicolson, who wrote serious histories of decorum following what they saw as the "crisis of Western civilization" in the hope that the "necessity of manners" would counteract militarism and even improve international relations. It was in the age of reeducation in the late 1940s and 1950s that etiquette books assumed their place in the broader re-civilizing process of turning belligerent Europeans into peaceful citizens.[38]

At first the renaissance of manners manuals after the war may not seem so surprising. The publishing history of such books has shown that they tend to enjoy booms following wars and revolutions, periods when the fabric of everyday life has been radically altered. Often they were written as an attempt to restore order to a world turned upside down. This is not to say that they were necessarily conservative or backward-looking. The outpouring of communist advice books in the new Soviet Union during the 1920s, which focused on how to live in a revolutionary society (to say nothing of their Viennese or German *proletkult* equivalents), is an obvious example. The peak periods of European etiquette book production were the 1820s, the 1920s, and the 1950s. In Germany alone over 800 etiquette books were published between 1870 and 1970, approximately 150 of which were printed in West Germany between 1948 and 1965. From the late 1950s and 1960s the Soviet Union published 50 to 100 new titles a year.[39]

What made Europe's post-1945 production of advice books so unique was its political situation. The physical destruction and loss of life meant that the traditional means of transmitting class taste, family artifacts, and social standing were severely disrupted by the war, rendering the surviving young generation—as the guidebooks often noted—cut off and unschooled, without adequate moral guidance and cultural compass. The authors of these guidebooks sought to address these concerns that a postwar generation was unsure how to live and behave after the war.

Etiquette books were written in this new spirit, and as such served as a kind of self-generating civilizing industry in post-1945 Europe across the Iron Curtain. At issue was not simply relearning table manners. Fundamental to the advice books was reeducating the self, retraining the body and mind to live in a new postwar world, and reschooling militarized societies in the values of peace, dignity, and personal honor. That Germany served as the Cold War's first ideological battleground between East and West also lent these guidebooks a certain utopian edge in willing a brave new German world of post-fascist civic culture, whether liberal or communist. The divided country's superpower patrons were quite supportive of this reform zeal, as the cultural campaign to remodel civilian life was part of the broader crusade to reeducate a hyper-militarized former enemy into the ways of law, order, and propriety. German etiquette books serve as the focus of this section, but the main themes were widely shared across the continent.

Let's start with the West German guides. In them one could find a combination of old and new. Common to all were tips about how one should introduce someone correctly, greet strangers, behave in a theater and in public transportation encounters, and how to dress and use proper speech in every situation. Many of these guidelines were aimed at young women, and concerned tips on dress, flirting, courting, choosing partners, and preparing to run a household. Others were directed at young men as special targets of the need to civilize former warriors and boys who were unparented during the war. Attention centered on hygiene, clean haircuts, smart clothes, and polished shoes. The modern elements—how to act in the cinema, how to answer the phone—were for the most part extensions of older eighteenth-century cultural codes. There were also elements that betrayed a world recovering from catastrophe, as evidenced in the pages dedicated to how to react to family death announcements, behaving tactfully at funerals, and how to address a widow. The main thrust was still toward bringing social interaction up-to-date with the modern world, but in a way that Germans could express themselves without simply imitating foreigners. While offering praise of the English gentleman as the exemplar, one West German guidebook insisted that "Germans should not slavishly ape foreign customs and mores. Nonetheless, the notion of the Gentleman is something that has spread over the whole world and thus is equally valid for us." It went on to discuss proper modes of address, how and on what occasions to wear hats, when to use *Sie* or *Du*, how to dress sensibly and eat properly, as well as how to write a fetching letter as befitting a polite and modern German citizen. Equally striking was the complete absence of the US in these sources. While fascination with the American way of life was palpable elsewhere in West German culture, it did not find its way into these etiquette books at all.[40]

What made this West German language new was its strong emphasis on individual dignity and respect. As one 1949 West German guidebook called *Proper Behavior at Work and in Private: A Useful Guide for Young People* put it, the task of such books is to "ascertain the moral substance beneath the outward appearance of behavior, helping young people to understand that the norms governing social interaction are a key part of the social and cultural battle for humanity itself." In this case, this "social and cultural battle" was painted as the key drama of the century, to the extent that the struggle for personal civility was much bigger than simply one's private decorum: "It cannot be reduced to a matter of private interest, since it touches on vital economic, national and social concerns in addressing the decisive cultural issue of the century—that is, the honor and dignity of the individual, as well as his liberty and relation to the whole [of humanity]." One could detect echoes of the UN Charter and West Germany's new provisional constitution (the so-called Basic Law) in this passage, as the dignity and honor of the individual was put center stage as an emblem of progress and civilization.[41]

The effort to break from the Nazi past could also be seen in the postwar preoccupation with social distance and a clear demarcation of public and private. In them the emphasis was on polished comportment and relaxed yet reserved expressions of interaction, ones in which emotions were to be kept under strict control. The strong emphasis on retaining the formal address (*Sie*) instead of the informal (*Du*) in these books was intended to restore and preserve propriety as the basis of postwar social interaction. The defense of class culture in the face of political upheaval was present in German conservative guidebooks of the 1920s, but what distinguished their post-1945 successors was a strong disinclination toward any sense of *Volkskultur* or the dissolution of the individual into any larger collective, be it nation, class, or race. The affirmation of cultivated individuality was a common trait of West European culture after the war, as social distance itself was depicted as the precondition for the proper functioning of liberal society.[42]

These guidebooks did not encourage readers to shun public life and retreat into private havens of coffee and cake. Many of them were noticeably concerned with reeducating German youth for life at the office. Tips on work life were also directed at women, and this is one of the distinctive features of post-1945 etiquette books across Europe. Advice was given to young West German and Dutch professional women about how to reconcile career, office life, and femininity. But in those books targeted at young men, women hardly figure at all in discussions about good behavior at the office, as seen for example in G. von Hilgendorff's 1953 *Good Behavior, Your Success*. And if women at work are mentioned, this is where much of the most sexist language surfaced. W. A. Nennstiel's 1949 *Proper Behavior at Work and in Private* likened women in the office to "warm gulf streams" that helped heat human relations. While such language tended to disappear by the early 1960s, good behavior at work was related to proper comportment at home or in town. What made these tips about proper office behavior so striking was their relationship to the military past. Nennstiel described the barracks as the counterfoil to civilized life: "Military discipline plays no role in the social world that one encounters at work or in one's private life." The need to eradicate rude military habits became even more direct in other sections: "While receiving instructions or assignments, one needs to avoid military behavior, be it standing upright with hands pressed against your sides, straightened knees, clicked heels and 'Yes sir, Commander!'; instead it is better to be civil, even 'bourgeois.'"[43]

Other elements distinguished these postwar advice books. In the United States, religious tolerance found its way into the world of American etiquette books as a new social virtue. Amy Vanderbilt's

1952 *Complete Guide to Etiquette* included a section on "Interfaith Courtesy and Understanding," and aimed to explain Jewish and Catholic rituals and holidays to Protestant America. Such views reflected the Eisenhower-era ideal of "tri-faith America" as the backbone of Judeo-Christian civilization. By contrast, a new trait of Western European advice literature was the immigrant experience. The most celebrated instance from an immigrant perspective is the work of Hungarian-born British journalist and humorist George Mikes, who moved to Britain in 1940. His 1946 book *How to Be an Alien: A Handbook for Beginners and More Advanced Pupils* became an instant bestseller in Britain on the strength of its wit and gentle send-up of the difficulties associated with mastering the quirkiness of British culture as a foreigner. Featured are tips on how to queue, drink tea, talk about the weather, and try to understand the differences between British and continental intimacy: "Continental people have sex lives; the English have hot-water bottles." Mikes went on to write some forty travel books on a variety of humorous and serious topics, ranging from *How to Be Inimitable: Coming of Age in England* (1960) to a 1957 BBC television program titled *The Hungarian Revolution*. His work was exploited as Cold War propaganda: Radio Romania seized on his *How to Be an Alien* as an "anti-British tract," serializing segments on the alleged hypocrisies of capitalist cultural life. In any case, Mikes's travel books and light satires of various countries traded on a common midcentury experience of European immigration, parochial nationalism, and the desire for cultural assimilation.[44]

The arrival of non-European immigrants to European metropoles became another instance of the civilizing mission, especially toward women. For example, from the early 1950s French social workers associated with the organizations Aid to Overseas Workers and the North African Family Social Service targeted Algerian women living in Paris, Metz, Lille, and Marseilles for home economics courses on French civilization, which included lessons on sewing and how to knit, wash, keep a tidy home, cook nutritious food, do household shopping, speak proper French, and transmit French values to the entire family. And for the 180,000 mixed-race Indisch Dutch people who arrived in the Netherlands from the Dutch East Indies after independence, the Dutch government developed a "resocialization and assimilation" program to help new arrivals adjust to living in Holland, which even included lessons on how to behave on the boats coming over. These new immigrants were then given courses on good housekeeping, bookkeeping, and the avoidance of indebtedness as part of their successful assimilation. Whereas these colonial education practices of uplift and control were standard fare since the late nineteenth century, they were now being reintroduced in the metropole for newcomers from former colonies in the name of nation-building and cultural integration.[45]

Communist regimes provided their own versions of these etiquette books, and took them even more seriously than the West. Just as socialism was in part aimed at civilizing capitalism, so too did state socialism take measures to civilize communism. Morality itself was deemed crucial in assuring that socialist society would stay true to its lofty goals and steel itself from turning into its ideological enemy. The emphasis on "the satisfaction of material and cultural needs" first articulated in Stalin's 1936 Constitution was later included verbatim in the civil codes of all socialist republics after 1945, and was intended to check the demons of surplus value and irrational consumerism. There was no shortage of utterances from the Kremlin that "the idea of overproduction as an unlimited bounty of personal property was alien to communism," or that communism stood in opposition to the "morality of bourgeois society, which raises the concept of 'mine' as its highest principle." The Soviet Union's 1961 Moral Code of the Builder of Communism affirmed the collectivist virtues of socialism, including "love for the Socialist Motherland," "elevated consciousness of social duty," "honesty and fairness, moral purity, simplicity and modesty in one's social and personal life." The moral code was posted at schools, and students were often required to memorize it. Socialist manners manuals were produced in the dozens per year. A. Dorokhov's *It Does Matter* (1961) and the anonymous *Aesthetics of Behavior* (1963) went through print runs in the hundreds of thousands in the Soviet Union. Their content shifted from handy hints of make-do-and-mend to exploring new possibilities of citizen behavior and comportment, in which the central concerns of 1920s manners books—hygiene and self-education—were slowly replaced by exhortations of proper table manners, elegant dress, and refined speech. A recycled *kul'turnost'* ethic from the 1930s maintained that the supposedly private qualities of tact and discretion would be observed at home and at work. Even so, this was delicate business. I. S. Runova's *We Must Struggle with Petty-Bourgeois Vulgarity* (1962) sought to curb the danger of petty bourgeois values by discouraging the acquisition of "lumpy great beds with a super-abundance of nickel-plated knobs, plush tablecloths, oversized sideboards and the like."[46]

Likewise, first secretary of East Germany's ruling Socialist Unity Party Walter Ulbricht propagated his prescriptive Ten Commandments of Socialist Morality in 1958, with emphasis on performance, loyalty, cleanliness, and decency. These commandments were widely published in the media, and mass-produced in card form to be carried around in wallets or displayed on the mantelpiece at home. Functionaries and schoolteachers were to promote the virtues of pursuing a career, founding a family, and working diligently for the good of the country. In his keynote speech at the Eleventh Plenum in 1965, Secretary of Education—and later general secretary of the Socialist Unity Party—Erich Honecker proclaimed that "our GDR is a clean state, in which there are unshakable standards of ethics and morality, of propriety and decorum." These views dovetailed with the incessant discussion of creating new "socialist personalities" for socialist state and society. As in Stalin's Soviet Union, the new virtues of socialist behavior implied a transformation of public values, effecting the transition from militant revolutionary asceticism to controlled individual consumption based on upstanding private life and civilized conduct.[47]

Although fewer guides were published in the East, they enjoyed robust circulation and full state backing. Karl Smolka's 1957 *Gutes Benehmen von A bis Z*, or *Good Behavior from A to Z*, went through ten reprintings by 1974, whereas W. K. Schweickert and Bert Hold's 1959 *Guten Tag, Herr von Knigge! Ein heiteres Lesebuch für alle Jahrgänge über alles, was 'anständig' ist* (*Good Morning, Herr Knigge! A Humorous Book for Everyone About What Is Proper*) was already in its twentieth reprint by 1969. Unlike in the West German guides, the war hardly figured at all in the East German counterparts. The tone was much more about the break with the capitalist past and the fascination with the socialist future. Nor was there any explicit reference to their Soviet partners as model citizens. Soviet influence in the cultural makeover of East German everyday life was certainly present, but tended to be confined to the sphere of political reeducation and pedagogy, especially child-raising. The world of décor and table manners, by contrast, was untouched by Soviet influence, mirroring the absence of American references in West German guides.[48]

There was no shortage of discussion on how everyday manners perfectly reflected the differences between East and West. East German manners manuals routinely condemned their West German opposites as brazen egotism dressed up as personal cultivation, whose main message was all about gaining a competitive edge and using manners for personal career advancement. The opening sentence of Hans Martin's 1949 West German guide, *Darf ich mir erlauben . . . ? Das Buch der Guten Lebensart*, or *May I Allow Myself . . . ? The Guide to a Good Style of Life*—"Good behavior is a key milestone on the road to success"—attracted particular ire. Karl Smolka's bestselling 1957 guide, *Good Behavior from A to Z*, attacked what he saw as the elitism and cloaked brutality of capitalist behavior celebrated in these West German books: "They are vital means for the 'better society' to distinguish themselves from the masses by demonstrating their legitimacy as the dominant class and social order." At stake, however, was more than simply trying to recast interpersonal relations in a new egalitarian manner. Smolka heralded the new dawn of socialist civility thus: "The vast majority of the population has been excluded from the rules of good form and the opportunity to apply them, just as they have been excluded from justice and education. For the first time in German history, in the Workers' and Peasants' State, our GDR, the working population is setting the tone. It is now in a position to acquire those things that were withheld for so long: education, knowledge—including knowledge of the rules of good form, which help to determine how people live together."[49]

Despite all the rhetoric about socialist difference, GDR guides betrayed a discernibly similar tone and message to their Western rivals. Like their West German counterparts, they were concerned with detailed instructions on how to sit, walk, court, and shake hands, when to take off your hat, how to set the table and dine properly, and which gifts should be brought to dinner parties, as noted in Figure 22. But there were some key differences: The world of work received much less coverage in GDR guides, while a good amount of space was devoted to the theme of how to get along with civil servants and bureaucrats. Not least, the whole topic of death (how to behave at funerals, console the bereaved, design a death announcement) went unmentioned. Nowhere were these petty bourgeois sensibilities more on display than in their attitudes toward women and girls. The promotion of socialist family values—much of which assumed that the wife/mother would bear the responsibility for housework and child-raising—flew in the face of vaunted socialist ideology about the full equality of the sexes. Guidebooks largely concentrated on the world after work, and it was here that they championed a host of traditional ideals, not unlike their West German equivalents. A passage from Kleinschmidt's *Don't Be Scared of Good Manners* was typical: "A lady who asks a gentleman to dance is as ridiculous today

Figure 22. Tips on proper handshakes and public greetings, East Germany, 1957. *Credit: Karl Smolka,* Gutes Benehmen von A bis Z *(Berlin: Verlag Neues Leben, 1957)*

as she was a thousand years ago." It was precisely at home and on the town where women and girls were to cultivate their femininity with grace and charm.[50]

Like in West Germany, the intended audience for these books was often young men. Karl Smolka's widely circulated 1964 *Junger Mann von heute*, or *Young Man of Today*, is a good example of this socialist approach. In particular, Smolka's book aimed to educate the socialist young man as an upstanding member of the community, taking pains to provide detailed advice on the importance of working well, serving in the military with honor, being a good friend, choosing a compatible partner, and enjoying sports. Where these books departed from West German equivalents was not only in a softer form of masculinity, replete with tips on sewing and attractive hairstyling. They were also distinguished by a more comprehensive approach to the young man's life. West German guides tended to limit their advice for young men to work, dress, and decorum for public life—the private home was more or less left untouched. Sexual intimacy was rarely discussed in West German manners guides until the late 1960s. In East German books, sexual education was a common topic, and enjoyed relatively extensive coverage from the early 1960s on. To the extent that Smolka's book was about socializing the young man into the ways of adulthood, ranging from love to ironing, its thrust was toward de-privatizing personal life in the name of socialism. In the socialist advice literature, social distance was not seen as a precondition to healthy political development. Manners, morals, and Marxism were all united, as one guidebook neatly expressed: "Man in socialist society" "will not dissemble, or bow or scrape, or swindle, neither will he eat fish off a knife, or drink champagne out of red wine glasses, any more than he will rob or exploit others."[51]

To dismiss Eastern European advice books as simply conservative and petty bourgeois misses the point, however, for there was a very modern sensibility at work in them—namely, the notion of social engineering. The advice book industry was firmly in keeping with this broader crusade to remake European society from top to bottom. This may explain too why socialist manners manuals in particular took on a more strident tone in the late 1950s and early 1960s. By that time, there was a growing sense that despite the eradication of capitalism and traditional political structures, socialist citizens in Eastern Europe had not been sufficiently transformed in terms of everyday life. This was no small admission, since it implied that Marx's classic formulation that the transformation of the base would necessitate a transformation of the superstructure (values, culture) had not come to pass as predicted. The survival of unwanted petty bourgeois attitudes supposedly seen in everything from rising youth crime to domestic violence all pointed up that socialist civilization was not automatically emerging, and justified more robust state intervention into everyday life. For this reason, the cottage industry of texts promoted the East German mission to build a new socialist society on new concepts of selfhood and civility.

The mass production of advice books across Cold War Europe reflected a shared compulsion toward developing codes of conduct and sets of rules for everyday citizens. It was one in which the gestures and small coin of everyday life—eating, drinking, dressing, and conversing—were fundamental elements of the common crusade to correct the crooked timber of humanity. This dimension of post-1945 life was in many ways a throwback to the nineteenth century, which witnessed a great flowering of etiquette books across the Western world, with Victorian England setting the tone. The idea that manners could hold a society together enjoys a venerable tradition. In his observations of early nineteenth-century America, Alexis de Tocqueville repeatedly noted the cohesive power of manners in the new republic, creating as they did patterns of belonging, thinking, and ways of behaving. For Europeans after 1945, this was certainly part of the drive to return to a world ruled by law and decency in the aftermath of war and destruction. The keen interest in publishing so many etiquette books after the war was an attempt to reassert the very thing that the Nazis had crushed beneath their jackboots and tanks—civil society.[52]

With political and economic stabilization the rude struggle for survival was slowly ending. The violence and chaos that had disfigured European everyday life since 1914, with brief exceptions, was giving way to an established social order in both halves of the continent. The 1950s mildness of manners was the fruit of political security and the pacification of everyday life. No less significantly, everyday interaction was a sphere in which Europeans could carry out their reeducation themselves, relatively removed from the direct influence of their respective superpower patron.

In the first two decades after World War II, the fields of science, humanitarian law, housing, and civility assumed their designated place in re-civilizing the continent by helping convert European warfare states into welfare states. What united them all was the common belief that civilization was synonymous with peace and progress. Other social groups, as we shall see in the next chapter, saw things differently, and interpreted civilization as intimately linked to European power and the reconquest of territory overseas.

five

EMPIRE RECLAIMED

O N MAY 8, 1945, THE DAY MOST OF THE WORLD CELE-brated the final defeat of Hitler, the French government wished to toast the Allied victory in newly reconquered Algeria. There, the festivities of this first V-E Day were designed to commemorate both France's liberation from Hitler's grip and its reassertion of imperial control in its former colonies. Things did not go according to plan. The Algerian town of Sétif became the site of violent confrontation between French troops and Algerian separatists. Sétif was a center of Muslim agitation and Algerian nationalism, and the townspeople were less than keen to see the return of their longtime colonial oppressors, who had occupied their country since 1830. Nationalists wanted to fly the Algerian flag together with those of the Allied powers, and to lay a wreath at the city's war memorial alongside those of the other political parties. Banners of local activists were emblazoned with the slogans "We want the same rights as you!" "Down with Colonialism," and "Long Live Algerian Independence." Police were instructed to seize the placards and to set up barricades to block the demonstration. Crowds gathered, and shots were fired amid the melee. For the next five days groups of separatists roamed the countryside with clubs and knives, militants were arrested, and martial law imposed. Agitation soon spread to the nearby towns of Guelma and Constantinois, and took the form of peasant insurrections. The French government's brutal suppression of the Algerian uprising lasted several days, ending with some 6,000 to 8,000 Algerian casualties and the death of 102 settlers. The event created a new generation of nationalists in Algeria. Writer Kateb Yacine, who witnessed the violence firsthand as a sixteen-year-old young man, wrote about the "shock which I felt at the pitiless butchery that caused the deaths of thousands of Muslims. I have not forgotten. From that moment my nationalism took definite form."[1]

So while France was meting out rough justice toward collaborators back home in the wake of V-E Day, French troops were imposing violent order in the colonies at the same time. Such jarring coincidences of anti-imperialism at home (against Nazi occupation) and imperialism abroad were not uncommon after the war. Yet it is the dramatic combination of national liberation on the continent and recolonization overseas in 1945 that makes this moment so significant. The end of one empire in Europe—Hitler's Third Reich—was accompanied by the recouping of older ones by France, the Netherlands, and Belgium.

This chapter puts the restoration of European empires at the center of midcentury European history and draws attention to the violent side of Europe's new civilizing mission. It focuses on the legacy of fascism, the Greek Civil War, the dream of Eurafrica, and the reception of reclaimed empire at the United Nations in the 1950s and 1960s as staging posts of the remaking of Western Europe. Ideas of civilization undergirded newly emerging geopolitical relations between Western Europe and the United States, as well as those between the Western European imperial powers and their colonies. The year 1945 is often seen as the beginning of the end of the European Era, marking the historical decline of Europe's half-millennium dominance on the world stage. The twin events of May 8, 1945, in Europe and North Africa show that the end of the war in no way spelled the end of empire. In fact, all the wars around the world after 1945 were either colonial or anticolonial wars, and the reclaiming of empire created conditions of further violence. Viewed globally, the second half of the twentieth century was no less bloody than the first—between 1945 and 1983 it is estimated that some 19–20 million people were killed in around 100 serious military conflicts waged around the world. But mid-twentieth-century European wars of reconquest—with several notable exceptions, such as the Algerian and Vietnam Wars—have been largely forgotten.[2]

The denial of European empire is in part connected to the self-congratulatory tale of the European Union. The still-reigning mythology is that after World War II the Western European imperial powers abandoned their colonies and overseas interests, turning toward one another rather than abroad in the name of peace and prosperity. The affirmative story of West European integration culminating with the 1957 Treaty of Rome, which gave birth to the European Economic Community, is usually depicted as one of renewed self-possession, wherein Western Europeans nobly shed their violent imperialist ways of old. Walter Lipgens, one of the first and most influential historians of European integration, famously portrayed Western European solidarity as a reaction to the "racial arrogance of Nazism" and totalitarianism, against which "people came to their senses and returned to the true European tradition" of comity and cooperation. Necessity was turned into a virtue, as decolonization was interpreted as the moral reassertion of European civilization.[3]

When the European Union was awarded the Nobel Peace Prize in 2012, Europe's imperial history after 1945 went unmentioned. José Manuel Durão Barroso, president of the European Commission, and Herman Van Rompuy, president of the European Council, called their Nobel Prize lecture "From War to Peace: A European Tale." They used the occasion to sing the praises of the EU as a force for good and world peace, one in which the EU was a "new legal order, which is not based on balance of power between nations but on the free consent of states," "the quest for a cosmopolitan order, in which one person's gain does not need to be another person's pain." They ended their speech by saying that precisely because the EU is "a community of nations that has overcome war and fought totalitarianism, we will always stand by those who are in pursuit of peace and human dignity" and will "help the world come together." And yet, four of the original six members of the European Economic Community that signed the Treaty of Rome—France, Belgium, the Netherlands, and Italy—were still imperial powers at the time, and in 1957 these countries insisted on having their overseas territories associated with the new union, which included French Algeria, the Belgian Congo and Rwanda, Dutch New Guinea, and Italian Somalia. This is hardly ancient history: today's map of the European Union still features France's Guadeloupe, Réunion, and Martinique; Portugal's Azores and Madeira; and Spain's Canary Islands—all officially dubbed the "outermost regions of the EU." At the time of the signing of the 1957 treaty—and ever since—these territories were rarely discussed as colonies or protectorates. And yet the place and significance of empire was crucial to the redefinition of Western Europe in the first decade and a half after the end of World War II.[4]

THE SUCCESSFUL REFASHIONING OF EUROPE AS A PEACE-LOVING continent was predicated on another dimension of postwar reconstruction—burying the specter of fascism. Even though fascism had been defeated and discredited in 1945, the work of laying to rest its toxic legacy went far beyond meting out rough justice toward fascist authorities and collaborators in the immediate aftermath of the war. Closely connected with this international campaign to destroy fascism was the European conversion of the history of resistance from allegedly treasonous wartime activity to the moral foundation of post-fascist Europe. The Nazi occupation of Europe served as the testing ground for a new European civilization built on antifascist ideals. Even those fascists still around in the 1950s dramatically changed their tune. They denounced war and devoted their conferences and journals to espousing a more pacific image of postwar Europe based on firm immigration quotas, all but abandoning interwar fascism's central plank of the racially motivated, avenging-warrior nation-state. Postwar fascists were generally less nationalist in orientation, and even became new Europeans of a sort. The in-house journal (founded in 1953) for former member of Parliament and neo-fascist Oswald Mosley's British Union Movement was tellingly titled *The European*.

More importantly, fascism's bundled values of war, imperial expansion, and civilization did not survive the cease-fire. This is in marked contrast to how the Central Powers reacted to wartime loss after 1918. From the beginning, Italian and German fascism were intent on winning back territories lost during the Great War (in Germany's case), or during the peace negotiations afterward (in Italy's case). Such resentment was not limited just to nascent fascists. The German public reacted angrily to the stripping of their colonies in Africa; in March 1919 the "undefeated" general Paul von Lettow-Vorbeck led a repatriated assembly of East African *Schutztruppen* in colonial uniform before cheering crowds through the streets of Berlin. The Weimar colonial movement took issue with Allied charges of German "uncivilized" misrule in the colonies of German South West Africa, linking the "lie" of colonial guilt with the outrage of the infamous war guilt clause of the Versailles Treaty. The 1920s saw the flowering of exhibitions, photographs, and media coverage devoted to highlighting the "illegal" deprivation of German colonial property and the illegitimacy of President Woodrow Wilson's Versailles *Diktat*. The Nazis traded on this popular outrage when they came to power, and feted these ill-treated "colonial heroes" in photography shows, public statuary, documentary films, and school observations of the fiftieth anniversary of the founding of German South West Africa.[5]

The defense of civilization was a favorite rhetorical tool of Italian fascists. In his first speech in Trieste on September 20, 1920, Mussolini connected fascism to ancient Rome, claiming that fascism was the heir to Rome's "universal civilization." Il Duce elaborated on this view in his second speech in Trieste on February 6, 1921, saying that "it is fate that Rome shall return to be the vector of civilization in all Western Europe. Let's raise the flag of the empire, of our imperialism, which should not be confused with the Prussian or English kind." Mussolini frequently spoke of the birth of a young fascist civilization that was replacing a dying liberal order. Writing in his newspaper *Il Popolo d'Italia* in August 1933, he boasted, "We have entered fully into a period which can be called the transition from one type of civilization to another," and that there "is nothing more auspicious and fascinating than the glow on the horizon of a new civilization." Fascist Italy even devoted great energy to condemning the "uncivilized" persistence of slavery still being practiced in Africa, in part as a means of diverting attention away from Mussolini's brutal domestic politics and to shore up the country's international reputation as a caring Catholic nation. Italy's invasion of Abyssinia in 1935 was justified to the international community as a humanitarian emergency intervention to halt the slave trade there, as slavery became the key metaphor of Ethiopia's supposed barbaric state and failed government. With it the classic nineteenth-century fusion of imperialism and humanitarianism was revived in the 1930s from a radical right-wing perspective.[6]

Mussolini topped up the civilization rhetoric after Italian troops defeated the Ethiopians in the Abyssinian War. In his speech on the fall of Addis Ababa on May 5, 1936, he crowed that "Ethiopia is Italian. Italian de facto, because it is occupied by our victorious armies, Italian de jure, because with the gladio of Rome, civilisation triumphs over barbarism." Such language was not just associated with the African campaign. During Italy's long-forgotten wartime conquest of Europe—when Italian troops occupied Corsica, parts of the French Alps, Slovenia, Montenegro, Croatia, Albania, Macedonia, and Greece—Mussolini bragged about Italy's new "aristocracy of civilization" and warrior elites who had brought revived glory to Rome after centuries of defeat and humiliation. What was called Italy's new "civilizing mission" was based on Fascist Italy's own racist version of "living space," or *spazio vitale*, in which the Italian "new man" would control the occupied territories—in the words of fascist ideologue Domenico Soprano—as "the custodian and bearer of a superior civilization." Even if these imperial dreams amounted to little in the end, they reflected fascist understandings of the union between civilization and war. Mussolini's last speech—given at the Teatro Lirico in Milan on December 16, 1944—pleaded for the defense against the "monstrous alliance between plutocracy and bolshevism," whose "barbaric war" is destroying "what European civilisation built in twenty centuries."[7]

Yet such rhetoric was not simply fascist bluster—it enjoyed popular Italian support. This was particularly the case with Il Duce's invasion of Ethiopia. Letters of congratulation poured in to local Italian authorities, extolling the chance to avenge past humiliations and to bring the grandeur of Italian Catholic civilization to a barbarous people. Italy's ignominious defeat there in 1896 was the first time that an African army defeated a modern European power. The Church provided support too, with cardinals, archbishops, and bishops offering public endorsements of the 1935 invasion in the press. One young telegraph operator from Montepulciano wrote in his diary about his "pride" after arriving in Ethiopia in late 1935 as one of the first "to bring the breath of civilization to this uncivilized land." Many others expressed similar views about serving fatherland and fascism. For one female twenty-year-old physics student from Padua who heard the news of Italian forces entering Addis Abada, the invasion signaled the rightful imposition "of the 'Roman peace' on the world," which "carried the greatest and most radiant of civilisations into the land of Africa, thus renewing the splendours of the ancient Latin empire!"[8]

The Third Reich frequently used the language of civilization. In Germany, the preferred terms were of course *Volksgemeinschaft*, *Kultur*, and *Abendland*; other more Western cognate terms—such as humanity—were often referred to derisively as *Humanitätsdüselei*, the sentimental and pernicious rhetoric of the Allies. Nevertheless, Hitler's regime also worked to co-opt the idea that Germany was the true defender of European civilization, or *Abendland*. Whereas the assertion that Nazism stood in opposition to the ideas of the French Revolution figured prominently in Nazi propaganda early on, the portrayal of Nazi culture as anti-Bolshevik became even more prevalent after the outbreak of war between Hitler and Stalin in 1941. Views of a Nazi-dominated united Europe drew on strong anti-Americanism among right-wing circles in the Weimar Republic, and further intensified after 1933. In Germany, anti-Western attitudes were stronger in the First World War than in the second, as the Third Reich portrayed itself as advancing the broader mission of Western civilization, albeit within a violent racial and anti-Semitic framework. Hitler's second Four-Year Plan, launched in October 1936, was mainly concerned with the growing power of the Red Army, and was described in terms of the threat of Bolshevism to European civilization. A good example was the 1937 Nazi pavilion at the World Exposition in Paris, where the regime's anti-Bolshevism was broadcast as a commonality with Western nations. The idea that Moscow was the real threat to Western civilization was particularly played up by German authorities in occupied France after 1940. The regime even used its notorious party rag, the *Völkischer Beobachter*, to trumpet the cultural claims of the Third Reich as the inheritor of European humanism, with special stress on the "Germanic" origins of Western culture.[9]

Fascist Italy and Nazi Germany also joined forces to build a new cultural order in Europe. In 1935 the Italians organized a Fascist International meeting in Montreux, Switzerland, to promote fascist modernism internationally. An "Italo-German revolutionary alliance against the West" was conceived as the cultural expression of the "Rome-Berlin axis" announced by Mussolini in 1936. The new cultural partnership between the fascist powers included lavish writers' festivals, musical events, and art exhibitions, as well as the creation of dozens of German-Italian Societies across Germany. The fascist powers were hailed for leading what one Italian publicist called their great "civilizations of the spirit." That the language of civilization was used to bridge their differences may at first seem puzzling. After all, in the First World War Italian propagandists had joined their French allies in drawing a clear distinction between German *Kultur* on one hand and Italian *civiltà* and French *civilisation* on the other. Germans too had expended great energy in extolling the unique qualities of German *Kultur* as the very foundation of Hitler's messianic mission. But over the course of the 1930s and especially after the outbreak of war, the Italians and Germans played down their differences and repositioned themselves as joint defenders of a new Europe against the threat of both the West and the East. "Europe" and "civilization" became the terms of choice to describe their solidarity. Just five days after Hitler's invasion of the Soviet Union in June 1941, Reich Minister of Propaganda Joseph Goebbels briefed the press about the new meaning of the war: "Europe marches against the common enemy in unique solidarity and rises up against the oppressor of all human culture and civilization. The birth hour of the new Europe takes place without demand or coercion from Germany." Bolshevism and Americanism were the enemies against which the fascists were waging their war for Europe. Goebbels's propaganda machine went into overdrive to ramp up the "civilization versus barbarism" theme with the British

bombing raids of German cities in 1942. A Goebbels press directive in March 1942 condemned the "barbarity of the British terror
raids," which were "unique in world history" for targeting "the most
valuable cultural centres of Europe"; a *Völkischer Beobachter* article
from April 26, 1942, following the British bombing of Rostock
screamed, "British Barbarism: Historical Monuments Bombed in
Rostock"; and damage to the Cologne Cathedral resulting from a
British raid in late May 1942 was denounced in the same newspaper as "England's assassination of European culture."[10]

The Nazi invasion of Poland in 1939 was couched in terms of
the civilizing mission. With it the "Germanization of the East" campaign during World War I was revived and radicalized after 1939.
The Third Reich's General Government in Poland was a zone of
experimentation for the expansion of German administration in the
East, and was partly based on the structures that Italy had tried to
establish in East Africa a few years before. Hans Frank, the notorious governor-general of occupied Poland, blithely admitted in an
interview in 1939 that Poland was now a "colony" whose inhabitants were "slaves of the Great German World Empire." Frank and
his government installed themselves at the Wawel Castle in Kraków,
the traditional residence of Polish kings. "My one ambition," Frank
reportedly said at one point, "is to elevate the Polish people to the
honour of European civilization." At the opening of Warsaw's newly
refurbished Skarbek Theatre in 1942, Frank boasted that "we, the
Germans, do not go to foreign lands with opium and similar measures like the English," but rather "we bring art and culture to other
nations," reflecting the great achievements of the German Volk. The
Third Reich's "civilizing mission" was linked to imperial conquest
elsewhere, often proudly documented in pictures. The regime, for example, provided copious documentary photographs of the resettlement of ethnic Germans from Latvia, Estonia, Galicia, Bessarabia,
and Bukovina at the beginning of the war as a celebrated "homecoming" to the greater Reich. The regime even organized various art

and photography exhibitions by Wehrmacht soldiers in occupied France to accentuate the cultural sensibility of the military conquerors. A new Baedeker guide of Nazi-occupied Warsaw published in 1943 exalted the architectural glories and scenic spots of the capital made great "predominantly through the efforts of Germans." This sense of entitled reconquest was one of the things that distinguished Nazi imperialism from its European rivals', who rarely claimed to be taking back what supposedly once had been theirs. In the Polish case, Goebbels commissioned German popular writer Edwin Erich Dwinger to report on alleged Polish atrocities committed against ethnic Germans living in Warsaw. In his 1940 book *Der Tod in Polen*, or *Death in Poland*, Dwinger framed the Nazi attack of Poland as a defensive cultural war, claiming that because of Poland's "unbelievable cultural disgrace" (*Kulturschande*) committed "against countless people of culture," in the future "there will be nothing that this people will be in a position to complain about, because it has erased itself from the rank of peoples of culture." Civilization served as a pretext for war and reprisal.[11]

Not surprisingly the Poles shot back, and tried to turn the language of civilization against the Germans in their international appeals for help. Germans and Poles had battled over cultural heritage and war damage during the Great War as well, but the devastation associated with the Second World War was of a different magnitude. In 1939 the Polish government in exile published a slim book in English called *The German Invasion of Poland: Polish Black Book*, made up of firsthand accounts and damning atrocity photographs detailing the "wickedness" perpetrated by the Germans. It argued that the Germans had violated the Hague Conventions by terrorizing civilians as well as conducting bombing raids of cities, churches, and cultural monuments, with supporting condemnations by President Franklin D. Roosevelt, Pope Pius XII, and Prime Minister Neville Chamberlain. Featured too were excerpts from a September 19, 1939, speech by Warsaw mayor Stefan Starzynski, who made no bones that this battle was "the struggle of right against might and of civilization against barbarism." A follow-up volume was published on *The German New Order in Poland* in 1941, documenting "massacres and tortures," concentration camps, religious persecution, as well as the "humiliation and degradation" of the Polish nation and its culture. It drew comparison between Belgium in 1914 and Poland in 1941 for international readers, even if this new version of "German crimes against divine and human law" was clearly of a new height of "systematic and boundless cruelty." After 1945 the Poles appealed to the international community for reparations, especially in relation to art and culture. A pamphlet produced in 1945 by the Polish Ministry of Culture and Art ended with a call for international acknowledgment, compensation, and a special indemnity toward Poland's decimated treasured artifacts and monuments. Poland's provisional communist government created an Office for the Reconstruction of the Capital, which quickly organized an exhibition in 1945 called *Warsaw Accuses* at Poland's National Museum, in which before-and-after photographs of ruined symbols of the country's "national civilization"—the Royal Castle, St. John's Archcathedral, and the Old Town Market Square—were displayed to represent the city as a "modern Pompeii"; the show traveled to the United States, and in it Nazi Germany was accused of intending to "kill culture and the nation."[12]

While these claims never found their way into court, such pleas illustrated just how central notions of civilization had become in interpreting international conflict during the Second World War. Civilization was a cherished term of identity and action not only for the liberal West, and had also been deployed by the Soviets as a language of solidarity during the Great Patriotic War. It was incorporated into fascist ideology just as readily, perhaps even more so, first in Italy and later in Nazi Germany. In various theaters of action, civilization became a condition for war as well as for the defense of national culture under attack. After 1945 the language of civilization played less of a role in international war-making, though it did maintain its presence in various civil wars and imperial adventures, as we shall see. The link between fascism, war, and civilization may have ended, but the connection between authoritarianism and a peacetime civilizing mission persisted in Southern Europe.

THE GREEK CIVIL WAR PLAYED A UNIQUE ROLE IN THE MAKING of Cold War Europe and recast the mission of Western civilization in dramatic ways. Once the German army had been defeated by the Allies there in 1944, the fundamental political question was whether the exiled King George II should reoccupy the Greek throne. Civil war began in 1944, as resistance against the occupying German army was transformed into a battle of national renewal led by the National Liberation Front (EAM) and its military wing, the Greek People's Liberation Army (ELAS), both of which were dominated by the Greek Communist Party. What made things difficult for these partisan fighters was that Stalin was not supportive for various tactical reasons. Greek partisans fought on regardless, refusing to concede to the forces of "monarcho-fascism," and pledged to challenge British efforts to reinstall the conservative monarchy. EAM's insurrection was principally supported by the Yugoslavs, who fanned the flames of civil war not only in Greece but also in Albania and Italy. After the right won the disputed election of March 1946, large amounts of Western aid and material tipped the balance against the liberation army, as the communists were unable to gain comparable support from Moscow or Belgrade. Conservative forces sponsored by the British and then the Americans eventually took control in Athens and around the country. Through the late 1940s Greek communists continued to be prosecuted and sentenced to death in large numbers. By the end of 1945 some 49,000 EAM supporters had been jailed, and many languished there through the late 1960s. The war tore apart Greek state and society and created a massive refugee problem, leaving lasting scars on the country for decades.[13]

Of greater relevance here is how the Greek conflict was transformed from a complicated civil war into a high-pitched Cold War drama with long-term effects on the redrawing of the geography of postwar Europe. The war not only marked the passing of global power from Britain to the United States, it also became a principal theater for staging the defense of Western civilization itself. As in the past, Greece was once again hailed as the cornerstone of the West, but now it represented a strategic flank of the Cold War Atlantic order as well. Where the fate of Greece had been a favorite cause of romantic nationalism for foreigners in the early nineteenth century, most famously associated with the exploits of Lord Byron, this time Western solidarity with menaced Greece was pure statecraft. Soviet meddling in Iran and the Turkish Straits in 1946 drew nervous Western attention to the region, and drove home the point that after the long and costly battle against Hitler's Germany, Britain no longer had the material capacity to protect the area from Soviet encroachment. On February 21, 1947, the British embassy in Washington dispatched a message to the US State Department announcing that the British government was unable to continue aiding Greece and Turkey, and implored Washington to take over as guardian of the region. The situation was grave enough to convince the new and erstwhile isolationist American president that intervention was urgent. Complicating things was that the Republican Party enjoyed a majority in Congress at the time, and was averse to large expenditures and overseas entanglements. Making a case to his domestic political rivals would not be easy, Truman realized, and he needed to prepare. To this end, Truman initially stressed that what was at stake was above all the preservation of democracy, not the protection of petroleum in the Middle East. His advisors urged him not to mention the Soviet Union by name in his speech, lest he unduly antagonize Stalin. Something grander needed to be offered.[14]

Truman told his advisors that aid to Greece would necessitate the "greatest selling job ever facing a President," as he needed to find a way to convince a skeptical Congress and American public about new American global responsibilities. A carefully planned press campaign was organized between the government and the *New York Times* to prepare the political ground several weeks before Truman's speech. The newspaper exaggerated Soviet strength and engagement in the region, while downplaying British and American meddling in the country. Details of Greek domestic fighting were soft-pedaled in favor of presenting the civil war as a direct conflict between the Soviet Union and United States. The American press loudly endorsed Truman's planned aid package in Greece and Turkey in the name of national security, and painted the distant civil war in epic proportions. As one journalist put it, "The course of history depends on our choice," for if Greece were "lost to the Western world," Turkey and Italy would be next. One *New York Times* article began by saying that communism was strong and growing in Italy and France, whereas democracy was fragile in the rest of Western Europe, creating a potentially dangerous situation since "nature and communism abhor vacuums." For this journalist, the stakes could not be higher: "The weakness of Britain and France, and the virtual dissolution of the rest of Western Europe means that the United States, and only the United States, is capable of sustaining Western civilization." Greece was now the new frontier of Western defense.[15]

In his historic speech to Congress on March 12, 1947, President Truman famously declared that it was now American policy "to support free peoples who are resisting attempted subjugation by armed minorities or by outside pressures," and that its first installment should be a massive aid package to Greece and Turkey. The battle, as he put it, was fundamentally between two ways of life, freedom versus totalitarianism. While first coined by Italian fascists in the 1920s to describe their ambitious antiliberal political program, totalitarianism now became a favorite Cold War term to tar the enemies of liberalism, be it fascist or communist. George Kennan, the highly influential diplomat and policy advisor under Truman, framed Washington's new uncompromising strategy to contain the totalitarian Soviet Union. Less well known is that he also dramatized Truman's American understanding of aid as a defense of Western civilization. In a presentation at Washington's War College two days after Truman's speech, Kennan warned about the dangers of not assisting these countries in need, for "in abandoning Greece we would be abandoning not only the fountainheads of most of our own culture and tradition; we would also be abandoning almost all of the other areas in the world where progressive representative government is a working proposition." Aid to Turkey was justified as part of the need to defend the fringes of the West. Such views were not limited to statesmen and politicians, as the recasting of the Greek Civil War as a new American crusade resonated in the press at the time.[16]

The reception of Truman's speech was mixed. On the one hand, King George of the Hellenes sent a telegram thanking Truman for his "inestimable assistance," as thousands reportedly shouted "Long live Truman" outside the American embassy in Athens, with shops festooned in American and Greek flags. On the other, the Greek communist leader, Nikos Zachariadis, interpreted Truman's speech as a perilous gesture, predicting that it would lead to "fresh ruins" and "an increase in the number of cemeteries." The wider communist world was consistent in its denunciation. Polish premier Józef Cyrankiewicz derided the speech as a bald "confession of imperialism" aimed to turn the Mediterranean countries into American colonies. Left-wing newspapers in France and Italy voiced similar objections. The Moscow newspaper *Izvestia* intoned that Truman's "threats of totalitarianism are singularly reminiscent of Hitler's screams about Bolshevism." In the US, the reception was not altogether ringing either. Left-leaning publications such as the *New Republic* and *Nation* were skeptical, and various members of Congress worried that this "new, world-wide Monroe doctrine" ended the comfortable habitus of isolationism in favor of engaging riskily in the affairs of Europe. Henry Wallace, Truman's former commerce secretary, added that Truman's words were effectively a "declaration of war" on the Soviet Union.[17]

Nevertheless, Truman's speech soon turned into American foreign policy doctrine. The Greek-Turkish aid bill became law on May 22, 1947, after which the language of civilization was routinely enlisted for legitimacy and grandeur. This was notably the case with Secretary of State George Marshall's announcement of the European Recovery Program (thereafter known as the Marshall Plan) a month later in June 1947. For Marshall, aid to Europe was "a matter which may largely determine the course of history—certainly the character of Western civilization—in our time and for many years to come." A report on "European Recovery and American Aid" of November 1947 argued that "in 1940, it seemed inevitable that a large part of what we call western civilization was irreparably lost," but that "now if we apply to the making of the peace the same spirit which triumphed in war, may we not see an equally dramatic vindication of the ideals and principles of free men everywhere?" CIA director Allen Dulles noted that "we saw as never before the magnitude of the task of saving Europe for Western civilization." It is no coincidence that Marshall reacted to the Prague coup of 1948 by calling for "urgent and resolute action" if the United States was to defend Western civilization in peril.[18]

The remaking of the Western alliance was directly connected to the Greek Civil War. It found its initial blueprint in Churchill's famed "Iron Curtain" speech in Fulton, Missouri, in 1946, delivered with Truman at his side, in which he signaled the arrival of a new and outward-turning Anglo-American partnership committed to the defense of "Christian civilization" and Western values. What distinguished Truman's March 1947 speech was that America was prepared to go it alone. The Soviet response to Truman's speech was predictably vitriolic. Soviet statesman Andrey Vyshinsky declared that the speech was but a call to war in a world now divided into two hostile camps. According to the American ambassador in the Soviet Union, Vyshinsky's speech about American saber rattling received wide coverage in Russia and caused great consternation about a possible war with the United States, to the point that "housewives [were] queuing up for sugar, laying down extra supplies of potatoes and buying or bartering to obtain extra warm clothes." The Cold War was now set in motion, a war in which subterfuge, propaganda, and culture were the new weapons of engagement. Like Churchill in 1944, Americans felt that restoring monarchy as a legitimate head of state would be the best way of maintaining order in Greece. From that point on the new Greek state rested on the army, monarchy, and American support, and became more of a counterrevolutionary regime than an outpost of liberal democracy. This is the reason why democracy itself was soft-pedaled as the justification for American engagement. Instead, civilization stepped into the breach to consolidate the new Atlantic Alliance. Greece and Turkey were both admitted to NATO in 1952, after which the US established sizable military bases in both countries.[19]

The cultural effects of American engagement in Europe were palpable in various ways. In the United States its new global role found cultural expression in the institutionalization of so-called Western Civilization courses at many universities in the 1940s and 1950s. While required classes in "Western Civ" were originally mooted after the First World War in Great Books programs at Columbia University and the University of Chicago, largely as a means of conveying to returning soldiers a sense of what they had fought for, they became a standard feature of American higher education from the 1940s through the 1980s and beyond. What underlay them was the effort to move beyond parochial nationalism, and to help students understand America's new place in the postwar world and in the sweep of world history. These courses were designed to blend international and national history, and to drive home the point that America was both the inheritor and guardian of Western civilization itself. Not for nothing was the course mocked by its critics as a feel-good American tale of Western history "from Plato to NATO." So whereas in Britain the academic field of global history evolved from imperial history, its American variant in the 1950s and 1960s explicitly grew out of these university foundation courses—the taught story of Western civilization was the American version of global history.[20]

In Western Europe the US stepped up its cultural influence. American agencies such as the Rockefeller and Carnegie Foundations poured money into Western Europe in the fields of higher education, intellectual exchange, and cultural diplomacy to braid American and European cultural interests. In the 1950s a raft of US government–sponsored American modern art exhibitions (featuring the work of Abstract Expressionists like Jackson Pollock and Mark Rothko) and jazz band tours (including Louis Armstrong and Miles Davis) were organized to celebrate American freedom, artistic individuality, and the American way of life, all presented as the antithesis to the buttoned-up dictates of Soviet-style socialist realism. The CIA-sponsored Congress for Cultural Freedom, founded in West Berlin in 1950 with branches in some thirty-five countries at its height, was another example of American Cold War engagement in Western Europe. It was both antifascist and anti-Stalinist in outlook, and gathered a dazzling list of writers and artists, such as Arthur Koestler, Bertrand Russell, Karl Jaspers, and Jean-Paul Sartre, to address the relationship between freedom and tyranny. Its aim was to help with the cultural reconstruction of devastated Europe in the name of liberal democracy and intellectual liberty. The Congress for Cultural Freedom organized countless conferences and cultural events in Western Europe, and founded journals like *Der Monat* in West Germany and *Encounter* in Britain to give popular credence to the mission of anti-Soviet cultural liberalism. Notably the language of engagement was not "Europe," which still had a bad smell to many intellectuals, especially on the left. As noted with Churchill's European Movement in the last chapter, the discourse on Europe was dismissed as a conservative project to block socialist welfare politics across Western Europe. The idea of united Europe and united European culture also had lingering fascist association for many Europeans, especially in France. As Jean-Paul Sartre remarked in 1947, "The word Europe" carried with it "the sound of boots of Nazi Germany" and "an odor of servitude and Germanism." During the occupation, the German-run Radio Bruxelles had signed off every night with a tune beginning "For the New Europe." Western civilization and the free West instead became the preferred terms of bridge-building in this period. The Truman Doctrine provided this new American-led Western alliance with its military cover and cultural purpose.[21]

The international effects of the American containment of the Greek Civil War were far-reaching in other ways. Not for nothing has it been called the "first shot of the Cold War." Firstly, it led to Stalin's crackdown in Eastern Europe, often carried out through terror, purges, and violence against political opponents. There was a kind of fearful symmetry between the treatment of communists in parts of Western Europe and the punishment meted out against noncommunists in Eastern Europe. The expulsion of communists from the governments in Italy, France, Belgium, and Luxembourg in 1947 found parallels in the fate of noncommunist political parties in Eastern Europe, and in both cases the superpowers were equally meddlesome, even if their methods differed significantly. Secondly, the events in Greece served notice to communists in France and Italy about the risks associated with trying to take control themselves and to deviate too far from Moscow. Perhaps most importantly, the civil war marked the beginning of the end of the British military presence in Europe and the Middle East. It was the first step in a War of British Succession, as the formerly British-controlled lands of the Ottoman Empire were being taken over by new superpowers. So cozy was the relationship between the American and Greek governments that the Americans actually drafted the Greek application for aid in connection with the Truman Doctrine. The effect was what Norwegian historian Geir Lundestad has suggestively called "empire by invitation," as Western Europeans explicitly encouraged the Americans to take a more active role in European affairs. French Atlanticists were the most insistent, and the defense of civilization was often the language of alliance. In March 1948 French foreign minister Georges Bidault implored Washington to fortify politically and militarily "the collaboration between the old and the new worlds, both so jointly responsible for the preservation of the valuable civilization." In the first three years after 1950 the American defense budget tripled in size as the US began to spread its military and ideological umbrella over Western Europe.[22]

The American guardianship of Greece as a new frontier of Cold War Europe was the moment in which the United States assumed the mantle as the principal defender of Western civilization itself. With the subsequent formalization of NATO as a new community of defense two years later, the United States broke from long-standing diplomatic tradition in committing itself to peacetime military alliance with European powers. But unlike the situation in Hungary, Italy, and Spain in the 1940s, as discussed in Chapter 3, Christianity played no role in the mission to defend Greece. On the contrary, this was strictly an anticommunist calculation of Cold War containment. Where that chapter described the emergence of Judeo-Christian civilization as the moral foundation of European integration, Western civilization now became a distinctly secular language of transatlantic alliance in a period of European vulnerability and transition.

THE BREAKDOWN OF THE STATE DURING THE SECOND WORLD War, followed by foreign superpower control of the continent, forced Western Europeans to think about sovereignty, political community, and Europe in fresh ways. The fifteen-year period between the end of the war and the end of empire is usually glossed over in mainstream accounts of postwar Europe as an awkward parenthesis, yet it was a pivotal moment of European imperial history. For starters, France invested more public funds in its colonial empire between 1947 and 1958 than it had between 1880 and 1940. While attention to Europe's reconquest abroad after 1945 usually concentrates on doomed French rule in Algeria, the restoration of empire was part of a broader trend. In fact, the early postwar period was more a replay of interwar developments, and cannot be easily consigned to an aberrant prehistory of the European Union. New European "civilizing missions" in Asia and Africa continued to shape Western Europe's relationship with the so-called Third World long before the wave of national liberation struggles in the 1960s.

One of the most talked-about plans for European reengagement with Africa was the controversial Eurafrica project. Its basic idea was that the great European powers would coordinate overseas colonialism to speed European recovery and to plug the yawning "dollar gap" with the United States. The call to pool overseas resources may sound unprecedented, but it was not. Europeans joined forces militarily in various colonial hot spots, such as in Qing-era China. The brutal crushing of the Boxer Rebellion (1899–1901) by an eight-nation alliance showed that Western powers could—and did—act together when common interests were threatened. After the Great War, the newly created League of Nations gave its blessings to international cooperation among the imperial powers to manage colonial development in the mandates, all the while maintaining a strict cultural hierarchy between imperial powers and colonial subjects: according to the League Covenant, the mandate system was based on a "sacred trust of civilization" in which the "tutelage of such peoples should be entrusted to advanced nations." For the League, empire, civilization, and development were inseparately bound.[23]

The dream of Europeanizing colonialism really took wing between the world wars, and was seen as a necessary means of fending off growing American power. It was closely associated with the influential Austrian Japanese politician and intellectual Count Richard Coudenhove-Kalergi. He was a tireless advocate for European integration, and founded the Pan-European movement in 1923 to promote the cause of European unification. For him Eurafrica was a geographical space that stretched from Norway's North Cape to the Congo, and would primarily provide Europe with wheat, rice, corn, copper, cotton, and rubber, among other commodities. Coudenhove-Kalergi's vision of Eurafrica was born from the fallout of the Great War, and in particular the economic weakening of Europe on the world stage. Even if the British and French empires were actually at peak power in the interwar years, in part thanks to the transfer of former German colonies to them as new mandates, Pan-Europeanists were convinced that combining European overseas resources was the best strategy to shore up European power in relation to the United States and the new Soviet Union. For Coudenhove-Kalergi, European integration, overseas expansion, and the renewal of European civilization were intimately connected. In his 1923 book, *Pan-Europe*, Coudenhove-Kalergi held that Pan-Europe was the "political expression of the European cultural community" as an "occidental nation," one that excluded the Soviet Union. In his eyes, European civilization was built on humanism, Christianity, and racial belonging, going so far as to say that "Europe's culture is that of the White Race, which sprang from the soil of Antiquity and Christianity." By the late 1920s he saw the stark choice facing Europe as nothing less than Pan-Europe or war—by which he meant that if Europeans continued to fight one another, it would lead to Europe's hasty exit from the world stage. Coudenhove-Kalergi developed these ideas further in his 1939 *Europe Must Unite*, in which he claimed that Europeans must be made aware that all the peoples of Europe "are children of a common civilization, a common race, and a common continent, heirs of a common tradition, bearers of a common mission, bound together forever in a community of destiny and life." Fascist Italy became one of the main advocates of Eurafrica in the 1930s, and during the Second World War the idea continued to inspire the writings of Vichy French Europeanists. From the 1930s onward, Coudenhove-Kalergi's Pan-European movement counted a range of notable supporters, among them Heinrich Mann, Albert Einstein, Konrad Adenauer, Aristide Briand, and Winston Churchill.[24]

After 1945 Coudenhove-Kalergi's Eurafrica scheme was dusted off and became a subject of serious discussion among Western policy makers and colonial administrators keen on reviving the fortunes of the continent. In 1950 Coudenhove-Kalergi was awarded the prestigious Charlemagne Prize in honor of his work on European unity, underlining that "the renewal of the Carolingian Empire in the spirit of the 20th century would be a decisive step toward the unification of Europe." The imperial powers also found the idea attractive after the war. Part of the reason why they set such great store in reclaiming their lost colonies was the shared perception that overseas territories had been indispensable to Allied victory. Old colonial ideas of Africa as the natural reserve of European foodstuffs and raw materials resurfaced, though now in the form of a collaborative Eurafrica guise to think beyond the fragility and limitations of the European nation-state, and to imagine alternative models of transregional integration. Eurafrica was also seen as a means of replenishing fast-diminishing dollar reserves in connection with the winding-up of Marshall Plan aid in 1952.[25]

European powers reacted differently to the scheme. Britain flirted with but then dropped the idea, turning instead toward the Atlantic Alliance as a more reliable source of security and prosperity. France, the Netherlands, Belgium, and Italy were more intent on the Eurafrica plan, and enthusiasm for it was expressed by various public intellectuals. For example, in his book tellingly titled *Afrika:*

Europas Gemeinschaftsaufgabe Nr. 1, or *Africa: The European Commu-nity's Number 1 Priority*, Austrian writer Anton Zischka argued that Franco-German coal and steel cooperation was the first step toward mining Africa's resources. Africa, so Zischka reasoned, should serve as "Europe's America at its backdoor," the exploitation of which would complement Western European economic and political in-tegration, as well as be a check on Soviet power. Similar views were circulated in West Germany and France as part of a broader effort to reimagine relations between Europe and Africa for a new post-war world. Conservative policy makers and thinkers in France, the Netherlands, and Belgium saw the future of a new united Europe as based on a shared colonial control of Africa. Even Oswald Mosley, the notorious founder of the British Union of Fascists, linked the recovery of Europe to the control of African resources. As he put it in a 1949 speech at Kensington Town Hall, a "new civilization will be born" if the "energies of Englishmen, Frenchmen, Germans and Italians" were "pooled and directed by common consent and purpose to win wealth from the richest Continent on Earth."[26]

Eurafrican ideas and national planning dovetailed most notably in France. The Second World War saw new welfare policies toward Africa, in a spirit similar to Britain's 1942 Beveridge Report. At a conference on postwar empire organized by the Free French in early 1944 in Brazzaville, the capital of French Equatorial Africa, the ob-ject of French colonial policy was announced to "assure the Africans of a better life by raising their purchasing power and improving their standard of living." In 1945 colonial subjects became citizens of the French Union, with elections held that year in French Africa for di-rect representation in the French National Assembly. The direction of French foreign policy had pivoted toward Africa. As the young Fourth Republic official François Mitterand wrote in 1957: "The Mediterranean, not the Rhine, is the axis of our security and our foreign policy." Others at the time, like the eminent French his-torian Alfred Grosser, recognized that the new mental geography of French national security "extended from the Paris-Algiers-Brazzaville axis," one in which French national security and the defense of the West "seemed to justify military action in Algeria." The point was that France did not feel compelled to choose between Europe and empire, but could have both. France was hardly alone in connecting renewed empire, European federalism, and the export of European civilization. At the ceremony christening the 1957 Treaty of Rome, Dutch foreign minister Joseph Luns proclaimed that it is "our firm conviction" that the treaty "permits the continuation of her grand and global civilizing mission."[27]

While the Eurafrica project was connected to imperial recovery for France and Belgium, for others it was linked to imperial decline. The Dutch effort to restore its empire was short-lived, and Amsterdam was looking for a way to win new overseas markets and influence after the loss of colonial Indonesia. The Dutch launched two major military offensives in July 1947 and December 1948 to try to win back its former colony, both of which failed. Between 1945 and 1949 over 150,000 Dutch troops fought in Southeast Asia in losing efforts; an estimated 5,000 Dutch troops and over 100,000 Indonesians died in these conflicts. Even so, the debates in the Dutch parliament in 1945 and 1946 revealed the extent to which the conservative Christian parties—such as the Roman Catholic State Party (RKSP) and the Catholic People's Party (KVP)—enunciated the "mission," "duty," and "calling" (*roeping*) of enforced Dutch authority. In their eyes, "binding the peoples of the Netherlands and the Indies in the Kingdom's calling" would be "fruitful to the great peoples' good of national freedom, fruitful to spiritual civilization, fruitful also to material wellbeing." Effective guerilla warfare, an insurrection led by the Communist Party of Indonesia, and the American threat of cutting off Marshall Plan aid to the Netherlands if Indonesian independence were not granted combined to force the Dutch to concede the defeat of their former holding—a full accord was signed, and Indonesia became fully sovereign in November 1949. (The Dutch held on to New Guinea until 1960 to keep some imperial foothold in Asia.) In the early 1950s the Netherlands thus became one of the drivers for the Eurafrica project, as its foreign policy pivoted toward European integration, links to Africa, and serving as a faithful ally within NATO and the transatlantic order.[28]

A forgotten prime mover of the Eurafrica project was none other than the newly formed Council of Europe. While we noted in Chapter 3 how the Council helped to give concrete form to European integration on the continent, it also insisted on the incorporation of Western overseas territories as part of council membership. Its Strasbourg Plan of 1952 codified the idea of tethering Western Europe and its overseas territories in a new Eurafrican community of trade. One journalist noted that it implied that there is "no reason to regard the Mediterranean as a dividing line between the continents of Europe and Africa," for the body of water could be seen as a "great inland sea in a stretch of mutually complementary territory running from Northern Norway to southern Africa" in a "true Euro-Africa." By 1958 some eighteen African countries had been brought into special relationship with the European Economic Community. The 1957 Treaty of Rome may have overtaken the Council of Europe's Eurafrica proposals, but associative membership was granted to the French and Dutch dependencies and the Belgian Congo as well as Italian Somaliland in the Rome treaty. Not everyone was so pleased with this neocolonial arrangement, especially the West Germans. But in this case, Belgian foreign minister Paul-Henri Spaak, whom we encountered in Chapter 3 as a great champion of European integration, played an instrumental role in convincing the West Germans to endorse the principle of overseas association in the 1957 treaty.[29]

The rebooted postwar version of Eurafrica was sharply criticized by the communist world. The Soviet Union condemned the scheme as nothing but European imperialism dressed up in new language.

One 1960 article in the Soviet monthly *International Affairs* argued that Black Africa was "increasingly becoming a preserve of collective colonialism by the imperialist powers." The East German press was especially vociferous, not least because it afforded the socialist regime the opportunity to chasten West Germany's *Eurafrika* plans as simply recycled nineteenth-century imperialism and Nazi-era *Afrikapläne*. The developing "common political front" between France and West Germany was denounced as an imperialist cabal to impede African liberation and growing relations with the socialist countries.[30]

The Eurafrica project was also championed by a number of Western European socialists. In Britain, Ernest Bevin's idea of an Anglo-French-led imperial "Western European Union" was part of his vision of how Europe could assert itself globally as a Third Force between the United States and the Soviet Union. The sterling crisis of 1947 meant that Labourite Britain was keen to seek partnership with France in exploiting their colonies in a common effort to ease their financial problems. Its attitude toward Africa was mostly an extension of the principles of "developmental imperialism" espoused by the Fabian Colonial Bureau, a largely autonomous socialist think tank founded in 1940, to the postwar period. French socialists championed the trans-European administration of empire too, citing as precedent the early 1930s Franco-German industrial cooperation in North Africa. French socialist Guy Mollet backed the idea of the Eurafrican community, specifically advocating "cooperation between Algerians and French to keep the union together." In the 1950s French socialists pushed for African development instead of independence, in part because they were skeptical about nationalism as progressive international politics. Most of the other Western European socialist parties were also on board with these development policies, though others were more critical. The West German Social Democratic Party, for example, harbored serious concern about the Eurafrica project and even lobbied for Algerian independence. The result was that the Eurafrica project opened up deep fissures between socialists in Western Europe, and perhaps more seriously, divided European socialists from their Asian and African counterparts around the issue of state sovereignty.[31]

With this in mind, one would assume that recycled Western European dreams of empire after 1945 would encounter wholesale resistance from African leaders, intellectuals, and policy makers. Ghanaian president Kwame Nkrumah likened the Treaty of Rome to the Congress of Berlin in 1885: "the latter treaty established the undisputed sway of colonialism in Africa, the former marks the advent of neo-colonialism in Africa." Guinean president Sékou Touré condemned Eurafrica as "just a European idea for Africa," "an extension of Europe to Africa." Tunisian president Habib Bourguiba saw France's war in Algeria as killing off any goodwill from the African side, darkly concluding that "Eurafrica will die in Algeria."[32]

Still, there was some sympathy among African leaders. A telling example was Léopold Sédar Senghor, then French deputy from Senegal in the newly elected French National Assembly and later the first president of independent Senegal. In the 1940s and 1950s—that is, the decade and a half before independence—Senghor spent a great deal of energy advocating for Senegal to stay in the newly renamed French Union, arguing that the country's best future would be as part of a French federal model. Above all he worried that independent Africa would be balkanized, not unlike the breakup of the Habsburg and Ottoman Empires at the end of the Great War. Opting to join a revamped European-African union makes more sense if we remember that newly independent countries had few places to turn to for badly needed aid after independence, apart from asking for alms from their former imperial overlords or delicately playing off the superpowers against each other to their own advantage, which many leaders effectively did. Through the 1950s aid was still mostly bilateral, and large international agencies like the World Bank played a comparatively little role at the time. The World Bank was a marginal international creditor in those days, furnishing not more than around

5 percent of all development aid by 1957. Only in the late 1960s did the bank shift its attention away from the industrialized nations. Senghor thus supported the *Eurafrique* idea because he saw closer European-African cooperation as a worthwhile venture, though he explicitly insisted on the political representation of peoples from "overseas territories" as the precondition for African participation. In the mid-1950s Senghor enthused that a "Eurafrican France of 88 million inhabitants would be in the first rank, as much by the number of its inhabitants as by the resources of all sorts it would control." For him the time was ripe to change France from an imperial republic to a democratic federation. Federalism thus potentially offered African connections with France and other African countries in a system of shared sovereignty beyond the nation-state.[33]

The conservative cultural vision of a united Western Europe remained prominent through the 1950s and helped create some cultural space free from American influence. By the late 1950s, the Eurafrican idea faded in prominence and was absorbed by broader regional entities like the EEC and the rash of post-imperial bilateral relations forged between Europeans and Africans. By the late 1940s, harder versions of regional solidarity solidified across the Cold War divide, best seen in NATO and the Warsaw Pact. Alternative federal ideas fared quite badly across Africa at the time: Kwame Nkrumah's Pan-African Union and Léopold Senghor's West African Federation both failed. With time the nation-state proved to be the sacrosanct foundation of the international order, though it was hardly foreordained or universally desired at the time.[34]

THE TRANSNATIONAL MODEL OF POLITICAL COMMUNITY THAT remained uppermost in the minds of contemporaries was of course empire. The international debate about it in the 1950s is usually cast as a crude antechamber to decolonization, yet it is worth reconsidering how it was tied up with an understanding of civilization at the time. The status and future of empire became a key talking point at the United Nations in the 1950s, years before the voices and agenda of the Third World exerted their majority position in that body. Historian Mark Mazower has shown that in its early years, the UN— like the League of Nations before it—tended to defend European imperial possessions, not challenge them. What remains overlooked is the way in which the old nexus of empire and civilization was confronted in the period.[35]

By the mid-1950s representatives to the UN from Latin America, India, the Soviet Union, and several African countries were raising objections to the practices of empire. The postwar restoration of empire sat uneasily with the wartime espousal of liberal values in general and the principles of the United Nations Charter in particular. British and French insistence on the infamous "colonial clause" in the UN Charter, which held that overseas colonies were exempt from the Charter's commitment to equality and justice, created an easy target for the Soviet Union and its allies to challenge the West during the early UN General Assemblies. Such criticism was often couched in the new language of human rights. In 1950 a Polish UN representative pointed to Western hypocrisy when he said those nations had insisted on the colonial clause "because they wish to perpetuate a position of inferiority, oppression, and arbitrary exploitation in their colonies." In 1951 Egypt and India used the shaming rhetoric of human rights to make anti-imperial arguments against the French in Morocco, and delegates from the Philippines and Chile demanded that the West's civilizing mission must come to an end.[36]

The new superpowers were drawn into the fray and made things awkward for the European imperial regimes. After all, both claimed that their own international identities were defined by anticolonialism. While the US proudly saw itself as the world's first successful colonial uprising, and lent support to anticolonial causes worldwide, the Soviet Union had loudly championed anti-imperial campaigns since the 1920s and in principle was committed to self-determination for all. Both of course were glaringly inconsistent in their policies. (The Soviet case will be addressed in Chapter 8.) Aside from the Suez Crisis, in which the Americans took issue against both the British and French in their struggle with Nasser's Egypt, Washington supported its Western European partners in debates about empire through the 1950s. President Eisenhower initially offered military support to Egypt after its 1952 revolution, yet he quickly changed his mind, supposedly because of a phone call from Churchill. The former British prime minister told the president, "My dear friend, surely you are not going to start your term in the White House by supplying arms to Egypt which may well be turned against the former comrades who fought under your command in the great battle for the liberation of Europe." However much Eisenhower voiced his desire to "be on the side of the natives for once," he continued to pledge allegiance to his NATO partners, and therefore voiced no public criticism of their colonial practices. By 1949 American officials had come to view Europe's colonies as vital to the European Recovery Program, insomuch as they would help address Western Europe's balance of payment deficit with the United States and increase productivity for African economies. Like the other colonial powers, Washington increasingly recognized that Western European economic recovery was dependent on African material development. As a consequence, Eisenhower's administration never cast a vote in the UN in favor of African independence or self-determination, and tended to side with its beleaguered European allies in Africa, including Belgium and Portugal. During a May 1960 visit to Lisbon, for example, Eisenhower made a point of supporting António de Oliveira Salazar's pariah Portuguese state, a NATO ally, saying that their two governments had "worked together without a single difference of opinion."[37]

Less well known is that the United Nations became a key forum for apologists of empire, who used the language of European civilization to defend a status quo under fire. By the late 1950s France and Britain were expressing their exasperation at the turn of opinion among newer members at the UN, including how the old language of civilization was becoming the stuff of accusation and ridicule. In 1956 a French official sniffed that these "newcomers" wish to "assure themselves the role of judge before our accused and uneasy civilizations" in an effort to "humiliate their old masters" and "deprive them of what remained of their overseas possessions."[38]

One of the most vociferous justifications for empire was Sir Alan Burns's *In Defence of Colonies*, published in 1957. Burns had been governor of the Gold Coast (modern-day Ghana) from 1941 to 1947 and spent decades before that in the British Colonial Service. He served as the British representative at the United Nations from 1945 to 1955, and heard criticism of the British Empire firsthand in those meetings. The first postwar decade saw the dramatic expansion of the British colonial presence in Africa, characterized by what some have called repressive developmentalism. In that period the British Colonial staff increased by 45 percent, a third of which were development specialists. Its bureaucracy also swelled, especially in the fields of agriculture, forestry, and surveying, with similar trends in the French colonies, such as Guinea. What is more, there was growing discomfort within the British Colonial Office about the changing tenor of the UN and its loud critics of colonialism. Sir Hilton Poynton, Britain's permanent under-secretary of the Colonial Office from 1959 to 1966, expressed concern that "a motley international assembly" might put the British Empire in question. Like all UN member states, Britain had agreed to the UN Charter, which said that all "administrative states" were to submit reports, hear petitions, and accept visiting missions to the trust territories, as well as to prepare them for independence. This implied a potential affront to sovereignty, but it was the 1956 Suez Crisis that changed the international community's moral views of the British Empire. That the botched British-French-Israeli invasion of Egypt took place at the same time as the Soviet invasion of Budapest effectively drew a moral connection between British, French, and Soviet imperial aggression in the eyes of many UN member states and anticolonial critics around the world.[39]

Burns's book was a riposte to charges of mismanagement, and he in turn accused his critics of inverted racism. "'Anti-colonialism' is merely a cover for intense racial feeling," Burns boldly began, "a colour prejudice in reverse which reflects the resentment of the darker peoples against the past domination of the world by European nations. In all cases 'anti-colonialism' is based on emotion rather than on reason." He went on to defend Britain's colonial record, which "though far from spotless" is "much better than is generally allowed." In his eyes the UN critics of empire were blatant hypocrites "whose governments are the most notorious for tyranny, inefficiency or corruption." The "victims of Soviet expansion" are less free than the inhabitants of British colonies, he continued, and the "Amerindians" enjoyed "no greater share in the government of their countries" than those in British dependent territories. What especially galled Burns about the UN debates was what he called the "Salt Water Fallacy": whereas the "expansion by a country over land, and the incorporation of large areas of territory inhabited by other races and peoples is apparently perfectly praiseworthy, the extension of one's jurisdiction over sea is stigmatised in certain quarters as 'Colonial imperialism' and the 'oppression of subject races.'" He added that if we "recognize Soviet sovereignty over the whole vast area of the Soviet Union" as "a single unit," then "equally we must insist that the British Colonial Empire, although split up by intervening oceans, is every bit as much of a single international entity as the Soviet Union." No less irksome to him was that the British, having brought "under their protection backward peoples and leading them toward civilization, prosperity, and self-government, should be classed as brutal imperialists."[40]

Much of the rhetorical firepower at the UN was directed at other colonial powers. Among the most attacked was Belgium, which may at first seem an unlikely focus of animus. Prior to the Second World War the Belgian Congo had been a relatively minor colony with a small number of settlers—17,000 in 1930, dropping to 11,000 in 1934—which enjoyed comparatively little popular support or interest back home. But after the war Belgium invested more money and manpower in the Congo as a means of reviving the Belgian economy. Substantial state investment was made in the Congo's social infrastructure, above all in education and health, areas which had long been confined to the work of Christian missionaries. The number of settlers also rose, from 24,000 in 1947 to 89,000 in 1959. In 1955 King Baudouin of Belgium made a triumphant tour of the colony to transmit a positive image of successful paternalism, declaring before 70,000 in the colonial capital that "Belgium and Congo form a single nation." In the eyes of the Belgian government, the modernization of its colony was in step with what Baudouin called "the civilizing role of Belgium." The Congo was a precious investment and asset (not least for its uranium deposits) that the Belgians were keen to protect.[41]

By the early 1950s Belgium's resurgent colonial policy was under scrutiny. The Belgian Communist Party and a conclave of Catholic bishops in the Congo supported Congolese independence. But it was the international criticism that stung the most, and Brussels mobilized its A-team of international diplomats to defend its colonial policy internationally. In 1953 the Belgian government took its case to the international community in a brochure revealingly called *The Sacred Mission of Civilization: To Which People Should the Benefits Be Extended?* The polemic featured speeches from prominent Belgian politicians and government representatives at the United Nations. The Belgian foreign minister, Paul van Zeeland, advanced the so-called *thèse belge*, which pivoted on Belgium's compliance with the Charter of the United Nations and the fact that Belgium had done great service in developing the material fortunes of the Congolese. Van Zeeland and others complained about unfair accusations toward Belgium, and claimed that the UN had been far too sympathetic to nationalist causes in Asia and Africa. Like Burns, they argued that most states had underdeveloped ethnic groups and areas in their midst, and therefore every state should be subject to the same criticism.[42]

Two senior Belgian UN representatives, Fernand van Langenhove and Pierre Ryckmans, sharpened Belgium's position in subsequent publications by invoking civilization as the parlance of defense. In 1954 van Langenhove published a 100-page pamphlet called *The Question of the Aborigines Before the United Nations: The Belgian Thesis*. A senior diplomat and the former president of the UN's Security Council, van Langenhove revived nineteenth-century language in saying that the "duty of a civilized State toward the backward indigenous people is not only a duty of protection," but also "a duty of civilization" predicated on "the betterment of conditions for the welfare and advancement of these peoples." Van Langenhove complained that the new independent African states were fomenting militant nationalism around the colonial world and thus vitiating the duty of civilization, which "consists in liberating from serfdom, destitution and the threat of complete extinction the most wretched of the aborigines." That same year a "Report from Belgium" was delivered to the United Nations by Pierre Ryckmans, former governor-general of the Belgian Congo and Belgium's delegate to the UN's Trusteeship Committee. Ryckmans openly defended Belgian sovereignty in the Congo, taking particular umbrage at a damning report by the International Labor Organization on *Living and Working Conditions of Aboriginal Populations in Independent Countries*, published the year before. For Ryckmans this "terrible book" erroneously claimed that the standard of life for the average Congolese was far inferior to that of Belgians back home. As a counterclaim, he too resorted to classic nineteenth-century rhetoric in reminding his audience that "the Congo of former days" was nothing but "a swarm of tribes, most of them as backward as the forest-dwelling peoples of the Amazonian basin." "Not until the arrival of the Whites did this continent at last, and for the first time," he went on, "know peace—a peace which, in the Congo, has reigned uninterrupted ever since." It was thanks to Belgium's duty of care that the present-day traveler "meets indigenous inhabitants who are educated and civilised." Not surprisingly such language met with great hostility from the international community. While Britain and France expressed polite support toward their Belgian colleagues, Brussels became increasingly isolated in its old-style defense of empire. Yet this did not deter Belgian ministers from insisting both domestically and internationally through the 1950s that "premature autonomy" would spell disaster for the Congolese, the West, and the UN itself.[43]

Plenty of criticism was also directed at a new member of the United Nations, Portugal. Portugal's was the oldest of all European empires, whose expansion abroad dated back to the capture of Ceuta in North Africa in 1415, and now counted Angola, Mozambique, Cape Verde, Macao, and Timor among its possessions. After his elevation as prime minister in 1932, António de Oliveira Salazar set out to construct his *Estado Novo*, or New State, an authoritarian regime that sought to modernize the country and strengthen ties to its colonies. Salazar made the glory of empire and the civilizing mission a point of national pride through schoolbooks, speeches, and holidays that extolled Portugal's contribution to civilization and the spread of Christianity. He stepped up his colonial policy after 1945, launching a new era of reforms based on welfare colonialism, Catholic engagement, and strong military control. As with the French and Belgians, the new emphasis on political assimilation and economic integration was seen as the best means of assuring imperial survival. In 1953 Salazar launched an ambitious six-year plan of economic expansion in Angola and Mozambique, which led to the construction of numerous roads, railways, ports, hotels, and factories. With it, emigration from Portugal to its African territories surged to over

100,000 between 1950 and 1960. The decade also saw the dramatic swelling of the political police, counterinsurgency militias, and the army in the overseas territories, along with the huge expansion of bureaucrats, administrators, technical planners, and intelligence officers. Church and missionary societies were also modernized and identified as powerful agents of the civilizing mission in step with the colonial bureaucracy.[44]

The Iberian country was admitted to the UN on December 14, 1955, after which its colonial policy was severely attacked by India, the Soviet Union, and others. As early as February 1956 the UN secretary-general dispatched a letter to the Portuguese government about the questionable welfare of the "non-autonomous territories" of Angola and Mozambique. In the ensuing UN debates, Iraq, Ghana, India, and Morocco led the charge against Portugal's colonial record. The Portuguese delegates were shocked by this rude reception, repeating that Portugal had built the "only successful multi-racial civilization that the world has ever seen." Portugal was taken off guard by UN criticism because until the mid-1950s the West had given its blessings to Salazar's regime. The Americans had set up military bases on the remote Azores islands as strategic military refueling stations for the potential rapid deployment of American troops to Europe, Africa, and the Middle East, and pledged support of Portugal. Lisbon had carefully negotiated these base rights in 1946, 1948, 1951, and 1957 in exchange for political protection, with the result that Portugal was firmly integrated into the American sphere of influence in Cold War Southern Europe. Salazar's regime also took part in the Marshall Plan and NATO, which provided economic assistance, military protection, and long-coveted international recognition, especially after the Soviet Union had vetoed Portugal's UN application in 1946.[45]

To stem the international outcry, the Portuguese government published a defense called *The United Nations and Portugal: A Study of Anti-Colonialism*. It was authored by Alberto Franco Nogueira, consul general in London who was eventually appointed as Salazar's foreign minister during the turbulent period of 1961 until 1969. Nogueira provided vital intellectual cover for Salazar's policies, and defended his country's empire in terms of civilization. The controversy over the Portuguese case centered on the interpretation of Article 73 of the UN Charter regarding "non-self-governing territories," which stated that all member states must "accept as a sacred trust the obligation to promote to the utmost" the "well-being of the inhabitants of these territories." This may look like just another dull legal clause, and was actually a recycled holdover from the 1920 League of Nations Covenant about the "sacred trust of civilization" for member states. Whereas the interwar clause was used to help reinforce empire, the UN's anticolonial advocates—led by India and the Soviet Union—reinterpreted it to mean that all colony-holding member states must provide evidence of good stewardship to scrutinizing UN committees. Nogueira countered that Portugal would not comply with this request. He claimed that the Portuguese constitution had been revised in 1951, after which its colonies were declared "overseas provinces" along the lines of the British Commonwealth and French Union. This meant that Portugal technically did not have any "non-autonomous territories," rendering Portugal's overseas territories a domestic matter, much like Algeria for France. Nogueira also claimed that there was no distinction between "civilised" and "uncivilised" in Portuguese law or in its language, and that all peoples living in overseas territories were treated equally as Portuguese.[46]

In UN General Assembly debates, Portugal portrayed itself as a victim, unfairly charged with racial discrimination. Its UN representatives pointed out that India's caste system denied "human rights" to large sections of its populations, and that no one objected to actions of the "largest and most ruthless and tyrannical colonial empire in the history of mankind," namely, the Soviet Union. Other Portuguese administrators argued that Portugal's "way of life" in its overseas territories was one in which "universal values are preserved," even as its record was being denigrated by the UN's Third World "tribal allegiance" fueled by "despotic racialism" and irresponsibility. If anything, so they maintained, Portugal should be commended for bringing "Christian humanitarianism" and its civilizing mission to the territories.[47]

Various intellectuals chimed in to trumpet the virtues of Portugal's civilizing mission, most prominently the well-known Brazilian sociologist Gilberto Freyre. Freyre was a prominent Latin American thinker who was a former student of Franz Boas at Columbia University, and best known for his 1933 anthropology book, *The Masters and the Slaves*. This was an influential study of races and cultures in Brazil, and championed the role of black heritage in Brazil as proof of the country's successful assimilation policy. With time his originally left-leaning anthropology grew more conservative, and soon Freyre became a defender of Salazar's imperial politics. In his writings, he coined the term *Luso-tropicalism* to describe Portugal's unique presence in the tropics. In his eyes, Portuguese imperialism was different from that of the other European powers because it was based on a more integrative model of intercultural assimilation that included native cultures in a higher form of civilization. Freyre saw Roman Catholicism's assimilation of non-Christians as an analog of Portugal's own policies in the tropics. Luso-tropicalism was therefore a hybrid civilization that combined precolonial and pre-Christian elements with European culture. For Freyre, this harmonious blend of Portuguese and indigenous cultures in Africa and Latin America sat in stark contrast to other European imperial regimes, which tended to eradicate indigenous cultural forms in agriculture, medicine, and the arts. For Freyre, it was no coincidence that the other European powers were now "retiring from the warm areas" because they never developed the "spirit" and "vigour" of composite modern civilizations. Only the Portuguese, so he argued, managed to adapt European values to the tropics in the form of successful multiracial societies whose cultural values transcended race and ethnicity. Freyre's work was constantly cited by Portuguese apologists in the face of growing international discontent about Lisbon's overseas possessions.[48]

Criticism of Western European imperialism also came from another source, the churches. In the 1950s, Catholic and Protestant theologians worked to forge a new common front of the ecumenical movement, as noted in Chapter 3; less known is that challenging traditional conceptions of Western civilization became one of their rallying issues. In the eyes of church leaders and lay writers, Western European federation and decolonization were legitimate historical responses to the perversions of European nationalism and imperialism. Empire was a morally indefensible institution, and global Christian engagement with brethren in Africa and Asia began with renouncing the church's association with imperial politics. In the 1930s a number of Protestant theologians and missionaries had discussed severing Christianity from Europe's civilizing mission, most visibly documented in the proceedings of the International Missionary Council conference in Tambaram, India, in 1938. Yet the wave of decolonization in the 1960s intensified the call for Christian anti-imperial mobilization. The campaign was led by Joseph Blomjous, the Dutch Catholic bishop of Mwanza, Tanzania, and Scottish Presbyterian bishop Lesslie Newbigin, both of whom asserted that the presence of new nations in Africa and Asia compelled Christianity to change tack, and to cut its long-standing ties to the brutal secular abuses of Western civilization for the sake of a new universal Christianity based on peace, ecumenicalism, and diversity. In 1960 the reformist Pope John XXIII moved in this direction by creating the Secretariat for Promoting Christian Unity as part of the preparation for the Second Vatican Council that opened in 1961. Five years later Blomjous and Newbigin founded the Committee on Society, Development and Peace, which coordinated the work of all major Christian charities and missionary organizations in a new spirit so as to free Christianity from colonial contamination. Now decolonization, not empire, represented the fulfillment of Christian mission and the moral renewal of Europe. Christian thinkers interpreted European federalism and overseas disengagement as twin expressions of a new globally oriented and rehabilitated Christian civilization, perhaps best articulated in Swiss writer Denis de Rougemont's influential *The Meaning of Europe*, published in 1963. While one could detect a lingering paternalism in de Rougemont's book, as noted with such passages as "Europe's political retreat coincides with the accelerated adoption of our civilization by the under-privileged nations," such books reflected a broader effort to break the bond between Christianity and Europe's old civilizing mission, to put the idea of a Christian civilization on a new moral footing that transcended confessional and old North-South imperial divides. The UN was therefore not the only major NGO against which Western European empires were struggling.[49]

History was not on the side of the Western European empires. Portugal's defense of empire was dismissed as an "intellectual sleight of hand" by Senegal's UN delegate, and as "premeditated dereliction" by Tunisia's delegate; Ghana's delegate went so far as to say that in Africa's colonial territories "radical surgery is required." In their campaign, African states received their most consistent backing from communist nations, as well as from noncolonial European states such as Sweden and Norway. The Soviets used the conflict to charge that Salazar's colonial "war of extermination" in Angola was "thanks to the support and assistance by the NATO allies." By the early 1960s there was rising anti-Portuguese nationalism in the territories—a guerilla war in Angola had been raging for several years, and there was unrest in Portuguese Guinea. The anti-Portuguese cause in Angola and Mozambique received support from independent African countries, as nationalist guerillas were trained in Algeria, Tunisia, and Mali. But however much these rebellions were brutally suppressed by Portuguese armed forces, and however much Lisbon encouraged white settlement to counter African disaffection, the rebels for independence would eventually win out. Europe's first and last overseas empire was dissolved in 1975, drawing to a close over 500 years of Lusophone imperial rule in the tropics.[50]

ONE OF THE MOST ENDURING MYTHS OF HISTORY-WRITING about Europe in the twentieth century is that the century can be neatly divided into a tale of two halves, with the first half made up of episodes of war, revolution, and mass violence, while the second is a tale of relative peace and prosperity. This crude interpretation gets us only so far, especially in light of the restoration of empire after 1945, to say nothing of the continuation of civil war (Greece), fascism (Spain), and authoritarianism (Portugal) in Southern Europe. The Second World War pointed up the suspension of Western European states and empires, after which France, the Netherlands, and Belgium sought to undo the effects of Nazi occupation by reclaiming their imperial holdings abroad. It exposed the dark side of Western Europe's re-civilizing story in terms of its imperial relationship to the wider world and in the redrawing of its geographical frontiers and national identities after Nazi Germany's surrender.

The changing terminology of civilization mirrored these historical transformations. While the defeat of the Third Reich may have destroyed the link between fascism, war, and civilization, the peacetime authoritarian regimes in Spain and Portugal continued to stylize themselves as advancing a Catholic civilizing mission, especially in the Portuguese colonies. Civilization remained a protective shield of imperial power and privilege for the likes of Belgium and Portugal, as these beleaguered European empires were slow to grasp how the world was changing. The passionate debates about empire and civilization helped transform the UN from a wartime alliance to a peacetime arbiter of international politics, playing host to the clash between old and new powers, imperialism and anti-imperialism. By the 1960s the rhetoric of civilization became more and more connected with the cause of decolonization. As the Cold War migrated south, so too did the remaking of civilization as part of the anti-imperial struggle.

What was new too after 1945 was how civilization was used to underwrite an American-led Atlantic Alliance based on a shared history and identity. It was part of American peacetime expansion and commitment to Western Europe, fueled by a secular sense of America's mission in the world. The Americanization of Western civilization marked a dramatic departure from the understanding of civilization in earlier chapters—whereas for many observers in 1945 civilization elicited loss, nostalgia, and the dream of prewar Europe, the militarization of the Western alliance turned the terminology of civilization from a defensive to an offensive rhetoric that combined geopolitical strategy with epic moral purpose. The Greek Civil War served as the go-to template for blending empire with cultural mission, one that shaped American foreign policy for decades. After North Korea attacked South Korea in 1950, for example, Truman declared that "Korea is the Greece of the Far East," and "if we stand up to them like we did in Greece three years ago, they won't take over the whole of the East." In relation to Vietnam, Henry Cabot Lodge, the American ambassador to the United Nations, later remarked that "we of the free world won in Greece," and "we can win in Vietnam." President John F. Kennedy drew the connection too, comparing the Vietnam War to "long struggles against Communist guerrillas in Greece and in Asia." Such logic anticipated the way American secretary of defense Donald Rumsfeld and the George W. Bush administration would invoke the Allied occupation of Germany after 1945 as the model for the occupation of Iraq after the Second Iraq War that started in 2003. For American policy makers looking for a new moral mission after 9/11, the apparent successes of the 1940s were seized upon for ready reference and historical guidance. But in the intervening decades, as discussed in the next chapter, the discourse of civilization was fundamentally transformed by non-Europeans with the coming of decolonization.[51]

six

DECOLONIZATION AND AFRICAN CIVILIZATION

Ghana, Algeria, and Senegal

O N MARCH 6, 1957, AT ACCRA'S OLD POLO GROUNDS, THE first prime minister and later first president of Ghana, Kwame Nkrumah, declared the country's long-awaited independence before a crowd of over 100,000 onlookers. Nkrumah had led the Convention People's Party since 1951 with the rallying slogan of "Self-Government Now," and spurred the people of the Gold Coast into political action over the course of the 1950s. He had been imprisoned by the British authorities for his revolutionary agitation in the early 1950s, which increased and legitimated his stature as an African nationalist. At the Pan-African Congress in Manchester, England, in 1945, Nkrumah had helped write the "Declaration to the Colonial Peoples of the World" that proclaimed the "rights of all peoples to govern themselves." Only "under conditions of political freedom," it went on, can colonial peoples devise their own economic plans and social legislation "as are now imperative for any truly civilized country." In 1957 the moment had arrived.[1]

While the motion for independence had been agreed to with the British government some six months before, this was the ceremonial handover of power. At the stroke of midnight the Union Jack was solemnly lowered, and the red, green, and gold flag of the new state of Ghana was raised to great cheers of "Freedom!" from the crowd. "To-day, from now on," Nkrumah proclaimed, "there is a new African in the world and that new African is ready to fight his own battle and show that after all the black man is capable of managing his own affairs." "We have done with the battle and we again re-dedicate ourselves," he continued, "in the struggle to emancipate other countries in Africa, for our independence is meaningless unless it is linked up with the total liberation of the African continent." Nkrumah's speech was followed by a minute of silence to mark the moment, after which the band played Ghana's national anthem.[2]

Ghana was the first sub-Saharan African country to achieve its independence, and for that reason held a special place in the drama of decolonization that unfolded over the coming decade. Journalists on hand described the event in epic tones. Accra's leading daily newspaper, the *Daily Graphic*, predicted that Ghana "will stand as a model for colonies everywhere," a country that will "show them that there is a peaceful road to independence and that brains not bombs win freedom." African American writer Richard Wright wrote that Ghana was a "kind of pilot project of the new Africa" watched by people around the world, while the renowned Trinidad-born journalist George Padmore extolled Ghana as a model African state that uniquely combined "black nationalism plus socialism." The independence celebration also occasioned the first encounter between Martin Luther King Jr. and the then vice president Richard Nixon, punctuated by King's acid remark that "I'm very glad to meet you here, but I want you to come visit us down in Alabama where we are seeking the same kind of freedom the Gold Coast is celebrating." For many well-wishers, Ghana marked what one historian called the "birth of a new civilization freed from the legacies of colonial rule and capitalist extraction," the harbinger of a new world.[3]

But for all the novelty and excitement associated with self-rule, there were thorny issues of transition. In his 1963 book, *Africa Must Unite,* Nkrumah reflected on the strangeness of the handover for the future of his country. The difficulty of redefining Ghanaian identity "seemed to be summed up in the symbolic bareness which met me and my colleagues when we officially moved into Christiansborg Castle, formerly the official residence of the British governor. Making our tour through room after room, we were struck by the general emptiness." "Except for the occasional piece of furniture," he continued, "there was absolutely nothing to indicate that only a few days before people had lived and worked there. It is as though there had been a definite intention to cut off all links between the past and present which could help us in finding our bearings. It was a covert reminder that, having ourselves rejected the past, it was for us to make the future alone." Nkrumah went on to reassure his readers (and perhaps himself) that "we in Ghana are making our plans and shall strive unremittedly to raise our people to such higher levels of civilised living as we are able to do by our own exertions." While these tabula rasa reminiscences were written long after the fact partly in an effort to justify some of his controversial political choices, they do draw attention to the complicated birth of new nations. Ghana was hardly a unique case, as parts of French Africa suffered a similar fate. Guinea, for example, had been the sole African territory that refused de Gaulle's 1958 offer of increased autonomy within a French Union of African States, and voted for independence. After the vote, French colonial technicians and civil officials were instructed to quit Guinea immediately, after which they destroyed all remnants of their colonial government in order to punish Guinea for its unexpected defiance. The new Guinean president, Sékou Touré, was left with the same impression as Nkrumah. In November 1959, Touré delivered a lecture at Chatham House in London in which he also noted that "we were left with nothing, not a document, not even the Legal Code." Similar developments took place in Kenya, where the most incriminating documents were flown back to London, while some were reportedly dumped in the sea; the same went for Algeria after the long war with France, as French Algeria's administrative archives were shipped back to France after independence, where they are still held and to this day remain a bone of contention between France and Algeria.[4]

Even so, there were strong continuities with the European past as these new leaders worked to forge a new map for the future. This uneasy inheritance affected all newly independent states in Asia and Africa at the time, whether these countries had won their independence through war or peace. It also had to do with the equally difficult challenge of reviving—or really, reinventing—indigenous cultural traditions as a foundation of political legitimacy. This chapter addresses the making of new national identities in Ghana, Algeria, and Senegal, in part based on conjoining a precolonial past with a postcolonial present. This may at first seem odd, since much of the scholarship on postcolonial Africa has worked within the parameters of modernity and modernization, and postindependence leaders were not shy in using large modern technological projects—most famously, the Aswan Dam in Egypt and the Volta Dam in Ghana—to showcase the coming of modernity and the long-wished-for rupture from the colonial legacy. The concept of civilization, by contrast, was—and still is—often seen as the awkward hangover from an unwanted colonial heritage.

Still, the language of civilization continued to inform European-African cultural connections even after the end of empire, and was co-opted by African anticolonial elites for new political purposes in the 1960s. Whereas the language of civilization had long been used to justify European expansion and empire, it was now seized and recast as an ideology of anti-imperialism, non-European sovereignty, and national identity for new African states. It was common knowledge that China and India possessed rich and ancient civilizations that had been recognized by international observers for centuries. However, similar recognition was not accorded to Africa outside Egypt, and thus the assertion of African civilization as separate and equally vibrant took on heightened political significance in former European colonies in the aftermath of decolonization. Such claims helped to strengthen the legitimacy of the new postcolonial states of Ghana, Algeria, and Senegal as modern polities rooted in the past. These examples may be quite disparate—one is Anglophone, two Francophone; one was shaped by the British doctrine of indirect rule, the others by French imperial republicanism. Two of them experienced peaceful handovers, while one was engulfed in bloody conflict for nearly a decade. But in each case, the long-maligned term civilization became a favorite rhetorical weapon to turn the tables on former European overlords and to redefine the relationship between Africa and Europe. How and to what extent the most European of ideologies was transplanted in Africa by Africans is the main question at hand.

NKRUMAH SOUGHT TO OVERCOME THE SENSE OF CULTURAL rupture by restoring the place of long-denigrated African traditions. For starters, the renaming of the Gold Coast as Ghana was intended to signal the rebirth of the region's ancient African Akan empire. Nkrumah was a committed nationalist and advocate for African political union, and was keen to forge a nonaligned cultural identity. Ghana hosted a series of pan-African conferences in the late 1950s with the aim of reviving the pan-African dream of continental unity from the interwar period. The Ghana-Guinea Union of the late 1950s was the first postcolonial confederation in Africa, as each country ceded some sovereignty over its territory in the name of greater union. The new Ghanaian president's mix of ideology and personal ruling style was so distinctive that the period gave rise to a neologism, *Nkrumahism*, understood as a blend of Ghanaian nationalism, African socialism, and pan-Africanism.[5]

Nkrumah took a keen interest in the cultural affairs of the state and the forging of a new Ghanaian national identity. He oversaw the creation of numerous cultural institutions and museums, and obsessively presided over the appointment of teaching posts at the University of Ghana at Legon. In his eyes, political independence had to be fortified by the decolonization of African culture. In his 1961 book, *I Speak of Freedom: A Statement of African Ideology*, he addressed the legacy of British imperialism in starkly psychological terms: "We were trained to be inferior copies of Englishmen, caricatures to be laughed at with our pretensions to British bourgeois gentility," making us "neither fish nor fowl. We were denied the knowledge of our African past and informed that we had no present." When he opened the First International Congress of Africanists in Accra in December 1962, Nkrumah intoned that European education "was directed at estranging us from our own cultures in order to more effectively serve a new and alien interest. In rediscovering and revitalizing our cultural and spiritual heritage and values, African Studies must help to redirect this new endeavour." The creation of the Institute of African Studies at the University of Ghana in 1961 was designed to fulfill this mission. Nkrumah opened the new institute by saying that its "essential function" was to "study the history, culture and institutions, languages and arts of Ghana and of Africa in new African centred ways—in entire freedom from the propositions and pre-suppositions of the colonial epoch." The institute, he believed, would attract those "who wish seriously to devote themselves to a study of Africa and African civilisations." Its library contained a substantial body of Arabic and Hausa documents that demonstrated indigenous scholarly production in Ghana, including royal "stool histories," oral traditions, and poetry in and beyond Ghana itself.[6]

Ghana's Independence Day celebrations endeavored to blend traditional culture and forward-looking modernity. Nkrumah's showcasing of African heritage and cultural unity was explicitly intended to downplay alternative tribal representations. Traditional dancing and drumming were featured at the festivities, but regional flags and emblems were not. Nkrumah himself was a member of a minority ethnic group—the Nazima, from the Western Region—and the Ga and Asante were the main ethnic groups in the country. Certain regional idioms were expressed in the featured dance events, but the explicit overall message was one of national unity. Promotion of indigenous culture was viewed as fundamental to the construction of Ghana's national and international identity. While Nkrumah himself wore a Western suit for the 1957 transfer-of-power ceremony, he donned a traditional chief's *kente* robes for high-level state occasions (like his speeches at the UN) to shore up his political legitimacy as the symbolic trans-tribal leader of the new African nation.[7]

Nkrumah's claim that the British simply taught Ghanaians to despise their traditions may have served his broader ideological agenda, but it was not strictly true, at least not in the cultural sphere. A good example of the cultivated preservation of traditional African art before independence was the pioneering Achimota School outside Accra, which trained an indigenous elite of Gold Coast political figures and artists, including Nkrumah himself, as well as Kofi Antubam, Amon Kotei, and Vincent Kofi. Even if the school was originally founded in 1927 by the British colonial administration, those Europeans hired to teach there did not simply peddle ahistorical ideas about African "primitive culture." Rather, they were convinced that modern African culture could combine indigenous heritage with European forms. Teachers at the school rejected the long-standing Christian denigration of traditional African art pieces as "fetish" objects and instead extolled the value of African tradition. Instead of the French ideal of assimilation, the school reflected the British approach of adaptation in training a new elite in the spirit of indirect rule. Achimota's curriculum devoted great energy to helping students recover indigenous African art forms in their studies, what one art historian has described as the "Bauhausing of West African crafts." The point is that there were strong continuities between colonial and postcolonial eras in art and culture, despite being downplayed or ignored by Nkrumah and Ghanaian cultural authorities at the time.[8]

The Ghanaian artist most associated with Nkrumah's cultural mission was Kofi Antubam. Antubam was a son of a chief, and a graduate of the Achimota School. Antubam studied at Goldsmiths College in London, and his work was featured in the 1947 *Neo-African Art* exhibition at the British Council in Accra. Antubam knew Nkrumah well, and shared his political outlook. In one speech Antubam lamented the way in which "our traditions and cultural patterns" have been "devoured in the wake of the ethnocentricism [*sic*] of the colonisers." For him the "time for the sort of grotesque, African art that belongs to the solitary shades of forest graveyards, or the mushroom grown shelves and galleries of dark ethnological museums," was "long past," and synthesizing the old and the new was the way of the future. Antubam was commissioned to design some of the most memorable political art at the Independence Day ceremonies, including the Asante Golden Stool for Nkrumah, which became a new national symbol of sovereignty, tradition, and power. Until that point, swords, royal seats, clothes, jewelry, and carvings had been part of the panoply of tribal regalia. And since Ghana had no tradition of the art of writing, the finery of Ghanaian chiefs assumed special significance. Antubam's specially designed presidential chair and other symbols of state for Nkrumah were modern versions of these traditional paraphernalia of power (Figure 23). Antubam also painted portraits of prominent Ghanaians, executed wood reliefs for Accra's Central Library and the main assembly hall of the Ghana Parliament building, and designed the immense mosaic featuring traditional Ghanaian figures for the exterior of the Accra Community Center. His work was the visual expression of Nkrumah's concept of the African Personality as a blend of old and new, and was inseparable from the country's first leader.[9]

Figure 23. President Kwame Nkrumah in Parliament, Accra, Ghana, 1960, with presidential seat designed by Kofi Antubam. *Credit: AFP, Getty Images*

After 1957 there was a flurry of initiatives to nationalize Ghanaian culture. The former Arts Council of the Gold Coast was renamed as the Arts Council of Ghana, whose aim was to "foster, improve and preserve the traditional arts and culture of Ghana." The cultural takeover could be seen in film too. In 1948 the British Colonial Film Unit had been established in the Gold Coast "to avail the Gold Coasters of British civilization and also the high standard of civilization that we [the British] ourselves enjoy." It was the first film school in West Africa designed to train film students in the British colonies. After independence the Colonial Film Unit was repurposed to burnish the image of Nkrumah's Ghana with similar colonial-era propaganda techniques. In the early 1960s the Arts Council founded a National Theatre Movement as well. Nkrumah was inspired by early Soviet models of taking socialist culture to the countryside after the Russian Revolution, and Ghanaian theater troupes were encouraged to do similar community-building work. Traveling theater troupes staged contemporary skits about the issues facing the country for rural audiences. As such they served as "living magazines" that transmitted urban fashions, highlife music, dance, and ideas to nonliterate sections of the vast countryside, and in so doing helped develop a sense of Ghanaian national culture as an idiom of modern civilization.[10]

Moving forward was not simply a matter of expunging the stain of imperialism—it was also predicated on reconnecting to the ancient past. In 1942 Nana Sir Ofori Atta I, a leading Gold Coast intellectual, published a book called *Chiefancy in Modern Africa, with Special Reference to the Gold Coast*. In it Atta I claimed that "I regard it as a great pity for any country which boasts of civilization to have no real foundation in its own tradition or to rely upon no traditional background. The people of such a country become, so to speak, 'characterless.'" The statesman and historian J. B. Danquah, in his 1944 book, *The Akan Doctrine of God: A Fragment of Gold Coast Ethics and Religion*, argued that inhabitants of the region were linked to the ancient kingdom of Ghana (Danquah is often credited with giving Ghana its name). While both men later became strong critics of Nkrumah's authoritarianism, Nkrumah furthered their ideas of grounding the new state in precolonial civilization. At the first Conference of Independent African States on April 19, 1958, he made clear that antiquity must form the basis of any new African identity, an antiquity that had been disregarded or misread by colonizers, European historians, and various indigenous rulers. For him there were "no limits to ways in which we on this African continent can enrich our knowledge of our past civilisations and cultural heritage through our cooperative efforts and the pooling of our scientific and technical resources."[11]

Ancient history was identified as an important source of political legitimacy for new nations. Efforts to reaffirm the value and achievements of African traditions had been present in the 1930s, perhaps most notably in Jomo Kenyatta's anthropological study *Facing Mount Kenya*, published in 1938. In it, Kenyatta, who eventually became the first leader of independent Kenya, celebrated traditional Kikuyu ways as the foundation of East African civilization. Western scholars also lent their support to the concept of African civilization. In the 1950s there were a number of books published on the theme of African humanity, its intellectual capacities and moral evolution, many by Francophone scholars. In the Anglophone world, Raymond Michelet's *African Empires and Civilisations* (1945) and J. C. de Graft-Johnson's *African Glory: The Story of Vanished Negro Civilizations* (1954), as well as the works by Georges Balandier, all challenged old ideas of African communities as "living fossils" and "frozen societies." In a special 1957 issue of *United Asia* dedicated to celebrate Ghanaian independence, British archaeologist Basil Davidson contended that it mattered little "whether or not the Akan are in direct descent from ancient Ghana. What matters is that they can reasonably claim to have inherited much of the tradition and civilisation of that notable African kingdom of the distant past." "And that is why the Gold Coast of today," Davidson continued, "can look back on twelve hundred years of history—on a pageant of humanity whose poverty and whose riches are one with the universal story of mankind." The repeated use of the word civilization was typical of the time, meant to dispel old colonial prejudices that Africans were peoples without history or culture. The reclamation of African civilization—by African leaders and intellectuals, with support from international experts—was evidence of sovereignty and arrival.[12]

In building a new Ghanaian culture around the ruins and symbols of the ancient past, there were other issues that complicated the construction of national identity. Nkrumah's melancholy recollection of the lack of any administrative handover was only one dimension of the transition—the other side was the enduring legacy of the colonial material inheritance itself, starting with the old seat of the Gold Coast's colonial administration, Christiansborg Castle. The castle was first built in 1652 as a small trading lodge by the Swedish African Company, and in 1661 was acquired by Danish merchants who rebuilt it as a castle from which they ran their commercial affairs until the British arrived in 1873 and refashioned it as their colonial headquarters. In 1957 it was taken over as the government seat of independent Ghana, making the building a symbol of precolonial, colonial, and postcolonial heritage all at once. These castles were presented as symbols of a colonial past that had been overcome. In the late 1950s the government devoted substantial resources to renovating ancient castles around the country for the sake of national culture and to generate tourist revenues, including Elmina and Cape Coast Castles. The endeavor to nationalize ancient artifacts could also be noted in a new ordinance passed by the country's Museums and Monuments Board that declared that ancient relics found during Nkrumah's extension of Christiansborg Castle in 1960 (pots, beads, and brasswork) would be managed by the national Board "in the interest of Ghana."[13]

Just as tricky was the colonial architectural heritage. Forging a new cultural identity from the ruins of empire was no easy task, not least because it wasn't at all clear what Ghanaian identity actually was. The commissioned new architecture of postcolonial Accra pointed up this problem, and tended to blend colonial and postcolonial styles. Some of the most high-profile new state buildings in Accra were designed by the famous British husband-and-wife team of Maxwell Fry and Jane Drew in the style they called Tropical Modernism. Fry and Drew opened a Department of Tropical Architecture at London's Architectural Association in 1955, and developed their Bauhaus-inspired ideas of a new universal approach to building in tropical climates by "interpreting applied science in humanistic terms." Theirs was a late-colonial aesthetic that drew on the Central European interwar International Style to modernize both British colonial architecture and indigenous building idioms, as evidenced in their work in Ghana, Nigeria, and India. For them, the point was not simply to impose a European style on Ghana, but rather to synthesize British and

Figure 24. Wesley Girls' School, Cape Coast, Ghana (Fry, Drew and Partners, c. 1953). *Credit:* Architectural Review, *May 1953*

African modernism. British tropical architecture exerted great influence on Ghanaian town planning both before and after independence. Such functionalist styling was read as the visual vocabulary of modernity and progress, with Fry and Drew combining a Fabian socialist sensibility with Nkrumah's notion of African socialism, as noted in Figure 24. Nkrumah may have been committed to the revival of African traditionalism, but he was also keen to exploit this modernist style as the face of his new forward-looking regime. His government constructed housing, hospitals, and schools as emblems of political legitimacy, social welfare, and effective self-rule. Science museums were built around the capital, including the Geology Museum (1964) and the Museum of Ethnography (1964), which explicitly conveyed a strong modern message. Local architects were also involved—London-trained Ghanaian architect John Owusu Addo designed several buildings at the Kwame Nkrumah University of Science and Technology in Kumasi. Yet

during Nkrumah's reign much of Ghanaian postcolonial architecture was influenced by the British Tropical Modernism school,
even if there was also a notable strain from Eastern Europe as well,
which will be discussed in Chapter 8.[14]

Perhaps the most telling example of the contradictory aspects of
the country's cultural identity was the National Museum of Ghana,
opened just a few days after independence in March 1957. It was a
consciously modern building designed by Fry and Drew, crowned
with an aluminum dome in recognizable International Style. It made
no reference to vernacular architecture, and was hailed as the visual
embodiment of democracy, modernity, and internationalism—the
foundational values of Ghana's new national identity (Figure 25).
Things were far less simple, however, when it came to choosing the
artifacts that went inside the museum. While the building's shell
was designed to communicate universalism and modernity, the objects on display were selected to connect independent Ghana to its
indigenous precolonial past. Complicating things was the fact that
the museum's collection was based on artifacts discovered during
commercial mining excavations in the 1920s and put together by
British ethnographers, which drew awkward continuities between
the colonial and postcolonial period.[15] Many of Nkrumah's political opponents were also skeptical of the link between socialism
and culture, and resisted his centralizing program at the expense
of regional power alignments. Various Ghanaian chieftains thus
did not want their regional or tribal artifacts displayed as part of
Nkrumah's larger narrative of a unified socialist nation, or even of
pan-Africanism. The first show that opened in Ghana's new national
museum was the *Man in Africa* display in 1957, whose centerpiece
was an ensemble of sixty Akan stools as the symbolic center of the
nation, but which represented only one of the four ethnolinguistic
groups in the country. It was precisely this problem of reconciling
tribal, national, and pan-African ideologies that bedeviled the new
museum and Nkrumah's larger cultural politics.[16]

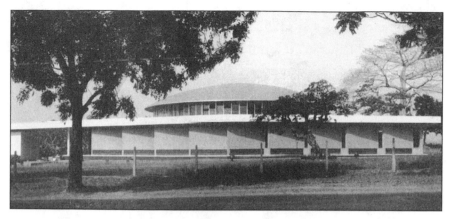

Figure 25. Maxwell Fry and Jane Drew, National Museum, Accra, Ghana, 1957. *Credit: "Works in the Tropics by Drake & Lasdun,"* Architectural Design, *February 1958, 78–79*

Even so, civilization was a usefully elastic term that could bridge divergent and at times contradictory identities associated with multiethnic postcolonial states. Ghana's effort to repurpose past and present was not unique, but rather was the first sub-Saharan attempt to give shape to what a postimperial African civilization might look like once the Europeans were gone.

ALGERIA WAS A RADICALLY DIFFERENT SITUATION, AND ITS WAR with France became one of the defining conflicts of the second half of the twentieth century. The Algerian War was inseparable from the emergence of militant Third Worldism at the international level, and served as the lightning rod for anticolonial radicalism around the globe. Arguments of civilization were militarized by both the French and Algerian sides to give meaning to their roles in the violent conflict. As one French diplomat posted in Algiers in the early 1960s put it, such anticolonial radicalism sharply "rejected the inertia of Western civilization and counted on the youth of the world, who sought to liberate themselves once and for all."

The war generated a huge amount of international attention, and was the most closely watched story of decolonization. For its part, the National Liberation Front, or FLN, was inspired by Nasser and Nkrumah's pan-African solidarity as well as Marshal Tito's non-aligned socialism. Egypt in particular played a pivotal role in lending military and moral support to the anti-French struggle, and Yugoslavia's military and humanitarian aid helped turn this French civil war into a cauldron of anticolonial struggle more generally. The war became a rallying point for much of Africa, and Frantz Fanon, the French West Indian psychiatrist who served as the FLN's roaming ambassador, inspired radicals in countries more associated with the peaceful transition of power, including Ghana.[17]

According to recent estimates, the war claimed the lives of between 300,000 and 500,000 Algerians and displaced many more. More than 2 million French armed forces personnel served in Algeria from 1954 to 1962, and around 25,000 French imperial soldiers and perhaps another 3,000 civilian European settlers died in the conflict. It was both an imperial and civil war at the same time, and its official designation as a "police action" or "pacification operation" did little to hide its brutal nature. Terrorism was practiced on both sides, and only intensified as the war went on. Torture, rape, and summary executions were common, as was the public display and parading of corpses. The main instruments of killing in this war—the knife, razor, and homemade bombs—bespoke the intimacy of brutal violence. So whereas Ghana was celebrated for its peaceful handover, the long and bloody struggle for Algerian independence marked a different kind of divorce between Europe and Africa. But like Ghana's fight for independence, the Algerian War was shaped by the demands of self-determination and the making of a postimperial identity—and the rhetoric of civilization was central to it.[18]

Algeria had been a favorite rallying point for international justice since the mid-nineteenth century. The French defeat of the Ottoman regency in Algiers in 1830 was celebrated as a victory of Christian civilization. After Algiers was conquered, a Te Deum of grace and a mass were celebrated at Notre Dame Cathedral in Paris and in the Casbah on July 11, 1830. The French commander in chief extolled the Christian victory in a speech before the chaplains: "You have just opened with us the door to Christianity in Africa. Let's hope that it will rekindle the civilization that has been extinguished." These nineteenth-century French offensives into Algeria raised the moral issue of the proper conduct of warfare, especially following the scorched-earth policy of Marshal Thomas Robert Bugeaud, which culminated in the deliberate smoke suffocation of 500 Algerians in 1845 in a grotto in Dahra. Alexis de Tocqueville, usually regarded as an apologist of French imperial expansion in Algeria, expressed misgivings during his Algerian sojourn, writing in his notebook, "I returned from Africa with the distressing notion that we are now fighting far more barbarously than the Arabs themselves. For the present, it is on their side that one meets with civilization." A century later the debate about France's imperial conduct in general and use of torture in particular during the Algerian War became one of the great moral controversies of midcentury international relations.[19]

By the late 1950s the Algerian War had become synonymous with revolutionary violence, and was given intellectual force by the war's principal theorist, Frantz Fanon. Fanon was a psychiatrist who originated from Martinique and joined the FLN army in 1955. His 1961 international bombshell, *The Wretched of the Earth*, became a touchstone text for Third World insurrectionary violence in the age of decolonization, calling for the colonial world's forceful emancipation from the physical and psychological yoke of settler colonialism and European civilization. In his writings he built on the work of the Martinique poet and publicist Aimé Césaire. Césaire opened his widely read *Discourse on Colonialism*, published in 1950, with a frontal attack on the violent hypocrisy of European civilization: "A civilization that proves incapable of solving the problems it creates is a decadent civilization," and a "civilization that chooses to use its principles for trickery and deceit is a dying civilization." In his eyes, "'Western' civilization" was unable to solve "the two major problems to which its existence has given rise: the problem of the proletariat, and the colonial problem; that Europe is unable to justify itself either before the bar of 'reason' or before the bar of 'conscience.'" Here Césaire blended Marxism and anticolonialism to condemn the original sin of European civilization, namely colonialism as a failed attempt to "civilize barbarism." Like Fanon, he saw colonial violence as not only damaging to its victims, but also to its perpetrators. Europe had ruined itself through its colonial enterprise, he wrote, to the extent that "colonization works to decivilize the colonizer." With rhetorical flourish he concluded that the great irony is that Europeans "thought they were only slaughtering Indians, or Hindus, or South Sea Islanders, or Africans." Instead, "they have in fact overthrown, one after another, the ramparts behind which European civilization could have developed freely."[20]

The Algerian War saw the fusion of the nineteenth-century ideology of the civilizing mission with French republicanism and welfare paternalism. The stalemate between French and Algerian forces in the early years of the war led to the call from the French conservative establishment and military elite to bring back Charles de Gaulle to take command of the war and save the Fourth Republic. With the general's return to power in 1958, the French government redoubled its civilizing mission of modernization and the winning-over of moderate Algerians. De Gaulle's so-called Constantine Plan was devised with this end in mind. While various reform initiatives had been circulating since the late 1940s, this plan was a much more comprehensive vision of social and economic reconstruction designed to reconcile republican values and the imperial state. It was a program of social engineering that would transform Muslim Algerians into productive modern Frenchmen, based in large measure on the resettlement of millions of Algerians in thousands of new labor camps and villages in the name of progress and pacification. Such militant colonial paternalism penetrated deep into the countryside and set out to remake the fabric of "backward" Algerian everyday life. It marked a new marriage of social planning and American-style social science aimed at breaking the cycle of underdevelopment in the region. As one official bulletin put it, Algeria "must conquer, by its labor and for all its inhabitants, its full participation in the civilization of the twentieth century." As historian James McDougall notes, the new civilizing mission was "indistinguishable from submission to a 'second conquest'—of their land and of themselves." The late 1950s plan for Algeria dovetailed with similar schemes rolled out in the metropole at the time aimed at integrating Algerians already living in French cities. From the late 1940s through to the end of the war in 1962, the French state offered expanded services (housing, language instruction, job training, and welfare benefits) to the 300,000 Algerian migrants residing in the metropole in an effort to maintain control of Algeria.[21]

Military strategy complemented economic policies. In fact, France's counterinsurgency campaign was also couched in the terms of a new civilizing mission in Algeria. Here the values of civilization were used to justify military brutality and the existential demands of the imperial republic. In his first General Directive as newly appointed government representative in Algiers in 1956, hardliner Robert Lacoste stated that the "war we are waging in this country is that of the Western World, of civilization against anarchy, democracy against dictatorship." In April 1959 Colonel André Lalande, adjutant to the chief of the general staff for psychological operations in Algiers, provided the rationale for counterterrorism in his indoctrination sessions of newly drafted soldiers: "We are defending France, our motherland, which is made not only of men and of goods but of the very values of our civilization, founded on the dignity and the development of Mankind; here, we are fighting in the vanguard of the free world." At stake was nothing less than French civilization itself, and printed versions of Lalande's lectures were distributed in the thousands to French troops. The passionate French defense of civilization was hardly confined to military circles, and had popular echoes. Jean Lartéguy's bestselling novel *The Centurions*, published in 1960, recounted the dedication and exploits of French paratroopers in Algeria who protected imperial France in the name of anticommunism and Western civilization. Many of the characters in the book found a new moral mission in Algeria after having fought in and been defeated in the Battle of Dien Bien Phu in French Indochina. This was hardly fiction: Colonel Marcel Bigeard recounted in his memoir how "every evening we sat around the light of the paraffin lamps, talking about Dien Bien Phu and our dead comrades," and "also spoke of the present war [in Algeria] and how we needed to win it very quickly." The humiliating French withdrawal from Indochina made the defense of French empire all the more vital in Algeria.[22]

By the late 1950s the war had become a burning issue at the United Nations and generated a good deal of debate about human rights in the General Assembly. In its first letters to the UN in 1955 and 1956, the FLN framed its struggle in the language of human rights violations and the right to self-determination, citing mass arrests, the outlawing of national political parties, the banning of newspapers, and the arbitrary seizure of homes as evidence of the French government's breaching of international law. The rebels were effective in winning support from other developing countries at the General Assembly on these grounds, citing the UN Charter as justification. Like their counterparts from imperial Belgium and Portugal whom we encountered in Chapter 5, French UN representatives were caught off guard. In response to Algerian charges of injustice, the French adamantly refused to discuss Algeria at the United Nations, deeming the conflict a domestic matter immaterial to the international body. Neither the General Assembly nor the designated Special Committee on Colonial Affairs agreed, as the admission of seventeen new UN members from Africa in 1960 tipped the balance of opinion away from France and the colonial powers. Newly independent Guinea and Mali led the attack against the savagery of French actions in Algeria. In protest the French angrily withdrew from any UN debate on Algeria after 1958, marking the first boycott lodged against the international body since the Soviet walkout over the nonrecognition of Mao's China in the Security Council in 1950.[23]

Instead, the French devoted great energy to launching an international media campaign to win over international public opinion. They enlisted members of their UN staff in New York to this task. The French embassy secured assurances from the *New York Times* that the newspaper would be supportive of the French, and arranged for delegations of *pied noirs* (French settlers who lived in Algeria during French rule) and Francophone Muslims to tour the US to defend the empire and draw attention to the dangers of Soviet encroachments in Africa. A 1956 French government memorandum dispatched to all its embassies stated that "our troubles in Algeria inscribe themselves in a great conflict that, since the end of the war, has set the East against the West. It is about more than a clash of different political visions: it is a clash of two civilizations." Western European press echoed this Francocentric version of the war as an epic defense of "Western Civilization" against "Islamic fanaticism." Growing American knowledge of the torture and bloodshed in Algeria, however, meant that French propagandists had to change tack. After 1958 French publicists shifted the propaganda for international audiences from the usual "civilization versus barbarism" to the benefits of development, modernization, and the virtues of continued integration.[24]

Even so, more and more information was being leaked back to France about what was happening in Algeria. Drip-feed public revelations of misconduct and atrocities by French soldiers stirred passionate debate and soul-searching about the fate of imperial France and its republican tradition. Details of the unsavory war were increasingly reported by mainstream press at the time, and disturbing photographic coverage spilled into bestselling outlets like *Paris Match* and *Life* magazine in the United States. While most of the discussion centered on the actions of French paramilitary fighters in Algeria, the capital did not go untouched by the direct violence of the war. On October 17, 1961, over 200 Algerians were killed and thrown into the Seine River, on the order of the notorious police prefect of Paris Maurice Papon, who was later convicted (in 1998) of crimes against humanity for his role in deporting 1,600 Jews to concentration camps during the Nazi occupation. By the late 1950s some of the biggest luminaries of the Left Bank intellectual scene were brandishing their pens against the war itself. Marguerite Duras, Jean-Paul Sartre, Albert Camus, and Simone de Beauvoir were involved in the Action Committee of Intellectuals Against the Pursuit of the War in Algeria. Camus later broke away, in part because he had grown up as a *pied noir* in Algiers and always considered Algeria integral to France. As he put it in 1955, "the choice in Algeria" was "between a marriage of convenience and a marriage of death for two xenophobias." All the way until his untimely demise in a car crash in January 1960, Camus defended the preservation of French Algeria, and pushed for political federation between the two countries as an emblem of the unity in diversity of two cultures. But his views were more of a diminishing minority taste, especially among intellectuals, and the split between Sartre, de Beauvoir, and their former friend Camus dramatized the combustible nature of the Algerian conflict across French intellectual life.[25]

By this time the Algerian War had become a battle over images of humanity and inhumanity, as both sides turned to the media to publicize their respective cause, often mobilizing the language of civilization for their ends. By the mid-1950s scandalous images of brutality were circulating in the French press, kicking off wide discussion about their veracity and significance. French and Algerians alike published pamphlets brimming with graphic photographs of atrocities, reminiscent of the media war over sensationalized killings during the Spanish Civil War. In the mid-1950s the French government produced a series of atrocity books, including *Documents sur les crimes et attentats commis en Algérie par les terrorists* (1956) and *Aspects véritables de la rébellion algérienne* (1957). They attempted to raise the moral stakes of the battle by accusing the rebels of transgressing civilization itself through their heinous acts. The 1956 *Documents* booklet chronicled the atrocities of "a few groups of terrorists directed by proven bandits" whose "barbaric" actions "have been nothing but an uninterrupted succession of crimes against humanity, against civilisation, against progress." The book makes for difficult reading, splashed as it is with dozens of gruesome photographs of mutilated, dismembered, and tortured corpses, often with slit throats, severed heads, and the amputated noses of unlucky teachers, women, children, and old people. The destruction of Algeria's material infrastructure was documented as well, as decimated French-built hospitals and schools "stand as a silent monument to the barbarism of a movement which claims to be the liberator of the people." The French military also included gruesome photographs in leaflets distributed to conscripts returning home from active duty in the late 1950s, not only to steel resolve but also to make soldiers aware of the global struggle "undertaken against the West by the ambitious leaders of pan-Arabism in the service of Soviet communism." French colonial minister Robert Lacoste reportedly mailed graphic photographs to influential editors and writers to enlist moral support. All told, the French state churned out no fewer than 1.65 million pages of propaganda after the Battle of Algiers, the FLN's urban guerrilla warfare campaign against French Algerian authorities in 1956–1957. This was a war waged in the international media as much as it was in Algerian cities and villages.[26]

The FLN responded in kind, printing its own shocking brochures to draw attention to its cause. The FLN established an

Algerian public relations office in New York to counter French propaganda. From 1958 to 1961, the FLN produced forty-six pamphlets on various aspects of the Algerian struggle and organized numerous media events in New York. Examples included *Genocide in Algeria* (June 1958) and *French Church Leaders Denounce Army's Excesses and Use of Torture in Algeria* (April 1959). In the 1958 brochure *Genocide in Algeria*, the FLN even used the term genocide to describe counterinsurgency. Another 1961 book claimed that French behavior in Algeria "seems to have developed into a consistent defiance of every humanitarian principle. All attempts to humanize it which have been made over the last seven years have been without success."[27]

But it was the issue of torture that caught the most attention, sparking passionate discussions of barbarism and civilization. In 1958 Sartre wrote that torture "is neither civilian nor military, nor is it specifically French: it is a plague infecting our whole era." Justification of torture emerged from the doctrine of revolutionary war developed by a group of French veterans of colonial wars, especially in Indochina. French field manuals issued for special operations in Indochina in the early 1950s permitted hostage-taking and disregard toward civilians in areas of Indochinese resistance. In a lecture at a training center for counterinsurgency in 1952, French colonel Charles Lacheroy breezily shrugged that "one does not fight a revolutionary war with the Code Napoleon." French colonial authorities viewed the Algerian liberation movement as a band of criminals, not legitimate soldiers, which placed them outside humanitarian law. One French colonel encapsulated the sentiment: "We don't take prisoners," for "these men are not soldiers." Under General Raoul Salan, who took charge of all French forces in Algeria at the end of 1956, this doctrine meant fighting the rebels with their own means—propaganda, guerilla tactics, and psychological warfare. In Salan's eyes, this war was no less than "the last battle for White Christian Civilization in the northern part of Africa."[28]

Accusations about torture started to circulate in the French press. In the early 1950s they had been occasionally aired in the mainstream press by the likes of Resistance veteran against Nazi occupation Claude Bourdet and Catholic writer François Mauriac, but revelations increasingly circulated after 1957, not least from demobilized reservists. Discussion spilled out from Left Bank cafés and literary journals into mainstream French society. The churches voiced their moral concerns about the conduct of the war by French soldiers, and the Vatican issued condemnations of French military behavior in the late 1950s; other church leaders defended the "sacred union" of the army, the state, and the Church. By the late 1950s, the issue of torture exploded as a major public issue in Paris.[29]

Henri Alleg's memoir, *The Question,* unleashed a storm of controversy when it was published in 1958. He had been a communist editor of the left-wing, pro-independence daily *Alger Républicain* from 1950 to 1955. Once the newspaper was banned, Alleg went into hiding and was arrested in Algiers by paratroopers in 1957 and then transferred to an internment camp outside the city. His book was an unvarnished chronicle of the beatings, electric torture, and brutality visited upon him by the French army in Algeria, and became an overnight sensation. It sold 60,000 copies in the first two weeks, and continued to enjoy massive sales in France. It was Alleg's distinctly dispassionate and nonjudgmental tone that made it so powerful, recounting at one point how he was "attached to a black board, streaked with humidity, and soiled with the sticky vomit undoubtedly left over by other 'clients.'" So controversial was the book that the reprinted run was seized by the police as treasonous in that it supposedly demoralized the serving army, marking the first time that a book was censored by the French authorities since the eighteenth century. Jean-Paul Sartre's follow-up defense of the book in the newspaper *L'Express* was also seized by the police by order of the minister of the interior. Most disturbing was Sartre's acid comment about the shallowness of French moral recovery after

Nazi occupation: "Appalled, the French are discovering this terrible truth: that if nothing can protect a nation against itself, neither its traditions nor its loyalties nor its laws, and if fifteen years are enough to transform victims into executioners, then its behavior is not more than a matter of opportunity and occasion. Anybody, at any time, may equally find himself victim or executioner." What he was describing was the de-civilization of the metropole.[30]

Another famous event was the trial of the Algerian young woman Djamila Boupacha, who lodged a court case against her torturers for their crimes. She had been arrested in 1960 and taken to the El Biar detention center, where she was tortured and raped by French forces. Wartime maltreatment of Algerian women was common, as homes and bodies were routinely searched, and rape was reportedly a routine occurrence. Captured FLN female fighters were subjected to physical torture and abuse as well. Boupacha was accused of having planted a bomb at the University of Algiers on behalf of the FLN. Since there were no witnesses, she was tortured to extract a confession. Her case became a cause célèbre, leading to the publication of another bestseller, *Djamila Boupacha*, edited by her lawyer Gisèle Halimi and Simone de Beauvoir. In the book, Boupacha recounted her thirty-three-day ordeal at the hands of French army soldiers as part of her legal defense, which included harrowing accounts of beatings, electric shocks, cigarette burns, and sexual assault. The book was supplemented by testimonies by leading French public figures, ranging from journalist Daniel Mayer to popular writer Françoise Sagan, several of whom pointed to the crisis of Judeo-Christian civilization or French civilization that the trial provoked. One contributor posed the question—isn't it now "impossible to persuade populations to remain French in the name of civilization which offers so macabre an image?" Sagan best captured the seamy underside of the trumpeted glories of civilization in writing that "I do not believe that the fanfares of grandeur could ever drown the screams of a young girl."[31]

While the FLN was winning in the court of public opinion, it was in the realm of humanitarian law where the FLN scored its greatest moral victory. The broader international debate on torture pivoted on the legal attempt to civilize warfare, which took the form of pressing for the application of the 1949 Geneva Conventions, discussed in Chapter 4. More than any other conflict, the Algerian War tested the limits of the Geneva Conventions, and it was the issue of legitimate warfare and the legal status of rebels that proved most controversial. The FLN went on the offensive to win over the international community—it began by claiming that it was a "nation-party" and thus the authentic voice of the Algerian people. Its struggle with the French, so it reasoned, was a war of national liberation whose fighters were entitled to protection by international legal norms. Part of the effort to underscore the rebels' moral legitimacy was to declare that the FLN was committed to upholding agreed international principles of war and justice. In 1958 the FLN released fifty prisoners as a gesture to prompt "the progressive humanization of the war on the French side." In its 1960 *White Paper on the Application of the Geneva Conventions of 1949 to the French-Algerian Conflict*, the provisional government of the Algerian Republic—the FLN's government-in-exile based in Cairo—included testimonies from French soldiers, Algerian Red Crescent reports, international press, and recent French publications that accused the French military of torture, reprisals, and summary executions. The FLN's own record of treatment of French POWs was hardly impeccable, but the International Committee of the Red Cross was permitted to visit and inspect FLN detention centers (the French refused access to theirs) in February 1958. Here the FLN and the Algerian Red Crescent were effectively converting the language of humanitarianism into usable political capital. Whereas the French balked that such international humanitarian norms were immaterial to this conflict, the FLN countered in its 1960 *White Paper* that such conventions "must govern and determine the treatment of man by man if *our* civilization is to be worthy of the name." Notably, the FLN invoked the idea of "our" shared civilization in the singular as a kind of international moral community suffering from imperial abuse. The cry of civilization was refashioned as a claim against the imperial powers by colonial peoples themselves.[32]

In 1960 the FLN stepped up its publicity campaign at the UN and Red Cross. It sent a permanent delegation to Geneva to argue its case for self-determination in the spirit of the UN General Assembly's resolution earlier that year, the Declaration of the Granting of Independence to Colonial Countries and Peoples, which had made self-determination a human right. When the Red Cross's 270-page report on allegations of French torture in Algerian detention camps was leaked to *Le Monde* in 1960, exposing the French mistreatment of Algerian prisoners at eighty-two detention sites (complete with names and details), it sparked a fresh media scandal. At first the French government denied the allegations, but soon was forced to concede the Red Cross findings, after which many of the centers were closed down. The French government was forced to acknowledge that the war was no longer strictly an internal matter, but had grown into a full-blown diplomatic crisis. The FLN succeeded not only in winning the international media battle and the war itself, but also in lending credence to the legitimacy of national liberation movements everywhere.[33]

However, the place and significance of French civilization in Algeria did not end with independence. On the contrary, the colonial patrimony enjoyed a strange afterlife in postcolonial Algeria. A telling example is the French artwork that had been shipped back to the Louvre during the final phase of the civil war. Among the items crated up and secretly dispatched to France were significant paintings by Monet, Renoir, Pissarro, Degas, and Delacroix, among others, amounting to the largest collection of European art in Africa. The works had been donated to the new art deco Fine Arts Museum in Algiers in 1930 on the occasion of the centenary of

France's conquest of the country in 1830. During the Algerian War, French authorities worried that these priceless artworks—including Orientalist nudes and Renaissance-era Christian paintings—might offend Muslim sensibilities and hence be targeted for destruction; they were therefore sent off to Paris in the early 1960s for safekeeping.

What is surprising is that the new independent Algerian government wanted this French artwork back. At first this may seem puzzling, given the militant language of the National Council of the Algerian Revolution's Tripoli Program, drawn up just a month before independence. It demanded a "definition of culture" that would do away with the hated "cultural cosmopolitanism and Western impregnation." The ensuing lawsuit over which state owned the French cultural property lasted a full seven years, after which the Algerian government finally won its case on a technicality included in the 1962 Évian Accords that drew the war to a close. The fate of the French art provoked wide discussion in France in the late 1960s. The director of French museums at the time, Henri Seyrig, suggested that these artifacts of France's cultural heritage might "inspire in Algerians an admiration and respect for French civilization." Others, mostly on the political right, saw the restitution as yet another betrayal of French Algeria. The contested artwork was repatriated to Algeria in 1969 amid great fanfare, and is still on display at the renamed National Museum of Fine Arts in Algiers. Striking too is that the Algerian government reclaimed these fine art pieces in the name of "our country's property," "our artistic patrimony," and civilization.

This reclamation of colonial-era artwork found no equivalent in Ghana or anywhere else in the former British Empire. It was indicative of the ways in which Algerians had internalized the old ideal of French republican civilization. Algeria's reappropriation of metropole culture was unique within France's former empire, and amply illustrates the deep cultural entanglement of French-Algerian relations since the nineteenth century, which continued long after the civil war. Even Algeria's ancient Roman legacy was claimed as national heritage in the early 1970s. This story of contested artwork calls attention to the ambiguous aftermath of decolonization more generally, and shows how these new postcolonial states—even revolutionary ones—often built their new national identities on a negotiated blend of old and new.[34]

LÉOPOLD SÉDAR SENGHOR'S SENEGAL IS PERHAPS THE MOST famous case of the remaking of African civilization in the wake of decolonization, certainly within the Francophone world. Senghor was one of the most prominent and charismatic African leaders in the 1960s, especially in international cultural circles. He was an established poet, one of the founders of *négritude*, and thought of himself as culturally French his whole life, even after independence. He exerted a controlling hand over the cultural affairs of newly independent Senegal, perhaps even more so than Nkrumah did in Ghana. And like in Ghana, the transition of power was a peaceful one, though relations with France remained closer. For Senghor's new republic, decolonization was never simply a matter of military, economic, and political independence, but pivoted on a new and unique fusion of European and African culture. In it, decolonization was bound up with Africans reclaiming their own national heritage as the cultural bedrock of newly won sovereignty. Senegal was a special case in the way that the precolonial past, long dismissed by the colonial powers, was now recast as the living heritage of modern Africa. Antiquity thus became the stuff of origin and patrimony in conceiving new histories of new African nations, and Senghor was at the forefront of this campaign.[35]

Senghor's ideas of African civilization were directly linked to his conception of *négritude*. At one point he defined it as "the entire values of the civilization of the black world as they are expressed in the life and in the works of Blacks," with the aim of creating in Africa and for Africans "a new civilization, which suits Africa and the new times." Nonetheless, Senghor also saw Europe as a prospective partner in this civilizational model, and sought to build bridges between France and Africa in what he sometimes called "Euro-African civilization." He expounded these views long before independence in 1960, and (as noted in Chapter 5) had been a deputy in the French National Assembly from 1946 to 1958. Senghor was even linked to postwar proposals for a federalist union with France that put France's colonies on a more equal political basis. In September 1946 Senghor gave an impassioned speech in the Assembly during which he insisted that "together we will create a new civilization, whose center will be in Paris," ushering in "a new humanism" on "a scale of the universe and of humanity." He went on to state that the prospect of a new federal democracy was first possible "if we rid ourselves once and for all of the seeds of imperialism that, at our invitation, Nazism planted within us. Hitler is dead; we must all kill the piece of him that lives within us." Only a "cooperation between civilizations," Senghor continued, assured a peaceful and viable future. This was a political philosophy of interdependence fortified by new ideas of blended civilization.[36]

Senghor's idea of *négritude* was less exclusionary or racist than often portrayed. On the contrary, it underpinned what he called the "Civilization of the Universal." As he put it, *négritude* "will again play its essential role in the edification of a new humanism, more human because it will have reunited in their totality the contributions of all continents, of all races, of all nations." While Senghor developed some of these universalist ideas in the 1930s, his two years as a prisoner of war in Nazi-occupied France—in particular at Stalag 230 in Poitiers, the camp reserved for colonial troops—proved transformative. There he read poetry, taught himself German, and immersed himself in the work of Goethe. In Senghor's telling, his prison time allowed him "to meditate on the 'Greek miracle' whose civilization was founded upon *métissage*"—a fruitful mixture of Hellenic culture with non-Hellenic cultural influences, such as Egyptian and Ethiopian elements. What his internment also taught him was the global condition of interconnected humanity, and even a sense of forgiveness toward historical injustices. His experience shaped his postwar view that imperial powers and colonized peoples alike had to acknowledge and remake their inescapable bonds as fellow human beings. On the occasion of a roundtable of African and European intellectuals in Rome in 1960, Senghor argued that Europe—like Africa—was a crossroads of influences from Asia, Africa, Egypt, and Israel; the flawed self-conceit of European civilization was that it had reduced its mixed world culture to the privileging of Greek rationality as the chief characteristic of its heritage. What was needed instead, so he continued, was to recognize that all cultures comprise a world fund of civilization. For him, the role of intellectuals was thus to "bring out the values of a civilization of the universal, where all cultures can fully play their role, in respect for their originality and their dignity." In his eyes, federalism was the most appropriate political expression of this existential *métissage* and hybrid heritage.[37]

Like other pan-Africanists of his generation, such as Aimé Césaire, Senghor pointed to 1930s French surrealism as a key broker of this new African thinking. Surrealism was identified as a place where African and European culture could be bridged on equal terms. The new European fascination with African antiquity after the Great War had reordered European-African relations for both metropole and colony, as Paris became the center of international anticolonial thought. What these colonial thinkers living in the French capital saw in surrealism was its revolutionary potential to upend playfully all political values and cultural hierarchies, as well as the long-standing imperial denigration of traditional African culture as primitive and naïve. Pivotal too was the work of German anthropologist Leo Frobenius. In his book *Kulturgeschichte Afrikas*, published in 1933 and translated three years later as *History of the African Civilization*, Frobenius asserted not only that Africans possessed a long and proud civilization—itself a radical claim to make in 1933—but that there was a "unity of human civilization" made up of interrelated and equal civilizations. Frobenius was hardly alone with his anti-primitivism. In an essay published in 1929, French anthropologist Marcel Mauss challenged the idea of a global hierarchy of civilization, countering that the world was made up of a "fairly large ensemble of societies" whose civilizations in the plural needed to be understood as a history of "borrowings" and "historical filiations, of techniques, of arts and institutions." The English historian R. H. Tawney, in a preface to a 1929 study of Maori economics, added that anthropologists had proved that "what are called primitive societies are not necessarily, it appears, uncivilized. Some of them," he continued, are "merely peoples with a different kind of civilization." In his 1952 essay *Race and History* French anthropologist Claude Lévi-Strauss went so far as to say that the real barbarian is the one "who believes in barbarism." In any case, Frobenius's views exerted great influence on African intellectuals living in Paris in the 1930s—Senghor later recounted that Frobenius's work was "like a thunderclap" on his generation, particularly the idea that the "barbarous Negro" was itself a European invention. What the German anthropologist did was to help African intellectuals reclaim the language of civilization for themselves as a new fighting term of pride and anticolonialism, reconnecting a pre-imperial past with a postimperial future. Even those critics of the rhetoric of civilization often adjusted their message in light of the trend toward repossession. The best example is Martinique poet Aimé Césaire, who wrote in his *Discourse on Colonialism* that civilization itself was not necessarily the problem, but rather the European manipulation of it—"I systematically defend our own Negro civilizations; they were courteous civilizations." While Frobenius's star declined dramatically in the field of anthropology over the decades, his influence was decisive on Senghor.[38]

Interest in the power, presence, and unity of African civilization was a strong trend in the 1950s and 1960s. After the famed Bandung Conference of 1955, the first major gathering of leaders of African and Asian states, Egypt's president Gamal Abdel Nasser launched an energetic propaganda campaign toward the rest of Africa, one that identified Egypt as the great ancient African civilization. Nasser even said that racial differences among Africans were merely imperialist propaganda, a view that gained adherents after British, American, and Israeli troops withdrew from the Suez Canal in 1956. Others dedicated great energy to proclaiming the essential cultural unity of Africa. In 1955 the Senegalese historian and anthropologist Cheikh Anta Diop published a book about the singularity of African civilization, one in which Egypt and sub-Saharan Africa were part of the same "black civilization." Diop was a leading figure in the budding ideology of Afrocentricity, and was widely read and debated at the time. He followed up with another book in 1960 comparing the political systems of Africa and Europe from antiquity to the formation of modern states around the themes of caste, state formation, technology, and migration, in effect making a strong statement of intercontinental cultural equality. In 1974 Diop further developed these themes in *The African Origin of Civilization: Myth or Reality*. Controversial as it was at the time, Diop's work on the origins of civilization reflected a broader trend to link the precolonial past with a modernizing present. Excitement toward writing African history afresh from a postcolonial perspective was reflected in the 1964 Ghanaian initiative to draft a new *Encyclopedia Africana*, which was launched by prominent African American intellectual W. E. B. Du Bois, who had moved to Ghana in 1961 at Nkrumah's invitation. In Du Bois's eyes the encyclopedia "would reveal the genius of [Africa's] people, their history, culture and institutions" from prehistory to the present.[39]

Such cultural trends were part of the growing interest in precolonial history among African leaders and intellectuals. This often pivoted on the issue of reclamation. It is generally forgotten that de-mands for the return of cultural property were a distinctive feature of the Bandung Conference, which sought to challenge the "indignity of imperialism's cultural chauvinism." This came in the form of de-mands that the imperial powers must relinquish artworks stolen from Africa and Asia. Some European countries cooperated as a gesture of postimperial goodwill, such as the Belgian return of Congo artifacts to Zaire, and the Dutch repatriation of colonial objects to Indonesia. While notions of Africa as the "cradle of mankind" and the "origins of civilization" emerged in the 1930s thanks to the work of figures like British paleoanthropologist Louis Leakey, the "cradle of mankind" argument was popularized and politicized in the 1960s as the foun-dation of Afrocentric history and heritage in the era of independence. The 1967 Pan-African Congress on Prehistory and Quaternary Stud-ies in Dakar, which included representatives from thirty-two coun-tries, began by affirming Africa as the "cradle of humanity." In the opening address, Senghor called for further archaeological research into "Africanité" and Africa's "progresse vers son unité totale."[40]

Senghor was keen to turn these trends to his advantage. During his reign, the state played a leading role in promoting cultural events. The centrality of culture for political thinking was something that he, Césaire, and others had developed in the 1930s, even to the point of insisting that politics must be put to the service of culture and not vice versa. Senghor busied himself with creating new institu-tions that would preserve the cultural heritage of the nation, such as the reorganization of the Mali Arts Center as the National Arts School for a new generation of Senegalese artists.[41] A good part of Senghor's cultural policy pivoted on rediscovering African antiquity. For him, the assertion of African civilization itself was part of the effort to decolonize the African mind and remind Africans of their great and glorious pasts. In 1961 Senghor gave his blessings to the archaeological excavation of the long-lost eleventh-century town of Aoudaghost, a former oasis in Hodh El Gharbi, Mauritania, at

Figure 26. Aoudaghost excavation, Mauritania. *Credit: Augustin F. C. Holl*

the southern end of a trans-Saharan caravan route. The project was spearheaded by French archaeologists Jean Devisse and Raymond Mauny along with twenty-four trained African students from the University of Dakar. This was the first such excavation connected to independent Senegal, and was accompanied by widespread news coverage. One magazine cover features the young French archaeologists working together with African students in a visual display of cooperation and mutual recognition (Figure 26). The text extolled the political significance of the discovery: "At a time when Africa, now independent, turns with passion to its past, for us this is an expedition of capital interest. Indeed, it appears that it allows for the veil that shrouded this historical enigma to be lifted."[42]

The opening of the high-profile First World Festival of Black Arts in April 1966 in Dakar best captured this shift of sensibility. This was a landmark show for African history—it was the very first

Figure 27. First World Festival of Black Arts, Dakar, 1966, catalog cover. *Credit: Ibou Diouf, Collection PANAFEST Archive, Musée du Quai Branly, Paris*

international show of African art to take place on African soil, and was explicitly designed, as one publicist put it, to allow "Africans to speak with their own voice." As noted in the commemorative catalog, the show "allowed the destruction of external prejudices and internal complexes by proving that the black world is not only a 'consumer of civilizations' but well and truly, a 'producer'" (Figure 27). The exhibition showcased Senghor's Senegal as a modern and cultured state as some 2,500 artists, musicians, performers, and writers gathered in Dakar to celebrate Black Art across continents. Among the star-studded cast were Senghor, Aimé Césaire, Langston Hughes, Josephine Baker, Duke Ellington, Wole Soyinka, and the Alvin Ailey American Dance Theater. Hughes and American dance choreographer Katherine Dunham helped oversee preparations. Representatives from thirty African countries were on hand, together with six significant African diasporic populations—namely the US, Brazil, Haiti, Trinidad and Tobago, the UK,

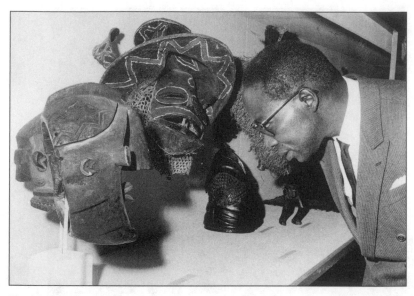

Figure 28. Senghor at First World Festival of Black Arts, Dakar, 1966.
Credit: Bridgeman Images

and France. On offer in Dakar was a huge variety of art, dance, drama, and musical performances.

Some 600 objects from over fifty museums and private collections in Africa, Europe, and North America were proudly displayed. The exhibition reunited many African objects across continents for the first time, and in this sense the show served as a spectacle of Senghor's idea of *négritude*. Senghor's celebration of pan-Africanism advanced a new cultural geography of African art, one that both spanned centuries from prehistory to the present and spanned continents, as noted in Senghor's welcoming of American jazz great Duke Ellington to open the festival (Figures 28 and 29). It was an image of *négritude* that foregrounded pan-African racial belonging above all. Classical African artifacts (such as sculptures and masks) were exhibited alongside a selection of works by Picasso, Léger, and Modigliani from the Museum of Modern Art in Paris to underscore Africa's influence on European modernism and the interconnectedness of Europe and Africa. The show was cofounded

Figure 29. Senghor shaking hands with Duke Ellington, Dakar, 1966. *Credit: Associated Press*

by Senegal, UNESCO, and France, and some 25,000 guests from around the world attended.[43]

The events of the 1966 festival were broadcast on radio for the Senegalese public, and some 300 press articles were published in the national daily newspaper, the *Dakar-Matin*. Dozens of folkloric dance troupes performed in the streets, though not officially as part of the festival. On display was art from the Dogon and the Baluba of Kasai, and the masterpieces of Benin. The catalog stressed too both the "diversity of Negro art" and "its underlying unity," one in which "Negro African art" served as "a leaven in the bread of humanity." The show was accompanied by a one-week colloquium showcasing world experts on African art and culture. Panels were devoted to highlighting the links between African culture and its offshoots in North and South America, as evidenced in Negro spirituals, Brazilian sculpture, and traditional African architecture. A panel on preservation ended with a call for more African studies in schools, the

305

creation of new museums, and the protection of artisans working in traditional craft areas. All these measures were identified as means to "lift the African past from obscurity" and protect ancient artifacts of African civilization for posterity.[44]

Senghor's idea of *négritude* as one of the "humanisms of the 20th century" was not subject to universal acclaim. In his *Wretched of the Earth,* Fanon condemned Senghor for being a typical westernized "colonized intellectual" who spoke in the name of "the people," though he had no real connection to them. For Fanon, the "bards of Negritude" obscured the fact that "every culture is first and foremost national," thus all these conferences on "Negro-African culture" and the "cultural unity of Africa" simply peddled false consciousness and conservative abstraction. The nation—not *négritude* or African civilization—was the key to resistance, sovereignty, and identity formation. South African exiled writer Ezekiel Mphahlele challenged the poetry inspired by *négritude* as being a romantic rhapsodizing of Africa—"Ancestors, naked feet, half-naked women and so on." Others dismissed Senghor's celebration of the emotive and rhythmic quality of reclaimed African-ness as reductive and even "self-primitivizing." For these critics, the claim to antique African civilization therefore carried with it the danger of reproducing— not rejecting—an unwanted colonial heritage.[45]

That said, Senghor developed the most articulate sense of African civilization in the first decade after independence. Like Nkrumah's Ghana, Senghor's Senegal fronted culture as a principal means of signaling the break from the past and giving voice to a new national cultural identity. But whereas Nkrumah tended to obscure the connections between colonial and postcolonial culture, Senghor embraced the links with the precolonial and colonial pasts as the foundation of the new Senegal. As noted, Senghor was long committed to French federal confederation, and only later advocated self-determination through peaceful change. He rejected the FLN's revolutionary violence, and even tried to broker a peace between

France and Algeria toward the end of the war. Senghor was keen to maintain a respectful relationship with Senegal's former imperial power. But Senghor was not necessarily inclusive—after all, it is worth remembering that his 1966 Black Arts extravaganza pointedly barred the Arab world, including the Maghreb, from participating, on the grounds that it did not count as black. The exclusionary politics of his pan-Africanism created rancor among his critics and opened up regional divisions among pan-Africanists. In this sense, the reclaimed language of civilization reflected the broader cultural realignments of newly independent African states, and Senghor's vision of a living African heritage was integral to them.[46]

BY THE MID-1960S MOST OF THE FIRST GENERATION OF THIRD World leaders had lost power or their lives: Sukarno in Indonesia, Ben Bella in Algeria, and Nkrumah were all overthrown in military coups between 1964 and 1966, and Nehru died in 1964. Already by the mid-1960s there was a cult of personality surrounding these "founding fathers" of Third World independence, and many of the initial dreams of democracy on the continent turned into harsh and often corrupt authoritarian regimes. Strict state control over the media, education, and cultural life in these postcolonial nations was quite typical. The use of culture—and especially indigenous heritage—as a means of broadcasting new political power and the break from the colonial past was closely associated with these new states, and often did not survive the first generation of leaders. So linked to Nkrumah was the iconography of Ghanaian presidential power that no succeeding Ghanaian head of state has ever used his presidential chair for the swearing-in ceremony. But in the blush of decolonization, civilization remained a decidedly secular language of thinking beyond the nation-state as well as toward the past and future. The African advocates of federalism, including Senghor, Guinea's Sékou Touré, and Mali's Modibo Keïta, were initially unsure whether the territorial state or more regional formations of "Negro-African civilization" should be the focus of their political attention. With time, the hardening of nationalisms and the nation-state system vitiated the aspirations of African federalism. Ideals of postcolonial African civilizations were arguably the last residue of these older dreams of political federation and pan-Africanism.[47]

Attitudes toward human rights in Africa are another indication of these larger shifts. In the 1940s and 1950s African intellectuals were the champions of universalism, working to force the European powers to make good on the Universal Declaration of Human Rights in their colonial territories. A rallying point of dissent was the controversial European Convention on Human Rights, which, as discussed in Chapter 3, regionalized human rights in 1950 around Western European ideas of liberal Christian individualism. This anticommunist European convention was seen as woefully conservative and hypocritical by anticolonialists. Senghor, then a socialist member of the French delegation to the Consultative Assembly of the Council of Europe, voiced his concern that the Convention "would transform the European Declaration of Human Rights into the Declaration of European Human Rights" to the exclusion of others. No less troubling was that human rights were being twisted toward special European interests. After decolonization, for example, human rights language was not infrequently enlisted by former imperial powers to protect white minorities (and their property) still living in Africa and elsewhere. It was only after the Algerian War that the French state ratified the European Convention so as to safeguard the European minority still living in Algeria. But by the late 1960s, Third World advocacy of human rights as a step toward democratization had faded. At the United Nations' International Conference on Human Rights in Tehran in 1968, the new priority among developing-world delegates was to make economic development a human right. Two-thirds of these delegates hailed from newly decolonized countries that had spurned democracy by 1968, and they wished to turn the spotlight away from homegrown authoritarianism. This was one of the hidden and conservative aspects of the slow replacement of the rhetoric of civilization by a more militant rights language of development. The claim to civilization had been key to the struggle of anticolonialism and postcolonialism across the continent, and was closely bound to assertions of sovereignty, regional identity, and independence. The emergence of rights and development politicking by these new African states was still tied up with international justice (international assistance and emergency relief in cases of civil war or famines), but the wider interests in the ancient past, cross-continent identities, and regional political unity began to drop away by the early 1970s.[48]

These developments should not obscure the ways in which the early years of decolonization dramatically reordered the relationship between Europe and Africa. These seismic historical transformations were not couched just in terms of the spreading of nationalism and independence movements, but also by the political assertion of indigenous heritage. Such claims became especially militant in the Algerian War, as the battle for military control was also waged on the moral terrain of civilization and barbarism. Sartre's comment on the implications of Alleg's memoir touched on the awkward fact that France, having been controlled and mistreated by Nazi occupying forces during the war, had seemingly learned few moral lessons from the Vichy experience, in that the French state was now perpetrating its own de-civilizing mission in Algeria. The colonial wars in British Kenya, the Belgian Congo, the Dutch East Indies, Portuguese Angola, and French Algeria were not only stories of brutal imperial violence and eventual loss of empire; they were also referenda on the myth of European civilization. Even those peaceful handovers of power—such as in Ghana and Senegal—targeted the undoing of the legacy of European civilization as the very ground of nation-building and cultural rebirth.

Changing ideas of civilization thus reflected Europe's changing relationship to the wider world. Where civilization only a decade and a half earlier served as a rallying cry for Europeans to reconstitute Europe morally after Nazism, the term was captured by anticolonial leaders and movements—including Nkrumah, the FLN, and Senghor—for their own national causes. As soon as the concept migrated southward and became fused with anticolonialism, it was all but abandoned by European leaders and intellectuals, in large measure because it no longer denoted European power and privilege. This abandonment, however, did not last as the concept was quickly reinvented in Europe for different purposes, as we shall see in the next few chapters. The inversion of the language of civilization during decolonization signaled a cultural divorce of Europeans from their former colonies. Into the breach stepped international organizations like UNESCO to help build new transcontinental bridges between Europe and Africa around the grand ideal of world civilization.

seven

WORLD CIVILIZATION

IN 1957 THE CELEBRATED SWISS WRITER MAX FRISCH PUB-
lished a novel, *Homo Faber*, in which he explored the themes of
physical dislocation, spiritual homelessness, and the limits of technology's mastery of modern life. The protagonist, Walter Faber, is
an accomplished Swiss engineer who travels across Europe and the
Americas as a technical expert for the United Nations Educational,
Scientific and Cultural Organization, or UNESCO for short. The
book is a kind of satire of the "one world" romanticism and do-gooder
development for all championed by the spin-off UN agency. In one
scene Faber is en route to South America to help build turbines in
Venezuela and strikes up a conversation with an acquaintance he
meets on the plane, which suddenly turns sour: "I only lost my tem-
per when Marcel started to talk about my work, that is to say about
UNESCO, saying the technologist was the final guise of the white
missionary, industrialization the last gospel of a dying race and living
standards a substitute for a purpose of living."[1]

Frisch was scarcely alone in his critical depiction, as UNESCO
was subject to bitter wrangling among various factions from the
beginning. Its agenda was ambitious—to strengthen, enrich, and
extend the United Nations' experimental foray into international

politics, providing what one commentator called the soul to the body of the UN. No other international agency did more to place itself at the heart of international cultural affairs amid an increasingly toxic international political atmosphere. The agency was founded in 1946 amid the blush of postwar idealism, and its career over the decades was marred by a series of protests and dramatic walkouts by various delegations. The agency's lofty dream was often ridiculed in the world press as woefully starry-eyed and out of step with a hard-edged world of Cold War power politics. By the late 1950s, UNESCO's own civilizing mission was pilloried as nothing but a "cavalry of hobby horses" and "pork barrel riding on a cloud."[2]

Such dismissive characterizations of UNESCO's record over-look its significant role in reconceptualizing European civilization after 1945. Like the United Nations Relief and Rehabilitation Administration discussed in Chapter 1, UNESCO was dedicated to binding the wounds of war, but it approached the issue differently. It did not dispense emergency humanitarian relief, as UNRRA did, but instead focused on the fields of education, science, and culture to further the cause of peace and international understanding. One of the agency's signature programs was the protection and preservation of world-famous artifacts of civilization threatened by war, neglect, and natural disaster. These included religious buildings, palaces, monuments, and other man-made cultural treasures from antiquity to the present. Looking after the world's precious material inheritance was considered too important to leave to state actors and volunteer organizations, so it was decided that a new secular international body should be entrusted to safeguard it. UNESCO led the way in protecting heritage sites in Europe and around the world, reflecting a shift of attitude among preservationists and liberal activists from a traditionally Eurocentric approach to a wider vision of preservation as synonymous with peace, equality, and shared patrimony. UNESCO served as a unique hub of international knowledge production both before and after decolonization, and was explicitly dedicated to overcoming cultural barriers between Europe and the developing world. It did so by means of soft power, aiming to spread international understanding through cross-cultural respect, general education, and above all the promotion of what it boldly called "world civilization."[3]

Today most people associate UNESCO with the management of World Heritage sites, which is a key part of its ongoing legacy. But its conception of world civilization was far more wide-reaching, to the extent that the agency set its sights on combating the scourges of nationalism, racism, and Eurocentrism in numerous ways, ranging from literacy campaigns to archaeology salvage projects. To this end UNESCO revised the very geography of civilization in working to bridge the West, East, and South in a spirit of peace and preservation quite unlike any other international organization at the time. What distinguished UNESCO was its serious attempt to give form to a new conception of world history and world civilization that transcended the nation-state system and Cold War division. The story of postwar Europe is one of ruin and renewal, and UNESCO helped shape the message and meaning of cultural reconstruction.

UNESCO WAS FOUNDED IN PARIS A YEAR AFTER THE CHRIS-tening of the United Nations in 1945. Its roots go back to intergovernmental organizations between the wars, such as the League of Nations' International Institute of Intellectual Cooperation and the International Bureau of Education based in Geneva, but its brief was much wider. It was given popular resonance by British prime minister Clement Attlee's famous phrase that "wars begin in the minds of men." The American poet and UNESCO delegate Archibald MacLeish subsequently embellished Attlee's phrase to coin the sentence that opens UNESCO's Constitution—"Since wars begin in the minds of men, it is in the minds of men that the defences of peace must be constructed." The agency was created to compensate for the shortcomings of the ill-starred League of Nations, which mainly concentrated on political matters in its effort to achieve some semblance of collective security. If war was ideological, so went the logic, then peace must be ideological too. The agency's task was to wage war on war itself. That a number of key figures associated with UNESCO had either spent time in concentration camps or were active in anti-Nazi resistance groups across Europe lent UNESCO a strong moral pedigree. Ideas for a new organization geared toward international understanding had been brewing in the US State Department since 1944, driven by President Roosevelt's conviction that "civilization is not national—it is international." At the San Francisco conference that gave birth to the United Nations, President Truman stressed the importance of a new international commitment to cultural and educational cooperation. With the dawning of the Cold War, UNESCO was seen as a possible platform for superpower dialogue, an aid to developing countries, as well as an instrument of transnational cultural diplomacy.[4]

The campaign was neatly reflected in its Parisian headquarters. Its first residence was at Hotel Majestic, where the agency resided from 1946 until 1958. The luxury hotel had hosted part of the Paris Peace Conference after World War I, and was commandeered a generation later as the Paris headquarters of the Third Reich's military high command, after which it was repurposed by the American military administration following the liberation of Paris. The takeover of the hotel for UNESCO was viewed as a sharp break from an unwanted militaristic and warring past. As the organization's first director-general, Julian Huxley, solemnly put it in his memoirs: "Thus my occupancy visibly symbolized the transition from war and racialism to peace and cultural co-operation." UNESCO's bid to help remake the modern world was visibly articulated in the styling and ethos of its newly built headquarters in Paris, opened in 1958. This high-profile concrete-and-glass edifice was designed by Bauhaus luminary Marcel Breuer, along with fellow interwar modernists

Pier Luigi Nervi and Bernard Zehrfuss, to serve as the engine room of international educational cooperation and global cultural exchange. This "symbol of the 20th century" was heralded as a great showpiece of international modernism, with works by Picasso, Miró, Calder, Henry Moore, and Isamu Noguchi gracing the interiors and gardens. The building incarnated the ideal of post-fascist universalism, where peace, rationality, and transparency were to replace nationalism, prejudice, and violence as the defining characteristics of the age.[5]

The new agency was first led by Julian Huxley, who was the grandson of Thomas Huxley, the friend and fervent champion of Charles Darwin and his ideas of evolution, as well as the brother of renowned writer Aldous Huxley. Julian Huxley cut quite a figure in his own right. He was an eminent zoologist and popularizer of science for mainstream British society, having written a slew of books on the subject of evolution and the relationship between science and society. During World War II he was a regular participant on the popular BBC radio program *The Brains Trust*, and was reportedly a household name by virtue of his frequent media appearances. Huxley was an outspoken liberal humanist in the scientific community, and a famous opponent of Nazism and its pernicious usage of scientific racism. In his 1946 primer, *UNESCO: Its Purpose and Its Philosophy*, he remarked that the guiding idea of the organization would be "world scientific humanism," based on a conception of evolution that would encompass all human endeavor and provide the full integration of science and culture. While his "world scientific humanism" philosophy met some resistance at the time, Huxley remained undeterred that UNESCO should facilitate "the emergence of a single world culture."[6]

Another key figure behind the scientific orientation of UNESCO was the renowned Cambridge biologist and historian of science Joseph Needham. It was Needham who was most responsible for the *S* in UNESCO. He is best known for his seven volumes on *Science and Civilisation in China*, published between 1954 and 2004 and long considered one of the towering monuments in the history of science. Needham argued that Chinese science was responsible for many of the world's scientific discoveries and technological break-throughs through the fifteenth century, and dedicated his work to returning China to its pivotal place in the broader history of scientific achievement. Needham was a colleague and close friend of Huxley's, and spent much of World War II in China as head of the special British Council mission to maintain links with the Chinese scientific community during Japanese occupation. His deep knowledge of Chinese science and culture was seen as a great asset in UNESCO's new world history initiative. Needham had already outlined what this history might look like in his short 1945 book *Chinese Science*, and hoped this primer would serve as a useful model. Like Huxley, Needham was convinced that science and technology should serve as the backbone of any history of humanity, since he believed that cultural interaction and the transfer of scientific knowledge accounted for much of what we call civilization. His plea was also well-timed: integrating science into UNESCO's brief was seen as especially urgent following the explosion of atomic bombs in Japan, which made imperative the managing of science and atomic energy. In a 1947 report, Needham wrote that "the natural sciences are the most international of all human activities," for "scientific men understand one another at once, from whatever corner of the world they come to meet together." While the idea of science as a unifier was prevalent in the nineteenth century, it got a new lease on life after 1945. By 1949 UNESCO had set up field scientific cooperation offices in the capitals of various underdeveloped countries (Montevideo, Cairo, Istanbul, Delhi, Jakarta, and Manila) with the aim of dispensing knowledge and mobilizing modern science for the sake of peace and international understanding. In many respects, this new scientific popular front was understood as a means of bridging what British novelist and chemist C. P. Snow famously called modernity's irreconcilable two cultures—the humanities and the sciences.[7]

UNESCO spearheaded various campaigns to promote literacy and the creation of libraries around the world. In the eyes of the agency, books served as major defenses of peace in their ability to foster sympathy, curiosity, and intercultural knowledge. Inspired by Goethe's idea of *Weltliteratur*, or world literature, UNESCO promoted common literary heritage as a means of bringing cultures together. To this end it publicized and translated a canon of world classics, and worked with the International Federation of Translators to help create a shared literary heritage. Between 1948 and 1994 the agency published 866 books from all over the world, originally written in ninety-one languages. In the early 1960s two centers for the free distribution of textbooks were created in Accra, Ghana, and Yaoundé, Cameroon, to combat illiteracy and spread international culture. In independent Congo, UNESCO agents worked to reopen schools after the Belgians departed, train new staff, and help reform the national educational system.[8]

UNESCO also set its sights on reviving damaged cultural traditions, especially in Europe. Despite proclaimed universalism, its early preservation campaign was expressly geared toward Europe, fueled by the need to shore up what was perceived as Western civilization in crisis. At the Conference of Allied Ministers of Education in London in 1944, education ministers from sixteen countries met to discuss postwar reconstruction as well as the rehabilitation of European heritage in the face of Nazi looting and destruction. The conference tipped its hand in declaring that "a concentrated effort is being made for the immediate protection and ultimate restitution of the cultural heritage of Western civilization." The early years of UNESCO continued this logic, as it developed an expansive notion of cultural reconstruction. This meant books for libraries, materials for schools, scientific equipment for laboratories, the distribution of musical instruments, and the creation of International Youth Camps. The agency also organized translations of the world's classics in the various languages of the member states of the UN.[9]

As part of its early world civilization mission, UNESCO promoted human rights. In June 1947 it sent out a questionnaire on human rights to dozens of international lawyers and public intellectuals across the world, including specialists in Chinese, Islamic, and Hindu law and custom. Respondents included Indian anticolonial nationalist Mahatma Gandhi, Italian philosopher Benedetto Croce, and English writer Aldous Huxley, among others. Most heartening to UNESCO was the fact that virtually all those asked affirmed the common idea—if not necessarily the vernacular terminology—of human rights. The well-known French Catholic human rights champion Jacques Maritain collected and edited the responses. In the introduction to the published report, Maritain noted with great relish that respondents agreed on a set of practical values and concepts (including the "right to live a life that is free from the haunting fear of poverty and insecurity") as a "sort of common denominator" of human rights. The thin volume was seen as a key conceptual breakthrough internationally, especially at a time when the drafting committee for the UN Declaration of Human Rights was making heavy weather of forging any concrete meaning of human rights for the international community. The answers to the questionnaire gave needed intellectual ballast and international blessing to UNESCO's search for a notion of common humanity.[10]

The agency's 1950 traveling exhibition on the history of human rights, *The Human Rights Album*, was the first major international show on the theme anywhere. A kit of photographs and captions was sent to all UNESCO national commissions for display and education. It was designed for schoolchildren as a kind of slideshow of human progress, highlighting the abolition of slavery and inhumane treatment, religious tolerance and mutual respect, the emancipation of women, rights of citizens (e.g., free speech, opinion, assembly, and the vote), economic and social rights (dignity of work, right to relief), as well as cultural rights (education, scientific research). The accompanying information packet stated plainly that "the same paths of liberty have been trodden, throughout the centuries and throughout the world, by civilizations that were very far apart—Vedantic India, Classical China, Greece, Islam, Medieval Europe, and so forth, up to modern times." The show insisted that "Human Rights, far from being arbitrary conventions, are in fact organic needs which are essential to the harmonious development of human life, and bear witness to the brotherhood of men," and that "World Peace depends on the concrete and universal application of Human Rights."[11]

Expressions of secular universalism were particularly pronounced in the agency's high-profile statements on race. From the very beginning UNESCO saw race as one of the great stumbling blocks to an understanding of world civilization. Julian Huxley's coauthored 1935 book, *We Europeans*, was a widely cited denunciation of racism from the vantage point of scientific inquiry, famously concluding that race should "be dropped from the vocabulary of science." Although his early views on race and eugenics were complicated and even quite conservative, Huxley did change with time, and headed an agency dedicated to eradicating racism in all forms. In the early 1950s it launched an international campaign to discredit scientific racism as a social myth that should play no role in judging human difference. This was most strikingly expressed in UNESCO's famed 1950 Statement on Race, written in large measure by renowned French anthropologist Claude Lévi-Strauss, which proclaimed that "all men belong to the same species, *Homo sapiens*." Lévi-Strauss's elegiac 1955 memoir on the fate of anthropology, *Tristes Tropiques*, captured this shift away from Eurocentrism toward a world of separate but interrelated civilizations. A few years later he ruminated on the crisis of anthropology after imperialism, and claimed that "the great civilization of the west" is "everywhere emerging as a hybrid," echoing the views of Senegalese poet and president Léopold Sédar Senghor and others, as discussed in the last chapter.[12]

Between 1950 and 1967 four major statements on race were issued, all of which stressed human equality and the specious nature of biological racism. UNESCO statements on race were distributed to scientists, science journals, and newspapers to publicize its findings. UNESCO established a three-book series on race—*The Race Question in Modern Science*, *The Race Question and Modern Thought*, and *Race and Society*—all published in pamphlet form in French and English and mass distributed through UNESCO's National Commissions around the world. Not that everyone was pleased—UNESCO publications were banned from Los Angeles public schools in the early 1950s for being anti-Christian, anti-American, and communist in spirit, and South Africa withdrew from UNESCO on the grounds that such publications were interfering with the country's domestic affairs. Even so, these interventions found warm reception in Eastern Europe and in developing countries, evidence that the organization was making good on claims of antiracism and world civilization. The same was true of the American civil rights movement, including the National Association for the Advancement of Colored People. As the Reverend Jesse Jackson recalled, "We went around the South giving speeches, holding up the UNESCO study, saying that blacks were not inferior. A world body had studied and concluded that we were not inferior. It was a big deal." In 1967 the US Supreme Court drew liberally on the UNESCO race statements in landmark decisions to strike down the ban on interracial marriage in various states as unconstitutional. Such actions helped transform the United Nations into a key advocate of antiracism worldwide, and thereafter were closely linked to the civil rights struggle among African Americans and anticolonialists in Africa, Asia, and Eastern Europe.[13]

UNESCO's IDEA OF WORLD CIVILIZATION SOON BECAME MIRED in controversy. A good example was the sticky problem of membership, best seen in the meeting of UNESCO's 1951 General Conference in Paris. On the agenda was expanding the list of member states, and there were some awkward applicants. At issue was the dilemma facing the Allies in the immediate aftermath of the war, namely what to do with the defeated Axis powers. UNESCO was the first major international body that endeavored to bring these former fascist countries back into the "family of nations" as equal partners. Seeking international forgiveness of former fascists was not easy at the time, as there was still a great deal of antipathy toward these countries from all quarters. Recall that the International Olympic Committee voted to exclude German and Japanese athletes from the London 1948 Games as punishment for the regimes' wartime atrocities, undermining for some the internationalist spirit of the Olympics. The politics surrounding the admission of West Germany, Japan, and Spain to UNESCO exposed rifts in what this idea of world civilization and post-fascist international community actually meant.

At first the campaign to include West Germany and Japan was greeted with skepticism and resistance. The Czech and Polish UNESCO observers were dead set against any agency presence in occupied Germany. It is worth noting here that while serving as a charter member of the UN, the Soviet Union did not join UNESCO until 1954, before which it routinely denounced the UN agency as simply a tool of American imperialists. Soviet criticism of UNESCO in the late 1940s was channeled through East European member countries—Poland, Czechoslovakia, Hungary, and Yugoslavia—which roundly argued that any UNESCO activity in Germany and Japan would seriously compromise the agency's principles of peace and cooperation. But these views were all but ignored— by 1950 UNESCO officials had descended on West Germany and Japan with a full education reform program in mind. In the defeated countries, international conferences were organized, libraries and museums were being reopened, and history textbooks were rewritten to expunge dangerous nationalism. The new agency desperately needed a few successful programs as good advertisements, and West Germany and Japan were identified as ideal candidates.[14]

Both the Japanese and West German governments understood the diplomatic importance of membership. In Japan the overtures to UNESCO first came through civil society. The Japanese chapter of the international association of writers, PEN, sought cooperation as early as 1947, and the Sendai Cooperative Association was the first UNESCO-sanctioned affiliate in the world. With time Japanese parliamentarians recognized the symbolic quality of building links to the UN agency as a means of connecting democratization with world peace and integration into the world community. A key figure who helped bring UNESCO and West Germany together was Konrad Adenauer's foreign secretary, Walter Hallstein. Hallstein's name is commonly associated with the inflexible West German foreign policy doctrine that bore his name, one that held that the Federal Republic would sever ties with any country that diplomatically recognized its rival German republic in the East. Yet it is worth recalling that Hallstein was rector of Frankfurt University until 1948, the founding chair of the German national UNESCO committee, and its president in the crucial period of 1949–1950. From June 1950 onward he also headed the West German delegation for the negotiation of the Schuman Plan, which proposed to place French and West German coal and steel production under one common authority, and helped draw up the Treaty of Paris in 1951 that gave birth to the European Coal and Steel Community. For him, all these issues were closely intertwined. Like others in Bonn, he knew that gaining admission to UNESCO (not unlike the Palestinian campaign for UNESCO admission in 2011) was the crucial first step toward full membership in the international community and a move toward full state sovereignty. True to his Cold War politics, Hallstein worked to make sure that East Germany's application to UNESCO was continually shelved, to the consternation of East German campaigners—it was not until 1972, after repeated applications, that the German Democratic Republic was admitted to UNESCO.[15]

By the time the vote was called at the 1951 UNESCO General Conference in Paris, there were surprisingly few dissenting voices, especially concerning Japan. It was held that UNESCO's vaunted universalism began with accepting all applicant states, regardless of past behavior. Particularly striking was the language used to explain why to incorporate former fascist states. The Panamanian representative spoke for the majority view in saying that in admitting Japan we "must forget the horrors of war and banish all feelings of rancor as well as all desire for vengeance and endeavour, to inculcate in each of those people, which in a moment of madness wished to impose upon the world a system of oppression and evil, all the noble feelings to which we have referred." As noted in Chapter 3, the Council of Europe was partly forged on forgetting, and Churchill's 1948 Hague speech demanded the forgiveness of West Germany as a precondition to building a strong and united Western Europe.

UNESCO extended this logic from Europe to the global community, and the theme of willful forgetting was particularly pronounced in regard to West Germany. Despite vocal objections from the Israeli representative that West Germany "does not give the impression of a community that has undergone the moral revolution without which no redemption is possible," those in the majority saw things differently. One supportive delegate boldly proclaimed that "Unesco's mission is essentially one of harmony, tolerance and to some extent, forgetfulness." After short deliberation, the vote in favor of both countries carried easily. The head of the UK delegation and permanent secretary in the Ministry of Education, John Maud, offered this stunning word of welcome to the Federal Republic, which is worth quoting at length: "Mr Director-General, you quoted to us some words of Flaubert that 'history like the sea is beautiful for what it washes away' and you added with your customary genius that you only agreed with that if you could add 'history is specially beautiful for what it confirms,' and what we have just done I think is a historic act of faith in the possibility of washing away those hateful doctrines of racialism and war which will always be associated with the Nazis and in the possibility of confirming the genius of the German people as artists, as thinkers, as contributors to civilization" and, Maud concluded, "it is the spirit and the voice of Leibnitz and Goethe, and I would like to think of the music of Beethoven, which we have within our family, now that we have Germany as a member of UNESCO." Rarely has such international blessing and the balm of selective memory been celebrated so openly; Hallstein, who was on hand for the ceremony, rightly recognized the moment as a fundamental "step towards the restoration of normal relations between ourselves and the rest of the world."[16]

The policy of benign forgetting toward fascism was not so easily accommodated with other applicants. Former fascist countries were one thing; current fascist countries were quite another. Whereas the discussion about Japan and West Germany was mostly confined to internal deliberations with scattered international press coverage, Spain's application in 1952 provoked fierce international debate. Newspapers from across the globe—especially in South America—mocked UNESCO's hoped-for moral rehabilitation of fascist Spain, while figures like French writer Albert Camus and Spanish cellist and conductor Pablo Casals implored the agency to withdraw its invitation. A *New York Times* article concluded that "Unesco's value as a 'symbolic and moral' force would be jeopardized if it were to admit to membership a notorious dictatorship." It did not help matters that during the debate Spanish dictator Francisco Franco had meted out death sentences to several Spanish trade unionists, causing uproar from international union leaders. Nevertheless, Spain was admitted without much fuss that year to uphold UNESCO's universalist attitude and ethos, thanks in part to consistent support from the international Catholic community. Franco wasted little time in capitalizing on this new tolerant spirit: the next year a concordat was signed with the Vatican and a mutual defense pact was signed with the US, after which his country was admitted into the United Nations in 1955. However, the agency was not always a soft touch for illiberal regimes, as there was little forgetting or forgiveness toward communist countries. In the 1952 debate on Romania's and Bulgaria's entry, the US delegation led the charge against them by citing their recent human rights records. The Czech and Polish delegations countered that the American attack was "not directed against the Rumanian people alone," but—far worse—"against the universality of UNESCO." But in its effort to stay above the ideological fray and maintain its universalist remit, UNESCO grudgingly admitted Bulgaria in 1956 and Romania in 1962.[17]

UNESCO then set its sights on a much more grandiose project to make good this philosophy of universalism. In the early 1950s it set out to write global history anew for a world emerging from the death and destruction of World War II. It embarked on a high-profile but now largely forgotten six-volume, multiauthored *History of Mankind* book series, which originated in the early 1950s and ran through the 1970s. The series included hundreds of contributors and consultants from across the globe, and never has a world history project generated such intense international interest and media attention.[18]

The UNESCO world history project was born of the perceived need to restore a lost sense of common humanity after 1945, and to reconsider Europe's relationship to the wider world. The project for a new "history of mankind" was driven forward by UNESCO director Julian Huxley as what he called a natural history of world civilization. According to Huxley, UNESCO's mission should be— acknowledging Wendell Willkie's 1943 bestselling American book of the same name—the creation of "One World in the things of the mind and spirit." Huxley subscribed to an idea of progress as a union of all separate traditions, conjoined in the advance of "world civilization." As he explained: "Civilization, because civilization implies peace, and is indeed in essence the technique of peaceful living. World civilization because peace must be global, and because civilization conferred to one section of humanity is not compatible with UNESCO's constitution, and is indeed provocative of violence and war; advance of world civilization because world civilization is in its infancy and because we need the dynamic appeal of a distant and ever-receding goal." The *History of Mankind* must "lay stress on the cultural achievements of the human race, and dealing with war and politics only in so far as they influenced cultural and scientific progress."[19]

The idea of writing global history has deep roots, though its emergence as a modern subject of inquiry arguably arose at the end of the nineteenth century and during the interwar years. English historian and politician Lord Acton described world history in 1898 as "distinct from the combined history of all nations" and stressed the "common fortunes of mankind"; in Germany historians Karl Lamprecht and Hans F. Helmolt championed similar ideas of world history at the same time, wherein international exchange instead of warfare was foregrounded. In the 1920s H. G. Wells wrote that world history was "something more and something less than the aggregate of the national histories." In his 1921 *The Salvaging of Civilization*, Wells argued that one particular book of world history, the Bible, had united Western peoples for centuries, and now a new book was needed to unite world peoples in a similar way. Spengler and Toynbee lent further popularity to the idea of world history, especially in an era of growing professionalization and emphasis on the nation-state. Most of these histories were written from the perspective of the West; in the case of Wells and Toynbee, their narratives tended to be tales of separate, distinct civilizations. Notably, the idea of universal civilization—even based on a Western model— found some resonance among Asian intellectuals in the Ottoman and Japanese Empires in the late nineteenth century, though these views were increasingly mooted after World War I, as the stress fell upon the primacy of distinct civilizations.[20]

A clear antecedent of UNESCO's world history is H. G. Wells's 1,100-page popular global history, *The Outline of History*, published in 1920. This book was the most popular work of history in the first half of the twentieth century, reportedly having sold over a million copies by 1931. It built its narrative around issues of evolution, ecology, and social Darwinism. Julian Huxley knew Wells, and even collaborated with him on the volume's companion piece, *The Science of Life*. It is not difficult to detect various themes that found their way into the UNESCO Mankind project: the endeavor to write a readable world history from the dawn of time to the present for a broad readership; the focus on the earth's prehuman history; pride of place to non-Western ancient civilizations, such as India, Egypt, and China; and science as the common thread. Wells's contention that the danger of nationalism lay in a "de-civilization of men's minds" and that "our true nationality is mankind" became cherished UNESCO principles.[21]

UNESCO's world history project gained additional luster from the involvement of several internationally famous historians. Arnold Toynbee served as a kind of consultant for the project, and lent his support to the idea of writing a world history from the perspective of science and technology. No less prominent was the great French historian Lucien Febvre. Febvre founded the famous journal *Annales d'histoire économique et sociale* in 1929, and was president of the committee overseeing a new *Encyclopédie française* in the 1930s. Febvre had been one of France's delegates to the UNESCO Preparatory Commission in London in 1946, and several French commentators credit him as the originator of the *History of Mankind* initiative. In a 1949 report, Febvre set out the objective of the project as "to act upon the minds of people in order to extirpate the fatal virus of war." He founded the *Journal of World History* in 1953, and in his foreword to the first issue Febvre boldly announced that UNESCO's world history would be composed "not of those so-called Heroes, those 'scourges of God,' who for thousands of years seem to have been brought into the world only to covet, kill, plunder and burn." Instead, this history "does not breed hatred. It does not tend to crush the so-called 'small nations' beneath the weight of the great ones. It considers them all as so many participants in a great common enterprise. . . . And that, to parody the slogan of that would-be Caesar who ended in the mud, in Sedan, we may say, and we repeat, 'History is peace.'" His was a direct challenge to standard Great Men of History narratives in which the history of warring elites would be replaced by chronicles of the peaceful exchanges of cultures—humanity on the move.[22]

History of Mankind's six volumes ranged from prehistory to the first half of the twentieth century. Febvre set the tone by saying that "there are no insignificant peoples, no poor or destitute civilizations that have not contributed in one way or another to the building of our great and overconfident civilizations that, in fact, survive by borrowing." The central task was then not only to write about peace, but to write world history as a record of cultural interaction and cross-fertilization. At first this may sound rather banal, especially given today's enthusiasm in the historians' profession about networks and flows as the basis of new transnational histories. However, UNESCO's view of history was quite novel in the late 1940s, not least because modern histories of civilizations (as with Spengler and Toynbee) had largely conceived civilizations as geographically and culturally distinct blocks with their own internal logic, life cycle, and achievements. Emphasis by contrast was placed on trade, travel, migrations, the exchange of ideas, and even war, but only insofar as war exerted influence upon cultural exchanges and interactions. Another controversial feature was a strong disavowal of Eurocentrism. Febvre's *Journal of World History* advanced a decidedly anti-Eurocentric perspective, and the appointment of the well-known Indian historian and diplomat K. M. Panikkar as one of the editors of volume 6 of *History of Mankind*, on the twentieth century, lent further credibility to this internationalist approach. Senghor served as a member of UNESCO's International Commission for the History of Mankind, alongside Lévi-Strauss and the Lebanese philosopher and human rights lawyer Charles Malik.[23]

For all these reasons, there was a good deal of excitement about this new world history. Indian scholars welcomed the project as a means to "correct the myopia of Western savants, so many of whom, unable to see beyond Greece, have withheld from the East and especially from India the credit for cultural priority." Decolonization was the departure point and framework for the project. In the last volume, on twentieth-century world history until 1960, Gandhi is given more coverage than Hitler, while Kwame Nkrumah and Jomo Kenyatta receive more attention than Stalin or Mussolini. For UNESCO, civilization and peace were synonymous, and this new history was to provide a record of civilian achievements of humanity in the past as an alternative history for a divided and belligerent Cold War world. Relatedly, UNESCO organized accompanying conferences that gathered teachers from areas where historical conflict was endemic—Germany and France, Japan and China, Mexico and the United States—to write new textbooks that challenged militant nationalism and stressed common histories in the name of political peace. Not for nothing did the *New York Times* hail this as a "grand and unparalleled publishing venture."[24]

Even before the volumes were published in the mid-1960s, the project ran into Cold War conflict. On the one hand, the Soviet Union and its communist allies felt that worker history had been underplayed in the draft volumes, especially in the last installment on the twentieth century. The Soviet delegate on the commission, Alexandre Zvorikine, duly returned over 500 pages of objections to the volume's characterization of communism, technological developments in the USSR, the Soviet economy, and its political system. On the other, religious leaders—be they Catholics, Protestants, or Jews—voiced disgruntlement with the project, on grounds ranging from the supposedly atheistic thrust of the project to the downplaying of Jewish history. The most trenchant criticism came from a seemingly unlikely source—the Catholic Church. Efforts were made to bring the Catholic Church on board early on: a permanent papal ambassador to UNESCO was appointed in 1949, and the papal nuncio in France, Angelo Giuseppe Roncalli (later Pope John XXIII), was invited to address UNESCO's General Conference in July 1951. By the early 1950s the Vatican had sent extensive criticisms of the early drafts of the histories. Christian skepticism toward UNESCO's world history project deepened in the wake of the traveling exhibition *The Human Rights Album* discussed above, in which Christianity barely featured and Jesus went unmentioned. Criticism toward the new world history volumes poured in from the Christian press across the world, ranging from France, Italy, Spain, Switzerland, Canada, Mexico, the US, and even Czechoslovakia. Sixteen conservative French deputies signed a letter accusing UNESCO of peddling "the influence of an anti-Christian ideology."[25]

The *History of Mankind* project may have been good politics, but not necessarily good history. Press reviews took issue with its version of history-writing. On offer was a kind of liberal Whiggishness, in which the past and present were read as unifying and reasonable, peaceful and peaceable—in sharp contrast to a dangerous Cold War world that offered little of this to most observers. Press reviews of volume 6, on the twentieth century, were decidedly mixed. While some greeted it as a "valuable and fascinating work," others were unconvinced. One Indian reviewer noted that the project ended up undermining its own objectives: "The idea was to develop international understanding. But what has been the reaction to the volumes already published? Some bad feelings were created among the peoples of different countries, especially of the Communist and newly independent and developing countries." The effort to exclude the world of violent emotions from history was damned by one *Guardian* reviewer: "The result is moderate consensual liberalism with several minority reports," and "if archaeologists unearth it in the remains of the UN headquarters, they are likely to find a new consensus: that it was the things this history omits, the emotions and angers of man, which led to violent destruction of the city-level at which it was found." Conservative American journalists railed against the world history project as a sinister plot to extinguish people's "individuality and their love of country in favor of the miasmic visions of a bunch of burocrats [*sic*] brought up on a globaloney diet." Muslim countries were displeased with the benign interpretation of the Christian Crusades, and there was criticism about the relative paucity of African and South American history.[26]

For all its hype and investment, UNESCO's two-decade, multivolume international history-writing enterprise never reached its intended goal and broad audience. In part this had to do with the fact that both UNESCO and the world had changed. Jaime Torres Bodet, the eminent Mexican diplomat and writer who succeeded Huxley as the second director-general, devoted the agency's energies to technical assistance to poorer countries, turning the attention away from world civilization toward more practical concrete tasks with tangible results. And in the period from 1946 to 1956 member states went from thirty to eighty—many of these new independent countries were suspicious of ideas of world civilization, preferring instead to mint new narratives of national arrival and nationalist achievement. Even the project's title—the *History of Mankind*—seemed woefully outdated, as "mankind" was viewed as a sexist holdover from an unreconstructed past. This world history project was a last gasp of the language and mission of civilization itself before it was politely replaced by "development" as the more politically correct watchword of First-Third World relations. Put differently, what was progressive in the 1940s—writing a new universal history of humanity—was greeted as conservative and even neocolonial by the mid-1960s. In fact, the Algerian War made some of UNESCO's integrationist policies seem rather backward-looking and imperial, especially in terms of the agency's claims that domestic racism (rather than colonialism)

was the real problem at hand. Yet UNESCO's mission of world civilization scored great successes in other areas.[27]

BY FAR THE AGENCY'S MOST SPECTACULAR PROJECT WAS THE
rescue of the Nubian monuments from the waters of Lake Nasser
that straddled southern Egypt and northern Sudan. No event better
exemplified its abiding mission to build and safeguard world civilization, and as such constituted an instructive tale of Cold War
internationalism. After 1945 the internationalization of the heritage industry was closely tied to projects of state-building and the
construction of new national identities, as seen with the national
reclamation of monuments, religious sites, and natural parks around
the world. UNESCO flew in the face of these trends, and made
great strides in bringing together international law, historical preservation, and intercultural awareness about the material heritage
of world civilization. The Nubian monument preservation project
played a special role in this cultural crusade, hailed as proof that
such a global heritage consciousness could and did exist despite
geopolitical antagonism and ideological difference. Given Gamal
Abdel Nasser's effort to speed along Egypt's Aswan High Dam
project in the early 1960s, the ancient land of Nubia played host to
a dramatic clash between progress and preservation that attracted
worldwide media coverage. The UNESCO International Campaign
to Save the Monuments of Nubia captured a distinctly postwar sensibility of humanity's shared but imperiled cultural patrimony. As
one contemporary commentator wryly put it: "Thus Nubia, poor,
forgotten and now doomed, commanded in its dying days the interest of mankind."[28]

Nasser's Aswan High Dam project began in 1960, and took ten
years to complete. While ideas of taming the Nile go back to phar-
aonic times, the modern era's effort to devise a reservoir to store
excess water from the Nile's great floods began with the building of

the first Aswan Dam between 1898 and 1902. It was designed by British engineers, and was intended mainly for cotton cultivation. The dam was raised in 1912 and then again in 1933 in order to meet Egypt's growing water demands. As the first dam construction was nearly finished, there was growing concern among Egyptologists and others about the fate of the ancient Nubian ruins and peoples once the area behind the dam was flooded. Hasty compromises were struck—the famous Philae monument, for example, was allowed to be half-submerged for five months of the year. In this case, the preservationists were largely overrun by the technocrats, who drove ahead with subjugating the Nile for agricultural and economic purposes.[29]

The conflict between old and new became even more pronounced in the wake of the Egyptian Revolution of 1952 to overthrow the monarchy. Regulating the Nile served as the political cornerstone of the fledgling United Arab Republic, and the dam was described as Nasser's latter-day pyramid for its central political symbolism. Nasser announced his intention to nationalize the Suez Canal in July 1956, expecting that revenues generated from this would help underwrite dam construction and the creation of a 300-mile-long artificial lake, Lake Nasser. With the outbreak of war later that year, Egypt was in urgent need of support, and in 1958 the Soviet Union offered financial assistance for the project, along with the requisite technicians and heavy machinery. The joint dam project became the source of great Cold War theater as a sign of a new Soviet-African axis, as well as a showcase of Soviet engineering (even if the Soviets simply modified an earlier West German design).

International safeguarding of cultural property had been devised a century or so earlier, often in reaction to the destructive capacities of war. In the wake of the Napoleonic Wars, for example, plunder became a key moral issue among nations, and international treaties (beginning with the 1874 Brussels "Project of an International Declaration Concerning the Laws and Customs of War") were expressly dedicated to redressing damage and destruction to state property of all kinds in times of war. The aftermath of the Great War saw renewed international attention toward preservation. The League of Nations and its new International Commission on Historical Monuments endeavored to create new legal instruments to protect cultural antiquities as a step toward international cooperation. The League's first attempt to set up a cultural heritage conservation initiative took place in 1922, on the back of the international excitement associated with the discovery of King Tutankhamun's tomb earlier that year. The League's International Museums Office was founded in 1926 to carry on the mission, and the final report of its high-profile conference in Athens in 1931 concluded that the "question of the conservation of the artistic and archaeological property of mankind is one that interests the community of States, which are wardens of civilization."[30]

After 1945 there was a move to rehabilitate and extend this interwar dream, even to the extent of rendering such destruction an internationally recognized criminal offense. At the Nuremberg Trial, the destruction of cultural property was declared a crime against humanity. Alfred Rosenberg—infamous head of the Third Reich's Center for National Socialist Ideological and Education Research—was singled out for his office's unlawful seizure of cultural treasures. UNESCO's heritage protection mission began to take shape over the course of the next decade. The massive earthquake in Cuzco, Peru, in 1950, which left some 30,000 homeless, launched the agency's first mission to save archaeological ruins. It sent out teams of international archaeologists, art historians, and technical experts to work with Peruvian locals to save the Aztec ruins, and by all accounts it was a very successful initiative. UNESCO's new global vision found further expression in the 1954 Hague Convention on the "Protection of Cultural Property in the Event of Armed Conflict," which was a fortified version of the Hague Conventions of 1899 and 1907. "Cultural property belonging to any people," so it proclaimed, is "also the cultural heritage of all mankind."[31]

Figure 30. Rescue of Nubian monuments, Abu Simbel, UNESCO, Egypt, 1965. *Credit: UNESCO Archive*

UNESCO needed a big project to showcase its new role as warden of world civilization, and the timing of the threat to the Nubian monuments could not have been more fortuitous. At a moment when Egypt had just removed British military forces after seventy years of occupation, UNESCO was viewed by Nasser as a nonpartisan intergovernmental alternative to Western institutions. There was growing interest in the Nubians among *National Geographic* photographers in the early 1950s, and the Save the Monuments of Nubia campaign looked to build on this international publicity. Proposals were solicited from various quarters of Europe, and eventually the experts selected a Swedish plan to have the temple facades and walls cut into big blocks that could be transported to a safe place and then rebuilt on higher ground. Rock temples were to be hewn from the cliffs and then transported in sections, while freestanding temples were dismantled, transferred, and reassembled (Figure 30). To drum up support, the Egyptian government organized an exhibition, *5,000 Years of Egyptian Art*, which started its world tour in Brussels in 1960.[32]

In March 1960 UNESCO's new director-general, Vittorio Veronese, kicked off the international appeal. He made his case for the higher cause of universal civilization: "These monuments, the loss of which may be tragically near, do not belong solely to the countries who hold them in trust," for they were "part of a common heritage which comprises Socrates' message and the Ajanta frescoes; the walls of Uxmal and Beethoven's symphonies." The language of rights and legal protections was gravitating to the center of this heritage campaign. Whereas the early twentieth-century preservation drive to save the famed Nubian monuments had been justified by Egyptologists for the study of biblical narratives and theories of racial diffusion, the 1960s campaign was animated by a decidedly secular ideal of universal civilization that linked the ancient past to the present around the ideas of science, culture, and peace. This initiative challenged state sovereignty in subtle ways. Until that point all monuments within states were of exclusively national concern and were to be cared for by individual states, but this time things were different. As UNESCO's director of the Monuments of Nubia Service, Ali Vrioni, remarked, "For the first time the world has seen organized international action to save monuments of archaeological wealth, which, in law, belong only to the two countries where they are located."[33]

The media campaign went into high gear. A number of publications were produced by UNESCO to help publicize the urgency of the campaign. In 1961 an exhibition of Tutankhamun treasures toured the US, helping generate interest in the endangered Nubian monuments. That same year President John F. Kennedy launched an impassioned plea before Congress to garner American assistance, and justified support with the language of civilization: "The United States, one of the newest civilizations, has long had a deep regard for the study of past cultures, and a concern for the preservation of man's great achievements of art and thoughts [sic]," and "by thus contributing to the preservation of past civilizations, we will strengthen and enrich our own." The US sought to make up for its failure to support the Aswan Dam project, heeding the call to rescue the ancient monuments by matching Egypt's $10 million financial commitment. Accompanying exhibitions took place both

Figure 31. Commemorative stamps for UNESCO's
Save the Monuments of Nubia campaign, Egypt
and Libya. *Credit: UNESCO Archive*

in the US and Europe, and a number of countries (such as Egypt
and Libya) issued commemorative stamps to keep the campaign in
the public eye (Figure 31). The European dimension was significant
too. The original Honorary Committee of Patrons for the Nubian
campaign was chaired by King Gustav VI Adolf of Sweden, flanked
by Queen Elizabeth of Belgium, Queen Frederica of Greece, Prince
Mikasa of Japan, UN secretary-general Dag Hammarskjöld, Julian
Huxley, and France's culture minister, André Malraux. Malraux
waxed lyrical about UNESCO's great mission to undo the corruption of time and to reconceive world history as a new "family of
man" dedicated to peace and concord. As he put it: "At the moment
when our civilisation divines a mysterious transcendence in art and
one of the still obscure sources of its unity, at the moment when we
are bringing into a single family relationship the masterpieces of so
many civilisations which knew nothing of or even hated each other,
you are proposing an action which brings all men together to defy
the forces of dissolution."[34]

At first Malraux's endorsement of the project might appear as
entirely in keeping with UNESCO's broader brief. UNESCO was
based in Paris and seen as a particularly French institution in terms
of the agency's campaign to define and defend the idea of world
civilization. Yet it is worth recalling that Malraux was hardly a figure
associated with progressive culture in the 1920s. In 1924 Malraux
was scandalously charged with stealing several stone Khmer statues

and bas-reliefs from the temple of Banteay Srei in Cambodia during his expedition to study ancient monuments of Khmer architecture. Reportedly he had been warned of the illegality of removing the sculptures, but ultimately justified his archaeological "recovery" on the grounds that the temple was in a state of total neglect and disrepair, and thus fell under the category of "abandoned property" (*res derelicta*) belonging to no one, given that it had not been officially classified by any legal authority at the time. Malraux and his assistant were detained while trying to transport a full ton of material to Saigon en route to Paris, and his trial in Phnom Penh became a major cause célèbre (the so-called Angkor Affair) about the international ownership of heritage, to say nothing of French-Indochina relations. The stolen pieces were eventually returned to the temple wall (where they are today), and ownership was transferred to the state. Such a figure espousing the importance of world heritage may seem hypocritical to some, but it can also be argued that Malraux's conversion to the universalist cause was symptomatic of a changed internationalist sensibility after 1945. His shift of attitude dramatically demonstrated that UNESCO's project was in large measure an effort to move archaeology (and indeed civilization itself) beyond the sphere of imperialism and nationalism once and for all. In his eyes, the whole rescue operation was "a kind of Tennessee Valley Authority of archaeology," the "antithesis of the kind of gigantic exhibitionism by which great modern states try to outbid each other."[35]

Egypt and the Sudan defended their national claims even as they cooperated with UNESCO. The Egyptian government funded around one-third of the project, even if its ideas diverged from UNESCO's in subtle ways. Sarwat Okasha, Egyptian minister of culture and national guidance, made clear that the Nubian monuments belonged to Egypt first. Nasser—who had shown no interest in the issue a few years earlier—suddenly changed his spots and made clear to whom the ruins belonged, saying, "We pin our hopes on the preservation of the Nubian treasures in order to keep alive monuments which are not only dear to our hearts, we being their guardians, but dear to the whole world which believes that the ancient and the new components of human culture should blend in one harmonious whole." The national dimension of this international rescue mission was underscored by Sudanese officials as well, who lauded the mission for having "sparked interest among the Sudanese in their own past and cultural heritage."[36]

In the race against time, some twenty-five countries sent archaeological teams to Nubia in a frantic effort to record, relocate, and salvage the monuments of Nubia before the Nile submerged them. Shifts worked frantically day and night to record and save the monuments, turning the temples into film studios of study and documentation. At Abu Simbel one could hear Arabic, English, German, French, Spanish, Italian, Swedish, and Polish being spoken, as archaeologists and engineers collaborated in apparent harmony and goodwill. Archaeological teams hailed from Spain, Scandinavia, Ghana, the United States, and a joint French-Argentinian mission, and included key missions from Great Britain, West Germany, and Italy. Support came from across the Cold War blocs, with missions from the USSR, East Germany, Hungary, Czechoslovakia, Poland, and Yugoslavia. The expedition from the Polish Academy of Sciences and National Museum of Warsaw made some of the greatest discoveries, uncovering an eighth-century cathedral built on the site of an ancient church, whose excavation yielded over 100 frescoes made between the eighth and eleventh centuries. Yugoslav newspapers generously covered the Nubian campaign, with special reference to the country's experts in Sudanese Nubia. In numerous publications the East European missions proudly boasted of their contribution. Added luster derived from the on-site presence of Crown Princess Margrethe of Denmark, who arrived in 1962 as part of the Scandinavian mission, and reportedly impressed everyone by refusing the luxury accommodation of the Nile Hotel in favor of living with members of the mission so as to get a taste of the "Nubian way of life."[37]

But it was less the glamour than the unique anti–Cold War spirit of international cooperation that struck journalists at the time. One *New York Times* reporter in 1961 marveled at the way the project brought together countries that officially did not recognize each other (such as Spain and the USSR) or were in political conflict (India and Pakistan); as he put it, "There seemed to be no Cold War in the Land of Kush," as Moscow and Washington, "so feverishly contesting the future of all Africa, are working hand in hand to protect its past." UNESCO director Vittorio Veronese could not resist plugging his agency's achievement, praising the way that "from a land which throughout the centuries has been the scene of—or the stake in—so many covetous disputes should spring a convincing proof of international solidarity."[38]

On March 10, 1980, the long-awaited consecration of two dozen of the most famous Nubian statues rescued from the waters of Lake Nasser took place with all solemn pomp and circumstance, crowning an unprecedented twenty-year international campaign to save the monuments. In the end the project involved the support of dozens of countries and NGOs, along with thousands of archaeologists, engineers, and volunteers, in a common enterprise of fundraising, political will, and technical virtuosity that transcended Cold War divisions. UNESCO's Save the Monuments of Nubia campaign can certainly be counted as a great success on archaeological terms. For one thing, it set in motion broader ideas and practices of international heritage protection. Reclaiming ancient ruins around the world as the property of humanity (managed by UNESCO) found formal expression in the organization's 1964 International Charter for the Conservation and Restoration of Monuments and Sites, known as the Venice Charter. By the late 1960s, the new concept of World Heritage sites as a common language of universal patrimony was fueled by the growing belief that defending world cultural heritage would help promote tolerance and international peace. The ideals of world civilization gained further credence with the formal passing of the 1972 Convention Concerning the Protection of the World Cultural and National Heritage, which boldly proclaimed that the international community "has an obligation to support any nation in discharging this trust if its own resources are not equal to the task." While in 1978 there were only 12 sites inscribed on the inaugural World Heritage list, today there are over 900 listed.[39]

UNESCO's success in this project became a pretext for salvage operations in other countries. Florence and Venice recovered from their respective floods in 1966 thanks in large part to UNESCO's international fundraising campaign. The Buddhist temple of Borobudur in Indonesia was cleaned and restored between 1970 and 1983 under UNESCO auspices. The Egyptian government donated four temples as tokens of appreciation—Debod to Spain, Taffa to Holland, Dendur to the US, Ellesiya to Italy—to be housed overseas as part of the "open air" worldwide Nubian museum. The Egyptian government built the Nubian Museum in Aswan and the National Museum of Egyptian Civilization in Cairo as a result of the project. In a very real sense, the Nubian rescue mission changed forever the practice of archaeology on a global scale. This really was—as one 1966 *Guardian* article put it—the "most spectacular archaeological rescue the world has seen," and has framed the way that heritage sites are managed around the world ever since.[40]

THE UNESCO MISSION WAS SIGNIFICANT IN A NUMBER OF WAYS. First, the early UNESCO debates afford a unique view into the call to "forgive and forget" on the international level, as UNESCO advanced a one-world vision of world civilization predicated on integrating former fascist enemies into the international community. In the case of West Germany and Japan, UNESCO played a supportive role in helping former fascist belligerents remake their identities as new "civilian power" regimes and exemplars of a new post-Axis world order. These UNESCO membership debates revealed the moment when one international system was quietly burying another, in this case, the specter of international fascism. With it the healing powers of internationalism neatly dovetailed with a new politics of national recovery advanced by the losers of World War II.

And in its various initiatives, the agency forged new links of co-operation across Cold War divides. From the 1940s on, the agency was a valued clearinghouse of new ideas about world affairs and cultural exchange across ideological camps, and helped to reconceive the relationship between Europe and the rest of the world after the war. For Western elites UNESCO served as a global platform to disavow Western cultural and racial supremacy through its championing of a unity-in-diversity model of world civilizations. Its archaeological and development projects around the world, together with its statements on race, did much to win the trust and confidence of new African and Asian elites, who increasingly looked to UNESCO for cultural support and material assistance in constructing the cultural infrastructures of new independent nation-states. The agency also sponsored a number of international conferences across Africa on prehistory in the 1960s, and was a strong patron of Senghor's Festival of Black Arts blockbuster exhibition in 1966 discussed in the last chapter. And as we shall see in the next chapter, UNESCO emerged as a vital contact point for elites from Eastern Europe and the developing world to share knowledge and expertise in the social sciences in a spirit of anti-Western political cooperation and socialist solidarity. Initial Eastern European skepticism toward UNESCO quickly evaporated, not least because the agency became an ardent critic of Western imperialism, racism, and apartheid. In this sense, the agency did much to rehabilitate the old European concept of civilization for non-Europeans as an ecumenical language of anticolonialism, mutual recognition, and regional identities in the Global South.

There were limitations to UNESCO's mission, however, and Cold War rivalries and chronic underfunding certainly played their part. While there was successful international cooperation to preserve various archaeological sites and material objects around the world in the name of world heritage, such cooperation crumbled when it came to writing a shared narrative of the past, best seen in the failed *History of Mankind* project. And even some of the highly touted salvage projects had serious downsides. The fanfare around the Nubian monuments preservation project obscured one extremely awkward issue: the evacuation of the Nubian peoples themselves. Some 100,000 Nubians were removed over a painful period of nine months starting in October 1963. They had been forced to relocate three times already before the 1963 resettlement—in 1902, 1912, and then again in 1933. This time they were relocated from Lower Nubia in the Sudan northward to Kom Ombo in Egypt, losing their ancestral land and social fabric with it. In the Sudan, riots broke out when news of the move was announced, and local Sudanese authorities were even taken hostage at one point. While some Nubians, especially young men, were in favor of resettlement, confusion and anger on the part of the Nubians were rife. In a 1955 letter, Jean Vercoutter, commissioner for archaeology in the Sudan just before the Nubian restoration campaign, wrote: "The attitude of the Nubians themselves was bitter. 'We would be better looked after if we were statues,' was a remark often heard." The debit side of the Aswan High Dam project was captured by a *National Geographic* photographer covering the rescue mission: "The new bustle struck me with special intensity, contrasting as it did with the dying land around us. Nubia had always been mostly empty space, and the Nubians had ever felt themselves to be denizens of the horizon. But after the modern Nubians were relocated to save them from the rising flood, the area lost its last trace of life. Not a soul, not a sail."[41]

UNESCO was nonetheless unique in the manner that it managed the past as much as the present, providing a vision of world civilization that had as much to do with willfully forgetting violent national pasts as about forging a new international community of

343

member states. It set out to show the world that Europe had learned the lessons of World War II, rejecting the violent legacy of racism and war in favor of peace, international cooperation, and mutual respect. What is more, UNESCO accepted the diminished place of Europe in the world, expressly acknowledging that Europe was just one civilization among many. Such views had been mooted in some ways since the Enlightenment, but UNESCO is the first international organization to give these ideas institutional expression and global force. UNESCO's renewal of ruins was inseparable from the moral renewal of ruined Europe itself. This is not to say that nationalism and Eurocentrism ever disappeared from the organization, as the politics surrounding the designation of World Heritage sites since the early 1970s attest. However, we should not lose sight of UNESCO's grand project—to break the long-standing equation of Europe with civilization, and to strip the story of civilization of its martial, imperial, and racial baggage. Peace and civilization were viewed as integral and synonymous, with peace itself identified as the most precious ruin in need of urgent care and preservation.

Interest in both the modernization and ancient history of the developing world was not confined to Western governments, business officials, and international agencies. The next chapter shows how Eastern Europeans were also keen to build their own relations with decolonizing Africa in the 1960s, and to this end established an elaborate network of cultural connections with various African countries under the banner of socialist civilization.

eight

SOCIALISM'S CIVILIZING MISSION IN AFRICA

O N January 6, 1961, Nikita Khrushchev delivered a
landmark speech on "For New Victories of the World Communist Movement" at the Institute of Marxism-Leninism in Moscow in which he hailed the "awakening of the peoples of Africa."
The Soviet premier proclaimed that it was the "historical mission" of
world communism to support "wars of liberation" around the world
so as to undo the injustice of colonialism. In his eyes, such support
was both appropriate and timely because "communists are revolutionaries, and it would be a bad thing if we did not take advantage of
new opportunities" or look "for new methods and forms that would
best achieve the ends in view." The speech signaled the end of the
Soviet Union's relative isolation since the end of the Second World
War, during which a battered USSR sought above all to heal and
protect itself from the devastation of war. Under Khrushchev the
Soviet Union looked to enlarge its global influence in relation to
the US, its Western allies, and an increasingly aggressive China. This
time the focus was not westward as during the endgame of the Second World War, but rather southward. As part of its turn abroad
in the 1960s, the Soviet Union portrayed itself as a role model of

anticolonialism, non-Western development, and speedy moderniza-tion. That a Soviet Sputnik had beaten the Americans to outer space in 1957 was further evidence that Moscow was successfully expand-ing the frontiers of communism by land and by air.[1]

Decolonization marked the opening up of new geographical and imaginative horizons, as observers around the world recognized the seismic shift in world history. "New frontiers" was a favorite buzz phrase of the era, most famously associated with American president John F. Kennedy. His 1961 State of the Union address was explic-itly devoted to the theme, especially in connection with the need to check what was worryingly viewed as Soviet encroachment on the New Africa. Kennedy had used the term repeatedly in his campaign speeches, and then in his presidential addresses, to galvanize Ameri-can engagement with the newly decolonized world. "Their revolution is the greatest in human history," he wrote, adding that "the great battleground for the defense and expansion of freedom today is the whole southern half of the globe." Kennedy's idea of America's New Frontier in Africa was a direct response to Khrushchev's new gaze southward. JFK studied Khrushchev's 1961 speech in great detail, and apparently read portions of it out loud during the first meeting of his National Security Council after taking office in late Janu-ary 1961. Kennedy's celebrated Peace Corps initiative was largely designed to counteract the growing presence of Eastern European doctors, engineers, teachers, and welfare professionals in Africa at the time, what Kennedy called the Eastern Bloc's "missionaries for international communism." The freshly installed president sought to move away from Eisenhower's indifference toward Africa by court-ing African nationalist leaders, hosting no fewer than twenty-eight African heads of state at the White House in his abbreviated ten-ure in office. Not for nothing was Kennedy's foreign policy team known as the New Frontiersmen. But independent Africa was not being eyed just by the superpowers, as the British, French, and in-creasingly the West Germans worked to peddle their influence in the aftermath of liberation. No wonder Tanzanian president Julius Nyerere cynically characterized the period as the "second scramble for Africa."[2]

Equally energetic were communist newcomers to the continent. Their growing presence was largely due to the fact that the international communist world was both expanding and fracturing at the time. The unexpected Chinese Revolution of 1949 was confirmation to them that world history was very much on their side, as "world communism" could count 830 million new members since 1945, including 80 million from Eastern Europe.[3] The communist world was also fracturing, as evidenced in the Yugoslav-Soviet split in 1948 and souring relations between the People's Republic of China and the Soviet Union from 1956 to 1966. This meant that the Soviet Union, China, Yugoslavia, Cuba, and Eastern Europe competed against both the West and themselves for the hearts and minds of the elites of newly independent countries. A new frontier mindset gripped the communist world as well. In the first decades of the twentieth century, communist thinking on frontiers had been closely linked to the shifting fortunes of the Soviet Union itself. But now the situation was changing, as virtually all the communist powers, including the USSR, China, and Yugoslavia, as well as smaller Eastern European states, were keen on looking beyond their borders. So much so that the period can arguably be understood as a kind of socialist version of the "frontier thesis" of political development and ideological regeneration. Originally the frontier thesis was articulated by American historian Frederick Jackson Turner in his 1893 classic booklet, *The Significance of the Frontier in American History*, in which he reinterpreted the dynamic relationship between politics and geography as a driver of American history. Turner argued that Americans did not learn to become democrats through institutions, schools, or civic ideology, but rather through their experience on the frontiers of the American West. In his telling, it was the frontier that turned settlers into Americans, and Americans into democrats. For Turner, the frontier afforded a "perennial rebirth" by means of expansion and exploration. Over the course of the 1960s, Africa became a dynamic hub of global encounters, whose frontier opened up new possibilities of East-South cultural interaction in unprecedented ways.[4]

For their part, Eastern Europeans devoted a great deal of public relations to insist that they arrived in Africa as the "other Europeans," innocent of the stain of imperialism. These two regions of the world may have enjoyed a few historical connections, but it was the Cold War that brought them in dramatic contact for the first time, both physically and virtually. Communists firmly rejected the whole ideological project of the civilizing mission, and never described their engagement with Africa in these terms. They lampooned the prejudicial framework of civilization and barbarity as irredeemable holdovers of the intellectual armory of Western imperialism and racism. The West too was changing its vocabulary of engagement, and tended to couch its rebooted mission in the more palatable language of development and human rights. Communists largely did the same thing, but they also invoked the causes of anti-imperialism and a socialist version of modernity as the basis of far-flung fraternity. The accent was placed on industrial modernization, independence, and solidarity as the shared goals of Eastern European and African elites. These links—both real and imagined—were not always geared toward a shiny technological future; crucial too were efforts to give form to what a transcontinental, postimperial civilization might look like from a socialist perspective. A blend of modernity and African antiquity emerged as a surprising point of cultural diplomacy between them in the era of decolonization.

In this respect, Eastern European elites built relations with their African counterparts around the policies of progress and heritage preservation, and cooperated with UNESCO and other international agencies in forging closer ties with the developing world. The result was a significant transformation of Eastern Europe's international place and presence across Africa from the 1960s onward.

Figure 32. Bolshoi Ballet performing in Cairo, Egypt; Kabul musicians playing in Moscow. *Credit:* To Know Each Other *(Moscow: Novosti Press Agency Publishing House, 1967)*

In 1967 the Soviet Union published a punchy brochure in English titled *To Know Each Other*. It sought to take advantage of a fast-changing political world, and aimed to further develop Soviet cultural networks with foreign countries. The stated mission of the Union of Soviet Friendship Societies was to promote "friendship among all nations of the globe" in the name of "peace and humanism." By the late 1950s the USSR had mounted numerous art shows of works from other Eastern European countries as well as other socialist lands, such as China, North Korea, Vietnam, and Mongolia. Such events were becoming common instances of Soviet cultural diplomacy from the mid-1950s onward, a trend worryingly noted by Western observers. By 1967 the Union of Soviet Friendship Societies had established contacts with no fewer than thirty-two African countries, fourteen Latin American countries, and seventeen countries in Southeast Asia and the Middle East. *To Know Each Other* went on to highlight a number of events on literature, art, dance, photography, and folk handicrafts, accompanied by photographs of exchanges—such as the renowned Bolshoi Ballet performing in Cairo and Kabul musicians playing in Moscow, as noted in Figure 32. *To Know Each Other* documented Soviet cultural activities and exchanges abroad, and was conceived in part as a means to help promote indigenous cultures everywhere.[5]

Khrushchev's cultural diplomacy echoed early Soviet initiatives. Linking foreign policy and culture formally began with the creation of the USSR's All-Union Society for Cultural Relations with Foreign Countries (VOKS) in 1925. VOKS was set up as an umbrella organization to convey a positive image of the Great Experiment to the West, and even brought over foreigners (especially Americans) to show off the country and its achievements. This tradition of cultural diplomacy was renewed after Stalin's death as part of the peacetime competition with both the West and China. The cultural offensive toward the developing world was designed to dovetail with Moscow's stepped-up soft power campaign in Eastern Europe in the

1950s and 1960s. Opening the Soviet state to the world also helped give expression to the belief that the future belonged to socialism, with the Soviet Union as the harbinger of progressive culture.[6]

The Soviet Union had been a loud advocate of anti-imperialism worldwide from its revolutionary beginnings and continued to champion the cause of emancipation through the 1930s. Anti-imperialists in the developing world praised the Soviet condemnation of Italian imperialism at the League of Nations during the Abyssinian crisis of 1935. Eastern European solidarity toward Ethiopia included League of Nations representatives from the Little Entente (Romania, Yugoslavia, and Czechoslovakia) and the Balkan Pact (Yugoslavia, Greece, Romania, and Turkey), who passionately defended Ethiopia's independence and sovereignty as a League member in the spirit of the organization's founding charter. The Italian assault on Ethiopia anticipated another international crisis three years later—the Nazi occupation of Czechoslovakia's Sudetenland, what Trinidad intellectual George Padmore called the "New Abyssinia"—which effectively conjoined the fate of Eastern Europe and Africa in the struggle against European fascist imperialism globally. In 1945, Moscow proclaimed its support of African anticolonial movements at the founding meeting of the United Nations in San Francisco in the face of a reconsolidated European colonial system.[7]

To extend support to the developing world, in 1955 Khrushchev traveled to India, Burma, Afghanistan, Egypt, and Indonesia—visiting some thirty-five countries in all. Diplomatic relations with heads of state from Africa were further formalized through prize-giving cultural ceremonies. In 1961 the Soviet Union awarded the Lenin Prize to Guinean president Sékou Touré, in 1962 to Ghanaian president Kwame Nkrumah, and in 1963 to Malian president Modibo Keïta. In the early 1960s, the Soviet Union became a member of over 200 international organizations, from the UN to UNESCO to the International Olympic Committee. Soviet publishing houses churned out some 100 million books per year to send to the developing world. Over 20,000 Soviet artists were sent to sixty countries from 1955 to 1958, more than half to nonsocialist lands; from 1961 to 1965 these numbers rose to 80,000 Soviet artists with as many foreign artists traveling to the USSR in this same period. In 1960 Moscow's Institute of Oriental Studies' popular monthly journal *Sovremennyi Vostok* (*Contemporary East*) was renamed *Aziia i Afrika Segodnia* (*Asia and Africa Today*), and used the new language of Afro-Asian solidarity organizations that now were being wooed by Soviet politicians. The magazine was intended to whet domestic interest in overseas cultures inaccessible to most Soviet citizens, and to help curb young people's abiding fascination with Western society. Images of interracial friendship between children and young people were featured as images of peace, often contrasted with pictures of racial strife in the American South. Moscow also hosted large-scale youth festivals as meeting places of international students. In the summer of 1957, for example, some 30,000 young people from across the world came to Moscow to take part in the Sixth World Festival of Youth and Students. For two weeks the Russian capital was a centerpiece for international youth, peace, modernity, and solidarity, during which all cinemas, circuses, exhibitions, sporting events, and public transport were offered free of charge, with Radio Moscow providing full coverage. Soviet filmmakers were sent to Africa in the early 1960s to celebrate the growing friendship of the Soviet Union with newly independent countries in a spirit of revolutionary romanticism, as evidenced in the films *Hello, Africa!* (1961) and *We Are with You, Africa!* (1963).[8]

Eastern European leaders such as Yugoslavia's marshal Josip Broz Tito, the GDR's prime minister Otto Grotewohl, and Romania's Nicolae Ceausescu also toured Africa in the 1960s and 1970s, and Ethiopia's emperor Haile Selassie, Touré, and Nkrumah were frequent visitors to Eastern European capitals. Eastern European leaders used these visits not only to communicate good relations between their countries and new African nations but also to help build

Figure 33. Marshal Tito and Ethiopian president Haile Selassie at the site of the 1896 Battle of Adwa, 1955; Tito and Egyptian president Gamal Abdel Nasser visiting Aswan Dam, Egypt, 1968. *Credit: Museum of Yugoslavia, Belgrade*

a sense of shared interest and political fellowship between countries that otherwise had little historical relation with one another. Tito's state visits to Africa were notable in this regard—the visual documentation of his meetings went far beyond handshakes, fraternal embraces, and diplomatic speechmaking. Lavish press coverage was devoted to other aspects of these cultural encounters, such as giving and receiving gifts, inspecting local crops, signing trade agreements, visiting historical sites, watching traditional dancing, and even going on safari hunts, which Tito undertook with characteristic gusto, as seen in Figure 33. As early as 1954 Yugoslavia started cultural cooperation with Egypt, sending a folklore troupe and art exhibition, while a delegation of Egyptian professors visited Yugoslavia that summer. Such initiatives were replicated across Eastern Europe. From the early 1960s the Czech government arranged economics-for-culture exchanges with Ghana in which economic assistance was sent in exchange for print materials and ethnographic objects for study by Czech Africanists. In 1964 some fifteen Czech musicians played in the Cairo Symphony Orchestra, whereas that same year the Czechs received an Indian children's troupe, the Cambodian royal ballet, a Guinean folk dance troupe, and a Nigerian jazz band.[9]

Such overtures from socialist countries were often welcomed by leftist African elites. Marxism exerted great influence on African intellectual thought from the 1930s through the 1950s—Césaire's *Discourse on Colonialism* was suffused with Marxist thinking, as was Frantz Fanon's *The Wretched of the Earth*. Nkrumah proclaimed himself a socialist, and enjoyed warm relations with the Soviet Union and other Eastern Bloc states. His 1960 book *Conscientism* reflected his broader effort to combine Marxism with decolonization, and he served as a polestar of postcolonial thinking. Touré published three books on African socialism and Guinean national development, while Senghor drew on Marxist humanism as a vital contribution to *négritude* and the repositioning of "Negro-African civilisation" as a "communitarian and socialist civilisation."

Not least, Nyerere's idea of African socialism—and in particular his *ujamaa* ideas of family-based communalism—were well known across Africa and abroad.[10]

On occasion the Soviet Union and its Eastern European allies faced suspicion from anticolonial elites. Delegates at the famed Bandung Conference in 1955 made no bones about criticizing the Soviet Union as an imperial power. Iraqi foreign minister Fadhel Jamali argued that "today the Communist world has subjected races in Asia and Eastern Europe on a much larger scale than any old colonial power." Ceylonese prime minister John Kotelawala added that "if we are united in our opposition to colonialism, should it not be our duty to declare our opposition to Soviet colonialism as much as to Western imperialism?" African American writer Richard Wright went so far as to say in 1956, "Black people primarily regard Russian Communists as white men. Black people primarily regard American, British, and French anti-Communists as white people." The Soviet Union and its allies were also heavy-handed in the way they used African liberation struggles to criticize the West, so much so that Touré implored the Eastern Bloc not to exploit decolonization for its own political purposes.[11]

The Hungarian crisis of 1956 deepened hostility toward Soviet imperialism. While the Soviet Union and Hungary insisted that this was a domestic matter and thus irrelevant to the international community, most observers remained unconvinced. Nor did they accept the Hungarian regime's official interpretation that its necessary crackdown had been waged against Western imperialists and domestic "counter-revolutionaries" seeking to spread reactionary capitalism back into Eastern Europe, even to the point of portraying itself in natural solidarity with Algerians fighting the French state. The 1956 Soviet invasion of Hungary tied the Soviet Union's hands on international crises of decolonization. Khrushchev's legendary shoe-banging moment at the UN General Assembly in October 1960 was in angry reaction to a Philippine delegate who accused the Soviet Union of being an imperial power in Eastern Europe. Equally, African and Asian delegates were not keen to endorse American efforts to tar the Soviets as "red colonialists," not least because the US had sided with France in Indochina, consistently placed NATO loyalty over African welfare (best noted in the defense of Portuguese African territories), and had not cut off links to apartheid South Africa. African delegates at the UN thus grew increasingly suspicious of both Moscow and Washington's motives, which opened some space for smaller Eastern European countries to build alliances with their counterparts in the Third World beyond the headline drama of superpower conflict.[12]

Relations between some of the smaller countries of Eastern Europe and new African nations were indirectly strengthened by China's aggressive anti-Europeanism on the continent. China strove to scuttle these budding Eastern European–Third World relations by playing the card of racial solidarity. In 1961 Mao reportedly told a Kenyan reporter that "Europeans are all the same" and "we non-whites must hold together." Mao repeatedly insisted to various African leaders that the Soviets, Eastern Europeans, and Yugoslavs were white Europeans who could not be trusted, a view that caused consternation across the Non-Aligned Movement. In a 1964 meeting with Algerian president Ahmed Ben Bella in Belgrade, Marshal Tito railed against China's insinuations that "all blacks are good and all whites are bad." Ben Bella agreed, in no small measure because of the support the FLN had received from Yugoslavia during its long colonial war against France, concluding that "ideas about continents and skin color need to be overcome because progressive forces exist all around the world." On another occasion Ben Bella supposedly told Tito: "We are white like you, maybe a little more brown." China's effort to turn Third World politics into a race war failed miserably, as Mao's post-Bandung efforts to paint the Soviet Union, Yugoslavia, and Eastern Europeans as sinister white missionaries of modernization not unlike their Western counterparts did not gain traction. The Soviet Union and its allies countered that they arrived in Africa as anticolonial Europeans with no imperial past. Cultural brokers from Eastern Europe even argued—especially those hailing from countries of the former Habsburg Empire—that they too had been subjected to colonial control first by the Habsburgs and then by the Nazis, which meant that they could relate to their African counterparts as equal partners on a global anti-imperial front. From the early 1960s the Non-Aligned Movement helped remake the Third World as a political project with unbounded membership rather than as the expression of non-Western, nonwhite identity.[13]

Culture was used to promote a softer side of these socialist regimes, expressly geared toward the mission of peace and anti-imperialism. African political leaders, students, and economic experts were invited to Eastern Europe to consult, study, and exchange ideas with their partner countries. The classic model of interaction between the Second and Third World was one in which Eastern European white-collar labor (such as doctors and engineers) was exported, while students (and later blue-collar labor) from the Global South were imported. The field of culture, by contrast, offered the possibility of genuine exchange and international contact in a decidedly postimperial context. That Eastern European cultural emissaries (archaeologists, curators, travel writers, filmmakers, and photographers) arrived as anti-Western internationalists went some way in holding out the promise of building different networks of "friendly relations." Such cultural diplomacy was also designed to shore up the legitimacy of the socialist state, and to help mobilize young Eastern Europeans for the global socialist cause. It also enabled certain socialist countries to overcome their international isolation. Most notably this was so for Yugoslavia following its 1948 split with Moscow, for Hungary after the uprising in 1956, as well as for East Germany suffering from West Germany's stringent foreign policy to sequester its rival republic.[14]

Cairo occupied a privileged place in the firmament of cultural relations between the Second and Third Worlds, and played host to international rivalry. The Egyptian capital was considered the cultural center of both the Arabic and African worlds, and the US, Britain, West Germany, the Soviet Union, Eastern Europe, and China all vied for influence there. In the 1950s and 1960s Soviet and Eastern European cultural diplomacy usually consisted of exporting high culture to the rest of the world. International tours of the Bolshoi Ballet were used to present a highbrow visage of Soviet culture, as the star-studded classical ballet troupe routinely performed in the United States at the time. While the US also sent its own modern dance teams and jazz musicians as cultural ambassadors to the Soviet Union, the turn southward for Soviet culture was more widely remarked at the time. Wide press coverage was dedicated to the Bolshoi Ballet's tours of Egypt in 1961, and Soviet composers, violinists, pianists, and opera singers performed hundreds of concerts as far afield as Argentina, Chile, Mexico, Cuba, and Uruguay. Other Eastern European regimes followed suit in dispatching their state orchestras to Africa, Asia, and Latin America. During Tito's visit to Cairo in 1959, for example, plenty of media attention was paid to Belgrade Opera performances in Cairo, both to showcase Yugoslav high culture and to challenge the predominance of their French and Italian counterparts. Czech and Polish orchestras performed in the Egyptian capital too, though by the end of the 1960s the GDR had taken the lead in developing the socialist opera business in Egypt. Classical music became a means for Eastern Europeans to compete with the West and with one another as inheritors of European musical heritage.[15]

The focus on Cairo was no happenstance. The concentration of attention on the city reflected old European attitudes toward the continent's cultural geography. Tellingly, Moscow never sent its orchestras or ballets to sub-Saharan Africa, betraying long-standing European prejudices about the cultural discrepancies between the

Maghreb and sub-Saharan Africa. These value judgments were not only European sentiments, as hierarchies of civilization within Africa were at times expounded by various African statesmen too. In his 1954 treatise on *The Philosophy of the Revolution*, published two years after the Egyptian revolution, Gamal Abdel Nasser wrote that Egyptians must not "relinquish our responsibility to help spread the light of knowledge and civilization to the very depth of the virgin jungles of the Continent." And from his jail cell in France in 1961, Algerian FLN leader Ahmed Ben Bella imagined that "in two or three generations, Arab civilization and the Arabic language could become the *point commun* of all the countries of Africa." The language of civilization carried within it mixed elements of imperialism, anti-imperialism, and postimperialism all at once.[16]

Attitudes toward the cultural life of sub-Saharan Africa were a source of divergence between the Soviet Union and other Eastern European countries, especially Yugoslavia. The smaller European communist countries directed more cultural attention to Africa beyond the Maghreb, building links with Ghana, Mali, Senegal, Guinea, and Tanzania on a range of cultural fronts. They were also all keen to make sure that these new relationships were not simply unidirectional, as African writers and artists were routinely invited to Eastern Europe as cultural emissaries. As early as 1962 there was an exhibition of contemporary Egyptian art in Belgrade, and the Cuban National Ballet performed in Romania in 1966. Cairo singers journeyed to Belgrade for specialist training with the Belgrade Opera, and the Yugoslav music-publishing industry mass-produced recordings of Egyptian composer Abu Bakr Khairat and other genres of Arabic music. The Eastern European cultural encounter with Africa challenged the more typical Soviet formula of exporting its high culture to the rest of the world while "folklorizing" other cultures for their reciprocal visits to the Soviet Union. Eastern European states by contrast were generally more interested in broadcasting relations of reciprocity to their Third World counterparts, and there were many joint ventures. In 1965 the Ghana Institute of Art and Culture sent drama students to the GDR, theater technicians to Czechoslovakia, and a dance band to tour Romania.[17]

The 1960s was the golden age of the cultural agreement as an emblem of mutual understanding and good relations between Eastern Europe and Africa, which typically functioned as the first step toward economic, diplomatic, and even military cooperation. What made them socialist was the way that they were generally forged as top-down official state-to-state relations, with no role accorded to civil society groups or nongovernmental organizations. These relations tended to be strictly bilateral, as each country tended to put forward its best and most distinguished cultural form. Eastern European countries were very keen to initiate these contacts, as they built up their international profiles as champions of small-state solidarity. More than that, these burgeoning networks greatly expanded the cultural geography of Eastern European socialism worldwide, into one that was not exclusively Moscow-centric in the development of these diverse transcontinental links. At times Eastern European enthusiasm toward creating cultural exchanges became heavy and excessive for receiver countries, largely because they often did not possess the resources to take part regularly. One internal Ghanaian government report warned that "exchanging performing troupes with socialist countries" may be desirable, but our "type of economy does not allow us to reciprocate the facilities offered by those countries." Even so, Western observers saw this Eastern European activity in the developing world as a dangerous development. A secret 1966 CIA report that monitored the dissemination of books, press, radio, film festivals, exhibitions, binational friendship societies, and economic aid in Africa, Asia, and Latin America concluded that communists were successfully exploiting "anti-Western prejudices" and presenting themselves "with an image of benevolence" to "disguise political indoctrination under a cultural cloak."[18]

THE COMMUNIST WORLD ALSO STROVE TO BUILD ITS INTERNA-
tional profile around high-tech collaborations and development aid,
such as the joint Egyptian-Soviet project to raise the Aswan Dam in
the early 1960s. These projects were used to craft Moscow's preferred
self-image as the capital of socialist modernity and a close friend
of the developing world. The spectacular Sputnik flight of 1957
strengthened the perception of the Soviet Union as the pacesetter
of technological progress worldwide. Dispensing high-profile gifts
to new partner countries based on no-cash grants, loans, or barter—
such as large technological enterprises and development projects—
helped sow goodwill among receiver countries. In the early 1960s, the
Soviet Union's Afro-Asian Solidarity Committee sponsored visits for
foreign leaders to see the development of the trans-Caucasian and
Central Asian republics. These visits—along with the accompanying publicity—helped to burnish the USSR's reputation as a champion of Central Asian development and culture, and to demonstrate
its credentials as a progressive "Asian power" to the non-European
world. To this end, Central Asian voices were mobilized to testify
that the Soviets were serious about educational uplift in local Asian
languages, economic investment in the Central Asian peripheries,
and safeguarding Central Asian culture and heritage.[19]

Eastern Bloc countries actively participated in this modernization drive in Africa in the 1960s, and often did so in competition with the Soviet Union, China, Yugoslavia, and one another.
Socialist assistance could include anything from weapons to powdered milk to sponsored film festivals. Interactions ranged from
science, medicine, technology transfer, military aid, trade, cultural
exchange, and student programs. Assistance toward Africa was a
popular cause in Eastern European countries, and found its way
into Eastern European everyday life, often through travel writing,
mass media, and solidarity drives at factories and schools. In these
instances, rapacious Western neo-imperialism was contrasted with
socialist assistance, solidarity, and goodwill.[20]

One of the most prominent fields of cooperation was modern architecture, especially in the redesign of African cities after decolonization. As noted in Chapter 6, avant-garde architecture was seen as fundamental to nation-building, as new African governments would address their countries' underdevelopment through state-led industrial planning, for which Eastern European countries offered ready assistance. Polish architects built in Ghana; Hungarian designers in Nigeria; East Germans in North Korea, Zanzibar, and Syria; Romanians in the Sudan and Libya; Yugoslavs in Libya and Egypt; and the Chinese in Guinea. Yugoslav architects and engineers were the most active and innovative, as Tito's republic emerged as a trendsetter in disseminating socialist architectural modernism to newly independent states. The proliferation of communist polestars (Moscow, Beijing, Havana) proved advantageous to African leaders, enabling them to build their own versions of modernity as a blend of old and new, international and indigenous. Ghana is a good example of these developments, as Nkrumah was keen to draw on Eastern European socialist modernism to stylize his new state. In 1961 he visited the socialist "new towns" of Dunaújváros in Hungary and Nowa Huta in Poland as part of an eight-week tour of the Soviet Union, Eastern Europe, and China, and a number of leading Ghanaian architects (such as A. W. Charaway and E. G. A. Don Arthur) were trained in Moscow. Accra's International Trade Fair Centre (opened in 1967) was designed by Polish architect Jacek Chryosz, and Ghana's government seat, Flagstaff House, was designed by Hungarian architect Károly Polónyi in 1964 (Figure 34). It was after his tour of Eastern Europe that Nkrumah steered the country in a more socialist direction of development, best noted in his Soviet-inspired party programs "For Work and Happiness" (1962) and "Seven-Year Development Plan" (1964). The blending of Western, socialist, and African modernism in the cityscape of Accra epitomized the diversity of postcolonial architecture in Ghana and elsewhere in Africa.[21]

Figure 34. Jacek Chyrosz, International Trade Fair Centre, Accra, Ghana, 1967. *Credit: Jacek Chyrosz Archive, Warsaw*

Architecture was used as a language of solidarity that could bridge the divergent historical experiences of Eastern Europe and Africa. Central European modernists had used architecture as a visual expression of national arrival after the breakup of the Habsburg Empire, as Polish and Czech architects in particular fused international-style modernism with vernacular nationalism after the Great War to help create new cultural identities. In the 1960s East European architects argued that their own postimperial experience helped them understand Africa's historical situation. Polanyi, for example, wrote that East-Central Europe shared a common "colonial experience" with Africa; as someone from the Carpathian region, he too had experienced colonization by external powers. The great Polish travel writer Ryszard Kapuściński expressed similar views in his books, in particular *The Shadow of the Sun*, in which he drew a connection between African postcolonial countries and his upbringing in "colonized" eastern Poland. (Many of his other books, such as his 1978 study of Ethiopian dictator Haile Selassie, *The Emperor: Downfall of an Autocrat*, were read as parables about the Polish state under Soviet imperial rule.) Similar views could be found in the Polish popular press too, such as the Polish youth magazine *Dookoła Świata*. One 1963 article, following the long romantic tradition of presenting Poland's historical fate as a series of martyrdoms, compared Poles to African nations in which Poland was "a European nation" that historically "has played the role of a 'White Negro', rather than that of a colonialist." Such imagined cultural affinities were not just European inventions. Ghanaian journalists covering the opening of Eastern Europe–made showpiece buildings in their country in the early 1960s drew links between the colonial past of Ghana and the history of Prussian, Russian, and Habsburg domination of Eastern Europe. African media coverage of Tito's high-profile tours of African countries in 1961 and 1970 similarly stressed the parallels between Yugoslavia's anti-imperial and anti-Soviet identity with their own stories of African freedom fighting and nonalignment. During Tito's visit to Ethiopia, for example, Ethiopian journalists highlighted the shared experience of Yugoslavia and Ethiopia as both having been targeted by Italian fascist aggression during World War II. In these instances, modern architecture not only rendered development visible, it also provided a shared Eastern European–African visual vocabulary of modernization.[22]

Eastern Europe's turn southward complemented its effort to build connections to the West. It was in this period that the Soviets and their allies devoted great attention to the idea of "socialist humanism" as the basis of post-Stalinist social values, as a number of thinkers across the West became interested in humanism as a point of convergence between the blocs. *Socialist Humanism: An International Symposium* in 1965 was a milestone in this cross-European thinking. The German-born American social psychologist and humanist intellectual Erich Fromm gathered a range of thinkers from Western and Eastern Europe, with some participants from Asia and Africa, including Senghor. The background of the symposium was growing popular interest in the recent publication of Marx's long-lost early writings, the so-called *Grundrisse*, which revealed the young Marx's early preoccupation with the causes and effects of alienation as a symptom of modern industrial life. The 1965 volume reflected a shared "opposition to dehumanization." The point of departure was to discuss what Fromm called "the renaissance of humanism in various ideological systems," a cross-bloc "belief in the unity of the human race" in reaction to the fear of the "enslavement of man by the machine and economic interests" as well as the "wholly new threat to mankind's physical existence posed by nuclear weapons." Socialist humanism was not directly invoked as an ideological term to bridge Eastern Europe and Africa, however, though it was used in Soviet publications in connection with the international campaign for peace and anticolonialism. Instead, the more expansive concept of socialist humanity became the more favored description of new bonds of geopolitical solidarity.[23]

Concern with the future also became an unlikely place where Eastern and Western Europeans put aside their ideological differences in the name of understanding a common "scientific-technical civilization." The coming of "post-industrial society" prompted renewed attention to the nature and meaning of social forecasting and the management of a shared technical future. Such thinking had been the stuff of speculation and science fiction for decades, but what was different in the 1960s was this new sense that the rational control of the future through careful planning was both possible and imminent. A new cottage industry of futurist prognosticators emerged about the fate of the individual, community, and civilization itself, and is generally associated with such figures as Norbert Wiener, Daniel Bell, Jacques Ellul, and others involved in the study of futurology. UNESCO also played a role in bringing these thinkers together, many of whom were linked to UNESCO's International Social Science Documentation Center in Vienna, led by Marxist philosopher Adam Schaff. The socialist world took part in these international debates about and planning industrial society, as evidenced by the founding of new journals as well as numerous conferences and transnational exchanges.[24]

A seminal publication was Radovan Richta's *Civilization at the Crossroads: Social and Human Implications of the Scientific and Technological Revolution*, published in Czechoslovakia in 1969. The book was the fruit of Richta's research team in Prague, and caused a great international stir when it was translated into English the following year. The main point was that current technological changes were challenging the "foundations of civilization" and "man's place in the world." What was striking was the surprisingly little attention paid to the differences between socialism and capitalism; on the contrary, Richta's book went even further in its exploration of "cybernation," alienation, and a world ruled by elite technocrats by saying that socialism had "to evolve in its own civilization base." His book was a blend of early Marx and systems theory, and his hypothesis of the new "socialist personality" shaped by new technological demands was not so different from notions of the coming of "technological man" popular in the West at the time. Even if these revisionist socialist ideas about pluralist futures—to say nothing of the fate of Richta's research project—were rolled back by Moscow's military clampdown on the Prague Spring in the autumn of 1968, after which such open-ended socialist futurology was banned, the wider point is that the language of technical civilization had served as a conceptual bridge uniting East and West. Ideas of modernity and historical time certainly connected Eastern Europe and Africa in a socialist story of development, but the terminology of a socialist technological civilization less so. Instead, Eastern European understandings of common socialist civilization with Africa were often geared toward the legacy of its ancient past.[25]

EASTERN EUROPEAN–AFRICAN COOPERATION WAS NOT LIMited to developing infrastructures and showcasing avant-garde modernist architecture. In fact, the communist world's focus wasn't always on the future, nor was it always on modernization. There was a flip side of this relationship that goes largely unremarked in what little literature exists on the subject, and this is the socialist attitude toward African heritage. It was here that the language of civilization resurfaced in surprising ways.

Decolonization served as the big bang for fresh interest in African history and heritage across the Soviet Union and the Eastern Bloc. This however was not so easy, since Marx and Engels had virtually nothing to say about Africa, and much the same went for Lenin. Moscow's attitude toward Africa was mostly drawn from recommendations drafted by the Negro Commission appointed in 1922 in connection with the Communist International, which strove to create a singular black solidarity movement across continents. Until the late 1950s neither the Soviet Union's Foreign Ministry nor the KGB had developed any departments for African affairs; in fact, there were few experts on Africa or Asia anywhere in the Kremlin. While there is a long tradition of German and Russian scholarship on Africa from the late nineteenth century through the 1950s, other Eastern European countries had comparatively little expert knowledge of the region. Even those countries with the richest tradition of knowledge—Russia and Germany—had to start afresh in devising a socialist approach to African studies. At a 1958 conference of Soviet Orientalists, the journalist Georgii Zhukov sounded the alarm that "life has left us behind, and we happen to be unprepared for creating a theory of dealing with Asian and African countries," adding that "we need our Soviet missionaries, our Soviet Doctor Schweitzers."[26]

Eastern European Africanists did not reject "bourgeois Orientalism" completely. Eastern European anthropology, archaeology, and ancient history were comparatively open to Western scholarship in this period, and there were many joint conferences across Cold War borders. A number of British Marxist Africanists, such as Gordon Childe, Basil Davidson, and Peter Shinnie, were approvingly cited in Eastern European publications, and the world-renowned Polish anthropologist Bronisław Malinowski remained a touchstone of Polish ethnography after 1945. As noted in the last chapter, UNESCO played a pivotal role in bringing together experts from Africa and Western and Eastern Europe in the name of world civilization, and its antiracism won over African and Eastern European elites to the

UNESCO cause. Experts from across Eastern Europe supported the UNESCO project on the Mutual Appreciation of Eastern and Western Cultural Values in the mid-1950s. Yet the communist world wanted to make its own distinctive contribution to the study of Africa.

New views began to circulate in the 1950s. In the *Great Soviet Encyclopedia* published in 1951, it was claimed that the Soviet perception of the Orient as an equal civilization broke sharply from views espoused in Western Europe and North America. "Bourgeois Orientology," so the entry read, "diametrically opposed the civilizations of the so-called 'West' with those of the 'East,' slanderously declaring that Asian peoples are racially inferior, somehow primordially incapable of determining their own fates, and that they appeared only as history's object, rather than its subject." The Soviet Union slowly began to use the concept of socialist civilization as an alternative to Western civilization in response to its encounter with the developing world. A *Pravda* report on a 1958 Tashkent conference of Asian and African writers took the opportunity to announce that while capitalist "civilisation" led to "economic colonisation of the peoples of Asia and Africa and strangled their forms of art," the "civilisation of socialism promotes the development of artistic values of different nationalities." Such language was now increasingly applied to cultural relations within the Eastern Bloc. As Khrushchev remarked in a speech in October 1958 about Russian-Polish relations: "The peoples of the Soviet Union and the Polish people are building a great socialist civilisation hand in hand, like brothers."[27]

The 1960s saw the Soviet Union and Eastern Europe engage in a crash course to acquire knowledge of Africa, as seen in the flourishing of new African studies departments in universities across the socialist world. A slew of new archaeology and anthropology institutions and journals were founded to study Africans and Asians, often in the name of celebrating a socialist humanism rooted in a shared premodern past and modernizing present. Take the Polish

Anglophone journal *Africana Bulletin*, which began life in 1964 at the University of Warsaw and was published in French and English. The journal's first issue made clear why this mattered: African history "has to be freed from the falsifications of the colonialist era." Special interest was geared toward Egyptology and archaeological projects in Egypt and the Sudan, and the journal covered findings by Polish teams in the Nile delta as well as joint African-Polish anthropological expeditions across the continent.[28]

Another example was the Czech magazine *New Orient: Journal for the Modern and Ancient Cultures of Asia and Africa*, which first appeared in 1960. It was published in English and covered history, archaeology, the arts, music and theater, literature, and folktales. It was dedicated to the appreciation of the ancient past, the so-called Old Orient; the word *new* in the title "should express our endeavor to approach the Orient without outdated prejudices, without an exotic, romantic or mysterious veil." Articles focused on various aspects of world culture, such as Chinese archaeology, ancient Indian medicine, Vietnamese theater, Congo masks, and UNESCO's rescue of the Nubian monuments. One 1960 issue featured short statements from experts in "Eastern Studies" from around the world, who all underlined the need to better appreciate other civilizations and promote world civilization, so as to combat stereotypical notions of these ancient cultures as "peoples without history." Polish Orientalists argued that it was easier for them to appreciate the idea of a shared world civilization given their own supposedly nonimperial history. Ananiasz Zajaczkowski, director of the Oriental Institute of Warsaw University, proudly asserted that "Since the Poles—and the Czechs—bear no trace of colonial psychology and, on the other hand, have much sympathy for the nations of Asia and Africa, they can find much easier a common language of understanding and common civilization with the East."[29]

The Soviet Union and its allies devoted great energy to show Africans that the communist world was deeply interested in their rich past and cultural accomplishments. As early as 1954 leading Soviet Africanists Ivan Izosimovich Potekhin and D. A. Ol'derogge published *The Peoples of Africa*, the first study of Africa written from a Marxist-Leninist perspective. In 1961 the leading Soviet Orientalist journals tellingly changed their names from *Contemporary East* and *Soviet Orientology* to *Asia and Africa Today* and *Peoples of Asia and Africa*, respectively, to best harness this wind of change. In them the language of civilization was used to build bridges to African counterparts by asserting that Africa was a "flourishing civilization before colonialism intervened." Numerous conferences and publications devoted to the ancient history of Africa took place in the 1960s, with a strong focus on class structure, slavery, and the life of common people. In part this was done as a means of distinguishing the communist world's attitude toward Africa and Asia from the old-style racist framework of Western European imperialism or its new guise as American modernization theory. In his 1960 booklet, *Africa Looks to the Future*, Potekhin pleaded for the building up of the academic fields of African history and African heritage to destroy the false scholarly claims of rival Western imperialists. He directly accused them of having destroyed "high African civilization, which, with the help of the Soviet Union, is there for the Africans to regain." His idea that Eastern European archaeologists could help Africans rediscover their own pasts was articulated even more forcefully in a late 1950s radio broadcast. In it Potekhin asserted that postcolonial African intellectuals "assisted by the progressive scholars" from Eastern Europe are now "unmasking the lie of imperialistic propaganda" that African people "do not have a history of their own. The obligation of Marxist historians is to help in the restoration of historical truth." For him, the truth pivoted on the explicit acknowledgment of African civilization itself.[30]

Anthropology communicated this solidarity. In reaction to the West's campaign to develop African rural countries according to American ideas of modernization, Eastern European anthropologists sought to win over Africans sympathetic to the socialist cause by defending traditional anticapitalist village life as a means of managing the slow transition to full development. Only socialism, so the argument went, held out the possibility of countering the destructive cultural power of American-style modernity by uniting humanism, internationalism, and revolution. Soviet Africanists extolled the role of folklore as a new hybrid cultural form that would help Africans cope with the transition to modernity. As one conference report from 1965 put it: "We Soviet Africanists" set our task in "preserving and developing the traditions of humanism and proletarian internationalism with respect to the peoples of Africa, traditions which have always been inherent in Russian revolutionary democracy and Marxism-Leninism." Klaus Ernst's widely cited 1973 book, *Tradition and Progress in the African Village*, was emblematic of this kind of socialist thinking, as premodern traditional village life—Mali in this case—was seen as the building block of Africa's future of "non-capitalist development."[31]

Eastern European promotion of folkish heritage was not something simply directed toward the non-European world. The aftermath of the Second World War saw a stepped-up campaign to resuscitate folk art in the Soviet Union and Eastern Europe as the foundation of international socialist culture that connected it with interwar communist ideology. Russian folk culture had first been treated by communist revolutionaries as an unwanted residue of antimodernity and peasant reaction against the new Bolshevik state, but Stalin soon recognized the ideological power of supporting folk culture for Soviet political legitimacy. In the 1950s a romanticized nineteenth-century worker folk culture was revived across the Soviet Union and Eastern Bloc in the form of music events, dance performances, and theater festivals, as well as in ceramics and the decorative arts—traditions that blended nationalism and socialism, peasant culture and multiethnic modernity. For example, the East German journal *Volkskunst*, or *Art of the People*, routinely extolled traditional

Figure 35. East German folk dancers, cover of *Volkskunst: Monatsschrift für das künstlerische Volksschaffen* (GDR), June 1952

arts and crafts, and featured folk dancers in traditional costume from around the world in a celebration of both the diversity and unity of socialist peoples' cultures, as evidenced in Figures 35 and 36.

Championing international socialist folk culture was not a rejection of modernity, but rather a powerful expression of it, in that it stitched together socialist states in a new family of nations that united past and present across geopolitical boundaries. By the early 1960s, the officious advocacy of traditional culture in socialist Europe was starting to be viewed as provincial, old-fashioned, and even embarrassing among those committed to modernizing socialist cultural life. Yet the folk culture movement got a new lease on life with decolonization, during which it was identified as a useful bridge to the Third World. Dance troupes from Senegal, Mali, Guinea, and elsewhere were regularly invited to tour Eastern Europe in the name of fraternity with indigenous cultures from around the world.[32]

Figure 36. International Socialist Folk Festival, cover of *Volkskunst: Monatsschrift für das künstlerische Volksschaffen* (GDR), Summer 1953

In this context, culture was often a more relevant term for Eastern European societies than civilization. Culture referred to the construction of a progressive national identity after 1945, one that elevated the moral and ideological mission of socialist state-making and aligned socialist societies to one another around a blend of tradition and modernity. It was the Soviet Union's encounter with the developing world that spurred ideological interest in the notion of socialist civilization as a bridge to the Global South. As Eastern European affirmations of African indigenous culture grew more common, the idea of a progressive and shared civilization with the colonial and postcolonial world emerged as a new ideological pillar of Eastern European foreign policy and soft power relations with independent African countries.[33]

Archaeology was no less important in this respect, and from the 1960s on there were a number of East European excavation projects in Tanzania, Kenya, and the Sudan. Archaeology was converted into a socialist political science, and this happened in two ways. First, archaeology was used to document long-standing African oppression by foreigners, and to drive home the point that the same dangers were still around. Secondly, archaeology was used to underpin new narratives for the present. When Nyerere announced his project of building "African socialism" in the early 1970s, East German archaeologists strove to show that Tanzania's hoped-for non-capitalist development could be built on its own centuries-old egalitarian traditions. One can detect echoes of prerevolutionary Russian populism here, when Russian intellectuals went to the countryside in the late nineteenth century to advise peasants on the virtues of rural socialism; this old European socialist tradition exerted some influence on the thinking of Nyerere, Bissau-Guinean revolutionary Amílcar Lopes Cabral, and even Frantz Fanon. The accent on the distant past carried a different sense of historical time, in that these Eastern European archaeologists suggested not only that Africans could draw on ancient precolonial pasts as they modernized, but that the traumatic wave of colonial violence from the nineteenth century through to recolonization in the aftermath of the Second World War was only a bracketed phase of African history. A premodern African past and non-Western present, so they reasoned, could then be joined in the name of socialist solidarity.[34]

Numerous joint archaeological excavations took place involving African and European teams dedicated to studying ancient African civilizations, such as the high-profile excavation of the eleventh century Aoudaghost site in Mauritania in 1961, as discussed in Chapter 6. Peter Shinnie, a Scottish communist who led archaeological teams at the University of Ghana on dozens of digs in the 1950s and 1960s, did much to publicize prehistoric Sudan and the ancient Nile delta city of Meroe as homegrown African civilizations. In his 1967 book *Meroe: A Civilization of the Sudan*, Shinnie concluded that "Meroe was an African civilization, firmly based on African soil, and developed by an African population. That an urban, civilized and literate state existed deep in the African continent and lasted nearly a thousand years in itself constitutes an achievement of outstanding importance." From 1960 to 1966 Shinnie was director of the University of Ghana's excavations at Debeira West and was part of UNESCO's Save the Monuments of Nubia collaborative project, after which he trained generations of African archaeologists. Over the decades he worked closely with prominent East German archaeologist Fritz Hintze, a fellow expert on ancient Meroean civilization. Eastern European archaeologists, anthropologists, and experts of African art worked to provide an alternative account of African history, stressing that the continent's cultures had rich and vibrant precolonial national pasts characterized by noncapitalist development. They too took part in international preservation projects that sidestepped Cold War antagonism in the name of world civilization.[35]

Other communist countries added their voices to this defense of traditional African civilization. The Romanian embassy in Conakry, Guinea, drafted a report in 1963 claiming that the colonial powers have destroyed "African civilization without inserting anything in its stead," thereby condemning Africans to "obscurantism and spiritual poverty." By contrast, the Romanian government voiced its commitment to the preservation of heritage and folklore in Guinea and Mali. In his *On the Spiritual Culture of African Peoples*, Constantin Ionescu-Gulian, the director of the Romanian Academy's Institute of Philosophy, denounced the "falsifications" of Western Orientalism and extolled the "flourishing civilizations" of ancient Africa that arose from the "strong social and moral traditions of the primitive commune." The language of civilization was even peddled by Chinese revolutionaries, who sought to compete with the Soviet Union. In 1956 China organized an Asian Writers' Conference in New Delhi, and maneuvered to position itself as the guardian of ancient tradition. Chinese government officials argued that the Chinese, Indians, Arabs, and Africans were all heirs of great ancient civilizations that had been corrupted by Western imperialism and therefore wished to lead the effort to create "a new civilization for all mankind" made up of the best traditions of each.[36]

Eastern European interest in traditional African art in the 1960s followed the same lines. European attention toward African art first developed in the late nineteenth century, enjoyed popularity after World War I within the French art world and beyond, and took off again after 1945 in Western Europe, best noted in the French journal *Présence Africaine*. Less known is that Eastern Europe also turned to African art in the 1960s, with the Soviet Union, Yugoslavia, the GDR, and Czechoslovakia leading the way. In this period the socialist world devoted great energy to celebrating traditional arts and crafts as a way of connecting Eastern Europe with Africa. Dozens of exhibitions on traditional African culture were organized, journals were created, and new museums founded to deepen this international solidarity around premodern material artifacts.[37]

The GDR was the most energetic. East German art critics condemned the West's, and particularly West Germany's, underhanded effort to destroy indigenous African art through the embrace of modernism and the cheap commercialization of African tourist trinkets—what was dismissively called "airport art." Support of traditional indigenous cultures around the world became an official plank of the GDR's cultural diplomacy in the early 1960s, as a number of East German exhibitions extolled the virtues of traditional African art. Art historian Burchard Brentjes opened his 1965 book *African Rock Art* by saying that generations of European plunderers had robbed Africans of the "artistic treasures of their ancestors" and "their sense of the past, their historical consciousness." He called on socialism to serve as the guardian of tradition, and in so doing rejected the way that Westerners were bent on cutting Africans off from their roots and killing off their revolutionary potential. East German Africanists challenged the view that African history began only with the colonial encounter by restoring a sense of history and accomplishment. In his popular 1968 book *From*

Schanidar to Akkad: 7,000 Years of Oriental World History, Brentjes advanced a radical conception of socialist time, armed with ancient maps and documentation of ruins, statuary, and masks. For him the point was to recall ancient history so as to better understand the limited temporal horizons of capitalism itself. From there he made the bold claim that from a long-term historical perspective there is only a "short transition phase between the original form of primitive communism to a highly industrialized version of communism." East German Africanists promoted ancient African civilization as a means of championing Africa's socialist past and potentially socialist future beyond the nation-state and pan-Africanism.[38]

The GDR's favorite African artist was the Ghanaian Kofi Antubam, whom we encountered in Chapter 6 as Nkrumah's exponent of independent Ghanaian culture. Antubam was both a socialist and traditionalist. In his remarks at the opening of Ghana's new national museum in 1957, he called for loosening the hold of "conservatism in Ghanaian traditions and customs" on the minds of the "Ghanaian chiefs and people," concluding that in "an age of socialism" it is "no longer fashionable and socially proper for the privileged few to maintain their so-called birth right to enjoy alone what they only hold in trust for the many." In 1961 Antubam was invited to East Berlin at Brentjes's request. There his work was exhibited as an example of an African artist who engaged with traditional art and culture, and who developed a synthesis of African heritage with European elements. During the visit Antubam praised the GDR's support and called on all African states to salvage the cultural legacy of "their indigenous ways of life." Antubam—lauded in Nkrumah's Ghana as a "missionary in the crusade of African rediscovery"— was lionized across the Eastern Bloc. The East German government commissioned him to put together a book on *Ghana's Heritage of Culture*. In the preface to the East German publication, president of the German-African Society Gerald Götting remarked that African culture and art, long denigrated as primitive by "so-called civilized apologists of colonial or neo-colonial policy," had now "got[ten] a new content" deeply "linked to tradition."[39]

But there were fears afoot. Some of this had to do with timing, given that the communist world became interested in African heritage precisely at the moment when new African states were using ancient heritage to construct new national and pan-African identities. For Eastern European Africanists, the problem was not just primordial nationalism, but also racism. The figure who generated the most animus was Léopold Sédar Senghor, the poet and president of Senegal. At first glance Senghor should have been a natural ally of Eastern Europe's culture initiative to extend a hand to Africa. Senghor frequently spoke about the importance of socialism and was an inspiring figure of anti-imperialism on the world stage, often insisting on the need to blend socialism with *négritude*. But his was a different kind of socialism, and one with specifically African roots. As Senghor put it at one point, "We had already realized socialism before the European presence," and now "have a vocation to renew it by helping it to restore its spiritual dimensions." Senghor chided the communist world's lack of religious and spiritual freedom, and pledged that his country would "never follow the Communist example." The spiritual dimensions of his socialism caused concern, and his Eastern European critics—especially those in the Soviet Union and the GDR, to say nothing of his communist critics within Senegal itself—felt that his idea of *négritude* was too ethnically based. The irony is that Senghor's *négritude* arguably was an African version of pan-Slavism, which was revived after 1945 (especially in archaeology circles) to link multiethnic communities across Eastern Europe in a cultural expression of regional socialist unity. In any case, Eastern European cultural elites rejected Senghor's pan-Africanism as racist and exclusionary, not least because they were the ones being rejected as outsiders. Race trumped class as the main language of a shared postcolonial African history and diasporic identity, and was used to help fend off Africa's heritage from Eastern Europe's geopolitical agenda.[40]

Eastern European Africanists were particularly ambivalent about Senghor's 1966 international arts festival. On the one hand, the Soviets produced a celebratory documentary film of the event, *African Rhythmus*, the only color film of the festival produced by any country. The Soviets also helped the Senegalese government ease its accommodation problem during the festival by lending one of its docked cruise ships to put up festival attendees. Guests staying on the Soviet liner were treated to an on-board exhibition on "Russo-Negro Brotherhood." An accompanying exhibition of African masks was mounted in Belgrade, Zagreb, and Ljubljana to complement Dakar's 1966 festival, as well as to promote African culture in Yugoslavia more generally. On the other hand, Soviet and East German art critics denounced Senghor's *négritude* as irredeemably Western, bourgeois, and racist. So even if the Soviet press called the festival "a significant event in the history of world culture" that "will play a big role in the cultural revival of Africa," Senghor's name passed unmentioned in *Pravda's* coverage; attention instead was heaped on Senegalese writer and filmmaker Ousmane Sembène as the more genuine socialist.[41]

Eastern Europeans recast African heritage to suit their political purposes. The Czechs had a long interest in African art, as noted with the rich collections of the Náprstek Museum of Asian, African and American Cultures in Prague, founded in 1862. The museum's centenary was celebrated in pages of *New Orient* extolling the museum for preserving "cultural values threatened with extinction in the rapid changes in civilization in our age." While old museums were being revamped, new ones were founded, such as the Museum of African Art in Belgrade in 1977. The Belgrade museum was the first one opened in Yugoslavia devoted exclusively to African art. The catalog stated that while there are bigger and richer collections elsewhere in the capitals of former colonial powers, the Belgrade Museum of African Art was the "product of friendship" and a "symbol of non-alignment" inspired by "a new attitude of appreciation toward the achievements of folk art," a consecrated, uniquely post-imperial museum space of nonexploitation and civilizational equality. Only in progressive Eastern Europe, so went the logic, could such progressive museum spaces have been created in the first place.[42]

How African leaders and intellectuals received this overture from the socialist world is not easy to gauge. Eastern European experts in ancient history were certainly invited by the governments of Ghana, Senegal, and other countries as project consultants to help them unearth and learn about their ancient pasts. Western specialists took part in various African conferences and symposia in the 1960s, such as those linked to Senghor's 1966 Dakar Black Arts festival. Eastern European Africanists were generally received as friends of independent Africa, and were welcomed at these cultural events. The term civilization—even more so than socialism—was used to join these cultures, as the socialist world expended far greater energy than the West in promoting the achievements of African antiquity. Modernity was of course the other preferred term, but in this case the rhetoric of civilization was used to block the future-oriented Americans as suitable cultural partners. While African intellectuals from Nkrumah to Nyerere remained suspicious of the claims of Western civilization, they tended to be more sympathetic toward the socialist world's anti-imperial ideas of equal and connected world civilizations in the 1960s.

EAST-SOUTH CULTURAL RELATIONS REMAIN A LARGELY FOR-gotten chapter of Cold War history to this day. Although recent years have seen new interest in the Global Sixties as well as the Socialist Sixties, the focus is usually on either First-Third World encounters or so-called South-South interaction. East-South encounters, by contrast, reveal the ways in which seemingly incongruous zones of the world were connected in a new map of Cold War international relations, one that underlined the agency of smaller states in forging partnerships across continents. These contacts helped to reinvigorate Eastern European socialist projects, and were often used to readjust Eastern Europe's relationship with the Soviet Union in a spirit of relative autonomy in foreign affairs. If these activities marked an expansion of socialist space, they also represented an alternative sense of socialist time. At issue was a romanticized view of the future based on technology and modernization, for which Eastern European socialists sought to provide ample support and a helping hand. And yet, it was also based on a selective vision of Africa's "proto-socialist" antiquity. An enlarged geography of socialist civilization was being promulgated at a moment when African elites were reclaiming their own heritage as markers of postcolonial arrival, be that of nationalism, federalism, *négritude*, or pan-Africanism. Eastern Europe's global vision of socialist civilization strove to complement local African narratives of collectivity, and offered an alternative reading of African history through the lens of socialist Orientalism.

Most importantly, this Eastern European–African encounter helped Eastern Europe to broadcast a new self-image as the better and more progressive Europe, dedicated to liberation struggles and the plight of the world's oppressed. From this perspective, such cultural diplomacy might be dismissed as largely public relations and soft power alliance-building to advance socialism's hard power agenda of economic aid, military assistance, and geopolitical influence. But this interpretation overlooks the ways in which the multiplication of cultural relations with the developing world signified Eastern European reengagement with the wider world in the 1960s, and with it the ideological renewal of socialism's global mission in the aftermath of empire. For many Eastern Europeans, these encounters were transformative in giving fresh meaning to the broader socialist cause worldwide, especially since political life back home was comparatively static and resistant to reform at the time. Excitement associated with solidarity in Africa was registered in memoirs of Eastern European doctors, journalists, schoolteachers, agricultural experts, and other socialist missionaries who spent years in Africa and Asia. The same went for the wide media coverage of Eastern European–Third World encounters back home. Visits by heads of states and foreign dignitaries, travel writing, art shows, cultural festivals, and student exchanges—all helped to make real socialist alliance with peoples from other lands, and the language of civilization was central to it.

But there were other hidden elements at play. Eastern Europeans drew on the once-denigrated idea of civilization not only to reject old European hierarchies and prejudices toward the rest of the world under the banner of equality and mutual respect but also to place Eastern and Western Europe on an equal cultural footing to overcome Eastern Europe's own sense of underdevelopment, isolation, and colonial complex toward its Western European rivals. What distinguished the world of culture from other modes of Eastern European contact with the developing world was that it made visible these encounters. Unlike economic or military relations, which often took place away from the glare of the media or were deliberately obscured from view, these many cultural events were always staged, performative, and closely tied to media coverage. They were designed to visualize solidarity, to bring close the achievements, struggles, and causes of distant strangers in a new politics of proximity. Their changing forms and contents reflected Eastern Europe's evolving understanding of its region's identity, geography, and cultural mission in the world.

Consciously inclusive concepts of civilization that incorporated diverse nations, regions, and peoples were a strong feature of progressive international politics in the early 1960s, but it did not last. The rest of the decade and beyond witnessed a blowback against such integrative ideals, as white minority-ruled regimes in Africa along with their conservative counterparts in Europe effectively reclaimed the mantle of civilization as a separatist cause in the name of race, religion, and reaction.

nine

RELIGION, RACE, AND MULTICULTURALISM

O NE OF THE MOST FAMOUS INSTANCES OF THE BACKLASH
against the counterculture of the 1960s was the landmark
thirteen-part BBC television series *Civilisation*, broadcast in 1969
by the eminent British art historian Kenneth Clark. Back in the
1930s Clark became the youngest director of London's National
Gallery, and went on to chair the War Artists Advisory Committee during the war. This body was responsible for archiving Britain's
artistic production, often by commissioning designated war artists
to document the effects of war on the British public. Clark oversaw
a related project soon after the outbreak of war in 1939, Recording
Britain, which recruited artists to record the life and spirit of the
country's towns and villages for posterity, lest they were destroyed
by Nazi bombing. Curating and protecting cultural patrimony at
risk was a central thread of Clark's career, and partly inspired the
Civilisation program. The series nimbly traversed the period from
the barbarian conquest of ancient Rome to the tumultuous 1960s,
with the threats of iconoclasm and civilization in crisis as its chief
themes. His was a story of fragility and luck, of how civilization as
we know it barely survived in the face of war, vandalism, and decay.

As he put it, civilization was "something which was worth defending, and something that was in danger."[1]

Civilisation struck a chord with viewers across the world. Television and accompanying book rights were sold to over sixty countries, and no BBC program ever equaled its ability to bring art to the masses. The series followed Mortimer Wheeler's *The Glory That Was Greece* (1959) and Compton Mackenzie's *The Grandeur That Was Rome* (1960), though Clark's series broke all viewer records. The program took three years to produce, staffed by a twelve-person crew who logged over 80,000 miles visiting eleven countries. Clark summarized the objective for the program thus: "I was determined to show Western man trying to discover himself," and "I was also determined to show that civilisation could die by its own inbred imperfection." Clark also wanted to convey the glories of the past in an era in which the "guides of coach parties" have become "the only surviving transmitters of traditional culture." For him, civilization was mostly a Mediterranean family history that included France and Italy, with Germany, Britain, Holland, and the US playing supporting roles. The episodes combined classical and Christian humanism, extolling "great men performing great deeds," and Clark delivered the series with authority and flair (Figure 37).

Its scope was very much of its time for the BBC—no Africa, Asia, Islam, or South America, nor any female artists either. Even so, the reception was overwhelmingly congratulatory—J. B. Preistley wrote that the series was "in itself a contribution to civilisation," while another reviewer dubbed Clark the "Gibbon of the McLuhan Age." By contrast, leftist critic Raymond Williams dismissed Clark's program as the "'old dinner-table style' of propaganda for an ignoble past, and a means of rejecting the world today." After all, 1969 was the height of the Vietnam War, the Nigerian Civil War, and the year of Woodstock. In the art world the 1960s saw strident efforts to lampoon the pious sanctity of Art with a capital *A*, ranging from pop art to arte povera. None of this impinged on Clark's

Figure 37. British art historian Kenneth Clark
filming his blockbuster *Civilisation* television series,
1969. *Credit: Radio Times, Getty Images*

story, however, as he revisited the great moments in Western art
from the late medieval period until the modern day. John Berger's
1972 four-part BBC series *Ways of Seeing* was a trenchant Marxist response to Clark's patrician Eurocentrism, and epitomized the
New Left attitude toward Clark's traditional conception of art, con-
noisseurship, heritage, and civilization.[2]

Clark's rearguard defense of civilization under assault was a
common position in the worlds of culture and international relations alike. Whereas the language of civilization was integral to the
anticolonial cause in the 1950s and 1960s, it was increasingly mobilized to preserve various ancien régimes and counterrevolutionary
causes from the mid-1960s onward. Across the West the student
revolts of 1968 challenged what were perceived as the false idols of
the reconstruction generation, openly mocking the heroic defense
of civilization as symptomatic of repressive Establishment values.

Everywhere the rallying cries of change were democracy, freedom, and civil rights. That some of the most violent regimes of the 1960s in Southern Europe—Franco's Spain and the Colonels' Greece—justified their political order in the name of protecting Christian civilization from the dangers of communism and modernity further compromised civilization's once-progressive platform in the eyes of young people. It was during this period that rights—both civil and human—supplanted civilization as the language of universalism, equality, and international solidarity. How the concept of civilization migrated from the campaigns of moral reconstruction, anticolonialism, and anti-Westernism to shore up various right-wing regimes under threat is the subject of this chapter. Over the course of the 1970s and 1980s, civilization rested at the heart of discussions about redrawing the religious and even racial boundaries of the continent, and was closely aligned to conservative causes, including apartheid, militant Catholicism, and the rejection of multiculturalism.

THE DEFENSE OF TRADITION UNDER SIEGE WAS THE STUFF OF West European thinking in the face of secularization, consumerism, and the American way of life in the 1960s, as discussed in Chapter 4. Apprehension was also directly linked to the end of empire, as the onset of decolonization generated conservative anxiety about civilization in crisis. British internationalist thinkers were particularly exercised by "the revolt against the West." In the early 1960s public intellectual Gilbert Murray defended the British Empire as one of the last great hopes for "Christian civilization," after which he predicted that "many great regions are likely to be rebarbarised" by those—led by the Muslim world—united against the West. Historian Hugh Seton-Watson also greeted decolonization not as "a glorious extension of democracy, but a tragic delay of civilization, similar to the decline of the Roman Empire, and followed by the same result, reversion to barbarism." Renowned international relations scholar Martin Wight went on to criticize the "Bandung Powers" of the Third World for turning the United Nations into "an organ of anti-colonial movement, a kind of Holy Alliance in reverse." In the estimation of these and other observers, decolonization represented a profound crisis for the West. Worries about the collapse of old Eurocentric "standards of civilization" in a rough-and-tumble international community continued through the 1970s as the erosion of Eurocentric values was seen to render international governance all but impossible in what political theorist Hedley Bull called the postcolonial "anarchical society" of international relations.[3]

Such dark predictions were hardly confined to the parlors of power in London and other European metropoles. The reactionary argument about barbarism unleashed by decolonization assumed garish proportions in the controversial 1967 Italian film *Africa Addio*, or *Farewell, Africa*, directed by Gualtiero Jacopetti and Franco Prosperi. Their film, originally conceived for audiences back in Europe, is a compilation of eyewitness footage from three years spent in various hot spots around the continent. Its release became a scandalous sensation, not least because its negative portrait of newly independent Africa boldly suggested that Africa was best served under European dominion. "The old Africa has disappeared," the narrative voiceover lamented, and "died amidst the massacres and devastations which we filmed." The New Africa by contrast "emerges over the graves of thousands of whites and Arabs, millions of blacks, and over those bleak boneyards that once were the game preserves." On show were gory segments of Mau Mau rebels killing their way through Kenya, mass graves of Arabs in Zanzibar, and mercenary executions in the Congo. Film posters featured taglines on African liberation struggles such as "Consumed by Savagery, Conceived in Blood!" or "Savagery! Brutality! Inhumanity! It bathed the World in Blood!" while another, in a knowing reference to the American civil rights movement, screamed that "This is Africa like it is! Where Black is beautiful, Black is ugly, Black is brutal!" (Apparently, the original Italian film title was rejected as too unmarketable in the US, so the American release was called *Africa: Blood and Guts*.) While some reviewers welcomed the film's "courage and sincerity," others condemned *Africa Addio* as an "orgy of sadism and fascist racism" that pictured Africans as irredeemably "monstrous and savage," or as a retrograde justification of European colonialism. Some twenty African embassies in Rome lodged a formal complaint to the Italian government, but to no avail. In any case, the wistful end of the European "civilizing mission" in Africa framed the film's narrative and reception.[4]

Elsewhere the defense of the old imperial regime took on military expression, as various right-wing political upheavals in the 1960s were legitimated through the rhetoric of civilization. We have already seen how authoritarian Spain and Portugal used the language to maintain order and bolster support domestically and internationally, as did France during the Algerian War. A new installment was the so-called Greek Revolution of April 21, 1967. National Greek elections were scheduled for that May, and many predicted that left-leaning liberals and communists would sweep into power, possibly throwing the country into constitutional crisis. As the election neared, right-wing army officers engineered a violent takeover to "save the nation," as tanks and paratroopers poured into the streets of Athens. Some 8,000 people were arrested in the first month of the coup alone. This Colonels' Coup, as the takeover came to be known, was driven by the desire to fend off the forces supposedly imperiling the country—communism, secularism, materialism, national division, and Western decadence. For inspiration, the leaders looked back to the authoritarian nationalism of Greek dictator Ioannis Metaxas, who ruled the country from 1936 to 1941. Metaxas advocated the rebirth of what he called Greece's "Third Hellenic Civilization" as a kind of corollary to Hitler's Third Reich. Colonel Georgios Papadopoulos, one of the leaders of the coup, justified the 1967 military intervention by saying that "we had arrived at a situation of anarchism in this country of Helleno-Christian civilization. We had become estranged from all ideals, from every Christian institution, from every written and unwritten law." Other colonels proclaimed that the crackdown was necessary because "Greece is a mission, and this mission consists of civilization." After the coup, Greek secondary school curricula were "purified" in the name of "Helleno-Christian" nationalism. Placards put up after the coup promulgated the guiding ideals of the putschists as "Tranquillity—Progress—Regeneration" and "Greece for the Christian Greeks." Even as late as August 1971—a full four years after the coup—the state passed a law to muzzle the press, calling on all journalists, including foreign correspondents, to respect Helleno-Christian principles. Fascist-style sporting events and martial pageantry from the 1930s were revived under the colonels in the form of ultranational "Festivals of the Polemic Virtue of the Greeks." The crusade against modernity was extreme—the colonels banned modern music, long hair for men, and miniskirts for women, as palace guards and ceremonial officials paraded around in traditional Greek costume.[5]

The Greek military coup was condemned by the international community. The Council of Europe suspended Greece's membership in 1969 in response to widespread reports of torture and other human rights violations. Such international condemnation was a dramatic departure from the Cold War politicking over Greece in the 1940s discussed in Chapter 5, when civil-war Greece became a dramatic pretext for the military consolidation of an America-led coalition in the name of Western civilization. This time the Greeks were reclaiming the language of civilization for themselves, reinventing their own traditions as ideological cover for right-wing military insurrection. But given the country's strategic geopolitical position, Greece's NATO partners supported the junta until its overthrow in 1974.

No issue, however, captured the international imagination regarding the interplay of civilization and barbarism more than South

African apartheid. By the early 1960s South Africa was routinely denounced at the UN and other international fora for its brutality and segregationist policies, especially after the Sharpeville massacre in 1960, during which sixty-nine people were killed. That apartheid was formally institutionalized the same year as the United Nations' Declaration of Human Rights—1948—foreshadowed the coming collision between Pretoria and the United Nations. Domestically, apartheid provided Afrikaner nationalism with a sense of purpose, and united Afrikaner and English settlers in moral mission and common defense against indigenous South Africans. After the electoral victory of the Afrikaner National Party in 1948 the policy of apartheid was presented as the best means to guarantee the security of white Christian civilization. In a letter to American churchmen in 1954, National Party leader D. F. Malan asserted that apartheid was "the deep-rooted colour consciousness of the white South Africans," which itself was the "physical manifestation of the contrast between two irreconciliable ways of life, between barbarism and civilization, between heathenism and Christianity." Prime Minister Hendrik Verwoerd sought to make light of the violent implications of apartheid by saying that segregation was synonymous with "good neighborliness" and mutually beneficial "separate development."[6]

The notion of white civilization drew on older transatlantic polemics about the so-called white man's burden as a chief justification of imperialism. Former American government official E. Alexander Powell's *The Last Frontier: The White Man's War for Civilization in Africa*, published in 1912, was one of many books at the time that addressed the perceived connections between race, expansion, and the civilizing mission. But these views were hardly one-dimensional or consensual, as other voices could be heard on the relationship between apartheid and civilization. In the 1930s Isaac Schapera's edited volume *Western Civilisation and the Natives of South Africa* addressed the interaction between market-driven European civilization and the tribal structure of African society, and concluded that both had been positively changed as a result. More critical views were registered by historian Arthur Keppel Jones's 1951 pamphlet, *Race or Civilisation? Who Is Destroying Civilisation in South Africa?*, in which he showed that race and civilization were not the same thing, to the extent that civilization was a higher value and more inclusive concept. Keppel Jones suggested that if "nonwhites" were not admitted into a more expansive notion of "civilisation," then the "verdict of history on the evanescent European civilisation in Southern Africa" would be "a flame that flickered for only a few generations, and then became a mere historical interlude between two Dark Ages." In a 1952 pamphlet South African philosopher E. E. Harris went further in demolishing the idea of "white civilization" as specious and immoral, and promoted gradual racial integration as the solution to race tensions in South Africa. South African Christian liberals also pledged to create a nonracial civilization in South Africa based on Western cultural values.[7]

The legitimacy of apartheid was put to the test during British prime minister Harold Macmillan's famous 1960 visit to Cape Town. There, on February 3, he delivered his landmark "Wind of Change" speech to both houses of the South African Parliament about the inexorable march of African nationalism. A few days before his speech, Macmillan sat down with two of South Africa's most prominent politicians, Prime Minister Hendrik Verwoerd and Foreign Minister Eric Louw. What transpired pointed up the growing gap between the imperial metropole and the beleaguered South African state. The South African politicians tended to invoke an older language of European civilization to win Macmillan's support. As Verwoerd saw it, "We call ourselves European. But actually, we represent the white men of Africa. They are the people, not only in the Union [of South Africa], but throughout major portions of Africa, who brought civilization here." For good measure, Verwoerd added that "if the United Kingdom and the United States could show greater confidence in what the Union Government" was "trying to do to further the Western cause," then the Union would help exert more pressure "on the other African states" to do the same. Verwoerd even attributed the international unpopularity of his regime to the lack of political support from Washington and London, and was particularly incensed by President Kennedy's effort to link anticolonial revolutionary movements in sub-Saharan Africa to the spirit of 1776. Macmillan, while polite, wasn't really listening. His "Wind of Change" speech only widened the chasm between the hosts and their guest; during the speech Verwoerd's face reportedly "grew slowly more pale and tense," not least because—in breach of protocol—an advance copy of the speech had not been supplied to the hosts. Nelson Mandela found Macmillan's speech "terrific," and African National Congress (ANC) leader Albert Luthuli praised it for providing "some inspiration and hope." Even so, Verwoerd provided a quick response to Macmillan at the conclusion of his speech, saying that while there were understandable differences of opinion, "there must not only be justice to the Black Man in Africa, but also to the White Man," and one mustn't forget that white South Africa served as a "bulwark against communism" that upheld the "values of Christian civilization." Here Verwoerd effectively fused republican nationalism and apartheid ideology, and carried the day in the South African press, as congratulatory telegrams streamed into the press offices. Even so, it was clear that South Africa was now in a defensive position, as reporters close to the government sounded the alarm about the high stakes in the West's apparent change of heart. Cape Town's *Die Burger* intoned that the "state of emergency we have been plunged into by this Western panic can only be fought with united forces. It is a struggle for civilization." Both the confrontation and Pretoria's dramatic withdrawal from the Commonwealth the following year had the effect of consolidating Verwoerd's hold on power, ushering in another two decades of "high apartheid" in the face of growing resistance.[8]

Antiapartheid activists exploited the language of civilization to call for the end of apartheid. A good example is Luthuli, chief of the Amakholwa people as well as president of ANC, who was awarded the Nobel Peace Prize in 1961. In his weekly columns for the Soweto-based tabloid *Golden City Post* during the 1960s, Luthuli took direct aim at the idea of white civilization. A staunch Christian and champion of nonviolence, Luthuli held a vision of civilization that echoed Senegalese president Léopold Sédar Senghor's views. In one 1961 article titled "What Is This White Civilization?" Luthuli insisted that "true civilization is neither white, black or brown," but rather a "synthesis." There was no such thing as white civilization, he concluded, and he advocated a UNESCO-inspired ideal of a "broad universal civilization" based on an integrated multiracial society as itself a kind of World Heritage. Antiapartheid activism from foreigners also lampooned the language of civilization. One example is the film work of the celebrated British antiapartheid activist Reverend Michael Scott. Between 1946 and 1948 Scott worked at a squatter settlement outside Johannesburg and helped produce a twenty-four-minute black-and-white film called *Civilization on Trial in South Africa*, released in the early 1950s. The film title was a knowing reference to Toynbee's 1948 booklet, *Civilization on Trial*, discussed in the introduction, and the film sought to scandalize viewers. It opened with scenes of Johannesburg's plush "civilization intended for whites only," in stark contrast to subsequent shots of run-down township areas and delapidated government housing. It was the first antiapartheid film made in South Africa, and used the hypocrisy of civilization to heighten its moral critique.[9]

By the early 1960s opposition to apartheid had emerged as a galvanizing human rights issue at the UN. India, Ghana, and the Soviet Union led the charge, and in doing so asserted their credentials as leading exponents of anticolonialism on the world stage. South African racism toward Indian workers had prompted the UN's first petition concerning human rights violations back in 1946, and pressure on the regime was mounting. Support also came from

African legal experts, who were quick to link apartheid to human rights and the rule of law. By 1961 South Africa was feeling more isolated, and even Britain that year at the UN General Assembly's sixteenth session joined the rest of the member states in assenting that apartheid was "now so exceptional as to be sui generis."[10]

Antiapartheid emerged as one of the most prominent transnational social movements of the second half of the twentieth century. It gave rise to a new politics of morality at the international level, creating new coalitions across continents and Cold War divisions. This included the presence of Scandinavian, British, Dutch, American, and Japanese NGOs that loudly criticized those states in league with Pretoria, and provided international moral and financial support. The British and Swedish antiapartheid movements—two of the earliest and most prominent—emerged from the churches, and became updated versions of nineteenth-century international campaigns to abolish slavery. With time antiapartheid became a rallying issue for Third World politics more generally, combining as it did anticolonialism and antiracism. African American civil rights activists, for example, carried the UN flag along with the Stars and Stripes in the 1964 Selma marches in opposition to the display of the Confederate flag.[11]

In the communist world, too, the link between antiapartheid and racial equality attracted widespread publicity. The Soviet Union maintained close relations with the African National Congress from the very beginning, and China used the issue to build networks with Third World radicals. Yet it was in the Eastern Bloc where the antiapartheid struggle was recast most dramatically. The satellite states organized dozens of academic conferences, exchanges, and cultural displays of solidarity with freedom fighters in South Africa that addressed the nexus of race and rights. Socialist countries suffering from international isolation either due to political crisis or nonrecognition by the UN—such as Hungary after the upheavals of 1956, and the diplomatically isolated German Democratic Republic—

quickly identified the apartheid issue as a means of improving their international reputation and influence. East-South and East-West solidarity were often mediated through the UN, and the designation of apartheid as a crime against humanity in the International Convention on the Suppression and Punishment of the Crime of Apartheid adopted by the UN General Assembly in 1973 received strong support from Eastern European delegates. UNESCO publications, such as the 1967 *Apartheid: Its Effects on Education, Science, Culture, and Information*, enjoyed broad circulation in Eastern Europe.[12]

East Germany was a special case in the antiapartheid campaign. On the one hand, it was keen to show that it had broken completely with the Third Reich's racial politics. On the other, antiapartheid became a means of undermining the legitimacy of the rival West German state. Publications like *The Bonn-Pretoria Alliance* accused "West German revanchists, militarists and neo-colonialists" of trying to "regain what they lost under Hitler by means of economic, diplomatic and military presence." The GDR championed the ANC's violent struggle, funneled financial support to its fighters, organized international conferences, published all the ANC's journals and pamphlets, such as *Sechaba* and *ANC Speaks*, and even flew wounded ANC soldiers to East Berlin for convalescence. The antiapartheid cause was featured in East German popular magazines and taught in East German classrooms. Such links could also be seen in the reception of renowned German playwright Bertolt Brecht in South Africa. There all-black troupes (such as the Serpent Players) performed Brecht plays in the early 1970s and in so doing cemented the link of Brecht and antiapartheid. South African playwright Athol Fugard directed a play in East Berlin as part of the GDR's international solidarity with South Africa, and Fana Kekana's 1976 antiapartheid play, *Survival*, drew on Brecht's epic theater techniques. Thabo Mbecki, longtime ANC activist and later second postapartheid president of South Africa from 1999 to 2008, reportedly had a particular fondness for Brecht's allegorical satire of the rise of Hitler, *The Resistible Rise of Arturo Ui*, which he saw performed by the Berliner Ensemble in London in 1970.[13]

While the antiapartheid cause helped to create a transnational civil society that transcended Cold War division, apartheid remained entrenched in South Africa as a bastion of Christian civilization, anticommunism, and economic liberalism. Such conservative identity politics even affected Pretoria's understanding of ancient history and archaeology. The Transvaal Museum in Pretoria came under political pressure when it mounted exhibitions detailing the history of human evolution in South Africa in 1952 and again in 1963. Archaeological interest in the Bantu Iron Age, which flourished on liberal English-speaking campuses from the 1960s, challenged white nationalist narratives that directly linked the spread of Christian civilization and progress to white settlement and the suppression of hostile local Africans. The University of Pretoria went so far as to shelve its own archaeological research into Mapungubwe, an extensive and prosperous African medieval precolonial kingdom from the area, since white supremacists refused to accept that this culturally rich kingdom was the product of indigenous African culture. African ruins that were celebrated in the 1960s for the causes of postcolonial nationalism, African civilization, and proto-communism were now either ignored or reread by apartheid apologists to legitimate white settler rule.[14]

Rhodesia was coming under similar criticism from the international community, and there too the language of civilization was mobilized to defend white privilege. Ian Smith, who became Rhodesia's prime minister in 1964 and oversaw the country's independence in 1965, was the last leader of white Rhodesia until the winning of universal suffrage in 1979, and often described his country as having established "a civilization of the highest standards." In a 1965 address to the nation at the hour of its sovereignty, Smith solemnly declared that "we have struck a blow for the preservation of justice, civilization and Christianity." In his autobiography, *The Great Betrayal*, Smith recounted the goodness of Rhodesia's settler society in unreconstructed colonial tones ("our blacks" were "the happiest souls on earth"); for him, Britain's war against Nazi Germany and the struggle to preserve white supremacy in Rhodesia were part of the same civilizing mission, to say nothing of his abiding admiration for the strong-arm tactics and colonial policy of Portuguese president António de Oliveira Salazar. In Smith's eyes, Rhodesia embodied the true Britain before its empire disintegrated. So strong were these beliefs that in a 1966 newspaper interview in the *Rhodesia Herald*, Smith opined that "if Churchill were alive today I believe that he would probably emigrate to Rhodesia—because I believe that all those admirable characteristics of the British we believed in, loved and preached to our children, no longer exist in Britain"; those values exist in Rhodesia "to a greater degree than they ever existed in the mother country." The rise of an anticolonial resistance movement under Robert Mugabe sparked wide international discussion, though many continued to support Smith's pariah state in Africa. One British Anglican minister entreated the international community in 1977 to rise up to defend "Christian civilization" in the face of the unwarranted "demands of black terrorist leaders."[15]

The regimes in Greece, South Africa, and Rhodesia used the rhetoric of civilization against the forces of democracy, equality, and human rights. The upshot was that the progressive, pluralistic, and secular character of civilization after 1945 was being reworked in the periphery and ex-colonies of Europe as a discourse of reaction, anticommunism, and white privilege. This mutation was not simply a reversion to old nineteenth-century imperial roots, for this time civilization was less a justification for expansion and social engineering than a defense of the status quo and European conservative interests. In these settings, civilization became the last stand of pariah states to protect right-wing and segregationist states.[16]

THE TWO KEY INTERNATIONAL EVENTS OF 1975—THE SIGNING of the Helsinki Accords and the death of Franco—marked a new era of European politics, one in which the forces of liberal civilization (the spreading of rights, the end of fascism, and economic liberalization) were reshaping international relations in a spirit of East-West détente and reform. The Mediterranean rim of Western Europe saw the demise of authoritarianism in Greece, Portugal, and Spain, each of which made the transition from dictatorship to democracy in remarkably bloodless fashion. The 1970s brought an end to the longest dictatorships in Europe—Salazar had ruled Portugal from 1932 to 1968, while Franco presided over Spain from 1936 until his death in 1975. In part these transitions were peaceful because these countries were members of NATO and an American-led Cold War West. Spain and Portugal's noninvolvement in World War II and strategic Cold War importance had enabled them to preserve their right-wing regimes unmolested by outside powers for decades. They had also abandoned economic autarky in the late 1950s in favor of rapid modernization so as to open up their relatively closed economies to Western European trade.

The rallying slogans driving mid-1970s Southern Rim reform were democracy and freedom, not civilization. This is not so surprising, given that the counterrevolutionary Southern European regimes had all constructed their Cold War identities as defenders of Christian civilization. Calls for regime change took aim at this sclerotic Mediterranean legacy of authoritarianism, international isolation, economic underdevelopment, and religious conservatism. That Portugal's revolution coincided with the emancipation of its last remaining colonies in Angola and Mozambique further strengthened the linkage of liberalization and anticolonialism. While Portugal's transition from dictatorship to democracy was short and sharp, Spain's was a slower negotiated transformation. Not that these dramatic 1970s changes signaled the victory of civil society, since in most of these countries—especially in Portugal—popular mobilization took place only *after* the revolution itself. The unlikely peaceful transitions in Spain, Portugal, and Greece prompted observers to christen the trend a new "southern paradigm," spurring a cottage industry of commentary linking democratic transitions in different parts of Europe as part of a larger tale of liberalism triumphant.[17]

The liberalization of Southern Europe put an end to the old prejudice that "Europe begins at the Pyrenees," after which these Mediterranean rim countries were economically and culturally better integrated into the rest of Western Europe. The high-profile accession of Greece to the European Union in 1981, followed by Spain and Portugal in 1986, was designed to help consolidate their political place in the family of liberal European nations. Perhaps the crowning cultural event in the reintegration of Spain into the international community was the repatriation of Picasso's *Guernica*, his iconic painting of the horrors of the Spanish Civil War that had been in exile at the Museum of Modern Art in New York since 1939 at Picasso's request. Picasso gave specific instructions that his masterpiece was not to be sent to Madrid until Spain did away with fascism. On September 10, 1981, *Guernica* was dispatched to post-Franco Spain as part of the country's "national patrimony," and was widely seen as what one *New York Times* journalist called a "moral endorsement of the country's infant democracy." No event better marked the expansion of "civilized Europe" southward at the time.[18]

The integration of these Mediterranean countries altered the cultural map of Europe. Southern Europe was no longer understood as the frontier of Christian Europe as it had been in the Cold War, but now assumed a more central place in the cultural geography of Western Europe. There had been some movement in that direction a decade earlier. By the mid-1960s, the Spanish tourist industry began to develop holiday charter flights and package tours for Americans and Western Europeans, linking tourism with modernization, political peace, and cultural diplomacy. By the end of that decade the consumer boycotts against Franco's Spain had dissipated, as Spain emerged as a favorite destination for what was called "mass leisure civilization." The intensification of tourism to the region in the 1970s as well as the rising number of Southern European migrants in France, West Germany, and elsewhere signaled the growing cultural presence of the southern fringe in a more pluralistic Europe.[19]

But if 1975 helped dissolve the old ideological boundaries between Southern and Northern Europe, even more dramatic changes were afoot on the frontiers between Western and Eastern Europe. The Helsinki Accords of 1975 registered a political earthquake in East-West relations, even if their power wasn't perceived as such at the time. The accords were the fruit of a large international conference that took place in the Finnish capital, attended by almost all European countries (save Andorra and Albania), as well as the US and Canada. The thirty-five-country conference was designed to resolve the political frontiers of Europe thirty years after the war. Unlike after the Great War, there was no equivalent peace conference to draw up and codify borders after 1945, and this conference aimed to settle these questions diplomatically. The Soviets were primarily interested in receiving international blessing for the de facto Red Army occupation of Eastern Europe. Borders were the first order of business and the first area of agreement; this was hailed as a great diplomatic coup for the Soviet Union, to the consternation of American conservatives, who felt that President Gerald Ford had blithely sacrificed the freedom of tens of millions of captive Eastern Europeans on the altar of *Realpolitik*. Yet it was the so-called Basket II and Basket III agreements that mattered more in the medium term. Basket II permitted more contact and cooperation between Eastern and Western Europe, in the form of sharing scientific and academic knowledge, increasing East-West cultural events, and expanding visiting rights for families divided by Cold War barriers. So whereas the Iron Curtain was now acknowledged as an international military fait accompli in the first part of the accords, the Basket II agreements in effect rendered the Berlin Wall more porous by encouraging traffic and exchange across the East-West frontiers. In this sense, the Accords built on West German chancellor Willy Brandt's *Ostpolitik*, or Eastern policy, which paradoxically was designed to overcome the status quo by officially acknowledging it.

The Basket III agreements on human rights were perhaps the most important aspect for subsequent developments. The Soviet and Eastern Bloc formal commitment to human rights—seen by the Eastern European signatories as a meaningless concession to the West, especially since the formal acknowledgment of the inviolability of national sovereignty trumped all—inspired Eastern European dissidents to push for change. Once these communist states signed the document and published the accords in national newspapers, reformers across Eastern Europe cut out and cited the accord to shame their governments into compliance. Soon thereafter human rights groups mushroomed across the region and developed contacts with other Eastern European dissidents as well as with West European activists. Examples ranged from Czechoslovakia's Charter 77 to the establishment of various Helsinki Watch groups in the Eastern Bloc. As with the mid-1970s regime changes in Southern Europe, the Helsinki language of reform was democracy and human rights, not civilization. The shared mid-1960s East-West language about the problems associated with technical civilization, as discussed in the last chapter, dipped from view.[20]

Not that the 1960s theme of civilization faded completely among East European intellectuals. The dissident Czech playwright and eventual president of postcommunist Czechoslovakia Václav Havel invoked the term often, generally in reference to the modern scourge of alienation and the dangerous side effects of what he called "technical civilization." Havel picked up the theme from his long-standing taste for German philosophy, especially Martin Heidegger. Civilization in crisis peppered Havel's famous 1978 essay on *The Power of the Powerless*, in which he wrote that "modern humanity"—from whatever ideological camp—is unable to fend off the onslaught of "technological civilization" and "industrial-consumer society." In 1984 Havel was awarded an honorary doctorate by the University of Toulouse, and in his lecture (which he was unable to deliver in person) he elaborated on the tragic role of the intellectual living in a "totalitarian country," though he was quick to point out that the dangers were the same in each half of Europe. Eastern Europe's "totalitarian systems of modern technical-industrial society," Havel concluded, were just the most visible instances of a much deeper malaise. As he suggestively put it, Eastern Europe served as "the avant-garde of a global crisis of this civilization, first European, then Euroamerican, and ultimately global."[21]

For Havel and other Eastern European dissidents, the new rallying term for East-West solidarity was a very old one—*Europe*. With it the long-cherished values of European civilization—rule of law, democracy, cultural engagement, and the leading role of intellectuals—were transformed into an imagined cultural geography that enabled activists to think beyond the confines of the nation-state and Cold War blocs. For Eastern Europeans, this was a striking development. After all, nineteenth-century European intellectuals were generally the champions of romantic nationalism and nation-building; in Central Europe intellectuals were the dreamers of nations long before these nation-states were created on the ground. It was the Russian Revolution that "europeanized" European intellectuals and turned many of them into internationalists of various stripes. Cold War division and Soviet occupation effectively returned most Eastern European intellectuals into spokespeople of their captive nations. But after Helsinki there was more international exchange and cross-Curtain thought, as the old ideological differences gave way to exploring what Europeans had in common. Such thinking reached its apogee in the 1984 essay by Czech writer Milan Kundera, who famously argued in the *New York Review of Books* that the real tragedy of Central Europe was its forgotten status as a "kidnapped West" suffering under the brutality and cultural imperialism of an unwanted

"Soviet civilization." As Kundera put it, "the deep meaning" of Central Europeans' resistance to Soviet hegemony "is the struggle to preserve their identity—or to put it another way, to preserve their Westernness," and for him this was why the "disappearance of the cultural home of Central Europe was certainly one of the greatest events of the century for all of Western Civilization." The clash of civilizations was thus being played out within Eastern Europe itself.[22]

The spread of human rights and Europeanism in the early 1970s in part reflected an era of growing détente and secularism on the continent. Across Europe and America, church pews were emptying out, as more and more people—especially the young—were turning away from religious life. The apparent decline of Christianity in the US prompted a *Time* magazine cover story in April 1966 on the theme "Is God Dead?," and a poll conducted in France in the late 1960s found that only 15 percent of French adults reported that they took weekly communion. By that time the ideal of Judeo-Christian civilization as the spiritual foundation of American liberalism was coming under fire. While several Jewish theologians back in the 1950s worried that the trumpeted early Cold War Jewish-Christian amity threatened the survival of Judaism, the hollowness of this "shared tradition" was subject to trenchant critique by the late 1960s. Arthur Cohen's polemic *The Myth of the Judeo-Christian Tradition*, published in 1969, countered that Jewish-Christian relations were better understood as a long and painful history of cultural antagonism, not common purpose; the 1970s shift toward the celebration of ethnic particularism further vitiated the 1950s politics of consensus. Similarly, the notion of Judeo-Christian civilization was increasingly denigrated during and after the Vietnam War by leftist thinkers as a racist ideology that legitimated the mistreatment of non-Western peoples around the world.[23]

The decline of Christian Europe was one of the most striking if silent revolutions of the 1960s. At the institutional level, the papacy and churches played no role at Helsinki, and the age of détente saw the decline of Christian militancy, especially within the Roman Catholic Church. Vatican II stood for peace and accommodation, and the long standoff between Catholicism and communism reached a surprising juncture of nonaggression. Pope John XXIII's 1963 encyclical *Pacem in Terris* announced the possibility of cohabitation with communism, setting in motion a new Vatican *Ostpolitik* that anticipated the coming political thaw. Communist states and the churches made a bargain in which the state would protect the church's rights on the condition that the churches had to recognize the state's secular authority, which included breaking ties with partner churches abroad. This had its echoes in the West, as Christian churches in the US and in Western Europe generally became less involved in international affairs, increasingly concentrating on national matters like school curriculum, abortion issues, and "family values."[24]

Erstwhile Cold War combatants like Hungarian cardinal Mindszenty became the awkward survivors from a bygone era. By the early 1970s the US felt that Mindszenty's fifteen-year exile within the American legation in Budapest was a stumbling block to warming Soviet-American relations, and in 1971 he was quietly transferred to his "second exile" at the Pázmáneum seminary in Vienna. His old supporters were hugely disgruntled by the humiliating turn of events. One biographer upbraided the Church for having lost its fighting spirit from the early days of the Cold War. While "early Christians were filled with reverence for their brothers who had suffered persecution for Christ's sake," nowadays "the decadent West would rather live in peace with pagans and murderers than with God Himself," as "the tears and blood of the persecuted are an embarrassment and hindrance to the deals of businessmen and the negotiations of diplomats." Not that Mindszenty's passing was forgotten, as his death in 1975 enjoyed wide coverage and commemorations among the Roman Catholic faithful. In Cleveland, Ohio, a city plaza was named after him, and in New Brunswick, New Jersey, home to tens of thousands of Hungarians who fled the country after the uprising in

1956, a ten-foot statue bearing his name was unveiled in Mindszenty Square; another memorial to him was erected in Santiago, Chile.[25]

A few years later the international profile of Roman Catholicism was dramatically transformed by the surprise election of the relatively unknown cardinal of Kraków, Karol Józef Wojtyła, as Pope John Paul II in October 1978. Wojtyła was the first non-Italian pope in over 450 years and the first Slavic pontiff, and at fifty-eight years of age also the youngest pope in over a century. His chosen name signaled the continuity with the Vatican II reforming popes, John XXIII and Paul VI. The new pope was bent on reviving the Church's mission in the world, one that explicitly combined a re-invigorated Catholicism, humanism, and what he repeatedly called "Christian civilization." Mindszenty's old crusade to couch the Church's struggle against communism in terms of human rights, Christian morality, and Christian civilization was seized by a new generation of Eastern European Catholic activists in the late 1970s and 1980s. In the 1950s Mindszenty's fate helped invent a new political conscience for Western Europe; now Mindszenty's legacy resurfaced as part of a new conscience of the East. The center of gravity for Catholic activism had shifted from Hungary and Italy to Poland and the Polish pope.[26]

John Paul II's week-long pilgimage to Poland in June 1979 was a seismic event that reverberated far beyond Poland. He delivered thirty-two sermons in six cities, before an estimated 13 million on-lookers, as noted in Figure 38. Special trains arrived every few minutes at Warsaw's station over the course of his visit, many packed with pilgrims and devotees from across Eastern Europe. Windows and porches in housing blocks along the pope's motorcade routes were transformed into makeshift shrines and altars decorated with flowers, flags, and photographs of the pontiff, and many Poles knelt roadside in shows of respect and gratitude. Needless to say, Wojtyła's spectacular return to Poland was a delicate issue for Polish communist authorities. Almost immediately after he was elected, he was invited by Polish Catholic leaders to return to his homeland in May 1979 for the 900th anniversary of the martyrdom of St. Stanisław, the Catholic patron of Poland executed in 1079 for opposition to the policies of King Bolesław the Bold. The state was nervous about the timing of events, and a compromise was eventually reached to postpone his visit until the following month. When he did arrive, the whole country changed. As British journalist Timothy Garton Ash observed, "For nine days the state virtually ceased to exist," as "everyone saw that Poland is not a communist country—just a communist state." Radio Free Europe reported that his election had sparked a "massive outburst of national pride and satisfaction," one in which the entire nation "suddenly acquired glory and prestige." The celebrated Polish journalist Adam Michnik remarked that even if Poles "do not want ambrosia from the heavens or military intervention," even if they do not "expect the Yalta accords to be invalidated overnight," the cardinal's elevation was a kind of "miracle."[27]

For his first major speech at Victory Square in Warsaw on June 2, 1979, a fifty-foot cross was erected directly in the center of the public space so that the new pope could celebrate an open-air mass with over a million congregants. On this occasion, John Paul II directly linked the history of Poland with that of Christ, declaring that "it is impossible without Christ to understand and appraise the contribution of the Polish nation to the development of man and his humanity." And in a sermon the next day at the ancient cathedral city of Gniezno, he posed the rhetorical question about Europe's true identity: "Is it not Christ's will" that "this Polish Pope, this Slav Pope, should at this precise moment manifest the spiritual unity of Christian Europe?" In another speech to young people of the Archdiocese of Gniezno that same day, he remarked that "Polish culture still flows with a broad stream of inspirations that have their source in the Gospel," approvingly citing the great Polish poet Adam Mickiewicz's statement that "a civilization truly worthy of man must be a Christian civilization."[28]

Figure 38. Pope John Paul II, Wadowice, Poland, June 7, 1979. *Credit: Associated Press*

In his sermons, encyclicals, and homilies, John Paul shifted Catholic doctrine into new territory, often co-opting what had long been a secular vocabulary. For starters, John Paul built on Vatican II's concept of the "right to culture," expanding it as a byword for identity, history, and spirituality, a kind of synonym for Christian civilization that transcended material concerns and political boundaries. The same went for his attitude toward human rights and its secular international defender, the United Nations. While Pius XII had harbored a deep distrust toward the UN, John XXIII saw it as a positive model, and believed that the 1948 UN Declaration of Human Rights was a "step in the right direction" toward a "juridical and political ordering of the world community." For John Paul II human rights began with the dignity of the person and religious freedom, a personalist doctrine very much in keeping with progressive Catholic theology from the 1940s and early 1950s, though his anticommunism was much less militant and aggressive. John Paul wished to bring the rights discussion back within the Church, to rebaptize human rights for a new age. No one failed to miss the message: as one commentator put it, it was the "Church, not communism, which now stood firmly on the side of man." The pontiff also expressed growing concern with the spiritual alienation and psychological disorientation that resulted from what he called technical civilization, echoing Havel and other Eastern European intellectuals. In his first encyclical, *Redemptor Hominis*, or *Redeemer of Man*, promulgated on March 4, 1979, the pontiff intoned that humankind "cannot become the slave of things, the slave of economic systems," for a "civilization purely materialistic in outline condemns man to such slavery, even if at times, no doubt, this occurs contrary to the intentions and the very premises of its pioneers."[29]

Eastern European press coverage of his visit was kept to a minimum to mitigate the magnitude of the tour. Local Polish radio and television were faced with a more difficult task, given the outpouring of support. Polish television crews tried to downplay the media effect by focusing exclusively on the pontiff while he was speaking in order to avoid any panning shots of the massive crowds in attendance, and camera coverage studiously conveyed the impression that his appeal was mainly among the elderly, nuns, and clergy. One French journalist remarked that the Polish state's bizarre media coverage was akin to televising a football match in which the cameras showed everything but the ball. Even so, the scale of the event surpassed all expectations.[30]

Less remarked is that John Paul was rewriting the cultural geography of Christian Europe. On one hand, he worked to initiate détente between the Western and Eastern branches of Christianity. To this end the pope built on Vatican II's Decree on Ecumenism, *Unitatis redintegratio*, issued on November 21, 1964, which recognized the rich heritage of the Eastern Orthodox churches and Roman Catholicism's debt to them in liturgy and doctrine. In 1980 the Eastern saints Cyril and Methodius were officially declared the co-patrons of the continent with St. Benedict. On the other hand, the pontiff took his message about the revival of Christian Europe on the road to the West in the early 1980s. During his 1982 pilgrimage to Santiago, Spain, John Paul entreated "you, old Europe" to "discover your origins. Give life to your roots," and implored Europe and Europeans that "you can still be the beacon of civilization and stimulate progress throughout the world." European identity, he continued, "is incomprehensible without Christianity," which has "ripened the civilization of the continent" and "all that constitutes its glory." This was no small rhetorical move, precisely because these broader terms of community—humanity, civilization, and human rights—were originally devised as explicitly secular concepts of universal fellowship, and here John Paul was making a concerted effort to bring them into the language of Christian mission.[31]

The pope was not the only one thinking about European civilization and identity in this period. Another outsize—if unlikely—figure was none other than the general secretary of the Communist Party of the Soviet Union, Mikhail Gorbachev. John Paul and Gorbachev headed two of the great antinational ideologies of the modern world—Catholicism and communism—and they both looked to blend their idea of internationalism with European identity. With his ascendancy to power in the spring of 1985, Gorbachev set his sights on radically reforming the ailing Soviet Union. His two-pronged reform campaign of *glasnost* (openness) and *perestroika* (restructuring) received great attention both domestically and internationally, as the new Soviet leader unleashed his own wind of change across the Soviet Union. Less remarked were the cultural implications of Gorbachev's "new thinking," and in particular his assertion about the "common European home" and the need to rejoin the Soviet Union to what he called "collective European civilization." While the rhetoric of a "common European home" had first been mooted by general secretary of the Soviet Union Leonid Brezhnev during his 1981 visit to Bonn, Gorbachev made it a central element of his cultural reform policy to imagine a common European identity and heritage beyond geopolitical division. As Gorbachev put it in his book *Perestroika*, after "pondering on the common roots of such a multi-form but essentially common European civilization, I felt with growing acuteness the artificiality and temporariness of the bloc-to-bloc confrontation and the archaic nature of the 'iron curtain.'" Gorbachev was an admirer of Czech communist reformer and former leader Alexander Dubček back in the late 1960s, as well as the liberalizing Western European Eurocommunists in the 1970s. He was especially attracted to what he called "the potential opportunities for a pan-European policy which lay in the 'spirit of Helsinki,' a unique achievement in itself." While Gorbachev's views were primarily designed to lessen the tensions between East and West in the spirit of a new détente, they did mark a shift of Soviet attitude. Whereas the 1960s and 1970s marked the communist thrust southward in the wake of decolonization, the 1980s witnessed a distinctive westward shift politically, economically, and culturally.[32]

That Gorbachev would compete with the pope on the terrain of civilization may seem at first quite surprising, given the Soviet Union's long-standing dismissal of the term civilization as bound up with imperialism and racism. And yet, as noted in the last chapter, the communist world's acceptance of the term—including the idea of socialist civilization—was in large measure the result of its encounter with the developing world. Like John Paul II, Gorbachev's invocation of civilization was not militant or exclusionary, but rather understood as an ideology of solidarity that bridged East and West, and less so North and South. Such language reflected the forging of new alliances and continental identities. In the last decade of the Cold War, John Paul and Gorbachev stood as the two champions of a reformed and more peaceable Europe.

THAWING EAST-WEST RELATIONS IN THE LAST DECADE OF THE Cold War transformed the cultural geography of the continent, but it came at the expense of other relations. For example, not everyone was pleased with Gorbachev's turn westward. Various African observers, for example, interpreted Gorbachev's "common European home" as the comeback of Eurocentrism and the socialist world's turn away from long-standing commitments to their continent.[33] The militant Third World movement in the early 1970s had been in part a reaction against warming East-West relations and the increasing abandonment of anticolonial struggles by the Soviet Union. Angola, Ethiopia, and Afghanistan all challenged détente by pleading to the Soviet Union that they were proper Marxist-Leninists in need of assistance, and in this sense helped reactivate Cold War antagonism. By the late 1970s, Eastern European–African exchanges began to slow down. With mounting economic problems in the USSR came a growing sense that resources were being squandered abroad, and by the late 1980s Gorbachev had cut back Soviet support for Latin American communist parties and leftist movements across the world. This is not to say that these exchanges withered completely, as Yugoslavia and East Germany remained committed to maintaining these solidarity initiatives. But in general, the missionary zeal of 1960s socialist internationalism had faded.[34]

East-West European détente was shaping new cultural identities. A European Festival of Friendship was organized in Bucharest in 1977 as a follow-up to the Helsinki Accords, and featured artists from across Europe performing a mixture of classical and folk music. The high-profile celebrations of the 2,050th anniversary of the first centralized Dacian state in Romania in 1980 and the 1,300th anniversary of the first Bulgarian medieval state the next year, showcased the central place of Romania and Bulgaria within European civilization through the storied ruins of antiquity. While the turn toward ancient national pasts (and an anti-Roman one at that in the case of Romania) was part of the socialist states' effort to mobilize patriotism in an era of economic downturn, it also signaled a break from solidarity with the Global South around the theme of international socialism. Eastern European archaeologists

411

began to use their work to portray Islamic and Turkish civilization as totally distinct from that of their European counterparts. A telling example of this Eastern European distancing from Africa was the famous "Letter of Six" written in the spring of 1989 by a half dozen former veterans of the Romanian politburo. In it they denounced the economic policies, administrative mismanagement, and degradation of Romania's international status under the reigning dictator Nicolae Ceaușescu. In particular they upbraided him for having taken their country "out of Europe" by not following the reformist lead set by their Eastern Bloc neighbors to the west as part of the Helsinki Process. Most revealing was that the Six explicitly rejected the country's 1970s turn toward Africa, reminding Ceaușescu that "Romania is and remains a European country" and "you cannot remove Romania to Africa."[35]

The same sensibility was taking shape from an African perspective. Consider the 1977 Second World Black and African Festival of Arts and Culture, or FESTAC 77, held in Lagos. With it, Nigeria assumed the center of a global "black imperium," showcasing Nigeria's growing economic and cultural power against its longtime rival Senegal. Several dozen African countries gathered "to ensure the revival and resurgence of Black and African cultural values and civilization" across the world. For the opening ceremony, national delegations paraded in traditional costume, with Guinea's contingent flying banners reading "No Whititude, No Negritude" and "To each people their culture." FESTAC 77 served as the inversion of Senghor's 1966 Black Arts festival discussed in Chapter 6, not least because the 1966 Dakar show explicitly excluded North Africa and the Arab world. Unlike Senghor's show, there were no invited Western experts, nor any real UNESCO presence. On the contrary, there were passionate calls to repatriate ancient African artworks now residing in foreign museums and private collections. This 1977 show also strove to provide a more inclusive all-African vision than the 1969 Pan-African Cultural Festival held in Algiers, which had peddled a more radical agenda to focus on Arab culture and anticolonial revolution. For the 1969 show, delegates from radical movements and art groups in Brazil, India, and Vietnam were on hand, as were Black Panther representatives from the United States. Soviets and Eastern Europeans were also invited to take part in the 1969 Algiers festival, and the Soviet Union opened an exhibition in the Soviet cultural center on *Africa Through the Eyes of Soviet Artists*. In the FESTAC 77 show, by contrast, the Soviet Union and Eastern Bloc countries were altogether absent, reducing the socialist world's role to well-wishing from the sidelines.[36]

Changing attitudes toward human rights in the 1970s and 1980s reflected this new fracturing of old transcontinental solidarities. As noted in Chapter 3, the 1950 Western European Convention on Human Rights signaled a Cold War regionalization of human rights, but this trend intensified internationally in the 1980s. A separate African Charter of Human Rights and Peoples' Rights was drafted by the Organisation of African Unity in 1981, and a Universal Islamic Declaration of Human Rights was drawn up by the Islamic Councils in London and Paris that same year. Likewise, the socialist world worked to put together its own Socialist Declaration of Human Rights as a collective initiative within the Warsaw Pact, focusing on socialist achievements in the areas of equality, welfare, employment, and anti-imperial solidarity. But this Eastern European cross-national initiative quickly broke down over national differences, confirming the limits of socialist internationalism. Others attacked the once-vaunted universalism of human rights as nothing but masked Western ideology. Saudi intellectual and UN delegate Jamil Baroody led the charge in the 1970s by proclaiming universalism as warmed-over cultural imperialism. For him the Universal Declaration of 1948 was nothing but a Western plot "to impose a concept of those rights shaped according to their own norms of civilization"; the hallmark value should instead be one of "relativity in the cultural, social and economic spheres, just as in the political sphere." The new defensive slogan was cultural relativism, which grew in strength in the 1990s across the non-Western world.[37]

The backlash against solidarity was in part an effect of the presence of foreign students and workers in Europe. In both Western and Eastern Europe, the mission to help modernize the economies and material infrastructures in the Global South included training a new cadre of technical elites. Education thus became one of the most important means of cultural exchange and bridge-building between the First, Second, and Third Worlds from the 1960s onward. While more students from Africa studied in Western Europe than in Eastern Europe, the Eastern European exchange programs received a great deal of publicity as emblems of socialist unity. Approximately 10,000 Third World students had studied in Eastern Europe by the mid-1960s. The USSR set up its high-profile Patrice Lumumba Peoples' Friendship University in Moscow, which opened in 1960, followed by the creation of similar educational facilities in Czechoslovakia, East Germany, and Bulgaria.[38]

Most foreign students from the developing world studying in the Soviet Union and Eastern Europe had positive experiences, and often expressed deep gratitude for the chance to study for free and learn from industrially advanced countries. There is still a good amount of nostalgia among those foreigners who studied or worked in Eastern Europe in this early period. Yet there were others who suffered, and they attracted attention. As early as March 1960, African students in Moscow wrote a public letter of complaint to the Soviet government about racist mistreatment. Expectations of lifestyle and adaptation proved a source of tension. Nigerian students, for example, expressed their displeasure with life in Moscow: "No cars, no cafes, no good clothes or good food, nothing to buy or inspect in the stores, no splash of color to relieve Moscow's damp gray," and "not a trace of the civilized pleasures of Paris—or even Dakar." In part some of the chafing was due to the fact that many of these African students came from relatively privileged backgrounds, and were shocked by the relative poverty and racism found in Eastern Europe. In May 1963 in Prague, African students were beaten up in public, apparently due to resentment against the alleged privileged status of African students. Soviet and East European authorities often blamed the foreign students, arguing that their discontent was due to their privileged social background and bourgeois morals. The arrival of tens of thousands of industrial workers from Asia in the 1980s (such as Vietnamese workers in Czechoslovakia) only exacerbated the racial tensions in Eastern European societies. Yet we need to be careful to take these reports at face value, since tales of unhappy foreign students in the Soviet Union and elsewhere in the Eastern Bloc became a mini–cottage industry in the West to score political points and shame Eastern European states. In any case, what made these exchanges important is that they were early tests of multiculturalism in formerly multiethnic nation-states violently purged of Jews and other minorities by both Hitler and Stalin.[39]

The intensification of pan-Islamism complicated these relations. Over the course of the 1970s the dream of Islamic civilization served as a guiding ideal of imagined Islamic kinship that transcended geopolitical divisions. The early 1970s saw more interest in thinking about Islamic humanism, as well as the regenerative role of tradition in Islamic thought. Illustrative was the Muslim world's growing reception of the British historian of world civilizations, Arnold Toynbee. Toynbee considered Islamic civilization one of the last civilizations to survive westernization, and his ideas about the power of pan-Islamism were widely respected. In the 1950s and 1960s Toynbee was invited to lecture in Cairo, Beirut, Kabul, Istanbul, and Islamabad, and his lecture tours enjoyed great press coverage around the region; many of his works were then translated into Arabic. Decades before, Oswald Spengler's 1918 classic, *The Decline of the West*, also influenced Asian, African, and Latin American intellectuals, not least because Spengler's book seemed to herald their own cultural emancipation. Spengler's text was greeted enthusiastically among Chinese nationalists and *négritude* writers in the 1920s and 1930s, many of whom were attracted to his idea (borrowed from eighteenth-century German philosopher Johann Gottfried Herder's notion of the *Volksgeist*) that every people enjoys a distinctive individual spirit or civilization. But it was Toynbee's critiques of Western materialism and demands to think beyond the international system of nation-states that resonated with those in search of a new cross-national Islamic identity.[40]

Pan-Islamism was born as a defensive reaction to late nineteenth-century Western imperialism and its accompanying ideology of cultural superiority, and became a mobilizing ideology in the 1920s with the loss of the Ottoman caliphate and the Allied carve-up of the Middle East after World War I. In the early 1920s, the Soviet Union reached out to Muslims to drive home the message that communism and Islam were compatible. For much of the post-1945 period, Muslims had been quite well integrated into socialist states and international socialist ideology in the aftermath of decolonization. The Soviet Union's friendly policy toward Islam intensified in the 1950s and 1960s, and was bound up with publicizing the religious freedom and institutional support that its Muslim citizens supposedly enjoyed. In both Soviet Central Asia and Yugoslavia, for instance, not only had mosque construction proliferated, but highly ranked communist Muslims were seen as vital instruments for the propagation of anti-imperialist or nonaligned internationalism. But while pan-Islamism remained a minor factor in the first half of the Cold War, things were shifting. The 1974 Second Islamic Summit Conference in Lahore, Pakistan, was a salient development of pan-Islamism, marking a pivotal moment of growing disenchantment among Muslim elites toward both liberalism and communism as international causes and the need for viable alternatives.[41]

Increasing cultural criticism was now directed at the West. The 1980s critique of the West as a mechanistic soulless civilization that had exerted undue corrosive influence on the developing world was famously articulated by the Iranian writer and intellectual Jalal Al-i Ahmad in his *Occidentosis: A Plague from the West*. Portions of this book were secretly printed in 1962, and then posthumously published in full form in Tehran in 1978. Al-i Ahmad's polemic was conceived as a diagnosis of Iran's decadent infatuation with the West, lampooning the effete pro-Western Iranian ("occidentotic") elite as a case study of cultural despair. Al-i Ahmad defined *occidentosis* as a cultural disease and a break with a traditional past, what he called "the aggregate of events in the life, culture, civilization and mode of thought of a people having no supporting tradition, no historical continuity, no gradient of transformation, but only what the machine brings them." The full version of the book was published only a year before the Ayatollah Khomeini's Islamic Revolution overthrew the shah, but it soon became a central point of reference in Persian cultural life after the establishment of the Islamic republic. Al-i Ahmad himself was a translator of Western literature, and he routinely cited Ionesco, Picasso, and Camus in the text, to the point that Camus's *The Plague* served as the inspiration for the title. Khomeini's regime stylized itself as the great defender of Islam against the creeping scourge of Western civilization, and Al-i Ahmad's call for the "return to Islam" marked out his generation.[42]

The Iranian Revolution of 1979 deepened the estrangement between Europe and Islam, though its effects were first registered in Eastern Europe. Initially, Eastern European elites, particularly in the Soviet Union, supported Khomeini and instructed the Iranian communist Tudeh Party to do the same. These Eastern Europeans believed that the anticapitalist economic program of the Islamist government would usher in the next stage of secular revolution, one that was also anti-American. Albania's Enver Hoxha, for example, saw the early years of the Iranian republic as holding out the prospect of longer-term anti-imperialist and Marxist potential. The regime's occupation of the US embassy, the seizing of American hostages, and the condemnation of the US as the "Great Satan" won sympathy in Eastern Europe, even if the Iranian republic expressly maintained a strict nonalignment, with the slogan "Neither East nor West." The revolution was also welcomed by socialist states for opening the door to new economic links and oil exchanges with the communist world. Yet East European observers were soon troubled by the lack of economic reforms, the attacks on leftist movements, and the regime's liberal use of political violence. Communist authorities increasingly viewed Arab students studying at Eastern European universities as potentially threatening agents of conservative ideology within socialist societies. After 1979, Eastern European state security services exercised greater vigilance toward Muslim citizens and pooled their intelligence across the Bloc to combat what they identified as a growing danger.[43]

The Soviet Union lost further credibility among Muslim publics with its 1979 invasion of Afghanistan. With the intervention, the Soviet Union squandered the good relations with the Arab world that specialists had built up since the early 1960s. While the Soviet Union redoubled its effort to repair the damage with Muslim elites, often in the form of stepped-up engagement and diplomatic discussions with various Muslim leaders, distrust and disillusionment spread. The specter of pan-Islam spooked socialist regimes with sizable Muslim minorities, such as Bulgaria, Yugoslavia, and the Soviet Union. Socialist security services (led by the KGB) believed that the international terrorist threat largely came from the Middle East and the rise of radical Islamic movements, and Arab nationalism was deemed the most troublesome element of these movements. Until the mid-1970s Eastern European regimes had identified nationalism as a necessary and positive dimension of the anticolonialism struggle of the 1950s and 1960s, yet the religious nature of extra-European nationalisms in the 1970s undermined their former progressive content, rendering them reactionary and retrograde in the eyes of communist authorities.[44]

For their part, Eastern European experts began to emphasize the dissimilarities between their own region and the Middle East, concluding that the Arab Middle East was driven by antiprogressive Islamic religious notions. Islamic regimes in Libya, Egypt, and Iran were increasingly viewed as violent, intolerant, and premodern zones of underdevelopment. Eastern European Orientalists—once committed to bridge-building between the Second and Third Worlds—now identified a newly emerging civilizational divide between a traditionalist Islam and modern, enlightened Europe and North America, judging political Islam as antithetical to socialist development. Claiming that Muslims were fifth columnists, Bulgaria targeted the Turkish community within its borders for reeducation. In 1985 Todor Zhivkov's government set out to force all Turkish Muslims to change their names to Bulgarian spellings, to strip them of their right to educate their young in their own language, and even to convert them forcibly to Eastern Orthodoxy. Such hardline policies eventually led to the expulsion of 300,000 Turks in the summer of 1989. In the late 1980s the Bulgarian government used ancient ruins to prove the origins of Christian Bulgaria in areas heavily populated by Muslim citizens, so as to support the claim that the region was Christian long before the Muslims arrived from the Ottoman Empire. This was part of a larger trend to affirm Eastern Europe's Christian heritage, and once again archaeology was enlisted to tell new political stories. In June 1987 King Juan Carlos of Spain visited Budapest and was taken to the sites at which Spanish troops fought for the liberation of Buda from the Turks in 1686, a ceremony designed to invoke a shared past between two of Europe's borderland nations, together with a shared responsibility to protect the continent's Christian heritage against the threat of Islam. The idea of the defense of Europe against a Muslim threat was thus being revived in the last decades of the Cold War in the socialist world, years before the more well-known

Eastern European realignments and identity politics against Muslim citizens in the postcommunist period.[45]

Such disturbing views found echoes in Western Europe too, though developments there were more slow-burning. In the 1980s the anxiety toward multiculturalism heightened across the West. Typically the main currents of 1970s European life were identified as economic slowdown, the growth of new social movements like feminism, environmentalism, and gay rights, and the rise of neoliberalism. The right-wing hostility to multiculturalism in the 1970s played a central role in undoing many of the 1960s dreams about integration and pluralism. Europe of course has long been defined in relation to external threats, ranging from the Crusades to the Ottoman Empire to the Bolsheviks. In the nineteenth century the presence of foreign populations within newly drawn nation-states also caused great worry, be it Basques, Germans, or Bretons in Third Republic France, or Danes, French, and Poles in Bismarck's Second Reich. But for Britain and France, the history of immigration is mainly an effect of decolonization, evidenced by the coming of Caribbean citizens to Britain in the late 1940s, or three generations of Algerians living in France. These were not of course the only newcomers. After 1945 the largest immigrant groups to Britain were the Irish, followed by the Poles who had fought the Nazis, German and Italian POWs, as well as other refugees from Eastern Europe. But in the public imagination the story of immigration was directly associated with people of color who arrived in the metropole. Between 1953 and 1961 some 240,000 Caribbeans arrived in Britain, spurring growing apprehension about their effect on British society. Such fear was piqued in Conservative MP Enoch Powell's infamous "Rivers of Blood" speech in 1968, in which he predicted that in "fifteen or twenty years' time the black man will have the whip hand over the white man." While Prime Minister Edward Heath summarily dismissed Powell on account that his words were "liable to exacerbate racial tensions," Powell maintained popular support. Grumblings about immigrant communities continued to simmer on the Right during the 1970s, yet the 1980s gave birth to full-blown national debates about the social consequences of immigration and ethnic diversity.[46]

Similar developments were taking place in France. French anti-Muslim prejudices were of course nothing new. After his first trip to Algeria, Alexis de Tocqueville wrote in 1843 that there "are in the entire world few religions with such morbid consequences as that of Mohammed. To me it is the primary cause of the now visible decadence of the Islamic world." While such attitudes percolated in French colonial circles through the Second World War and beyond, such animosity spiked dramatically during the Algerian War. Once the FLN took the war to the French capital in the late 1950s in the form of sabotage and police assassinations, French media traded on stereotypes of "Arab criminality" and Algerian barbarism. Such views hardened in response to large numbers of Algerians who emigrated to France after the end of hostilities. Between 1962 and 1965 over 111,000 Algerians moved to France, far more than the average of 11,000 emigrants a year during the Algerian War. By the time conservative president Valéry Giscard d'Estaing came to power in 1974, these figures were seen as unmanageable, after which his government endeavored to radically curb all immigration. D'Estaing even organized a massive campaign in 1979 to forcibly repatriate some 500,000 Algerians, though the measure was stopped in the face of protests from opposition political parties, trade unions, and the churches.[47]

Indicative of this growing unrest toward Algerians in France was the formation of Jean-Marie Le Pen's *Front Nationale*, founded in 1972. Le Pen served as a paratrooper in the Algerian War and headed a veterans' organization, the National Front of Combatants, in the late 1950s. He had long been accused of torturing Algerian victims during the war. His political movement was an effort to preserve what he saw as France's sacred ethnic monoculturalism. By the early 1980s immigration was moving to the center of French political discussion. So explosive was the issue in national political life that French Socialist presidential candidate François Mitterand and Giscard d'Estaing agreed not to address immigration during their televised debate in May 1981. In any case, Le Pen transformed Mitterand's language of the "right to difference" as a defense of greater regional autonomy and ethnic diversity into what he called a "justification of French cultural sovereignty." His guiding idea of "France for the French" garnered further support as a new voice of the radical Right after Mitterand's socialist victory in 1981. In Le Pen's eyes, immigrant claims on French citizenship impinged on "native" French ones in a zero-sum game of identity, and he repeatedly railed against the corrosive influence of Arab and Islamic culture on the soul of the French nation. He couched his conservative rhetoric in the defense of Western civilization against the decadence of multiculturalism. The National Front sounded the alarm about "western civilization in peril," posing the menacing question that if the "white race risks submersion by the third world, shouldn't one defend oneself?" Mainstream French press began to take the bait. The conservative *Le Figaro* magazine dedicated an October 1985 edition to the future of France, asking "Will We Be French in 30 Years?" and even promised to disclose the "secret numbers" behind current demographic trends that will "put in peril our national identity and determine the destiny of our civilization" in the years to come.[48]

By the end of the 1980s, growing skepticism about the benefits of multiculturalism had ignited into a full debate about civilization in crisis. While the term multiculturalism first emerged in the 1970s in the United States as a positive moniker of pluralistic societies, the 1980s witnessed a discernible retreat from this ideal across the West. With it the nonintegration of foreigners served as a staging post for new identity politics in Britain, France, and West Germany.[49] Islam was increasingly seen as antithetical to Western values and Euro-

Figure 39. Book burning of Salman Rushdie's *Satanic Verses*, Bradford, England, 1989. *Credit: Getty Images*

pean freedoms, with the result that the place and behavior of Muslims became a litmus test for the viability of multiculturalism. In Britain the infamous Salman Rushdie Affair in 1989 brought these issues to a head. His picaresque novel *The Satanic Verses* generated a huge amount of international controversy when it was published at the end of 1988. On January 14, 1989, some 2,000 angry Muslim residents of the West Yorkshire city of Bradford paraded through town and publicly burned his book, as noted in Figure 39, followed by similar book burnings in Bombay, Kashmir, Dacca, and Islamabad. A month later the Iranian leader Ayatollah Khomeini issued a *fatwa* against Rushdie, calling on Muslims to kill the author and his publishers for blasphemy against the prophet Muhammad. The death warrant drove Rushdie into hiding for a decade, but others associated with the book were not so lucky—a London bookstore that sold the book was firebombed, while his Japanese translator was stabbed and his Norwegian publisher shot. These events shocked and polarized British public opinion, and Muslim outrage was reported in the British media as evidence of the violent and aggressive nature of Islam, as well as the impossibility of ever integrating Muslim citizens into Western "open societies." Conservative British journalist Charles Moore stoked the debate by proclaiming in a newspaper editorial that "Britain is basically English-speaking, Christian and white," concluding with the provocation that if things don't change, then the "hooded hordes will win."[50]

That same year France became embroiled in its own controversy with Islam and the problems of multiculturalism. Several months after the Rushdie Affair, sisters Leila and Fatima Achaboun were sent home from a middle school in Creil outside Paris for refusing to take off their headscarves in class. Their defiance on religious grounds was interpreted as a challenge to the sacred quality of French republican *laïcité*, or secularism, because all schools and civic institutions were to be neutral spaces untouched by religious values or iconography. For many French republican critics, these traditional headscarves were sinister symbols of Islamic patriarchy, anti-Enlightenment values, and the refusal to integrate. The rescue and liberation of Muslim women now became a justification for state intervention. British and French reactions often put their concerns toward multiculturalism in terms of an assault on national identity, but others expanded the rhetoric to interpret these developments as the crisis of Western civilization itself. In this sense, the defensive language of a white minority culture under threat abroad in the ex-colonies of South Africa and Rhodesia now came home to the metropole in the guise of the preservation of monoculturalism for the religious and racial majority.[51]

In a different way, the United States was also embroiled in its own crisis of civilization in the late 1980s. In this case, the attack on multiculturalism was not driven by terrorism or the dangers of Islam. Rather, the anxiety reflected the new conservatism of the Reagan years, which sought to roll back the "excesses" of progressive education and to shore up an American identity under threat from leftist educators. The focus was on the universities. Secretary of Education William Bennett set the tone by railing against what he perceived as the militant nature of leftist changes to university curricula that undermined the very values of Western civilization as the cornerstone of higher education and good citizenship. This sensibility was close in spirit to Clark's *Civilisation* series, but Bennett had a number of like-minded conservative crusaders. Allan Bloom's *The Closing of the American Mind* and E. D. Hirsch's *Cultural Literacy: What Every American Needs to Know*, both published in 1987, were national bestsellers that lamented the decline of American "cultural literacy" and contempt for the past. For Bloom, faddish moral relativism based on what he called the "Nietzscheanization of the Left and vice versa" was proof of "how higher education has failed democracy and impoverished the souls of today's students," leading in his estimation to intellectual "nihilism, American style." Bennett, Hirsch, and Bloom were particularly perturbed that the long-cherished university foundation course in Western civilization was being diluted or replaced by postcolonial studies, feminist theory, and minority literature— Voltaire was out, Frantz Fanon and Toni Morrison were in. As discussed in Chapter 4, the Western Civilization course had been a fixture on the American university curriculum since the 1920s, and was designed to teach American students about their nation's place in the world as the guardian of Western culture. In the 1980s students at various elite universities, notably Stanford and Duke, led the fight back in the name of multiculturalism and progressive education. They countered that the country, the world, and the university had changed dramatically since the 1950s, and that university reading lists should reflect and explore the world beyond the hoary canon of "dead white European males." The national press covered the controversy with hyberbolic polemics; one *Newsweek* magazine story was headlined "Say Goodnight Socrates: Stanford University Puts an End to Western Civilization." Campuses across the country

425

Figure 40. Reverend Jesse Jackson in protest march against
Western Civilization course, Stanford University, 1987. *Credit:
Stanford University Libraries, Department of Special Collections
and University Archives*

joined in the protests, punctuated by American civil rights activist Reverend Jesse Jackson leading a chant at a 1987 rally of some
500 students at Stanford with the slogan "Hey hey, ho ho, Western
Civ has got to go" (Figure 40). Humanities departments effectively
fended off the right-wing campaign in the name of independence
and freedom of thought, but the debate marked a newly aggressive
conservative assault on the world of education and culture. If nothing else, it revealed that the United States was fighting its own flank
of the European culture wars over the relationship between Western
civilization and multiculturalism.[52]

UNLIKE THE FIRST HALF OF THE CENTURY, THE POST-1945
period witnessed no real territorial changes in the European state
system, and the Helsinki Accords cemented the de facto map of
postwar Europe for the international community. Eastern Europe
remained an extended barrack of Red Army occupation, while

the map of Western Europe all but returned to the geographical lineaments of Charlemagne's empire. But even if the geopolitical frontiers of Europe had not changed, the cultural geography of the continent underwent major transformation in the 1970s and 1980s. *Ostpolitik* and the Helsinki Accords rendered the Berlin Wall more porous, as people, goods, and ideas now traveled more easily across borders. The internal distinctions between Southern and Northern Europe were dissolving too, as Greece, Portugal, and Spain were integrated into Western Europe. The infamous Schengen Agreement, in which France, West Germany, and the Benelux countries dismantled their common frontiers in June 1985 so as to allow full freedom of movement for their citizens, did away with internal frontiers even more, auguring the return of passport-free Europe from the days before the First World War. Yet here, too, the removal of internal boundaries saw the construction of new external borders protecting Europe from outsiders in the form of tighter security checks and the policing of foreigners. As historian Tony Judt put it: "Civilized Europeans could indeed transcend boundaries—but the 'barbarians' would be kept resolutely beyond them." Good fences, after all, make good civilizations.[53]

The 1980s thus saw the comeback of conservative Europe, and the discourse of civilization registered widespread feelings of insecurity and identity crisis. The right-wing turn was a reaction against the dreams of détente and the liberal culture of the 1970s, closely associated with the loosening of social hierarchies, cultural norms, and sexual mores, as well as national borders. The forces of change in Europe and its former dominions—resurgent Catholicism and Islamism, the rejection of multiculturalism, and the defense of white privilege—were really the revenge of old ideologies, giving expression to what is sometimes called revolutionary traditionalism. Marxism and secular nationalism no longer commanded the same ideological appeal, as newly imagined cultural identities beyond national and regional boundaries became more pronounced.

In the 1970s and 1980s the physical and mental borders of Europe were being redrawn, and voices from both halves of the continent expressed concern about their vulnerability to foreign ideas and people from the developing world. Anxieties about a new crisis of civilization reflected growing right-wing worries about cultural decline and identity theft. Calls to protect the religious and racial heritage of European civilization under assault fueled the fears and fantasies of European conservatism in the last two decades of the Cold War and beyond.

Conclusion

NEW IRON CURTAINS

O N AUGUST 24, 2015, IRINA BOKOVA, THE BULGARIAN
director-general of UNESCO, issued a statement about the
Islamic State's ongoing destruction of Syria's ancient city of Palmyra
(Figure 41). In it she urged the international community "to stand
united against the persistent cultural cleansing" of the "diversity and
richness" of Syria's history and identity. Bokova was the first woman
and Eastern European to hold the UNESCO directorship, and she
used the organization to draw attention to ISIS's vandalism of cultural treasures in Iraq and Syria, and in particular to the circulation
of their videos boasting about the decimation of the ancient city of
Nimrud and the World Heritage site of Hatra. The destruction of
the Baalshamin temple at Palmyra occurred one week after ISIS be-
headed the elderly archaeologist Khaled al-Asaad, who had looked
after the ruins for forty years, and only several days after the razing
of the Mar Elian monastery in the Syrian town of al-Qaryatayn.
In March 2015 Bokova launched the Unite4Heritage initiative as
part of a concerted global campaign to combat "the destruction and
pillage of cultural heritage in conflict zones, most recently in Iraq."
Over 20 million people have followed UNESCO's Google blog
posts, and #Unite4Heritage has been a massive media campaign to

Figure 41. ISIS destruction of Palmyra, August 2015. *Credit: Pictures from History/Bridgeman Images*

raise awareness about ISIS's vandalism in the Middle East. As it had on many occasions since the late 1940s, UNESCO presented itself as the guardian of world civilization and its endangered heritage sites across the globe.[1]

Bokova described the gravity of these acts in classic UNESCO terms. In an address at Yale University in 2016, she remarked, "We know that Palmyra belongs to all Syrians, but I would say it belongs to the whole humanity. And this is why it matters that we bring the international community together." In a speech in Edinburgh a few months later, Bokova sharpened her language in saying that today "we see violent extremists seeking to destroy heritage, to erase layers of civilization"; Bokova insisted that "there is no clash of civilizations—but there is a divide between those who reject 'living together' and those who believe in humanity as a single community." Notable too was the way that she conjoined human rights and cultural desecration, significantly calling the dynamiting of Palmyra a "crime against civilization." These were not isolated or empty

Figure 42. Mariinsky Orchestra performing at Palmyra, Syria, 2016. *Credit: VASILY MAXIMOV/AFP via Getty Images*

phrases—international calls for justice led to the first prosecution in 2016 of the destruction of cultural heritage as a war crime at the International Criminal Court in The Hague. The defendant, Ahmad al-Faqi al-Mahdi, a member of a jihadist group linked to Al Qaeda who took part in ruining a number of precious ancient monuments in Timbuktu, Mali, ended the trial by begging for forgiveness and pleading that the people of Timbuktu "accept my regrets."[2]

The shocking images of ISIS's renewed vandalism of Palmyra in December 2016 spurred a further round of worldwide condemnation, but by then the line between terrorism and civilization had started to blur. On May 5, 2016, the ruins of an ancient Roman amphitheater in the World Heritage site of Palmyra had served as the dramatic background for a classical music concert by the Russian Mariinsky Orchestra. The concert was called "Praying for Palmyra—Music Revives Ancient Ruins," and featured pieces by Johann Sebastian Bach along with two Russian composers, Sergei

Prokofiev and Rodion Shchedrin (Figure 42). Russian conductor Valery Gergiev described the event as "our appeal for peace and concord. We protest against barbarians who destroyed wonderful monument's [*sic*] of [the] world's culture." But as archaeologist Lynn Meskell has argued, the concert was an overt celebration of Russian military victory over ISIS, one in which classical music was used to honor the "victims of extremists" and to showcase Russian president Vladimir Putin's triumph of civilization over barbarism. In large measure the message was designed to deflect international criticism of Russia's massive air-strike campaigns in Syria in support of the regime of Syrian president Bashar al-Assad. A live feed from Putin's Black Sea holiday redoubt enabled him to convey his message about the urgent need to "rescue modern civilization from this terrible menace—international terrorism." Konstantin Dolgov, Russia's Ministry of Foreign Affairs human rights chief, followed up with a tweet that the concert "is a spiritual response to those who want to destroy Syria" and to "deprive it of Christian principles."[3]

Such celebrations were premature, however. By the end of 2016 Palmyra had been recaptured by ISIS. To undo its humiliation by Russian forces six months before, ISIS razed part of the same ancient theater where the Russian musicians had played. What is more, they produced a video in retaliation to UNESCO's condemnation of their destruction of World Heritage sites as a war crime, saying, "We will destroy your artefacts and idols anywhere and Islamic State will rule your lands." This quid pro quo between the Russians and ISIS dramatizes how spectacles of civilization and barbarism were staged by both sides as military statements. Further complicating things was the offstage intensification of the lucrative black market in Syrian cultural plunder. As Bokova admitted in her Edinburgh speech, an alarming amount of antiquities from Syria and Iraq continued to be seized in a number of countries, including Finland, Turkey, France, the United States, and the United Kingdom. The looting business was so brisk, she continued, that British customs officials at Heathrow Airport confiscated some 3.4 tons of stolen objects between 2007 and 2009. The militarization and commercialization of civilization thus went hand in hand. That said, the international community stepped up its calls for reprisal and reparation. Accusations of barbarism were common fare at the time, echoing foreigners' observations of a devastated Germany back in 1945. But this time the theater of destruction was outside Europe, as the international community embraced these threatened ruins as world heritage.[4]

The tension between barbarism and civilization framed the 2018 eight-part BBC television series *Civilisations*, copresented by British historians Simon Schama, Mary Beard, and David Olusoga. It was a conscious update of Kenneth Clark's landmark 1969 *Civilisation* series. The title *Civilisations* in the plural expressly signaled the double break from Clark's singular designation and his Eurocentric framework, as these presenters put forward a global story of civilization from prehistoric times to the present that recounted the rich tapestry of world culture writ large. In various ways, Schama, Beard, and Olusoga dispensed with Clark's patrician curatorial gaze in favor of multiple thematic and geographical perspectives, highlighting issues of gender, class, race, and the politics of seeing. And yet, there were also continuities with Clark's original series. That the first episode—called "The Second Moment of Creation," narrated by Schama—opened with dramatic shots of ISIS's detonation of Palmyra echoed Clark's departure point of civilization in danger. Less explicit was the manner in which the program strongly promoted a UNESCO agenda of universalism, peace, inclusivity, and cross-cultural influence. Schama's voiceover of the videoed vandalism reminded viewers that this was an assault on all of us, since "we are all inheritors of an endless chain of memories."

Palmyra was by no means the only recent international episode that invoked the idea of civilization in crisis. Consider France in the wake of the November 13, 2015, terrorist attacks in Paris, for which ISIS claimed responsibility. Shock and confusion resulting from the events quickly evoked the themes of civilization and barbarism for a shaken polity. Prime Minister Manuel Valls sounded the alarm by painting the conflict in epic proportions—"C'est un combat de valeurs, c'est un combat de civilisations." To calm down the emotional rhetoric, Socialist President François Hollande assured the French public and international community that "we are not in a war of civilizations, because these assassins don't represent one," clarifying that "we are in a war against jihadist terrorism, which threatens the entire world." Hollande's follow-up speech at UNESCO two days later—where he had been invited to give the keynote address to celebrate the organization's seventieth anniversary—endeavored to place ISIS's cultural desecration in a broader context. "UNESCO is the moral conscience of humanity," and what "underpinned its foundation was the promotion of the diversity of cultures," a "diversity anchored in the recognition of the equal dignity of cultures, as every people has a special message to bring to the world." Even so, for Hollande and the French, the coordinated terrorist assault was an attack on both French civilization (based on its values of *laïcité*) and world civilization at the same time.[5]

Other European heads of state were summoning a similar vocabulary of civilization under threat, but in different contexts. Since the dissolution of the Soviet Union in 1991, Russian presidents from Boris Yeltsin to Vladimir Putin have revived the idea of Eurasianism based on a distinctive Eurasian civilization as a chief principle of Russian foreign policy, especially in response to the eastward expansion of NATO. In 2015 the Hungarian prime minister Viktor Orbán made a name for himself by taking a hardline policy against the tide of refugees fleeing from Syria, Afghanistan, and elsewhere, erecting razor-wire fences to keep them out of the country. Orbán claimed to have taken this step in the name of Christian civilization. During the tense EU debate on the Mediterranean crisis, he maintained that these "immigrants" would forever alter "Europe's civilization." In a speech in September 2015, he rejected international calls for Hungary to take its share of Syrian refugees, saying that those arriving "have been raised in another religion, and represent a radically different culture." "Europe and European culture have Christian roots," he continued, and something must be done to secure the borders precisely because "Europe's Christian culture is barely in a position to uphold Europe's own Christian values." In a more incendiary speech at the Kötcse civic picnic on September 17, 2017, Orbán proclaimed the era of hypocritical "liberal babble" was over. In language strongly reminiscent of Enoch Powell, he declared that "we are inundated with countless immigrants: there is an invasion, they break down fences," against which Hungary's "borders must be protected, and [its] ethnic and cultural composition must also be protected." In Hungary—and elsewhere in Eastern Europe—the myth of an ethnically homogeneous region unburdened by colonialism has been used by right-wing elites to deny any responsibility to settle non-European, non-Christian refugees.[6]

Open borders, long proclaimed by the supporters of the fabled revolutions of 1989 as the very expression of freedom and human rights, are now identified as the very causes of insecurity. Widespread perceptions of the influx of migrants as undermining national identity are closely connected to a demographic pincer movement—huge out-migration of "native" Eastern Europeans toward France, Germany, and especially Great Britain for work purposes, coupled with the immigration of migrants from the Middle East and North Africa, despite the small number of these people in countries like Poland, Hungary, and Serbia. This has led to a virulent renationalization of politics across the old East-West divide, one that is leading to what some call a "browning" of European society—both in terms of immigrant skin color and neofascist sympathies. Liberalism's focus on the rights of minorities has been replaced by populist claims about the rights of the majority. Orbán, leader of Poland's Law and

Justice Party (PiS), Jarosław Kaczyński, and other leaders in Central Europe have led the charge against the Western siren songs of secularism, free movement, and multiculturalism, dismissing the West's long-touted universalism as nothing but the particularism of the rich. Some Polish conservatives have even denounced cosmopolitan Western liberalism as a "civilization of death" for its advocacy of gay rights and abortion. The call of civilization now means the defense of white Christian identity and the closure of borders to immigrants. In the minds of these new nativists, Central Europe is the "true Europe" and its last bulwark. While the language of civilization has experienced great historical variation from the nineteenth century through decolonization and beyond, its main meaning since the 2015 refugee crisis has been commandeered by conservatives as an ethnically based language of purity and pollution. Like communism before it, liberalism is dismissed as another god that failed.[7]

It would be tempting to suggest that this conservative drift in Eastern European politics is mainly due to the fall of communism. Certainly 1989 did much to remake the political landscape of the region, though it is worth pointing out that the language of civilization was largely absent from the upheavals. This was not the case several months before. In early 1989 Jerzy Urban, the spokesman for Poland's Council of Ministers, conceded that the "superiority of Western civilization had become obvious to everybody," and in March of that year Gyula Horn, the last communist foreign minister of Hungary, remarked that the choice before the nation lay between "catching up with the civilized countries or becoming irremediably banished to the peripheries of world developments." But during the uprisings that summer and autumn, the rallying cries were about freedom, rights, and the independence of long-captive nations. On occasion, Czechs and Slovaks declared that they were bringing about a "new civilization" in the autumn of 1989, but they were largely alone in employing this language. Other developments that year illustrated the changing meaning of European civilization.

436

For example, the martyrdom of Cardinal Mindszenty returned to Hungarian public awareness. In 1989 his case was reopened, and the celebrity cardinal was officially exonerated of all charges leveled by the Communist government. Mindszenty's bones were reburied in Esztergom Cathedral, the seat of the Catholic Church in Hungary, located some fifty miles northwest of Budapest, and his resting place has become a pilgrimage site. Two films about Mindszenty were released in Hungary in 2010—Gábor Koltay's *The White Martyr* and Zsolt Pozsgai's *I Love You, Faust*, both of which portray the cardinal as a double victim of German National Socialists and Hungarian communists. The enduring popular fascination with the imprisoned cardinal has been exploited by Orbán's regime to rewrite Hungarian history as a story of Christian martyrdom and national regeneration.[8]

Perhaps the most dramatic episode that indicated the changing shape of European politics was the meeting on December 1, 1989, between Pope John Paul II and Mikhail Gorbachev at the Vatican's Apostolic Palace. Here two towering Cold War figures came face-to-face—Pole and Russian, cardinal and communist, Christian and Marxist. It was the first-ever diplomatic meeting between the leader of the world's first communist state and the head of the Roman Catholic Church. Each represented the allegiances of a large swath of the globe, though by this time Gorbachev's empire was fast disintegrating, especially in Eastern Europe. A reporter on hand wrote that these two Slavs who had "done more than anyone else to usher in a new order in Europe" now sat together in quiet conversation. Gorbachev surprised his listeners by renouncing seven decades of militant atheism and the persecution of religion, declaring the right of all Soviet believers to "satisfy their spiritual needs." Earlier that year Gorbachev had even confessed to having been baptized as a child, and on this occasion the two leaders pledged their support for the Helsinki Process, affirming that there was common space for both Catholic and Communist worldviews in the fields of cultural and humanitarian issues. The long-forgotten encounter was part of

Gorbachev's larger mission to "make the Soviet Union a full partner in a common European civilization." A decade earlier such a meeting would have been inconceivable. Back in 1979 Soviet minister of foreign affairs Andrei Gromyko satirically likened John Paul II's homecoming to Poland to Khomeini's triumphant return to Iran earlier that year, but Gromyko was more prescient than he realized in terms of what role religion would play in events in Poland—and across the region—just ten years later.[9]

The fallout of 1989 not only revealed the enduring power of religion and nationalism in Eastern Europe but also signaled the decline of internationalism. At first this claim may seem counterintuitive, not least because one of the strongest myths of 1989 was that it brought with it the re-internationalization of the long-cosseted rust-belt economies of Eastern Europe. The 1990s witnessed the stark arrival of many symbols of the West, ranging from Harvard MBAs to McDonald's, NATO to Pizza Hut. But Americanization is, of course, hardly the same thing as globalization. Since the mid-1950s, Eastern Europe had been engaged with the Global South in countless ways, as evidenced in the spheres of trade, labor training, military assistance, education, cultural promotion, and humanitarian assistance. Some have even argued that the socialist world was more open than the West in terms of international trade and interaction for much of the Cold War, to the point that post–Cold War neoliberalism arguably has its real roots in socialist Eastern Europe. What we are witnessing now is the effects of these severed economic and political linkages with the Global South since the fall of communism, coupled with the retribalization of Eastern European politics in new ways.[10]

Gorbachev's 1980s rhetoric of a "common European home" played a key role in rethinking European identity beyond Cold War borders. The growing sense of East-West European solidarity in the Global North often came at the expense of a long-fought-for North-South allegiance, and as discussed in the last chapter, by the late

1980s Gorbachev had cut back Soviet support for Latin American communist parties and leftist movements across the world. Some African observers interpreted his idea of the "common European home" as a new defense of Eurocentrism and the marginalization of their continent. The uprisings of 1989 in Eastern Europe only accelerated these distancing trends. After all, many labor migrants from Asia and Africa who had studied and worked in Eastern Europe for years were suddenly sent home in 1989 as figures of an unwanted socialist internationalism. Up to 80,000 contract workers from Vietnam, Angola, Mozambique, and Cuba were forced to leave during the collapse of the East German regime, since Bonn did not want them to settle in Germany, and the Czechoslovak government expelled some 37,000 Vietnamese labor migrants in late 1989. Such actions reflected larger international realignments. Nigerian major general Joseph Garba, who was president of the United Nations General Assembly from 1989 to 1990, openly expressed concern in a series of speeches at the UN that 1989 would spell bad news for Africa, as Europeans formerly separated by the Cold War divide now were turning toward one another at the expense of the Global South. Garba pointed out how events in Eastern Europe were already having an impact on the fortunes of the region's long-standing trade and political partners in the Southern Hemisphere, coupled with the fact that Western aid and food supplies were being dramatically diverted from Africa to "the emerging (and white) democracies in Eastern Europe." In his eyes, "the cold war is over, but Japan won, Eastern European States reaped the benefits, and Africa lost."[11]

The identity of Europe was being challenged in other ways. The Bosnian War of the early 1990s marked a new identity crisis for the continent, not least because the war witnessed the harrowing return of "ethnic cleansing" and genocide to Europe for the first time since World War II. With it came a changing moral understanding of human rights and civilization. For one thing, the war saw the transformation of human rights into a just cause for military strikes against Serbia in the late 1990s, radically altering—and some say fatally compromising—their old universalist appeal and mission of peace; after the NATO bombings, such rights talk was increasingly condemned by international critics as simply Western warmaking by other means. The militarization of human rights was also aligned with the defense of civilization, which further hollowed out the 1960s pacific reorientation of the concept. French intellectuals, led by Bernard-Henri Lévy and André Glucksmann, were quick to redefine the gravity of the war as a crisis of civilization. In 1992 Lévy proclaimed that besieged Sarajevo was a symbol of the fate of the European values of peace and cohabitation; for him, Sarajevo "is a civilized city, this is a European city. If Europe means openness, tolerance and cosmopolitanism, Sarajevo is no doubt one of the greatest capitals, not only of Balkan Europe, but of Europe itself." Glucksmann characterized the Yugoslav People's Army's bombardment of the Croatian cities of Vukovar and Dubrovnik in late 1991 as "Europe as a civilization being crucified" and a "moral Pearl Harbor." Yet it was the genocidal massacre of Srebrenica in July 1995—in which Serbian troops under General Ratko Mladić overtook a small contingent of Dutch peacekeepers guarding the UN-designated "safe area" and then brutally killed over 8,000 Bosnian Muslims—that captured international attention as grim proof of civilization in crisis. Harrowing stories and photographs of Bosnian victims drew connections with the Holocaust in the minds of many. Tadeusz Mazowiecki, Polish politician and special rapporteur for the former Yugoslavia for the UN's Commission on Human Rights, was shocked by UN inaction and incompetence in the war; in his letter of resignation to the commission's chair on July 27, 1995, he raised the stakes of the tragedy by saying that the "very stability of international order and the principle of civilization is at stake over the question of Bosnia."[12]

The terrorist attack on the United States on September 11, 2001, further intensified this rhetoric of civilization in crisis, and fundamentally changed American engagement with the world. The 1990s mission to spread democracy gave way to emotional calls for the defense of civilization, though they were combined in the discourse of regime change in Iraq and Afghanistan. President George W. Bush led the charge in numerous speeches on the "war on terror." A week after the attack, he insisted that this "is not, however, just America's fight. And what is at stake is not just America's freedom. This is the world's fight. This is civilization's fight." In November of that year he ratcheted up the bellicose rhetoric, declaring that "we wage a war to save civilization." By the end of the month, Bush had painted a stark picture of the new era—"there is a great divide in our time—not between religions or cultures, but between civilization and barbarism." Over the period from September 11, 2001, to May 2004 Bush made use of the terms civilization or civilized sixty-two times in speeches, interviews, and addresses.[13]

The renewed interest in the post–Cold War mission of civilization was linked to conservative discussions about the dawning of an American-style Pax Romana. After 9/11 the discourse shifted to justify a new American unilateralism that took on the role of global policeman and moral enforcer of world affairs. American conservative Robert Kagan, in his 2003 book *Of Paradise and Power: America and Europe in the New World Order*, justified American intervention in Iraq in direct reference to growing cultural differences between Europe and America. He famously argued that "on major strategic and international questions, Americans are from Mars and Europeans are from Venus." The rebranded international relations lexicon of "civilization versus barbarism" emerged as a common lens through which to see America's relationship to the rest of the world. More recent books, such as Niall Ferguson's 2011 *Civilization: The Six Killer Apps of Western Power*, continue to lament the decline of Western civilization and to call on the West to reclaim its global leadership and "killer apps" of competition, science, property, medicine, consumerism, and work ethic.[14]

America's aggressive foreign policy in the wake of 9/11 met resistance in Europe. Prominent European intellectuals Jacques Derrida and Jürgen Habermas sought to turn anti-Americanism into a new continental virtue, asserting in a February 15, 2003, joint letter published in the German weekly *Die Zeit* that the massive demonstrations in Paris, London, Rome, Madrid, and Berlin against the American invasion of Iraq—the largest mass mobilization since the Second World War—marked the dawning of a New Europe and European public sphere. They called on Europeans to "counterbalance the hegemonic unilateralism of the United States in the international arena and within the United Nations." For Habermas and Derrida, Europe was a collection of civilian states undergirded by respect for law and human rights. What emerged, however, were new fissures between Western and Eastern Europe. A good example was the so-called Letter of Eight published in January 2003, which openly supported the US-led invasion of Iraq. Signatories included Czech Republic president Václav Havel along with Prime Ministers Leszek Miller of Poland and Péter Medgyessy of Hungary, and they made their case by invoking the defense of shared values of "democracy, individual freedom, human rights and the rule of law." After a follow-up letter of support from the so-called Vilnius Group of more than ten Eastern European countries, French president Jacques Chirac snapped that the new members of Europe missed a "good opportunity to keep quiet." Old and New Europe seemed at loggerheads. Polish journalist Adam Krzemiński took issue with Habermas and Derrida's Western European arrogance, reminding them that homegrown Eastern European civil society had long ago brought down communism, acidly adding that "no one in the West rejoiced after the East-Central European 'Autumn of the People.' In Paris or London there was actually a great deal of embarrassed discontent arising from German unification and the feared influx of the poor to the West. Even fourteen years later, there is obviously no feeling of joy within 'core Europe' over the EU's eastward expansion." Internal European squabbling may have pointed up the deep regional differences within Europe, but it also revealed that the language of civilization played little role among either the European supporters or critics of the Iraq War.[15]

Instead, civilization resurfaced in relation to the crisis of multi-culturalism resulting from growing security concerns after 9/11. In the wake of the rising tensions across Europe, multiculturalism was judged a failure by various Western European leaders. At a Christian Democratic Union meeting in 2010, German chancellor Angela Merkel declared that "the multicultural concept is a failure, an absolute failure." A few months later French president Nicolas Sarkozy also called it a "failure," saying that "in all our democracies, we've been too concerned about the identity of the new arrivals and not enough about the identity of the country receiving them." In a speech on February 5, 2011, British prime minister David Cameron added his voice to the shift in values. "Under the doctrine of state multiculturalism, we have encouraged different cultures to live separate lives, apart from each other and apart from the mainstream," to the point that "we've even tolerated these segregated communities behaving in ways that run completely counter to our values." For a growing choir of cultural commentators, Europe's policy of multiculturalism was condemned for abetting the development of separatist ethnic identities and producing homegrown extremists. There was certainly some resistance, as figures like British Pakistani intellectual Tariq Modood campaigned for multiculturalism and pointed out how fears of Islamic terrorism had become a serious test case for democratic citizenship. Yet the mood music in Western Europe was clear, as Islam was increasingly interpreted as incompatible with "British values," German liberalism, and French republicanism. The language of Judeo-Christian civilization also made a comeback. As noted in Chapter 3, this early Cold War term served to bridge Judaism and Christianity in the name of liberal democracy and anticommunism. In more recent debates about the Islamic menace,

443

Dutch far-right politician Geert Wilders has called on Europe to defend "Judeo-Christian culture" in the face of Islamic invasion. Michel Houellebecq's novel *Submission* (2015), which centers on the possible effects of a radical Muslim political party winning the 2022 French presidential election, was a sort of updated version of Jean Raspail's bestselling 1973 novel, *The Camp of Saints*. Raspail's story pivoted on an imaginary invasion from the Third World, in which a million immigrants on a hundred ships from Calcutta arrived on the southern coast of France, seized the country, and in short order brought about the "death of the white race." Raspail's novel has long been a touchstone text for right-wing extremists across Europe and North America.[16]

Anxiety toward Islam and multiculturalism was not an issue just within individual nation-states, but also resonated in debates about the expansion of the European Union, especially regarding possible membership for Turkey. The 9/11 terrorist attacks overshadowed the discussions about Turkish accession, which began in September 2005. Liberals saw Turkey as a potential bridge between the West and the Muslim world, a possible means of overcoming a hardening clash-of-civilizations mentality. Conservatives countered that Turkey and Islam were too alien, proof of the intrinsic incompatibility of the EU, democracy, and Islam. Here again the language of civilization was used to fortify the cultural borders of Europe. Anti-Muslim sentiment even gave opportunities for Eastern European countries to reinvent their national identities and war records. Some Serbian intellectuals, for example, exploited the controversy surrounding the Danish publication of cartoons of the prophet Muhammad in 2005 to legitimize earlier violence against Bosnian and Kosovar Muslims during the 1990s Bosnian War by positioning Serbia as one of the great defenders of Western civilization.[17]

Just as alarming is the way that paranoia about the crisis of "white civilization" has taken roots in "alt-right" circles in a number of countries. As noted in the last chapter, such rhetoric began to surface in the 1960s, ranging from the Greek Colonels' Coup to Enoch Powell's "Rivers of Blood" speech. In 1968 in Nice, several dozen far-right French activists created the Research and Study Group for European Civilization, usually known by its French acronym, GRECE. The group promoted its ideas under the rubric of the *Nouvelle Droite*, or the New Right, and vehemently espoused the superiority and defense of Western civilization. In 1977 one of its founders, Alain de Benoist, proclaimed "the gradual homogenization of the world, advocated and realized by the two-thousand-year-old discourse of egalitarian ideology, to be an evil." More bellicose white civilization rhetoric of late can be traced to the writings of another far-right French thinker, Renaud Camus, and in particular to his notorious theory of *le grand remplacement*. Camus (no relation to the French Nobel Prize writer) is the president and cofounder of the National Council of European Resistance, dedicated to fighting "the invasion and the destruction of the Europeans of Europe," and *Le Grand Remplacement* (*The Great Replacement*) is the title of his 2011 book. The book is a call to arms to overturn the way in which native "white" Europeans have been "reverse-colonized" by black and brown immigrants "flooding the Continent," threatening white civilization with possible extinction. The key issue for him and his followers is the apocalyptic specter of "ethnic and civilizational substitution." Camus's reactionary ideas have attracted a large following in the international alt-right "identitarian" community in the last few years.[18]

Such language haunts the speech of right-wing thinkers and activists. President of France's National Rally party Marine Le Pen, in the run-up to French national elections in 2017, was not shy in warning her followers that French civilization was under threat from immigration, and that Frenchmen "feel strangers in their own country." Camus even sent an open letter to Orbán in late April 2018, congratulating him on his reelection victory and praising Hungary as a "living fortress of European Resistance," whose leaders understand that "invasion, colonization and ethnic substitution" is a "matter of life and death for European civilization." Camus's ideas directly inspired the radical right-wing Unite the Right rally in Charlottesville, Virginia, on August 11, 2017, where marchers chanted "Jews will not replace us!" And in the mosque shootings in Christchurch, New Zealand, on March 15, 2019, killing fifty-one people, the white supremacist murderer claimed in a Facebook manifesto that he was acting to stop "white genocide" and to protect "white civilization" under threat. Other right-wing parties have used the revival of civilization as their rallying cry. When historian Thierry Baudet recently founded the extreme right-wing Dutch party Forum for Democracy, he described Holland as being in the "milieu des ruines d'une belle civilisation." On May 18, 2019, Italian deputy prime minister Matteo Salvini hosted a rally in Milan flanked by leading right-wing figures like Marine Le Pen, Geert Wilders from the Netherlands' Party for Freedom, and Jörg Meuthen from Germany's Alternative für Deutschland, in which anti-immigration and the protection of European civilization served as their shared platform. The potent brew of nationalism, religious conservatism, and racism in Europe is a reaction to the onslaught of neoliberalism and economic austerity in the 1990s, and right-wing parties in both Western and Eastern Europe have exploited widespread feelings of alienation, frustration, and being left behind by mainstream political parties. The defense of both the beleaguered nation and European civilization continues to mobilize new and popular alt-right outlets.[19]

Moral alarm has been increasingly sounded in the United States too. President Trump's infamous speech in Krasinski Square in Warsaw on July 6, 2017, referred to the defense of civilization five times, entreating Europe and the United States to join forces in the fight against terrorism and the "new barbarians" amassing at the fragile frontiers of the West. In this speech, there was no mention of the right-wing Polish government's recent crackdown on judges and journalists, nor of Warsaw's refusal to accept more migrants—the two main issues that exercised Poland's EU partners at the time. Trump openly recycled the clash-of-civilizations theme, one that President Barack Obama had studiously avoided lest it play into the hands of radical extremists in framing the conflict as one of the West versus Islam, not just jihadists. In Trump's words, "I declare today for the world to hear that the West will never, ever, be broken," and "Our values will prevail. Our people will thrive. And our civilization will triumph." Most disquieting to listeners was his statement that "the fundamental question of our time is whether the West has the will to survive," to the extent that his speech was designed to steel possible military resolve about imminent battle. Small wonder that one *Washington Post* reporter called him a "crusader in chief." Striking too was how civilization supplanted other, more familiar terms. Whereas President George W. Bush's Warsaw speech in 2003 referred to democracy thirteen times, Trump by contrast mentioned it just once; human rights went totally unremarked. In Trump's parlance, civilization replaced democracy and human rights as sources of allegiance and identity. And in his inaugural address on January 20, 2017, Trump pledged to defend the "civilized world" against terrorism. Gone was the concept of the "free world," which had been standard in presidential speeches since Truman. This linguistic difference may seem small, but it reflected a changing tenor of identity politics that connected conservative leaders in Europe and America. The day after Trump's surprising electoral victory in November 2016, Orbán crowed during an interview with the British *Daily Mail* that "this is the second day of a historic event, in which Western civilisation appears to successfully break free from the confines of an ideology."[20]

THE RIGHT'S TAKEOVER OF THE TERM IS A RELATIVELY NEW development, and has not gone uncontested. In the era between 1945 and the late 1960s, ideas about the reconstruction of civilization were not confined to Europe nor to the imperial powers, and were associated with causes from across the political spectrum. Its makeover served as a mainstay of progressive political thinking through the era of decolonization from a variety of perspectives. After 1945 the career of the concept was shadowed by its nemesis—barbarism—and for this reason civilization was closely tied to the larger problem of to what extent ideology justifies exclusion and violence. In response, a central strand of the new mission of civilization was universalist and inclusive, and often associated with international organizations dedicated to peace, cosmopolitanism, and cross-cultural dialogue, such as the United Nations and UNESCO. They may no longer command the same authority they once did, but they still offer a powerful alternative vision of ruin and renewal.

Notable too are the patterns of representation. For example, the immediate aftermath of the war saw efforts to visualize the destruction and reconstruction of European civilization, as evidenced in the photography of rubble and the charitable activities of humanitarian relief workers dispensing aid to needy survivors across the continent. The visual focus on civilization then moved to political agitation for peace and the emblems of prosperity, ranging from antinuclear marches in Britain and West Germany to new housing, buildings, and shiny consumer objects as the symbols of recovery and arrival. The visual connection of civilization to war and conquest—which was common from the Age of Imperialism through the Second World War—rarely resurfaced in Cold War Europe. The obvious exception was the colonial wars, and the Algerian War in particular, when atrocity images were exploited by both sides to win support from the international community for their respective cause. Harrowing images of violence and de-civilization returned to Europe in the Bosnian War of the early 1990s, and more recently with the terrorist attacks in Paris and elsewhere in Europe. But from the 1960s until the early 1990s, the visual expression of civilization under threat all but disappeared, as the focus of debate and representation moved to other fields. This is part of the reason why this book opens with the destruction of Europe at the end of World War II and closes with the detonation of Palmyra. In each case, foreigners arrived to help salvage a civilization in ruins—in 1945 this included British, American, and French humanitarian workers alongside Allied military authorities in Germany and across war-torn Europe, whereas in 2016 the roster of arrivals was made up of European-based international agencies and volunteer groups. Between these two disasters arose a wide variety of calls to reclaim ruined cultural inheritance for a new postwar world.

No less striking is the gender representation of civilization in crisis. As discussed in Chapter 1, female relief workers after the war played a significant role in the early reconstruction period, and served as some of the first builders and narrators of liberated Europe. Women were also directly involved in the peacetime make-over of the continent in myriad ways, from housing and design to public health, work life, and everyday culture on both sides of the Iron Curtain. Intellectuals like Simone de Beauvoir and Hannah Arendt penned trenchant critiques of Europe's culture of prosperity, especially in terms of the dangers of American civilization. But with the stabilization of Europe in the 1950s, the various discourses of civilization largely passed to male elites connected to power, be they leaders of states, administrations, the churches, or social organizations. Significantly, growing agitation for women's equality seized the language of rights and freedoms, not civilization. The campaign for women's rights in Western Europe in the 1960s—together with its more muted corollaries in Eastern Europe—centered on overcoming social boundaries and political barriers; by contrast, civilization (at least after the mid-1960s) increasingly became a conservative justification for border construction and social control so as to protect a majority culture supposedly at risk from immigrants and asylum seekers.

If the changing tenor of civilization was partly bound up with gender, it was also related to race. This is why the discussion on

Europe's ex-colonies is so important. The co-optation of the European idea of civilization in Ghana, Algeria, and Senegal demonstrates how the ideological heritage of Europe was reconfigured outside Europe at the end of the European Era of world history. The fusion of civilization and ethnic violence shaped the relationship between Europe and the wider world from the Age of Imperialism through fascism and the Second World War. The brutal expulsions of ethnic Germans in Czechoslovakia and Poland in 1945, along with the French and Dutch restoration of empire in the 1940s (to say nothing of the continuation of British, Belgian, and Portuguese overseas empires at the time), amply illustrate that this violent legacy in no way ended with the cease-fire in 1945. With time African elites managed to turn the rhetoric of European civilization against the Europeans, while at the same time broadcasting new notions of Afrocentric civilizations as assertions of political sovereignty, nation-building, and cultural arrival.

In the 1960s old European ideas of a fixed hierarchy of races and civilizations gave way to fresh views of civilization linked to peace and bridge-building, as noted by the endeavors of African nationalists, UNESCO preservationists, and Eastern European Africanists. But this inclusive moment did not last. European colonies in Africa, such as South Africa and Rhodesia, also reclaimed the language of civilization for their own purposes, in this case to defend apartheid and white minority rule. The 1960s effort to overturn the nineteenth-century equation of civilization with privilege and exclusion was reversed by the end of the decade, as ideologues in these European outposts in southern Africa returned the idea of civilization back to its imperial and racist beginnings. What happened next was something unexpected: this colonial logic to revive the rhetoric of civilization to bolster white minority rule in southern Africa caromed back to mainland Europe in the 1970s. Now the defense of civilization was employed to warn white majoritarian culture (in both Western and Eastern Europe) about the dangers of "reversal colonization" by immigrants who had arrived from Europe's ex-colonies and trade partners a decade or more before.

Such restrictive and right-wing redefinitions of civilization were challenged by more inclusive voices and visions of Europe. In 1999 Václav Havel wrote an article on the tenth anniversary of the fall of the Berlin Wall called "The Search for Meaning in a Global Civilization." In it he took stock of the world in the wake of colonialism and communism, and diagnosed the era as suffering from a loss of spiritual compass and moral direction: "The world of our experiences seems chaotic, disconnected, confusing. There appear to be no integrating forces, no unified meaning, no true inner understanding of phenomena in our experience of the world. Experts can explain anything in the objective world to us, yet we understand our own lives less and less." Such a predicament was in no way confined to Europe, nor was Havel's piece a paean to pessimism. For Havel, the "central political task of the final years of this century" remains "the creation of a new model of coexistence among the various cultures, peoples, races and religious spheres within a single interconnected civilization."[21]

Recasting world history as a story of interconnectivity and mutual influence was long ago present in the writings of Senghor and others, as discussed in Chapter 6. Yet it is worth remembering that these were bold and controversial views at the time, and met a good deal of resistance in an age of nationalism. A telling example is the recently discovered unpublished 1950 book manuscript written by two of France's most influential historians, Lucien Febvre, a professor at the Collège de France and one of the leading lights of the Annales school, and his junior colleague François Crouzet, a scholar of economic history at the Sorbonne. Their manuscript was provocatively titled *Origines internationales d'une civilisation: Eléments d'une histoire de France*, and provided a revisionist account of French history as the product of global influences over the centuries. Their main contention was that the French had always been a mixture of peoples, including Turks, Arabs, and Africans; for them, the point

was that "We Are All of Mixed Blood." The same influx of influences from beyond France characterized the country's flora, fauna,
and foodstuffs. In what eventually became known as the UNESCO
approach to the rewriting of world history, Febvre and Crouzet
maintained that France's history was a long tale of endless borrowings from all parts of the world, underlining how the French were
"heirs of a diverse past." In this case, the connection to UNESCO
was direct in that their project was commissioned by the agency
as a means of challenging conventional nation-centered histories.
Their spirited antinationalist French history was to encourage international understanding and to help overcome the scourge of ethno-
nationalism and Eurocentrism in the classroom. However, their
history was too radical for UNESCO in 1950, and its publication
was blocked by those who felt that Febvre and Crouzet had gone
too far in dispensing with the centrality of both the nation-state
and Europe's global supremacy. The manuscript was abandoned by
its authors and languished in an attic for decades until its rediscovery sixty years later. Its belated publication may at first suggest
that we live in more globalized times in which antinationalist and
non-Eurocentric histories are routinely published, to the point of
becoming almost de rigueur in the academy these days. Yet the language of civilization has been scrubbed from today's accounts of the
globalizing past. For the left, the terminology of civilization remains
a source of chagrin and loathing, an unwanted hangover from the
era of imperialism. Febvre and Crouzet's story draws attention to
the discomfort antinational and anti-Eurocentric histories caused,
and still cause for the wider public.[22]

Today these musings from Havel, Febvre, and Crouzet seem like
visitors from another epoch. The 9/11 attacks and the refugee crisis
have fueled the comeback of right-wing nationalism, tribal populism,
and anti-Muslim xenophobia, and the perceived crisis of civilization
has helped to justify the pulling up of the drawbridge. No better
proof of our changing world is the feverish construction of walls

in Europe, and elsewhere. Recent years have witnessed the erection of over 745 miles (1,200 kilometers) of fences and new borders in Eastern and Southeastern Europe, mostly in reaction to the refugee crisis that started in 2015. For many Eastern Europeans, elitist cosmopolitan values of free movement are seen as a threat, not a source of identity. The democratic revolution of 1989 has been followed by a demographic counterrevolution against the openness of 1989. Similar wall construction can be noted in the Middle East, Central Asia, Southeast Asia, the Far East, and North America. At least sixty-five countries—one-third of the world's nation-states—have built new barriers along their borders in the last two decades, and half of all those erected since World War II have been constructed since 2000. Demands to protect civilization under threat have accompanied the fortification of new Iron Curtains, serving as both the political cause and effect of new boundary-making.[23]

So there is a new specter haunting Europe, and it goes by the old name of civilization. Today's Europe-wide deployment of the term as an ideological retaining wall against the coming of "new barbarians" risks undoing the decades-long work of peacemongering organizations that put forward more universalist, postimperial ideals of shared world civilizations. The early 1950s associations of civilization with science, comfort, rights, and protecting civilians in war zones have long dropped away, as have the connections to housing, consumer goods, and etiquette books. The same goes for the old ideas of using civilization to link continents in international solidarity, apart from UNESCO, Amnesty International, and sundry NGOs. Instead, civilization is being narrowly redefined as a story of religious identity, cultural defense, and sometimes military expansion—a return to its nineteenth-century forerunner. And as in the nineteenth century, these views are not confined to the West, as strong-arm leaders across the world—from Hungary to Turkey, Russia to Egypt, China to the United States—have deployed the term to bolster their conservative political outlook. Renewed interest in "civilizational essences" has percolated for two decades in response to both globalization and the effects of September 11, 2001. Such defensive identities can be seen in the celebration of "Asian values," Sinocentrism, Afrocentricity, religious fundamentalism of all stripes, and even a revived Eurocentrism. As opposed to an understanding of the world based on interaction and mutual influence, recent understandings of civilization have focused on sharp boundaries, differences, and ethnic homogeneity in the name of cultural autonomy and managed modernization.[24]

But the ongoing recasting of civilization is not simply a story of doom and gloom, saber rattling, and beefed-up border construction. Chinese sociologists, for example, are rethinking the history of "communist civilization," with an eye toward understanding the relationship between state and market from an international communist perspective.[25] UNESCO and its far-flung national commissions dotted around the world continue their preservation work under the banner of world civilization, and a new generation of environmental historians—and environmentalists—have opened the scope of global history and international politics far beyond the nation-state to study the development and effects of borderless industrial civilization worldwide. While critical green voices were first heard in the 1960s and 1970s in protest of the debit side of postwar industrialization, this field has grown exponentially in the last two decades. Some—especially in China—now talk about the coming of a sustainably managed "ecological civilization" as a step toward a better future. The outbreak of the coronavirus pandemic at the end of 2019 has prompted anxious international concern about a much deeper global crisis of civilization, and has brought with it a renewed one-world planetary consciousness about the mortality of humanity and civilization itself. Whether this will lead to concerted action based on more universal values to preserve a future of our species is impossible to say at this stage. The point is that the overheated militarization and racialization of civilization in recent political language is certainly a serious development, but it may not last, and it is by no means the only iteration of civilization on offer nowadays.[26]

Over the centuries the term has shifted and mutated dramatically according to context and advocacy group, and this book has attempted to track its postwar shape-shifting across the continent and beyond. As Toynbee noted many years ago, civilization is "a movement and not a condition, a voyage and not a harbour." There is no reason to expect its future to be any less central or mercurial, for it remains to this day a highly charged descriptor of identity, possibility, loss, and longing precisely because it is so political.[27]

Here it may be worth reflecting on V. S. Naipaul's words on civilization thirty years ago. On October 30, 1990, the Trinidad-born Nobel laureate writer delivered the Walter B. Wriston Lecture in Public Policy at the Manhattan Institute in New York on the theme of "Our Universal Civilization." Naipaul opened by admitting that this was a "rather big title," and that he felt "a little embarrassed by it." Even so, he went on to defend the idea of universal civilization because it made possible his "journey from the margin to the center, from Trinidad to London," for "in spite of my ancestry and Trinidad background," "I was part of a larger civilization." For Naipaul, this was no easy story, since universal civilization "wasn't always as attractive as it is today. The expansion of Europe gave it for at least three centuries a racial taint, which still causes pain. In Trinidad, I grew up in the last days of that kind of racialism. And that, perhaps, has given me a greater appreciation of the immense changes that have taken place since the end of the war, the extraordinary attempt of this civilization to accommodate the rest of the world, and all the currents of that world's thought." While not everyone would subscribe to the positive or accommodating character of civilization described here, Naipaul's speech underscores the multiple interpretations, experiences, and meanings of civilization after 1945 for many people around the world, and not just in Europe. Whether Naipaul's words are the past or the future of "universal civilization" is impossible to say, but both are possible.[28]

The rescue of civilization in danger was a central element in glossing the continent's cultural, social, and political transformation after World War II, and renewed anxiety about its embattled place in the world has intensified across Europe in our times. The events of 9/11 and the current predicament of Europe in relation to the crises of terrorism and refugees have reactivated the civilization-in-crisis theme in ways not seen since the early Cold War, providing ideological pretext for an emotional language of fear, insecurity, and collective identity. Mobilizing this language to support border guards or assault troops will of course make peacemaking and intercultural understanding all the more difficult once the geopolitical conflicts are over, as noted with the quid pro quo violence surrounding Palmyra. In the end, potentially universal concepts like civilization—or its equally beleaguered cousin, humanity—may be the only language we have left to imagine the prospect of peace and international cooperation. How civilization will be used to narrate political fear and transformation is an open question, but it continues to define a continent that feels itself under threat.

AFTERWORD AND ACKNOWLEDGMENTS

I HAVE BEEN CARRYING THIS BOOK IN MY MIND FOR MANY years, in some form or another. Part of it is a result of my training at Haverford College and the University of Chicago back in the 1980s and 1990s. Both of these history departments were firmly committed to the Great Books Western civilization curriculum that was first introduced at various American universities after the Great War in order to help returning GIs understand the place and mission of the United States in a changing global world. The University of Chicago (along with Columbia University) spearheaded this initiative, and requisite "Western Civ" courses were embedded in most American colleges and universities from the mid-1950s onward. By the time I graduated from Haverford in the mid-1980s and then went on to Chicago for graduate school a few years later, the canon was under fire across the country as part of the Reagan-era cultural wars about American identity and historical purpose, and the hopes, blind spots, and controversies surrounding this foundation course have shaped this book in various ways. So too did the approach of one of my professors at Chicago, Reinhart Koselleck, whose pioneering work on

Begriffsgeschichte started me thinking about the history of concepts as political forces in their own right.

I first heard the word *civilization* in my primary school in Phoenix, Arizona, in the early 1970s, most likely in connection with the purple mimeographed homework exercises on the great achievements of Aztec, Egyptian, Chinese, and European civilizations. Civilization was probably the longest word I knew at the time, and no doubt the heaviest. Perhaps the deeper and less obvious origin of this project is a strong memory from Mrs K.'s sixth-grade English class. Mrs. K. was an old-fashioned and much-appreciated primary school teacher, who took her job seriously as a transmitter of knowledge and tradition. Like all primary school teachers, she covered all the basic subjects, yet grammar was something she pursued with missionary fervor. She devoted fastidious attention to laying bare the deep structure of language in elaborate diagrams teeming with the alien elements of subject, verb, predicate, modifiers, and auxiliary words. In response to a classmate who dared to ask why anyone should care about this, she coolly replied that proper English represented the thin line that separated civilization from barbarism. Education in her eyes was an evangelism of uplift and refinement, and the correct use of language was what connected those of us in the former Mexican territories with the rest of the country and even to England itself in a shared heritage of Western civilization. Such elevated meaning was of course completely lost on me at the time, but the words continued to resonate. My West Phoenix primary school was a jumbled mix of Hispanic, Native American, and Anglo pupils, and even then I remember wondering whether her defense of proper English language usage was aimed at all of us, or only at some. What struck me, however, was something else that I have never forgotten: as she stood there in front of the blackboard, chalk in hand, off to her right on a butcher's hook hung a large worn wooden paddle at the entrance of the classroom, a reminder of teacherly authority that was not infrequently used by teachers at the school. It was the stark visual juxtaposition of grammatical instruction and corporal punishment that stayed with me. The image of her framed by both the rules of proper linguistic practice and the threatening paddle dramatized the two faces of civilization that inform this book—education and pacification, culture and violence.

I would also like to record my thanks to those institutions and people who made this book possible. First, I am extremely grateful for having been awarded a Leverhulme Senior Research Fellowship in 2018–2019, which granted me the time needed to complete the research and writing of this book. I was also coinvestigator of a large collaborative Arts and Humanities Research Council/UK grant project (2014–2017) on "Socialism Goes Global: Cold War Connections Between the 'Second' and 'Third Worlds,'" and some of the material from it (especially in Chapters 8 and 9) was researched as part of that generous grant. The history faculty at Oxford and St. Antony's College also supported me in important ways. The staffs of the National Archive in London; the Public Records and Archives Administration Department in Accra, Ghana; the Imperial War Museum in London; Cambridge University Library's Special Collections; the Staatsbibliothek in Berlin; and the Bodleian Library in Oxford were very helpful. Parts of Chapter 2 were published in "The Polemics of Pity: British Photographs of Berlin, 1945–1947," in *Humanitarianism and Media: 1900 to the Present*, ed. Johannes Paulmann (Oxford/New York: Berghahn, 2018), 126–150; parts of Chapter 3 were published in "Religion, Science and Cold War Anti-Communism: The 1949 Cardinal Mindszenty Show Trial," in *Science, Religion and Communism in Cold War Europe*, ed. Paul Betts and Stephen A. Smith (London: Palgrave, 2016), 275–307. A section of Chapter 4 was published in "Manners, Morality and Civilization: Reflections on Postwar German Etiquette Books," in *Histories of the Aftermath: The Legacies of the Second World War in Europe*, ed. Frank Biess and Robert Moeller (Oxford/New York: Berghahn, 2010), 196–214; parts of Chapter 7 were published in "Humanity's New

Heritage: UNESCO and the Rewriting of World History," *Past &
Present* 228, no. 1 (August 2015): 249–285, and "The Warden of
World Civilization: UNESCO and the Rescue of the Nubian Mon-
uments," in *Heritage in the Modern World*, ed. Paul Betts and Corey
Ross, *Past & Present* 226, supplement 10 (2015): 100–125. I thank
all the publishers for allowing me to reproduce them.

I am indebted to a number of friends and colleagues who gave
their valuable time, feedback, and support. In July 2019 I held a
manuscript workshop to go over a first full draft, and I am grateful for the constructive criticism of those present: Patricia Clavin,
Anne Deighton, Martin Conway, Steve Smith, and Saul Dubow.
Saul has read many of the chapters over the years, and the manuscript is much better thanks to his sharp editorial eye. Anne Deighton provided generous comments on several early chapter drafts;
Steve Smith read a few versions of the introduction, and I am grateful for his advice and encouragement. Corey Ross, Lynn Meskell,
Nick Stargardt, Jane Caplan, Martin Geyer, Monica Black, Kate
Skinner, Ruth Harris, Alon Confino, and Stefan-Ludwig Hoffmann kindly read parts of the manuscript, to my great benefit. Bob
Moeller deserves special mention, since he read every chapter (several twice) and has been a remarkably attentive reader and friend
over the long haul. David Priestland, Faisal Devji, Dace Dzenovska,
and Yaacov Yadgar helped me think through the opening. I owe a
debt of gratitude to Giovanni Cadioli for his research assistance on
various themes, especially Russian and Italian language sources. The
project also benefited from stimulating conversations with Margaret MacMillan, Eugene Michail, and Johannes Paulmann. I am also
grateful to all my colleagues at the European Studies Centre, St.
Antony's College, for their support and solidarity. My agent Felicity
Bryan and subagent George Lucas have been helpful and encouraging at every turn, and I felt privileged to work with both of them.
Sadly, Felicity passed away before the book was published, and her
energy, wit, and professionalism will be sorely missed. Thanks go to

Andrew Franklin at Profile and Lara Heimert at Basic for taking on the project, and I am indebted to my editors—Connor Guy at Basic and Cecily Gayford at Profile—for their skillful editorial engagement and guidance about writing for a broader audience. Heartfelt thanks to the production teams at Basic and Profile. Calah Singleton cleared the illustrations with speed and savvy; during the production of the book, Roger Labrie and Susan VanHecke were expert line and copy editors, respectively, and I thank them both for their meticulous work.

My greatest debt is to my family. My daughters, Lucie and Anna, probably heard more about the project than they wished, and provided good pointers, welcome distraction, and perspective. My sister, Sharon Stella Betts, and my brother-in-law, David Leven, were always there, and shared their perceptive impressions on an early draft of the introduction. My mother, Petra Betts, took interest in the project from the beginning, and sadly my father, Charles Betts, passed away before it was completed. My wife, Sylvie, has been there at every step with ideas, advice, reassurance, and a wider view of things, and so much more besides. To her, Lucie, and Anna this book is dedicated.

NOTES

Introduction: Old World Made New

1. Tanja Collet, "Civilization and Civilized in Post-9/11 US Presidential Speeches," *Discourse and Society* 20, no. 4 (2009): 455–475, and www.white house.gov/briefings-statements/remarks-president-trump-people-poland; www .lemonde.fr/politique/article/2015/06/29/la-guerre-de-civilisation-de-valls-rejouit -la-droite_4663488_823448.html; "Refugees Threaten Christian Roots, Says Hungary's Orban," *Reuters*, September 3, 2015, and Andrew Rettman, "Orban Says Migrants Will Change European Civilization," *EU Observer*, June 2, 2015; Constantine Pleshakov, *The Crimean Nexus: Putin's War and the Clash of Civilizations* (New Haven: Yale University Press, 2017); Habib Afram, president of the Syriac League of Lebanon, asserted that ISIS is "not destroying our present life, or only taking the villages, churches, and homes, or erasing our attired future—they want to erase our culture, past and civilization," drawing a parallel to the Mongol invasion of the Middle East, in Kareem Shaheen, "Outcry Over Isis Destruction of Ancient Assyrian Site of Nimrud," *Guardian*, March 6, 2015.

2. Jürgen Osterhammel, *The Transformation of the World: A Global History of the Nineteenth Century*, trans. Patrick Camiller (Princeton: Princeton University Press, 2014 [2009]), 826–873; Tony Judt, *Postwar* (London: Random House, 2005), 5.

3. Hannah Arendt, "Nightmare and Flight," in *Hannah Arendt: Essays in Understanding, 1930–1954*, ed. Jerome Kohn (New York: Harcourt, Brace & Co., 1993), 134; Dan Diner, "Den Zivilisationsbruch erinnern: Über die Entstehung und Geltung eines Begriffs," in *Zivilisationsbruch und Gedächtniskultur: das 20.*

Jahrhundert in der Erinnerung des beginnenden 21. Jahrhunderts, ed. Heidemarie Uhl (Innsbruck: Studien Verlag, 2003), 17–34.

4. Brett Bowden, *The Empire of Civilization: The Evolution of an Imperial Idea* (Chicago: University of Chicago Press, 2009).

5. Samuel P. Huntington, *The Clash of Civilizations and the Remaking of World Order* (New York: Simon & Schuster, 1996), 28; Stig Jarle Hansen, Atle Mesoy, and Tucany Kardas, eds., *The Borders of Islam: Exploring Samuel Huntington's Faultlines, from Al-Andalus to the Virtual Ummah* (New York: Columbia University Press, 2009).

6. Arnold J. Toynbee, "Post-War Paganism Versus Christianity," *The Listener*, January 20, 1937, 124; Toynbee, *A Study of History*, abridgement of volumes I–VI by D. C. Somervell (New York: Oxford University Press, 1947), 1–11, 35–42, 567–578; Toynbee, *Christianity and Civilisation* (London: Student Christian Movement Press, 1940); Toynbee, *Civilization on Trial* (London, 1948), 24; William H. McNeill, *Arnold J. Toynbee: A Life* (Oxford: Oxford University Press, 1989), 205–234.

7. Kenneth Clark, *Civilisation: A Personal View* (London: John Murray, 1969), 1; Felipe Fernández-Armesto, *Civilizations* (London: Macmillan, 2000); Reinhold Niebuhr, "Culture and Civilization," *Confluence: An International Forum* 1, no. 1 (March 1952): 67; Claude Lévi-Strauss, *Tristes Tropiques* (London: Jonathan Cape, 1973 [1955]), 448.

8. Mary Beard, *Civilisations: How Do We Look? The Eye of Faith* (London: Profile, 2018), 203.

9. Régis Debray, *Civilisation: Comment nous sommes devenus américaine* (Paris: Gallimard, 2017), 11; Martin Conway, "Democracy in Western Europe after 1945," in *Democracy in Modern Europe*, ed. Jussi Kurunmäki, Jeppe Nevers, and Henk te Velde (New York: Berghahn, 2018), 231–256.

10. Lucien Febvre, "Civilisation: Évolution d'un Mot et d'un Groupe d'Idées," in *Civilisation: Le Mot et L'Idée*, ed. Lucien Febvre et al. (Paris: Renaissance du Louvre, 1930), 1–55; Fernand Braudel, *A History of Civilizations*, trans. Richard Mayne (London: Penguin, 1993 [1987]), 3–23, and Raymond Williams, "Civilisation," in *Keywords: A Vocabulary of Culture and Society* (London: Fontana, 1988), 57–60; Norbert Elias, *The Civilizing Process*, vol. 1: *The History of Manners* (New York: Urizen Books, 1978 [1939]).

11. Philippe Bénéton, *Histoire de mots: Culture et civilisation* (Paris: Presses de la fondation nationale des sciences politiques, 1975), 40–41, 81–82, 104–105; Stuart Woolf, "French Civilization and Ethnicity in the Napoleonic Empire," *Past & Present* 124 (August 1989), 105–106; Jörg Fisch, "Zivilisation, Kultur," in *Grundliche Grundbegriffe: Historisches Lexikon zur politisch-sozialen Sprache in Deutschland*, ed. Otto Brunner, Werner Conze, and Reinhart Koselleck, Bd. 7

(Stuttgart: Klett-Cotta, 1992), 679–774; Fred Bridgham, ed., *The First World War as a Clash of Cultures* (London: Camden House, 2006).

12. John Horne and Alan Kramer, *German Atrocities, 1914: A History of Denial* (New Haven: Yale University Press, 2001), 214–217, and Barbara Besslich, *Wege in der 'Kulturkrieg': Zivilisationskritik in Deutschland, 1890–1914* (Darmstadt, Germany: Wissenschaftliche Buchgesellschaft, 2000); Thomas Mann, *Reflections of a Non-Political Man*, trans. Walter Morris (New York: Frederick Ungar, 1983), 23; Vejas Gabriel Liulevicius, *The German Myth of the East: 1800 to the Present* (Oxford: Oxford University Press, 2009), 131–147.

13. Paul Valéry, *Variété* (Paris: Editions de la Nouvelle revue française, 1924), 11–12.

14. Prasenjit Duara, "The Discourse of Civilization and Decolonization," *Journal of World History* 15, no. 1 (March 2004): 1–5; C. E. M. Joad, *For Civilization* (London: Macmillan & Co., 1940); James McMillan, "War," in *Political Violence in Twentieth-Century Europe*, ed. Donald Bloxham and Robert Gerwarth (Cambridge: Cambridge University Press, 2011), 5054, 6869.

15. Richard Overy, *The Morbid Age: Britain and the Crisis of Civilization, 1919–1939* (London: Penguin, 2009), 42–44, 182–183.

16. Margrit Pernau, Helge Jordheim et al., eds., *Civilizing Emotions: Concepts in Nineteenth-Century Asia and Europe* (Oxford: Oxford University Press, 2015).

17. Vera Micheles Dean, *The Four Cornerstones of Peace* (London: McGraw-Hill, 1946), 54; *"We the People..." United Nations Conference on International Organisation: The Story of the Conference in San Francisco* (London: UN Information Organisation, 1946), 6–13; Clyde Eagleton, "The Charter Adopted at San Francisco," *American Political Science Review* 39 (October 1945): 935; Virginia Crochcron Gildersleeve, *Many a Good Crusade* (New York: Macmillan, 1954), 316; Glenda Sluga, *Internationalism in the Age of Nationalism* (Philadelphia: University of Pennsylvania Press, 2013), 88.

18. Irving Norman Smith, "San Francisco First Steps to Peace," *Behind the Headlines* 5, no. 6 (September 1945): 1, 31.

19. *Charter of the United Nations: Report to the President on the Results of the San Francisco Conference by the Chairman of the US Delegation, the Secretary of State, June 26, 1945* (Washington, DC: Department of State, 1945), 11, 19; Gildersleeve, 331–332; Harry Truman, Verbatim Minutes of the Opening Session, April 25, 1945, in *UNIO, Documents* (New York: United Nations, 1945), 425, and *The United Nations Conference on International Organization: Selected Documents* (Washington, DC: US Government Printing Office, 1946), 939.

20. Edward Keene, *Beyond the Anarchical Society: Grotius, Colonialism and World Politics* (Cambridge: Cambridge University Press, 2002), 136–140; "Peace Terms for Italy: A Letter from Benedetto Croce," *Manchester Guardian*, September 10,

1945, 4; *The San Francisco Conference and the Colonial Issue: Statement by the Council on African Affairs, April 1945* (New York: Council on African Affairs, Inc., 1945), 4–5; Paul Gordon Lauren, "First Principles of Racial Equality: History and the Politics and Diplomacy of Human Rights Provisions in the United Nations Charter," *Human Rights Quarterly* 5, no. 1 (1983): 21; Sluga, 91.

21. *Women's Share in Implementing the Peace: United Women's Conference, San Francisco, May 19, 1945* (San Francisco: United Women's Conference, 1945); Johannes Morsink, "Women's Rights and the Universal Declaration," *Human Rights Quarterly* 13 (1991): 229–256; Marika Sherwood, "'There Is No New Deal for the Blackman in San Francisco': African Attempts to Influence the Founding Conference of the United Nations, April–July 1945," *International Journal of African Historical Studies* 29, no. 1 (1996): 93; Mark Mazower, *No Enchanted Palace: The End of Empire and the Ideological Origins of the United Nations* (Princeton: Princeton University Press, 2009), 7–62, quotation 63.

22. Martti Koskenniemi, *The Gentle Civilizer of Nations: The Rise and Fall of International Law, 1870–1960* (Cambridge: Cambridge University Press, 2009); Gerrit W. Gong, *The Standard of "Civilization" in International Society* (Oxford: Clarendon Press, 1984); Mark Mazower, "The End of Civilization and the Rise of Human Rights," in *Human Rights in the Twentieth Century*, ed. Stefan-Ludwig Hoffmann (Cambridge: Cambridge University Press, 2010), 29–44; Tony Judt, *Postwar* (London: Allen Lane, 2005); Mark Mazower, *Dark Continent: Europe's Twentieth Century* (London: Penguin, 1998); Konrad Jarausch, *Out of Ashes: A New History of Europe in the Twentieth Century* (Princeton: Princeton University Press, 2015); Ian Kershaw, *Roller-Coaster: Europe, 1950–2017* (London: Penguin, 2018).

1. CALL TO ALMS

1. Stephen Spender, *Ruins and Visions* (London: Faber & Faber, 1942); Spender, *European Witness* (London: Hamish Hamilton, 1946), 21–22. See Florian Alix-Nicolaï, "Ruins and Visions: Stephen Spender in Occupied Germany," *The Modern Language Review* 109, no. 1 (2014): 54–74.

2. Spender, *European*, 23–24, 68, 109.

3. Keith Lowe, *Savage Continent: Europe in the Aftermath of World War II* (New York: Viking, 2012), 3–6; William Shirer, *Twentieth-Century Journey: A Native's Return, 1945–1988* (New York: Simon & Schuster, 1990), 9; William Peters, *In Germany Now: The Diary of a Soldier* (London: Progress Publishing Company, 1945), 8; B. Gorbatov and M. Merzhanov, "We Talk to Berlin's Cave Dwellers," May 2, 1945, in *What We Saw in Germany with the Red Army to Berlin, by Thirteen Leading Soviet War Correspondents* (Moscow: Soviet War News, 1945), 55.

4. William Shirer, *End of a Berlin Diary* (New York: Knopf, 1947), 160; Janet Flanner, "Letter from Cologne," *Janet Flanner's World: Uncollected Writings, 1932–1975*, ed. Irving Drutman (London: Secker & Warburg, 1980), 98; William I. Hitchcock, *Liberation: The Bitter Road to Freedom, Europe, 1944–1945* (London: Faber & Faber, 2008), 192.

5. Klaus Mann, *Stars and Stripes*, quoted in Susan T. Pettiss, with Lynne Taylor, *After the Shooting Stopped: The Story of an UNRRA Welfare Worker in Germany, 1945–1947* (Victoria, Canada: Trafford, 2004), 74; Theodor Plievier, *Berlin: A Novel* (London: Hammond, 1956), 9; Arnold Zweig, "Fahrt durch die Ruinenstadt" (1948), cited in *Berlin 1945: A Documentation*, ed. Reinhard Rürup (Berlin: Wilhelm Arenhövel, 1995), 66.

6. Spender, *European Witness*, 235, and Isaac Deutscher, *Reportagen aus Nachkriegsdeutschland* (Hamburg: Junius, 1980), 114, quoted in Rürup, 62.

7. Letter of August 9, 1945, in Grigor McClelland, *Embers of War: Letters from a Quaker Relief Worker in War-Torn Germany* (London: IB Tauris, 1997), 49; letter of May 25, 1946, in McClelland, 173–177; Walter Kempowski, *Swansong 1945: A Collective Diary from Hitler's Last Birthday to VE Day*, trans. Shaun Whiteside (London: Granta, 2014 [2005]), 312, 337, 394, 414.

8. Dwight D. Eisenhower, *Crusade in Europe* (London: William Heineman Ltd., 1956 [1950]), 446; *Atrocities and Other Conditions in Concentration Camps in Germany* (Washington, DC: United States Government Printing Office, 1945), 15; Mavis Tate, MP, "More on Buchenwald," *Spectator*, May 4, 1945, 402–403; George Gallup, "Public Says U.S. and Germans Should See Nazi Horror Films," *Washington Post*, May 20, 1945, 5B; Benjamin A. Lindsey, "'Organized Crime Against Civilization': The Congressional Investigation of Liberated Concentration Camps in 1945" (master's thesis, University of Vermont, 2012).

9. *The Relief of Belsen, April 1945: Eyewitness Accounts* (London: Imperial War Museum, 1991), 11; Douglas Botting, *From the Ruins of the Reich, Germany, 1945–1949* (New York: Meridian, 1985), 45–46; Ben Shephard, *After Daybreak: The Liberation of Belsen, 1945* (London: Jonathan Cape, 2005), 72.

10. Freddie Knoller, with John Landaw, *Living with the Enemy: My Secret Life on the Run from the Nazis* (London: Metro Publishing, 2005), 209; Brian Urquhart, *A Life in Peace and War* (New York: Harper & Row, 1987), 85; *Conditions of Surrender: Britons and Germans Witness the End of the War*, ed. Ulrike Jordan (London: German Historical Institute, 1997), 95; Dan Stone, *The Liberation of the Camps: The End of the Holocaust and Its Aftermath* (New Haven: Yale University Press, 2015), 104.

11. Richard Bessel, *Germany 1945: From War to Peace* (London: HarperCollins, 2009), 6.

12. Hans Ostwald, *Sittengeschichte der Inflation: Ein Kulturdokument aus den Jahren des Marktsturzes* (Berlin: Neufeld und Henius Verlag, 1931), 7–8, and

Bernd Widdig, *Culture and Inflation in Weimar Germany* (Berkeley: University of California Press, 2001).

13. Dagerman, 5, quoted in Werner Sollors, *The Temptation of Despair: Tales of the 1940s* (Cambridge: Harvard University Press, 2014), 114.

14. Sharif Gemie, Fiona Reid, and Laure Humbert, *Outcast Europe: Refugee and Relief Workers in an Era of Total War, 1936–1948* (London: Continuum, 2012), 234; Zorach Warhaftig, *Relief and Rehabilitation: Implications of the UNRRA Program for Jewish Needs* (New York: Institute of Jewish Affairs of the American Jewish Congress and World Jewish Congress, 1944), 90; Lowe, 35–39, 24; Alice Bailey, *The Problems of the Children in the World Today* (New York, 1946), 9–10.

15. Szabolcs Szita, *Trading in Lives? Operations of the Jewish Relief and Rescue Committee in Budapest, 1944–1945* (Budapest: Central European University Press, 2005); *Aiding Jews Overseas* (New York: American Jewish Joint Distribution Committee, 1942), 13; Amy Zahl Gottlieb, *Men of Vision: Anglo-Jewry's Aid to Victims of the Nazi Regime, 1933–1945* (London: Weidenfeld & Nicolson, 1998), 178–182.

16. Paul Weindling, "'For the Love of Christ': Strategies of International Catholic Relief and the Allied Occupation of Germany, 1945–1948," *Journal of Contemporary History* 43, no. 3 (July 2008): 477–492, quotation 481.

17. John W. Bachman, *Together in Hope: 50 Years of Lutheran World Relief* (Minneapolis: Kirk House, 1995), 13–35; Lyn Smith, *Pacifists in Action: The Experience of the Friends Ambulance Unit in the Second World War* (York, UK: William Sessions Ltd., 1998).

18. Robert Collis and Hans Hogerzeil, *Straight On* (London: Methuen, 1947), 28; Gemie et al., 170; Rhoda Dawson, "The Stagnant Pool: Work among Displaced Persons in Germany, 1945–1947," 19, typed manuscript, file: Mrs. R.N. Bickerdale 95/26/1, Imperial War Museum, London.

19. Eryl Hall Williams, *A Page of History in Relief: London—Antwerp—Belsen—Brunswick. Quaker Relief: 1944–1946* (York, UK: Sessions Book Trust, 1993), 45, 51.

20. Clifford Barnard, *Binding the Wounds of War: A Young Relief Worker's Letters Home, 1943–1947* (London: Pronoun Press, 2010), 69; Roger C. Wilson, *Quaker Relief: An Account of the Relief Work of the Society of Friends, 1940–1948* (London: George Allen & Unwin, 1952), 322; Margaret McNeill, *By the Rivers of Babylon: A Story of Relief Work among the Displaced Persons of Europe* (London: Bannisdale, 1950), 100.

21. Gemie et al., 200; McNeill, 77; Juliane Wetzel, "An Uneasy Existence: Jewish Survivors in Germany After 1945," in *The Miracle Years: A Cultural History of West Germany, 1949–1968*, ed. Hanna Schissler (Princeton: Princeton University Press, 2001), 137; Hannah Arendt, "The Aftermath of Nazi Rule: Report from Germany," *Commentary* 10 (October 1950): 342–343; Robert Moeller, *War*

Stories: The Search for a Usable Past in the Federal Republic of Germany (Berkeley: University of California Press, 2001).

22. Carson, 79; McNeill, 152, 154.

23. Grace Fox, "The Origins of UNRRA," *Political Science Quarterly* 65, no. 4 (December 1950): 561–584; Rana Mitter, "Imperialism, Transnationalism, and the Reconstruction of Post-war China 1944–7," in *Transnationalism and Contemporary Global History*, ed. Matthew Hilton and Rana Mitter, *Past & Present* 218, supplement 8 (2013): 51–70; *Helping the People to Help Themselves: The Story of the United Nations Relief and Rehabilitation Administration* (London: United Nations Information Organisation, 1944), 2.

24. Philip Noel-Baker, foreword, Leonard Woolf, introduction, Julian Huxley, "Relief and Reconstruction," H. J. Laski, "The Machinery of International Relief," in *When Hostilities Cease: Papers on Relief and Reconstruction Prepared for the Fabian Society*, ed. Julian Huxley et al. (London: Victor Gollancz, 1943), vii, 11–13, 17, 21, 33, 39; see too the International Labour Office report by Eugene M. Kulischer, *The Displacement of Population in Europe* (Montreal: International Labour Office, 1943).

25. Jessica Reinisch, "Internationalism in Relief: The Birth (and Death) of UNRRA," in *Postwar Reconstruction in Europe: International Perspectives, 1945 1949*, ed. Mark Mazower, Jessica Reinisch, and David Feldman, *Past & Present* 210, supplement 6 (2011): 269.

26. Gary J. Bass, *Freedom's Battle: The Origins of Humanitarian Intervention* (New York: Knopf, 2008), 273.

27. Laure Humbert, "French Politics of Relief and International Aid: France, UNRRA and the Rescue of European Displaced Persons in Postwar Germany, 1945–1947," *Journal of Contemporary History* 51, no. 3 (2016): 606–634.

28. Jessica Reinisch, "'Auntie UNRRA' at the Crossroads," in *Transnationalism and Contemporary Global History*, ed. Matthew Hilton and Rana Mitter, *Past & Present* 218, supplement 8 (2013): 92; Marshall MacDuffie, *The Red Carpet: 10,000 Miles Through Russia on a Visa from Khrushchev* (London: Cassell & Co., 1955), 197–214; Andrew Harder, "The Politics of Impartiality: The United Nations Relief and Rehabilitation Administration in the Soviet Union, 1946–7," *Journal of Contemporary History* 47, no. 2 (2012): 358.

29. *Times* (London), January 21, 1944; Hitchcock, 220; Harder, 366; Reinisch, "'Auntie UNRRA,'" 87, 97.

30. *The Story of UNRRA* (Washington, DC: Office of Public Information, UNRRA, 1948), 30–31.

31. Susan Armstrong-Reid and David Murray, *Armies of Peace: Canada and the UNRRA Years* (Toronto: University of Toronto Press, 2008); Hitchcock, 222; Francesca M. Wilson, *Aftermath: France, Germany, Austria, Yugoslavia, 1945 and 1946* (London: Penguin, 1947), 28; Shephard, *The Long Road Home: The Aftermath of the Second World War* (London: Bodley Head, 2010), 59.

32. McNeill, 228; Paul Weindling, "'Belsenitis': Liberating Belsen, Its Hospitals, UNRRA, and Selection for Re-emigration, 1945–1948," *Science in Context* 19, no. 3 (2006): 401–418; Tara Zahra, *The Lost Children: Reconstructing Europe's Families After World War II* (Cambridge: Harvard University Press, 2011), 71, 91.

33. Wilson, *Aftermath*, 10, 41, 51, 253.

34. Kathryn Hulme, *The Wild Place* (Boston: Little, Brown, 1953), x–xi, 107; Gemie et al., 201; Pettiss, 7–8, 50.

35. Heide Fehrenbach and Davide Rodogno, eds., *Humanitarian Photography: A History* (Cambridge: Cambridge University Press, 2015), 1–21.

36. Dean Acheson, *Present at the Creation: My Years in the State Department* (New York: W. W. Norton, 1969), 201; Silvia Salvatici, "Sights of Benevolence: UNRRA's Recipients Portrayed," in Fehrenbach and Rodogno, 200–210.

37. McNeill, 130; *Poland, 1946: The Photographs and Letters of John Vachon*, ed. Ann Vachon (Washington, DC/London: Smithsonian, 1995), 53; Anna Holian, *Between National Socialism and Soviet Communism: Displaced Persons in Postwar Germany* (Ann Arbor: University of Michigan Press, 2011), 48–50.

38. Dawson, 63; Gemie et al., 195.

39. McNeill, 107; Shephard, *Long Road*, 146.

40. Lorna Hay, "Can UNRRA Relieve the Chaos in Europe?," *Picture Post*, September 15, 1945; Hitchcock, 226; Shephard, *Long Road*, 177.

41. Peter Gatrell, *The Making of the Modern Refugee* (Oxford: Oxford University Press, 2013), 90.

42. G. Daniel Cohen, *In War's Wake: Europe's Displaced Persons in the Postwar Order* (Oxford: Oxford University Press, 2011), 2; Hulme, *Wild Place*, 44; Bessel, 256–257; Dawson, 229; Eleanor Roosevelt, *On My Own* (New York: Harper, 1958), 50.

43. Zorach Warhaftig, *Relief and Rehabilitation: Implications of the UNRRA Program for Jewish Needs* (New York: Institute of Jewish Affairs of the American Jewish Congress and World Jewish Congress, 1944), 21; Cohen, 11, 127–129; Bartley Cavanaugh Crum, *Behind the Silken Curtain: A Personal Account of Anglo-American Diplomacy in Palestine and the Middle East* (New York: Simon & Schuster, 1947), 145; Pettiss, 62.

44. W. Arnold-Forster, "UNRRA's Work for Displaced Persons in Germany," *International Affairs* 22, no. 1 (January 1946): 1–13; Wilson, *Quaker Relief*, 118–126; Martha Branscombe, "The Children of the United Nations: UNRRA's Responsibility for Social Welfare," *Social Service Review* 19, no. 3 (September 1945): 310, 316, 323.

45. Cardinal Aloisius Muench, "One World in Charity," reprinted in Suzanne Brown-Fleming, *The Holocaust and Catholic Conscience: Cardinal Aloisius Muench*

and the Guilt Question in Germany (Notre Dame, IN: University of Notre Dame Press, 2006), 45, 140–145.

46. *Investigation of Starvation Conditions in Europe and the Report of the Emergency Economic Committee for Europe, January 29, February 1 and 7, 1946* (Washington, DC: US Government Printing Office, 1946), 8, 12–13, 22–24, 29; Lucius D. Clay, *Decision in Germany* (Garden City, NJ: Doubleday, 1950), 265.

47. Cohen, 67. In the end, UNRRA reportedly aided 7 million displaced Soviet laborers and POWs, 1.6 million Poles, 1.8 million French, 696,000 Italians, 389,000 Yugoslavs, 348,000 Czechs, and 285,000 Hungarians. Zahra, 7, 19; *The Story of UNRRA*, 47; Harder, 363; Hitchcock, 247; Reinisch, "'Auntie UNRRA,'" 87–89.

48. "Trümmerfrauen: Contested Memories of Germany's 'Rubble Women,'" OpenLearn, September 4, 2017, www.open.edu/openlearn/history-the-arts /history/trummerfrauen-contested-memories-germanys-rubble-women; Elizabeth Heineman, "The Hour of the Woman: Memories of Germany's 'Crisis Years' and West German National Identity," *American Historical Review* 101, no. 2 (April 1996): 354–395.

49. Edmund Wilson, *Europe Without Baedeker: Sketches Among the Ruins of Italy, Greece and England* (London: Secker & Warburg, 1948), 86–87, 120.

2. PUNISHMENT AND PITY

1. Mary Fulbrook, *Reckonings: Legacies of Nazi Persecution and the Quest for Justice* (Oxford: Oxford University Press, 2018), 213; Bradley F. Smith, *The American Road to Nuremberg* (Stanford, CA: Hoover Institution Press, 1982), 199.

2. Lawrence Douglas, *The Memory of Judgment: Making Law and History in the Trials of the Holocaust* (New Haven: Yale University Press, 2001), 13; Philippe Sands, *East West Street: On the Origins of "Genocide" and "Crimes Against Humanity"* (London: Weidenfeld & Nicolson, 2017), 281.

3. Douglas, 85; Hartley Shawcross, "On the Law of the Charter on Crimes Against Humanity, July 26, 1946," reprinted in *The Nuremberg War Crimes Trial, 1945–46: A Documentary History*, ed. Michael Marrus (Boston: Bedford, 1997), 189; John W. Dower, *Embracing Defeat: Japan in the Wake of World War II* (New York: Norton, 1999), 443–484.

4. John Haynes Holmes, "The Judgment of the Court," in *The Case of Civilization Against Hitlerism* (New York: Robert Ballou, 1934), 143, 145; and *New York Times*, March 8, 1934, recounted in Peter Fritzsche, *Iron Wind: Europe Under Hitler* (New York: Basic Books, 2016), 26–27; Pierre Van Paassen and James Waterman Wise, eds., *Nazism: An Assault on Civilization* (New York: Harrison Smith and Robert Haas, 1934), vii.

5. Christiane Wilke, "Reconsecrating the Temple of Justice: Invocations of Civilization and Humanity in the Nuremberg Justice Case," *Canadian Journal of Law and Society* 24, no. 2 (2009): 181–201; H. G. Wells, *The Rights of Man, or What Are We Fighting For?* (London: Penguin, 1940), 101; Charles de Gaulle, "Oxford Speech," in *War Memoirs*, vol. 1, *The Call to Honor 1940–1942, Documents* (New York: Viking, 1955), 313, 320; Michaela Hoenicke Moore, *Know Your Enemy: The American Debate on Nazism, 1933–1945* (Cambridge: Cambridge University Press, 2010), 298; Frank Ninkovich, *Modernity and Power: A History of the Domino Theory in the Twentieth Century* (Chicago: University of Chicago Press, 1994), 2–8, 120–122; Konrad H. Jarausch, *After Hitler: Recivilizing Germans, 1945–1995* (Oxford: Oxford University Press, 2006), 47.

6. V. I. Lenin, "What Is to Be Done?," in *Collected Works* (Moscow, 1960–1977), vol. 5, 373; V. I. Lenin, "The Socialist Party and Non-Party Revolutionism," in *Collected Works* (Moscow, 1960–1977), vol. 10, 76; J. V. Stalin, "On an Article by Engels, July 19, 1934," in *Works* (Moscow, 1946–1954), vol. 14, 17; J. W. Stalin, *Werke* (Berlin: Dietz Verlag, 1953), Bd. 10, 211, quoted in S. Datlin, *Afrika unter dem Joch des Imperialismus* (Berlin: Dietz Verlag, 1953); Trotsky's full speech: www.marxists.org/archive/trotsky/1932/11/oct.htm. I thank Steve Smith for this reference.

7. V. Kemenov, "In Defence of Civilization Against Fascist Barbarism," and Hewlett Johnson, "The Soviet Peoples Are Carrying Civilization's Banner," in *In Defence of Civilization Against Fascist Barbarism: Statements, Letters and Telegrams from Prominent People* (Moscow: VOKS, 1941), 5–9, 102.

8. "Avantyura fashisma neset emu gibel," *Pravda*, June 24, 1941, 4; "Krasnaya armiya zashchishchaet mirovuyu zivilizaziyu," *Pravda*, August 30, 1941, 3; "Znamya pobedi vodruzheno pod Berlinom!," *Pravda*, May 3, 1945, 1; "Velikoe torzhestvo sovetskoi kulturi," *Pravda*, June 16, 1945, 1. I thank Giovanni Cadioli for these and subsequent Russian language sources.

9. James Brown Scott, ed., *The Proceedings of the Hague Peace Conferences: The Conference of 1899* (Buffalo: William S. Hein, 2000), 15, 461, and 714, cited in Marco Duranti, *The Conservative Human Rights Revolution: European Identity, Transnational Politics, and the Origins of the European Convention* (Oxford: Oxford University Press, 2017), 23; Arthur Eyffinger, *The 1907 Hague Peace Conference: "The Conscience of the Civilized World"* (The Hague: Judicap, 2007).

10. Ilya Ehrenburg, *We Come as Judges* (Moscow: Soviet War News, 1945), and Ian Buruma, *Year Zero: A History of 1945* (London: Atlantic Books, 2013), 225–226.

11. Ilya Ehrenburg, *We Will Not Forget* (Washington, DC: Embassy of the USSR, 1944); Keith Lowe, *Savage Continent: Europe in the Aftermath of World War II* (New York: Viking, 2012), 55; Miriam Gebhardt, *Crimes Unspoken: The Rape of German Women at the End of the Second World War* (London: Polity, 2017), 13–22.

12. Lowe, 248; István Deák, Jan T. Gross, and Tony Judt, eds., *The Politics of Retribution in Europe: World War II and Its Aftermath* (Princeton: Princeton University Press, 2000), 134–135; Fabrice Virgili, *Shorn Women: Gender and Punishment in Liberation France*, trans. John Flower (Oxford/New York: Berghahn, 2002), 173–189.

13. Francine Hirsch, "The Soviets at Nuremberg: International Law, Propaganda, and the Making of the Postwar Order," *American Historical Review* 113, no. 3 (June 2008): 701–730; Kim Christian Priemel, *The Betrayal: The Nuremberg Trials and German Divergence* (Oxford: Oxford University Press, 2016), 109; "Protsess glavnykh nemetskikh voyennykh prestupnikov v Nyurnberge," *Pravda*, January 9, 1946, 9; A. Leontev, "Proiskhozhdeniye i kharakter vtoroy mirovoy voyny," *Pravda*, April 1, 1946, 3; "Nemetsko-fashistskim prestupnikam net poshchady!," *Pravda*, August 2, 1946, 1.

14. Wilke, 199.

15. Douglas, 83, 85.

16. Ulrike Weckel, *Beschämende Bilder: Deutsche Reaktionen auf alliierte Dokumentarfilme über befreite Konzentrationslager* (Stuttgart: Franz Steiner, 2012), 52; Dan Stone, *The Liberation of the Camps: The End of the Holocaust and Its Aftermath* (New Haven: Yale University Press, 2015), 29–39; Douglas, 23–30, 69. The film's close link to the Hollywood film industry could be seen in the fact that the camps film was spliced in as a set piece in Stanley Kramer's 1961 film *Judgment at Nuremberg*.

17. Kevin Reynolds, "That Justice Be Seen: The American Prosecution's Use of Film at the Nuremberg International Military Tribunal" (PhD thesis, University of Sussex, 2011), esp. 115–154; Janet Flanner, "Letters from Nuremberg," in *Janet Flanner's World: Uncollected Writings, 1932–1975*, ed. Irving Drutman (London: Secker & Warburg, 1980), 99; Weckel, "Watching the Accused Watch the Nazi Crimes: Observers' Reports on the Atrocity Film Screening in the Belsen, Nuremberg and Eichmann Trials," *London Review of International Law* 6, no. 1 (March 2018): 45–73.

18. Richard Bessel, *Germany 1945: From War to Peace* (London: HarperCollins, 2009), 209; Priemel, 149; Richard Overy, "Interwar, War, Postwar: Was There a Zero Hour in 1945?," in *The Oxford Handbook of Postwar European History*, ed. Dan Stone (Oxford: Oxford University Press, 2012), 62; Werner Sollors, *The Temptation of Despair: Tales of the 1940s* (Cambridge: Harvard University Press, 2014), 187–188.

19. Hirsch, 720, 725–726, 730.

20. Carl Schmitt, *The Nomos of the Earth in the International Law of the Jus Publicum Europaeum*, trans. G. L. Ulmen (New York: Telos, 2006 [1950]), 228.

21. Lowe, 123; A. J. P. Taylor, *The Course of German History* (London: H. Hamilton, 1968 [1945]), 21; James Jay Carafano, *Waltzing into the Cold War:*

The Struggle for Occupied Austria (College Station: Texas A&M University Press, 2002), 63.

22. James F. Tent, *Mission on the Rhine: Reeducation and Denazification in American-Occupied Germany* (Chicago: University of Chicago Press, 1982), 46 and 254–311; Maria Höhn, *GIs and Fräuleins: The German-American Encounter in 1950s West Germany* (Chapel Hill: University of North Carolina Press, 2002), 61–66.

23. Douglas Botting, *From the Ruins of the Reich, Germany, 1945–1949* (New York: Meridian, 1985), 161; Patricia Meehan, *A Strange Enemy People: Germans Under the British, 1945–1950* (London: Peter Owen, 2001), 161, 165; Gabriele Clemens, *Britische Kulturpolitik in Deutschland, 1945–1949* (Stuttgart: Franz Steiner, 1997).

24. Timothy R. Vogt, *Denazification in Soviet-Occupied Germany: Brandenburg, 1945–1948* (Cambridge: Harvard University Press, 2000), and Norman M. Naimark, *The Russians in Germany: A History of the Soviet Zone of Occupation, 1945–1949* (Cambridge: Harvard University Press, 1995), 38, 401–466.

25. F. Roy Willis, *The French in Germany, 1945–1949* (Stanford, CA: Stanford University Press, 1962), 16.

26. Willis, *The French in Germany*, 75, 78, 148–151, 179, 247; Alan Milward, *The European Rescue of the Nation-State* (London: Routledge, 2000), 335; F. Roy Willis, *France, Germany, and the New Europe, 1945–1963* (Stanford, CA: Stanford University Press, 1965), 35; Tent, 313.

27. Atina Grossmann, *Jews, Germans, and Allies: Close Encounters in Occupied Germany* (Princeton: Princeton University Press, 2007), 17–22.

28. Lisa Haushofer, "The 'Contaminating Agent': UNRRA, Displaced Persons, and Venereal Disease in Germany, 1945–1947," *American Journal of Public Health* 100, no. 6 (June 2010): 993–1003; Carafano, 65; Meehan, 150–151.

29. William I. Hitchcock, *Liberation: The Bitter Road to Freedom, Europe 1944–1945* (New York: Faber & Faber, 2008), 179–181.

30. Quoted in Meehan, 40, 89.

31. *Pocket Guide to Germany* (Washington, DC: Army Information Branch, US Army, 1944), 2–3, 18, 32; *Germany: The British Soldier's Pocketbook* (London: Political War Executive, 1944), 2–5, 31, 41.

32. Percy Knauth, "Fraternization: The Word Takes on a Brand-New Meaning in Germany," *Life*, July 2, 1945; Buruma, *Year Zero*, 24, 28.

33. Bessel, 177–181; Willis, *French*, 248–249; Naimark, *Russians in Germany*, 31; Jessica Reinisch, *The Perils of Peace: The Public Health Crisis in Occupied Germany* (Oxford: Oxford University Press, 2013), 293.

34. Leonard Mosley, *Report from Germany* (London: Victor Gollancz, 1945), 114–115, 122, 123–124; "British Wives in Germany," *Times* (London), October 10, 1946, 5.

35. Petra Goedde, "From Villains to Victims: Fraternization and the Feminization of Germany, 1945–1947," *Diplomatic History* 23, no. 1 (Winter 1999): 1–20; Ann Elizabeth Pfau, *Miss Yourlovin: GIs, Gender, and Domesticity During World War II* (New York: Columbia University Press, 2013), 157–164.

36. Carafano, 125–129; Heide Fehrenbach, *Race After Hitler: Black Occupation Children in Postwar Germany and America* (Princeton: Princeton University Press, 2005), 17–45; Höhn, 91–93; Robert Knight, "National Construction Work and Hierarchies of Empathy in Postwar Austria," *Journal of Contemporary History* 49, no. 3 (July 2014): 491–513.

37. Perry Biddiscombe, "Dangerous Liaisons: The Anti-Fraternization Movement in the US Occupation Zones of Germany and Austria, 1945–1948," *Journal of Social History* 34, no. 3 (Spring 2001): 611–647; John Willoughby, "The Sexual Behavior of American GIs during the Early Years of the Occupation of Germany," *Journal of Military History* 62, no. 1 (January 1998): 166–167.

38. Bessel, 205.

39. Martha Gellhorn, *The Face of War* (New York: Atlantic Monthly Press, 1988), 162, and Ira A. Hirschmann, *The Embers Still Burn: An Eye-Witness View of the Postwar Ferment in Europe and the Middle East and Our Disastrous Get-Soft-with-Germany Policy* (New York: Simon & Schuster, 1949), 94–95.

40. Phillip Knightley, *The First Casualty* (London, 1978), 322, quoted in Martin Caiger-Smith, *The Face of the Enemy: British Photographers in Germany, 1944–1952* (London: Dirk Nishen, 1988), 9; Ludger Derenthal, *Bilder der Trümmer- und Aufbaujahre: Fotografie im sich teilenden Deutschland* (Marburg, Germany: Jonas, 1999), 44–45; Stefan-Ludwig Hoffmann, "Gazing at Ruins: German Defeat as Visual Experience," *Journal of Modern European History* 9, no. 3 (2011): 340–341; Tom Allbeson, "Ruins, Reconstruction and Representation: Photography and the City in Postwar Western Europe, 1945–1958" (PhD thesis, University of Durham, 2012).

41. David Shneer, *Through Soviet Jewish Eyes: Photography, War, and the Holocaust* (New Brunswick, NJ: Rutgers University Press, 2011); Dagmar Barnouw, *Germany 1945: Views of War and Violence* (Bloomington: Indiana University Press, 1996), 25 and related images on 14, 23, 30, 31.

42. Margaret Bourke-White, *Dear Fatherland*, 38–39, and Lee Miller, "Germans Are Like This," *Vogue*, June 1945, 192, cited in Sollors, 62–63; Charles E. Egan, "All Reich to See Camp Atrocities: Allies Want Billboard in Each Community to Teach Germans They Have Guilt," *New York Times*, April 24, 1945, 6; Richard Bessel, *Lee Miller: Deutschland 1945* (Cologne: Greven Verlag, 2018), 1–29.

43. *Life*, October 15, 1945, 107–115.

44. Kevin Jackson, *Humphrey Jennings* (London: Picador, 2004), 310–313.

45. Caiger-Smith, 7; Norman Clark, "25,000 Seek Food Every Day at the Gates of Berlin," *News Chronicle*, August 24, 1945, 1, 4.

46. Lorna Hay and Haywood Magee, "Report on Chaos," *Picture Post*, September 8, 1945, 9; Lorna Hay and Haywood Magee, "Can UNRRA Relieve the Chaos in Europe?" *Picture Post*, September 15, 1945, 16–19, 26.

47. Charles Bray, "Retribution...It Falls on Women and Children," *Daily Herald*, August 24, 1945, 2.

48. *Picture Post*, December 1, 1945, cited in Barnouw, 152; Conway Hall Speech, October 8, 1945, MS Bonham Carter 355, fos. 88–101, Bodleian Library, Oxford.

49. Andrew Chandler, *The Church and Humanity: The Life and Work of George Bell, 1883–1958* (Farnham, UK: Ashgate, 2012); A. C. Grayling, *Among the Dead Cities: The History and Moral Legacy of the WWII Bombing of Civilians in Germany and Japan* (London: Bloomsbury, 2006), 179–180; A. Chandler, "The Church of England and the Obliteration Bombing of Germany in the Second World War," *English Historical Review* 108, no. 429 (October 1993): 920–946; Bishop of Chicester, *If Thine Enemy Hunger* (London: Victor Gollancz, 1946), 3, 4 and 8.

50. Benjamin Frommer, *National Cleansing: Retribution Against Nazi Collaborators in Postwar Czechoslovakia* (Cambridge: Cambridge University Press, 2005), esp. 33–62, 95–267, quotation 42; Norman M. Naimark, *Fires of Hatred: Ethnic Cleansing in Twentieth-Century Europe* (Cambridge: Harvard University Press, 2002), 108–139, and Peter Gatrell, *The Unsettling of Europe: The Great Migration, 1945 to the Present* (London: Penguin, 2019), 23–25, 92.

51. *New York Times*, November 13, 1946, 26; "The Sudetenland," *Manchester Guardian*, June 15, 1945; "The Watch Tower," *Record*, September 21, 1945, quoted in Matthew Frank, *Expelling the Germans: British Opinion and Post–1945 Population Transfer in Context* (Oxford: Oxford University Press, 2008), 179; "Church Council Warns Against Vengeful Peace: Victors Urged to Alter Their Outlook," *Chicago Daily Tribune*, February 26, 1946, 9, quoted in Sollors, 123.

52. *The Land of the Dead: Study of the Deportations from Eastern Germany* (New York: Committee Against Mass Expulsion, 1947), 3–5, 32; Lora Wildenthal, *The Language of Human Rights in West Germany* (Philadelphia: University of Pennsylvania Press, 2013).

53. Julian Hochfeld, "An Open Letter from a Polish Socialist to a Friend in the Labour Party," quoted in Frank, *Expelling*, 95, 223, and 241.

54. George Bilainkin, *Second Diary of a Diplomatic Correspondent* (London: Sampson Low, Marston & Co., 1947), diary entry for August 14, 1945, 181.

55. Victor Gollancz, *What Buchenwald Really Means* (London: V. Gollancz, 1945), 16; Ruth Dudley Edwards, *Victor Gollancz: A Biography* (London: Victor Gollancz, 1987), 404–405.

56. Matthew Frank, "The New Morality—Victor Gollancz, 'Save Europe Now' and the German Refugee Crisis, 1945–1946," *Twentieth-Century British*

History 17, no. 2 (2006): 238. Victor Gollancz, *Leaving Them to Their Fate: The Ethics of Starvation* (London: Victor Gollancz, 1946), 34, 43; Gollancz, *Leaving*, 1, 21, 30–32.

57. Victor Gollancz, *Our Threatened Values* (London: Victor Gollancz, 1946), 7, 116, 155, 156.

58. Victor Gollancz, *Is It Nothing to You?* (London: Victor Gollancz, 1945), 2–3.

59. Shephard, *Long Road*, 253; Reinisch, *Perils*, 153.

60. Frank, *Expelling*, 147–149; *UNRRA, Gateway to Recovery* (Washington, DC: National Planning Association, 1944), 9. *New York Times*, November 22, 1943.

61. Gollancz, *Leaving*, 11; *Save Europe Now, 1945–1948: Three Years' Work* (London: Victor Gollancz, 1948), 5, 9.

62. Peters, *In Germany Now*, 105; Franz Burger, *Gollancz's Buchenwald Never Existed* (London: Hutchinson, 1945), 3; Edwards, 548, 623; Frank, "New Morality," 254.

63. Konrad Adenauer, *Memoirs, 1945–1953* (London: Weidenfeld & Nicolson, 1966), 60; Edwards, 458–462.

64. Lynn Hunt, *Inventing Human Rights: A History* (London: W. W. Norton, 2007); *The Book of Needs* (Paris: UNESCO, 1947); Heide Fehrenbach, "Children and Other Civilians: Photography and the Politics of Humanitarian Image-Making," in Heide Fehrenbach and Davide Rodogno, eds., *Humanitarian Photography: A History* (New York: Cambridge University Press, 2015), 167–187; *Children of Europe*, photos by David Seymour (Paris: UNESCO, 1949); *The Family of Man*, ed. Edward Steichen (New York: Museum of Modern Art, 1955), 4.

3. FAITH AND FRONTIERS

1. István Rév, "The Suggestion," *Representations* 80, no. 1 (Fall 2002): 64.

2. Paul A. Hanebrink, *In Defense of Christian Hungary: Religion, Nationalism, and Antisemitism, 1890–1944* (Ithaca: Cornell University Press, 2006), 228; Hansjakob Stehle, *Eastern Politics of the Vatican, 1917–1979*, trans. Sandra Smith (Athens: Ohio University Press, 1981), 258.

3. "A Cardinal on Trial: Charges against the Hungarian Primate," *Times* (London), February 3, 1949, 5; Jonathan Luxmoore and Jolanta Babiuch, *The Vatican and the Red Flag: The Struggle for the Soul of Eastern Europe* (London: Geoffrey Chapman, 1999), 43; József Cardinal Mindszenty, *Memoirs*, trans. Richard and Clara Winston (London: Weidenfeld and Nicolson, 1974), 75–77.

4. Nicholas Perry and Loreto Echeverría, *Under the Heel of Mary* (London: Routledge, 1988), 231–257; James Baaden, "Post-War Saints, 1945–1960," *History of European Ideas* 40 (2014): 1–20; Ruth Harris, *Lourdes: Body and Spirit in the Secular Age* (London: Allen Lane, 1999), 249–255.

5. David Blackbourn, *Marpingen: Apparitions of the Virgin Mary in Bismarck-ian Germany* (Oxford: Clarenden, 1993), 378; Monique Scheer, "Catholic Piety in the Early Cold War Years; or, How the Virgin Mary Protected the West from Communism," in *Cold War Culture: Perspectives on Eastern and Western European Societies*, ed. Annette Vowinckel, Marcus M. Payk, and Thomas Lindenberger (Oxford/New York: Berghahn, 2012), 131, 134, 138; Mary Vincent, "Made Flesh? Gender and Doctrine in Religious Violence in Twentieth-Century Spain," *Gender & History* 25, no. 3 (November 2013): 678–680; Monica Black, "Miracles in the Shadow of the Economic Miracle: The 'Supernatural '50s' in West Germany," *Journal of Modern History* 84, no. 4 (December 2012): 836, as well as Black, *A Demon-Haunted Land: Witches, Wonder Doctors, and the Ghosts of the Past in Post–World War II Germany* (New York: Metropolitan, 2020), chapter 7.

6. Perry and Echeverría, 238; Damian van Melis, "'Strengthened and Purified Through Ordeal by Fire': Ecclesiastical Triumphalism in the Ruins of Europe," in *Life After Death: Approaches to a Cultural and Social History of Europe During the 1940s and 1950s*, ed. Richard Bessel and Dirk Schumann (New York: Cambridge University Press, 2003), 231–242.

7. Nicholas Boér, *Cardinal Mindszenty and the Implacable War of Communism Against Religion and the Spirit* (London: BUE Limited, 1949), 215–216.

8. *Documents on the Mindszenty Case* (Budapest: Atheneum, 1949), 7–11.

9. Mindszenty, *Memoirs*, 114–116; Jószef Mindszenty, *Four Years Struggle of the Church in Hungary: Facts and Evidence Published by Order of Josef, Cardinal Mindszenty*, trans. Walter C. Breitenfeld, intro. Christopher Hollis (London: Longmans, 1949), xi–xiii; Boér, 287; *New York Times*, February 17, 1949.

10. Charles Gallagher, "The United States and the Vatican in Yugoslavia, 1945–1950," in *Religion and the Cold War*, ed. Dianne Kirby (London: Palgrave, 2002), 118–144.

11. Peter C. Kent, *The Lonely Cold War of Pope Pius XII: The Roman Catholic Church and the Division of Europe, 1943–1950* (Montreal: McGill-Queen's University Press, 2002), 156–170; Jonathan P. Herzog, *The Spiritual-Industrial Complex: America's Religious Battle Against Communism in the Early Cold War* (New York: Oxford University Press, 2011), 64; Stephen D. Kertesz, "Human Rights in the Peace Treaties," *Law and Contemporary Problems* 14, no. 4 (Autumn 1949): 627–646.

12. Melissa Feinberg, *Curtain of Lies: The Battle over Truth in Stalinist Eastern Europe* (New York: Oxford University Press, 2017), 3–12.

13. So pervasive were these media images of the martyred archbishop that Mindszenty himself opened his 1974 memoirs by correcting *The Prisoner* film's inaccuracies and misleading scenes, ranging from the wrongly featured "luxurious" furniture in his prison cell to what he called the film's wrongful emphasis on the

courtesy of the sentries, the prison's good food, and supposedly "pleasant and congenial" conversations with guards. Mindszenty, *Memoirs*, xxvii–xxviii.

14. Dianne Kirby, "Harry Truman's Religious Legacy: The Holy Alliance, Containment and the Cold War," in Kirby, 77–102; Myron C. Taylor, ed., *Correspondence Between President Truman and Pope Pius XII* (New York, 1953), 9–10; Herzog, 78, 99–100; Kent, 192; William Inboden, *Religion and American Foreign Policy, 1945–1960: The Soul of Containment* (Cambridge: Cambridge University Press, 2008), 257.

15. Patrick Thaddeus Jackson, *Civilizing the Enemy: German Reconstruction and the Invention of the West* (Ann Arbor: University of Michigan, 2006); Konrad Adenauer, "Christian Civilization Is at Stake," in his *World Indivisible: With Liberty and Justice for All* (New York: Harper & Brothers, 1955), 12–13.

16. Kent, 228–229; "Roman Catholics' Strong Protest: Denial of Human Rights Denounced," *Manchester Guardian*, February 8, 1949, 5; Enda Delaney, "Anti-Communism in Mid-Twentieth Century Ireland," *English Historical Review* 126, no. 521 (August 2011): 892; Boér, 9–10; "Atlantic Pact and Western Union," *Round Table: The Commonwealth Journal of International Affairs* (1948): 105–110; Luxmoore and Babiuch, 95; "Communists Make Martyr of Cardinal," *Life*, February 21, 1949, 27; Francois Honti, *Le Drame Hongrois: Une Grande Bataille de la Civilisation Chrétienne* (Paris: Editions du Triolet, 1949), esp. 118–184.

17. Zoltán K. J. Csáky, *Ich schwöre, dass Kardinal Mindszenty unschuldig ist* (Zurich: Thomas Verlag, 1949), and R. P. Jérôme Szalay, *Le Cardinal Mindszenty: Confesseur de la Foi, Defenseur de la Cité* (Paris: Mission Catholique Hongroise, 1950); *The Trial of Jószef Mindszenty* (Budapest: Hungarian State Publishing House, 1949), 4, 5, 11.

18. J. Fred MacDonald, "The Cold War as Entertainment in 'Fifties Television," *Journal of Popular Film* 7, no. 1 (1978): 1–27; Tony Shaw, "Martyrs, Miracles, and Martians: Religion and Cold War Cinematic Propaganda in the 1950s," *Journal of Cold War Studies* 4, no. 2 (Spring 2002): 15–17.

19. Feinberg, 83–85.

20. Wolfram Kaiser, *Christian Democracy and the Origins of European Union* (Cambridge: Cambridge University Press, 2007), 181; Stehle, 296; John Pollard, "The Vatican, Italy and the Cold War," in Kirby, 103–117.

21. "Plot to Drug Mindszenty Revealed," *Washington Post*, January 23, 1949, M3.

22. The phrase was attributed to Bela Fábián, former leader of the Hungarian Independent Democratic Party, in "Mindszenty Trial Held Soviet Farce," *New York Times*, February 10, 1949, 5; "Spellman Warns," 1–2; Boér, 287.

23. Edward Hunter, *Brainwashing in Red China: The Calculated Destruction of Men's Minds* (New York: Vanguard, 1951), 12, 233; the British Ministry of Defence published its own report on the brainwashing of British POWs in the

Korean War, though it was mocked in the British press and not taken very seriously. Ministry of Defence, *The Treatment of British POWs in Korea* (1954), cited in Cyril Cunningham, "'Brainwashing,'" *RUSI Journal* 118, no. 3 (1973): 39–43.

24. Susan L. Carruthers, "Redeeming the Captives: Hollywood and the Brainwashing of America's Prisoners of War in Korea," *Film History* 10, no. 3 (1998): 275–294.

25. "'Truth Serum' Ban Is Dropped in UN," *New York Times*, April 1, 1950, 3.

26. John M. Crewson, "Files Show Tests for Truth Drug Began in OSS," *New York Times*, September 5, 1977, 1; John Marks, *The Search for the "Manchurian Candidate": The CIA and Mind Control* (New York: W. W. Norton, 1979), 11, 24–25.

27. US Central Intelligence Agency, "Security Research Section: Interrogation Techniques of Unfriendly Countries, #184367," February 24, 1949, 1–3; "Communist 'Confession' Techniques, #144891," May 1949, 5, 17; "Proposed Memorandum for the Secretary of Defense, #144688," January 1952, 5, 20. All part of MKULTRA Collection, CIA Archives, Washington, DC (hereafter cited as MKULTRA).

28. "Mind-Control Studies Had Origins in Trial of Mindszenty," *New York Times*, August 2, 1977, 16; Marks, 25, 31; "Assistant Director, Scientific Intelligence to Deputy Director for Central Intelligence, Memo: Project Artichoke, #144689," February 4, 1952, 1, 5, MKULTRA; Crewson, 1; "Out of Soviet Laboratories—Brainwashing, #146095," 1955, 3, MKULTRA; Martin A. Lee and Bruce Schlain, *Acid Dreams: The CIA, LSD, and the Sixties Rebellion* (New York: Grove, 1985); Giles Scott-Smith, "Interdoc and West European Psychological Warfare: The American Connection," *Intelligence and National Security* 26, nos. 2–3 (April–June 2011): 355–376; Jens Gieseke, *Mielke-Konzern: Die Geschichte der Stasi, 1945–1990* (Stuttgart: Deutsche Verlags-Anstalt, 2001).

29. Timothy Melley, *The Covert Sphere: Secrecy, Fiction, and the National Security State* (Ithaca: Cornell University Press, 2012), 44–72; W. H. Lawrence, "Why Do They Confess? A Communist Enigma," *New York Times*, May 8, 1949; David Seed, "Brainwashing and Cold War Demonology," *Prospects* 22 (October 1997): 535–573; J. Edgar Hoover, *Masters of Deceit* (New York: Pocket, 1958), 75.

30. Mary Dudziak, *Cold War Civil Rights* (Princeton: Princeton University Press, 2000), 19–46.

31. Christopher Dawson, *The Judgment of the Nations* (New York: Catholic University of America, 1942), 185–186; Inboden, 39; Samuel Moyn, *Christian Human Rights* (Philadelphia: University of Pennsylvania Press, 2015).

32. Jacques Maritain, *Humanisme Intégral: Problèmes temporels et spirituels d'une nouvelle chrétienté* (Paris: Aubier, 1968), 10; Jacques Maritain, *The Twilight of Civilization*, trans. Lionel Landry (London Sheed & Ward, 1946), 11, 15–16, 45–46.

33. "Roman Catholics' Strong Protest: 'Denial of Human Rights' Denounced," *Manchester Guardian*, February 8, 1949, 5; Pope Pius XII, "The Mindszenty Trial," in *Vital Speeches of the Day*, February 15, 1949, 265–266; John Epstein, *Defend These Human Rights: Each Man's Stake in the United Nations: A Catholic View* (New York: The America Press, 1947), 47–53; Canon John Nurser, "The 'Ecumenical Movement' Churches, 'Global Order,' and Human Rights: 1938–1948," *Human Rights Quarterly* 25, no. 4 (November 2003): 841–881.

34. "Loss of Human Rights in East Europe: Sir Hartley Shawcross's Plain Speaking at the UN," *Times* (London), October 7, 1949, 4; "May Cardinal Mindszenty's Martyrdom Not Be in Vain Says Sir David Maxwell Fyfe," *Catholic Herald*, April 29, 1949, 1.

35. *Trial*, 15; "The Cardinal's Sentence," *Times* (London), February 10, 1949, 4; Kertesz, "Human Rights in the Peace Treaties," 627–646.

36. Inboden, 157, 186; Samuel Moyn, *Christian Human Rights* (Philadelphia: University of Pennsylvania Press, 2015); this regionalization of human rights spurred similar efforts elsewhere, as noted in the 1970 Latin American Human Rights Convention and the 1981 African Charter on Human and Peoples' Rights.

37. James Chappel, *Catholic Modern: The Challenge of Totalitarianism and the Remaking of the Church* (Cambridge: Harvard University Press, 2018), esp. 22–107; Giuliana Chamedes, "The Vatican, Nazi-Fascism, and the Making of Transnational Anti-Communism in the 1930s," *Journal of Contemporary History* 51 (April 2016): 261–290; www.vatican.va/offices/papal_docs_list_it.html; Udi Greenberg, "Catholics, Protestants, and the Violent Birth of European Religious Pluralism," *American Historical Review* 124, no. 2 (April 2019): 519.

38. Mindszenty, *Four Years Struggle*, 178.

39. Paul Hanebrink, "Islam, Anti-Communism and Christian Civilization: The Ottoman Menace in Interwar Hungary," *Austria History Yearbook* 40 (2009): 114–124; Rosario Forlenza, "The Enemy Within: Catholic Anti-Communism in Cold War Italy," *Past & Present* 235, no. 1 (May 2017): 227.

40. Hanebrink, *A Specter Haunting Europe: The Myth of Judeo-Bolshevism* (Cambridge: Harvard University Press, 2018), 224–225; Mark Silk, "Notes on the Judeo-Christian Tradition in America," *American Quarterly* 36, no. 1 (Spring 1984): 65; Herzog, 66, 69.

41. Kevin M. Schultz, *Tri-Faith America: How Catholics and Jews Held Postwar America to its Protestant Promise* (New York: Oxford University Press, 2011), 15–42, 68–96.

42. Waldemar Gurian, "In the Face of the World's Crisis: A Manifesto by European Catholics Sojourning in America," *Commonweal*, August 21, 1942, 415–418; Carl J. Friedrich, "Anti-Semitism: Challenge to Christian Culture," in

Jews in a Gentile World: The Problem of Anti-Semitism, ed. Isacque Graeber and Steuert Britt (New York: Macmillan, 1942), 1–18; for discussion, Udi Greenberg, *The Weimar Century: German Émigrés and the Ideological Foundations of the Cold War* (Princeton: Princeton University Press, 2014), 1–75, 120–165.

43. Elena Aga Rossi and Victor Zaslavsky, *Stalin and Togliatti: Italy and the Origins of the Cold War* (Stanford: Stanford University Press, 2011), 131–157; Rosario Forlenza, "The Politics of the Abendland: Christian Democracy and the Idea of Europe After the Second World War," *Contemporary European History* 26, no. 2 (2017): 230–240.

44. Judith Keene, *Fighting for Franco: International Volunteers in Nationalist Spain During the Spanish Civil War, 1936–1939* (London: Continuum, 2004), vii; Giuliana Chamedes, *A Twentieth-Century Crusade: The Vatican's Battle to Remake Christian Europe* (Cambridge: Harvard University Press, 2019), 182–183; David Brydan, *Franco's Internationalists: Social Experts and Spain's Search for Legitimacy* (Oxford: Oxford University Press, 2019), chapter 5.

45. Michael Lang, "Globalization and Global History in Toynbee," *Journal of World History* 22, no. 4 (December 2011): 747–783; Richard Overy, *The Morbid Age: Britain and the Crisis of Civilisation, 1919–1939* (London: Penguin, 2009), 271–275, 294; Herzog, 15–16.

46. Quoted and perceptively discussed in Marco Duranti, *The Conservative Human Rights Revolution: European Identity, Transnational Politics, and the Origins of the European Convention* (Oxford: Oxford University Press, 2017), 133, 147.

47. Winston Churchill, "Something That Will Astonish You," Zurich, September 19, 1946, in *Blood, Toil, Tears, and Sweat: Winston Churchill's Famous Speeches*, ed. David Cannadine (London: Cassell, 1989), 312; Duranti, *Conservative*, 143; E. H. Carr, "A Voice from Zürich," *Times* (London), September 20, 1946, in Duranti, *Conservative*, 146.

48. Greenberg, "Catholics," 511–536.

49. Kent, *Lonely*, 157; Philippe Chenaux, *De la chrétienté a l'Europe: Les catholiques et l'idee européenne au XXe siècle* (Tours, France: Éditions CLD, 2007), 9; Paul-Henri Spaak, "The Integration of Europe: Dreams and Realities," *Foreign Affairs* 29, no. 1 (October 1950): 94–100, and "The West in Disarray," *Foreign Affairs* 35, no. 2 (January 1957): 184–190; A. W. Brian Simpson, *Human Rights and the End of Empire: Britain and the Genesis of the European Convention* (Oxford: Oxford University Press, 2001), 569.

50. Vanessa Conze, *Das Europa der Deutschen: Ideen von Europa in Deutschland zwischen Reichstradition und Westorientierung (1920–1970)* (Munich: Oldenbourg, 2005), 27–56; Forlenza, *Politics,* 261–286.

51. Robert Schuman, "L'Europe est une communauté spirituelle et culturelle," *L'Annuaire européen* (1955), 17–23; Forlenza, *Politics,* 269; Maria Mitchell, "Materialism and Secularism: CDU Politicians and National Socialism, 1945–1949,"

Journal of Modern History 67, no. 2 (June 1995): 278–308; Richard Couden-hove-Kalergi, *An Idea Conquers the World*, with a preface by Winston Churchill (London: Hutchinson, 1953), 310, cited in Forlenza, *Politics,* 268; Jean Monnet, *Mémoires* (Paris: Fayard, 1976), 339.

52. Christoph Hendrik Müller, *West Germans Against the West: Anti-Americanism in Media and Public Opinion in the Federal Republic of Germany, 1949–1968* (New York: Palgrave, 2010); Greenberg, *Weimar,* 158; Jackson, *Civilizing,* ix, 93, 126.

53. K. H. Schmolz, *Der Dom zu Köln, 1248–1948* (Düsseldorf: L. Schwann, 1948), and Hermann Schnitzler, *Der Dom zu Aachen* (Düsseldorf: L. Schwann, 1950); Tom Allbeson, "Visualising Wartime Destruction and Postwar Recon-struction: Herbert Mason's photograph of St Paul's Re-Evaluated," *Journal of Modern History* 87, no. 3 (September 2015): 532–578; Michael Meng, *Shattered Spaces: Encountering Jewish Ruins in Postwar Germany and Poland* (Cambridge: Harvard University Press, 2011).

54. William McNeill, *Arnold J. Toynbee: A Life* (New York: Oxford University Press, 1989), 213–217; Duranti, *Conservative,* 100, 108, 114, 176.

55. Marco Duranti, "'A Blessed Act of Oblivion': Human Rights, European Unity and Postwar Reconciliation," in *Reconciliation, Civil Society, and the Politics of Memory,* ed. B. Schwelling (Bielefeld, Germany: Transcript, 2012), 115–139; James Sloan Allen, *The Romance of Commerce and Culture: Capitalism, Modernism, and the Chicago-Aspen Crusade for Cultural Reform* (Chicago: University of Chi-cago Press, 1983), 147–200; Duranti, *Conservative,* 193.

56. Duranti, *Conservative,* 301.

57. "Mindszenty Urges UN to Assist Hungarians," *Milwaukee Journal,* No-vember 12, 1956, 1; Victor Conzemius, "Protestants and Catholics in the German Democratic Republic, 1945–90: A Comparison," *Religion, State and Society* 26, no. 1 (1998): 56.

58. Letter from Mindszenty to John Foster Dulles, November 8, 1957, in *His Eminence Files: American Embassy Budapest,* ed. Árpád Ádám Somorjai (Budapest: Magyar Egyháztörténeti Enciklopédia Munkaközössége, 2008), 30.

59. Mindszenty, *Memoirs,* 235; József Közi-Horvath, *Cardinal Mindszenty: Confessor and Martyr of Our Time,* trans. Geoffrey Lawman (Williton: Cox, Sons and Co., 1979), 7.

60. Paul-Henri Spaak, *Combats Inachevés,* vol. 1 (Paris: Fayard, 1969), 149.

4. Science, Shelter, and Civility

1. Ivor Montagu, *What Happened at Wrocław: An Account of the World Confer-ence of Intellectuals for Peace, 1948* (London: British Cultural Committee for Peace, 1949), 15, 26.

Notes

2. Feliks Topolski, *Confessions of a Congress Delegate* (London: Gallery Editions, 1949), 10, 14, 17; Vladimir Dobrenko, "Conspiracy of Peace: The Cold War, the International Peace Movement, and the Soviet Peace Campaign, 1946–1956" (PhD thesis, London School of Economics, 2016), 65–66; *Six Hundred Millions for Peace: A Report on the World Congress for Peace, Paris, April 20th to 25th, 1949* (London: British Cultural Committee for Peace, 1949), 3, 12.

3. Lawrence S. Wittner, *The Struggle Against the Bomb*, vol. 1, *One World or None: A History of the World Nuclear Disarmament Movement Through 1953* (Stanford: Stanford University Press, 1993), 58; Paul Boyer, *By the Bomb's Early Light: American Thought and Culture at the Dawn of the Atomic Age* (New York: Pantheon, 1985), 179–240; Jussi Hanhimäki and Odd Arne Westad, eds., *The Cold War: A History in Documents and Eyewitness Accounts* (Oxford/New York: Oxford University Press, 2003), 142.

4. Quoted in Barton Bernstein, ed., *The Atomic Bomb: The Critical Issues* (Boston: Little, Brown, 1975), viii; *Times* (London), November 20, 1945; Wittner, 109; Boyer, 37.

5. Joseph Preston Baratta, *The Politics of World Federation* (Westport: Praeger, 2004), 304–305; Wittner, 161; Mark Mazower, *Governing the World: The History of an Idea* (London: Penguin, 2012), 230–243.

6. Wittner, 59; Larry G. Gerber, "The Baruch Plan and the Origins of the Cold War," *Diplomatic History* 6, no. 1 (January 1982): 69–96; Dexter Masters and Katharine Way, eds., *One World or None, a Report to the Public on the Full Meaning of the Atomic Bomb* (New York: McGraw-Hill, 1946).

7. Christoph Lauch, "Atoms for the People: The Atomic Scientists' Association, the British State and Nuclear Education in the Atom Train Exhibition, 1947–1948," *British Journal for the History of Science* 45, no. 4 (December 2012): 591–608; Kenneth Osgood, *Total Cold War: Eisenhower's Secret Propaganda Battle at Home and Abroad* (Lawrence: University of Kansas Press, 2006), 161, 179.

8. Joseph Rotblat, *Science and World Affairs: History of the Pugwash Conferences* (London: Dawsons of Pall Mall, 1962), 6; David Holloway, "Nuclear Weapons and the Escalation of the Cold War, 1945–1962," in *The Cambridge History of the Cold War*, vol. 1, ed. M. P. Leffler and O. A. Westad (Cambridge: Cambridge University Press, 2010), 383; "Plamennii Priziv: Prishlo Vremya Deistvovat!," *Pravda*, July 12, 1962, 1.

9. "Vashnaya i pochetnaya rol uchenih v borbe za mir," *Pravda*, September 4, 1962, 1; Yale Richmond, *Cultural Exchange and the Cold War: Raising the Iron Curtain* (University Park: Penn State University Press, 2003), 96–101.

10. Jean S. Pictet, *Commentary: The Geneva Conventions of 1949* (Geneva: International Committee of the Red Cross, 1952), 8, 16; Helen M. Kinsella, *Image Before the Weapon: A Critical History of the Distinction between Combatant and Civilian* (Ithaca, NY: Cornell University Press, 2011), 112n48.

11. Kinsella, 57; Jean S. Pictet, "The New Geneva Conventions for the Protection of War Victims," *American Journal of International Law* 45, no. 3 (July 1951): 464, 475.

12. P. H. Vigor, *The Soviet View of War, Peace and Neutrality* (London/Boston: Routledge & Kegan Paul, 1975), 174–175.

13. *Final Record of the Diplomatic Conference of Geneva of 1949*, vol. 2, section B, 495–509; Boyd van Dijk, "'The Great Humanitarian': The Soviet Union, the International Committee of the Red Cross, and the Geneva Conventions of 1949," *Law and History Review* 37, no. 1 (February 2019): 209–235.

14. Timothy Johnston, "The Soviet Struggle for Peace, 1948–54," *The Slavonic and East European Review* 86 (April 2008): 259–282.

15. Young-Sun Hong, *Cold War Germany, the Third World, and the Global Humanitarian Regime* (Cambridge: Cambridge University Press, 2017); Péter Apor, "War and Peace," in *When Socialism Went Global: Connecting the Second and Third Worlds*, ed. James Mark and Paul Betts (forthcoming).

16. Michael Howard, *The Invention of Peace* (New Haven: Yale University Press, 2000), 100; Paul Betts, "When Cold Warriors Die: The State Funerals of Konrad Adenauer and Walter Ulbricht," in *Between Mass Death and Individual Loss: The Place of the Dead in Twentieth-Century Germany*, ed. Alon Confino, Paul Betts, and Dirk Schumann (New York/Oxford: Berghahn, 2008), 151 176.

17. Christopher Driver, *The Disarmers: A Study in Protest* (London: Hodder & Stoughton, 1964), 58; Bertrand Russell, "A Fifty-Six Year Friendship," in *Gilbert Murray: An Unfinished Autobiography* (London: Allen & Unwin, 1960), 209; Holger Nehring, *The Politics of Security: British and West German Protest Movements and the Early Cold War, 1945–1970* (Oxford: Oxford University Press, 2013), 28–30, 160–161; Andrew Oppenheimer, "West German Pacifism and the Politics of Solidarity, 1945–1974," in *Peace Movements in Western Europe, Japan and the USA During the Cold War*, ed. Benjamin Ziemann (Essen, Germany: Klartext, 2008), 41–60.

18. Ian Kershaw, *Roller-Coaster: Europe, 1950–2017* (London: Allen Lane, 2018), 26; Celia Donert, "From Communist Internationalism to Human Rights: Gender, Violence and International Law in the Women's International Democratic Federation Mission to North Korea, 1951," *Contemporary European History* 25, no. 2 (May 2016): 320; *We Accuse! Korea: Report of the Commission of the Women's International Democratic Federation in Korea, May 16 to 27, 1951* (Berlin: WIDF, 1951); Katharine McGregor, "Opposing Colonialism: The Women's International Democratic Federation and Decolonisation Struggles in Vietnam and Algeria, 1945–1965," *Women's History Review* 25, no. 6 (2016): 1–20.

19. Quoted in Richard Kuisel, *Seducing the French: The Dilemma of Americanization* (Berkeley: University of California Press, 1993), 37–38.

20. Sarah Fishman, *From Vichy to the Sexual Revolution: Gender and Family Life in Postwar France* (Oxford: Oxford University Press, 2017), 130; Frank Trentman, *Empire of Things: How We Became a World of Consumers, from the 15th Century to the 21st* (London: Penguin, 2016), 301; *When the War Was Over: Women, War and Peace in Europe, 1940–1956*, ed. Claire Duchen and Irene Bandhauer-Schöffmann (London: Leicester University Press, 2000).

21. *Design and Cultural Politics in Postwar Britain: The Britain Can Make It Exhibition of 1946*, ed. Patrick J. Maguire and Jonathan M. Woodham (London: University of Leicester Press, 1998), 3–66; Nicole Rudolph, *At Home in Postwar France: Modern Mass Housing and the Right to Comfort* (New York/Oxford: Berghahn, 2015), 53–86; Rebecca J. Pulju, *Women and Mass Consumer Society in Postwar France* (Cambridge: Cambridge University Press, 2011), 95–142; Katarzyna Jezowska, "Imagined Poland: Representations of the Nation State at the Exhibitions of Industry, Craft and Design, 1948–1974" (PhD thesis, University of Oxford, 2018).

22. Paolo Scrivano, "Signs of Americanization in Italian Domestic Life: Italy's Postwar Conversion to Consumerism," *Journal of Contemporary History* 40, no. 2 (2005): 317–340; Greg Castillo, *Cold War on the Home Front: The Soft Power of Midcentury Design* (Minneapolis: University of Minnesota Press, 2010), 67–69; Paul Betts, *The Authority of Everyday Objects: A Cultural History of West German Industrial Design* (Berkeley: University of California Press, 2004), 197–198, and Michael Meng, *Shattered Spaces: Encountering Jewish Ruins in Postwar Germany and Poland* (Cambridge: Harvard University Press, 2011), 2, 124–126; Herbert Nicolaus and Alexander Obeth, *Die Stalinallee: Geschichte einer deutschen Strasse* (Berlin: Verlag für Bauwesen, 1997), 171–220.

23. Christina Varga-Harris, *Stories of House and Home: Soviet Apartment Life during the Khrushchev Years* (Ithaca, NY: Cornell University Press, 2015), 24–52; Katherine Lebow, *Unfinished Utopia: Nowa Huta, Stalinism, and Polish Society, 1949–1956* (Ithaca, NY: Cornell University Press, 2013).

24. Karal Ann Marling, *As Seen on TV: The Visual Culture of Everyday Life in the 1950s* (Cambridge: Harvard University Press, 1994), 278; Mary Nolan, "Consuming America, Producing Gender," in *The American Century in Europe*, ed. R. Laurence Moore and Maurizio Vaudagna (Ithaca, NY: Cornell University Press, 2003), 251.

25. Erica Carter, *How German Is She? Postwar West German Reconstruction and the Consuming Woman* (Ann Arbor: University of Michigan Press, 1997); M. L. Roberts, *Civilization Without Sexes: Reconstructing Gender in Postwar France, 1917–1927* (Chicago: University of Chicago Press, 1994); Victoria de Grazia, *How Fascism Ruled Women: Italy, 1922–1945* (Berkeley: University of California Press, 1992), 41–115; Elizabeth D. Heineman, *What Difference Does a Husband*

Make? Women and Marital Status in Nazi and Postwar Germany (Berkeley: University of California Press, 1999), 17–74; Fishman, 15, 72–73, and Till van Rahden, "Fatherhood, Rechristianization, and the Quest for Democracy in Postwar West Germany," in *Raising Citizens in the "Century of the Child": The United States and German Central Europe in Comparative Perspective*, ed. Dirk Schuman (New York/Oxford: Berghahn Books, 2010), 141–164.

26. Robert G. Moeller, *Protecting Motherhood: Women and the Family in the Politics of Postwar West Germany* (Berkeley: University of California Press, 1993), 109–141; R. H. S. Crossman, *Socialist Values in a Changing Civilisation* (London: Fabian Publications, 1950), 5, 16.

27. Ina Merkel,...*und Du, Frau an der Werkbank: Die DDR in den 50er Jahren* (Berlin: Elefanten Press, 1990), 76–105.

28. Barbara Einhorn, *Cinderella Goes to Market: Citizenship, Gender and Women's Movements in East Central Europe* (London: Verso, 1993); Donna Harsch, *Revenge of the Domestic: Women, the Family, and Communism in the German Democratic Republic* (Princeton: Princeton University Press, 2006).

29. Nina Witoszek, "Moral Community and the Crisis of the Enlightenment: Sweden and Germany in the 1920s and 1930s," in *Culture and Crisis: The Case of Germany and Sweden*, ed. Nina Witoszek and Lars Trägardh (New York/Oxford: Berghahn, 2002), 58; Thomas Etzemüller, *Alva and Gunnar Myrdal: Social Engineering in the Modern World* (Lanham, MD: Lexington, 2014); Francis Sejersted, *The Age of Social Democracy: Norway and Sweden in the Twentieth Century* (Princeton: Princeton University Press, 2011), 241–332.

30. James Sheehan, *Where Have All of the Soldiers Gone? The Transformation of Modern Europe* (Boston: Houghton Mifflin, 2008), 172–197; Ronald Inglehart, *The Silent Revolution: Changing Values and Political Styles Among Western Publics* (Princeton: Princeton University Press, 1977).

31. Jeffrey Herf, *Reactionary Modernism: Technology, Culture, and Politics in Weimar and the Third Reich* (New York: Cambridge University Press, 1984), and Mary Nolan, *Visions of Modernity: American Business and the Modernization of Germany* (Oxford: Oxford University Press, 1994); Judt, *Postwar*, 353.

32. Victoria de Grazia, *Irresistible Empire: America's Advance through 20th Century Europe* (Cambridge: Harvard University Press, 2005), 10; Helmut Klages, *Technischer Humanismus: Philosophie und Soziologie der Arbeit bei Karl Marx* (Stuttgart: Ferdinand Enke, 1964).

33. Jean Améry, *Preface to the Future: Culture in a Consumer Society*, trans. Palmer Hilty (New York: Ungar, 1964), 298; Jean-Jacques Servan-Schreiber, *The American Challenge*, trans. Ronald Steel (London: Hamish Hamilton, 1968), 298; de Grazia, *Irresistible Empire*, 336–376.

34. Servan-Schreiber, 34.

35. Günther Anders, *Die Antiquiertheit des Menschen*, vol. 2, *Über die Zerstörung des Lebens im Zeitalter der dritten industriellen Revolution* (Munich: Beck, 1987 [1956]), 23, 25.

36. A. Dirk Moses, "*Das römische Gespräch* in a New Key: Hannah Arendt, Genocide, and the Defense of Republican Civilization," *Journal of Modern History* 85, no. 4 (December 2013): 867–913; Hannah Arendt, *The Human Condition* (Chicago: University of Chicago Press, 1958), 59, 137.

37. De Grazia, 11.

38. Arthur M. Schlesinger, *Learning How to Behave: A Historical Study of American Etiquette Books* (New York: Macmillan, 1946), and Harold Nicolson, *Good Behavior: Being a Study of Certain Types of Civility* (New York: Constable, 1955).

39. Horst-Volker Krumrey, *Entwicklungsstrukturen von Verhaltensstandarden: Eine soziologische Prozessanalyse auf der Grundlage deutscher Anstands- und Manierenbücher von 1870–1970* (Frankfurt: Suhrkamp, 1984), 27; Catriona Kelly, *Refining Russia: Advice Literature, Polite Culture, and Gender from Catherine to Yeltsin* (Oxford: Oxford University Press, 2001), 403.

40. Hans-Otto Meissner and Isabella Burkhard's *Gute Manieren stets gefragt: Takt, Benehmen, Etiquette* (Munich: Verlag Mensch und Arbeit, 1962), 44–51; Wilhelm Von Ginök, Lebenskunst: Ein Buch vom guten Benehmen für jedermann (Krefeld: Verlag 'Lebenskunst,' 1950), 15.

41. W. A. Nennstiel, *Richtiges Benehmen, beruflich und privat: Eine nützliche Anleitung für junge Menschen* (Mannheim: Max Rein, 1949), 3, 5.

42. Hans Martin, *Darf ich mir erlauben...? Das Buch der Guten Lebensart* (Stuttgart: Walter Hädecke, 1949), 109, and W. von Hilgendorff, *Gutes Benehmen, Dein Erfolg* (Vienna: Humboldt Taschenbuch, 1953), 160–161; Cas Wouters, *Informalization: Manners and Emotions Since 1890* (London: Sage, 2007), 64–69.

43. Cas Wouters, *Sex and Manners: Female Emancipation in the West, 1890–2000* (London: Sage, 2004), 43–46; Nennstiel, 17, 25, 33, 37, 46.

44. Kevin M. Schultz, 84; George Mikes, *How to Be an Alien* (London: Penguin, 1971 [1946]).

45. Amelia H. Lyons, *The Civilizing Mission in the Metropole: Algerian Families and the French Welfare State During Decolonization* (Stanford: Stanford University Press, 2013), 104–105; Elizabeth Buettner, *Europe After Empire: Decolonization, Society, and Culture* (Cambridge: Cambridge University Press, 2016), 216–221.

46. Varga-Harris, 132; Kelly, 315, 318–321, 342, 347, 403.

47. *Kahlschlag: Das 11. Plenum des ZK der SED 1965: Studien und Dokumente* (Berlin: Aufbau Verlag, 1991), 241; Deborah A. Field, *Private Life and Communist Morality in Khrushchev's Russia* (New York: Peter Lang, 2007), and Anna-Sabine Ernst, "The Politics of Culture and the Culture of Everyday Life in the DDR in the 1950s," in *Between Reform and Revolution: German Socialism and Communism*

from 1840 to 1990, ed. David E. Barclay and Eric Weitz (New York/Oxford: Berghahn, 1998), 489–506.

48. Ernst, 503n7.

49. Karl Smolka, *Gutes Benehmen von A–Z* (Berlin: Verlag Neues Leben, 1974 [1957]), 16.

50. Smolka, 7–8; Kleinschmidt, 233.

51. Karl Smolka, *Junger Mann von heute* (Berlin: Verlag Neues Leben, 1964), 8; Dagmar Herzog, *Sex After Fascism: Memory and Morality in Twentieth-Century Germany* (Princeton: Princeton University Press, 2007), 184–219, and Josie McLellan, *Love in the Time of Communism: Intimacy and Sexuality in the GDR* (Cambridge: Cambridge University Press, 2011); W. K. Schweickert and Bert Hold, *Guten Tag, Herr von Knigge: Ein heiteres Lesebuch für alle Jahrgänge über alles, was 'anständig' ist* (Leipzig: VEB Friedrich Hofmeister, 1959), 8.

52. Andrew St. George, *The Descent of Manners: Etiquette, Rules and the Victorians* (London: Chatto & Windus, 1993), xi.

5. Empire Reclaimed

1. Jean-Louis Planche, *Sétif 1945: Histoire d'un massacre annoncé* (Paris: Perrin, 2006); Jean-Pierre Peyroulou, *Guelma, 1945: Une subversion française dans l'Algérie coloniale* (Paris: Éditions la Découverte, 2009), 103–141; James McDougall, *A History of Algeria* (Cambridge: Cambridge University Press, 2017), 179–180; Martin Evans and John Phillips, *Algeria: Anger of the Dispossessed* (New Haven: Yale University Press, 2007), 52.

2. Niall Ferguson, *The War of the World: History's Age of Hatred* (London: Penguin, 2009), 613.

3. Walter Lipgens, *A History of European Integration*, vol. 1 (Oxford: Oxford University Press, 1982), 46.

4. www.consilium.europa.eu/media/26207/134126.pdf; Peo Hansen and Stefan Jonsson, *Eurafrica: The Untold History of European Integration and Colonialism* (London: Bloomsbury, 2014), 1–7.

5. Britta Schilling, *Postcolonial Germany: Memories of Empire in a Decolonized Nation* (Oxford: Oxford University Press, 2014), and Jared Poley, *Decolonization in Germany: Weimar Narratives of Colonial Loss and Foreign Occupation* (Bern: Peter Lang, 2005); Susan Pedersen, *The Guardians: The League of Nations and the Crisis of Empire* (Oxford: Oxford University Press, 2015), 32, 115, 196, 330.

6. www.mussolinibenito.net/discorso-di-trieste/; www.mussolinibenito.net/secondo-discorso-di-trieste/; Mussolini continued with this "vector of world civilization" theme in his Milan Speech, Piazza Duomo, October 25, 1932, www.mussolinibenito.net/discorso-di-milano-1932/; Benito Mussolini, "The Birth of a New Civilization," in *Fascism*, ed. Roger Griffin (Oxford: Oxford University

Press, 1995), 72–73; Amaila Ribi Forclaz, *Humanitarian Imperialism: The Politics of Anti-Slavery Activism, 1880–1940* (Oxford: Oxford University Press, 2015), esp. chapters 4 and 5.

7. www.lorien.it/x_inni/pg_canzoni-d/Disc_BM/Discorso_BM_1936-05 -05.html; Davide Rodogno, *Fascism's European Empire: Italian Occupation During the Second World War* (Cambridge: Cambridge University Press, 2006 [orig. Italian 2003]), csp. 44–53, 145–157; www.mussolinibenito.net/lultimo-discorso-del -dvce-dal-teatro-lirico-di-milano/. I thank Giovanni Cadioli for these Italian sources.

8. Christopher Duggan, *Fascist Voices: An Intimate History of Mussolini's Italy* (London: Vintage, 2013), 253, 267, 275.

9. Christian Helfer, "Humanitätsdüselei—zur Geschichte eines Schlagworts," *Zeitschrift für Religions- und Geistesgeschichte* 16, no. 2 (1964): 179–182; Lorna Waddington, *Hitler's Crusade: Bolshevism and the Myth of the International Jewish Conspiracy* (London: I. B. Tauris, 2008); Philip Gassert, "No Place for 'the West': National Socialism and the 'Defence of Europe,'" in *Germany and "The West": The History of a Modern Concept*, ed. Riccardo Bavaj and Martina Steber (New York/ Oxford: Berghahn, 2015), 216–229; David B. Dennis, *Inhumanities: Nazi Interpretations of Western Culture* (Cambridge: Cambridge University Press, 2012), esp. 359–451.

10. Benjamin G. Martin, *The Nazi-Fascist New Order for European Culture* (Cambridge: Harvard University Press, 2016), esp. 1–4, 16, 74, 80, 119, 151, 186–187, 246–255; Nicola Lambourne, *War Damage in Western Europe: The Destruction of Historic Monuments During the Second World War* (Edinburgh: Edinburgh University Press, 2001), 102–103.

11. Philippe Sands, *East West Street: On the Origins of Genocide and Crimes Against Humanity* (London: Weidenfeld & Nicolson, 2016), 216, 222, and 238; Elizabeth Harvey, "Documenting *Heimkehr*: Photography, Displacement and 'Homecoming' in the Nazi Resettlement of Ethnic Germans, 1939–1940," and Julie Torrie, "Visible Trophies of War: German Occupiers' Photographic Perceptions of France, 1940–44," both in *The Ethics of Seeing: Photography and Twentieth-Century German History*, ed. Jennifer Evans, Paul Betts, and Stefan-Ludwig Hoffmann (New York/Oxford: Berghahn Books, 2018), 79–107 and 108–137, respectively; Jane Caplan, *Jetzt Judenfrei': Writing Tourism in Nazi-Occupied Poland* (London: GHIL, 2013); Mark Mazower, *Hitler's Empire: Nazi Rule in Occupied Europe* (London: Allen Lane, 2008), 181; Edwin Erich Dwinger, *Der Tod in Polen: Die volksdeutsche Passion* (Jena, Germany: Diederichs, 1940), 123–124.

12. Ewa Manikowska, *Photography and Cultural Heritage in the Age of Nationalisms: Europe's Eastern Borderlands (1867–1945)* (London: Bloomsbury, 2019), 165–191; *The German Invasion of Poland: Polish Black Book* (London: Hutchinson & Co., 1939), 75, 125; *The German New Order in Poland* (London: Hutchinson

& Co., 1941), 17–18; Wacław Borowy, *General Observations on the Problem of Reparations with Regard to Art and Culture* (Warsaw: Ministry of Culture and Art, 1945); Michael Meng, *Shattered Spaces: Encountering Jewish Ruins in Postwar Germany and Poland* (Cambridge: Harvard University Press, 2011), 69–70.

13. Loring M. Danforth and Riki Van Boeschoten, *Children of the Greek Civil War: Refugees and the Politics of Memory* (Chicago: University of Chicago Press, 2012); Mark Mazower, ed., *After the War Was Over: Reconstructing the Family, Nation, and State in Greece, 1943–1960* (Princeton: Princeton University Press, 2000).

14. André Gerolymatos, *An International Civil War: Greece, 1943–1949* (New Haven: Yale University Press, 2016), 258–259.

15. Daniel Chomsky, "Advance Agent of the Truman Doctrine: The United States, the *New York Times*, and the Greek Civil War," *Political Communication* 17, no. 4 (2000): 415–432; Anne O'Hare McCormick, "The British Retreat in the Mediterranean," *New York Times*, March 3, 1947, 20; Hanson W. Baldwin, "Survival of Western Civilization Is Held to Depend on Our Actions," *New York Times*, March 2, 1947, 4.

16. Patrick Thaddeus Jackson, *Civilizing the Enemy: German Reconstruction and the Invention of the West* (Ann Arbor: University of Michigan Press, 2006), 150, 153–155, 160, 164–165.

17. "A 'Confession of Imperialism,'" *Manchester Guardian*, March 15, 1947, 6; Alexander Werth, "Moscow Starts Attack on Truman," *Manchester Guardian*, March 15, 1947, 5; Alistair Cook, "Mr Gromyko Wins Support on Greece," *Manchester Guardian*, April 9, 1947, 6; C. P. Trussell, "Congress Is Solemn: Prepares to Consider Bills After Hearing the President Gravely," *New York Times*, March 13, 1947, 1.

18. Igor Lukes, "The Czech Road to Communism," in *The Establishment of Communist Regimes in Eastern Europe, 1944–1949*, ed. Norman Naimark and Leonid Gibianskii (New York: Routledge, 2018), 265n70.

19. *Foreign Relations of the United States, 1947*, vol. 1 (Washington, DC: US Department of State, 1947), 76–79.

20. Daniel A. Segal, "'Western Civ' and the Staging of History in American Higher Education," *American Historical Review* 105, no. 3 (June 2000): 770–805; Gilbert Allardyce, "Toward World History: American Historians and the Coming of the World History Course," *Journal of World History* 1, no. 1 (1990): 23–75, and Katja Naumann, "Teaching the World: Globalization, Geopolitics, and History Education at US Universities," *German Historical Institute Bulletin Supplement* 5 (2008): 123–144.

21. Serge Guilbaut, *How New York Stole the Idea of Modern Art: Abstract Expressionism, Freedom, and the Cold War* (Cambridge, MA: MIT Press, 1990), and Penny M. Von Eschen, *Satchmo Blows Up the World: Jazz Ambassadors Play the Cold*

War (Cambridge: Harvard University Press, 2004); Martin, 274; Mazower, *Hitler's Empire*, 564.

22. Norman Stone, *The Atlantic and Its Enemies: A Personal History of the Cold War* (London: Allen Lane, 2010), 17; Geir Lundestad, "Empire by Invitation? The United States and Western Europe, 1945–1952," *Journal of Peace Research* 23, no. 3 (September 1986), 267; Georgette Elgey, *La république des illusions, 1945–1951* (Paris: Fayard, 1965), 382.

23. Gilbert Rist, *The History of Development: From Western Origins to Global Faith* (London: Zed Books, 2008), 47–79.

24. Sven Beckert, "American Danger: United States Empire, Eurafrica, and the Territorialization of Industrial Capitalism, 1870–1950," *American Historical Review* 122, no. 4 (October 2017): 1161–1162; Dina Gusejnova, *European Elites and Ideas of Empire, 1917–1957* (Cambridge: Cambridge University Press, 2016), esp. 69–97; Richard Coudenhove-Kalergi, *Pan-Europe* (New York: Knopf, 1923), 29; Richard Coudenhove-Kalergi, *Europe Must Unite* (Glarus, Switzerland: Paneuropa Editions, 1939), 19–20; Julia Nordblad, "The Un-European Idea: Vichy and Eurafrica in the Historiography of Europeanism," *European Legacy* 19, no. 6 (September 2014): 711–729; Hansen and Jonsson, 26–27, 31, 41.

25. Beckert, 1168; Arnold Rivkin, *Africa and the European Common Market* (Denver: University of Denver, 1964), and P. N. C. Okigbo, *Africa and the Common Market* (London: Longmans, 1967).

26. Anne Deighton, "Entente Neo-Coloniale? Ernest Bevin and the Proposals for an Anglo-French Third World Power," *Diplomacy and Statecraft* 17, no. 4 (2006): 835–852; Anton Zischka, *Afrika: Europas Gemeinschaftsaufgabe Nr. 1* (Oldenburg, Germany: Gerhard Stilling, 1951), 9–59; Gustav-Adolf Gedat, *Europas Zukunft liegt in Afrika* (Stuttgart: Steinkopf, 1954), and Pierre Nord, *L'Eurafrique, notre dernière chance* (Paris: Arthème Fayard, 1955); Robert Skidelsky, *Oswald Mosley* (London: Macmillan, 1975), 485–486.

27. Irving Wall, *France, the United States, and the Algerian War* (Berkeley: University of California Press, 2001), 21; Alfred Grosser, "France and Germany in the Atlantic Community," *International Organisation* 17, no. 3 (Summer 1963): 558; U. W. Kitzinger, "Europe: The Six and the Seven," *International Organization* 14, no. 1 (1960): 31; Hansen and Jonsson, 238.

28. Elizabeth Buettner, *Europe After Empire: Decolonization, Society, and Culture* (Cambridge: Cambridge University Press, 2016), 91, 94; Carl Romme, Catholic People's Party, *Handelingen der Staten-Generaal: 1946–1947, II, 29ste Vergadering*, December 16, 1946, 860. See too the comments of Johann Logemann (Dutch Independent Socialist minister) in *Handelingen der Staten-Generaal: Tijdelijke zitting 1945, II, 5de Vergadering*, October 16, 1945, 86, and Hendrik Tilanus (CHU), *Handelingen der Staten-Generaal: 1946-1947, II, 29ste Vergadering*,

December 16, 1946, 893. I thank Pieter-Jan Sterenborg for his research assistance on this point. H. L. Wesseling, "Post-Imperial Holland," *Journal of Contemporary History* 15, no. 1 (January 1980): 125–142.

29. R. W. Heywood, "West European Community and the Eurafrica Concept in the 1950's," *Journal of European Integration* 4, no. 2 (1981): 199–210, quotation 207.

30. Jakov Etinger, *Bonn greift nach Afrika* (Berlin: Dietz Verlag, 1961), 72, 99–100.

31. W. R. Louis and R. Robinson, "The Imperialism of Decolonization," *Journal of Imperial and Commonwealth History* 22, no. 3 (1994): 462–511; Guy Mollet, *Bilan et perspectives socialistes* (Paris: Plon, 1958), 35, 45–46; Talbot C. Imlay, "International Socialism and Decolonization During the 1950s: Competing Rights and the Postcolonial Order," *American Historical Review* 118, no. 4 (October 2013): 1124, and Anne-Isabelle Richard, "The Limits of Solidarity: Europeanism, Anti-Colonialism and Socialism at the Congress of the Peoples of Europe, Asia and Africa in Puteaux, 1948," *European Review of History* 21, no. 4 (July 2014): 519–537.

32. Quotations from Hansen and Jonsson, 270–271.

33. Frederick Cooper, "French Africa, 1947–1948: Reform, Violence, and Uncertainty in a Colonial Situation," *Critical Inquiry* 40, no. 4 (Summer 2014): 476; Guiliano Garavini, *After Empires: European Integration, Decolonization, and the Challenge from the Global South, 1957–1986* (Oxford: Oxford University Press, 2012), 22; L. S. Senghor, *Liberté*, vol. 2 (Paris: Sevil, 1977), 91; Gary Wilder, *Freedom Time: Negritude, Decolonization, and the Future of the World* (Durham, NC: Duke University Press, 2015), 7.

34. Hansen and Jonsson, 158–166, 182; Frederick Cooper, *Citizenship between Empire and Nation: Remaking France and French Africa, 1945–1960* (Princeton: Princeton University Press, 2014), Chapter 4.

35. Mark Mazower, *No Enchanted Palace: The End of Empire and the Ideological Origins of the United Nations* (Princeton: Princeton University Press, 2009).

36. Mr. Altman (Poland), "General Assembly, Third Committee, Summary Records," General Assembly document A/C.3/SR.295, 1950, 158, in Roger Normand and Sarah Zaidi, *Human Rights at the UN: The Political History of Universal Justice* (Bloomington: Indiana University Press, 2008), 231–232; Evan Luard, *A History of the United Nations,* vol. 2, *The Age of Decolonization, 1955–1965* (Basingstoke, UK: Palgrave, 1989), 78–79.

37. Dwight Eisenhower, *The White House Years: Waging Peace, 1956–1961* (New York: Doubleday, 1969), 34; Philip E. Muehlenbeck, *Betting on the Africans: John F. Kennedy's Courting of African Nationalist Leaders* (Oxford: Oxford University Press, 2012), 8.

38. Quoted in Jessica Lynne Pearson, "Defending Empire at the United Nations: The Politics of International Colonial Oversight in the Era of Decolonisation," *Journal of Imperial and Commonwealth History* 45, no. 3 (2017): 530–531.

39. William Roger Louis, "Public Enemy Number One: The British Empire in the Dock at the United Nations, 1957–1971," in *The British Empire in the 1950s: Retreat or Revival?* ed. Martin Lynn (London: Palgrave, 2006), 186–213.

40. Sir Alan Burns, *In Defence of Colonies* (London: George Allen & Unwin, 1957), 5, 17–19; the idea of the "Salt Water Fallacy" derives from Sir Hilton Poynton's speech at the Fourth Committee of the General Assembly at the UN, October 3, 1947, as noted by Burns.

41. Buettner, 171; "The Belgian Congo: From Wilderness to Civilization," special issue of *Les Beaux-Arts*, 1955.

42. *The Sacred Mission of Civilization: To Which People Should the Benefits Be Extended? The Belgian Thesis* (New York: Belgian Government Information Center, 1953), 7, 16–17, 28.

43. Fernand van Langenhove, *The Question of the Aborigines Before the United Nations: The Belgian Thesis* (Brussels: Royal Colonial Institute, 1954), 44, 94; Pierre Ryckmans, *Report from Belgium* (Brussels: Belgian Ministry of Foreign Affairs and External Trade, 1955), 4, 7; Guy Vanthemsche, *Belgium and the Congo, 1885–1980* (Cambridge: Cambridge University Press, 2012), 121–142, 203–204.

44. Buettner, 198; Miguel Bandeira Jerónimo and António Costa Pinto, "A Modernizing Empire? Politics, Culture, and Economy in Portuguese Late Colonialism," in their coedited *The Ends of European Colonial Empires* (London: Palgrave Macmillan, 2015), 51–80.

45. Patricia Wohlgemuth, *The Portuguese Territories and the United Nations* (New York: Carnegie Endowment for International Peace, 1963), 7–12, 24–25; Luís Nuno Rodrigues, "The International Dimensions of Portuguese Colonial Crisis," in Bandeira Jéronimo and Costa Pinto, 243–267.

46. Alberto Franco Nogueira, *The United Nations and Portugal: A Study of Anti-Colonialism* (London: Tandem Books Limited, 1964), 50, 57, 178; George Martelli, "Portugal and the United Nations," *International Affairs* 40, no. 3 (July 1964): 453–465.

47. Wohlgemuth, 26–27; Adriano Moreira, *Provocation and Portugal's Reply* (Lisbon: Bertrand, 1961).

48. Gilberto Freyre, *Portuguese Integration in the Tropics* (Lisbon: Realizacao Grafica, 1961), 12–13, 23, 31, 74–75. For discussion, Buettner, 194–195.

49. This paragraph summarizes Udi Greenberg, "Protestants, Decolonization, and European Integration, 1885–1961," *Journal of Modern History* 89 (June 2017): 314–354, and his "Catholics, Protestants, and the Violent Birth of European Religious Pluralism," *American Historical Review* 124, no. 2 (April 2019): 519; Denis de Rougemont, *The Meaning of Europe* (London: Sidgwick & Jackson, 1965), 96.

50. Wohlgemuth, 32–34.

51. Quotations in Gerolymatos, 295–296.

6. DECOLONIZATION AND AFRICAN CIVILIZATION

1. June Milne, *Kwame Nkrumah: A Biography* (London: Panaf, 1999), 57–74; Kwame Nkrumah, *Towards Colonial Freedom: Africa in the Struggle Against World Imperialism* (London: Heinemann, 1962), 42.

2. Kwame Nkrumah, *I Speak of Freedom: A Statement of African Ideology* (New York: Frederick A. Praeger, 1961), 107.

3. "How Britain Saluted Our New Nation," *Daily Graphic*, March 7, 1957, 10; Kevin K. Gaines, *American Africans in Ghana: Black Expatriates and the Civil Rights Era* (Chapel Hill: University of North Carolina Press, 2006), 81; Jeffrey S. Ahlman, *Living with Nkrumahism: Nation, State, and Pan-Africanism in Ghana* (Athens, OH: Ohio University Press, 2017), 3, 11, 14.

4. Kwame Nkrumah, *Africa Must Unite* (London: Heinemann, 1963), xiv, xv; Philip E. Muehlenbeck, *Betting on the Africans: John F. Kennedy's Courting of African Nationalist Leaders* (Oxford: Oxford University Press, 2012), 25; Ed Naylor, introduction to his edited *France's Modernising Mission: Citizenship, Welfare and the Ends of Empire* (London: Palgrave, 2018), xix; Todd Shepard, "'Of Sovereignty': Disputed Archives, 'Wholly Modern' Archives, and the Post-Decolonization French and Algerian Republics, 1962–2012," *American Historical Review* 120, no. 3 (June 2015): 869–883.

5. Letters from Nkrumah to S. G. Ikoku, March 2, 1964, and to Kodwo Addison, March 9, 1964, RG 17/1/380, Public Records and Archives Adminstrative Department (hereafter cited as PRAAD), Accra, Ghana.

6. Nkrumah, *I Speak*, 48; *Philosophy & Opinions of Kwame Nkrumah*, ed. Kofi Yeboah Tuafo (Accra: Africanstories Press, 2016), 202; Osagyefo Dr. Kwame Nkrumah, "The African Genius," Speech Delivered at Opening of the Institute of African Studies, October 25, 1963, Bodleian Library, Oxford University; Takyiwaa Manuh, "Building Institutions for the New Africa: The Institute of African Studies at the University of Ghana," in *Modernization as Spectacle in Africa*, ed. Peter Jason Bloom, Stephen Miescher, and Takyiwaa Manuh (Bloomington: Indiana University Press, 2009), 270–279.

7. Harcourt Fuller, *Building the Ghanaian Nation-State: Kwame Nkrumah's Symbolic Nationalism* (London: Palgrave, 2014), 74–79; Nkrumah, *Africa Must Unite*, 49; Paul Schauert, *Staging Ghana: Artistry and Nationalism in State Dance Ensembles* (Bloomington: Indiana University Press, 2007), 39–77.

8. G. A. Stevens, "The Future of African Art: With Special Reference to Problems Arising in the Gold Coast Colony," *Africa: Journal of the International African Institute* 3, no. 22 (1930): 150–160; Shoko Yamada, "'Traditions' and

Cultural Production: Character Training at the Achimota School in Colonial Ghana," *History of Education* 38, no. 1 (January 2009): 29–59; Rhoda Woets, "The Recreation of Modern and African Art at Achimota School in the Gold Coast, 1927–52," *Journal of African History* 55, no. 3 (2014): 445–465.

9. H. Nii Abbey, *Kofi Antubam and the Myth Around Ghana's Presidential Seat* (Accra: Studio Brian Communications, 2008), 44–45; Kofi Antubam, *Ghana's Heritage of Culture* (Leipzig: Koehler and Amelang, 1963), 20–21; Jean Marie Allman, *The Quills of the Porcupine: Asante Nationalism in an Emergent Ghana* (Madison: University of Wisconsin Press, 1993), 9–11, 45–49; Fuller, 69–71; in his obituary in the *Ghanaian Times* on April 6, 1964, Antubam was described as a "missionary in the crusade of African rediscovery" and a "great disciple of Nkrumahist-socialism," whose works "were a reflection of African renaissance," as noted in Nii Abbey, 44–45.

10. Kwame Botwe-Asamoah, *Kwame Nkrumah's Politico-Cultural Thought and Policies: An African-Centered Paradigm for the Second Phase of the African Revolution* (London: Routledge, 2005), 149–176; Janet Hess, "Exhibiting Ghana: Display, Documentary, and 'National' Art in the Nkrumah Era," *African Studies Review* 44, no. 1 (April 2001): 59–77, and Peter J. Bloom and Kate Skinner, "Modernity and Danger: *The Boy Kumasenu* and the Work of the Gold Coast Film Unit," *Ghana Studies* 12 (2009): 121–153; Cati Cole, *Dilemmas of Culture in African Schools: Youth, Nationalism, and the Transformation of Knowledge* (Chicago: University of Chicago Press, 2005), 53–86.

11. Magnus J. Sampson, foreword to D. A. Sutherland, *State Emblems of the Gold Coast* (Accra: Government Printing Department, 1954), 3; Kwame Nkrumah, *I Speak of Freedom: A Statement of African Ideology* (London: Heinemann, 1961), 129.

12. Alex Quaison-Sackey, *Africa Unbound* (New York: Frederick A. Praeger, 1963), 37; V. Y. Mudimbe, *The Invention of Africa: Gnosis, Philosophy, and the Order of Knowledge* (Bloomington: Indiana University Press, 1988), 88–89; Basil Davidson, "Historical Inheritance of Ghana," *United Asia: International Magazine of Asian Affairs*, special issue on "Ghana and African Nationalism," 9, no. 1 (1957): 14.

13. Ghana Museum and Monuments Board, Memorandum on Renovation of Old Castle, to Ministry of Education, January 9, 1959, file page 55, RG 11/1/245, PRAAD; letter from director of Ghana Museum and Monuments Board (illegible signature) to minister of education, Accra, December 6, 1960, file doc. number 248, RG 11/1/245, PRAAD, Accra.

14. Maxwell Fry and Jane Drew, *Tropical Architecture in the Humid Zone* (London: Batsford Ltd., 1956), 20; Iain Jackson and Jessica Holland, *The Architecture of Edwin Maxwell Fry and Jane Drew: Twentieth Century Architecture, Pioneer Modernism and the Tropics* (London: Ashgate, 2014), 147–182; Manuel Herz, "The

New Domain: Architecture at the Time of Liberation," in *African Modernism: The Architecture of Independence*, ed. Manuel Herz, with Ingrid Schröder, Hans Focketyn, and Julia Jamrozik (Zurich: Park Books, 2015), 4–15.

15. "National Museum for Ghana," *Times* (London), March 11, 1957, 8; Agbenyega Adedze, "Museums as a Tool for Nationalism in Africa," *Museum Anthropology* 19, no. 2 (1995): 58–64, and Arianna Fogelman, "Colonial Legacy in African Museology: The Case of the Ghana National Museum," *Museum Anthropology* 31, no. 1 (2008): 19–26.

16. Richard Rathbone, *Nkrumah and the Chiefs: The Politics of Chieftaincy in Ghana, 1951–1960* (Oxford: James Currey, 2000), 89–149; Fuller, 89–90; Mark Crinson, "Nation-Building, Collecting and the Politics of Display: The National Museum, Ghana," *Journal of the History of Collections* 13, no. 2 (2001): 231–250.

17. Jeffrey James Byrne, *Mecca of Revolution: Algeria, Decolonization, and the Third World Order* (Oxford: Oxford University Press, 2016), 3; Jeffrey S. Ahlman, "The Algerian Question in Nkrumah's Ghana, 1958–1960: Debating 'Violence' and 'Nonviolence' in African Decolonization," *Africa Today* 57, no. 2 (Winter 2010): 66–84.

18. James McDougall, *A History of Algeria* (Cambridge: Cambridge University Press, 2017), 232–233; Marnia Lazreg, *Torture and the Twilight of Empire: From Algiers to Baghdad* (Princeton: Princeton University Press, 2008), 53–54; Martin Thomas, *Fight or Flight: Britain, France, and Their Roads from Empire* (Oxford: Oxford University Press, 2014), 289.

19. Lazreg, 191; Cheryl B. Welch, "Colonial Violence and the Rhetoric of Evasion: Tocqueville on Algeria," *Political Theory* 31, no. 2 (April 2003): 235–264, quotation 248.

20. Aimé Césaire, *Discourse on Colonialism*, trans. Joan Pinkham (New York: Monthly Press Review, 1972), 1–2, 5, 75.

21. Alice L. Conklin, *A Mission to Civilize: The Republican Idea of Empire in France and West Africa, 1895–1930* (Stanford, CA: Stanford University Press, 1997); Muriam Haleh Davis, "'The Transformation of Man' in French Algeria: Economic Planning and the Postwar Social Sciences, 1958–62," *Journal of Contemporary History* 52, no. 1 (January 2017): 73–94; James McDougall, "The Impossible Republic: The Reconquest of Algeria and the Decolonization of France, 1945–1962," *Journal of Modern History* 89, no. 4 (December 2017): 807; Amelia H. Lyons, *The Civilizing Mission in the Metropole: Algerian Families and the French Welfare State During Decolonization* (Stanford, CA: Stanford University Press, 2013).

22. Matthew Connelly, "Taking Off the Cold War Lens: Visions of North-South Conflict During the Algerian War for Independence," *American Historical Review* 105, no. 3 (June 2000): 757; McDougall, "Impossible," 792–793; Daniel

Just, "The War of Writing: French Literary Politics and the Decolonization of Algeria," *Journal of European Studies* 43, no. 3 (2013): 227–243; Robert Gildea, *Empires of the Mind: The Colonial Past and the Politics of the Present* (Cambridge: Cambridge University Press, 2019), 92.

23. Arnold Fraleigh, "The Algerian Revolution as a Case Study in International Law," in *The International Law of Civil War*, ed. Richard Falk (Baltimore: Johns Hopkins, 1971), 226; Mohamed Alwan, *Algeria Before the United Nations* (New York: Robert Speller & Sons, 1959).

24. Matthew Connelly, *A Diplomatic Revolution: Algeria's Fight for Independence and the Origins of the Post–Cold War Era* (Oxford: Oxford University Press, 2002), 107, 127–134.

25. Lazreg, 5; James D. Le Sueur, *Uncivil War: Intellectuals and Identity Politics During the Decolonization of Algeria* (Philadelphia: University of Pennsylvania Press, 2001), 98–99; David Carroll, "Camus's Algeria: Birthrights, Colonial Injustice, and the Fiction of a French-Algerian People," *Modern Language Notes* 112 (1997): 517–549.

26. Emma Kuby, "A War of Words over an Image of War: The Fox Movietone Scandal and the Portrayal of French Violence in Algeria, 1955–1956," *French Politics, Culture & Society* 30, no. 1 (Spring 2012): 46–67; *Documents on the Crimes and Outrages Commited [sic] by the Terrorists in Algeria* (Algiers: Societé d'Editions et de Regie Publicitaire, 1956), 5–6, 88; McDougall, "Impossible," 791; Connelly, *Diplomatic Revolution*, 127–128.

27. Fabian Klose, *Human Rights in the Shadow of Colonial Violence: The Wars of Independence in Kenya and Algeria* (Philadelphia: University of Pennsylvania Press, 2013), 212, 214; *Genocide in Algeria*, FLN brochure, June 1958, unpaginated; Mohammed Bedjaoui, *Law and the Algerian Revolution* (Brussels: International Association of Democratic Lawyers, 1961), 211.

28. Pierre-Henri Simon, *Contre la torture* (Paris: Editions du Seuil, 1957), 24; Alastair Horne, *A Savage War of Peace: Algeria 1954–1962* (London: Macmillan, 1996 [1977]), 196, 485–489; Klose, 100, 124; Byrne, 50.

29. François Méjean, *Le Vatican contre la France d'Outre Mer* (Paris: Librarie Fischbacher, 1957); Lazreg, 194–195; Darcie Fontaine, *Decolonizing Christianity: Religion and the End of Empire in France and Algeria* (Cambridge: Cambridge University Press, 2016), 106–145.

30. Lazreg, 117; Jean-Paul Sartre, preface to Henri Alleg, *The Question*, trans. John Calder (London: John Calder, 1958), 12, 13–14. This is an English translation of Sartre's *L'Express* article published two weeks after the book's release.

31. Neil McMaster, *Burning the Veil: The Algerian War and the "Emancipation" of Muslim Women, 1954–62* (Manchester: Manchester University Press, 2009), 209–216; Simone de Beauvoir and Gisèle Halimi, *Djamila Boupacha: The Story*

of the Torture of a Young Algerian Girl Which Shocked Liberal French Opinion, trans. Peter Green (London: Andre Deutsch, 1962), 12–21, 246.

32. *White Paper on the Application of the Geneva Conventions of 1949 to the French-Algerian Conflict* (New York: Algerian Office, 1960), 12, 15, 58; Jennifer Johnson, *The Battle for Algeria: Sovereignty, Health Care, and Humanitarianism* (Philadelphia: University of Pennsylvania Press, 2016), 104, 110, 115–116, 124–157.

33. Bedjaoui, 215; *Le Monde*, January 5, 1960, 1; Evan Luard, *History of the United Nations*, vol. 2, *The Age of Decolonization, 1955–1965* (Basingstoke, UK: Macmillan, 1989), 75–103; Johnson, 157–191.

34. These two paragraphs build on the excellent article by Andrew Bellisari, "The Art of Decolonization: The Battle for Algeria's French Art, 1962–1970," *Journal of Contemporary History* 52, no. 3 (2017): 625–645; Paul-Albert Février, *Art de l'Algérie antique* (Paris: E. de Boccard, 1971).

35. Daniel Herwitz, *Heritage, Culture, and Politics in the Postcolony* (New York: Columbia University Press, 2012), 1–25.

36. L. S. Senghor, *Liberté I: Négritude et humanisme* (Paris: Seuil, 1964), 124; Gary Wilder, *Freedom Time: Negritude, Decolonization, and the Future of the World* (Durham: Duke University Press, 2015), 49–73, 143, 206–240.

37. Senghor, "La Négritude," 108, quoted in Wilder, 52; Janet G. Vaillant, *Black, French, and African: A Life of Léopold Sédar Senghor* (Cambridge, MA: Harvard University Press, 1990), 243–271; Nancy Jachec, "Léopold Sédar Senghor and the Cultures de l'Afrique Noire et de l'Occident (1960): Eurafricanism, Négritude and the Civilisation of the Universal," *Third Text* 24, no. 2 (March 2010): 201; Kahuidi C. Mabana, "Leopold Sédar Senghor and the Civilization of the Universal," *Diogenes* (July 2013): 1–9.

38. Michael J. C. Echeruo, "Negritude and History: Senghor's Argument with Frobenius," *Research in African Literatures* 24, no. 4 (Winter 1993): 1–13; Marcel Mauss, "Civilisations, Their Elements and Forms (1929/1930)," in Marcel Mauss, *Techniques, Technology and Civilisation*, ed. Nathan Schlanger (New York/Oxford: Berghahn, 2006), 61–62; Keith Thomas, *In Pursuit of Civility: Manners and Civilization in Early Modern England* (New Haven: Yale University Press, 2018), 267; Léopold Sédar Senghor, "The Lessons of Leo Frobenius," in *Leo Frobenius: An Anthology*, ed. Eike Haberland, trans. Patricia Crampton (Wiesbaden: Franz Steiner, 1973), vii; Césaire, *Discourse*, 10.

39. Tareq Y. Ismael, *The U.A.R. in Africa: Egypt's Policy Under Nasser* (Evanston, IL: Northwestern University Press, 1971), 36, 103; Cheikh Anta Diop, *Nations nègres et culture: De l'antiquité nègre-égyptienne aux problèmes culturels de l'Afrique noire d'aujourd'hui* (Paris: Éditions Africaines, 1955); Cheikh Anta Diop, *L'Afrique noire précoloniale: Étude comparée des systèmes politiques et sociaux*

de l'Europe et de l'Afrique noire, de l'antiquité à la formation des états modernes (Paris: Présence Africaine, 1960); Mudimbe, 89–97; Manuh, 270.

40. Vijay Prashad, *The Darker Nations: A People's History of the Third World* (New York: New Press, 2007), 45; Sarah van Beurden, "The Art of (Re)Possession: Heritage and the Cultural Politics of Congo's Decolonization," *Journal of African History* 56, no. 1 (March 2015): 143–164, and Cynthia Scott, "Renewing the 'Special Relationship' and Rethinking the Return of Cultural Property: The Netherlands and Indonesia, 1949–79," *Journal of Contemporary History* 52, no. 3 (July 2017): 646–668; Robert Ardrey, *African Genesis* (London: Collins, 1961), and Richard E. Leakey, *The Making of Mankind* (London: Michael Joseph, 1981), 11–15; Saul Dubow, "Henri Breuil and the Imagination of Prehistory: 'Mixing Up Rubble, Trouble and Stratification,'" *South African Archaeological Society* 12 (2018): 1–13; *Congrès panafricain de préhistoire, Dakar 1967*, ed. Henri J. Hugot (Dakar: Les Imprimeries Réunies de Chambéry, 1967), 18–19.

41. Senghor, "La Négritude comme culture des peuples noirs, ne saurait être dépassé," in his *Liberté* 5, 95; Tracy D. Snipe, *Arts and Politics in Senegal, 1960–1966* (Trenton, NJ: Africa World Press, 1998), 43–49; Senghor, "Socialisme et culture," *Liberté II*, quoted in Wilder, 216; Sékou Touré, "Le Leader politique considéré comme le représentant d'une culture," in *Présence Africaine* 24–25 (February–May 1959): 115; Senghor, "Éléments constructifs d'une civilisation d'inspiration négro-africaine," *Présence Africaine* 24–25 (February–May 1959): 279.

42. Augustin F. C. Holl, "Worldviews, Mind-Sets, and Trajectories in West African Archaeology," in *Postcolonial Archaeologies in Africa*, ed. Peter Schmidt (Santa Fe, NM: School for Advanced Research Press, 2009), 135–139.

43. *Premier festival mondial des arts nègres*, exhibition catalog (Dakar, 1966), unpaginated; Engelbert Mveng, "Signification africaine de l'art," in *Colloque: Fonction et signification de l'art nègre dans la vie du people et pour le people, 30 mars–8 avril, 1966* (Paris: Présence Africaine, 1967), 8; L. S. Senghor, "Fonction et signification du Festival mondial des Arts nègres," in *Liberté III*, 58–63; David Murphy, "Introduction: The Performance of Pan-Africanism," in *The First World Festival of Negro Arts, Dakar 1966: Contexts and Legacies*, ed. David Murphy (Liverpool: Liverpool University Press, 2016), 1–40.

44. L. S. Senghor, foreword, Georges-Henri Riviere, preface, Engelbert M'Veng, introduction to *L'art nègre: Sources, evolution, expansion* (Dakar/Paris: Réunion des Musées Nationaux Français, 1966), xiv, xxxviii, xxiv–xxxi, respectively; Herbert Pepper, "La notion d'unité, notion clé de l'expression négro-africaine," in *Colloque*, 231–241; Ekpo Eyo, "La préservation des oeuvres d'art et d'artisanat," in *Colloque*, 624 and 632.

45. Frantz Fanon, *Wretched of the Earth*, 10–13, 151–154, 170; Elizabeth Harney, *In Senghor's Shadow: Art, Politics, and the Avant-Garde in Senegal, 1960–1995*

(Durham: Duke University Press, 2004), 9, 45; Jacques Louis Hymans, *Léopold Sédar Senghor: An Intellectual Biography* (Edinburgh: Edinburgh University Press, 1971), 129; R. Depestre, *Bonjour et adieu à la négritude* (Paris: Laffont, 1980), 198.

46. Vaillant, 275–279, 289, 291–292.

47. Frederick Cooper, *Citizenship Between Empire and Nation: Remaking France and French Africa, 1945–1960* (Princeton: Princeton University Press, 2014), 434.

48. A. W. Brian Simpson, *Human Rights and the End of Empire* (Oxford: Oxford University Press, 2004), 739; Talbot C. Imlay, "International Socialism and Decolonization During the 1950s: Competing Rights and the Postcolonial Order," *American Historical Review* 118, no. 4 (October 2013): 1105–1132; Roland Burke, *Decolonization and the Evolution of International Human Rights* (Philadelphia: University of Pennsylvania Press, 2010), 94–108.

7. WORLD CIVILIZATION

1. Max Frisch, *Homo Faber*, trans. Michael Bullock (London: Penguin, 1974 [1957]), 55.

2. James Sewell, *Unesco and World Politics: Engaging in International Relations* (Princeton: Princeton University Press, 1975), 119, 135; Marian Neal, "United Nations Technical Assistance Programs in Haiti," *International Conciliation* 468 (February 1951): 102–111, and Glenda Sluga, *Internationalism in the Age of Nationalism* (Philadelphia: University of Pennsylvania Press, 2013), 108–111.

3. Akira Iriye, *Cultural Internationalism and World Order* (Baltimore: Johns Hopkins Press, 1997), 131–176; UNESCO, Preparatory Commission, *Conference for the Establishment of the United Nations Educational, Scientific and Cultural Organization, Held at the Institute of Civil Engineers, London, from the 1st to the 16th November, 1945* (London: Preparatory Commission UNESCO, 1946), 87.

4. Chloé Maurel, "L'Histoire de l'humanité de l'UNESCO (1945–2000)," *Revue d'Histoire des Sciences Humaines* 22 (2010): 165; Iriye, 93; Walter H. C. Laves, "Can UNESCO Be of Aid in World Crisis?" *Foreign Policy Bulletin* 38, no. 4 (November 1, 1958): 29–31.

5. Julian Huxley, *Memories II* (London: George Allen & Unwin, 1973), 23–24; Luther Evans, Françoise Choay, and Lucien Hervé, *Unesco Headquarters in Paris: A Symbol of the Twentieth Century* (Paris: Vincent Fréal, 1958), and Christopher Pearson, *Designing UNESCO: Art, Architecture and International Politics at Mid-Century* (Burlington, VT: Ashgate, 2010).

6. Julian Huxley, *UNESCO: Its Purpose and Its Philosophy* (Washington, DC: Public Affairs Press, 1947), 17, 61.

7. Joseph Needham, *Chinese Science* (London: Pilot Press, 1945); letter from Needham to Huxley, October 13, 1948, NCUAC 54.3.95, D161, Joseph Needham

Papers, University of Cambridge (hereafter cited as JNP); Patrick Petitjean, "Giving Science for Peace a Chance," in *Sixty Years of Science at UNESCO, 1945–2005* (Paris: UNESCO, 2006), 55; *Science Liaison: The Story of UNESCO's Science Co-Operation Offices* (Paris: UNESCO, 1954), 9–10; C. P. Snow, *The Two Cultures* (New York: Cambridge University Press, 1959).

8. Céline Giton, "Weapons of Mass Distribution: UNESCO and the Impact of Books," in *A History of UNESCO: Global Actions and Impacts*, ed. Poul Duedahl (London: Palgrave, 2016), 51–53, 57; Josué Mikobi Dikay, "Education for Independence: UNESCO in the Post-Colonial Democratic Republic of Congo," in Duedahl, 171.

9. *Allied Plan for Education: The Story of the Conference of Allied Ministers of Education* (London: UN Information Organisation, 1945), 29, 33; *Report of the Director General on the Activities of the Organisation in 1947: Presented to the Second Session of the General Conference at Mexico City, November–December 1947* (Paris: UNESCO, 1947), 6–7.

10. Jacques Maritain, introduction to *Human Rights: Comments and Interpretations* (London: Wingate, 1949), 10; Mary Ann Glendon, *A World Made New: Eleanor Roosevelt and the Universal Declaration of Human Rights* (New York: Random House, 2001), 73–78.

11. Exhibition of Human Rights, conspectus of the display, April 1949, 1–2: 342.7 (100) A066 "54," UNESCO Archives, Paris (hereafter cited as AUP).

12. Julian S. Huxley and A. C. Haddon, *We Europeans: A Survey of "Racial" Problems* (London: Jonathan Cape, 1935), 107; Glenda Sluga, "UNESCO and the (One) World of Julian Huxley," *Journal of World History* 21, no. 3 (2010): 397–414; "Statement on Race," in UNESCO, *The Race Concept: Results of an Inquiry* (Paris: UNESCO, 1952), 496–501; Michelle Brattain, "Race, Racism, and Antiracism: UNESCO and the Politics of Presenting Science to the Postwar Public," *American Historical Review* 112, no. 5 (December 2007): 1386–1413; Claude Lévi-Strauss, *Tristes Tropiques* (London: Jonathan Cape, 1973 [1955]), 436–448; Lévi-Strauss, "The Crisis of Anthropology," *UNESCO Courier*, November 1961, 12–17.

13. Anthony Q. Hazard Jr., *Postwar Anti-Racism: The United States, UNESCO and "Race," 1945–1968* (London: Palgrave, 2012), 63–84; Paul Duedahl, "Out of the House: On the Global History of UNESCO, 1945–2015," in Duedahl, 5–6; Penny Von Eschen, *Race Against Empire: Black Americans and Anticolonialism, 1937–1957* (Ithaca, NY: Cornell University Press, 1997), 69–95.

14. John A. Armstrong, "The Soviet Attitude Toward UNESCO," *International Organization* 8, no. 2 (May 1954): 217–233.

15. Takashi Saikawa, "Returning to the International Community: UNESCO and Post-War Japan, 1945–1951," in Duedahl, 117–121. See too Liang Pan, *The United Nations in Japan's Foreign and Security Policymaking, 1945–1962* (Cambridge, MA: Harvard University Press, 2005).

16. Eighth Plenary Meeting, June 21, 1951, *Records of the General Conference, 6th Session, Paris 1951: Proceedings* (Paris: UNESCO, 1951), 112–116.

17. E1/164 Press Review, 1947–1953, June 27, 1952, October 17, 1952, UAP; Sewell, 151; *Records of the General Conference, 7th Session, Paris 1952: Proceedings* (Paris: UNESCO, 1953), 46–53.

18. Sluga, "UNESCO," 393–417, and Poul Duedahl, "Selling Mankind: UNESCO and the Invention of Global History, 1945–1976," *Journal of World History* 22, no. 1 (2011): 101–133.

19. T. V. Sathyamurthy, *The Politics of International Cooperation: Contrasting Conceptions of UNESCO* (Geneva: Librairie Droz, 1964), 98; Julian Huxley, "The Advance of World Civilization," *UNESCO Courier* 1, no. 10 (November 1948): 1–6; Huxley, *Memories II*, 69.

20. Cemil Aydin, "Beyond Civilization: Pan-Islamism, Pan-Asianism and the Revolt Against the West," and Dominic Sachsenmeier, "Searching for Alternatives to Western Modernity: Cross-Cultural Approaches in the Aftermath of the Great War," *Journal of Modern European History* 4, no. 2 (2006): 204–223 and 241–260, respectively; Michael Adas, "Contested Hegemony: The Great War and the Afro-Asian Assault on the Civilizing Mission Ideology," *Journal of World History* 15, no. 1 (March 2004): 31–63.

21. H. G. Wells, *The Outline of History: Being a Plain History of Life and Mankind* (London: Cassell and Company, 1934 [1920]), 1144–1147.

22. Arnold Toynbee, personal paper to special joint committee on UNESCO Project for a Scientific and Cultural History of Mankind, February 20, 1950, ED 157/30, National Archives, London (hereafter cited as NAL); Charles Morazé, "Obituary of Lucien Febvre," *Cahiers d'Histoire Mondiale/Journal of World History* 3 (1956): 553–557; UNESCO General Conference, 4th Session, "Present Position of the Project Concerning the 'Scientific and Cultural History of Mankind,'" Paris, August 30, 1949, 4: NCUAC 54.3.95, D163, JNP; Lucien Febvre, foreword to *Cahiers d'Histoire Mondiale/Journal of World History* 1, no. 1 (July 1953): 7–9.

23. Patrick Petitjean, "The Ultimate Odyssey," in *Sixty Years*, 86; Michael Lang, "Globalization and Global History in Toynbee," *Journal of World History* 22, no. 4 (2011): 747–783.

24. Walter H. C. Laves and Charles A. Thomson, *UNESCO: Purpose, Progress, Prospects* (Bloomington: Indiana University Press, 1957), 400.

25. "A World History for World Peace," *The Reconstructionist* 17, no. 20 (February 8, 1952): 5–6; letter from UNESCO secretary-general Guy Métraux to Gottschalk, June 20, 1956, box 17, folder 9, Louis Gottschalk Papers, University of Chicago; *Gazette* (Montreal), January 18, 1950, as well as "L'Unesco Raye-t-Elle Christ?," *La France Catholique*, April 5, 1951; Marco Duranti, *The Conservative Human Rights Revolution: European Identity, Transnational Politics, and the Origins of the European Convention* (Oxford: Oxford University Press, 2017), 318, 320.

26. M. K. Haldar, "History Under UNESCO," *Thought* (India), February 25, 1967; Alex Comfort, "All Those in Favour?," *Guardian*, November 25, 1966; "UN Goes into the History Business," *Chicago Daily Tribune*, December 24, 1951; Duedahl, "Selling," 123–125.

27. Duedahl, "Selling," 130; Todd Shepard, "Algeria, France, Mexico, UNESCO: A Transnational History of Anti-Racism and Decolonization, 1932–1962," *Journal of Global History* 6, no. 2 (2011): 273–297.

28. Philip L. Kohl and Clare Fawcett, *Nationalism, Politics, and the Practice of Archaeology* (Cambridge: Cambridge University Press, 1995); Tom Little, *High Dam at Aswan: The Subjugation of the Nile* (London: Methuen, 1965), 157.

29. Hussein M. Fahim, *Dams, People and Development: The Aswan High Dam Case* (New York: Pergamon Press, 1981), 7–15; David Gange, "Unholy Water: Archaeology, the Bible, and the First Aswan Dam," in *From Plunder to Preservation: Britain and the Heritage of Empire, c. 1800–1940*, ed. Astrid Swenson and Peter Mandler (London: British Academy, 2013), 93–114.

30. Michael Elliott and Vaughn Schmutz, "World Heritage: Constructing a Universal Cultural Order," *Poetics* 40, no. 3 (June 2012): 262–263; Sarah M. Titchen, "On the Construction of Outstanding Universal Value: UNESCO's World Heritage Convention (Convention Concerning the Protection of the World Cultural and Natural Heritage, 1972) and the Identification and Assessment of Cultural Places for Inclusion in the World Heritage List" (PhD thesis, Australian National University, April 1995), 15–35.

31. Elliott and Schmutz, 265; *Cuzco: Reconstruction of the Town and Restoration of Its Monuments* (Paris: UNESCO, 1952). For discussion, Lynn Meskell, *A Future in Ruins: UNESCO, World Heritage, and the Dream of Peace* (Oxford: Oxford University Press, 2018), 18.

32. Fekri A. Hassan, "The Aswan High Dam and the International Rescue Nubia Campaign," *African Archaeological Review* 24, no. 3 (January 2007): 79; George Rodger, *The Village of the Nubas* (London: Phaidon, 1955); for alternative design plans, Lucia Allais, *Designs of Destruction: The Making of Monuments in the Twentieth Century* (Chicago: University of Chicago Press, 2018), 219–254.

33. "March 8 Appeal by Vittorio Veronese, Director-General of Unesco," *Unesco Courier* 13 (May 1960): 7; Gange, 112–114; Ali Vrioni, "Victory in Nubia," *Unesco Courier* 17 (December 1964): 5.

34. Message of Mr. John F. Kennedy, president of the United States of America, delivered to the US Congress on April 7, 1961, concerning the participation of the United States of America in the international campaign to save the monuments of Nubia, CUA/107/ Annex II: CLT/CIH/MCO box 28, UAP; André Malraux, "TVA of Archaeology," *Unesco Courier* 13 (May 1960): 10.

35. Walter G. Langlois, *André Malraux: The Indochina Adventure* (London: Pall Mall Press, 1966), 3–51, and Herman Lebovics, *Mona Lisa's Escort: André*

Malraux and the Reinvention of French Culture (Ithaca, NY: Cornell University Press, 1999); André Malraux, "TVA," 10.

36. Statement by President Gamal Abdel Nasser on the safeguarding of the Nubian monuments, June 5, 1961, CUA/107/ Annex 1: CLT/CIH/MCO box 28, UAP; Negm-el-Din Mohammed Sherif, "Victory in Nubia: The Sudan," *Unesco Courier*, special issue on "Victory in Nubia," February–March 1980, 19, and Meskell, 55.

37. Torgny Säve-Söderbergh, ed., *Temples and Tombs of Ancient Nubia: The International Rescue Campaign at Abu Simbel, Philae and Other Sites* (Paris: Thames & Hudson and UNESCO, 1987), 68; Little, 164; March 17, 1964, 4, E1/ 168, 1947–1966, UAP; Friedrich W. Hinkel, *Auszug aus Nubien* (East Berlin: Akademie-Verlag, 1978); Hassan, 320.

38. C. L. Sulzberger, "No Cold War in the Land of Kush," *New York Times*, March 20, 1961, 28; "March 8 Appeal by Vittorio Veronese, Director-General of UNESO," *Unesco Courier* 13 (May 1960): 7; Zbynek Žába, "Ancient Nubia Calls for Help," *New Orient* 1, no. 3 (June 1960): 9.

39. Sewell, 246; Kemal Baslar, *The Concept of the Common Heritage of Mankind in International Law* (The Hague: Martinus Nijhoff, 1998), xix–38.

40. John A. Larson, *Lost Nubia: A Centennial Exhibit of Photographs from the 1905–1907 Egyptian Expedition of the University of Chicago* (Chicago: Oriental Institute, 2006), x; Fred Wendorf, ed., *The Prehistory of Nubia*, vols. 1 and 2 (Dallas: Southern Methodist University Press, 1968); Hassan, "High Dam," 81; February 11, 1966, 3, E1/168, 1947–1966, UAP.

41. Little, 135–139; Hussein M. Fahim, *Egyptian Nubians: Resettlement and Years of Coping* (Salt Lake City: University of Utah Press, 1983), 40–41; Säve-Söderbergh, *Temples*, 73; Georg Gerster, "Saving the Ancient Temples at Abu Simbel," *National Geographic Magazine* 129, no. 5 (May 1966): 709.

8. Socialism's Civilizing Mission in Africa

1. *Analysis of the Khrushchev Speech of January 6, 1961: Hearing Before the Subcommittee to Investigate the Administration of the Internal Security Act and Internal Security Laws of the Committee on the Judiciary United States Senate, 87th Congress, First Session* (Washington, DC: US Government Printing Office, 1961), Appendix, 52–73, quotations 69 and 71; Philip E. Muehlenbeck, *John F. Kennedy's Courting of African Nationalist Leaders* (Oxford: Oxford University Press, 2012), xii; Jeremy Friedman, "Soviet Policy in the Developing World and the Chinese Challenge in the 1960s," *Cold War History* 10, no. 2 (2010): 247–272.

2. Thomas J. Noer, "New Frontiers and Old Priorities in Africa," in *Kennedy's Quest for Victory: American Foreign Policy, 1961–1963*, ed. Thomas Paterson (Oxford: Oxford University Press, 1989), 253–283; Muehlenbeck, xi–xv, 48, and Odd

Arne Westad, *The Global Cold War: Third World Interventions and the Making of Our Times* (Cambridge: Cambridge University Press, 2007), 110–157.

3. Zbigniew Brzezinski, introduction to his edited *Africa and the Communist World* (London: Oxford University Press, 1964), 5.

4. Frederick Jackson Turner, *The Significance of the Frontier in American History* (London: Penguin, 2008 [1893]), 2.

5. Frederick C. Barghoorn, *The Soviet Cultural Offensive: The Role of Cultural Diplomacy in Soviet Foreign Policy* (Princeton: Princeton University Press, 1960); Yale Richmond, *Cultural Exchange and the Cold War: Raising the Iron Curtain* (University Park: Pennsylvania State University Press, 2003); B. Smirnov, *To Know Each Other* (Moscow: Novosti Press Agency Publishing House, 1967), 1–8.

6. Michael David-Fox, *Showcasing the Great Experiment: Cultural Diplomacy and Western Visitors to the Soviet Union, 1921–1941* (Oxford: Oxford University Press, 2012); Patryk Babiracki, *Soviet Soft Power in Poland: Culture and the Making of Stalin's Empire, 1943–1957* (Chapel Hill: University of North Carolina Press, 2015); Alvin Z. Rubinstein, *The Soviets in International Organizations: Changing Policy Toward Developing Countries, 1953–1963* (Princeton: Princeton University Press, 1964), 36.

7. Chanakya Sen, *Against the Cold War: A Study of Asian-African Policies Since World War II* (London: Asia Publishing House, 1962), 125–126.

8. Tobias Rupprecht, *Soviet Internationalism After Stalin: Interaction and Exchange Between the USSR and Latin America During the Cold War* (Cambridge: Cambridge University Press, 2015), 5, and Anne E. Gorsuch, *All This Is Your World: Soviet Tourism at Home and Abroad After Stalin* (Oxford: Oxford University Press, 2011); Pia Koivunen, "The 1957 Moscow Youth Festival: Propagating a New, Peaceful Image of the Soviet Union," in *Soviet State and Society Under Nikita Khrushchev*, ed. Melanie Ilic and Jeremy Smith (London: Routledge, 2009), 46–65.

9. Radina Vučetić, "Tito's Africa: Representation of Power During Tito's African Journeys," in *Picturing Solidarity: Tito in Africa*, ed. Radina Vučetić and Paul Betts (Belgrade: Museum of Yugoslav History, 2017), 12–45; 1959 Report, Teritoriální odbory—obyčejné, Guinea, 1945–1959, karton 1, Archive of the Ministry of Foreign Affairs, Prague (hereafter cited as AMZV); Teritoriální odbory—obyčejné, Etiopie, 1945–1959, karton 1, AMZV; Report 19, April 1963, Fond 02/1, sv. 17, ar.j. 18, 14, Bod, Czech National Archive, Prague (hereafter cited as CNA); Report 15 April 1965, Fond 02/1, sv. 107, ar.j. 110, 6, Bod, CNA. I thank Alena Alamgir for these Czech references.

10. Senghor, "Éléments constructifs d'une civilisation d'inspiration négro-africaine," *Présence Africaine* 24–25 (February–May 1959): 277; V. Y. Mudimbe, *The Invention of Africa: Gnosis, Philosophy, and the Order of Knowledge* (Bloomington: Indiana University Press, 1988), 91–95.

11. Roland Burke, *Decolonization and the Evolution of International Human Rights* (Philadelphia: University of Pennsylvania Press, 2010), 28; John Kotelawala, *An Asian Prime Minister's Story* (London: Harrap, 1956), 186–187; Richard Wright, foreword to George Padmore, *Pan-Africanism or Communism? The Coming Struggle for Africa* (London: Dennis Dobson, 1956), 12; A. G. Mezerik, ed., *Colonialism and the United Nations* (New York: International Review Service, 1964), 9.

12. James Mark and Quinn Slobodian, "Eastern Europe," *The Oxford Handbook of the Ends of Empire*, ed. Martin Thomas and Andrew S. Thompson (Oxford: Oxford University Press, 2018), 351–373; D. N. Sharma, *Afro-Asian Group in the U.N.* (Allahabad: Chaitnya Publishing House, 1969), 74–81, 106; Jeffrey James Byrne, *Mecca of Revolution: Algeria, Decolonization, and the Third World Order* (Oxford: Oxford University Press, 2016), 93; Mary Ann Heiss, "Exposing 'Red Colonialism': U.S. Propaganda at the United Nations, 1953–1963," *Journal of Cold War Studies* 17, no. 3 (Summer 2015): 82–115.

13. W. A. C. Adie, "China, Russia and the Third World," *China Quarterly* 11 (1962): 200–213; Jeffrey James Byrne, "Beyond Continents, Colours, and the Cold War: Yugoslavia, Algeria, and the Struggle for Non-Alignment," *International History Review* 37, no. 5 (2015): 924; Jeffrey James Byrne, *Mecca of Revolution*, 268.

14. William Glenn Gray, *Germany's Cold War: The Global Campaign to Isolate East Germany, 1949–1969* (Chapel Hill: University of North Carolina Press, 2003).

15. Richmond, 124–125; Cadra Peterson McDaniel, *American-Soviet Cultural Diplomacy: The Bolshoi Ballet's American Premiere* (Lanham, MD: Lexington Books, 2015); Clare Croft, *Dancers as Diplomats: American Choreography in Cultural Exchange* (New York: Oxford University Press, 2015); Penny M. Von Eschen, *Satchmo Blows Up the World: Jazz Ambassadors Play the Cold War* (Cambridge: Harvard University Press, 2006); Ilya Prizel, *Latin America Through Soviet Eyes: The Evolution of Soviet Perceptions During the Brezhnev Era, 1964–1982* (Cambridge: Cambridge University Press, 1990).

16. Both quoted in Byrne, *Mecca*, 214–215.

17. "Tour of Rumania by the Ghana Workers Brigade Band No. 2," press release by J. Benibengor Blay, Esq. MP, minister of art and culture, June 7, 1965, RG 3/7/13, PRAAD; "Marionetten und Pantomimen: Kairoer Puppenspieler auf der Reise durch die sozialistische Staaten Europas," *Märkische Union* (Potsdam), December 24, 1964, in DR1/24025, Bundesarchiv, Berlin (hereafter cited as BAB). I thank Radina Vucetic for the Yugoslavia references.

18. F. Morisseau-Leroy, National Organiser, Drama & Literature, Protocol Proposals, January 27, 1965, files pp. 269–271, RG 3/7/13, PRAAD; https://cia.gov/library/readingroom/docs/DOC_0000313542.pdf.

19. Artemy M. Kalinovsky, "Writing the Soviet South into the History of the Cold War and Decolonization," in *Alternative Globalizations: Eastern Europe and the Postcolonial World*, ed. James Mark, Artemy M. Kalinovsky, and Steffi Marung (Bloomington: Indiana University Press, 2020); Eren Tasar, "Islamically Informed Soviet Patriotism in Postwar Kyrgyzstan," *Cahiers du monde russe* 52, nos. 2–3 (2011): 387–404.

20. David Caute, *The Dancer Defects: The Struggle for Cultural Supremacy During the Cold War* (Oxford: Oxford University Press, 2003).

21. See the special issue on "Cold War Transfer: Architecture and Planning from Socialist Countries in the 'Third World,'" edited by Łukasz Stanek, in *Journal of Architecture* 17, no. 3 (2012); Cole Roskam, "Non-Aligned Architecture: China's Designs on and in Ghana and Guinea, 1955–1992," *Architectural History* 58 (2015): 261–291; Martino Stierli, "Networks and Crossroads: The Architecture of Socialist Yugoslavia as a Laboratory of Globalization in the Cold War," in *Toward a Concrete Utopia: Architecture in Yugoslavia 1948–1980* (New York: Museum of Modern Art, 2018), 11–26; Łukasz Stanek, *Architecture in Global Socialism: Eastern Europe, West Africa, and the Middle East in the Cold War* (Princeton: Princeton University Press, 2020), 35–96.

22. Ákos Moravánszky, "Peripheral Modernism: Charles Polónyi and the Lessons of the Village," *Journal of Architecture* 17, no. 3 (2012): 333–359; Ryszard Kapuściński, *The Shadow of the Sun* (New York: Knopf, 2001), 40; *Dookoła Świata* 44 (1963): 3–4, 10. I thank Hubert Czyzewski for this reference. Stanek, *Architecture*, 56–62; Paul Betts, "A Red Wind of Change: African Media Coverage of Tito's Tours of Decolonizing Africa," in Vucetic and Betts, 47–77.

23. Y. P. Frantsev, *Istoricheskiy materializm i sotsial'naya filosofiya sovremennoy burzhuazii* (Moscow, 1960), 13–25; V. M. Chkhikvadze, *Sotsialisticheskiy gumanizm i prava cheloveka: Leninskiye idei i sovremennost'* (Moscow, 1978), 110–115, 150–162, 260–265; "Strana Oktyabrya—Vernyi Drug Narodov Azii i Afriki," *Pravda*, November 4, 1960, 1. I thank Giovanni Cadioli for the Russian references in this section. Erich Fromm, ed., *Socialist Humanism: An International Symposium* (London: Allen Lane, 1967), ix–xiv.

24. Jenny Andersson, *The Future of the World: Futurology, Futurists, and the Struggle for the Post–Cold War Imagination* (Oxford: Oxford University, 2018), 131, 138–139.

25. Radovan Richta, *Civilization at the Crossroads: Social and Human Implications of the Scientific and Technological Revolution* (Prague: International Arts and Sciences, 1969), 13, 51, 250–251; Andersson, 123–129.

26. From 1955 to 1957 the USSR sent 48 experts to underdeveloped countries via the UN; contrast this with the 924 sent from the US, 683 from France, and 1,143 from the UK. "From the History of Studies of African Problems in the Soviet Union," in *Africa in Soviet Studies: 1968 Annual* (Moscow: 'Nauka'

Publishing House, 1969), 145–152; Sergey Mazov, *A Distant Front in the Cold War: The USSR in West Africa and the Congo, 1956–1964* (Stanford, CA: Stanford University Press, 2010), 18.

27. *Great Soviet Encyclopaedia* (Moscow: USSR Academy of Sciences, 1951); "Bogatstvo Kulturi Sozialisticheskih Nazii," *Pravda*, October 14, 1958, 1.

28. Editorial Board, "Presentation," *Africana Bulletin* 1 (1964): 7; Elzbieta Dabrowska-Smektala, "Polish Excavations in Egypt and Sudan," *Africana Bulletin* 2 (1965): 102–112; Tadeusz Dzierzykray-Rogalski, "The Joint Arabic-Polish Anthropological Expedition in 1958–1962," *Africana Bulletin* 4 (1966): 105–107.

29. Zbynek Žába, "Ancient Nubia Calls for Help," *New Orient* 1, no. 3 (1960): 5–9; "Eastern Studies Today," *New Orient* 1, no. 4 (1960): 1.

30. Alexander Dallin, *The Soviet Union at the United Nations* (London: Methuen, 1962), 21; Pieter Lessing, *Africa's Red Harvest* (London: Michael Joseph, 1962), 33–34, 126; Ivan Potekhin, *L'Afrique regarde vers l'avenir* (Moscow: Editions de Littérature Orientale, 1962), 70–81.

31. Kirill Chistov, "Folklore, 'Folklorism' and the Culture of an Ethnos," in *Ethnocultural Development of African Countries* (Moscow: USSR Academy of Sciences, 1984), 119–139; V. S. Solodovnikov, "Opening Address at the Conference on the Historical Relations of the Peoples of the Soviet Union and Africa, May 19, 1965," in *Russia and Africa* (Moscow: USSR Academy of Sciences, 1966), 7–15; Klaus Ernst, *Tradition and Progress in the African Village: The Non-Capitalist Transformation of Rural Communities in Mali* (London: C. Hurst, 1976 [1973]).

32. Teresa Brinkel, *Volkskundliche Wissensproduktion in der DDR* (Vienna: LIT, 2010), 39–76.

33. Frank J. Miller, *Folklore for Stalin: Russian Folklore and Pseudofolklore of the Stalin Era* (Armonk, NY: M. E. Sharpe, 1990); Yitzhak M. Brudny, *Reinventing Russia: Russian Nationalism and the Soviet State, 1953–1991* (Cambridge: Harvard University Press, 1998), and Christine Varga-Harris, *Stories of House and Home: Soviet Apartment Life During the Khrushchev Years* (Ithaca, NY: Cornell University Press, 2015), 43.

34. Mikhail Miller, *Archaeology in the USSR* (London: Atlantic Press, 1956), 132–168; G. S. P. Freeman-Grenville, *The Medieval History of the Coast of Tanganyika, with Special Reference to Recent Archaeological Discoveries* (Oxford: Oxford University Press, 1962); Dieter Graf, *Produktivkräfte in der Landwirtschaft und der nichtkapitalistische Weg Tansanias* (Berlin: Akademie Verlag, 1973); P. L. E. Idahosa, *The Populist Dimension to African Political Thought* (Trenton, NJ: African World Press, 2004).

35. P. L. Shinnie, *Meroe: A Civilization of the Sudan* (London: Thames & Hudson, 1967), 168–169; Fritz and Ursula Hintze, *Alte Kulturen im Sudan* (Leipzig: Leipzig Verlag, 1966); *Nichtkapitalistischer Entwicklungsweg: Aktuelle Probleme in Theorie und Praxis* (Berlin: Akademie Verlag, 1973).

36. Work Plan of the Romanian Embassy, Conakry, February 7, 1963, MFA, 70/1962, Guinea; Constantin I. Gulian, *On the Spiritual Culture of African Peoples* (Bucuresti: Editura Stiintifica, 1964), 8, 81. I thank Bogdan Cristian Iacob for the Romanian references and translated passages. Richard Lowenthal, "China," in *Africa and the Communist World*, ed. Zbigniew Brzezinski (London: Oxford University Press, 1964), 157; John Cooley, *East Wind over Africa: Red China's African Offensive* (New York: Walker, 1965), 16.

37. Tibor Bodrogi, *Afrikanische Kunst* (Leipzig: VEB E.A. Seemann, 1967); W. and B. Forman, *Kunst ferner Länder* (East Berlin: Artia Verlag, 1956); Ferdinand Herrmann, "Die afrikanische Negerplastik als Forschungsgegenstand," in *Beiträge zur Afrikanische Kunst, Veröffentlichungen des Museums für Völkerkunde zu Leipzig*, Heft 9 (Berlin: Akademie-Verlag, 1958), 3–29.

38. Christian Saehrendt, *Kunst im Kampf für das "Sozialistische Weltsystem": Auswärtige Kulturpolitik der DDR in Afrika und Nahost* (Göttingen: Franz Steiner, 2017), 40, 75; Burchard Brentjes, *African Rock Art* (London: J. M. Dent, 1969 [1965]), 1; Burchard Brentjes, *Von Schanidar bis Akkad: Sieben Jahrtausende orientalischer Weltgeschichte* (Leipzig: Urania-Verlag, 1968), 5–6; *Der Beitrag der Völker Afrikas zur Weltkultur*, ed. Burchard Brentjes (Halle, Germany: Martin-Luther-Universität Halle-Wittenberg Wissenschaftliche Beiträge, 1977).

39. Kofi Antubam, *Ghana's Heritage of Culture* (Leipzig: Koehler & Amelang, 1963), 24, 207; Brentjes saw connections between his sculpture and that of the celebrated German artist Käthe Kollwitz, probably due to the fact that the German antifascist Vladimir Meyerowitz taught both Kollwitz and Antubam; Nii Abbey, 44–45; Roselene Decho, *Kofi Antubam: A Ghanesian Artist*, with an introduction by Burchard Brentjes (Berlin: Deutsche Akademie der Künste zu Berlin, 1961); Gerald Götting, preface to Antubam, *Heritage of Culture*, 11.

40. L. S. Senghor, *On African Socialism* (New York: Frederick A. Praeger, 1964); Senghor, *Rapport sur la doctrine et le programme du parti: Congrès Constitutif du Parti de la Féderation Africaine (Dakar, 1-3 juillet 1959)* (Paris: Présence Africaine, 1959), as well as "Éléments constructifs d'une civilisation d'inspiration négro-africaine," *Présence Africaine* 24–25 (February–May 1959); Mazov, 149; Wilbert J. LeMelle, "A Return to Senghor's Theme on African Socialism," *Phylon* 26, no. 4 (1965): 330–343; Ludomir R. Lozny, *Archaeology of the Communist Era: A Political History of Archaeology of the 20th Century* (Berlin: Springer, 2016), and Bruce Trigger, *A History of Archaeological Thought* (Cambridge: Cambridge University Press, 2006), 207–242.

41. Murphy, introduction to *First World Festival*, 8, 31–32; G. Abramov and P. Kaminskii, "Isskustvo Derevnee, Vechno Zhivoe," *Pravda*, April 20, 1966, 5.

42. Erich Herold, "The Centenary of the Naprstek Museum," *New Orient* 3, no. 6 (December 1962): 177; Živorad Kovačević, "The Opening of the Museum

of African Art—a Significant Cultural and Political Event," in *Museum of African Art: The Veda and Zdravko Pečar Collection* (Belgrade: Museum of African Art, 1977), 1–2.

9. Religion, Race, and Multiculturalism

1. Kenneth Clark, *Civilisation: A Personal View* (London, 1969), 1; Chris Stephens and John-Paul Stonard, eds., *Kenneth Clark: Looking for Civilisation* (London: Tate Britain, 2014), 13–29, 101–114, 123–131.

2. James Stourton, *Kenneth Clark: Life, Art and Civilisation* (London: HarperCollins, 2016), 326, 341–342, 345–346; Clark, 2.

3. Ian Hall, "The Revolt Against the West: Decolonisation and Its Repercussions in British International Thought, 1945–1975," *International History Review* 33, no. 1 (March 2011): 43–64; Hedley Bull, *The Anarchical Society: A Study of Order in World Politics* (London: Macmillan, 1977).

4. *Africa Addio*, film by Gualtiero Jacopetti and Franco Prosperi, text by John Cohen (New York: Ballantine, 1966), 7, 24–25; Marie-Aude Fouéré, "Film as Archive. *Africa Addio* and the Ambiguities of Remembrance in Contemporary Zanzibar," *Social Anthropology* 24, no. 1 (February 2016): 82–96.

5. James Becket, *Barbarism in Greece: A Young American Lawyer's Inquiry into the Use of Torture in Contemporary Greece, with Case Histories and Documents* (New York: Walker and Company, 1970); Gonda Van Steen, "Rallying the Nation: Sport and Spectacle Serving the Greek Dictatorships," *International Journal of the History of Sport* 27, no. 12 (August 2010): 2121–2154; Richard Clogg, "The Ideology of the 'Revolution of 21 April 1967,'" and Helen Vlachos, "The Colonels and the Press," both in *Greece Under Military Rule*, ed. Richard Clogg and George Yannopoulos (London: Secker & Warburg, 1972), 36–58, and 73, respectively; Tony Judt, *Postwar: A History of Europe Since 1945* (London: Allen Lane, 2005), 507.

6. Quotations and discussion in Saul Dubow, *Apartheid, 1948–1994* (Oxford: Oxford University Press, 2014), 13, 30, 279.

7. E. Alexander Powell, *The Last Frontier: The White Man's War for Civilization in Africa* (London: Longmans, Green and Co., 1912); Isaac Schapera, ed., *Western Civilisation and the Natives of South Africa* (London: Routledge & Kegan Paul, 1967 [1934]), ix; Arthur Keppel-Jones, *Race or Civilisation? Who Is Destroying Civilisation in South Africa?* (Johannesburg: South African Institute of Race Relations, 1951), 12; E. E. Harris, *"White" Civilization: How It Is Threatened and How It Can Be Preserved in South Africa* (Johannesburg: South African Institute of Race Relations, 1952).

8. Saul Dubow, "Macmillan, Verwoerd, and the 1960 'Wind of Change' Speech," *Historical Journal* 54, no. 4 (December 2011): 1087–1114; Ryan M.

Irwin, *Gordian Knot: Apartheid and the Unmaking of the Liberal World Order* (Oxford: Oxford University Press, 2012), 18–19; Philip E. Muehlenbeck, *Betting on the Africans: John F. Kennedy's Courting of African Nationalist Leaders* (Oxford: Oxford University Press, 2012), 179–180.

9. A. Luthuli, "What Is This White Civilization?" *Golden City Post,* March 5, 1961, quoted and discussed in Scott Everett Couper, "Chief Albert Luthuli's Conceptualisation of Civilisation," *African Studies* 70, no. 1 (April 2011): 55–57; Rob Gordon, "Not Quite Cricket: 'Civilization on Trial in South Africa': A Note on the First Protest Film Made in South Africa," *History in Africa* 32 (2005): 457–466; Christabel Gurney, "'A Great Cause': The Origins of the Anti-Apartheid Movement, June 1959–March 1960," *Journal of Southern African Studies* 26, no. 1 (March 2000): 213–244.

10. *The United Nations and Apartheid, 1948–1994* (New York: United Nations, 1994), 10–16; International Commission of Jurists, *African Conference on the Rule of Law, Lagos, Nigeria, January 3–7, 1961: A Report on the Proceedings of the Conference* (Geneva: International Commission of Jurists, 1961).

11. Håkan Thörn, *Anti-Apartheid and the Emergence of a Global Civil Society* (Basingstoke, UK: Palgrave, 2006); *A Global History of Anti-Apartheid,* ed. Rob Skinner and Anna Konieczna (London: Palgrave, 2019); Thomas Borstelmann, *The Cold War and the Color Line* (Cambridge: Harvard University Press, 2001), 189.

12. I. I. Filatova and A. B. Davidson, *The Hidden Thread: Russia and South Africa in the Soviet Era* (Johannesburg: Jonathan Ball, 2013); V. G. Shubin, *ANC: A View from Moscow* (Johannesburg: Jacana Media, 2008); Ian Taylor, "The Ambiguous Commitment: The People's Republic of China and the Anti-Apartheid Struggle in South Africa," *Journal of Contemporary African Studies* 18, no. 1 (2000): 91–106.

13. *The Bonn-Pretoria Alliance: Memorandum of the Afro-Asian Solidarity Committee of the German Democratic Republic* (Dresden: Zeit im Bild, 1967), 3–4; Loren Kruger, *Post-Imperial Brecht: Politics and Performance, East and South* (Cambridge: Cambridge University Press, 1994), 236, 238, 286–287.

14. Saul Dubow, "Global Science, National Horizons: South Africa in Deep Time and Space," *Historical Journal* (March 2020): 1–28.

15. Bill Schwarz, *The White Man's World* (Oxford: Oxford University Press, 2011), 396–397, 414, 421; the role of "white civilization" as the unspoken ideological justification with which whites learned "to live with the colour bar in all its nuances and implications" is directly addressed in Doris Lessing's first novel, *The Grass Is Singing* (London: Michael Joseph, 1950), 27; *Rhodesia's Finest Hour: The Prime Minister of Rhodesia Addresses the Nation* (Salisbury, Rhodesia: Government Printer, 1965); Elizabeth Buettner, *Europe After Empire: Decolonization, Society, and Culture* (Cambridge: Cambridge University Press, 2016), 67–68; Ian Douglas Smith, *The Great Betrayal* (London: Blake, 1997), 25, 72–73; Brian

David Williams, *What Rhodesia Must Do Now: The Threat to Christian Civilization in Africa* (Glastonbury, UK: Abbey Press, 1977).

16. Talbot C. Imlay, "International Socialism and Decolonization During the 1950s: Competing Rights and the Postcolonial Order," *American Historical Review* 118, no. 4 (October 2013): 1105–1132.

17. Nikos Poulantzas, *The Crisis of the Dictatorships: Portugal, Greece, Spain*, trans. David Fernbach (London: NLB, 1976); Samuel P. Huntington, *The Third Wave: Democratization in the Late Twentieth Century* (Norman: University of Oklahoma Press, 1991), 3–30; Richard Gunther, Nikoforos Diamandouros, and Hans-Jürgen Puhle, eds., *The Politics of Democratic Consolidation: Southern Europe in Comparative Perspective* (Baltimore: Johns Hopkins University Press, 1995), and Juan J. Linz and Alfred Stepan, *Problems of Democratic Transition and Consolidation: Southern Europe, South America, and Post-Communist Europe* (Baltimore: Johns Hopkins University Press, 1996).

18. Grace Glueck, "Picasso's Antiwar 'Guernica' Quietly Leaves U.S. for Spain," *New York Times*, September 10, 1981, and James M. Markham, "Spain Says Bienvenida to Picasso's 'Guernica,'" *New York Times*, September 11, 1981.

19. Sasha D. Pack, *Tourism and Dictatorship: Europe's Peaceful Invasion of Franco's Spain* (London: Palgrave, 2006), 83–135.

20. Daniel C. Thomas, *The Helsinki Effect: International Norms, Human Rights, and the Demise of Communism* (Princeton: Princeton University Press, 2001).

21. Václav Havel, *The Power of the Powerless: Citizens Against the State in Central-Eastern Europe* (London: Routledge, 2010), 56; Václav Havel, *Politics and Conscience* (Stockholm: Charter 77 Foundation, 1984), 12–13.

22. Tony Judt, "Nineteen Eighty-Nine: The End of Which European Era?," *Daedalus* 123, no. 3 (Summer 1994): 1–19; Milan Kundera, "The Tragedy of Central Europe," *New York Review of Books* 31, no. 7 (1984): 33–38.

23. Sarah Fishman, *From Vichy to the Sexual Revolution: Gender and Family Life in Postwar France* (Oxford: Oxford University Press, 2017), 117; Hugh McLeod, *The Religious Crisis of the 1960s* (Oxford: Oxford University Press, 2007), 188–213; Mark Silk, "Notes on the Judeo-Christian Tradition in America," *American Quarterly* 36, no. 1 (Spring 1984): 80–83.

24. Andrew Preston, "Universal Nationalism: Christian America's Response to the Years of Upheaval," in *The Shock of the Global: The 1970s in Perspective*, ed. Niall Ferguson (Cambridge, MA: Harvard University Press, 2011), 306–318.

25. József Közi-Horvath, *Cardinal Mindszenty: Confessor and Martyr of Our Time* (Chichester, UK: Aid to the Church in Need, 1979), 7, 128–130.

26. Pedro Ramet, *Cross and Commissar: The Politics of Religion in Eastern Europe and the USSR* (Bloomington: Indiana University Press, 1987), 66.

27. George Weigel, *Witness to Hope: The Biography of Pope John Paul II* (London: HarperCollins, 1999), 292; Timothy Garton Ash, *The Polish Revolution* (New

Haven: Yale University Press, 2002), 32; J. B. Weydenthal, "Poland's Politics in the Aftermath of John Paul II's Election," *The Pope in Poland* (Prague: Radio Free Europe Research, 1979), 10; Jonathan Luxmoore and Jolanta Babiuch, *The Vatican and the Red Flag: The Struggle for the Soul of Eastern Europe* (London: Geoffrey Chapman, 1999), 205.

28. *Return to Poland: The Collected Speeches of John Paul II* (London: William Collins & Sons, 1979), 43–44, 48.

29. Luxmoore and Babiuch, 119, 121, 211, 215, 235; Samuel Moyn, *Christian Human Rights* (Philadelphia: University of Pennsylvania Press, 2015); Christian Caryl, *Strange Rebels: 1979 and the Birth of the 21st Century* (New York: Basic Books, 2013), 344.

30. "How the Eastern European and Soviet Media Viewed the Papal Visit," *Pope in Poland*, 107–128; Weigel, 322.

31. Henry Kamm, "Pope, in Spain, Urges Europe to Be 'Beacon of Civilization,'" *New York Times*, November 10, 1982.

32. Mikhail Gorbachev, *Perestroika: New Thinking for Our Country and the World* (New York: Harper & Row, 1987), 194–195; Gorbachev, *Memoirs* (New York: Doubleday, 1996), 429; Marie-Pierre Rey, "'Europe Is Our Common Home': A Study of Gorbachev's Diplomatic Concept," *Cold War History* 4, no. 2 (2014): 33–65.

33. Charles Quist-Adade, "From Paternalism to Ethnocentrism: Images of Africa in Gorbachev's Russia," *Race and Class* 46, no. 4 (2005): 88.

34. Jeffrey James Byrne, *Mecca of Revolution: Algeria, Decolonization, and the Third World Order* (Oxford: Oxford University Press, 2016), 296; Odd Arne Westad, *The Global Cold War: Third World Interventions and the Making of Our Times* (Cambridge: Cambridge University Press, 2007), 364–395.

35. Denis Deletant, "Romania's Return to Europe: Between Politics and Culture," in *Europe and the Historical Legacy in the Balkans*, ed. Raymond Detrez and Barbara Segaert (Brussels: Peter Lang, 2008), 83–99; Bogdan C. Iacob, "Together but Apart: Balkan Historians, the Global South, and UNESCO's *History of Humanity*, 1978–1989," *East Central Europe* 45, nos. 2–3 (2018): 270; Vladimir Tismaneanu, *Stalinism for All Seasons: A Political History of Romanian Communism* (Berkeley, CA: University of California Press, 2003), 227–229.

36. Andrew Apter, *The Pan-African Nation: Oil and the Spectacle of Culture in Nigeria* (Chicago: University of Chicago Press, 2005), 52–75; Kofi Akumanyi, "The Festival of Arts, Culture," *Daily Graphic*, January 15, 1977, 5; Samuel D. Anderson, "'Negritude is Dead': Performing the African Revolution at the First Pan-African Cultural Festival (Algiers, 1969)," in *The First World Festival of Negro Arts, Dakar 1966: Contexts and Legacies*, ed. David Murphy (Liverpool: Liverpool University Press, 2016), 133–150; L. Pochivalov, "Isskustvo za Rubezhom. Prazdnik v Lagose," *Pravda*, February 24, 1977, 5. I would like to thank Giovanni Cadioli for this Russian reference.

37. Ned Richardson-Little, "The Failure of the Socialist Declaration of Human Rights: Ideology, Legitimacy, and Elite Defection at the End of State Socialism," *East Central Europe* 46, nos. 2–3 (2019): 318–342; Roland Burke, *Decolonization and the Evolution of International Human Rights* (Philadelphia: University of Pennsylvania Press, 2010), 137–139.

38. Abigail Judge Kret, "'We Unite with Knowledge': The People's Friendship University and Soviet Education for the Third World," *Comparative Studies of South Asia, Africa and the Middle East* 33, no. 2 (August 2013).

39. Rupprecht, 217–218, and Thomas Kunze and Thomas Vogel, eds., *Ostalgie International: Erinnerungen an die DDR von Nicaragua bis Vietnam* (Berlin: Ch. Links, 2010); Maxim Matusevich, "Probing the Limits of Internationalism: African Students Confront Soviet Ritual," *Anthropology of East Europe Review* 27, no. 2 (2009); Maxim Matusevich, *No Easy Row for a Russian Hoe: Ideology and Pragmatism in Nigerian-Soviet Relations, 1960–1991* (Trenton, NJ: Africa World Press, 2003), 84; S. V. Mazov, *A Distant Front in the Cold War: The USSR in West Africa and the Congo, 1956–1964* (Stanford, CA: Stanford University Press, 2010), 234.

40. M. Dia, *Essais sur l'Islam*, vol. 1, *Islam et humanisme*, vol. 2, *Socio-Anthropologie de l'Islam*, vol. 3, *Islam et civilisations negro-africaine* (Dakar: Nouvelles editions africaine, 1977–1981); A. H. Ba, *Aspects de la civilisation africaine* (Paris: Présence Africaine, 1972); Toynbee, *Civilization on Trial* (New York: Oxford University Press, 1948), especially the chapter on "Islam, the West and the Future"; *The Toynbee Lectures on the Middle East and Problems of Under-developed Countries* (Cairo: National Publications House, 1962); Michael Goebel, *Anti-Imperial Metropolis: Imperial Paris and the Seeds of Third-World Nationalism* (Cambridge: Cambridge University Press, 2015), 258; Cemil Aydin, *The Idea of the Muslim World: A Global Intellectual History* (Cambridge, MA: Harvard University Press, 2017), 193–197.

41. John Riddell, *To See the Dawn: Baku, 1920—First Congress of the Peoples of the East* (New York: Pathfinder, 1993); Alexandre Bennigsen and Chantal Lemercier-Quelquejay, *Islam in the Soviet Union* (New York: Praeger, 1967); Aydin, 199–226; Brenna Miller, "Faith and Nation: Politicians, Intellectuals, and the Official Recognition of a Muslim Nation in Tito's Yugoslavia," in *Beyond Mosque, Church, and State: Alternative Narratives of the Nation in the Balkans*, ed. Theodora Dragostinova and Yana Hashamova (Budapest: CEU Press, 2016), 129–150.

42. Jalal Al-i Ahmad, *Occidentosis: A Plague from the West*, trans. R. Campbell (Berkeley, CA: Mizan Press, 1984), 34.

43. Maryam Panah, *The Islamic Republic and the World: Global Dimensions of the Iranian Revolution* (London: Pluto Press, 2007), 65–69; Jeremy Friedman, "The Enemy of My Enemy: The Soviet Union, East Germany, and the Iranian Tudeh Party's Support for Ayatollah Khomeini," *Journal of Cold War Studies* 20,

no. 2 (Spring 2018): 3–25; Jordan Baev, "Infiltration of Non-European Terrorist Groups in Europe and Antiterrorist Responses in Western and Eastern Europe (1969–1991)," in *Counter Terrorism in Diverse Communities*, ed. Siddik Ekici (Amsterdam: IOS Press, 2011), 60.

44. Baev, 58–74.

45. Zachary T. Irwin, "The Fate of Islam in the Balkans: A Comparison of Four State Policies," in *Religion and Nationalism in Soviet and East European Politics*, ed. Pedro Ramet (Durham: Duke University Press, 1989), 378–407; Lolita Nikolova and Diana Gergova, "Contemporary Bulgarian Archaeology as a Social Practice in the Later Twentieth to Early Twenty-First Century," in *Archaeology of the Communist Era: A Political History of Archaeology of the 20th Century*, ed. Ludomir R. Lozny (Berlin: Springer, 2016), 177–188.

46. Robert Gildea, *Empires of the Mind: The Colonial Past and the Politics of the Present* (Cambridge: Cambridge University Press, 2019), 123; Rita Chin, *The Crisis of Multiculturalism in Europe: A History* (Princeton: Princeton University Press, 2017), 92.

47. Joan Wallach Scott, *The Politics of the Veil* (Princeton: Princeton University Press, 2007), 46; Neil MacMaster, *Colonial Migrants and Racism: Algerians in France, 1900–62* (London: Macmillan, 1997), 198; Chin, 66, 75, 120.

48. Miriam Feldblum, *Reconstructing Citizenship: The Politics of Nationality Reform and Immigration in Contemporary France* (Albany: State University of New York Press, 1999), 36–39, 42.

49. Chin, 7–17.

50. Talal Asad, "Multiculturalism and British Identity in the Wake of the Rushdie Affair," *Politics and Society* 18, no. 4 (1990): 455–480; Gildea, 165, 167.

51. Chin, 192–236; Francis Depuis-Déri, "L'Affaire Salman Rushdie: Symptôme d'un 'Clash of Civilizations'?" *Études Internationales* 28, no. 1 (1997): 27–45.

52. Allan Bloom, "Western Civ—and Me: An Address at Harvard University," *Commentary* 90, no. 2 (August 1990): 15–21; Richard Bernstein, "In Dispute on Bias, Stanford Is Likely to Alter Western Culture Program," *New York Times*, January 19, 1988.

53. Judt, 534.

Conclusion: New Iron Curtains

1. "The Right Head for UNESCO," *New York Times*, September 28, 2009; http://whc.unesco.org/en/news/1254.

2. Irina Bokova, "Preservation of Cultural Heritage: Challenges and Strategies" (address, Global Colloquium of University Presidents, hosted by Yale University, New Haven, CT, April 11, 2016), http://unesdoc.unesco.org/images

/0024/002448/244824e.pdf; Irina Bokova, "Cultural Cleansing—the Imperative of Protecting Cultural Heritage and Diversity" (address, Royal Society of Edinburgh, UK, November 20, 2016), http://unesdoc.unesco.org/images/0024 /002466/246668E.pdf; www.loc.gov/law/foreign-news/article/unesco-palmyra -temple-bombing-deemed-a-war-crime/; Marlise Simons, "Extremist Pleads Guilty in Hague Court to Destroying Cultural Sites in Timbuktu," *New York Times*, August 22, 2016.

3. www.youtube.com/watch?v=9b0hFIf4Zaw; Lynn Meskell, *A Future in Ruins: UNESCO, World Heritage, and the Dream of Peace* (Oxford: Oxford University Press, 2018), 176–194; "Praying for Palmyra: Russian Maestro Leads Orchestra in Ruins of Ancient City," *RT*, May 5, 2016, www.rt.com/news /341983-russia-gergiev-orchestra-palmyra/.

4. Meskell, 176–182, 296n22; Bokova, "Cultural Cleansing," 10; Benjamin Isakhan and Lynn Meskell, "UNESCO's Project to 'Revive the Spirit of Mosul': Iraqi and Syrian Opinion on Heritage Reconstruction After the Islamic State," *International Journal of Heritage Studies* 25, no. 11 (2019): 1–16.

5. www.lemonde.fr/politique/article/2015/06/29/la-guerre-de-civilisation -de-valls-rejouit-la-droite 4663488_823448.html; www.nytimes.com/live/paris -attacks-live-updates/hollande-says-france-is-at-war/; https://en.unesco.org/news /french-president-francois-hollande-invokes-unity-all-cultures-unesco-s-leaders -forum.

6. Andrei P. Tsygankov, "Finding a Civilizational Idea: 'West,' 'Eurasia,' and the 'Euro-East' in Russia's Foreign Policy," *Geopolitics* 12, no. 3 (2007): 375–399; Peter J. Katzenstein and Nicole Weygandt, "Mapping Eurasia in an Open World: How the Insularity of Russia's Geopolitical and Civilizational Approaches Limits Its Foreign Policies," *Perspectives on Politics* 15, no. 2 (2017): 428–441; Andrew Rettman, "Orbán Says Migrants Will Change European Civilisation," *EU Observer*, June 2, 2015; Ian Traynor, "Migration Crisis: Hungarian PM Says Europe in Grip of Madness," *Guardian*, September 3, 2015; "Refugees Threaten Europe's Christian Roots, Says Hungary's Orban," Reuters, September 3, 2015; www.kormany.hu/en/the-prime-minister/the-prime-minister-s-speeches/viktor -orban-s-speech-at-the-14th-kotcse-civil-picnic.

7. Ivan Krastev, *After Europe* (Philadelphia: University of Pennsylvania Press, 2017), 19, 36–76; Ivan Krastev and Stephen Holmes, *The Light That Failed: A Reckoning* (London: Allen Lane, 2019), 46, 52, 57, 68; James Mark, Bogdan C. Iacob, Tobias Rupprecht, and Ljubica Spaskovska, *1989: A Global History* (Cambridge: Cambridge University Press, 2019), 284; Rogers Brubraker, "Between Nationalism and Civilizationism: The European Populist Moment in Comparative Perspective," *Ethnic and Race Studies* 40, no. 8 (2017): 1191–1226.

8. Both quoted in Mark, Iacob, Rupprecht, and Spaskovska, 126; James Krapfl, *Revolution with a Human Face: Politics, Culture, and Community in*

Czechoslovakia, 1989–1992 (Ithaca, NY: Cornell University Press, 2013), 17; Attila Leitner, "Mindszenty Cleared Posthumously," *Budapest Times*, March 30, 2012.

9. Michael Dobbs, "Gorbachev, Pope Meet, Agree on Diplomatic Relations," *Washington Post*, December 2, 1989; Felix Corley, "Soviet Reaction to the Election of Pope John Paul II," *Religion, State and Society* 22, no. 1 (1994): 40–43.

10. Johanna Bockman, *Markets in the Name of Socialism: The Left-Wing Origins of Neoliberalism* (Palo Alto, CA: Stanford University Press, 2011), 189–214; Zsuzsa Gille, "Is There a Global Postsocialist Condition?" *Global Society* 24, no. 1 (January 2010): 9–30.

11. Odd Arne Westad, *The Global Cold War: Third World Interventions and the Making of Our Times* (Cambridge: Cambridge University Press, 2007), 370; Charles Quist-Adade, "From Paternalism to Ethnocentrism: Images of Africa in Gorbachev's Russia," *Race and Class* 46, no. 4 (2005): 88; Mark, Iacob, Rupprecht, and Spaskovska, 165; Fatima Nduka-Eze, ed., *Joe Garba's Legacy: Thirty-Two Selected Speeches and Lectures* (New York: Xlibris, 2012), 288–292, 310, 330–331; "Communism Collapses in Eastern Europe; the West Cheers, Africa Despairs," *The Economist*, April 7, 1990, 15.

12. George P. Fletcher and Jens David Ohlin, *Defending Humanity: When Force Is Justified and Why* (Oxford: Oxford University Press, 2008); Michael Barrett, *Empire of Humanity: A History of Humanitarianism* (Ithaca, NY: Cornell University Press, 2011), 186; Nadège Ragaru, "Missed Encounters: Engaged French Intellectuals and the Yugoslav Wars," *Südosteuropa* 61 (2013): 498–521; Norman M. Naimark, *Fires of Hatred: Ethnic Cleansing in Twentieth-Century Europe* (Cambridge, MA: Harvard University Press, 2001), 139–184; "The Fall of Srebrenica and the Failure of UN Peacekeeping," *Human Rights Watch*, October 15, 1995, unpaginated.

13. Tanja Collet, "*Civilization* and *Civilized* in Post-9/11 US Presidential Speeches," *Discourse and Society* 20, no. 4 (2009): 455–475.

14. Cullen Murphy, *Are We Rome? The Fall of an Empire and the Fate of America* (Boston: Houghton Mifflin, 2007); Ali Parchami, *Hegemonic Peace and Empire: The Pax Romana, Britannica and Americana* (Abingdon, UK: Routledge, 2009); Robert Kagan, *Of Paradise and Power: America and Europe in the New World Order* (New York: Vintage, 2004), 3–4; Mark B. Salter, *Barbarians and Civilization in International Relations* (London: Pluto, 2002); Niall Ferguson, *Civilization: The Six Killer Apps of Western Power* (London: Penguin, 2011), 324.

15. "United We Stand," *Wall Street Journal*, January 30, 2003, 10–11; Padraic Kenney, *The Burdens of Freedom: Eastern Europe Since 1989* (London: Zed, 2006), 154; Jacques Derrida and Jürgen Habermas, "February 15, or, What Binds Europeans Together: Pleas for a Common Foreign Policy, Beginning in the Core Europe," and Adam Krzeminski, "First Kant, Now Habermas: A Polish Perspective on 'Core Europe,'" in *Old Europe, New Europe, Core Europe: Transatlantic Relations*

After the Iraq War, ed. D. Levy, M. Pensky, and J. Torpey (London: Verso, 2005), 4, 146–147.

16. Tom Henegan, "Sarkozy Joins Allies Burying Multiculturalism," Reuters, February 11, 2011; Robert Gildea, *Empires of the Mind: The Colonial Past and the Politics of the Present* (Cambridge: Cambridge University Press, 2019), 133, 215, 220; Tariq Modood, *Multiculturalism: A Civic Idea* (London: Polity, 2007); Arun Kundnani, *The Muslims Are Coming! Islamophobia, Extremism, and the Domestic War on Terror* (London: Verso, 2014); Paul Hanebrink, *A Specter Haunting Europe: The Myth of Judeo-Bolshevism* (Cambridge, MA: Harvard University Press, 2018), 281.

17. Selcen Öner, "Turkey's Membership to the EU in Terms of 'Clash of Civilizations,'" *Journal of Interdisciplinary Economics* 20, no. 3 (2009): 245–261, and Catherine MacMillan, "One Civilisation or Many? The Concept of Civilisation in Discourse for and Against Turkish EU Accession," *Balkan Journal of Philosophy* 4, no. 2 (2012): 215–217; Karmen Erjavec and Zala Volčič, "'We Defend Western Civilization': Serbian Representations of a Cartoon Conflict," *Islam and Christian-Muslim Relations* 19, no. 3 (July 2008): 305–321.

18. Tom McCulloch, "The Nouvelle Droite in the 1980s and 1990s: Ideology and Entryism, the Relationship with the Front National," *French Politics* 4 (2006): 158–178.

19. Harriet Agnew and Anne-Sylvaine Chassany, "Le Pen Steps Up Anti-Immigration Rhetoric Ahead of French Election," *Financial Times*, April 18, 2017; Renaud Camus, "An Open Letter to Viktor Orbán," National Council of European Resistance, April 20, 2018, www.cnre.eu/en/open-letter-viktor-orban; Thomas Chatterton Williams, "The French Origins of 'You Will Not Replace Us,'" *New Yorker*, December 4, 2017; Nafeez Ahmed, "'White Genocide' Theorists Worm Their Way into the West's Mainstream," *Monde Diplomatique*, March 25, 2019; Jean-Pierre Stroobants, "Aux Pays-Bas, percée inattendue d'un nouveau parti de droite nationaliste," *Le Monde*, March 22, 2019, 3; Angela Giuffrida, "Far-Right Leaders Unite in Milan with a Vow to 'Change History,'" *Guardian*, May 19, 2019, 30–31.

20. Michael Hirsh, "Team Trump's Message: The Clash of Civilizations Is Back," *Politico*, November 20, 2016; www.whitehouse.gov/briefings-statements/remarks-president-trump-people-poland/; Eugene Robinson, "Trump's Dangerous Thirst for a Clash of Civilizations," *Washington Post*, July 6, 2017; Gideon Rachman, "Trump, Islam and the Clash of Civilizations," *Financial Times*, February 13, 2017; "Donald Trump's Election Victory Marks the 'End of Liberal Non-Democracy,' Declares Hungary's Prime Minister," *Daily Mail*, November 10, 2016.

21. Václav Havel, "The Search for Meaning in a Global Civilization," *English Academy Review* 16, no. 1 (December 1999): 3–7.

22. Lucien Febvre and François Crouzet, *Nous sommes des sang-mêlés: manuel d'histoire de la civilisation française* (Paris: Albin Michel, 2012); David Motadel, "Globalizing Europe: European History After the Global Turn," unpublished manuscript.

23. Krastev, *After Europe*, 19, 36–76; Tim Marshall, *The Age of Walls: How Barriers Between Nations Are Changing Our World* (New York: Scribner, 2018), 2–3; Peter Andreas and Timothy Snyder, eds., *The Wall Around the West: State Borders and Immigration Controls in North America and Europe* (Lanham, MD: Rowman & Littlefield, 2000), esp. 153–228.

24. Sebastian Conrad, *What Is Global History?* (Princeton: Princeton University Press, 2016), 174–184; Stephen Hopgood, *The Endtimes of Human Rights* (Ithaca, NY: Cornell University Press, 2013), 53–54.

25. Aurore Merle, "Towards a Chinese Sociology for 'Communist Civilisation,'" *Chinese Perspectives* 52 (March–April 2004): 1–16.

26. Eileen Crist, *Abundant Earth: Toward an Ecological Civilization* (Chicago: University of Chicago Press, 2019); Arran Gare, *The Philosophical Foundations of Ecological Civilization: A Manifesto for the Future* (London: Routledge, 2016); Jiahua Pan, *China's Environmental Governing and Ecological Civilization* (Heidelberg: Springer, 2016); Kim Stanley Robinson, "The Coronovirus Is Rewriting Our Imaginations," *New Yorker,* May 1, 2020.

27. Arnold J. Toynbee, *Civilization on Trial* (Oxford: University Press, 1948), 55.

28. V. S. Naipaul, "Our Universal Civilization," *City Journal,* Summer 1991, unpaginated, www.city-journal.org/html/our-universal-civilization-12753.html.

INDEX

Index

Index

Index

Index

527

Index

Index

Index

Index

Index

Index

ANNA BETTS

PAUL BETTS is a professor of European history at St. Antony's College, Oxford, and the author of several books, most recently *Within Walls: Private Life in the German Democratic Republic*, which won the Fraenkel Prize in Contemporary History. He lives in Oxford, England.